The
NETWORK
MANAGER'S
Handbook
1999

John M. Lusa, *Editor*

CRC Press
Taylor & Francis Group
Boca Raton London New York

CRC Press is an imprint of the
Taylor & Francis Group, an **informa** business

First published 1999 by CRC Press
Taylor & Francis Group
6000 Broken Sound Parkway NW, Suite 300
Boca Raton, FL 33487-2742

Reissued 2018 by CRC Press

Library of Congress Cataloging-in-Publication Data

The network manager's handbook / John M. Lusa, consulting editor. - 1999 ed.
    p.   cm.
  Includes bibliographical references and index.
  ISBN 0-8493-9990-4 (alk. paper)
    1. Computer networks–Management–Handbooks, manuals, etc.
  I. Lusa, John M.
  TK5105.5.N466217 1998
  658'.0546-dc21   98-46525

A Library of Congress record exists under LC control number: 98046525

ISBN 13: 978-1-315-89808-7 (hbk)
ISBN 13: 978-1-351-07718-7 (ebk)

Visit the Taylor & Francis Web site at http://www.taylorandfrancis.com and the
CRC Press Web site at http://www.crcpress.com

Contributors

DAVID AXNER, *Industry Analyst/Consultant and President, DAX Associates, Oreland, PA*

DOUGLAS R. BALLOU, *President, Ballou Consultants Inc., Lancaster, OH*

RICHARD A. BELLAVER, *Associate Professor, Center for Information and Communication Sciences, Ball State University, Muncie, IN*

DR. PHYLLIS BERNT, *Associate Dean of the College of Communications, Ohio University, Athens, OH*

DR. THOMAS A. BROWDY, *Program Director, Information Management Programs, Washington University, St. Louis, MO*

PETER BROWN, *Vice President, Information Technology, PRI Automation, Billerica, MA*

CHRISTOPHER S. CLEVELAND, *Senior Consultant, KPMG Peat Marwick LLP, Radnor, PA*

DR. S. ANN EARON, *President, Telemanagement Resources International Inc., Skillman, NJ*

PHIL EVANS, *Director of Telecommunications, Perot Systems Corp., Plano, TX*

JOHN FISKE, *Consultant, johnffiske.com, Prides Crossing, MA*

DR. FRANK M. GROOM, *Professor, Center for Information and Communication Sciences, Ball State University, Muncie, IN*

KEVIN M. GROOM, *Senior Technical Associate, AT&T, Cincinnati, OH*

JEFF C. HAFER, *Telecommunications Manager, GPU Service Inc., Reading, PA*

KENNETH HARNISCH, *former Offer Manager, AT&T Managed Network Solutions, New York, NY*

DALE HIBNER, *Manager, Whittman-Hart Inc., Chicago, IL*

ANTOINETTE Z. HUBBARD, *Principal, Leadership by Design, Cincinnati, OH*

DR. RON KOVAC, *Associate Professor, Center for Information and Communication Sciences, Ball State University, Muncie, IN*

DR. HANS KRUSE, *Director, J. Warren School of Communications System Management, Ohio University, Athens, OH*

LARRY L. LEARN, *Director of Technical Planning, OCLC Online Computer Library Center Inc., Dublin, OH*

JOHN M. LUSA, *Principal, International Communications, Dayton, OH; and Adjunct Faculty, Center for Information and Communication Sciences, Ball State University, Muncie, IN*

Contributors

THOMAS OSHA, *Director, Executive Communications, Cincinnati Bell Telephone, Cincinnati, OH*

BRYAN PICKETT, *Vice President, Enterprise Networks, Training and Documentation, Nortel, Richardson, TX*

ARLYN S. POWELL, JR., *Group Editorial Director,* Cabling Installation and Maintenance *magazine, PennWell Publishing Co., Nashua, NH*

KIMBERLY RUSSO, *Director of Marketing, Tele-Tech Services, Summerville, SC*

ED SIMONSON, *President, TeleDesign Management Inc., Burlingame, CA*

DR. GEORGE THOMAS, *Associate Professor, Electrical Engineering, University of Southwestern Louisiana, Lafayette, LA*

COLIN WYND, *WorldWide Channel Marketing Manager, NetMetrix Division, Hewlett-Packard Co., Palo Alto, CA*

BILL YAMAN, *Vice President, Solutions Management, Candle Corp., Santa Monica, CA*

MICHAEL G. ZIVICH, *Consultant, Ballou Consultants Inc., Lancaster, OH*

Contents

Contents

Introduction

We are proud and happy to be able to present the second edition of *The Network Manager's Handbook*. The great response to our first edition was gratifying.

It is no secret that the world of information technology is one of rapid change and innovation, and we are well aware that the management of computer and voice network must constantly deal with this fact of life. Thus, we dedicate this new book to those changes.

There is hardly a business or organization today of any size that does not employ some form of advance telephony, networking, or computer technology. Keeping up can be a daunting task for those in charge of using this technology within their enterprises. For those who are just entering or aspire to a career in information technology it must seem even more bewildering.

At the core of much of this technology is a blossoming career field that has essentially been created during the past 5 or 6 years. For simplicity's sake and for purposes of this book, we generically use the title of network manager. The position may actually be a vice president, director, manager, supervisor, or some other title. The title infrastructure manager has been used as well.

The focus of this edition is on that corporate position with overall responsibility for the computer and telephone network within the enterprise or organization. Reporting to this position may be people with direct responsibility for network engineering, help desks, data networks, local area network (LAN) administration, Internet and intranet systems, voice systems, World Wide Web administration, etc., depending on the size of the organization and its network. In many organizations, such as the larger airline companies, the budget for network operations may reach into the hundreds of millions of dollars. Here you may find vice presidents reporting to vice presidents.

A network manager generally reports to the chief information officer or someone with the responsibility for technology deployment within the organization. This reporting structure occurs in about 80% of the situations.

I know of some organizations in which the network manager is on the same level as the chief information officer (CIO). In other situations, where the organizations have not joined the modern world, the network manager, sometimes known as the telecommunications manager, is still reporting to the facilities manager. You may be able to ascertain the importance of the network to top management by where the network operation is positioned within the organizational chart.

This book is designed to help those hardworking networking professionals who constantly put their careers on the line as they investigate and employ new systems that come onstream with great rapidity; and, in many instances, they operate without the full and unequivocal support of top management. The trend, though, is in favor of new technology. Top management can no longer ignore the benefits of technology within their operations. Depending on background of the top executives, they may actually take a leading role in the employment and use of technology to ensure a strong competitive posture for their enterprise.

The inspiration for this book originally came from decades of experience in the computer and telecommunications industries as a writer, editor, and publisher for a number of business periodicals in these fields. Over the years I have seen tremendous changes. I have been there when momentous developments were announced or I have had the privilege to interview and meet firsthand many of those movers and shakers in the business and scientific world who made it happen, on both the user and provider sides.

As many of us have learned, keeping track and keeping up with the changes is no easy task. Much happens and it happens quickly. It is not only in the new technology but also in the marketing, distribution, and application of information and communications technology. To add to the perplexity, literally hundreds of vendors have come and gone during the past three decades.

I have heard others refer to this avalanche of information as information overload. It may be difficult at times to keep up with this constantly changing picture, but we, being humans, will always continue to try.

What really brought my thinking to a sharper focus was teaching a graduate-level class on telecommuncations management, essentially networking management, at the Center for Information and Communication Sciences, Ball State University, Muncie, IN. This course was not meant to make a network manager out of a student in one 3-hour semester course, but to cover as many as possible of the more important management tools used by a network manager. When I took possession of the course, I also took possession of its textbook and reading assignments. Being well researched, this wealth of information did a good job of providing reference material for the course. However, I found it still necessary to provide supplementary reading material.

By combining my decades of experience in the computer and communications field with my teaching undertaking, I felt the need to outline a book especially for network managers. Also, in realizing my own limitations, I knew that for assistance I could call on many experts in the various facets of networking, most of whom I have met over the years as an editor and a publisher of business publications directed toward the interests of network managers.

The next step was to contact my many associates in the field. The response was gratifying. *The Network Manager's Handbook* came together as an optimum mix of user, vendor, and academia input. You, as the reader, are offered a combination of both researched knowledge and real-world experience. What you read in this book is the result of a total of hundreds and hundreds of hours of work on the part of many—the chapter authors, their associates, and the talented editors and graphics artists at Auerbach division of CRC Press.

This book is designed as a compendium of technology, management techniques, and related information of interest to organizational network managers to assist them in their daily, as well as their longer term strategic business activities. It will also be a valuable and convenient desk-side reference that covers a wide range of topics for aspiring new network managers, and experienced executives who need to be refreshed on various topics.

The first section deals with the structure of the organization and how the network manager fits in it. In Chapter 1, Thomas Browdy of Washington University points out that the new breed of technological managers must effect a balance between technology, its application, and resources within an enterprise. He adds that the data processing (DP) manager of yesterday has been replaced with a multitalented executive who must step out and lead his or her enterprise technologically.

In Chapter 2, Phil Evans of Perot Systems Corp. points out that the network managers of the 1990s have more choices of services and equipment from more vendors than ever before. Because of the global nature of business, they have the opportunity to employ their choices in more locations than in the past.

The next section deals with maintaining the network. In Chapter 3, Peter Brown writes about the importance of quality management. He relates that the implementation of a quality program takes time, patience, training, and dollars; when it is done appropriately, the payback is a higher level of service, happier employees, and satisfied customers for fewer dollars. Chapters 4 through 6 provide a host of ideas and tools to manage and monitor the network and the applications running on it. Colin Wynd of Hewlett-Packard Co. in Chapter 6 writes that users are starting to expect error-free network connectivity with guaranteed uptime and response times.

At the basic level a network is cabling, according to Arlyn Powell of *Cabling and Installation Maintenance* magazine, and he writes that this is where most of the network failures occur. This section goes on to give ideas on how to set up a help desk operation from Jeff Hafer of GPU Service Inc. An entirely new chapter on network design was written by Kevin Groom and Frank Groom, a professor at Ball State University, who has a wealth of experience in the telecommunications industry.

Without the public carriers of all types there would be no private network. The next section tells who they are, how to deal with them, and how they are regulated. Phyllis Bernt of Ohio University in Chapter 10 writes that network managers have had to understand the complexities of regulation to fully grasp the range of options available for getting effective services at optimum rates. In Chapter 11, Kimberly Russo gives advice on whom they are and how to deal with local and exchange carriers in the U.S. Also, in this section, Christopher Cleveland, consultant for KPMG Peat Marwick LLP, covers the global and international aspects of telecommunications. He deals with the telecommunications environment throughout the world and with the effects of deregulation.

The section on the data network provides the basics of data communications in Chapter 13 by Dale Hibner of Whittman-Hart Inc. He begins by describing LANs and takes the reader out to the wide area network (WAN). Chapter 14 by David Axner of DAX Associates deals with network security.

Historically, voice systems were separate from data networks. With the digitizing of the network, as well as the voice system, it has made good sense to merge the operation of voice and data at some level. The section on voice systems deals with the voice network and its integration with computer systems, planning a cutover of a major voice system, and how to protect against toll fraud. Ed Simonson, president of TeleDesign Management Inc., offers a five-step, proactive solution for fraud prevention.

The next section on new technologies covers a wide range of topics. They include the new high-speed asynchronous transfer mode (ATM) and digital subscriber line (DSL) networks, the Internet as a corporate alternative, wireless networks, telecommuting, and videoconferencing. The network manager now has alternatives in technology and versatility in solving user problems only dreamed about just a few years ago. In Chapter 19, Larry Learn of OCLC Online Computer Library Center Inc., writing about the Internet, exclaims that now is not the time to be *faint of heart*. This new technology, if used correctly, presents unprecedented opportunities for new and improved global marketing and sales, greatly enhanced customer and user support, and greatly facilitated communications within an organization.

The section on the support for network managers focuses on a number of management tools that are available to the network manager. Invaluable tips are given on how to use outsourcing, requests for proposals (RFP), consultants, budgeting, and project management. In Kenneth Harnisch's Chapter 23 on outsourcing, he writes that the technological revolution now under way will undoubtedly accelerate the trend toward outsourcing because the need to manage sophisticated networks requires expertise and resources that many large organizations do not and will not possess. Douglas Ballou gives advice on writing RFPs, and Michael Zivich tells how to select a consultant. Ron Kovac and Antoinette Hubbard are welcomed as new writers in this edition. Ron explains the importance of budgeting as a management tool, while Antoinette details the importance of project management, a widely used tool. Richard Bellaver adds a new chapter on data warehousing and explains its impact on the network.

In the last section, readers are advised about educational opportunities in information and network management in higher education institutions throughout the U.S. and Canada. It is noted that these institutions are excellent recruiting sources for entry-level information system and networking professionals. Finally, Chapter 30 provides tips on sources of information that will help current professionals keep up with changes in information and networking technologies and their related industries.

The book closes with what should be three helpful appendices. The first two provide lists of industry vendors and publications, along with contact information, and the third is a comprehensive glossary of many industry terms and acronyms.

John M. Lusa
Consulting Editor
E-mail: jmlusa@compuserve.com

Chapter 1

The Corporate Information and Communications Hierarchy: Technological Management in Modern Enterprises

Thomas A. Browdy

INTRODUCTION

The impact of technology has changed the way businesses have operated since the 1950s. Accounting machines (precomputers) revealed the ability for technology to efficiently replace processes that were tedious and time-consuming. As these devices grew in impact across the enterprise, their management became much more complex. The data processing (DP) manager of the 1960s and 1970s was concerned with identifying and conquering new processes with automation. The balance for his decision making was between serving a frenetic demand with a two-pronged talented team of analysts and programmers. The analysts were listeners and communicators who could translate what someone wanted into models programmers could understand. Programmers took this new understanding and created workable systems using a "standard" set of computers.

Today the traditional DP manager, with his "one size fits all approach," has almost become a relic. It is no longer a single technology that needs to be managed for process efficiency gains, but multiple technologies that could be critical for business survival or growth. The chief information officer (CIO), or perhaps a team of decentralized information systems (IS) directors, has replaced the traditional DP manager and, in some cases, provides a new way for leadership to interact.

Telecommunications networks, data exchange, satellites, microwave, local area networks (LANs), wide area networks (WANs), switches, fiber optics, twisted pair, private branch exchanges (PBXs), cellular communications, transborder information automation, and a variety of telecommunications standards and proposed standards have all been thrown into a multiplicity of computing environments, creating a mixture that requires a whole new management orientation.

The new technological management orientation should include ways for planning, assessing, and deploying technology within and across enterprises. CIOs or IS leadership teams need to balance technological capability with enterprise capability to become or to stay a modern organization that has a chance of survival. Survivability means not only staying competitive in existing markets but also learning how to adjust quickly to dynamic markets whose changes are founded in unclear global business opportunities and processes, as well as technological innovations.

A continuing challenge is to ensure that the technology infrastructure is in place that services existing and new demands. This is coupled with a push by leaders at the very top of an organization looking for stable growth, along with the disgust of middle managers at not getting all they want from an information services organization (due to lack of budget or skill availability).

A power struggle ensues. Computing is pushed down the line until every department has a computing resource to manage, but little experience in managing it. In such a situation, the CIO or IS leadership team steps in to bring particular rationality to situations that often become irrational (incompatibility of computing devices, networks that do not "talk" to one another, etc.) The power struggle between top leaders, the CIO, and middle business managers has become more than one of budget. It is a struggle about who can make decisions about particular information resources.

ENTERPRISE EFFECTIVENESS

Results of this three-party struggle will contribute to the enterprise's effectiveness. If any one role constantly wins, they all lose. If top leadership wins the case for controlled stable growth, the next technological paradigm shift will be missed and a competitor will quickly pull ahead (airline reservation systems were not a part of a stable growth strategy by many now defunct airlines). Most incumbents in existing markets miss innovation-based para-

Section I
The Management Team

Exhibit 1.   Leadership Imbalance Results

digm shifts, and usually suffer the consequences of losing all or significant pieces of their businesses.

If middle-level business management always wins, there will be a constant changing of direction and technology learning will be stifled (Exhibit 1). Learning will never be able to reach a maturity level, which could spell the difference between enterprisewide effectiveness and point solutions that seldom contribute to the mission. If the CIO always wins, there will be a sophisticated technological infrastructure that no one uses. When one of these positions is weakened by organizational design, private power struggles, or ignorance, then the enterprise becomes less effective and its survival could even be threatened. A balanced power struggle is healthy.

Managing telecommunications within an enterprise is a formidable task. The swirl of technology coupled with the ever-changing business context creates a situation that demands high creativity and sharp intellectual acuity. Along with these characteristics the individual manager is also expected to actually get something done. Being creative and smart is just not enough.

This chapter presents frameworks that should sharpen one's intellectual capability about managing telecommunications; however, more than that, through usage of five case examples, it shows how these frameworks can be creatively applied to actually get something done. The frameworks are provided as a way to understand the parameters of effective technological management (Exhibit 2).

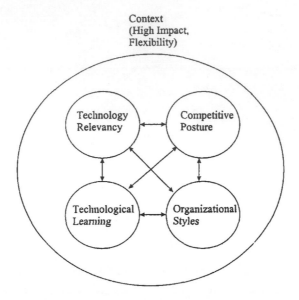

Exhibit 2. Parameters for Technological Management

These parameters include technology context (high expectations of impact, and extreme flexibility), technology relevancy, competitive posture, technological learning, and organizational styles. The effective technological manager can quickly assess the "values" these parameters take on and see how they interact to create a unique but understandable technological environment.

CASE EXAMPLES

Not all enterprises are created equal. This is illustrated by briefly describing five institutions. These institutions will be used throughout the chapter to highlight technological and organizational issues.

MasterCard International Inc.

At MasterCard International a group of potential customers are escorted through the machine room and given a presentation on how networks are managed to ensure fast and efficient processing of information. Pride is clearly intoned by the head network administrator as he comments on how often they identify WAN problems of commercial carriers before the carriers themselves know. MasterCard's expertise about networking has grown since the very beginning of its business. The technology used to keep the network functioning in a reliable manner is aging quickly, and there have been various projects to replace the equipment.

Movement around the halls is fast and furious. People are coming and going to various meetings and conferences. The human resources department has just posted jobs for all varieties of IS positions, and a new management team tries to create a portfolio of projects that will keep the enterprise up to date. Some of these projects are large and aggressive. Even though similar projects have failed in the past, there is still a penchant to strive for success in large projects. Large projects have been international in scope due to purchasing–behavioral differences of cardholders between countries. Internet initiatives have become a serious endeavor, but exactly how to handle this new technology is still an open issue.

The customers for MasterCard are primarily banks, while cardholders are customers of the banks. MasterCard International adds value to its customers by supplying various information products, network services, and advertising. It is owned and operated by its customers—a group of banking and other financial card-issuing institutions.

Smooth Ride Trucking (SMRT)

SMRT, a small- to medium-sized trucking firm nestled in the heart of mid-America, is run by a former driver. As tours are given to existing and potential customers, oohs and aahs can be heard in the plush balcony that overlooks a gymnasium-sized "war room" located behind a one-way glass window. People, quietly seated behind the glass in the hush of semidarkness, overlook the dispatchers' war room. The war room is a beehive of activity and, with its sophisticated information displays, reminds one of the movie *War Games*. The room contains an impressive array of 15-sq ft video projected images showing summary load distributions, individual truck locations, and weather conditions across North America.

The war room is both a function for dispatchers and a marketing device for potential customers. By building on the tradition of transporting soda bottles without breakage, this enterprise continues to move all sorts of delicate cargo. Specially equipped trailers and attention to driver care for cargo have remained parts of their tradition. SMRT handles delicate loads with routes that primarily go north and south to Canada and Mexico. For the southern routes trailers are usually dropped off just over the border, and drivers from Mexico take the cargo to its final destination. After losing equipment through various pilfering schemes, contracts were negotiated with the Mexican trucking firms on penalties for lost goods (including cargo, trailers, and trailer equipment).

One of the competitive edges the enterprise has is accurate and efficient dispatching. Trucks across the U.S. and parts of Mexico and Canada are constantly monitored to make sure few of them are without loads between destinations. It is not good business to have empty trailers traveling too far without a load. Ideally for every load that is dropped off the trailer is re-filled for a new destination. Each dispatcher has earned his stripes behind the wheel. The owner and president, being a former driver, maintains the rule that dispatchers have to know how drivers are thinking to make the drivers' jobs efficient.

Coupled with dispatcher expertise is a set of medium-sized computers that supports war room activities. Drivers are given cellular phones for official and private use. Each truck also has a telecommunications device that provides positioning information to dispatchers. The sophistication that has provided a competitive advantage is now becoming available to small independent trucking enterprises. This company feels compelled to take on the next network or computing challenge to maintain its market position. It hears the competition on its heels.

Big Auto Leasing (BIGAL)

From humble beginnings as a small dealership to one of the largest available fleets in the world, BIGAL competes aggressively on renting, selling, and leasing autos. It is a privately held company that has experienced exponential growth. BIGAL is within the top 10 companies that buy and "move" autos from manufacturing to ownership.

Local offices are opened with assistant managers learning their craft by washing autos—it is often heard on the lots that this is a company where "everyone starts from the bottom." An army of drivers, mostly part-time workers, are constantly moving autos from one location to another—sometimes to fulfill customer demands, sometimes in anticipation of demand (a large convention), and other times to level out the fleet across geographic locations (multiple states could be involved in any of these).

One of the biggest problems the company faces is knowing vehicle location. Each branch office has a significant number of vehicles. Operational decisions need to balance an ever-aging fleet (moving out older models) against individual and dealership customers who may want to buy, rent, or lease. An individual dealership purchase of a fleet of "program" cars from BIGAL is a critical part of this company's business.

BIGAL has one of the largest medium-sized computer environments in the world (housing a multitude of medium-sized computers in one location). Its communication technology is primarily satellite-based microwave. Using this communication capability each office reports its activities during the day to aid decision making about its multitude of vehicles.

Washington University (WU)

While strolling the Washington University campus, gothic architecture and the appearance of students and professors elicit a vision of great minds at work. WU is a private research and education-based institution of higher learning located in St. Louis, MO. Freshman students make decisions about attending WU vs. other institutions such as Yale, Stanford, Princeton, Cornell, Northwestern, and Carnegie-Mellon. Along with high value comes a high cost. However, each of these institutions has endowments that support scholarships for those whose qualifications add quality to each admitted class. Students are housed in campus dorms and in various individually leased or rented apartments located nearby.

The university includes schools of arts and sciences, engineering and applied science, medicine, business, social work, law, fine arts, and architecture. There is also a first-class library and supporting libraries in most of the schools. Departments of computer science and information management are housed in the engineering school.

The university is operated in a decentralized fashion with each school responsible for its own budget, academic viability, and services. Some services are provided through central administration, including development, physical plant, accounting and finance, human resources, and computing. Each school also has its own small version of the central services, including computing. Schools have their own computing lab environments that may attach to central administration services. Even some departments run their own computer labs. The central administration is also responsible for an electronic network and communications, including one of the first major Internet sites. Dorms and offices are wired for network communications.

The dean of the library holds the CIO position for the university. Administrative systems are very old (most written in the 1970s), and there has been little interest in investing in such systems.

Both full- and part-time students make up the university community. Part-time students take courses in the evening usually taught by adjunct faculty. Distance learning has been discussed, but the strategy is to maintain a classroom environment with classes taught by highly qualified faculty.

Amazon.com

This Internet-based business is one of the most popular examples cited for electronic-commerce. The quick and almost immediate success of Amazon.com has been both exciting to e-commerce entrepreneurs and feared by many traditional businesses. Started just a few years ago, this business provides a specialized link between book purchaser and publisher.

Because Amazon.com is able to establish partnerships with publishers and book warehouses, it is able to offer a tremendous variety of books from a single source, which can be accessed at anytime, and almost from anywhere. While it has no actual storage of books, the ability to present a book

9

to a potential customer, along with ancillary services such as reviews and titles of similar books, has created a very powerful business. Special services are provided in terms of preference searches, as well as searches by author, topic, and title. Links to other services such as chat rooms are also provided.

Because of its success, and the potential of e-commerce, Amazon.com has become a well-known brand name for bookstores—even though it has no frontal footage in any mall or along any street. It has given "bookstore" a new meaning. One might say its telecommunications environment is its real business, along with adequate computing power to service Internet requests. Amazon.com must also pay attention to traditional front and back office information systems to carry out its business.

Defining Characteristics

Each enterprise possesses a set of defining characteristics, including people, business or market, location, size, structure, culture, and technology. The combination of these characteristics creates a unique enterprise not to be replicated anywhere. It is easy to forget this principle of uniqueness when common measures such as financial performance, market share, and service performance are used for comparison purposes. These comparisons can lead to actions that mimic those taken by another company in an attempt to achieve a similar outcome.

However, what MasterCard does to be successful will not be the same as SMRT, as BIGAL, or as WU. What is common between enterprises is not as great as what is different. Yet, we can speak in generalities about enterprises to understand how to manage them. Technology relevance is one of these generalities.

TECHNOLOGY RELEVANCY AND COMPETITIVE POSTURE

Network managers are expected to provide key insights on telecommunications technology investment for their enterprises. One way to gain insight into telecommunications investment is to consider the current vs. future enterprise relevancy of telecommunications technology. The importance of telecommunications technology varies according to type of industry, how an individual enterprise competes in that industry, and the impact of industry changes. A given level of telecommunications usage may or may not be appropriate for where an enterprise is now. The same can be said about the future. If future events are envisioned that require additional telecommunications capability, then these kinds of projects need to be considered today. Exhibit 3 shows a relevancy grid for telecommunications technology. Determining where one is positioned on this grid may spell the difference between future success or failure.

Future Relevance

	Low	High
Present Relevance Low	Support	Transitioning
High	Sustaining	Strategic

Exhibit 3. Telecommunication Relevancy Grid

Future Relevance

	Low	High
Present Relevance Low	Universities	Trucking
High	Auto Leasing	Financial

Exhibit 4. Industry-specific Telecommunications Orientations

Industries, in general, may be placed on the relevancy grid. This gives one a place to start when considering an individual company (Exhibit 4).

Because each enterprise has a unique way it competes, blindly assigning an enterprise to a position on the relevancy grid strictly on the grounds of industry type may be unwise. Traditional market competitive analysis says that an enterprise can compete on *cost*, *differentiation*, or *niche*. The combination of industry technology relevancy, competitive posture, and available expertise provides guidance for where a particular enterprise falls on the grid. See Exhibit 5 for where our five case examples fall.

The example cases are completely predictable by industry type according to Exhibit 5. However, with a little more detail on one of the cases we can see how it could change positions. Suppose at WU we decided to initiate distance learning, begin recruiting freshmen through the Internet or

11

Future Relevance

		Low	High
Present Relevance	Low	WU	SMRT
	High	BIGAL	MasterCard Amazon

Exhibit 5.   Telecommunication Relevance For Case Examples

multimedia, and initiate research consortia through electronic sharing of research results that may include nontext-based medical diagnostic documents. The ability for multiple researchers at multiple locations to share information quickly is assumed to create the synergy to drive the research toward early conclusions and perhaps more funding.

At WU, future telecommunications technology capability will play a key role. Hence, the relevancy moves from *support* to *transitioning*. Relevancy should be coupled with a competitive posture to make clearer what, in particular, needs to be planned. Coupling relevance with competitive posture permits us to see what technology may be applicable. For example, if WU is a low-cost provider, then telecommunications technology can be used to increase volume. If WU is competing by *differentiation*, then one way to apply technology would be to use the Internet to increase the quality of the freshman class (Exhibit 6).

Support relevance suggests there is little need for planning significant changes to the telecommunications infrastructure. *Sustaining* indicates the current level of investment must continue, and the network manager needs to ensure contributions to the business remain visible so that they may continue. A *transitioning* enterprise means the network manager will be required to identify projects and gather resources to raise the telecommunications environment to a new plane. For *strategic*, the current investment needs to remain visible and future investment opportunities need to be identified and planned (Exhibit 7).

The big challenge looming before us in the business world is to be able to choose between learning our businesses as they continually evolve, which implies looking for competitive advantage through technology; or responding to transmutations of business segments, which implies using technology to create and compete in dynamic markets.

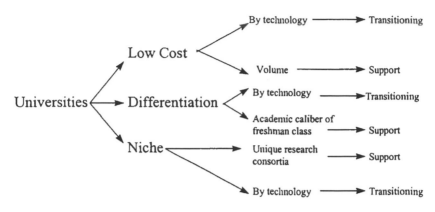

Exhibit 6. Telecommunication Relevancy for WU

Exhibit 7. Investment Posture by Telecommunications Relevancy

Telecommunications Relevancy	Investment Posture
Support	Keep budget
Sustaining contribution	Keep attention focused on current
Transitioning	Plan new telecommunications portfolio
Strategic portfolios	Balance between current and future

Due to globalization of businesses—including production and market implications, and innovative connectivity technologies such as the Internet—markets have become much more dynamic in this decade and will continue to do so well into the next. One of the general goals of many companies has been to strive for competitive advantage using technology. Since markets have become so dynamic, this goal may need to be replaced with one that utilizes technology to create and participate in dynamic markets. To illustrate this point, consider Amazon.com books and Britannica Encyclopedia.

With Amazon.com, what was a very traditional market became much more dynamic with the use of the Internet to sell books. One needs only to access Amazon.com on the Internet at anytime from anywhere, use a provided search mechanism, order a book or books, wait a few days, and it or they arrive at your doorstep. Responses by Barnes and Noble and others are bringing their own new added dimensions to selling books. This has become a changing market.

The ease of customers choosing between companies and products, customers who may visit at any time from almost anywhere, and integrative services contribute to this new era of dynamic markets. The next three characteristics present demands on those who expect to compete. First, the new ease that customers have to choose among companies means brand identity of the company will become more important and in new ways open cross-selling approaches (e.g., buying music compact discs [CDs] as well as books at Amazon.com). Second, customers visiting at any time from almost anywhere means there has to be a sustainable connectivity and responsiveness capability. Third, integrative services means bringing together in one place responses to direct as well as tangential customer needs and interests (e.g., getting a loan from the same place you purchase an auto).

Britannica did not consider the three demands of customer ease of choice, potential ubiquitous access, and integrated services, which resulted in it getting driven from the market by a lower quality product partnered with a personal computer operating system (i.e., Encarta and Windows). Britannica had brand identity, but it failed to understand the interests of customers to look up information with ease and the ability to integrate that information with other tasks (e.g., using it while writing a term paper). These new demands require a leadership that can think about future possibilities, as well as an appropriate technology infrastructure. Although there are other considerations in analyzing the negative outcome of Britannica, failure to realize the dynamic nature of its market contributed significantly to a disaster from which the company may never recover.

OVERALL TECHNOLOGY IMPACT

Modern planning practices have shifted from reducing everything to the lowest level of control, toward understanding what "containing whole," or context, the enterprise is a part of. To this end we should consider in which technology sea our enterprise finds itself afloat. Two important context issues are stability and flexibility of the environment, and technological synergistic effects.

Regardless of an enterprise's position on the relevancy grid almost every enterprise will have to deal with telecommunications technology in some form. What we have experienced, and will experience for some time, is the impact of technological component synergy. Technological component synergy occurs when mutually dependent, yet independently developed, technologies come together in a way that creates something new.

The DC 3 aircraft is a prime example for commercial aviation. Independent development of retractable landing gear, flaps, wing structure, and powerful engines, coupled with a desire from the public to travel at faster rates from coast to coast, came together in the DC 3. The importance of component interdependencies was not realized until the idea of commercial air travel became a problem someone thought solvable.

The personal computer was also a result of technological component synergy. The combination of computer on a chip, display devices, electrical printers, word processing, and eventually spreadsheet software, along with an increasing demand in office environments, led to a computing sea change.

Technological component synergy is also driving telecommunications technology. Components that are a part of this synergistic effect are fast switches, installed communication links, standards, communications interfaces (e.g., the Navigator browser from Netscape Communications Corp.), and Internet feeding frenzy by the general public. Few enterprises will be immune from the effects of this new technological component synergy. This means not just understanding where you are now technologically speaking, but where you want to be in the future.

The new imperative of modern enterprises is flexibility within constraints of intense competition. To become a *low-cost producer* means acquiring that capability usually through repeated trial and error refinements (continuous process improvement, as an example). However, to continue to improve the processes that are in place means to entrench the enterprise farther into what is *currently* important. Enterprise flexibility requires a focus on the future and could result in changing the way of doing business—the business product or products, the target customers, the suppliers, the workers, the geographic location, etc. To compete by *differentiation*, flexibility means finding new ways to make product or products different. Flexibility for a *niche* strategy could mean making or finding a new niche within which to compete.

Constant exploration of what can be done and creative solutions to problems of work force integration, coupled with the wisdom of controlled expansion, characterize modern organizations. The new era of flexibility requires telecommunications technology be managed to achieve the connectivity necessary to compete and remain agile. In fact, the agility of many enterprises is their ability to establish a multiplicity of communications modes, while in others it is a more narrowly focused telecommunications approach.

TECHNOLOGY LEARNING

Every significant technology goes through a learning process. If one can decide where he fits on a technology learning curve, then actions can be taken to move to a more mature usage of the technology. The learning curve has four distinct phases (flex points on the curve). Phase I is an initial exposure of the technology to a select group; phase II is expanded usage with contagious effects within and across enterprises. In phase III there is a recognition that the uncontrolled nature of experiences needs to be controlled so standards for usage are put into place, and phase IV is widespread assimilation. How much one pays attention to enterprise learning issues depends on how relevant the technology is to the enterprise.

15

Exhibit 8.   Learning Curve Attention

Relevancy Position	Learning Phases			
	Phase I Initiation	Phase II Expansion	Phase III Control	Phase IV Assimilation
Strategic	High	High	High	High
Transitioning	High	High	High	Low
Sustaining	High	High	Low	Low
Supporting	High	Low	Low	Low

Exhibit 8 relates technology relevancy to effort expended within each phase. Phase I needs to be traversed no matter the relevancy position, while high effort for phase IV is suggested for only the strategic relevancy condition.

Exhibit 9 shows how managerial actions differ by what phase of learning an organization is in with respect to telecommunications technology. Management's job will shift as the enterprise becomes more and more aware of how telecommunications technology will affect the organization. There is little doubt that everyone will eventually go through phases I and II. Phases III and IV should be traversed by those who see telecommunications technology as becoming critical for their enterprise.

Exhibit 9.   Managerial Action Examples

Action	Organic Style		Mechanistic Style	
	Phase I Initiation	Phase II Expansion	Phase III Control	Phase IV Assimilation
Projects	Experimental projects (some fail) For example, provide connections to the Internet Information exploration projects	Establish connections with various users For example, home pages on the Internet Online catalogs with phone numbers and e-mail responses	Connected LANs, client/server projects For example, implementation of intranets	Interorganizational systems For example, knowledge sharing among professionals Integrated supplier and buyer chain
Key decisions	Initiate a special project team Educate small group Outsource LAN install (learn) Secure WAN connectivity	Hire telecommunications expertise Negotiate WAN capability Install additional LANs	Develop network management function Become a telecommunications-enabled buyer (electronic data interchange [EDI])	Provide a secure telecommunications environment—both physically and logically

ORGANIZATIONAL STYLE

Where telecommunications technology fits in the enterprise depends on the current organizational style and what enterprise contribution telecommunications will have in the future. Organizational style may be characterized as *organic* or *mechanistic*. Mechanistic organizations are command- and control-centric, hierarchically run, concerned with production efficiency (both service or product), structured planning and control techniques, and monolithic in how projects are approached (not given to an experimental and research orientation). Organic organizations are loosely controlled, group- or team-oriented, flat chain of command, and concerned with intra- and inter-enterprise boundary spanning.

Mechanistic enterprises are very good at continuous process improvement (usually leading to low cost) because they can enact the standards that come with operational efficiencies. Telecommunications technology can enable mechanistic organizations to behave in flexible ways, contributing to long-term survival. Cross-functional networked teams can reach into the heart of an enterprise and provide a new view of what could be done and is being done. Such teams have been used to initiate new businesses, to attack immediate problems, as well as to seek out new ways in which a business can reintegrate itself internally among divisions, departments, and staff; as well as externally with markets, customers, and other institutions. This is using telecommunications to enable an organic overlay on a mechanistic organization to keep it competitive.

Changes are incremental by nature within mechanistic enterprises; hence, planning is a critical issue. Plans should be of two varieties: one dealing with infrastructure and the other, with penetration of the effect of telecommunications on the enterprise's products and services. (This is a telecommunications relevancy issue as discussed earlier.) Managing telecommunications in such an environment means providing "official" mechanisms by which telecommunications capabilities are installed, maintained, and supported. For the network manager, it means trying to stay ahead of the demand curve both in volume and sophistication.

This may be done with official surveys (not terribly popular with participants), help facilities (resource laden), sponsorship of events depicting the next wave of telecommunications capability during which individuals discover a viable usage for the technology, or initiating projects that may seem risky due to complexity of the technology involved.

Projects that use sophisticated technology do not lend themselves to planning, but they may be a necessary organic overlay to sustain a competitive posture. Organic overlays for the mechanistic structure of Master-Card are critical moves to keep its telecommunications technology relevant. The company overlays include running large projects with fairly loose controls.

Organic organizations, due to their nature, often need to provide a "control overlay" so technology can mature beyond phase II of learning. Organic organizations, while flat, usually have a residual hierarchy that serves to integrate teams or groups; and provide a communication mechanism for top leadership, owners, or board of directors. Teams or groups are enabled by a participant from the team or group representing them, to the residual hierarchy. A committee made up of these representatives, when required to meet regularly, can function as a mechanistic overlay to the organic organization. One of the functions of this committee is to provide a control point for technological decisions.

For network managers, this committee is critical. Otherwise, each team or group may enact its own standards and technology infrastructure sometimes serving to disintegrate activities that, through telecommunications technology, could be integrated for the good of the enterprise. The issue is not to remake an organic organization into a mechanistic one, but to engage the enterprise in control activities that mature telecommunications to phase IV. Phases III and IV are critical for organizations whose telecommunications technology is transitioning the technology or is of strategic relevance.

WU requires a committee, appointed by deans of its respective schools, to make sure there is telecommunications compatibility that reaches within the schools. While students have majors in each school and departments within schools all support particular programs, the push for across school eclectic experiences by students is very real. Also, departments are sharing intellectual resources to conduct research and secure research funding. For the organic WU enterprise this committee provides a mechanistic overlay that reinforces the mission of education and research.

For an enterprise such as BIGAL that is experiencing phenomenal growth, the organizational style is moving from organic to mechanistic. To survive, a more mechanistic structure is needed to control the vast numbers of people and resources. Telecommunications projects are critical because information needs to be consolidated and used for effective decision making. Telecommunications decision making, as well as other decision making, becomes more centralized in keeping with the move toward a more mechanistic structure. Hence, planning for telecommunications has been a part of the core planning process for the business.

SUMMARY

The parameters of technology context (expected impact and flexibility), technology relevance, competitive posture, technological learning, and or-

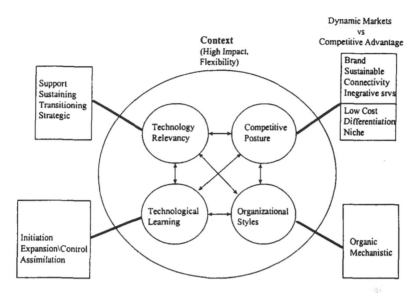

Exhibit 10. Parameters and Values for Technological Management

ganizational styles each have "values" they take on. For instance, one could be managing telecommunications technology with a transitioning relevancy, in a differentiation posture, in a flexible and high technological impact context, at an expansion phase (phase II) of learning, and within a mechanistic organization. Given these values, one manages differently in terms of planning and control, kinds of projects initiated, and how much relative attention to spend in a particular phase of learning.

There are over 300 possible "solutions spaces" given these parameters and their respective values. One cannot learn them all (and some parameters are undoubtedly missing), but one can develop the agility to manage according to what the possibilities are. It will take high creativity and sharp intellectual acuity, along with the energy to actually get something done (Exhibit 10).

The new reality for technological managers involves flexibility while remaining competitive. This calls for a flexible style of organization, led either directly, or indirectly through overlays, by a powerful technological management. The new breed of technology managers should be able to think abstractly through such frameworks as presented in this chapter and others. The new breed of technology managers can participate to effect a balance between technology, its application, and resources within an enterprise. Also, they ought to understand implications for various technologies, take up the slack for novice management of other computing resources, be advocates for particular technological solutions, and generally be held accountable for how technology affects the enterprise. The DP manager of yesterday has been and is being replaced with multitalented executives who step out and lead their enterprises technologically.

Chapter 2
The Changing Role of the Network Manager
Phil Evans

INTRODUCTION

Over the past three decades the role of the network manager has changed in many aspects while remaining fairly consistent in others. Throughout this period the network manager and telecommunications staff of most companies have been viewed rather consistently by executive management as "necessary overhead" that, while necessary, is extraneous to the core business and therefore to be minimized.

Attitudes are slowly changing as corporations have become absolutely dependent upon pervasive, effective communications to profitably run the business, but that change in attitude often results in the telecommunications function being outsourced to a company whose core business is technology. At the same time, the changes wrought by technology advancements and telecommunications legislation/regulation have created a dynamic new environment unparalleled in business history.

The network managers of the '90s have more choices of services and equipment from more vendors than ever experienced, and because of the global nature of business they have the opportunity to employ their choices in more locations than ever. The 1990s are indeed exciting times in all facets of Information Technology, but none more so than in telecommunications management.

Within this chapter we will trace the evolution of the network manager through the decades of 1970s, '80s, and '90s, and review the inexorable changes in technology, global business/political issues, telecommunications legislation/regulation, and the corresponding responses by the telecommunications industry as they all combine to direct and change the role of the network manager.

Through these three decades the whole telecommunications world has been turned upside down, primarily because of the growing pervasiveness of technology. As technology advanced, business was forced to either embrace change and adapt for competitive advantage, or face extinction as it was left in the wake of its competitors. The combination of business and technology forces brought so much pressure to bear on legislative and regulatory bodies that deregulation of the "natural monopoly" of telecommunications (the breakup of the Bell System) became a reality in the United States in the mid '80s, and soon was being followed by governments of developed nations around the world.

With deregulation came vast opportunities for entrepreneurs who envisioned new ways of applying telecommunications-enabled technology solutions to business as markets rapidly progressed from local to national to global. Caught up in all this change, much like a surfer who is engulfed in a monstrous wave, is the network manager, along with the telecommunications staff, who are responsible for the design, engineering, provisioning, operation, maintenance, and administration of the corporate networks.

Simply stated, the functions of the network manager have remained somewhat consistent through the three decades as:

Manager   Staff, networks, terminal equipment, budget
Engineer   Networks, terminal equipment, facilities
Innovator Adaptation of new services and equipment
Negotiator Doing more with less

Over the course of time, however, the role of the network manager within these functions has changed dramatically as the forces mentioned above, and described in the following sections, have become manifest.

THE 1970s: MONOPOLY/SCARCITY/INNOVATION/FRUSTRATION

Background

Network managers of the 1970s had a relatively uncomplicated existence. The "natural monopoly" telephone services were engineered and manufactured to provide service life measured in decades, effectively stifling technological advances. A limited number of telecommunications equipment and service options were obtained from a menu of tariffed offerings from the Bell System and a handful of independent telephone carriers that served the less-populated areas.

Because there were limited telecommunications options, and because business was generally regional or national in scope, the corporate telecommunications staffs were usually small in number. Of course there were exceptions, such as the major petroleum companies that constructed their own radio and microwave systems to serve remote areas in which they operated but where commercial services were nonexistent.

For the most part, however, network managers concerned themselves with the voice and message services provided by the monopoly carriers, and with the fledgling data services that were beginning to emerge. Limited services, and even more limited service monitoring/reporting capabilities, teamed to frustrate the network manager and telecommunications staff in the early to mid 1970s, but relief began to emerge and the profession took on new meaning by the latter days of the decade.

Voice Services

Interconnection of the company PBXs in the various geographical locations around the nation was a routine function of the network manager of the '70s. Such "tandem trunking" required engineering of the PBXs to accommodate the mix of in-bound, out-bound, and two-way trunks as well as administration of the dialing plans that numerically specified the dialing patterns. Traffic engineering — the allocation of the required number of proper trunks to accommodate demand — basically was nonexistent due to absence of accurate and timely usage reports.

The telephone company occasionally would run "busy studies" to determine how many calls were blocked due to inadequate trunks, but such studies were few and far between and of little value in engineering system capacities. Likewise, the telephone company occasionally would provide a "service observer" to monitor PBX operator efficiency, thereby providing some additional insight into the adequacy of the PBX services, but very little insight, indeed. User complaints were the normal impetus for making changes; proactive planning was only a dream for network managers.

The best source of usage information, or user demand, was the detailed billing records provided by the telephone companies. Unfortunately, the bills were generally several months in arrears and consisted of reams of printed paper, with billing data ordered and summarized by individual. Analysis of the data to determine traffic patterns by month, day, and hour amounted to tedious sifting through the volumes of paper to get some indication of what happened months ago. Ability to respond to the present telecommunications needs of the company personnel was therefore minimal.

Rotary-dial telephones in your choice of black, green, or tan were available in single-line, key (multiple lines), and Call Director (greater capacity multiple lines) models to sit behind a limited number of PBX models that varied by trunk/station line capacity and operator features. Touch-tone phones in models comparable to the rotary-dial phones were available at additional cost. As the 1980s approached, electronic PBXs with enhanced features and functions, and Centrex services, began to appear, providing network managers choices and capabilities of expanded proportions.

WATS (Wide Area Telephone Services) lines were introduced to the delight of the business community, for with WATS came discounts on long-distance telephone service, a concept previously untried by the Bell System. The nation was divided into six inter-state zones that radiated in progressively larger concentric circles from the various cities/states throughout the nation, plus a seventh zone for intra-state calls. Zone 6, the most expensive service, included the entirety of the contiguous 48 states; Zone 5, the next most expensive service, included all but the states most distant from the city in question; Zone 4 included still fewer states, etc. Zone 1 included only those states that were contiguous with the city/state in question.

WATS service was available in either full-time (24 hours/day, 31 days/month) or measured-time (set number of hours per month plus per hour charges for excess usage) options. The WATS zone pattern was different for every state. Users behind PBXs theoretically would compare the area code of the number they were about to dial to the lowest numbered WATS Zone that included that area code, and thereby use the most economical service.

Users had to dial a different access code for each WATS Zone, and since there were a limited number of WATS lines being contended for by numerous users, busy signals were common. Users quickly learned to dial progressively higher (and more expensive) WATS access codes as they sought to gain access to complete their toll calls. There initially were no monitoring devices to control user access, and no ways of monitoring calls to ascertain they were legitimate business calls. Network managers were faced with rapidly rising costs and no effective means to control them.

In response to the out-of-control WATS cost escalation, several companies designed and made commercially available computer-controlled telephone access devices to force calls on to the least expensive available WATS line. It also recorded who called what number at what time by day, date, the duration of the call, the WATS trunk over which the call was completed, the total traffic served by each WATS trunk, and other data relevant to almost real-time control of corporate telecommunications assets. The Action WATSBox and the Data Point Infoswitch were two popular models that enabled network managers, for the first time, to not only control use of corporate assets, but to also bill by usage to individuals grouped by cost centers, and to determine when the WATS lines were not functioning properly and so notify the telephone company.

Other entrepreneurs, encouraged by the successes of the WATS control systems, developed and introduced systems for monitoring and managing all services through the PBX, including computerized call accounting. AIOD (Automated Identification of Out-dialed Numbers) empowered the network manager to ensure efficiency through accurate and real-time system usage information. Service improvements and cost reductions were dramatic, and the latter days of the '70s were some of the best for network managers.

Message and Data Services

TTYs (teletypewriters) were the message and data terminals of the early to mid '70s. NASA put the first man on the moon using TTYs for telemetry relays from stations around the world. They were slow and feature-limited, but they were extremely reliable. TTY models provided either five-level Baudot or eight-level ASCII code, and they came with and without keyboards, paper tape punches, and paper tape readers, depending on the particular models. Three-hundred baud was the typical transmission rate.

Network managers engineered the message and data systems based on user requirements, traffic volumes, location of corporate offices, and the line expenses associated with connection of the TTYs. Hubs were generally provided in the corporate message center to receive — in punched paper tape format — messages from foreign offices, and to relay the messages to the addressed offices via punched paper tape readers. Such "hubbing" obviated the need for expensive connections from foreign offices to all domestic offices. International message service providers were few, consisting primarily of ITT Worldcom and RCA Globecom. Negotiating favorable price and service contracts was a challenge, since the international record carrier options were few.

Data frequently was transmitted via TTY at the 300 baud transmission speed, but dumb terminals and 1.2- and 2.4K-bps modems were appearing on the business scene. By the mid '70s, 9.6K-bps modems the size of small refrigerators were being rolled into corporate computer rooms on dollies, and network managers were thrilled with the new high-speed capabilities. With the increased speed, however, came the necessity for "clean" transmission lines, and the corresponding requirement for methods to monitor line performance. Network monitoring systems and line "conditioning" became a requirement to ensure optimal data throughput, and so the network manager and telecom staff were faced with new challenges.

From these new data services emerged the dedicated data networks that progressively occupied the network manager's attention. Additionally, networking became more complicated and expensive, since there were now three networks interconnecting corporate locations: a voice network, a message network, and a data network. With such network segmentation came territorial disputes within many companies.

The Data Processing Department claimed ownership of the data network, which was generally originated by the Office Services Department. Data Processing frequently won the territorial battle for data networking. When such segregation occurred, two network managers and two telecommunications staffs resulted, and territorial disputes grew in frequency and intensity. Network managers were forced to add arbitration to their skill set by the close of the decade of the 1970s.

THE 1980s:
DEREGULATION/CONFUSION/COMPETITION/OPPORTUNITY

Background

Technological advancements stimulated by the successes of the space program, a healthy business climate that was expanding globally, and the willingness of business to invest in data processing and automation systems combined to create an atmosphere of discontent with the restrictiveness of the "natural monopoly" position of the telephone companies. At the same time, a company that has been called "a law office with a microwave tower," MCI, was attracting a lot of attention with its reduced pricing for services that competed, to a limited degree, with the Bell System. Pressure built for both federal and state legislation that would deregulate the Bell System and stimulate competition.

By the mid '80s such legislation was forthcoming, and the Bell System was broken into seven RBOCS (Regional Bell Operating Companies) plus the AT&T, Western Electric, Bell Labs consortium. Through the latter portion of the 1980s competitive services and enhanced, computer-based telecommunications systems were introduced at an ever-increasing rate. Never had network managers had so much choice, both in terms of systems/services, and from so many sources. The magnitude of choice was a blessing and a curse because it was now incumbent on the network manager to pick "the best" solution from a growing number of available solutions that were being continually enhanced and/or obsoleted by new technology models. How to stay current and efficient while maintaining compatibility and protecting embedded investments became the dominant issue for network managers.

Voice Services

Through the first half of the 1980s, voice services remained a combination of PBX trunks and private lines/OPXs (Off Premise eXtensions), often augmented by private microwave systems that connected offices with high volumes of traffic between them. Network managers had the continuing challenges of quality of service, availability of service, and the cost-effective mix of various types of services necessary to satisfy user demands. Full-time vs. measured-time WATS services by zones, OPXs, one-way vs. two-way PBX trunks, and other line options were in continual need of evaluation as corporations expanded, contracted, added, and deleted various office facilities.

Likewise, PBX models as compared to Centrex systems were frequently being evaluated for meeting the needs of the business. Fortunately, the computer-based call accounting systems and network monitoring systems cited above were becoming more affordable as they were simultaneously becoming more capable in terms of features, function, and capacity. Cost control, allocations by usage, and network engineering statistics were all within the network manager's reach; and fortunately so, as a new service called "voice mail" was being employed at an ever-increasing rate. The trunking requirements, systems training, and management of voice mail systems occupied much of the network manager's time within numerous companies during the '80s.

In the latter half of the 1980s, T1 services, and the associated muxs (multiplexers), were introduced at rates that were extremely attractive to large businesses. Network managers felt one of their main prayers had been answered: voice and data could be mixed on the same transmission system, and at a fraction of the price of competing services. The "rule of thumb" was that a T1 line was affordable if there were six dedicated voice and/or data lines between two locations, and T1 provided the equivalent capacity of 24 voice lines.

The appeal was irresistible, and network managers busied themselves engineering T1 connections across their networks. Unfortunately, the T1 services, and the associated muxs of the 1984-1986 era, were prone to frequent service disruptions; and to a user, there is nothing subtle about network disruptions, especially during phone conversations. Exacerbating this nightmare for network managers was the inability to monitor T1 lines in a nondisruptive manner.

If you wanted the line checked by the providing telephone company, you had to move all users from the line and turn it over to repair for an undetermined period of time with only slim hopes the problem would be detected and repaired. What had appeared to be the answer to the prayers of network managers had, during its first two years of its introductory stage, become a curse of severe magnitude, and no small number of network managers lost their jobs because of the disparity between what had been promised and what was delivered.

For those network managers who survived the T1 debacle of the mid-'80s, conditions improved significantly with the 1986-1988 introduction of three successive telecommunications services brought on by the irresistible forces of technology and competition: fiber-optic cabling was installed across the nation by WilTel and Sprint, thereby motivating AT&T to do likewise for competitive equality. Extended SuperFrame was incorporated into T1 networks and into associated DSU/CSU hardware; and switched digital services were introduced. These three service enhancements had a profoundly positive impact on the whole telecommunications industry. Fiber-

27

optic networks are basically immune to most of the perturbations inherent to copper, coax, and microwave transmission systems, and therefore provide a quality of service only dreamed of before.

Extended SuperFrame, or ESF, as it is commonly called, provided a non-intrusive means of monitoring T1 lines. Switched digital lines provided 56K-bps and T1 connections that could be employed as needed, such as in migrating users off a dedicated T1 line when the T1 was beginning to suffer degradation, or providing extra capacity during periods of high user demand or in disaster recovery situations. These and similar improvements across the entire tele-processing industry provided the basis for the movement of information processing from computer-centricity to network-centricity.

Message and Data Services

"Smart" terminals that were network-connected to mainframe computers soon replaced the TTYs as business progressively embraced the numerous benefits wrought by technology and competition. Local area networks (LANs) grew in importance while wide area networks (WANs) continued to spread across the nation and into the far corners of the earth, thanks to increasingly reliable, affordable, and capable telecommunications networks and support systems. SNA/SDLC transmission protocol that replaced Bisync was soon being replaced itself by TCP/IP.

Network managers found themselves running hard to stay abreast of the rapid developments in the data world, both in the WAN and LAN environments, and new e-mail services were beginning to appear with their own set of capability and compatibility issues. The technologically advanced new world of competitive tele-processing offered significant opportunities, and significant challenges.

Facsimile, or "fax" as it is commonly known, languished for decades because of the presence of proprietary transmission protocols that precluded one manufacturer's machines from "talking" to the machines of another manufacturer. When standards finally emerged to enable all machines to communicate among themselves, the fax business exploded for a while, challenging the network managers to engineer effective networks and create efficient means of message management. E-mail and computer-based traffic has diminished the value of fax, but it still is a service commonly found in all businesses and many homes.

Staffing Challenges

All of the rapid advances in tele-processing strained the network manager's staff to maintain familiarity with new service offerings and the features/functions and costs associated therewith. During the late '80s the network manager's prime focus began to shift from network engineering/design and operations to staffing, training, cost modeling, and self-education to stay familiar with the rapid onslaught of new service and equipment offerings. Engineering and technical responsibilities were progressively absorbed by the telecommunications staff.

The telecommunications staff now had to be able to intelligently evaluate competitive data transport systems and recommend the one best suited for the company's present and future applications. Issues of capacity, compatibility, monitoring and reporting capabilities, vendor support, and other features/functions had to be weighed against cost and equipment availability to select the best multiplexers, modems, DSU/CSUs, and network monitoring systems from among many competitive choices.

Training had to be provided to enable staff members to competently work with new hardware and software systems as they were introduced into the corporate network, and new staff members with different skill sets had to be recruited. All of these demands forced the network manger to spend progressively more time creating business cases and making proposals to executive management, and in attempting to explain why such "increased overhead" was actually beneficial.

Network Performance

Although network performance was relatively poor during the early part of the '80s, low-speed data running robust protocols seemed to satisfy most user needs of the day, and voice was acceptable, as were message services. As time progressed, however, the needs created by technology advances in mainframes and network-connected computers and terminals, and the corresponding dependency of business on fast and reliable networking, forced network managers to seek improvements continually.

Speed improvements became available through advances in modems and multiplexers at a rate much faster than the network improvements required to accommodate the higher-speed equipment. Everyone associated with information processing was pressing the network manager to improve network performance, which was typically one errored bit in every one hundred thousand bits transmitted, or "one in ten to the minus fifth" BER (bit error rate). With the rapid deployment of fiber-optic cables across the nation, network performance did improve significantly toward the end of the 1980s. "One in ten to the minus sixth" BER, an order of magnitude improvement, was common by the late '80s. And with corresponding improvements in multiplexers and DSU/CSU terminating equipment, "one in 10 to the minus eighth" BERs were achieved.

With the attainment of progressively fast and reliable tele-processing systems and services, business applications were being developed to take advantage of the performance improvements, and such applications proliferated as the cost of the services decreased under competitive pressures. For the network manager, the times were good as competition teamed with technological advancements to enable provisioning of increasingly fast and reliable systems at progressively reduced costs.

Between 1986 and 1990, it was possible for network managers to expand their network capacities fourfold and improve performance fivefold, and still reduce their network costs by as much as a third. The euphoria of the network manager was somewhat mitigated, however, by the rapidly growing number of manufacturers and systems that offered an almost overwhelming variety from which to select. With competition comes choice; with choice comes confusion.

Competitive Pricing Plans

Competition definitely rewarded major businesses with reduced prices for telecommunications services. To compete with MCI's SCAs (Special Contract Arrangements) and similar pricing schemes from other carriers, AT&T won approval from the FCC for special pricing under its Tariff 12 pricing scheme.

Network managers became very occupied with inventorying their networks and associated hardware components, auditing bills to ensure accuracy — or more commonly, to catch inaccuracies — and planning/engineering expansions of their data and e-mail networks and disaster recovery plans, as well as their call center expansions/modifications, so as to be ready to negotiate with AT&T and MCI for the best packaged contract over the next one to five years. Those who negotiated carefully achieved handsome savings and improved service commitments. Thus, in the latter part of the 1980s, the network manager became more of a negotiator than ever before.

The Dark Side

While network managers were busily taking advantage of the numerous opportunities afforded by technology and competition, business gurus were also busy preaching the benefits of focusing on "core business" and "re-engineering" the corporation through the formation of "empowered teams" that could bring about improvements and savings through "downsizing." The coincidence of these two conditions was good news for the corporate executives and bad news for network managers.

Beginning in the late '80s, and continuing until today, executives have had the opportunity to evaluate the corporation's stable and cost-effective networks and to determine the relative worth of the telecommunications management and staff as compared to outsourcing the functions. Network managers who remained with the corporation were required to justify their existence and that of their staff on a recurring basis. Such led to morale problems and resulted in an unstable environment with a high turnover rate of qualified personnel, and consequently made the network manager's job that much more difficult.

THE 1990s: CHOICE/COMPLEXITY/CONVERGENCE/CONFUSION

Background

Change has continually accelerated through each year of the decade of the 1990s, as the global forces of technology, capitalism, and privatization/deregulation combine to shake governments, businesses, and individuals to their very core.

Everything has been digitized; video, data, image, and voice all look the same in digital transmission systems: a string of ones and zeros; global access to the Internet enables small businesses in the far corners of the earth to compete in major world markets through electronic commerce, and e-mail has become common to people throughout the world for both personal and business communications. Network-based call centers allow small businesses to provide levels of customer service once available only to the major corporations. Content, computing, and communications are all converging into network-based services, and wireless communication is expanding in service areas and capacities in unprecedented fashion.

Standards that once took years to negotiate are now being established in short order as companies that are the fiercest of competitors come together to cooperatively agree upon the way information will be processed, transported, and stored. These same competitors are joining forces, in cases where it makes sense, to cooperatively bid on jobs; a phenomenon referred to as "coopetition." Local access, always the exclusive domain of the "natural monopoly" local exchange carriers, has been opened to competition, and local number portability will allow individuals to retain their telephone and cell phone and pager numbers should they decide to change to a competitive carrier.

In the vortex of this "tornado" of rapid and expansive change is the network manager and the telecommunications staff, attempting to mitigate business vision/objectives to the telecommunications and information processing advances while simultaneously maintaining compatibility among systems and protecting investments.

Voice Services

For the past 20 years pundits have predicted that the volume of data traffic transported over public telecommunications networks would surpass voice traffic "next year." Data volumes have certainly grown in impressive proportions, but voice continues to be the dominant form of transported traffic. Since almost all voice traffic is now digitized — transported as a string of ones and zeros, just like data and video — network managers have had the opportunity to employ technology to "squeeze" more and more simultaneous voice conversations onto a single 64K-bps voice grade circuit.

Up until the early 1980s, voice was transmitted at 64K bps. But with advances in technology and employment of T1 circuits, it became possible to "fit" multiple conversations into the 64K-bps circuit. First two, at 32K bps bandwidth; then four, at 16K bps. The compression algorithms and digital technology advances have continued to improve so that it is now possible to send voice over the Internet and over frame-relay networks, thereby enabling network managers to continually provide for their employer's voice demands, and at greatly reduced costs.

Frame relay, originally intended exclusively for data transport, is now being used for voice transmissions when there is spare capacity on the network, and where it is economically attractive, as in international applications. Network managers have the opportunity to capitalize on advancements in compression algorithms and prioritization schemes to effectively "fill" unused portions of the frame relay network with voice traffic that rides along with the data traffic. Such multiplexing is the 1990s equivalent of T1 multiplexing in the 1980s, and the economic incentives are of similar magnitude.

Call Centers

The combination of powerful, expansive, affordable telecommunications networks and teleprocessing hardware/software systems enabled telecommunications carriers to provide network-based call center capabilities. This could be shared by numerous businesses that were too small to afford their own stand-alone call center operations. With such capability now affordable, network managers of smaller companies joined the network managers of the major corporations in turning their attention to the numerous networking issues involved in maintaining an efficient call center operation.

Such issues included number and location of call centers, hours of operation, load-sharing between centers, CTI (Computer Telephone Integration) to enhance the effectiveness of agents, 1+800 service lines, Internet accesses, inbound/outbound trunking, and numerous other related details. Because of the rapid enhancements that were continually forthcoming through the 1990s, special groups were often established within the corporate telecommunications department to focus on maintaining call center operations at peak performance.

Message and Data Services

The 1990s took on a whole new meaning for messaging and data services with the rapid growth in capabilities and speed of the telecommunications networks, and with the hardware and software components attached thereto in ever-increasing numbers. The Internet, and all the associated electronic-commerce and electronic-mail features and functions certainly made — and continues to make — its mark in almost every dimension of modern life.

Frame relay became, after a few years of watching and waiting by the more timid telecommunications staffs, the accepted transmission protocol for data. And with the introduction of additional capabilities, frame relay began to be employed for some voice applications, especially over international circuits. ATM (asynchronous transfer mode) was also making its appearance on the telecommunications scene, with promises to be the "be all, end all" protocol of the foreseeable future. Add to all of that PCs that continued to rapidly advance in features and capabilities while either remaining stable in cost, or diminishing in cost, plus new and enhanced software suites, and the glazed eyes of the network managers of the 1990s become more understandable.

With frame relay came a new breed of networking equipment from numerous vendors, each with their own unique set of strengths and weaknesses. Bridges, hubs, gateways, routers, FRADs (frame relay access devices), and NICs (network interface cards) began taking the place of modems, muxs, and DSU/CSUs, and the network manager and telecommunications staff had to learn the particulars of all of them in short order to perform their jobs effectively.

With frame relay also came "packetized" transmission protocol, automatic alternate routing, discarded packets, and over-subscription of "committed information rates" when "bursting" was experienced. In other words, the data transport world with which the telecommunications staff was familiar and comfortable was being overtaken by a whole new data transport world, and they had to learn it quickly to take advantage of the opportunities it offered.

E-mail in the early '90s was suffering from a malady like that of early facsimile: proprietary protocols that precluded one vendor's e-mail system from communicating with that of another vendor. Fortunately, clever conversion packages became available to enable communications between dissimilar systems, and with that came a rapid growth in e-mail between businesses and their associated customers and suppliers. Security also became more of an issue than ever before, as tele-processing systems were opened to the public for electronic commerce.

Internet access and all the related usage, security, addressing, and service considerations demanded a lot of the network managers in the 1990s. Obtaining corporate Internet address schemes and administering them throughout the corporation is no small task. Selection of the most desirable ISP (Internet service provider) in terms of network platform, capacity, help desk services, cost, maintenance, and commitment to QoS (Quality of Service) is also a daunting challenge. But these are components of the job description of the network manager in the current decade.

Video Services

As with all other telecommunications-based services, video has been the beneficiary of advanced hardware and software products along with dramatically enhanced network services. Videoconference facilities were almost the exclusive domain of carriers until the late 1980s. But with the introduction of fiber-optic networks and switched digital services, and new codecs (COder/DECoders) and compression algorithms, private videoconferencing systems became both practical and affordable.

By the mid 1990s, desktop systems that utilized miniature cameras and PC monitors along with specialized software packages were running on LANs and WANs in both one-way and two-way modes. Once again, the network manager had a new "opportunity" in design, engineering, and management of another new system.

Wireless Services

Two cellular carriers had been available in all the major metropolitan areas for voice services, and two wireless data providers were likewise present, but there was little interest in the services due to limited availability of applications, slow speeds, high costs, and limited service areas. Of all the wireless services, paging was the one most utilized. In the mid '90s, however, things changed dramatically.

The FCC auctioned off masses of previously unavailable radio spectrum, and major carriers with deep pockets bought both spectrum rights and established wireless companies. During this same period a commercially available service that provided translation capabilities between dissimilar wireless data services emerged, thereby providing application developers one platform to which to write their software as opposed to being forced to re-write the application for each different platform. Additionally, LEOS (low earth orbiting satellites) were being introduced along with GPS (geo positioning satellites), thereby enabling both the establishment of new businesses and enhancements to existing ones. Paging enhancements were also forthcoming, including two-way paging, short messaging service, and receipt of broadcast information like stock quotes.

While wireless had been basically a nonissue at the beginning of the 1990s, it suddenly became a hot one, and network managers had to scramble to learn all the nuances surrounding up to seven wireless carriers and several paging services in major metropolitan areas. Wireless PBXs and LANs were also emerging and creating still more opportunities for the telecommunications staff and the network manager.

Staffing Challenges

Concurrent with the rapid advancement of new and improved technologies, and all the associated hardware and software systems and networking alternatives, was the drive by corporate leaders to eliminate "all excess." To network managers, "all excess" translated to staff and budget. The marching orders of the 1990s to those telecommunications staffs that were not outsourced was, "Do more with less!" One part of their dilemma was reconciliation of executive expectation for state-of-the-art tele-processing systems to the denial of funds to hire, train, and retain staff; another part of their dilemma was maintenance of widespread networks without travel funds.

Staff members with good skills knew they easily could find employment at other companies because there were so few technically qualified personnel for the volumes of projects that were crying for attention. So in cases where training and advancement opportunities were being denied, turnover of personnel began to rise. "Between a rock and a hard place" took on new meaning for many of the contemporary network managers.

Competitive Pricing Plans

Competition continued unabated into the 1990s, and network managers continued playing one carrier against another for the best deals available. It was not uncommon for major corporations to use two or more competitive carriers to ensure continuity of service in the event one carrier suffered a catastrophic network outage and to keep the dominant carrier "honest" in their pricing and delivery of service. Since all carrier networks were based on fiber-optic platforms, all services were essentially the same. It therefore became necessary for carriers to distinguish themselves through the package of services they could provide and through marketing.

AT&T and MCI continued to be dominant, with Sprint and WorldCom tied for a somewhat distant second tier. Each tried to provide a "one-stop" shopping concept in that they tried to provide local access, long-distance, international, cellular, paging, satellite, Internet access, and financing along with consulting services and outsourcing. Separating the facts from the hype so as to intelligently evaluate the competing carriers started taking more and more of the network manager's time.

SUMMARY

As stated in the Introduction to this chapter, the functions of the network manager have remained somewhat constant over the past thirty years: Manager, Engineer, Innovator, and Negotiator. But what is managed, engineered, and available for innovation and negotiation, and the framework surrounding all of that, has changed dramatically.

The platforms upon which the telecommunications infrastructure rests are now fiber-optic and wireless. The protocols in primary use are packet- and cell-based; network transport speeds and network quality has increased by orders of magnitude. Business is global, and in most cases national economic systems are based on capitalism to one degree or another.

Telecommunications carrier companies that were formally "natural monopolies" have been, for the most part, deregulated and privatized, and the few services that were offered only under fixed tariffed rates have given way to a vast variety of services available at whatever price you are capable of negotiating. Desktop computers now have more processing and storage capabilities and communications capabilities than mainframe computers of 20 years ago.

Section II
Maintaining the Network

Chapter 3

Quality: The Key to a Successful Telecommunications Infrastructure

Peter Brown

INTRODUCTION

To be able to instill quality thinking in your staff, you must first understand quality. There are two complementary definitions that are frequently used when working with people. The first is a high-level or 50,000-foot view of quality which simply states: "Quality is:

"... **Meeting or exceeding all customer requirements** *(both explicit and implicit)."*

The second definition of quality, a quote by former U.S President George Bush, ties together a clear definition of quality with the customer and with the need for quality in business (i.e., to survive in the international competitive market).

"In business, there is only one definition of quality — **the customer's definition**. With the fierce competition of the international market, quality means survival."

To manage an organization that is trained in and practices quality in its daily operations means that the organization is well-versed in — and practices — measurement. It is often said that "if you can't measure it, then you won't be able to manage it." A few real-life examples will quickly demonstrate to you why metrics/quality are important to you as you deal with your customers, your people, and your suppliers.

0-8493-9990-4/99/$0.00+$.50
© 1999 by CRC Press LLC

Imagine meeting with an irate customer who recently called your manager because according to him, his LAN was down "all the time." You arrive with your quality charts demonstrating that in the last six weeks the LAN has been down once for a total of 22 minutes. It is just amazing how facts eliminate emotional outburst and help put events in a more realistic perspective.

Now one of your more challenging employees files a grievance against you because she claims that she has been denied appropriate training which others in the department have received. Having a comprehensive quality program in place, your human resources section of the quality plan includes comprehensive training records of all employees, thus enabling you to demonstrate with facts to the union steward and, more importantly, to your employee, that she has actually received more training than anyone else in the department and definitely sufficient training to accomplish her job.

Finally, you are sitting down with your IXC to negotiate a new contract. You bring your quality folder with you, with a Pareto chart that demonstrates this supplier has eight times as many billing errors as the competition and that it has been consistently late for the past 12 months with 28% of the frame relay orders. Your data also clearly illustrates that its supplier-related frame relay outages — which again are worse than its competitor — are primarily caused by LEC outages. Based on the above, you are able to get contractual commitments regarding billing improvements, a repayment clause for cost incurred by late orders, and an agreed-to "get well" plan for the frame outages which, if not met, lets you exit the contract without penalty.

In the above three examples, you can see why Quality is needed in every organization. It enables you to manage with fact and not emotions. A comprehensive quality program helps you address HR issues. Finally, a well-documented set of facts enabled by an aggressive metric management program lets you deliver dollars directly to the bottom line of your company.

GETTING STARTED

Implementation of a quality program takes time, patience, training and dollars, but done appropriately the payback is a higher level of service, happier employees, and satisfied customers for fewer dollars!

Before you can instill quality thinking in your staff, you need to *prepare yourself* and your team for what entering on the quality journey really means. As we all know in this day of downsized staffs and increased work required from the Telecommunications/Infrastructure staffs, the majority of our employees already see themselves overworked. If you introduce quality as one more program, it will be viewed as "the program of the year"

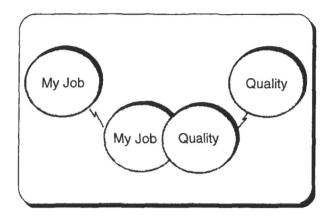

Exhibit 1.   Merging Job With Quality

and will be given lip service but not real commitment. Usually when you first introduce the concept of quality to an organization, people will indeed see it simply as incremental work or another project.

People have "their work" which, in their minds, generally fills their day 110% of the time. Then management introduces a new activity called quality, which represents in their mind a completely separate, added set of work! Is it any wonder people initially fight the thought of a quality program? They see it as adding to their already overburdened set of tasks.

This is exactly why it is extremely critical for you to carefully plan out the introduction of the quality program. A quality program starts with a definition of your organization's mission and objectives. You must meet with your internal customers to determine how they define their mission, how they measure their quality and obtain consensus on what your customers see as (acceptable/good) output for your group. Next, you need to measure your processes and develop a "level set" of what is being delivered today. After this research or homework, you will be positioned to craft people's goals in such a fashion that their work begins to merge with the new quality program (Exhibit 1).

Ultimately, when the quality program is fully introduced an individual's work will become coincident with or completely overlap the work elements of the quality program (Exhibit 2).

Developing a set of goals to lead people to the position that the quality program is a piece of their daily work is the role of management.

Now for some history about how and where the quality effort started, evolved to, and why it is important to you.

The Goal: Set goals, measure, and lead people so they have these circles coincident.

Exhibit 2.   Job and Quality Merged

HISTORY

In today's rapidly changing technological world, the concept of quality has become an expectation in the manufacturing world, but it is just starting to be adopted into the complex world of services, particularly information technology services. Quality as a discipline has its roots in discrete manufacturing, where lines were set up to produce high volumes of products, usually with limited mix.

Many of the basic elements of "quality" as a discipline were created in the early 1940s as a method of ensuring products produced in America in support of the World War II effort met certain criteria consistently. Quality's early and lifelong champion, Dr. Edward Deming, met significant resistance within the U.S. after WWII as he attempted to get American industry to accept and embrace many of the basic quality principles.

Surprising as it may sound, Deming's ideas on quality, as a critical piece of manufacturing processes, were first adopted in Japan. People that can remember the first products that were exported from the reindustrialized Japan in the 1950 will recall a product that was thought of as inferior, or of poor quality.

Yet by the mid to late 1960s, the world witnessed a dramatic turn around; we all saw Japan exporting products that were world-class — products that had fewer defects and were highly reliable and more resilient than those manufactured in the old industrial parts of the world (i.e., the U.S. and Europe). What brought about this dramatic change in the output of Japan? The principal item that enabled Japan to proceed in the global market place was quality — quality in its products, and quality in its processes — which resulted in unprecedented customer satisfaction.

Quality was born and matured in the discrete manufacturing world. Americans embraced quality during the late 1970s to mid 1980s as they raced to regain market share which had been lost to offshore competition. Simultaneously, within the American economy, a dramatic shift was beginning to happen.

Our economy was being transformed to that of a service-driven economy instead of a manufacturing-driven economy, and we faced a new challenge: How do you build customer loyalty, deliver increased value, and consistently make money in the service business? Though difficult to accomplish, the answer is straightforward — introduce quality as a formal discipline within the service industry or discipline to enable the consistent delivery of services that meet or exceed customer expectations.

In an operating telecommunications or infrastructure group, what do we mean by quality? How do you know if you are running/managing an operation in which quality is evident? Quality is important to you as both an employee and operating manager because the results of a comprehensive quality program enable your department to simultaneously:

- Increase customer satisfaction.
- Decrease per unit cost of services delivered.
- Reduce time to market.
- Increase employee satisfaction.

What is quality in an operating telecommunications/infrastructure environment? Some people might simply call it "back to basics." If your department is closely tied to your customer, knows his/her expectations, consistently meets or exceeds these expectations, then your people either are implicitly doing their task in quality fashion or have been trained in the quality discipline. After knowing and understanding your customer, the next critical attribute present in every organization that demonstrates quality is attitude.

If one walks around and visits with people where the group is implicitly committed to quality as a discipline, you find each member of the organization willing to help his/her peers; you find people making decisions that are correct for the company, not sub-units; you find people consistently trying to improve their processes; and probably more importantly, you find people working as a team and using established processes. A quality-oriented organization is "process"-driven and not dependent on individuals or star performers.

Finally, a quality-driven organization makes decisions based on facts and ensures that measurements are in place to enable people to measure three things: (1) Customer satisfaction as seen by the customer (i.e., his/her ability to reach an application when he/she needs access to the application); (2) Technical attributes needed to determine within the department if certain technical pieces of the telecommunication systems/infrastructure are performing as needed (i.e., is the router directing packets correctly); and (3) Processes of the department within control and expected limits (i.e., is the order management system within the department functioning as planned... all orders received are processed with "n" hours.) To be successful and deliver high customer satisfaction at lower per-unit costs in a timely fashion, a telecommunications/infrastructure operating unit must be well understood, and have easy-to-use, repeatable process.

QUALITY TOOLS AND HOW TO USE THEM

There is a set of five basic tools which you and your team need to master and use to measure the technical elements of your business, and usually you will need to master a seventh, to better measure and understand your customer. The fundamental tools that are associated with measurement in the quality world are:

1. Pareto Charts
2. Flow Charts
3. Fishbone or Ishikawa Charts
4. Run-Time Charts
5. Correlation diagrams

The sixth tool, usually associated with customer satisfaction, is a survey or an interview. To understand in-depth what the customer needs usually requires a series of interviews and perhaps a professionally prepared survey. Accomplishing your customer satisfaction planning requires as much or more training as does mastering the measurement of your technical business. This often is an area that technically oriented people tend to gloss over, and then they never do understand what their customers define as success or good performance.

Run-Time Charts

A run-time chart is simply a graphical depiction of how data in a given process occurs over time. These data points may be measurements, counts or percentages of a product or service characteristic. Exhibit 3 gives an example of a monthly graph of the number of supplier orders which were delivered late to schedule. Also note on the graph, the Goal line — to have a successful quality program, all graphical measures should have the actual data, a goal and an industry benchmark (to be discussed later).

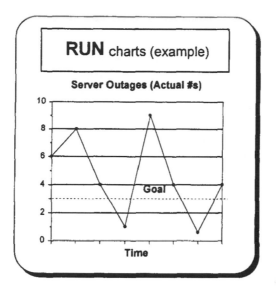

Exhibit 3. Run-time Chart

Pareto Charts

Perhaps the most critical tool or chart for people to use in the quality environment is the Pareto Chart. It is named after the Italian economist who originally postulated that 80% of the wealth in Italy was held by 20% of the people. Pareto's work was later generalized through investigation of problems (conditions) to reveal that a "vital few" conditions cause the majority of the problems, and the remainder of the problems result from the "trivial many" causes. The rule is often referred to as the 80/20 rule, in which 80% of the problems are the result of 20% of the causes.

The Pareto Chart itself is a bar chart (Exhibit 4) which illustrates problem causes in order of severity by frequency of occurrence, cost or performance. A few examples of where the Pareto law is often found at work are as follows: a few customers accounting for the majority of sales, specific defects accounting for the majority of customer complaints, or particular product lines accounting for the majority of profits.

It can be extremely helpful to join these two tools (Run-time charts and Pareto diagrams) into a single reporting device that gives you the performance of the current week or day on a run chart, and a Pareto chart of this week's fault/sales/occurrences, so that you can reference this week's performance to other weeks and then quickly see the reason for the faults or outages. Add to this some action-planning steps (i.e., How to correct the

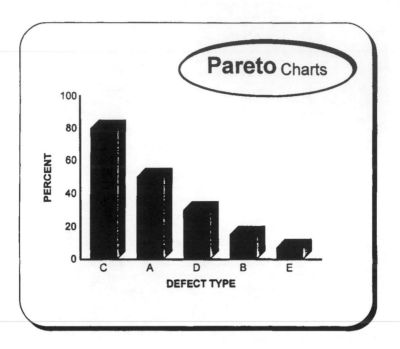

Exhibit 4.   Pareto Chart

faults), and you have a very useful daily/weekly/montly reporting form (Exhibit 5).

Fishbone Charts

One of the basic principles of quality is to find the "root" or fundamental cause of the problem and fix it instead of simply fixing the symptom or "non-root" cause and having the problem repeat itself again and again. A good example of this would be a PBX malfunction due to a collection of dust and simply blowing out the dust rather than checking for the root or main cause which is a missing filter.

The Fishbone Chart (Exhibit 6) or cause and effect diagram, originally invented by Kaoru Ishikawa to be used as a process-analysis or -control tool, is the method or chart used to identify possible causes of a problem and isolate those that are most likely responsible for the problem at a given time. Construction of the Fishbone Chart does not solve a problem but

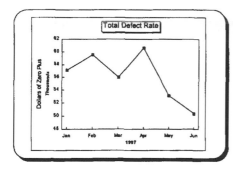 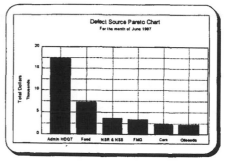

Exhibit 5. The Metric on the Left Measures Calling-card Usage via Zero Plus, Which is not the Cost-effective Method. The Metric on the Right Indicates the Source of the Defective Usage

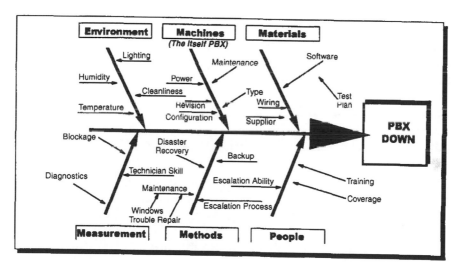

Exhibit 6. This Illustrates How a Fishbone Chart "Cause and Effect Diagram" Can be Built to Analyze a Down PBX

instead ensures that you do not easily overlook a cause or apply fixes where not necessary. The Ishikawa or Fishbone Chart usually has six main "bones," these being the generic areas of people, methods, measurement, materials, machines and environment. Each of these bones have many supporting spines or bones.

Flow Charts

Flow charts are an example of control or quality devices, which are a direct transferal from the manufacturing industry. A flow chart is a diagram of the product or workflow through each process. Flow charts are used to detect obvious redundancies and inefficiencies in work flow, to identify places within a process for data collection, and for setting up channels for communicating process controls by using control charts to help solve problems.

By inserting certain measurement criteria at various points in this flow process, you could easily determine information such as: (1) Number of calls the help desk receives; (2) Number of calls escalated to various levels in this process; (3) How responsive internal experts are to the support processes, and (4) How long it takes external suppliers to respond to support situations. Again the flow chart or process flow diagram is aimed as an aid to assist you in understanding your business and in selecting key measurement points with the process.

A sample control chart is shown in Exhibit 7, with data measured from measurement points A and B. The stated goal of the local help desk is to resolve 80% of the received calls locally. Looking at the control chart in Exhibit 7 one observes the goal and the associated upper and lower "Control Limits," where control limits simply indicate when the results of a given process are either "in or out-of control." Looking at Exhibit 7 one can see that for weeks 3, 4, and 5 there is a significant negative trend and the process clearly is "out of its control limits." Use of control limits and flow charts enables your team to spot performance trends, and by invoking timely corrective action you are able to maintain high levels of customer service.

Six Sigma — What It Is

"Six Sigma" is a term utilized in the pursuit of quality to mean two things: first it is a concept about how to approach quality and measurements and second, it is a mathematical measurement that is directly applicable to the number of defects or errors found in a given process.

First let's describe the measurement side of Six Sigma σ. In statistics there are two metrics terms that are often discussed in relation to process and quality control issues. These two terms are the mean and deviations from the mean which are called Sigma represented by the Greek Letter 8. To appropriately use the concepts of the median and sigma all references are to a normal deviation. The subjects of statistics, medians and sigmas are far more in-depth than will be covered in this book.

Exhibit 8 illustrates both the median, and the standard deviation or sigma for a normal distribution. The basic objective in the world of quality

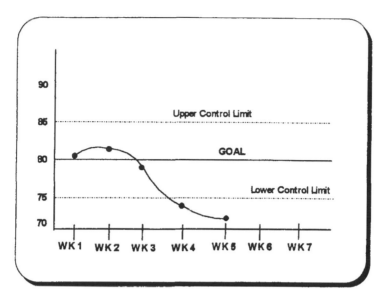

Exhibit 7. Sample Control Chart

is to establish a process, measure it in terms of deviation or sigma from the median of the process and to ultimately define your service process "tight" or well-defined enough that when defects in the process occur that they happen very infrequently. To be specific, a process defined so that it operates at 6 Sigma mathematically means that there would be less than 3 errors per million opportunities.

Let's take the mathematics "jibberish" and make it real through the use of a couple examples. Your office's PBX processes thousands of calls daily. We all know that the PBX processes those calls through a core set of internal logic. If you measured your call-volume for two weeks, and on average you were processing 100,000 calls per day for a total of 1,000,000 calls, and to the best of your knowledge you had three "high and dry calls" and all other calls completed as far as the PBX was concerned, it, as a process, functioned at a level of 6 Sigma, with three or less errors per million opportunities. Now you are asking the age-old question: "Do I really need or is it possible to achieve 6 Sigma performance within my computing/telecommunication environment?" The answer is yes! Every time you set goals of poorer performance you are costing your company money!

It is really done through two approaches. First is attitude — no detail is too small to check. Items such as the safety checklist are always faithfully executed, maintenance is carefully checked and monitored by a federal

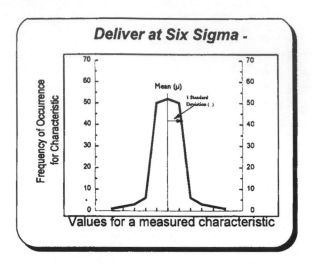

Exhibit 8. Frequency of Occurrence/Values for a Measured Characteristic

agency, etc. Second is redundancy: many of the airplane's systems are redundant, which is simply a identified cost of doing business. And all of this quality is built into a delivery system that we all find acceptable from a cost-of-service standpoint.

Examples of Real-life Uses of 6 Sigma

Six Sigma is used in many daily information technology operations. One example is illustrated in Exhibit 9, which shows a weekly graph of frame relay outages for a large international operation. The goals in this chart are calculated to a 6 Sigma and a 5 Sigma level. The result of this weekly measurement is discussed at least monthly with the interexchange carrier involved.

The overall goals in this chart start from the presumption that the only acceptable goal is zero outages. If you have an outage, then the duration of that outage should be kept below 6 Sigma measured in minutes or seconds. The goal is calculated as follows (24 hours/per day × 60 minutes/hour × 60 seconds per minute × number of available circuits).

BENCHMARKING: ITS PLACE IN QUALITY

In recent years there has been a significant amount published regarding benchmarking various processes within your enterprise. No quality program is completed without benchmark efforts. Benchmarking simply allows you to compare a given process within your company with a similar process in

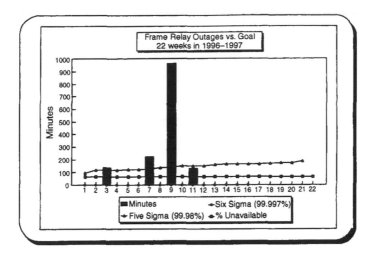

Exhibit 9. Frame Relay Outages vs. Goal

another company. An accurate set of benchmarks prepares your organization to establish meaningful goals to improve your internal processes.

When entering into a benchmarking activity you can benchmark the same processes within your company, benchmark between people within your industry, or seek out companies that are best-in-class in a specific process on a global basis. Each of these approaches has merit, and you must decide your overall goals for the benchmark activity to decide which approach is best for your company.

After selecting who you want to benchmark with, you then need to perform the following activities:

- Define common performance metrics for your process.
- Collect data.
- Analyze the data — determine gaps.
- Identify practices leading to superior performance.
- Communicate your results.
- Set goals and action plans.
- Implement your plan.
- Monitor progress and change in your processes.
- Recalibrate with benchmarking partner(s).

One caution when entering into a benchmarking exercise: Be prepared for a significant amount of detailed work before meaningful comparative data is achieved. Forming common performance-metric definition is time-consuming, hard work. Also, collection of data, even though metrics are agreed to, often requires modification of internal processes and again takes time and effort.

MANAGEMENT'S ROLE IN QUALITY

Quality as an approach will be successful only when management demonstrates a strong leadership example and plays its role of leading, encouraging, rewarding the behavior it expects from employees. Management must also change its behavior for the quality program to be successful.

The management behavior that is most critical to the implementation of a quality program is ensuring that metrics are established, asking the right questions, demonstrating patience, and giving feedback to employees. Here are the management roles:

- Establish the program.
- Establish the vision.
- Produce education programs.
- Ensure metrics are established.
- Ask the right questions.
- Review the metrics.
- Remove road blocks.
- Coach your employees.
- Demonstrate patience.
- Give feedback.
- Establish and use rewards.

We will discuss these specific roles in more depth. Without metrics there is no quality program. It is management's job to ensure that the appropriate metrics are developed and reviewed.

The review piece of this role cannot be over emphasized. Imagine what message you are sending to your people when you establish a comprehensive set of "quality metrics" to measure various elements of your operation and then instead of reviewing these metrics, call Joe or Sally in the Operations Center to determine the number of orders in backlog for frame relay circuits! Review of metrics dovetails directly with management's responsibility to "ask the right questions." Asking the right questions refers to your new approach, a quality approach to management.

It means asking "data-driven questions"; it means asking questions that are directly related to the way your team is now managing the enterprise. It means asking questions such as "what was the root cause of this outage." It means challenging your team to do complete analysis of the event. And it means understanding the behavior you want and then asking questions that will cause people to behave in the manner you want.

Let's examine an example. You are interviewing the manager of your billing department. For the last three months your department has been late in issuing bills. Your first question, based on quickly reviewing his monthly report, is how can you keep Joe as the accounting manager when he has consistently been late for the last three months?

If you had looked at the UNIX server outage you would have realized that there had been a conic problem with the accounting server for two months and the HR turnover report showed that three of the four people in accounting had left the company (this was no reflection on Joe — you learned that the three left to start their own software company). In this example, your actions of ignoring the new metrics severely undercut the efforts of your new quality program.

Patience and feedback also go hand in hand in building your team and teaching the team members to use their new tools, to do complete analysis and to use data-driven arguments with suppliers, both internal and external, to resolve problems in a more cost-effective manner. Patience is perhaps the most critical element of developing a comprehensive quality program. It is required in the areas of employee education, careful investigation and goal-setting.

Patience is needed because many of these quality tools and data-driven analyses will be new to your employees. In the past, often the loudest person or the person that made a heroic effort was your star. With a quality approach, you, as the leader, must demonstrate to the teams that investigative analysis yields the desired results — lower cost-per-unit and higher reliability/availability.

SUMMARY

To summarize, let's look at how you would use the new tools we have studied, where in the organization you should set quality goals, and some day-to-day examples of quality goals you might want to establish across your organization. Your understanding and frequent use of the quality tools we studied and others will enable you to move to "management by fact" and away from "management with emotion;" these tools equip you to formally sort through the numerous problems in your computing/telecommunication environment and separate the "vital few" that you should focus on from the "trivial many" that can easily overload your staff.

These tools, when used consistently, allow you and your staff to spot trends in network and system performance before outages occur. Instead they let you react proactively to trends, thus preventing them instead of fixing them. Quality attitude and tools help in the search for "root causes" of problems. In summary, a well-managed quality program moves you from being reactive to being proactive.

Many people struggle with the question: "To what level in the organization do I set goals?" Every person in an infrastructure organization should have quality measures. These measures range from technical quality measures such as TCP/IP latency response time, router availability, call center abandonment rate, server availability time, orders delivered on time, to financial metrics to customer satisfaction results.

A well-managed, carefully planned quality program enables you to engage your entire management team, to move to a proactive approach to operations, to lower your unit cost and simultaneously increase your customer satisfaction.

Chapter 4
Managing Applications on the Network

Bill Yaman and John Fiske

INTRODUCTION

Businesses today depend on the availability of decentralized, multiplatform systems and network resources. Smooth-running, reliable networks are essential in today's business environment, but yesterday's systems management strategies are not sufficient nor effective in today's distributed client/server computing environments.

New, advanced management solutions now help you, the network manager, CIO, or IT architect, manage your company's large and complex systems. As your systems increase in size and complexity, you must find the optimal, and most time-, cost-, and resource-efficient way to manage your information technology.

IT managers now realize that to make their client/server systems perform as intended, they need to have control over distributed applications. Usually the applications offer symptoms of a network malfunction; an improperly functioning application is the first indicator of a network problem. By using the application as an access point into your network, you can look into your IT infrastructure to find out what is causing the application not to perform.

Until recently, most network systems and management strategies involved monitoring and managing the technology that supports applications, not the applications themselves. Network and systems problems were not viewed from the applications perspective. In a change, companies are finding that application management supports the business; in fact, ensuring network/application availability has become a top business objective.

Application management was not addressed in centralized host environments because mainframes had embedded application monitoring facilities that could easily address issues involving application health, response time and administration. But now applications are deployed across multiple platforms nationally and internationally, and administrators are realizing that not being able to monitor or benchmark remote applications leaves them very vulnerable to problems that are hard to diagnose and even harder to solve.

Systems have become far too complex and heterogeneous to be managed with existing systems. In the "old days" when the entire enterprise ran off a single mainframe and attached dumb terminals, it was comparatively simple to look at the applications, and the network, such as it was. Systems management itself is not capable of providing a complete view of an application's journey through the enterprise. Nor do existing systems management devices allow the IT managers to look into the system from a single point.

DISTRIBUTED COMPUTING ENVIRONMENT

As managers gain control of their distributed computing environment, they have found application management produces multiple benefits. Well functioning networks with well functioning applications allow end users to be more productive by relieving them of the time-consuming headaches of managing desktops; it provides application consistency across the enterprise and helps ensure interoperability; and in addition, electronic software distribution yields cost savings.

Managing from a business perspective means keeping your "eye on the prize," with the prize being your most critical applications. Since all systems are not equal, an effective method of application management is to isolate and monitor those things in your IT that are most important. It is a way to simplify a very complex environment.

Today, with distributed applications and client/server networks connected to the reliable old mainframes through middleware, the network has become a new kind of hybrid creature. And to complicate matters further, the distinction between application and network is no longer clear. Consider for a moment: Is e-mail an application or a network? Or both?

THE PARADIGM

Application management should be focused on business value and must have end-user or customer perspective. This means the system and applications must be available when they are needed. So, applications management is about providing availability. What is availability? Availability is:

> Managing real-time behavior of applications and essential systems, subsystems, middleware and network resources to ensure their operational reliability, accessibility and performance in support of critical business processes.

The high cost of lost business means companies cannot afford network slowdowns. If finding the one percent of faults means an x percent increase in market share, monitoring will be done. Yet problems in today's complex, distributed networks are harder to find and more costly then ever to fix. To ensure network problems do not threaten application availability you need to:

- Determine quickly and accurately the source of network problems.
- View the health of your entire network from a single point.
- Control IS costs by leveraging staff productivity and managing software distribution.
- Protect applications from expensive threats to availability.
- View only the information you need to manage users, groups, or specific areas of your network.
- Simplify complexity by managing workloads, groups, and resources across multiple platforms.
- Manage expansion as your systems and applications grow.

As your company places more reliance on distributed mission-critical applications, your need for application management will intensify.

Application management is about providing and ensuring availability. The application management strategy requires a total application life cycle perspective that includes design, development, and operations of applications.

Managing applications is a new and huge challenge. The three main approaches to application management are measurement, modeling, and vendor management tools attached to enterprise applications. What follows is a discussion of each approach.

INSTRUMENTATION

The initial effort in application management has been to instrument applications with fish tags and hooks located inside the application to give, for example, end-to-end response time. As an application is written, the instruments are written into the code.

While instrumentation intuitively is the approach you would want to use to monitor your applications and network, it requires a great amount of labor to construct. And often instrumentation looks at areas of your network that are not "mission-critical."

Consider a hypothetical situation in which an insurance company buys a sales management tool that runs with an Oracle database on an AIX server. The sales management tool is expected to perform well, and the company naturally wants to interface the database with the claims system on a mainframe. The mainframe is a legacy system. And a middleware pipe is built between the new sales tool and mainframe.

To instrument the new middleware and the new sales tool through to the mainframe would require people to rewrite the legacy code. It might also require that the newly acquired application be "undone."

Although it is technically simple to write and insert the code, it is a very laborious task, and then it needs to be maintained. And when the company adds more applications to the system, with more middleware and other supporting software and hardware, still more code would have to be written.

To monitor application and system health you need a sample of what is going on at all times. Ideally you would want to be able to instrument the entire system, but as we have seen, this is impractical.

IT people need an alternative. A good alternative is modeling.

MODELING

Modeling is a top-down external method to monitor applications with the focus on the external view. The idea is to isolate mission-critical packets of IT and create models of situations that can occur in other areas of the IT architecture. Viewing your IT from the "top," at the end-user application, you establish, through experience, those situations "down" in the IT system that affect the performance of the top, user-interface application. By its nature, because it uses predictions rather than actual measurements, modeling is not as precise as instrumentation. But by looking at specific packets in the network you get a business view of what is going on in the system. Modeling is about prioritizing to the things that are critical to your system. You organize around your critical business components, not around technology.

Modeling operates according to an 80/20 rule which predicts that if you can model 20% of the applications you get 80% impact, and subsequent operational improvement. Rather than looking at everything, which is impractical, modeling monitors for symptoms that show at the application level.

Modeling is a noise filter. It allows you to focus on the mission-critical aspects of your IT, without your having to look at every last little bit of the system. It is simply a more efficient way of doing your business.

Although modeling is an efficient alternative to instrumentation, customizable, thoroughbred application management systems give systems operators even better control over their enterprisewide IT. Several excellent application management programs, provided by third-party vendors, combine the techniques found in instrumentation and in modeling to give the best kind of application management available.

OUT-OF-BOX VENDOR-SUPPLIED MANAGEMENT SOFTWARE

Vendor-supplied application monitoring products wrap monitoring around the application. The vendors provide the monitoring tools. In almost every case, the vendors partner with the system/application provider to develop the monitoring system. The partnership is advantageous to the application provider because the provider's expertise is more in developing the application, and not as much in command and control.

A Short Example

SAP R/3 is a large-scale client/server package to run a business. It runs order processing, general ledger, accounts payable, accounts receivable, inventory, manufacturing, production control, currency exchange, and other applications all integrated together. SAP was the first vendor to introduce this kind of system for the client/server environment. R/3 is built on a 3-tier architecture:

- Client (Windows, MacOS, OS-2, UNIX).
- Network connection to application servers UNIX boxes HP 6000.
- Database server (Oracle). Application programs to run business on servers. Clients become terminals.

SAP created a Computer Center Management System (CCMS) to provide application and system management for R/3 at the same time it created R/3. At the time there were no third parties with monitoring equipment for R/3. CCMS was essentially a requirement for SAP to be able to sell R/3.

But as it has turned out, CCMS has not been a long-term adequate solution for companies with more than one SAP system, nor has it been able to keep up with R/3's advancing technology. Most companies have multiple SAP systems. Additionally, SAP has often been interfaced with a legacy mainframe. CCMS looks only at SAP, but an open system command center can look into the whole network.

A third-party vendor, such as Candle Corp., Tivoli, and others can supply the open environment command system you need to manage the applications on your network.

In the above example, the key challenge to application management was to create an application-oriented view of the distributed computing environment. As it turns out, this is the emerging challenge for all application management systems.

APPLICATIONS ORIENTATION

The Hurwitz Group, a management consulting and software research firm in Massachusetts, says an applications orientation is the key to successful application management. It sounds confusing, but it means that you use the user interface application to look inside your IT.

The Hurwitz Group identifies the criteria for effective applications management:

- The ability to relate logical application components to the underlying technology infrastructure, such as a key application service or a file system running on a specific server node, and
- The ability to monitor discrete application software components, such as application servers and database tables.

Systems management strategy should focus on system resources availability. Application management is the access port into the health of your systems. If, for example, a daily sales report application is blank, yielding no data, something somewhere in the system is wrong. Your applications are the first place you will find out that something is not right — unless you have a coordinated systems management strategy and the tools in place to support it.

The first criterion enables management systems to identify which logical application components are affected by the failure of specific infrastructure elements. To meet this criterion, all information about a particular application must be gathered, and all objects representing parts of the infrastructure must be logically mapped to the application components that use them.

System administrators must be able to monitor discrete application components in order to know what the actual impact of the component failure is on the application. For example, if an application accesses multiple databases and one of the database servers goes down, the failure may not prevent the application from continuing to provide other functions that do not require the failed database. To fully understand the health of the application, the administrator must be able to determine what happened to the application because of the failure. In many companies a typical application stack would look like Exhibit 1.

Exhibit 1. A Typical Applications Stack

- Application
- Application Services (SAP R/3, *Lotus Notes*)
- Middleware (MQSeries)
- Database (SQL, Com/Engine)
- Operating systems NT Server
- Network (Com/Middleware)

An application failure almost always indicates a failure somewhere in the stack. To meet the second criterion, a system must provide administrators with a full understanding of the application components and how they interrelate. An application can consist of many components that execute on different devices. These components, or processes, can be dependent or independent depending on how the application was written. If the processes are independent, a single failure of an infrastructure component may not affect all the processes. Therefore, a management system that merely maps infrastructure components can give false readings of an application's true state of health; that system is not performing adequate or thorough application management.

The management system also needs to be expandable and flexible in order to accommodate the constant changes in the stack. At any time new hardware may be added and old equipment may be taken off-line. These changes can and do alter the operation of your IT infrastructure, but they can be managed with the right equipment.

Application management requires:

- The ability to map logical application components to the underlying IT infrastructure
- The ability to monitor the discrete application components and their interdependencies
- *Navigation capability to allow administrators to drill down through the stack for problem determination*

To manage applications adequately, a management system must have the ability to correlate (map) logical application software components to one another and to the underlying technology infrastructure. It requires very advanced correlation capabilities that do not exist in all management systems. It also requires an understanding of the application architecture and the ability to view discrete logical components of the application as it executes in a distributed environment.

Navigation indicates the ability to "drill down" from application into the IT stack to identify the faulty components. A graphical user interface (GUI) can reduce problem determination time. As previously mentioned, system down-time can cost your company millions of dollars. Your objective is to prevent whole applications from crashing.

Vendor-supplied management systems provide the ability to monitor discrete things and the interdependencies. The system helps you probe into important areas of your stack to map it back to the higher level application. Discrete monitoring of application components and the components of the infrastructure enables you to know that when something is wrong at the high level, something else is wrong down below.

So, what do you do if you find out that you have only 15 minutes until a disk-full that brings down a mission-critical Oracle database? With a good navigation tool, you would drill down to find out, as an example, it is on an NT server in the Boston office. You simply log-on from your remote location and delete some data to save the day.

Your job is to ensure system availability, and you want to prevent the system from going down, or you want to be able to find the trouble, correct it, and bring it back up quickly before (a) end users, irate, start calling you and, (b) before time elapses and business and dollars are lost.

To have this capability you need broad coverage either with your own product or other products with open interface to accept information from other sources. Legacy systems cannot be changed easily; it is easier and simpler to configure the monitoring system to work with what is already in place. New client/server systems are designed to be monitored with user- or manager-interface management systems, but the legacy systems, which were not, must be somehow connected through in order to be "seen" through the client/server management system. A device sometimes called an "alert adapter" makes the technical links to accommodate the inevitable heterogeneity of today's complex client/server, mainframe and legacy systems. Alert adapters are must-have tools.

RULES AND THRESHOLDS

In out-of-box vendor-supplied application management systems, rules and thresholds are customizable for each application and the underlying IT components in the stack. Typically, you develop sets of event/statistics values for specific functions, such as response time or other operating characteristics. Then you monitor for exceptions (if response time is greater than x...).

Rules are written within application products for each platform. Your sales management tool will have rules written to accommodate its location on the many different UNIX boxes, for example:

Rules are customized by platform by application:

Platform A/application X
Platform B/application X

Platform A/application Y
Platform B/application Y

Platform A/application Z
Platform B/application Z

And so on, with almost limitless variations.

Rules should be designed to say, if (a), and if (b), and if (c), then (result). This paradigm recognizes the interdependencies between hardware and software on all the layers within the stack. The rules are the critical operating elements in the management system, and they must be embedded or captured into the system.

In a GUI control system, when the rules are triggered, an alert goes to a screen at a central location. The nature of the alert is indicated by color (green = OK; yellow = problem incipient; red = failure). Alerts can also be sent by beeper, pager, fax alert, or phone call.

COMMAND AND CONTROL

After finding the location of the failure, the next step, obviously, is to correct it. This is usually done manually, though in some cases automatic controls work.

In an example of manual control, with five applications on one mainframe or UNIX machine during a period of high load, the control system warns of an incipient failure. The computer operator or manager, using the control system's tools locates the problem and issues commands to correct the problem. In this case, the IT manager makes a decision on which application shall be put temporarily down. The manager decides on a non-customer-interface application and announces "for next hour payroll (or accounts) receivable will be down."

To translate manual procedures into automated task functions you need a history to predict what might happen. With the history you know that when a problem occurs, and you know it takes a-b-c-d to fix the problem, it becomes a simple matter to have the computer issue the commands. The advantage to automated control is much quicker response time. The challenge is defining all of the a-b-c-d operations to fix all the potential failures that can occur within a system.

E-MAIL

An example of the diffuse line between application and network is email. Increasingly, e-mail is becoming a critical application. Companies simply run on e-mail.

E-mail is more than simply a communication device. In some companies, customer orders are entered by attaching the order to an e-mail message. Customer orders are attached to e-mail, and the orders get placed into an orders mailbox.

E-mail can also be fantastically complex. You rarely find a company with one e-mail system. A large corporation's e-mail systems may likely be a combination of Lotus Notes, CCMail, Eudora Pro, the Internet and other e-mail applications. If internal e-mail is not complicated enough, it becomes more so when you have to talk with another company (a vendor, a partner, a contractor), and you do so on the Internet, and your message goes into another wholly different e-mail architecture. E-mail is sent across internal networks through routers at each location. Network with NetWare (OS) with post office.

How do you manage this? There are individual products that look at mail routers, post offices, Lotus Notes, POP 3, and other applications. You still need an umbrella that looks at all the infrastructure, the routers, the hubs, the underlying operating systems, Windows NT, NetWare, UNIX, in a bottom-up approach.

Other products use a top-down approach. The control application sends an e-mail message through the network from point A to point B, and/or C, and/or D. If the test message gets through to the desired recipient location(s), the system is healthy, as far as it has been tested.

If not, something is not working correctly: for example, a message transfer agent's software is down. Or someone sent a 10MB CAD file and it was stored temporarily on a disk, but the disk was full and the disk crashed. Or perhaps someone changed an Internet Protocol address and the network segment cannot see the recipient server because the address changed.

E-mail should be treated as a mission-critical application/system. With its own complexities, your e-mail system needs its own customizable management tools.

CONCLUSION

Application management provides, manages, and ensures availability through monitoring, using flexible, customizable rules and thresholds, manual and automated command and control in a heterogeneous network from a single command point.

Efforts to develop new systems on lower cost machines have led to the explosive growth of network-based computing. This has led to dramatic growth in the information that is processed and shared both across a corporation and among its trading partners. In some cases, distributed architectures have been appropriate, while in others, more traditional approaches may have been a better solution. The reality, however, is that technology infrastructures now consist of a vast array of new products and services that take advantage of network-oriented environments.

Two types of system and application monitors exist presently: GUI and scripted language. The GUI, as employed by Candle Corp.'s Command Center, is fast and easy to use. It requires, as do all GUI applications, a dense amount of code. The scripted language interface, as employed by Tivoli's

TME 10, is more flexible and is not as much work to write the front end. But it is somewhat slower to use than a GUI because the operator has to read the information on the screen.

The most important component of your IT, from the business perspective, is the end-user application. It could be a complicated cross-platform application sitting on top of a stack. The top layer is the most important, but the problems occur down in the stack. The application may have a code problem, but it has presumably been tested. Within the stack, a hard drive could fill up and crash, or a server address could corrupt. These problems, however buried, cause the application at the top to malfunction.

The assortment of distributed solutions is likely to grow. Laptops, palmtops and other mobile computing devices will serve as clients connect to the network through a variety of wireless communications media. The increasing need for greater bandwidth will continue to reshape the distributed computing infrastructure. Although the "network computer" promises to lower many costs, its simple existence adds to the complexity of enterprise computing and furthers the need for effective systems and application management.

REFERENCES

Wreden, Nick. "Mission: Control," *Communications Week*, Oct. 28, 1996.

Stafford, Jan. "Client-Server's Missing Link," *Var Business*, February 1997.

Grygo, Eugene M. "Find the Application (Then Manage It)," *Client/Server Computing*, December 1996.

Sobel, Ken. "Navigating the Application Hype," *Hurwitz Balanced View*. 1996.

Sobel, Ken. "Creating an Applications Management Strategy," *Hurwitz Balanced View Research Bulletin*, Oct. 24, 1996.

Dravis, Paul J. *The Systems Management Challenge*, Robertson Stephens & Co. Institutional Research, Dec. 10, 1996.

Interviews with Bill Yaman, Barry Ader, David Caddis and Carl Kotalik of Candle Corp., February–April 1997.

Chapter 5
Tools to Manage Network Elements

Hans Kruse

INTRODUCTION

Before we can begin our discussion of network management systems, we have to define the functions that we want such a system to assist us with. Network management processes are commonly grouped into five categories:

1. *Accounting Management* This category contains information collection activities that lead to some sort of measurement of resource usage by user (or group of users). These activities may or may not lead to the actual issuing of invoices or charge-backs. In a voice network, the collection of station message detail recording (SMDR) is an accounting management function.

   In most data networks, accounting information is usually collected for planning purposes, rather than for direct charge-back. This is related to the problem of accounting data collection in packet-switched networks. While it is relatively easy to gather usage data on classes of users or activities (for example the total number of balance inquiries initiated in a bank's automated teller network), it is often very difficult to track usage by individual users or even departments, since that information typically is not carried in data packets.

2. *Performance Management* While accounting management functions focus on resource usage by users or applications on the network, performance management activities are aimed at measuring the degree to which the network is able to perform its intended functions. For example, one may collect statistics on abandoned calls in a customer service center (i.e., callers who gave up while on hold in a queue). In a data network, one typically wants to know the percentage of available bandwidth that is used by the active applications.

   In transaction networks (as for example in the automated teller network) one tracks the response time per transaction (how long before the answer to the balance inquiry comes back to the cus-

0-8493-9990-4/99/$0.00+$.50
© 1999 by CRC Press LLC

tomer). Note that the resource usage on a network is necessarily time-dependent. Data must be collected continuously, and processed appropriately into average traffic loads for different times of the day (and day of the week).

3. *Security Management*   The network manager must ensure — in real time — that the network is "secure" in the sense of the following definitions: The network must be available to authorized users at the agreed-upon levels of service; network resources must not be accessible to unauthorized users; data in the network and its attached devices must be kept confidential, i.e., accessed only by authorized users; the network must ensure data integrity, i.e., data must not be altered in any way during network transit; finally, the network may need to provide a way to authenticate data, i.e., provide a way to prove that the data was sent by the stated originator.

   Due to the wide variety of requirements, activities and processes in this area range from toll fraud detection to diverse routing of redundant circuits, and from hacker and virus detection to encryption and digital signature mechanisms.

4. *Configuration Management*   Activities in this area begin with the tracking of equipment inventory and the cable and wire plant. Equally important, each device in the network must be given a set of option settings upon startup (e.g., clocking and framing for a T1 channel service unit (CSU)), as well as addressing and routing information.

   The network manager should at all times have access to the current as well as intended options, address, and routing settings for each device in the network. Current information can assist in diagnosing problems, or can locate available capacity for a new applications request. Intended settings for a device also assist in troubleshooting when compared with the actual settings; of course the intended settings are crucial if a failed device must be quickly replaced with a properly configured spare.

5. *Alarm Management*   Almost all devices in a network are capable of signaling the detection of a problem in some fashion. Alarms created by network devices are used to identify the source of a network outage or to prevent an outage by detecting deterioration in a resource prior to failure. In addition to local audible and visual alarms, most devices can report alarms to network management systems. Many devices can also activate pagers or other remote alert options.

   In all but the smallest of networks, the network manager faces the problem that a single network resource failure may trigger alarms from many different devices, creating information overload. Network operators can easily be overwhelmed by too many alarms, which actually hinder rather than help the problem isolation process. In addition, it is normal for even a perfectly operating network

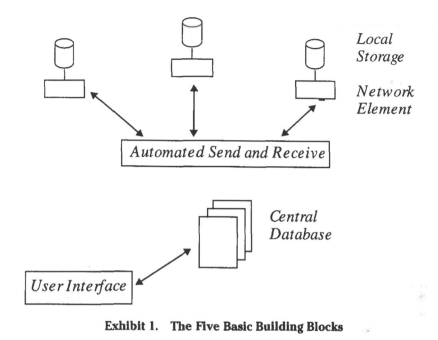

Local Storage

Network Element

Automated Send and Receive

Central Database

User Interface

Exhibit 1.   The Five Basic Building Blocks

to create a steady stream of low-level alarms. Again the problem is to recognize when an alarm can be ignored (or at least action deferred until a convenient time).

STRUCTURE OF NETWORK MANAGEMENT SYSTEMS

A Network Management System is supposed to assist in and sometimes automate some or all of the management functions we have just outlined. Although there are many different commercial implementations, they all include the five basic building blocks shown in Exhibit 1.

Managed Network Elements

Much of the difficulties surrounding network management systems arises from the fact that almost anything you attach to or insert into your network becomes by definition a manageable network element. Clearly we would expect to include modems, CSUs, and multiplexers in our network management system, as well as local area network (LAN) hubs and switches.

In addition, repeaters, bridges, and routers in our data network must be managed. In the voice network, PBXs and ACDs are the most visible part of the network. Increasingly, however, we need to also be concerned with applications and the platforms they operate on. Therefore, the network

69

management system should be able to address LAN-attached printers, database servers, file servers, voice mail and interactive voice response (IVR) systems, and possibly even end-user workstations.

Local Information Storage

If you review the definition of network management functions we covered earlier, you will see that the decisions to be made by the network manager require information about the current status of the each network element and some historical information about the amount of information that has passed through the element recently. The status information is derived from operational data that must be present in the device anyway (such as routing tables). Historical information is most easily and reliably assembled within each device as information flows are processed.

For this reason, most network elements have local storage capability for network management information. Indeed, in a small network, this information may never leave the element. Instead, the network manager may retrieve needed information directly at the device, using either a built-in keyboard and display or by attaching a simple display terminal to the device.

As the number of elements in a network grows and as these elements are distributed over a wider geographic area, direct access to each element may no longer be practical. It may be possible to attach a modem to each network element and use dial-up access to retrieve information and set configuration options. At some point, however, it will become imperative to collect the information from the network elements at a central site.

Centralized Database

By creating a centralized database the network management function can be improved in two ways: first, the collection of data from the local storage in the network elements can be automated; second, the network manager now has access to data from multiple network elements at the same time. This assists the network manager in those functions that require correlation of information from more than one place in the network.

Many network management functions require that the network manager insert information into the network element (e.g., configuration information). The network management database must therefore be able to send changes to the network element as well as collect information from the element.

Transport Network

As we discussed earlier, network elements can be managed locally, usually via a directly attached access device, such as a display terminal. If data from the network elements is to be collected into a central network management database, we need a transport network which covers the same geographic area as the actual network being managed (we will refer to the latter as the *information network*).

Two designs are possible for the transport network of the network management system. In many cases, it is possible to collect network management information over the information network; this is referred to as an in-band management system. It is also possible, and sometimes necessary, to transmit network management information over a separate management network designed specifically for this purpose. We refer to this as an out-of-band system.

Neither design has a principal advantage over the other one. The in-band network management network is usually less expensive, since it requires no additional circuits or equipment. The out-of-band system continues to operate (usually) even when the information network has failed and is therefore usable during network restoration activity. This is a large advantage for wide area networks where it may be impractical to physically reach an isolated device in a reasonable time. For that reason, LANs are usually managed using in-band systems, while wide area networks usually have at least an out-of-band option (such as a modem and a phone line attached to the maintenance port of each critical device), even if they normally operate in an in-band mode.

User Interface

Once our network elements are attached to the central database via the transport network, the network manager needs a convenient way to access the information collected in the central database and to make database modifications, which the network management system will transmit to the affected network element(s). This user interface may be located on the same computer as the database, or a distributed architecture may be used. In the latter case, the network manager can activate as many network management consoles as needed in different locations or for different network management functions.

The choice of single-console vs. a distributed user interface is usually made based on network size and price; systems with distributed user interfaces tend to be more expensive, while single-console ones become too restrictive once the network grows beyond the point where it can be handled by one operator. One should note that "web" technology may change this statement. Since it is becoming more and more common to enable database access via a World Wide Web server to distributed users with Web browsers, the same design can be used for network management.

This is certainly convenient for monitoring of network operations parameters. If security considerations are dealt with properly, the same technology can be used to make database changes.

Network management interface designers seem to have settled on the "map metaphor" for the user interface. That is, most network management systems will present the user a network map (often overlaid over a building blueprint or a geographic map) as the starting point for management operations. The map is used by the network operator to select network elements to operate on, and the network management system uses changes in color and/or different icons to convey to the operator the current status of each network element.

Care must be taken when purchasing a network operating system with a "map metaphor." Even a modest network can completely fill a 17- or even 21-inch computer screen with icons once all the network elements are accounted for. Good user interfaces allow the network manager to group icons either by function or by geography. A wide area network management screen may, for example, show initially only buildings; individual devices are revealed only after a specific building has been selected. A LAN map may show only "high level" devices, such as servers and routers, unless the operator specifically requests the display of other device classes (e.g., hubs).

The user interface must perform an additional, much less visible function. The central network management database simply collects data from the attached network elements. There is usually too much data to allow a simple examination or display of the data. The user interface must instead summarize and otherwise process the data for "human consumption." In the simplest case this involves the use of tabulation (e.g., create a report showing the percentage of bandwidth used on all LAN segments attached to a specific hub) and the use of thresholds (a toll fraud detection system may for example alert an operator if voice call volumes exceed 150% of the historical average usage for the current time of day).

High-end network management systems will also attempt to assist the network operator in performing certain tasks. The alarm management component of the system may for example attempt to examine alarms as they are received and correlate them into a probable problem diagnosis. Such a system is usually based on a rules-based "artificial intelligence," or AI, method. Even though the product literature may emphasize the AI aspect, the principle is relatively simple. Rules-based AI systems can very quickly compare a set of inputs (alarms in this case) to a large set of rules, and attempt to either prove that a particular explanation is likely or rule it out. After this process, there are often a small number of possible explanations left, which are then presented to the operator.

Rules-based AI systems are also frequently used to prevent configuration errors in the network. As the operator requests changes in device configuration, the network management system will examine its configuration rules and alert the operator of inconsistent settings (for example, two CSUs are on opposite ends of the same T1, but only one CSU is configure for B8ZS clear-channel operation). The system may also be able to suggest correlated configuration changes to avoid the inconsistency.

Because the functions we have outlined here require a fair amount of computing power, most network management systems are designed around workstation class computers, usually running various flavors of the UNIX operating system. In many cases, the native UNIX system is invisible to the network operator, who only sees the user interface of the network management system. If a UNIX-based network management station is attached to a LAN, however, all of the security precautions required to secure any UNIX workstation will also apply to the network management station. Properly securing a UNIX system is not something a first-time UNIX administrator should attempt without expert assistance.

CAN ONE SYSTEM REALLY DO ALL THIS?

We have described a wide range of functions that we want to perform centrally on all the network elements that make up our voice and data networks. Can a single network management system really perform in that role? In a word: no. The designers of network management systems face overwhelming difficulties in the design of such an all-encompassing system.

It is perfectly possible to create a system that can cover all the network management functions described if they are to be applied to a single class of devices, preferably all from the same vendor. It is not as easy, but still feasible, to perform a few functions on a large variety of device types from different vendors. Combining these two scenarios has not been accomplished yet.

In a typical network environment, the network manager will encounter many different device types. In all but a few networks, quite a few different vendors will be represented. In this type of network, the central integrated network management systems available today are designed to perform alarm and configuration management. Some systems have been developed by large equipment vendors. These systems are understandably very good at managing that vendor's devices. To be useful, however, any network management system must be able to deal with a multivendor network. Since the manufacturer of the network management system has no control over the local storage or the transport connectivity options of the managed devices, this requirement becomes the central problem in network management.

There are two common solutions implemented in today's systems. One is that the network management system can incorporate device-specific interface modules that query specific devices and translate the data into the structure required for the central database. This approach is very general and flexible in the range of devices it can support. It does, however, require a large amount of configuration work to set the system up, and the user may have to purchase special interface modules for network elements that the system does not already support.

An alternative approach involves the use of a standard network management protocol. Such a standard will define the type and structure of data that each type of device will hold in local storage. The standard will also define the transport options and the commands to be used to retrieve the data and to send configuration changes to the device. If all network elements support one of these standards, the setup and maintenance of the network management system will be considerably simpler. A potential negative to this approach (other than the question of how to deal with nonstandard devices) is that the standard data held in the device may only be a subset of the data the device vendor's proprietary structure holds. In that case, the standards-based management system may not have access to all the device options.

Since the central, integrated network management system cannot perform all the required network management functions, the system will then need to be supplemented with other tools to cover all the network management functions. Some of the more common supplemental tools are described below:

Cable tester

During installation of new service or after troubleshooting procedures point to a physical link as the likely problem source, cable testers permit out-of-service testing of physical wiring. This is the lowest level of test, and it is usually performed on-site.

Protocol analyzer

Many data communications problems result from equipment misconfiguration. Alarms and other diagnostics collected by the network management system can sometimes point to the source of the problem. However, many times it is necessary to actually "look into" the data stream to see the content of the transmission. A good protocol analyzer will present the data in human readable form, correlate separate data packets that are part of the same transaction, and allow the user to filter out unwanted traffic. Many protocol analyzers contain tools that specifically assist in problem resolution, such as two devices configured with the same address.

Since a protocol analyzer must be able to read all data on the network, its use should be carefully controlled for security reasons. Any unencrypted transmissions are vulnerable to unauthorized interception by a protocol analyzer. That may include passwords for some protocols, the content of electronic mail, etc.

Toll Fraud Detector

Detection of toll fraud on a customer-owned switch becomes necessary any time the PBX can at least, in principle, connect inbound and outbound trunks (regardless of the number of passwords and codes used). Hackers are very creative in finding ways to create these inbound to outbound "loops," so it is usually wise to assume that toll fraud is possible. A toll fraud detector is inserted into the SMDR stream (it receives the SMDR data from the PBX, processes it, and passes it on to the call accounting system). It keeps running averages of call volumes, and triggers an alarm if the call volume exceeds the threshold set for the current time of day. The alarm can go to a number of places, such as pagers, e-mail, voice announcers and other audible alarms, and of course the network management system. Some toll fraud detectors can even disconnect the PBX trunks or shut the PBX down entirely.

Security Auditing Tools

Data networks, especially LANs and Internet-connected networks are vulnerable to a wide variety of security threats. Most of these threats involve theft of service and unauthorized access to sensitive data. A good suite of network management tools will include security auditing tools appropriate to the types of networks that are in use in the corporation. These tools will probe the network using known lines of attack and report areas where these simulated attacks succeeded. There are also tools which will scan computer and voice mail systems for signs of past break-ins. This category of tools also contains scanners for known computer viruses, and those scanners should be kept up-to-date on all workstations.

Call Accounting

Integrated network management systems are not normally used for monthly reporting and billback operations (even though they may provide some input into such tools, for example records of completed work orders, or lists of features installed in a user's device). Call accounting systems are usually aimed at voice networks, where bill-back is common. They are highly specialized billing systems that can efficiently process a month's worth of call records and produce end-user bills, as well as departmental summaries. Good billing systems will also assist in reconciling actual call records with the invoices received from the carriers.

Cable and Wire Database

Although network management databases contain good device connectivity information, they are not usually designed to represent the detailed physical cable plant in a corporation's buildings. A cable and wire database directly tracks physical cable runs (of different media such as twisted pair and fiber), including spare capacity. If cable runs pass through intermediate points, these are also tracked in the cable and wire database.

Disaster Recovery Planning Tools

Disaster recovery deals with continued availability of critical resources even after significant network disruption. Proper planning and a detailed cost/benefit analysis are essential in the preparation of an effective and cost-justified disaster recovery plan. Disaster recovery planning systems are available from many of the large hot-site providers and are tailored towards tracking of critical resources, maintaining contact lists of key personnel, and keeping checklists that ensure that all parts of the network have been examined.

AN EXAMPLE OF A STANDARD: SNMP

The Simple Network Management Protocol (SNMP) was developed within the context of the Internet. It technically belongs into the Transmission Control Protocol/Internet Protocol (TCP/IP) family and requires an IP network to provide the transport between local storage and the central database. We should note that the Open Systems Interconnection (OSI) has standardized a competing network management protocol (CMIP). At this time, the TCP/IP protocols are much more widely deployed than OSI protocols. Without making any value judgment on SNMP and CMIP, we can conclude that SNMP is currently of more practical importance to the network manager, especially in networks that provide IP transport.

SNMP attempts to overcome the considerable problems inherent in managing a multivendor network with a variety of device types. The SNMP definitions cover a very formal definition of the content of local storage, and a specification of possible interactions between network management stations and the managed devices. We will very briefly describe how SNMP approaches these areas:

Local Storage Structure

SNMP defines the content of local storage as a collection of "managed objects," or variables. Every device type will clearly need a different set of variables; and even the same device type from two manufacturers may contain different, vendor-specific variables. SNMP defines a unique object name to each collection of variables. To manage the assignment of identifiers, a hierachial naming system is used. An SNMP object may be accessed via a (long) series of numbers, such as (1 3 6 1 4 1 879 32 55). In this example, the first number identifies that the ISO controls assignment of this type of object, the (3 6 1) point to Internet standard objects, the (4 1) following that identifies that this is a vendor-specific object. Conceptually, the object identifiers form a tree of increasingly more specific descriptions. This design makes it easy to delegate authority for the assignment of identifiers below a certain level in the tree, and it also makes it easy to add new identifiers.

Each object identified in this way can contain any number of variables that facilitate the management of the device in question. The network management station makes some assumptions about which objects a device may contain. It can make an access request to the device and find out from the device's response whether the assumption was indeed correct. The protocol also defines a way for the network management station to "scan" the device to learn about all objects supported by the device.

The SNMP design is attractive, since an update of a managed device does not impair the network management function; one simply cannot use any new capabilities until the network management system has been updated. At the same time, an older device can still be managed, since the network management system will "learn" that the older devices does not contain certain objects.

Protocol Functions

SNMP keeps the actual protocol functions very simple. The interaction between managed devices and the management system is based on a connectionless protocol, which requires little network resources. The protocol defines three retrieval functions: GET, GET-NEXT, GET-BULK. Respectively, these retrieve a specific object, scan for the next object, and retrieve all objects.

For device control, the protocol has the single SET functions, which modifies local storage variables for which this operation is allowed. Even functions such as "reset interface" or "reboot the device" are accomplished by storing specific values in a local storage variable. There is one function that allows the managed device to contact the management system, called a TRAP. The device can send such a message to alert the management system that something unusual has happened and that it should query the device to find out the specifics.

Security

Unfortunately, SNMP contains very little security. Standards designers are still struggling with possible approaches to this problem. Anyone who can intercept the network management traffic can discover the access codes used to interact with the devices in the network. Most device manufacturers have developed ways to work within the shortcomings inherent in SNMP's lack of security. Unfortunately, in some cases this means that critical device functions cannot be controlled via SNMP, since unauthorized access to these functions could severely disrupt the network.

SUMMARY

The features and capabilities of network management systems are updated at such a rapid pace that it is not practical to discuss specific systems here. In addition, the needs of each network are different. There are, however, a number of general recommendations that should help the network manager select a network management system.

Prepare for Multivendor Environments

Even if the current network is small and based on devices from a single vendor, this will most certainly not continue to be the case. Plan ahead and implement a system that is capable of supporting a wide variety of devices. If interface modules need to be developed, ensure that the vendor of the management system will continue to supply needed interface modules and at what price.

Insist on Standards Support, Including SNMP

Due to the current growth of the Internet, there has been considerable interest in, and vendor support of, the SNMP network management standard. Most LAN devices now offer SNMP support. Many traditional wide area network devices, such as CSU/DSUs, can also be obtained with SNMP support. Any network management system should support this standard and be capable of accessing the SNMP-compliant information in the network elements.

What is a Usable User Interface?

Look past the map-based, icon-covered screen. A good system will allow a hierarchy of displays, allow the user to customize the displays, and provide a wide variety of list-oriented reports. Look at how alarms are reported and acknowledged. If the system can correlate alarms, ensure that the rules in its AI system will work properly for the network to be managed.

Make Your Network Management System Redundant

Once a central network management system is in place, it is just as important to the organization as the network it manages. Therefore, the network management system must be redundant. There should be at least two geographically separate locations where the user interface is accessible.

The computer housing the central database is crucial to the entire system; the database needs to be maintained in at least two different locations. Modern database technology makes an almost real-time duplication of the database feasible. Finally, the paths to the managed network elements must not be lost, even during a network outage. Backup facilities, such as dial-up lines, must be available, especially if the network management system uses in-band transmission.

Security Considerations

A good network management system is a powerful tool, allowing the network manager to control a large network from a central site. This same tool in the wrong hands becomes an equally powerful tool that can deny network service to the legitimate users and facilitate unauthorized network access.

First, the central database and access to the user interface must be secured as one would secure the most critical of corporate information. Remote access to the central database should be heavily filtered so that only a very small number of workstations can gain access. The locations where these workstations are located must be secured with physical access restrictions (such as key cards) and monitored.

Second, access to the local storage in the network elements must be carefully password-protected. Clearly any attempts to write to the local storage must be accepted only from the central database site (most devices allow such restrictions). However, even the retrieval of information from the network elements must be restricted. Although it may seem harmless (since the device operation cannot be changed), information from the device may give an intruder information needed to penetrate the network security measures.

REFERENCES

These are a few examples of resources for more in-depth information on this subject.

Marshall T. Rose. *The Simple Book: An Introduction to Network Management*, Prentice Hall, 1996. This book provides a brief introduction into the structure of network management systems, and a detailed explanation of SNMP.

Gilbert Held. *Network Management*, John Wiley & Sons, 1992. This book focuses on management practices and on specific management tools.

William Stallings. *Practical Network Management*, Addison–Wesley, 1996. Stallings focuses on the standard network management protocols.

Not surprisingly, the Internet has many resources for the network manager. Any attempt to catalogue them would unfortunately be fleeting and futile. However, some examples may be useful:

The News Group — comp.dcom.net-management — is the best starting point. There are many other newsgroups for specific protcols, technologies, and operating systems.

An archive of the comp.dcom.net-management group, along with other resources, is at http://netman.cit.buffalo.edu/index.html.

One of the many mailing lists for network managers is net-troubleshooting@aggroup.com (send subscription requests to net-troubleshooting-request@aggroup.com); this list focuses on packet-level tracing and debugging of network problems.

Chapter 6
Enterprise Network Monitoring and Analysis

Colin Wynd

INTRODUCTION

In today's fast moving and highly competitive global business environment, the growing trend for industry is to invest in information technology (IT) to gain a competitive advantage in the marketplace. Corporations are now dependent on IT to perform their day-to-day business. As technology has evolved, one consequence has been an increase in the complexity of an IT environment.

This complexity is illustrated with the rapid deployment of intranet technologies. Client/server applications are being used in more mission-critical manners than ever before. With these two- and three-tier architectures, the boundaries of transactions are difficult to define, and the number of technology components and their relationships that must work together to provide a service are an order of magnitude higher than those used in the traditional mainframe systems.

This increased dependency has been especially apparent in the network arena. Networks have also had the largest change in complexity—evolving from a simple method for engineering departments to communicate to having the potential for everyone in a corporation to not only communicate with everyone else in the same organization but also with everyone connected to the Internet.

To respond to this new challenge of highly complex dependent networks, IT departments have adopted management products that are aimed at operational management and focused on ensuring the intranet (a corporation's network) is being monitored and analyzed for problems.

This chapter discusses the role that network monitoring and analysis takes in administrating networks. We start by explaining network monitor-

0-8493-9990-4/99/$0.00+$.50
© 1999 by CRC Press LLC

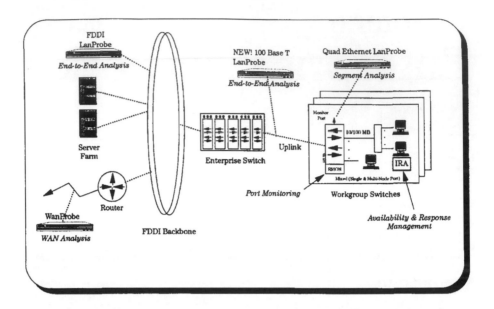

Exhibit 1.   Remote Monitoring Agents Installed on a Large Enterprise Network

ing and where it fits into the IT management arena before showing the range of functionality that network monitoring brings to the IT manager's arsenal.

NETWORK MONITORING AND ANALYSIS DEFINED

Distributed network monitoring is the ability to view a remote network and perform monitoring and analysis on that remote network as if it were local. In the past, portable devices were carried out to remote sites and placed onto the network when problems were occurring on that segment. Having a network-monitoring device on a segment only when there are problems means that the segment is not being monitored 99% of the time. Monitoring devices permanently placed on mission-critical segments can constantly monitor traffic. This means that analysis can be performed over and above fault management.

Exhibit 1 shows an example of remote monitoring agents installed on a large enterprise network with a variety of media types such as wide area networks (WANs), switches, and media types such as fiber distributed data interface (FDDI) and Ethernet.

The agents or "probes" reside on the remote segments and collect information of the traffic that they see. The segments can be of any media type from various local area network (LAN) media types such as Ethernet, FDDI, Token Ring, or some WAN protocols such as frame relay and asynchronous transfer mode (ATM). The segments can be geographically dispersed, but in general they must be interconnected. Polling of the interconnect devices can also take place. The network management console contains a suite of applications that collect the network information from these remote agents and by polling other devices, and then interprets them using power graphical user interfaces.

With this configuration network administrators can use tools to view and manage the whole network.

Some functions that the network administrator can perform are:

- Network performance management   This is the ability to continuously monitor certain network statistics to ensure adherence to the service level agreement and to set network thresholds to identify anomalies and the creation of baselines to aid in determining "normal" network performance.
- Network security monitoring   This is ensuring that only authorized users are accessing the network. This includes both monitoring the effectiveness of firewalls as well as internal security monitoring.
- Fault management and availability   This is being able to troubleshoot network problems in a timely fashion and to monitor the availability of servers from the end-user perspective.
- Capacity planning   Traffic profile modeling allows the network manager to do a quick "what if" analysis before reconfiguring network resources. Having the appropriate data of past network trends determines what changes need to be made in the future to handle the ever-growing network growth.

NETWORK MONITORING AND ANALYSIS IN THE IT ENVIRONMENT

The IT management environment covers the whole scope of devices that reside on the network as well as the network itself that enable business end users to function. We can break this down into four categories:

- Systems management is concerned with the performance of the computers on the network and usually deals with issues such as database performance and disk use on file servers.
- Element management is concerned with managing the various networking devices, such as bridges, routers, and hubs. Typical management issues deal with configuration tables, throughput, link states, and port partitioning. A device management application usually shows a picture of the device on your screen, complete with installed cards and indicator lights.
- Desktop management is concerned with the end-user workstations and personal computers (PCs). The management issues are PC configuration files, disk use, application support, etc.

- Network monitoring and analysis is primarily concerned with the activity on the wire itself. It is looking at the flow of data across the network in an effort to understand network performance and capacity, and to resolve problems related to networking protocols.

Service level management (SLM) is the strategy of defining, controlling, and maintaining the desired levels of IT service for the business end user. Business end users define with the IT department the level of service that is needed to support the end users. The level of service is turned into a set of objectives that the IT department can then monitor.

Network monitoring and analysis allows the IT department to manage one part of the end-to-end management picture. System, database, and application management issues are not discussed in this chapter.

Standards Overview

Network monitoring has benefited from several standards. The main standard currently in use for network monitoring is the remote monitoring (RMON) standard, which defines a method of monitoring traffic up to the data link layer (Layer 2) in the Open Systems Interconnection (OSI) stack. The RMON2 standard that currently has not yet been ratified by the Internet Engineering Task Force (IETF) defines how to monitor traffic at the network layer (OSI Layer 3) and some portions of the application layer (Layer 7). There are several proposed standards:

- Simple network management protocol (SNMP)
- RMON standard
- Remote monitoring version 2 (RMON2) standard

Why Do Network Monitoring?

As part of an IT department service level agreement (SLA) with its business end users, IT must maintain a certain level of network service. To be able to do this, the network must be monitored to ensure error-free connectivity, responsiveness, and level of throughput. If the network is not monitored, then it would be impossible for the IT department to guarantee any level of service.

In today's competitive environment, new client/server applications are quickly appearing in business environments; some examples are the World Wide Web, Lotus Notes, and networked games. If the network is not being monitored, then the effect of adding one of these network-intensive applications is unknown and eventually one will bring the network to its knees. If the environment is being monitored, then network bandwidth can be monitored and traffic trends analyzed to ensure that network bandwidth will always exceed future growth.

The ability to monitor trends changes the IT department from being reactive (waiting until something breaks before resolving the problem) to being proactive (resolving potential issues before they break). IT can now blend into the background allowing business end users to focus on their own function.

Who Does Network Monitoring?

Since there are many areas to network monitoring, many people are involved. Here are some generic descriptions:

- Network manager   This person is responsible for long-term strategic decisions concerning the network, and is involved in looking at new technologies such as 100Base-X or ATM, deciding where and when to modify bandwidth. This person also tends to look at network trends, performing forecasting, and capacity planning.
- Network engineer   This person is responsible for day-to-day operations of the network, and upgrades network devices and adds capacity. He also acts as a second line of support for problems that the operations center engineer cannot resolve.
- Operations center engineer   Most large corporations have a centralized monitoring center staffed with "level 1" engineers that attempt basic troubleshooting on problems. These engineers monitor for events that are triggered by servers, workstations, or network devices that can alert the operations center on potential problems. These engineers are the first line of support and are constantly in reactive mode.

What Data Is Provided?

Monitoring the network means that information on every single packet on every single segment can be gathered. Since it is impractical and costly to do this, network monitoring really means deciding which data is important and should be gathered and which data is redundant. Corporations with a large complex network need to decide on only a few critical pieces of information to collect, monitor, and analyze; otherwise the cost of monitoring the network will exceed all budgets. Some of the most critical measurements that should be gathered are:

1. Utilization   Segment utilization information should be gathered to generate trends for capacity planning purposes, baselining purposes, and performance information.
2. Error rates   Total error rate information can give performance indicators; baselining the error rate of the network and correlating it with utilization can give indicators of physical layer network problems.

3. Protocol distribution   This can generate trends for changing application mixes, monitoring the usage of new applications and the effect of new applications on the network.
4. Top talkers   These can also give indications on the performance of the network, performance of machines, load of application, and services on the network. Top talkers can also indicate potential new applications that are unknown to the network department (new Internet applications such as PointCast have been discovered using this method).
5. Latency measurements (echo tests)   These lead to trends in performance.

How Does Network Monitoring Work?

Network monitoring is a large subject, and there are many proprietary protocols that are involved. We are only going to cover standards-based protocols, plus the most widespread proprietary protocols.

SNMP. The SNMP was a draft standard in 1988 and was finally ratified in April 1989. SNMP is described by request for comments (RFC) 1098. SNMP has three basic components:

- Agent   This is a software program that resides in a managed element of the network such as a hub, router, or specialized device.
- Manager   This communicates with the agent using the SNMP commands.
- Management information base (MIB)   This is a database that resides with the agent and holds relevant management information.

Exhibit 2 shows the relationship between the three components (agent, MIB, and manager).

There are five types of SNMP commands called protocol data units (PDUs):

- Get request   A manager requests (from the agent) the value of a variable stored in the MIB.
- Get-next request   This is used by the manager to request information on multiple variables and is used to reduce network traffic. If one variable is not available, no values are returned. This request is also used to retrieve unknown rows if available.
- Set request   The manager instructs the agent to set an MIB variable to the desired value.
- Get-response   This is sent by the agent as a response to a SET or get-next command as either an error or identical to the SET to show it was accepted, or to a get-next with the value portions of the request filled in. The manager checks its list of previously sent requests to locate

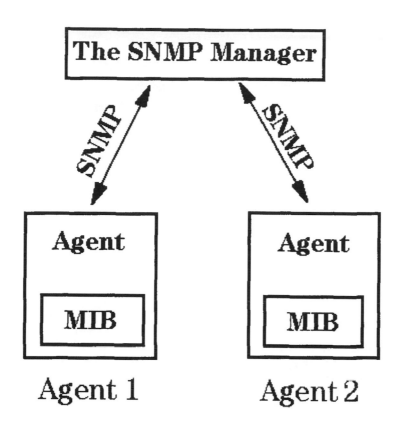

Exhibit 2. Relationship Between Agent, MIB, and Manager

the one that matches this response and if none are found, the response is discarded; otherwise it is handled.

- Trap   This is one of two unsolicited messages sent from the agent to the manager, often used for event notification.

MIB Tree. MIBs are hierarchical in nature; this allows unique identifiers for each MIB variable (or object). Some MIBs of interest are

- RFC1213   MIBII—basic system information and basic level statistics
- RFC1757   RMON
- RFC1513   RMON extension for Token Ring

There are several advantages that network management applications have with SNMP:

- The protocol is easy to implement.
- The protocol requires few resources to operate.

- The protocol is mature, stable, and well-understood.
- The protocol is widely available (on most computers), and most network devices have some form of agent or MIB embedded within them.

However, as networks have grown and the need for network management has become more imperative, several disadvantages with SNMP have become apparent; some of these disadvantages are

- Limited security
- Lack of a block transfer
- Polling-based protocol
- Trap limitations

SNMPv2 is a proposed standard that will address the preceding issues. Currently all issues have been addressed apart from the security issue but have caused the final version of the SNMPv2 standard to be delayed in the standards process.

RMON Protocol. The RMON standard is a specific standard for performing remote monitoring on networks. The RMON standard is defined by two standards, RFC 1757 and RFC 1513. The standard defines an MIB that is broken down into ten groups; the first nine define monitoring of Ethernet networks, and the tenth defines extensions for Token Ring. There are currently no standards for monitoring FDDI, 100Base-X, or WAN networks. RMON vendors have added their own proprietary extensions for these additional media types. RMON is limited, as it gives visibility only up to the data link layer (Layer 2) in the OSI stack. Exhibit 3 depicts a diagram of the RMON standard:

- Statistics group   This group contains many segment statistics in 32-b counters such as packets, dropped packets, broadcasts, and multicasts. These are just counters and not studies.
- History group   This group contains segment history statistics for various counters such as broadcasts, errors, multicasts, packets, and octets. These numbers are for certain time periods. RMON defines two default time periods—5 and 1800 s. The meaning follows.
- Alarms group   This covers threshold monitoring and trap generation when that threshold has been reached and allows alarms to be set of various counters and patch match. Traps can start and stop packet capture.
- Host group   This contains host table and traffic statistic counters, plus a timetable of discovery.
- Host top N   This contains studies for X time and X hosts, listing top talker for the study group.
- Traffic matrix group   This contains matrix of media access control (MAC) layer (Layer 2) conversations. Included is information such as error, packets, and octets sorted by MAC address.

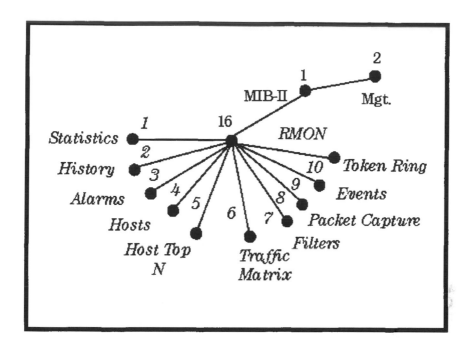

Exhibit 3.   The Hierarchical Nature of MIBs

- Packet capture and filter group   These two groups are used together. Packet capture group contains the packets that have been captured. Multiple instances can be created.
- Token Ring Group   This contains specific information about Token Ring such as ring order, ring station table, and packet size distribution for history studies.

The RMON standard has been widely deployed by embedding it into hubs, switches, and routers. Most implementations of this standard are "lightweight" or "partial" RMON, since they do not implement all the groups (in most cases only four of the nine groups). However, this means that IT managers can gather quite a bit of useful information about the state of their network without investing in stand-alone data collectors. This reduces the overall cost of network monitoring and analysis.

RMON2 Protocol. The RMON standard brought many benefits to the network monitoring community, but it also left out many features. The RMON2 standard attempts to address these issues by allowing the monitoring of Layer 3 (network layer) information as well as protocol distribution up to Layer 7 (application layer). Exhibit 4 shows the new standard. Just as RMON is, RMON2 is broken into different groups.

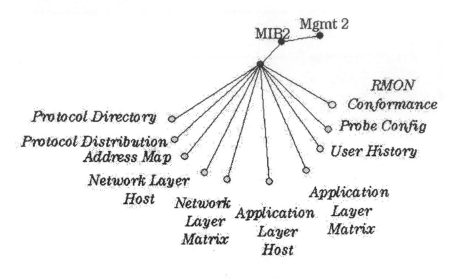

Exhibit 4.   RMON2 New Standards

It takes about ten times more processing power and memory to implement RMON2 than it does to implement RMON. Due to the competitive nature of hubs, switches, and routers, there has been little effort by the interconnect-device vendors to embed RMON2. This has significantly delayed the deployment and acceptance of RMON2 by the industry, although this is slowly starting to change. Exhibit 5 compares RMON to RMON2 to the Hewlett-Packard Co. NetMetrix Extensions in the network stack. Note that most vendor extensions still cover more of the stack than the RMON and RMON2 standards.

FUNCTIONS OF THE NETWORK ADMINISTRATOR

Network Performance Management

Performance management means being able to monitor segment activity as well as intrasegment traffic analysis. Network managers must be able to examine traffic patterns by source, destination, conversations, protocol and application type, and segment statistics such as utilization and error rates. Network managers must define the performance goals and how notification of performance problems should happen and with what tolerances. Some objectives that network managers are faced with are

- Baselining and network trending   With these they can determine the true operating envelope for the network by defining certain measurements (such as segment utilization, error rate, and network latency) to check your service level objectives and out-of-norm conditions which,

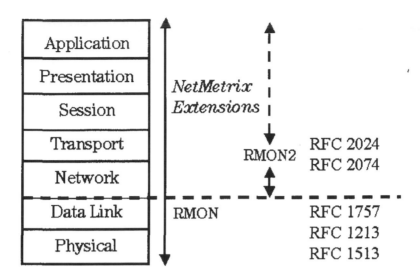

Exhibit 5. RMON, RMON2, and HP NetMetrix Extensions

if gone unchecked, may have drastic consequences on networked business users productivity.

- Application usage and analysis   These help managers answer questions such as, "What is the overall load of your Web traffic?" "What times of the day do certain applications load the network?" These also allow network managers to discover important performance information (either real-time or historic) that will help define performance service level objectives for applications in the client/server environment.
- Internetwork perspective   Is traffic between remote sites and interconnect devices critical to your business? With internetwork perspective capabilities, you can discover traffic rates between subnets and find out which nodes are using WAN links to communicate. It can also help you define "typical" rates between interconnect devices. Internetwork perspective can show how certain applications use the critical interconnect paths and define "normal" WAN use for applications.
- Data correlation   This allows you to select peak network usage points throughout the day and to discover which nodes were contributing to the network load at that peak point in time, which nodes they were sending traffic to, and which applications were running between them.

Exhibit 6 shows an example of traffic flow between several segments. The thickness of the line indicates the volume of traffic. With this information it is easy to identify potential WAN bottlenecks.

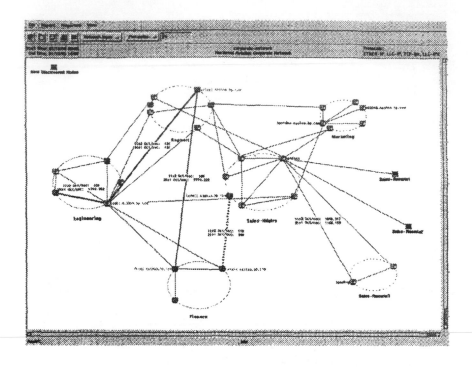

Exhibit 6. Traffic Flow Between Several Segments

Exhibit 7 shows clients/servers correlated with a time graph. Being able to determine how much one particular server affects the network can help in the positioning of that server and again improve performance.

Network Security Monitoring

Security management encompasses a broad set of access control policies that span network hosts, network elements, and network access points (firewalls). Consistent policies are the key here; the objective is to support access and connectivity that is appropriate to the business need, while restricting clearly inappropriate network-based access. As in other activities, constant monitoring for specific violations is critical, as is a notification mechanism. For certain conditions, immediate, automatic action maybe required, (i.e. "shut down this connection" or "shut down the fire wall"). Monitoring should include both passive and active monitoring (probing).

Access level monitoring ensures that the controls and security that are in place are actually performing to expectations. Monitoring the traffic flow to or from a firewall, for instance, ensures that no intruders are accessing

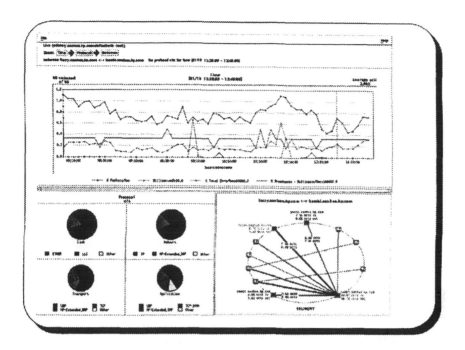

Exhibit 7.   Clients and Servers Correlated with a Time Graph

internally. Access level monitoring polices the "police" and ensures that nothing has been overlooked by the security.

Fault Management and Availability

Fault management is the continuous monitoring of the network and its elements and the detection of failures within the network environment. When a failure is detected, then notification of the failure must occur in a timely fashion. The failure must be qualified with respect to other failures and prioritized.

Fault management systems include software bundles to detect and notify a centralized system of these failures. The centralized system normally includes some form of discovery and mapping software that allows the network manager to have a graphic view of the network. These notifications must be correlated so that event storms are eliminated. A trouble ticketing system can also be incorporated so that a document trail is kept of the problem and allows a mechanism to communicate the status of the problem to the end users.

Another aspect to fault management is availability. This is the monitoring of servers from the business end user perspective to ensure that the

93

machine is available to the end user. Tracking and notification of any inter-ruption of client/server access are critical parts of the IT department func-tion.

Capacity Planning

Network demand is growing at unprecedented rates. New applications such as SAP and the Web are encouraging extensive use of the network. Graphics are now sent regularly over the network (either through a corpo-ration intranet or over the Internet). As network managers increase band-width, new capabilities for the network (such as voice-over-Internet Protocol [IP] or multimedia) become viable. This causes another spurt of demand for the network.

Capacity planning allows the network manager to look forward by look-ing at the past and helps the manager to forecast what the demand will be. This means that the IT department can keep one step ahead in demand.

Network Health and Availability Reporting

Network reporting is how we measure the quality of network services being provided by the IT department. This quality metric can be a complex value composed of information obtained from different parts of the intra-net fabric. Being able to report on the quality of the network being provid-ed also means that we have to continually monitor the fabric, and to understand which parts of the network are being used to provide overall IT services.

Reports can be generated from the RMON and RMON2 data being pro-vided. The typical information that interests us is

1. Network health reports show the network utilization, error rates, etc. These reports show how busy the network is, and therefore we can trend to predict future quality (or lack of).
2. Top consumer of the network can be the top consumer of a segment; however, due to switching, it is more valuable to have global reports showing the consumers of a building, site, or enterprise.
3. Application mix and usage are important for knowing the applica-tions running over the network and also for showing the changing mix of applications over time.
4. The client/server availability is being able to show the performance of the network between clients and servers, and the availability of servers from a client's perspective will indicate the application re-sponse time due to the network. If this is too high, end users will start to complain and productivity will decrease.

It is important that any reports are generated automatically; otherwise reports will not be generated or the effort to generate them will be too substantial to make it worthwhile.

Limitations of Network Monitoring and Analysis

Monitoring the network with the RMON standard means that only data link layer (Layer 2) information is collected. This is not high enough in the OSI stack to gather information about traffic trends of client/server applications.

The RMON2 standard defines a method of monitoring up to Layer 7 at certain times. RMON2 does not define continuous monitoring of all Layer 7 traffic, and RMON2 does not define any metrics for performance management.

Both the RMON and RMON2 standards were developed before switching and cell-based networks were widely distributed. Fundamental to RMON and RMON2 is that by distributing data collectors around the network, network monitoring and analysis can easily be achieved. Switching by its very nature makes it difficult to deploy data collectors in such a manner that complete visibility is easy to achieve. Network managers must now rethink how they deploy their RMON and RMON2 data collectors to achieve maximum visibility into the workings of the network.

SUMMARY

Enterprise network monitoring and analysis exist in a fast changing environment. From the early days (just a few years ago) of monitoring the physical layer of the networks to the future of application layer service level management, the whole arena is helping IT management take control of the distributed environment that it spans.

The move to have these tools on the NT platform will also speed the development of these tools as well as help bring down the cost of deploying these tools in the network environment.

Network monitoring and analysis will always have several aspects that have been described in this chapter, and the tools for implementing service level agreements between business end users and IT departments are quickly maturing.

However, network monitoring is only part of the total end-to-end solution that must include the whole environment that business end users operate. This means that systems, databases, and application monitoring tools must be deployed in conjunction with the network monitoring tools so that the whole environment can be viewed. Some tools such as Hewlett-Packard's OpenView family of products are just being released that for the first time can seamlessly integrate database, application, network, and system information on a single pane of glass for the end-to-end view that is necessary in this complex environment that IT must now work.

REFERENCES

Peter Phaal *LAN Traffic Management*, Prentice Hall, ISBN: 0-13-124207-5.
Dah Ming Chiu and Ram Sudama, *Network Monitoring Explained*, Ellis Horwood, ISBN: 0-13-614-710-0.
Nathan Muller, *Focus On OpenView* CBM Books, ISBN: 1-878956-48-5.
Marshall T. Rose, *The Simple Book*, Prentice Hall, ISBN: 0-13-812611-9.

Chapter 7
The Cable Plant

Arlyn S. Powell, Jr.

INTRODUCTION

The Open Systems Interconnection (OSI) reference model of the International Standards Organization (ISO — Geneva, Switzerland) divides the functions involved in the exchange of information between computer systems into seven layers, with the physical layer at the bottom and the application layer at the top. The physical layer, as its name implies, comprises the cable, connectors, and other passive components included in the cable plant that link computers and other networked end-user devices to the hubs, bridges, routers, and other active devices in the local area network (LAN).

Although the cable plant is often viewed by network managers as the simplest and least glamorous part of the network, it is worthy of further study and greater understanding — if for no other reason than that the surveys published in networking magazines consistently identify the cable plant as the place where the majority of network failures occur.

Let's take a brief tour of the cable plant, after which we will look at some of the technical issues that impact it.

Cabling Media

The basic component of any cable plant is clearly the cable itself. Although there are only four major cabling media — coaxial, shielded or screened twisted-pair, unshielded twisted-pair, and optical fiber — there are variations within each medium to serve the many tasks that cable is called upon to perform. A few of these variations include:

- *Backbone or riser cable* The large, multipair or multifiber cable that runs from the computer or equipment room to the telecommunications closet is called backbone cable. Because it ascends the shafts between floors in high-rise buildings, it is also sometimes called riser cable.
- *Composite cable* A recent manufacturing trend in the cabling industry has been to include both copper wire and optical fiber within the same overall jacket. Such mixed-media cables are called composites.

0-8493-9990-4/99/$0.00+$.50
© 1999 by CRC Press LLC

- *Horizontal cable*   The cables that connect the telecommunications closet on a building's floor with a workstation are called horizontal cables because they typically run horizontally rather than vertically.
- *Hybrid cable*   Although there has been some confusion in the nomenclature, hybrid cable is coming to be defined as a cable that includes both multimode and singlemode optical fiber within the same outer jacket.
- *Indoor/outdoor cable*   There have historically been marked distinctions between the characteristics of inside wire vs. outside-plant cable, but some manufacturers have recently introduced cable types that can meet the requirements of both, eliminating the need for an interconnect where the cable enters a building.
- *Inside wire*   Used within a building, inside wire is often characterized by stringent fire-resistance requirements that apply to its jacketing and materials.
- *Outside-plant cable*   Although outside-plant cable is usually associated with the large trunk cables installed by long-distance telecommunications service providers, it is also used in campus environments such as business parks, hospital complexes, military installations, and school and college campuses. It must provide protection from moisture, rodents, ultraviolet light, and other environmental conditions that installers of inside wire need not be concerned with.
- *Plenum cable*   Any indoor cable that is placed in an air-handling space, or plenum, must meet special fire-resistance requirements because of the role plenums can potentially play in spreading building fires.

Coaxial cable has a reputation among network managers as being a medium in decline, but it continues to find use in legacy data networks and has been recently identified by the cable-television industry as one of the two important residential cable types to be used in hybrid fiber-coax (HFC) installations.

Coaxial cable has higher bandwidth than any cabling medium except optical fiber, exhibits low attenuation so it can be run for long distances, and is by nature a shielded transmission path. Among its disadvantages, it is less familiar than twisted-pair technology and is more difficult to install and terminate. It is also more expensive than other copper-based media.

Shielded twisted-pair (STP) cable, like coaxial cable, is most familiar to those who have worked with mainframe or minicomputer systems, since the most common type of shielded cable in the U.S. has been IBM Type 1. However, a recent initiative in the European Community limiting electromagnetic (EMI) and radio-frequency (RFI) interference has given a variation of STP, *screened twisted-pair (ScTP),* a new lease on life.

There are several different cable designs vying for supremacy in the U.S. and Europe, but all configurations have in common a shield much like coaxial cable's outer braid that limits emissions both from and on to the cabling within. The need for grounding, as well as the extra materials required in ScTP designs for the shielding, make this medium larger, stiffer, and more difficult to terminate than unshielded media. ScTP cables also are more expensive. Proponents of the medium argue, however, that it offers more bandwidth than its unshielded counterpart, and its immunity to emissions justifies its use in such sensitive environments as factory floors and hospitals.

Unshielded twisted-pair (UTP) cable has become the dominant medium in data communications in recent years because it is a familiar format to network managers and it has the reputation of being rugged, inexpensive, and simple to install. UTP cable depends on electrical balance between signals transmitted over a wire pair to substitute for the shielding employed by other copper cabling media to prevent the noise and interference that lead to transmission errors.

Designed originally for voice lines, UTP cable's benefits for high-speed data networking have recently been called into question by critics who point out that the Category 5 UTP cable required for transmission at 100 MHz or above is more expensive, less rugged, and more difficult to install than twisted-pair telephone wire. In addition, the four-pair cable specified for most horizontal data wiring has acknowledged bandwidth limitations compared to optical fiber, even though manufacturers of so-called enhanced-performance Category 5 cable are already warranting it for transmission of asynchronous transfer mode (ATM) at 155M bps. A typical Category 5 cable is shown in Exhibit 1.

In addition, researchers are predicting that Gigabit Ethernet (at 1000 M bps) successfully can be carried on this medium. Left unresolved at this time are the complex encoding schemes, sensitive network electronics, standards and testing issues, and electrical characteristics to be specified before UTP cable can operate at 1G bps.

Unlike the three copper media, *optical fiber* transmits light instead of electricity and so operates on completely different principles, which in turn lead to a unique set of advantages and disadvantages. *Multimode optical fiber* is larger in diameter, permitting more light paths (or modes) in the fiber core, while *singlemode optical fiber* has a core so small that only a single light path is present. Even so, singlemode fiber provides the greater transmission bandwidth.

Because of its great bandwidth, optical fiber has been used for some years in long-distance telephone trunk lines, and while copper-wire manufacturers are experimenting with 1G-bps transmission over UTP, optical-fiber experimenters are working an order of magnitude higher, at 1T bps. For this reason, optical fiber is already the preferred medium for network

Exhibit 1. Four-Pair, Unshielded Twisted Pair (UTP) Category 5 Cable
This sample from Montrose/CDT is identified by each four pairs and lettering giving the standards it meets and name of manufacturer. (Photo courtesy of Monstrose/CDT)

backbones, and it is rapidly finding its way to the desktop for high-speed applications. Multimode fiber is specified for most backbones today, but far-sighted network managers are already installing hybrid cables containing multimode and singlemode fibers, using the former for current applications while leaving the latter "dark" or unused for projected future networking protocols.

Among its drawbacks, optical fiber has a reputation for being expensive, fragile, and difficult to install. Comparisons have shown, however, that it is no more fragile than Category 5 UTP, and manufacturers have done much in recent years to make fiber-optic cable simpler to terminate and install. The cost of fiber-optic cable and passive components has also come down considerably, even though the cost of the active electronics that converts light to electricity and electricity back to light remains a stumbling block to widespread fiber-to-the-desktop (FTTD).

CONNECTORS

As one might suspect, the popularity, pros, and cons of the connectors used with various cabling media are reflected by the use, advantages, and disadvantages of the media themselves. Coaxial connectors, for example, are larger, bulkier, more expensive, and more complicated to attach than their twisted-pair counterparts, and the same may be said of shielded or screened components. This results in part because the cabling media themselves are larger, stiffer, and made from more expensive materials, and it is also due in part to the complications in installation created by the need for grounding and the requirement that the cable link have an unbroken shield from end-to-end.

Four-pair UTP cable, on the other hand, is terminated for the most part using small, inexpensive, plastic eight-pin modular connectors — sometimes mistakenly called RJ-45 connectors. These connectors can be wired in a number of different patterns — the most common being labeled T568A and T568B. Often viewed as the weak link in a cable run because of the attenuation and crosstalk they can potentially contribute to a high-speed data line, they are designed by manufacturers to include compensating circuitry using several different engineering techniques. In addition, it requires manual skill to field-terminate a four-pair Category 5 cable to specification, leading some network managers to order their cabling factory-terminated and tested. Tools required to terminate an eight-pin modular connector include wire cutters, strippers, and crimpers.

More than a dozen different fiber-optic connectors have been in use over the last decade, among them the ST, SC, SMA, biconic, mini-BNC, FDDI, ESCON, FC, and D4. Each has its own story, as well as advantages and disadvantages, but the winner in the fiber-optic connector derby appears to be the SC, which is now recommended in both domestic and international cabling standards. In addition, the ST connector, which has a wide installed base, is being permitted to remain in use in existing installations. A typical coaxial BNC connector is shown in Exhibit 2.

Traditional fiber-optic connectors are noted for the time, effort, and skill required to attach them to optical fibers. Many come in multipiece kits that must be assembled in the field using ultraviolet- or heat-curing ovens needing an electrical outlet to operate. In addition, special tools, such as fiber cleavers and polishing pucks and films, must be used.

Manufacturers have worked hard in recent years, however, to both reduce the number of assembly steps required and to cut down on the special equipment that must be used. Several manufacturers now offer so-called quick-connect fiber-optic connectors that are crimped rather than epoxyed to the fiber. Such connectors are more expensive today than conventional designs, but they provide savings in installation time and the

Exhibit 2   Coaxial BNC Connector
The Quick Termination model from ITT Cannon. (Photo is courtesy of ITT Cannon)

need for specialized equipment. Most quick-connect connectors, though, still require cleaving and polishing.

OTHER CONNECTION SCHEMES

In addition to attaching connectors to the ends of equipment cords, patch cords, and horizontal cables, there are two other connection schemes that are found mostly — although not exclusively — in computer and equipment rooms or telecommunications closets: Crossconnection and interconnection.

A *crossconnect* includes movable patch cords or jumper cables that populate a patch panel. The *patch panel* in a telecommunications closet, for instance, is used to connect horizontal cable runs ending at workstations with riser cable originating in the computer room. The patch panel, which was developed to serve data communications needs, is noted for its flexibility, since moves, adds, and changes can be implemented simply by unplugging and plugging in patch cords.

The *interconnect* depends on direct connection of a wire, the most common method being *insulation-displacement connection (IDC)* found in telephone systems. With an IDC connection, the wire is forced into an ever narrowing groove until its insulation is penetrated and electrical contact established. Nicknamed a *punchdown block* because of the technique used to force the wires into the grooves, this device is noted for durable, lasting connections and it is not employed where flexibility in wiring is required.

Patch cords, as well as equipment cords, have copper-wire or fiber-optic connectors at each end that are attached in the same way that other cables are connectorized. Sometimes fiber-optic patch cords are also called *jumpers*. If a patch cord has one type of connector at one end and a different type at the other, it may be called an *adapter cable*. Connections between balanced cabling, such as UTP, and electrically unbalanced cabling, such as coaxial cable, is accomplished by using *baluns* (a shortening of "balanced/unbalanced").

Most LANs are built using single pieces of wire or fiber — that is, a four-pair Category 5 cable is pulled from telecommunications closet to workstation where it is cut to length and terminated at each end. A single, unbroken backbone cable then connects the workstation to the computer room, where it is connected to the network. In larger cable plants — on university campuses, for example — there may be a need for still one more type of connection: splicing.

Splicing of large-pair-count copper backbone cables is usually the province of a specialist in outside-plant wiring, but splicing optical fiber, which comprises most campus and building backbones anyway, has become a less technical procedure that may involve a network manager and his staff. For temporary repair of cut fiber-optic cables, a *mechanical splice*, which operates in much the same way as a fiber-optic connector, can be used. Permanent splices, which actually fuse the two glass ends of the fibers together, are made using a *fusion splicer*, an expensive, high-technology device that requires specialized training and, in some cases, a climate-controlled operating environment.

RACKS AND ROUTING

Although IDC blocks are often mounted on plywood attached to the wall of the telecommunications closet or equipment room, most data-communications equipment today is housed in racks or enclosures. *Racks* of standardized dimensions are little more than a series of horizontal shelves supported by legs, but they offer great flexibility in mounting both active equipment, such as hubs and routers, and passive components, such as patch panels. Racks are usually open in front and back to permit access to network components, but this open format can be a disadvantage if security, an aesthetic appearance, or protection from dust are required. In cases where more security or protection is needed, an *enclosure* may be the answer. A four-sided enclosure, however, will need a heat-dissipation capability for active electronics and will be more expensive than a rack of corresponding capacity.

Within buildings communications cabling is usually supported by some sort of distribution system that is designed to protect or isolate the cable

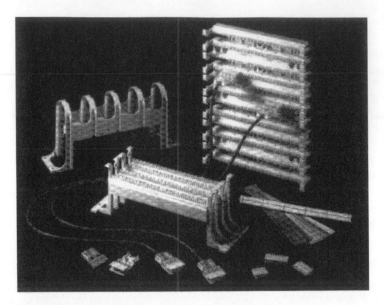

Exhibit 3. Punchdown System for Category 5 Cable
(Photo courtesy of Panduit Corp.)

runs while routing them flexibly to different destinations. The simplest such system probably consists of *cable-hanging hardware* such as bridle rings, which are used above suspended ceilings. Since both fiber-optic and Category 5 cables can be degraded in performance by bending, kinking, and crushing, such cable-hanging systems must be carefully designed and expertly installed if used for high-speed data networks. A punchdown system for Category 4 cable is shown in Exhibit 3.

If more support or protection is needed, *cable troughs, raceways, or wireways* can be installed. These systems can consist of three-sided, U-shaped channels (with optional lids); openwork wire or plastic modular units; or color-coordinated and decorator perimeter raceways designed to blend in with building interiors. The mechanics of joining system components together, their flexibility in turning left or right (or up and down), cost per foot, strength, appearance, and durability are all factors to consider in selecting a system.

For horizontal runs to the workstation, where only one or a few cables are involved, electrical or telephone *conduit* may suffice. Also, modular furniture systems, so popular in open-office work environments these days, often have their own built-in cable-routing features.

Most cable plants need a generic cable-grouping or management device, a need which is usually filled by the plastic *cable tie*. Applied by hand or using a simple device, these ties must not be cinched too tightly or they may crush the cables they hold. Crushing and other forms of mishandling can cause microbending in optical fibers, which degrades its performance; such practices can also disturb the uniformity of the twists in twisted-pair cable, which can again limit throughput.

In fact, conduit and other routing hardware may have a prescribed percentage of fill that is allowed, and both fiber-optic and Category 5 cabling have minimum bend radiuses, stripping and untwisting limitations for termination, and other handling and installation guidelines that, if not adhered to, may degrade the performance of the cable plant. In most cases, minimum guidelines are outlined in the relevant cabling standards.

CABLE PROTECTION AND MANAGEMENT

The Telecommunications Industry Association (TIA of Arlington, VA) has published a standard it labels TIA/EIA-606, which details the administrative requirements of identifying, labeling, and documenting each cable, connection, and passive component of an organization's network.

This standard has led to the vigorous development of a number of *cable management software (CMS)* packages, as well as a proliferation of cable marking and labeling equipment. In some cases, the CMS package will drive a computer printer to produce all the labels needed to tag various system components. Some cable-management software systems integrate into network management software, while others have a graphic capability stemming from compatibility with standardized computer-aided design (CAD) software.

CMS packages can also aid in hardware inventorying, trouble-ticketing and repair, and disaster planning and recovery.

Marking and labeling systems, as noted, can depend on CMS packages for input, or they can consist of portable, handheld labeling devices which can be used at a construction site. Labels can be made from a number of different materials — for instance, paper, plastic, or metal — and can be attached by adhesive, shrink-wrapping, or lamination. Labels can be color-coded, and they may be suitable for outdoor and hazardous-environment as well as indoor use.

Although not necessarily considered a part of the traditional cable plant, both firestopping devices and power conditioning and protection equipment are rapidly becoming vital considerations for the cable-plant manager.

Firestopping devices and materials normally are required by the local building code any time a cable run penetrates a firewall or fire-rated floor or ceiling. Various firestopping systems are offered by a number of different manufacturers, but each system must be rated by Underwriters Laboratories (UL of Oak Brook, IL) or another qualified testing laboratory. Fire ratings can be given in the number of hours it takes a fire of specified temperature to burn through a firestop, or the time it takes to reach a particular temperature, or both; the requirements for any given locale are found in the building code and enforced by the building inspector or some other official.

As sensitive network equipment has been connected to the telephone network (through modems) and the electrical power-distribution system (through power cords), issues of grounding and bonding, surge protection and suppression, and uninterruptible power supply have arisen. Lightning strikes, utility brownouts, and ground loops can burn out motherboards, shut down computer equipment, and even present an electrical-shock hazard to workers.

These eventualities have led the TIA to publish a grounding and bonding standard, TIA/EIA-607, just as they have brought makers of surge-suppression devices and uninterruptible power supplies (UPSs) into the networking market. *Surge suppressors or protectors* work something like fuses, sacrificing themselves when a power surge caused by a lightning strike enters a buildling and threatens the electronic equipment operating there.

An *uninterruptible power supply* can both condition utility power, removing its fluctuations, and supply back-up power in the case of a blackout or other power failure. With data networks operating 24 hours a day in many businesses and assuming critical roles in their financial success, network managers are being required to install power protection from the mainframe level right down to the individual personal computers at workstations.

Cabling Standards

Many data-communications and related organizations — the Institute of Electrical and Electronic Engineers (IEEE of New York City), the ATM Forum, the Gigabit Ethernet Alliance — have produced (and continue to produce) transmission standards that support specific applications. The Telecommunications Industry Association is unusual, however, in attempting over the past decade to produce a set of standards covering generic requirements for cabling systems so that they will support all relevant applications.

The organization's approach has been to set various levels of performance, called Categories, for which cable and connector specifications can be established. For example, with UTP cable three permissible maximums have been established for near-end crosstalk (NEXT), an electrical property relating to the spillover of signal from one wire pair to another measured at one end of a cable. The highest NEXT value is permitted for Category 3 cable, which is rated to 10 MHz and is currently used most often for voice lines. A more stringent NEXT requirement applies to Category 4, rated to 16 MHz, an interim category that is now almost defunct. The most rigorous requirement is for Category 5 cable, rated to 100 MHz, which has proved to be by far the most popular of the three cabling classifications.

Cabling and component manufacturers are responsible for having their products verified as meeting the relevant category specifications by an independent testing laboratory. In this scenario, if a network manager purchases only verified Category 5 cable and components and installs them properly, the network should operate to a bandwidth of 100 MHz, regardless of whether one manufacturer makes the cable and another the connectors. The need to purchase end-to-end proprietary systems is averted, and the end-user can rest assured that advertised performance will be actual performance.

The TIA's standards committees meet quarterly to consider technical issues that should be incorporated into future revisions of its standards, so it is impossible to be completely up-to-date. However, here is a list of core telecommunications-cabling standards that are in effect as of this writing:

- TIA/EIA-568A: Commercial Building Telecommunications Cabling
- EIA/TIA-569: Commercial Building Standard for Telecommunications Pathways and Spaces
- EIA/TIA-570: Residential and Light Commercial Telecommunications Wiring Standard
- TIA/EIA-606: Administration Standard for the Telecommunications Infrastructure of Commercial Buildings
- TIA/EIA-607: Commercial Building Grounding and Bonding Requirements for Telecommunications

In addition, the TIA recently has published two Telecommunications Systems Bulletins that are expected to be incorporated into future versions of the core standards. They are:

- TSB-67: Transmission Performance Specifications for Field Testing of Twisted-pair Cabling Systems
- TSB-72: Centralized Optical Fiber Cabling Guidelines

Other areas of the telecommunications industry covered by TIA standards are fiber optics, wireless communications, and telephone equipment. The TIA itself does not publish and maintain its standards; instead, it works through a document clearing house, Global Engineering Documents (GED of Englewood, CO), that sells TIA documents in both hardcopy and CD-ROM formats. Network-licensed versions also are available.

The cable plant supporting a local area network is a very broadbased undertaking, and its design, installation, and maintenance is governed, directly or indirectly, by a large number of standards bodies, both domestic and international. Some of these documents are available through GED, but many must be obtained individually from the organizations setting them. The best procedure for identifying all relevant standards and codes in a particular area is to contact a local cabling consultant.

TESTING AND TEST EQUIPMENT

It is important to set performance standards for the physical plant of local area networks, just as it is vital to ensure that the manufacturers of cabling and components adhere to the specifications included in such standards. However, neither of these activities will necessarily assure the network manager that the cable plant he has installed will operate to promised capacity. Such a guarantee can only be provided by testing.

Verification testing has, in fact, become the final, vital step in most cable-plant installations, with the expected test results included in the request for proposals (RFP) and specified in the installation agreement with the cabling contractor. As one might expect, the testing scenarios for fiber-optic cable and UTP copper cable are quite different.

Surprisingly, the testing of fiber-optic components and systems is the more stable and mature of the two areas. The TIA and its parent organization, the Electronic Industries Association (EIA of Arlington, VA) have maintained a series of test procedures for fiber-optic systems, the TIA/EIA-526 series, for a number of years. The corresponding series of test procedures for fiber-optic cable and components, the TIA/EIA-455 series, now numbers more than 130 procedures and continues to grow.

Until recently, the users of fiber-optic test equipment were almost exclusively telephone service providers, but in the last few years, as optical fiber has become the recommended medium for campus and premise backbones, these devices have gained importance in data communications and local area networking. To better serve this growing market, manufacturers of fiber-optic test equipment have aggressively reorganized their product lines.

The mainstay of the telephone service provider, for instance, has been the *optical time-domain reflectometer (OTDR)*, an expensive, sophisticated test instrument that can detect fiber breaks, as well as less severe problems, over great distances. High power, great sensitivity, and sophisticated features are less important in LANs, however, leading OTDR manufacturers to introduce a few years ago a very simple device using the same technology called an *optical fault finder*.

However, it quickly became apparent that network managers were not satisfied to know only that there was a break in an optical fiber — and perhaps how far down the fiber that break was. As verification testing has become a vital step to the acceptance of any cable-plant installation by the network manager, the need for test printouts, in the form of OTDR traces, for each fiber has arisen.

The solution has been the *mini-OTDR*, a compact, durable field tester with many of the capabilities a mainframe OTDR boasted of only five years ago, but at a fraction of the price. To capitalize on the proliferation of personal computers, some OTDR manufacturers have even offered specialized *OTDR boards* fitting into PCs or attaching to laptops that perform OTDR functions.

The OTDR, as its name implies, operates by sending a laser pulse down the fiber and measuring the time intervals until reflections are returned; these time intervals are then converted into distances. A much simpler, and hence less expensive, fiber-optic tester is the *optical-loss test set (OLTS)*, which consists of a *light source* and a *power meter.*

The light source, powered either by laser or light-emitting diode (LED), sends a pulse of known strength down the fiber and the power meter at the other end calculates attenuation on the basis of received signal strength. Some experts in fiber-optic data communications suggest that, because of the short distances and simple links involved, an OLTS, much less expensive than an OTDR, is really the only fiber-optic device needed for LAN testing.

Another fiber-optic device that will probably find a place in the cable-plant manager's tool kit, however, is the *optical talk set.* The equivalent of a telephone butt set, it permits technicians to talk to one another over one optical fiber while testing or repairing another.

Until the advent of the TIA's category system, the basic test tools for copper-wire networks were also fairly straightforward and simple. From the telephone industry came the *butt set,* a telephone handset that can be clipped on to voice circuits to both test and talk over them. Also coming from the telephone industry are the *tone generator* and *inductive probe,* a pair of tools used to trace wires in the maze found in many telecommunications closets and equipment rooms. The tone generator sends a signal down a wire to be traced and the inductive probe is used to find it at its other end.

To test and measure the various electrical properties of copper wire, a *multimeter* was the device of choice until recently. As its name implies, such a device, the current version of which is the *digital multimeter (DMM),* can measure multiple electrical characteristics, and might include an ammeter, voltmeter, ohmmeter, and other devices. If the distance to a break or fault in a wire must be measured, a *metallic time-domain reflectometer (MTDR)* may be needed if this function is not provided in an all-purpose device. A typical multimeter is shown in Exhibit 4.

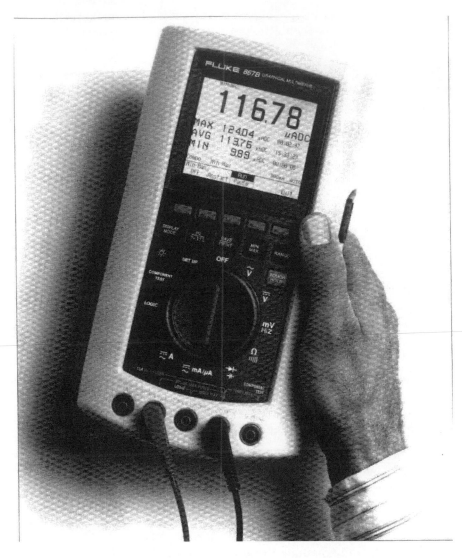

Exhibit 4.   Multimeter from Fluke Corp. Offers a Large Graphical Display (Photo courtesy of Fluke Corp.)

Although such telephone and electrical test equipment can be useful in maintaining LANs, the real mainstay of data-communications testing is the *LAN cable tester*. These devices focus on the electrical properties of copper wiring that is vital to data communications, with a small subset of them providing information to the 100-MHz limit established for Category 5.

In fact, most *Category 5 LAN cable testers* have, over the last year, been advertised to have extended capabilities above 100 MHz, in response to cable manufacturers who have introduced so-called extended-performance Category 5 cable that is claimed to be suitable for 155M-bps ATM and even faster protocols. Network and cable-plant managers examining such claims, however, should be aware that the TIA has not yet established cabling standards or test procedures beyond the Category 5 limit.

PROFESSIONAL ORGANIZATIONS, TRAINING, AND OTHER RESOURCES

The communications cabling industry as a distinct specialty, separate from electrical contracting, the telephone network of the Bell System, and proprietary data-communications systems, is arguably only about a decade old. Even so, it has developed a central standards-making body in the Telecommunications Industry Association and a professional organization in BICSI (Tampa, FL).

Although BICSI no longer spells out its name in its official literature, the acronym stands for Building Industry Consulting Services International. This is important only because it indicates BICSI's roots in the telephone industry, and specifically among that industry's building industry consultants (BICs). Today, however, this rapidly growing nonprofit telecommunications association has expanded its scope and finds that data communications and networking are its fastest growing sectors.

BICSI has established the essential credential for any professional designing telecommunications distribution systems, the Registered Communications Distribution Designer (RCDD) designation, and only last year launched a corresponding training, testing, and registration program for cabling installers. The organization also maintains the handbook of the cabling industry, the *Telecommunications Distribution Methods Manual (TDMM)*, which has recently been supplemented by a *LAN Design Manual* whose mastery can lead to a LAN Specialist designation appended to the RCDD.

Holding three regional conferences in the U.S. each year and offering extensive training through the BICSI Institute, the organization recently partnered with *Cabling Installation & Maintenance* magazine (Nashua, NH) to launch the first trade show for the cabling installer, Cabling Installation Expo.

Cabling Installation & Maintenance, one of several trade publications serving the industry, also offers training videos, an extensive website on the Internet, and a comprehensive annual "Buyer's Guide" issue that details the classroom, textbook, audio, and video training available in this rapidly changing and highly technical industry. The Buyer's Guide also provides information on the manufacturers and distributors of all the cable and components discussed here.

111

SUMMARY

Even though the cabling industry has only recently jelled from the telecom-munications and data-communications marketplaces, it is already a multi-billion-dollar industry in the U.S. and is expanding at a double-digit rate both domestically and worldwide. These are important facts for network and cable-plant managers because they indicate that both the complexity of the cable plant and the competitiveness of the vendors who provide for it will continue to increase well into the next century.

The only way to keep up with this complexity and change will be to rec-ognize the importance of the physical layer of the OSI model and stay informed of the many technical and business developments that impact it.

Chapter 8
Designing Enterprise Networks

Kevin M. Groom and Frank M. Groom

INTRODUCTION

Experienced network designers often describe their craft as being equal parts art and science. Where network structures exist and nodal statistics have been collected for traffic flow analysis, scientific conclusions can be drawn by designers concerning the flow of communications.

When a designer has collected reasonably accurate information about the probable need for future network growth, based on traffic patterns and a knowledge of business needs, sufficient capacity can often be provisioned. However, frequently the designer of a network has only general assumptions on which to base a plan and thus must employ principles that have proved effective in past design efforts. This represents the "artistic" side, where a combination of instinct and experience can aid a designer in satisfying present data networking needs while also preparing for future needs. The combination of technical flow statistics with a designer's skill and experience is the best assurance that a satisfactory network can be provided to the customer.

NETWORK DESIGN PRINCIPLES

There are a number of factors that should be considered in designing a network for optimum performance:

1. The principle of parsimony dictates that the more simple a structure is, the more likely it is to work and the easier it is to repair, change, and manage. Thus, the simpler the network design, the more options the designer will have to modify or expand it over the long term.
2. The design should minimize protocol conversion and frame encapsulation whenever possible. In most cases, transmission is likely to begin with the encapsulation of Transmission Control Protocol (TCP) packets within Internet Protocol (IP) packets, which then are encapsulated within a Layer 2 packet (such as an Ethernet packet). Thus, whenever the option exists to refrain from performing

additional encapsulation or segmentation, we should choose to avoid doing so.

3. The design should be both hierarchical (in that there should be several clearly defined layers, each having its own purpose specific to that layer) and modular (in that there should be several different components; i.e., subgroups of users). Each level of the hierarchy should house individual and separate modules. Moreover, each of these modules should provide specifically defined levels of connectivity performance for a specified set of users or for lower level modules.

4. The design should allow for the scalability of both components and transport speed. The ability to add additional switches and line connections—as well as faster lines and ports—is required due to the likely imprecision of the original design and the changes that occur over time due to the needs of the business in question.

5. Since all technology fails at some point, and because it usually occurs when the organization is most vulnerable to failure, the node components of the network should be chosen to contain Simple Network Management Protocol (SNMP) agents with management information bases (MIBs) for packet counts, traps, and trigger events.

6. The design should provide more than enough capacity to handle the anticipated initial traffic load, as well as be scalable enough to accommodate incremental modules that allow for the adjustment (and increase) of traffic load and the growth of the number of connected users.

7. The design should provide for stable performance under a varying traffic load, should have minimum potential for failure, and should have redundant links and nodes or standby replacement components.

8. The design should be for an affordable, but not necessarily least-cost, alternative.

9. The design should be for the support of the network while it is up and running. This should include installation of additional components, access for support and operational people, provision for replacement and growth parts for the network, and means to store and deliver them. This provides diagnostic tools and the capacity for their operation, as well as devising methods for the continual testing of the performance of the network.

10. The designer should also have a contingency plan for the recovery of all parts of the network should a serious disruption occur.

A basic principle of design is to construct an overall diagram that portrays the various separate functional modules, as well as their means of interconnection and the dependencies between each of them. Exhibit 1 presents a conceptual view of the layers of module functionality.

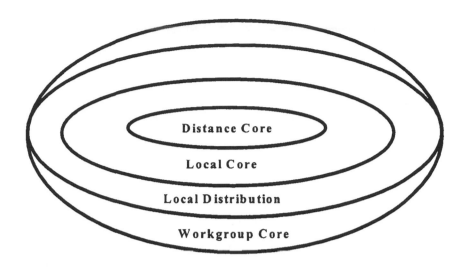

Exhibit 1. Conceptual Layered Network Design Model

The role of the *workgroup core layer* is the interconnection of a group of office workers to one another and to a set of office printers and file servers. The role of the *local distribution layer* is to interconnect modules of work group networks to each other, to a set of building servers, and to a gateway node that connects to sites beyond the building. The role of the *local core layer* is to interconnect individual buildings on a campus for connection to a central data processing site, or to access a wide area network (WAN) or the Internet for transport of traffic to a distant site. The role of the *distance core layer* is to provide the WAN or Internet connection to remote metropolitan, regional, national, or international sites.

This abstract network design model is displayed in a more detailed form as a hierarchical set of modular subnetworks, including the wide area intersite network, the campus interbuilding network, the building interfloor network, and the workgroup or floor and office network. The interconnection of these modular networks in a hierarchy, cross-connected by the WAN, is portrayed in Exhibit 2.

When designing networks, one must consider all the alternatives for transmission. In the local office, the transmission path may be a bus-oriented, shared-use path. However, as the transmission leaves the local office, a floor or building switch may choose alternative paths. The designer must choose a switch that will provide the desired number of paths to the selected destination. When a router is employed to interconnect floors or buildings, alternative paths are provisioned and the routers must be provided

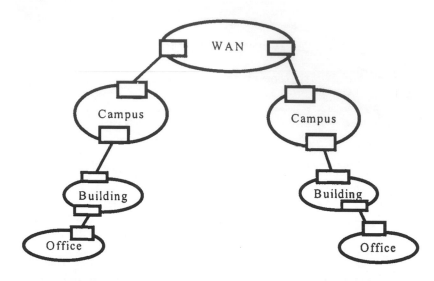

Exhibit 2.   A Detailed Hierarchical Model of an Enterprise Network

with various information to help it determine primary and alternative routing paths to the appropriate destination.

Advanced routing protocols provide the ability to split the paths to a specific destination and to send traffic down each path, thus balancing the traffic load among the available paths to the destination. Furthermore, because network traffic often needs to be sent to a variety of distant locations, the designer must choose between converting protocols (translating addresses at edge routers to the wide area protocol) or "tunneling" the traffic by means of encapsulation.

The use of switched networks makes possible the reservation of virtual circuits across the network. These provide guarantees for the characteristics of transmission speed, variations in speed due to latency in network nodes, and packet or cell loss minimization. Cell loss can be defined for both peak and average offered packet transmission loads. As routed networks move from our current IP version 4 addressing scheme to the next generation version 6, users will be able to prereserve bandwidth across the routed network, which will provided a quality of service guaranteed to accommodate a predefined traffic load.

OFFICE DESIGN

There are a number of options available for connecting workers in an office setting. The basic office connectivity local area network (LAN) choices currently being deployed include the following:

116

- 16M-bps Token Ring LANs for office workers who are closely tied to IBM mainframe systems, particularly those connected by means of IBM Systems Network Architecture (SNA) networks
- 10M-bps Ethernet for minimum to moderate packet transmission amounts, the most common and easily implemented LAN solution
- 100M-bps Ethernet, the emerging standard for higher volume office packet traffic with 100M-bps network interface cards (NIC) priced at the same level as 10M-bps cards, most being set at either 10- or 100M-bps rates
- 25M-bps asynchronous transfer mode (ATM) to deliver multimedia with pre-Pentium and low-speed Pentium machines whose internal bus cannot transfer at faster than rates of 8 to 30M-bps
- 51M-bps ATM and 100M-bps ATM, slower ATM speeds that were specified early in the protocol's development, but are seldom implemented
- 155M-bps ATM as the standard connection speed for users requiring heavy multimedia use, graphic media creation and transmission, and continuous client/server interactivity, as well as for computer-aided design, engineering, or manufacturing (CAD/CAE/CAM)
- Fiber distributed data interface (FDDI) to the desktop is no longer being considered viable for most designs, because 100M-bps Ethernet and 155M-bps ATM are able to match its performance, while the cost of network components is significantly lower with either option

When estimating the appropriate size for an office network, one needs to consider the volume of the source traffic from each user PC and its associated destinations. There are many varieties of potential traffic to consider; traffic can be sent to another PC in the office, to an office server, to a destination outside the office but in the same building, to another campus building, or to a distant location. Exhibit 3 contains a common worksheet for tallying these volume estimates. A standard Ethernet packet size of 1500 bytes is used, as well as standardized file sizes for e-mail, client requests, file transfer sizes, and prints submissions.

Another common tally for estimating how many of these standard packet volumes might be delivered from a user PC in a unit of time at average and at peak transmission levels is presented in Exhibit 4.

BUILDING DESIGN

A model building network is portrayed in Exhibit 5. The networked building has five floors, each of which has multiple work groups with its own local network supported by a distributed hub (D-Hub) or small switch. A smart hub (S-Hub) interconnects the various offices on a floor. At the floor hub all users gain access to a core building backbone network, which interconnects the floors of the building. This building backbone is supplied by a set of routers or switches (R/S) and the inter-floor links. By accessing the

COMMON PACKET VOLUMES		
TYPE	BYTE COUNT	PACKET COUNT
E-mail	300B- 1500B	1
Client request	200B	1
File transfer	50,000-500,000	30- 300
Print submit	2,500- 25,000	2- 18
Internet request	60 B	1

Exhibit 3.   Common Byte and Packet Counts for Typical Usage

FLOOR TRAFFIC WORKSHEET			
WkGrp Sw1	Destination Sw2	Peak Hr Vol.	Ave Hr Vol.
	Destination SwN	Peak Hr Vol.	Ave Hr Vol.
WkGrp Sw2	Destination Sw1	Peak Hr Vol.	Ave Hr Vol.
	Destination SwN	Peak Hr Vol.	Ave Hr Vol
WkGrp Sw3	Destination Sw1	Peak Hr Vol.	Ave Hr Vol.
’	Destination SwN	Peak Hr Vol.	Ave Hr Vol
WkGrp Sw4	Destination Sw1	Peak Hr Vol.	Ave Hr Vol.
	Destination SwN-1	Peak Hr Vol.	Ave Hr Vol
WkGrp SwN	Destination SwN-1	Peak Hr Vol.	Ave Hr Vol.

Exhibit 4.   Cross Workgroup Traffic Analysis Worksheet

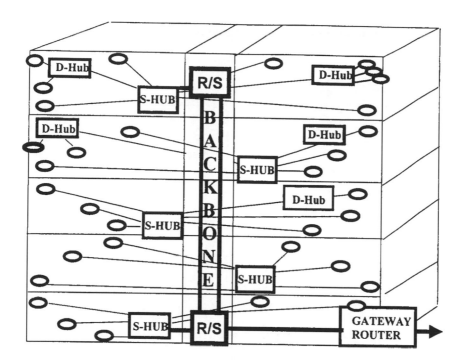

Exhibit 5. **A Building Network Design Showing the Gateway, Backbone, and Floor Nets**

building backbone, each user can gain access to a gateway router to leave the building network and enter the campus network, through which he can also access the enterprise's WAN or the Internet.

Building backbone network choices rarely include 10M-bps Ethernet or 16M-bps Token Ring, but 100M-bps Ethernet or 155M-bps ATM are often chosen for their higher speeds and increased capacity. In the past, it was common for 80% of user traffic to remain on the same floor as the group of users and their local file servers. The current trend is for 80% of traffic to leave the building and for a large portion of the traffic exiting the building to leave the campus for distant locations.

In cases where e-mail, remote printing, and moderate client/server access to remote application servers are the only requirements, 100M-bps Ethernet is satisfactory for the backbone. However, in cases where increased use of multimedia, heavy access to application servers, desktop videoconferencing, and time-sensitive transmission are required, many companies are installing 155M-bps ATM for building backbones. In some cases, companies are moving to 1G-bps Ethernet for heavy traffic between floors and for cross-campus connectivity. The faster connection costs approximately two to five

BUILDING BACKBONE REQUIREMENT			
Orig.WkGrp Sw1	Destin. Sw2	Peak Hr Vol.	Ave Hr Vol.
Orig.WkGrp Sw2	Dest. Sw2	PeakHrVol.	AveHrVol.
----	----	----	-----
Total Port Req. to/from Sw2		Peak	Ave
----	----	----	----
– –	– – –	– –	– –
Total BackPlane Requirement		Peak	Ave

Exhibit 6. Building Backbone Traffic Analysis Worksheet

times as much as 100M-bps Ethernet, but it offers the equivalent of real-time connectivity.

In cases where bursty data is most common, the usual choice is to stay with Ethernet, most likely at 100M-bps. Where large amounts of multimedia are interchanged, 155M-bps ATM (with LAN emulation of floor Ethernets) is frequently employed. FDDI was the backbone of choice in the early 1990s, but it is being replaced by 100M-bps Ethernet or 155M-bps ATM due to their cheaper cost, manageability, potential for further scalability, and plug-and-play operation. Exhibit 6 presents a typical worksheet to be used for recording the traffic flows and capacity requirements for connectivity among workgroup switches on various floors of a building.

ROLE OF A ROUTER

Routers are used in a network to perform a variety of functions. Their main function is to choose a route from a set of alternatives based on a Layer 3 IP address included in each packet and a routing protocol used to build and maintain the tables used to determine the routing. However, routers are also performing many new functions. Among these are

1. Subnet addressing   By using the host portion of the IP address, traffic can be routed to a switch or hub close to the destination user's PC. From there, the packets can be switched to their final destination

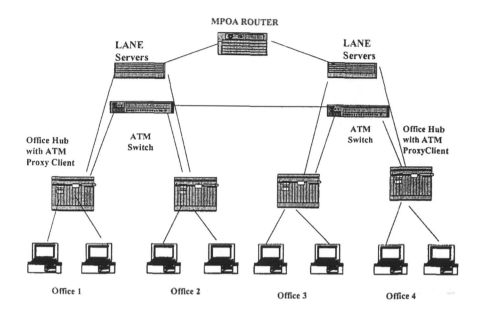

MPOA ROUTER

LANE Servers

LANE Servers

Office Hub with ATM Proxy Client

ATM Switch

ATM Switch

Office Hub with ATM ProxyClient

Office 1   Office 2   Office 3   Office 4

Exhibit 7.   MPOA Router Interconnecting ATM LANE Switching Networks

---

using the Layer 2 media access control (MAC) address burned into the NIC card of the PC.

2. VLAN identification   Routers can be used to allow users who are located on different floors of a building and on different LANs to occupy a "virtual LAN" (VLAN). These users can broadcast across a wider set of switches and hubs as if a single switch connected them. The placement of a router between the floor switches allows the recognition of tags placed on submitted packets that identify them as belonging to a specific VLAN.

3. Multiprotocol over ATM (MPOA)   In instances where an ATM backbone network is used to interconnect users on Ethernet or Token Ring LANs, the preexisting LANs are emulated or bridged by employing a proxy ATM client at the edge of the Ethernet. LAN emulation (LANE) servers are then used to assist in the route determination. However, when the emulated LANs reach between 750 to 1000 users (or one large building of workers), a router may be employed between the ATM backbone networks to determine when it is necessary to switch between the separate ATM backbones. First, a route between the backbones is determined, and then a cut-through path for subsequent cell forwarding is employed. Exhibit 7 portrays this set of ATM backbone switches, LANE servers, and MPOA routers for path determination between them.

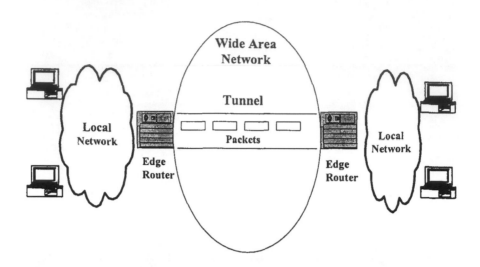

Exhibit 8.   Tunneling Packets by Encapsulation Across a Wide Area Network

---

4. Gateway tunneling function   Routers can also be placed at the edge of an enterprise campus of buildings for the purpose of accessing a WAN. The router can translate LAN addresses to the wide area addressing scheme or follow one of a set of encapsulation techniques (termed tunneling) to place the local packet inside the wide area packet and deencapsulate it at the destination edge router. This is portrayed in Exhibit 8.

CAMPUS DESIGN

The most important decision for the designer of a campus network is whether to deploy a routed or a switched network. In either case, the network will most likely have IP packets, operating over a choice of Ethernet, Token Ring, FDDI, ATM switches, hubs, or routers. Exhibit 9 portrays a campus switched Gigabit Ethernet backbone network, interconnecting buildings that are served by 100M-bps Ethernet backbones and 10M-bps Ethernet floor and office networks.

To calculate the required capacity for the campus backbone network, one needs to estimate the proportion of the traffic entering and exiting each given building. These two capacities are added to determine the total capacity for the building connection and backbone switch port. Furthermore, the amount of traffic that needs to exit the campus destined for distant locations must be estimated from the sum of all campus backbone entry traffic, minus all building destination traffic, to correctly size the access line to the campus edge router.

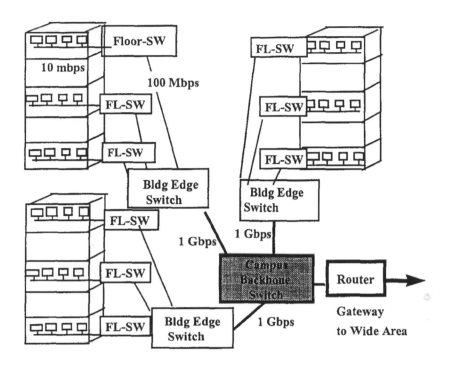

Exhibit 9.   Building Switches Accessing the Core Campus Switch and WAN

An additional tally sheet for estimating these sources and destinations over the campus backbone network is presented in Exhibit 10.

The options for campus backbones today are 100M-bps or 1G-bps Ethernet, or 155M- or 622M-bps ATM. Historically, 100M-bps FDDI was the campus backbone of choice. As with building backbones, however, FDDI has fallen into disfavor due to its higher cost, inflexibility in bandwidth allocation, and problems handling video and multimedia.

WIDE AREA ACCESS DESIGN

With the distribution of production plants and offices throughout the country and across the globe, quite frequently an enterprise's workers at one site must be connected to workers at another site, to a central and distant data processing site, and to the Internet. The edge router is the standard device deployed at the edge of a campus to bridge campus users to a WAN service or private line connection. Routers employ a flexible combination of bridging, protocol translation, and specialized serial modules for connection to telephone company circuits. An edge router bridging a campus to a WAN is portrayed in Exhibit 11.

123

CAMPUS BACKBONE TRAFFIC REQUIREMENT			
Orig.Bldg Sw1	Dest..BldgSw2	Peak Hr Vol.	Ave Hr Vol.
Orig.Bldg Sw2	Dest. BldgSw2	PeakHrVol.	AveHrVol.
----	-----	----	-----
Total Port Req. to/from Bldg.1		Peak	Ave
----	----	----	----
Total Switch Backplane/Reqt		Peak	Ave

Exhibit 10.   Enterprise Campus Backbone Traffic Requirements Worksheet

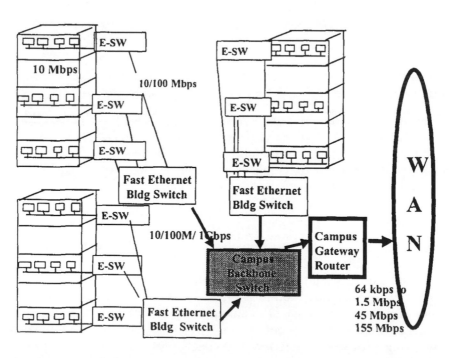

Exhibit 11.   Traffic Exiting a Campus Network to Access External Networks

EXISTING	ACCESS	INCREASE	NEW ACCESS
10 Users	1-64 kbps PL	+10 Users	2-64 kbps PLs or
2 Dest. Sites		+2 Dest. Sites	1-128 kbps PL

Exhibit 12.   Estimates of Proportionate Increase

Wide Area Source Traffic

There are generally two approaches to ensuring that sufficient bandwidth exits on the wide area access line. In many cases, some mode of external communication already exists, such as a dial-out modem (at 28 to 56K bps) or a 64K-bps subchannel of a T1. If an outside connection already exists, the existing capacity can be used as a base to estimate the new requirement. Exiting traffic packet counts, the number of users transmitting, the number of potential users, the number of potential destination sites, and the number of actual destination sites associated with recent packet counts are all variables that should be examined. Then new requirements can be estimated using the existing statistics as a benchmark, and the transport capacity may be increased in proportion to the expected volume increase. An example of a simple proportionate increase is presented in Exhibit 12.

Similarly, should one choose to upgrade his campus backbone from 10M to 100M-bps, it is likely that he would also need to upgrade the WAN access link as well. This is because a portion of the traffic volume that drove the need for the campus increase would also need to be placed on the WAN access line. Thus, an increase from 10M to 100M bps on the campus backbone would likely necessitate an increase from a 64K-bps access line to a 128K-bps access line for WAN connectivity—or increase an existing 1.544M-bps T1 line to a pair of T1s.

Since many enterprises now use the Internet for e-mail and nonessential traffic transport, current and prospective traffic statistics should be tallied on a campus worksheet as portrayed in Exhibit 13. This worksheet can then be used as a tool for making estimates based on existing traffic patterns, as well as for estimating requirements for new locations.

Most corporations tend to have a central site that houses a significant portion of the services used by their various distributed sites (or supplier and customer sites). A composite tally sheet is often employed to summarize the traffic from each location (regardless of destination), providing a

TRAFFIC TO AND FROM THE WAN OR INTERNET		
WAN TRAFFIC		
Campus Edge Router	PeakOutVol	AveOutVol
	PeakInVol	AveInVol
	Hourly Peak and Ave	
	Daily Peak and Ave	
	Weekly, Monthly, Yearly Peak and Ave	
INTERNET TRAFFIC		
Campus Edge Router	PeakOutVol	AveOutVol
	PeakInVol	AveInVol
	Hourly Peak and Ave	
	Daily Peak and Ave	
	Weekly, Monthly, Yearly Peak and Ave	

Exhibit 13. Worksheet for WAN and Internet Traffic Statistics

total arranged by source–location traffic pattern. The entire load of traffic is then analyzed in terms of individual destination sites, providing a listing of total traffic load received by each destination. Such a worksheet is presented in Exhibit 14. This sheet is used to size the local access lines that will carry the combined traffic to its various locations. In addition, at each destination location, the combined traffic (peak and average) can be estimated so that an access line or lines can be leased with capacity sufficient to carry all traffic to the server or administration site.

Wide Area Destination Traffic

When determining the traffic to be delivered to destination sites, we must also consider how much traffic is destined for mission-critical corporate servers and how much is store-and-forward e-mail traffic that is headed for a corporate e-mail server. Transactions to corporate application, database, and World Wide Web servers usually generate a substantially larger set of response transactions. The designer must estimate the response traffic from the servers, as well as the original and simpler request transactions.

WAN Choices: Private Line, Frame Relay, ATM

The most common WAN of choice today for most corporations is a carrier's frame relay service. The carrier offering the service first leases an ac-

126

WAN TRAFFIC ESTIMATES			
Location 1	**To Loc 2**	PeakOutVol	AveOutVol
		PeakInVol	AveInVol
	From Loc 2	PeakOutVol	AveOutVol
		PeakInVol	AveInVol
Location N	**To Loc N**	PeakOutVol	AveOutVol
		PeakInVol	AveInVol
	From Loc N	PeakOutVol	AveOutVol
		PeakInVol	AveInVol

Exhibit 14.   WAN Traffic Estimates by Location and Totals to and from Locations

cess line from the local Regional Bell Operating Company (RBOC) to the carrier's edge frame relay switch as portrayed in Exhibit 15. Alternatively, the carrier can lease this access line for the subscriber. Such access lines can be in multiples of 64K bps up to a full T1 at 1.544M bps, a DS3 at 45M bps, or 155M-bps fiber synchronous optical network (SONET) access line (which might be employed in connecting to ATM WAN service).

The most common option is for many dispersed sites to access one central site that contains a set of core enterprise servers (such as application, database, or Web hosts) and e-mail servers. Each of the distributed sites accesses the frame relay network by means of the local leased line, and has its traffic switched over the frame relay network to the switch closest to the destination. In cases where the shared common destination is a set of servers, a high-speed connection or set of connections is leased to connect locally to the site of the servers. This is portrayed in Exhibit 16.

To properly size the access lines and frame relay committed information rates, the source and destination traffic flows must be determined. In practice, packet counts are taken at edge devices for building and campus networks to calculate precise traffic flow. Alternatively, the speed of the connections emanating from buildings and traveling across campus can be used to identify the maximum traffic potential, and estimates of traffic

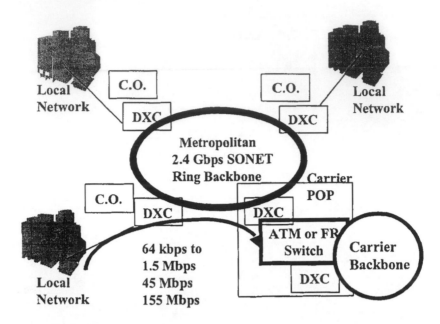

Exhibit 15.   RBOC Leased Line Access to a Carrier's Frame Relay Service

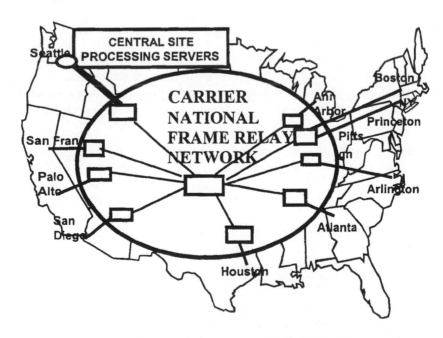

Exhibit 16.   Connecting to a Central Site by Means of National Frame Relay Service

leaving the LAN and entering the WAN can be approximated from the LAN traffic and capacity.

RBOC WAN Access Lines

The telephone industry provides only a limited number of connection alternatives for wide-area services. This short list includes

- 56K-bps modem service
- Integrated Services Digital Network (ISDN) dial access at up to 128K bps
- Asymmetrical digital subscriber line (ADSL) from 64 to 640K-bps access
- T1 and subchanneled T1 at 64K bps up to 1.544M bps
- DS3 connections at 45M bps
- Fiber SONET links at 51M and 155M bps

Cable modem access is on the horizon but will be limited to these same access speeds from the cable head end.

The basic approach for designing a WAN is to first determine the access line capacity required (including bidirectional requirements) from all the various sites. Then the common destination access line capacity is determined from the sum of the expected source average and peak traffic. To do this, one must translate the local LAN or direct the host's expected transmission capacity into the approximate bursty packet capacity of a T1 private line, which is the basic unit of telephone company transmission. Then the designer applies those access statistics to the national frame relay, ATM, or leased-line IP network one wishes to configure.

Where current wide area transmission already exists from the distributed sites, or from any subset of these sites, a set of variables (the current bandwidth, the offered load, and the amount of increased load as a percentage of the current load) are determined and applied proportionately to the other sites. However, in many cases the WAN must be configured without the analysis of previous traffic to set the benchmark.

Since T1 capacity is designed for 24 continuous voice channels, some approximations must be used to apply bursty packet data flows to T1s. Generally, a T1 can carry 1.544K bps. The standard packets to be transmitted contain 12,000 b (1500 bytes) plus addressing and control bits. Thus in a single second, about 125 packets can be transmitted by a T1. Experience has shown that a reasonably loaded 10M-bps Ethernet LAN serving about 24 users, whose performance (due to collisions, etc.) degrades to about 3M bps, can be effectively bridged to a distant location with a single T1 private line. This translates to 250 packets every other second for the 24 users. The upper limit for such active T1 bridging is to serve about 100 users who may be locally bridged through a hub serving 100 hosts or a set of switches. About 100 active Ethernet hosts can deliver 250 packets every second. Alternatively, up to 500 local hosts could transmit if only a small portion is active at any point in time and if an even smaller portion is transmitting packets destined for WAN transport.

T1s can be obtained at channel ranges from 64K bps (56K bps with an additional 8K bps for overhead), in successive increments up to 1.544M bps. If necessary, a designer can scale down the required access transport from a full 1.544M-bps T1 in proportional steps of 64K bps to a minimum connection of 64K bps (which might serve one host or occasionally be used by 5 to 8 hosts). A 64K-bps private line can support 1/24 the transmission of a full T1. Given all this, a designer can analyze the number of user hosts, the speed of their local connection, and the consistency of their transmissions over the WAN to determine the necessary amount of T1 capacity to access the WAN and to transmit between desired sites.

At the destination site, the normal approach to determining necessary capacity is to accumulate all information about the source access capacity and their frame relay committed information rates (CIR). A combined traffic load can then be determined, and full capacity can be provisioned at a level close to the accumulated amount of CIR capacity or about one half of the sum of the access line capacity. This can be adjusted up or down based on analysis of peak and average anticipated traffic offerings from the sources.

The general assumption is that the CIR for frame relay transmission (which is the level of service a customer is guaranteed by the carrier) should be about one half of the access line speed. Most current frame relay service offerings by the carriers are for permanent virtual circuit (PVC) service (the equivalent to a full or partial T1). Individual CIR links can be determined by analyzing each source access capacity, dividing it in half, and providing a frame relay CIR to the central destination. Should other destinations also be provided through the common source access line, the CIRs can be divided up proportionately.

Exhibit 17 presents a range of RBOC access line transport speeds and the frame relay CIRs that are generally appropriate for those speeds. Because frame relay service is normally purchased to supplant T1 capacity, frame relay capacity can be estimated based on T1 estimates. Furthermore, the actual CIR can be somewhat below the peak rate of traffic, allowing the carrier (or customer) to lease access lines at both ends at peak rate (or close to it); and the CIR of the frame relay service can be purchased at about one half or more of the peak rate. This is acceptable to many customers given that, when traffic is low and capacity is available, frame relay will allow them to "burst" above their CIRs. Usually, customers can increase traffic to only double their CIR s; this is, nevertheless, double their paid rate, making this an attractive option. Exhibit 17 presents a range of access line rates and the associated frame relay CIRs that normally are considered appropriate.

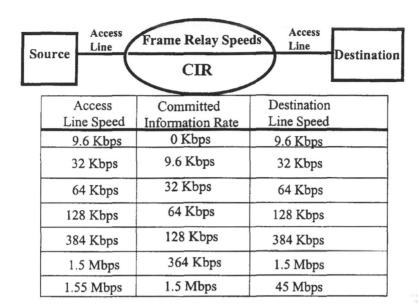

Access Line Speed	Committed Information Rate	Destination Line Speed
9.6 Kbps	0 Kbps	9.6 Kbps
32 Kbps	9.6 Kbps	32 Kbps
64 Kbps	32 Kbps	64 Kbps
128 Kbps	64 Kbps	128 Kbps
384 Kbps	128 Kbps	384 Kbps
1.5 Mbps	364 Kbps	1.5 Mbps
1.55 Mbps	1.5 Mbps	45 Mbps

Exhibit 17.   The Range Of Access and Frame Relay Transmission Alternatives

For the designer to determine the appropriate frame relay CIR to order from each location, the type, number, and speeds of the LANs at each source location should be tabulated. Then the total number of hosts must be determined, as well as the number of hosts at peak traffic times, and those that tend to transmit over the WAN simultaneously. Many enterprises tend to use frame relay service to connect many locations to one central site at a set of corporate servers. As such, the designer should sum up all the peak and average traffic loads from all the source sites and determine the number of T-1s required to carry all the traffic from the frame relay network to the destination servers (and the responses back from them). The following worksheet, presented in Exhibit 18, is used to amalgamate the source load potential and the total destination load.

When the source and destination traffic is from an ATM LAN, wide area ATM service may be chosen instead of frame relay service. Both employ circuits requiring carrier access and backbone network. However, ATM service is provided at a higher speed (and at a higher cost). Access links are provisioned at T1, DS3, and SONET transmission rates and multiplexed over the carrier's backbone network facilities.

IP NETWORK DESIGN

A network architecture that has been consistently deployed is the standard, router-based, IP network. In IP routing, destination routes are specified by

	Location 1	Location 2	Destination
Source Enterprise Net Type/Speed	Ethernet/IP 10 Mbps	Token Ring/ IP 16 Kbps	ATM 155 Mbps
Source Access Link Speed	64 Kbps	1.5 Mbps	1.5 Mbps
Source Access Transmit Speed	32 Kbps	128 Kbps	32/ 512 Kbps
Burst Peak Acccess Rate	64 Kbps	512 Kbps	512 Kbps
FR CIR	32 Kbps	128 Kbps	128 Kbps
FR Maximum Burst	64 Kbps	512 Kbps	1.5 Mbps
Destination Link Speed	64 Kbps	512 Kbps	1.5 Mbps
Destination Burst Rate	64 Kbps	512 Kbps	512 Kbps

Exhibit 18.   Source and Destination Frame Relay Worksheet

the IP address of each packet. The router examines each packet's destination IP address and compares it to entries in a routing table to determine the output port via which the packet is sent across the network to the next sequential router. Separate autonomous subnets can be created, and each can use the routing protocol most appropriate for its size and traffic load. A list of commonly used routing protocols follows:

- The routing information protocol (RIP) should be employed for smaller networks with 15 or fewer routers along a path and similar links connecting the routers. The path with the fewest routers along the way provides the shortest and best route.
- The open shortest path first protocol (OSPF) should be used for larger networks that employ a diverse set of linkage types.
- The Extended Interior Gateway Routing Protocol (EIGRP) is used if load balancing among routes is important and particularly when employing all Cisco Systems Inc. routers, since EIGRP is Cisco's proprietary protocol.
- Border Gateway Protocol (BGP) is used to route between autonomous networks. BGP can be employed regardless of which protocol is used in each autonomous subnetwork.

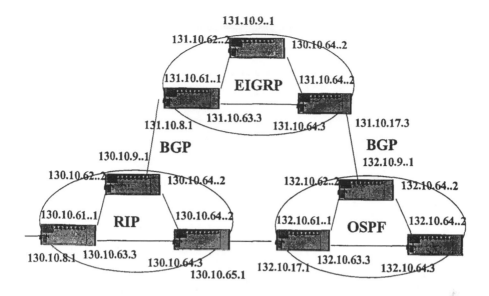

131.10.9..1

131.10.62..2   130.10.64..2

131.10.61..1   **EIGRP**   131.10.64..2

131.10.8.1   131.10.63.3   131.10.64.3   131.10.17.3

BGP   **BGP**

130.10.9..1   132.10.9..1

130.10.62..2   130.10.64..2   132.10.62..2   132.10.64..2

130.10.61..1   **RIP**   130.10.64..2   132.10.61..1   **OSPF**   132.10.64..2

130.10.8.1   130.10.63.3   132.10.63.3

130.10.64.3   132.10.17.1   132.10.64.3

130.10.65.1

Exhibit 19.   A Set of Three Autonomous IP Networks

Exhibit 19 portrays three autonomous IP networks, using RIP, OSPF, and EIGRP for routing protocols. BGP is used to route between these autonomous networks. Each port of each router must have its own unique IP address (such as 131.10.62.2).

With the emergence of frame relay and the Internet, these IP networks are usually overlaid on either frame relay private networks or virtual private networks (VPN) using the Internet as its underlying physical structure.

MANAGING THE INTERNET AND VIRTUAL PRIVATE NETWORKS

Corporations are increasingly placing information on extranet servers attached to the public Internet. Extranet servers are corporate Web servers placed outside the corporation's firewall and thus are relatively unprotected. Extranet servers may employ passwords where necessary. However, where the protection of sensitive information is required, the corporation places the Web server inside the firewall (on an intranet). In addition, the access of individual users may be a restricted limited set of sites, IP addresses, and a limited set of protocols (such as the restriction of Telnet).

In cases where an enterprise wishes to use the Internet as a corporate network alternative, it employs VPN components. These include encryption at both ends, special IP tunneling at the edge router, and authentication procedures at the destination Web server. Exhibit 20 presents the set of processes that are generally present in the operation of a VPN over the Internet.

133

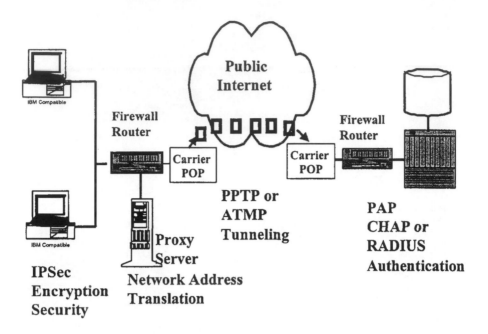

Exhibit 20. Components of a Corporate VPN Using the Internet

The use of VPNs, intranets, extranets, and the Internet as a corporate network is limited in that no one enterprise can manage the public Internet. Packet tracing can be performed to observe the sequence of routers traversed by a packet en route to a destination, but enterprise SNMP messaging is blocked. Thus, the enterprise must live with the performance achieved at any given moment or contract with a company such as UUNet Technologies, which provides private IP links as well as IP links to the public Internet.

MANAGEMENT AND TROUBLESHOOTING

All networks will eventually incur some level of failure, whether it is exhibited as a slow response, a packet volume increase, or the outright failure of a link or node. To observe the network, test it, and troubleshoot it, appropriate operational personnel must be trained, a centralized management platform must be deployed, and the nodes of the network should be purchased with appropriate SNMP agents and storage capacity to collect statistics.

Network Nodes with SNMP Agentry

The network designer must make sure that every network node placed has an appropriate SNMP agent included. The designer should determine

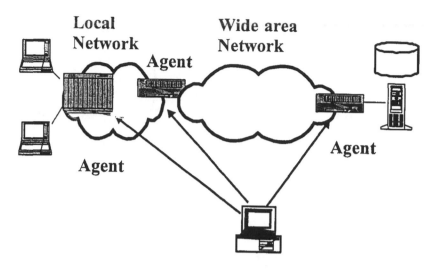

Central SNMP-based Network Monitoring and Analysis

Exhibit 21.   Monitoring SNMP Agents from a Central Network Management Station

which ports on a node, plug-in cards, backplane traffic, and events need to be captured. Exhibit 21 portrays the ongoing monitoring of selected network nodes by a central network management station. The central workstation sends Internet Control Message Protocol (ICMP) messages to the agent of a particular node requesting that the contents of a particular register be returned to the central site for analysis.

Node MIBs

Each node in the network (including hubs, switches, and routers) should be equipped with an SNMP agent and a set of registers generally referred to as MIBs. MIB-II is the current implementation and has been extended with remote monitoring (RMON MIB). The MIB contains general purpose registers with identification, up time, location, interfaces and types, address translations, IP information, TCP and User Datagram Protocol (UDP) group information, transmission, linkage, attributes, access attributes, and protocols. There are also options for special purpose user-defined registers and functionality. These MIB registers are the primary means by which the network is monitored on a consistent basis, and they must be configured for the specific network that has been constructed to allow the network to remain functioning as designed.

135

Network Management Workstation

Historically, the Sun Microsystems Inc. UNIX-based workstations were the device of choice for central site management of a large network. However, Windows NT-based stations have been replacing these as the more common devices. Sun NetManager, HP OpenView, and SNA Manager have been the most prevalent SNMP software packages for managing networks. Cisco's CiscoWorks, Cabletron's Spectrum, and Bay Network's Optivity have all been used in many implementations, either alone or combined with the traditional packages.

Operation and Support Groups

It is important for a well-designed network to have trained individuals monitoring the network and available for remote and on-site troubleshooting and correcting problems as they occur. Furthermore, a set of experienced installers must be available to add capacity to the network as the number of users and their traffic requirements increase. Ultimately, the performance of the technical support group over time determines the satisfaction of users with their network. These individuals not only fix problems when they occur but also anticipate capacity requirements and seek to scale the network to the changing requirements of a dynamically changing organization.

CONCLUSION

The prevailing trend of network design involves an IP protocol operating over a local network such as Ethernet; a wide area service such as frame relay or ATM; or a routed network using a serial, private-line connection. Each of these designs requires an estimate of likely traffic volume, source to destination traffic flow, and server location and service offerings. Networks should be designed not only to satisfactorily handle offered traffic but also to be relatively simple to install and maintain, as well as to manage and diagnose problems. Furthermore, the emergence of the Internet provides a public slow-speed alternative to be included in the overall connection technologies required by a corporation.

The hallmark of network designs in the future will be based on a collection of technologies, each appropriate for a subset of the corporation's users, tied together by a common reliance on an IP network protocol for addressing and packetization. The interconnection of such network protocols and the emergence of gigabit transmission speed will be enabled by the ability of all network technology to support IP as the networking glue that rides on top of each of the uniquely appropriate transmission media and connection protocols.

Chapter 9
Operating a Network Help Desk

Jeff C. Hafer

INTRODUCTION

Would you consider buying a car if you had no idea whom to call when you had problems? That is the feeling users get in some corporations when they use telecommunications and computers. There are two aspects to maintaining a reliable system. The network (highways and secondary roads) should be monitored and maintained to a satisfactory level without user (driver) involvement. The end user devices and applications (automobiles) require a call from the user to request help from the customer service organization (auto repair shop). Keep this analogy in mind when trying to design and operate a network help desk.

HISTORY OF THE HELP DESK

In many organizations, the help desk was created as a central point of contact for users of the data processing services. These users have accurately been referred to as customers. Users that experienced problems prefer to call a single phone number and have help desk personnel assist in resolving the problem or question. High level technical support could be called when needed. As personal computers, LANs and WANs became part of the data processing picture, the role of help desk became more difficult.

After the divestiture of AT&T, telecommunications functions such as PBXs, voice mail, interactive voice response (IVR) and interconnection circuits became the responsibility of the information technology group in many companies. Add videoconferencing and the diversity of services continues to grow into a complex web. Speaking of the World Wide Web, the expansive use of the Internet has introduced more variables into the equation.

MISSION OF THE HELP DESK

Before one can set up and operate an effective help desk, it is necessary to determine the mission of the help desk. There is no set formula for every company, network or organization. Some of the basic questions that must be asked are:

- What systems and networks are to be supported by the help desk?
- Will the help desk provide technical support or referral and tracking of problems?
- Is it important for the help desk to provide support 24 hours per day, seven days a week?
- How will second and third level support be obtained (in-house or external)?

If you do not know what you are trying to accomplish, you will never know when you have reached your destination. The best procedures, people and management will not be able to overcome the lack of planning. It has been said that no amount of planning can replace dumb luck. But a successful help desk operation depends on continuous improvement, and it is not possible if there are no goals to work toward or measure against as you move forward.

COST JUSTIFICATION

Building the cost justification for a help function is similar to justifying a set of encyclopedias for your house. It has value, it is expensive, but is it worth the cost? This dilemma is not lost on senior management. Most companies require some form of customer service function, which faces the same difficult task of balancing the cost against the value provided and impact on the business. However, in the case of the help desk, it is the information technology organization that must build the business case.

Since the cost of a quality help desk will be high, it is important to break it down into smaller numbers. What you need to sell to senior management is the product, not the process. In other words, it will be more effective to break down the cost into a per user cost rather than into individual components of the help desk operation. You must estimate the cost of each part of the operation to determine the total cost. Once the total cost is determined, you can divide it by the number of users (customers) that could use the service to create a unit cost value equation. That sounds easy, right? Well, it is not quite that simple.

Suppose the help desk supports telephone systems, voice mail, IVR, videoconferencing, host computer operations and client/server computer networks. Not all users will use all of these systems. And those that do will not use them to the same degree or place the same value on a 24-hour/day help desk operation. Knowledge of the users and their needs is important when trying to determine the unit cost.

Let's say you estimate the total annual cost of the help desk operation to be $1 million and there are three thousand users in the company. A quick calculation would tell you that the unit cost is approximately $333/user. If the average employee costs the company $45,000 per year with benefits, this would equate to about 15 hours of work. In order for the help desk to be cost justified it would have to save each user 15 hours of work per year. It is highly unlikely that management would believe that to be the case.

WHAT LEVEL OF SUPPORT MANAGEMENT?

A better approach would be to decide what level of support management would consider the bare minimum. It would be easy to get agreement that there must be someone to call when employees experience problems. By determining the cost to provide this minimum level of service, a base line can be established. If management accepts the base line, your role as a network manager is to justify the *additional* expense that would improve the service above the minimum acceptable level.

In this case it may be decided that the minimum level of help function available to users would cost $700,000. The remaining $300,000 would then be the differential that must be justified above the minimum level of acceptable service. By taking this approach, you can state to management that it will cost $700,000 to operate a help desk that can support the users at the minimum level. Additional services could be provided for an additional cost of $300,000 per year. It is important to show what basic and additional services would be provided for each level of service.

Incremental services that would provide value to some companies are listed below. Each company is different. Some may find value in all of these and many more. Others will not benefit from all of them.

- Expanded hours of operation.
- Reduced response time for second and third level support by using in-house personnel or provisions in contracts with outside contractors.
- Including real-time alarm monitoring for help desk personnel to be more proactive in problem identification.
- Obtaining or developing a robust problem tracking system that will allow help desk and technical personnel to monitor outstanding problems and provide status that is available to everyone.
- Increasing the skills of first level support — those that answer the help desk phone — to improve initial support.

If your company uses a charge-back method for services, the level of support can be based on a willingness of the user to pay. Just as bank cards are available in standard, gold and platinum, the level of help desk can be tailored to the needs and desires of the user. In companies where this method is possible, it may be easier to justify the cost to increase coverage hours, tools to improve support and response time to problems.

MANAGING THE HELP DESK PERSONNEL

Depending on the mission of the help desk, the people in the function will have different skills, motivations and compensation. Those factors play a role when determining the best method to manage help desk personnel. Another factor is whether all support is provided from within the organization or if outside groups are used to provide some of this support.

If help desk personnel are company employees, management must ensure that career opportunities are available to those employees. People who answer the phones when customers call must have a combination of technical, communications, and interpersonal skills to handle the myriad of questions and complaints that will arise on a daily basis. It is important for these people to see opportunity for growth in the position to keep the level of motivation high. Although no manager appreciates losing good people to another organization, it is important that the employees working in the help desk function understand that it is not a dead-end job.

Operational improvement will occur only if the people responsible for the help desk are given additional responsibilities. Not only will this reduce the amount of second and third level support required, but also the people will see it as an opportunity to expand their individual skills. Those people that do not recognize the value of increased responsibility should be a concern to management.

Frequent team meetings are an excellent method of improving teamwork and broadening the knowledge base of the individuals on the team. This is described in more detail later in the chapter. It is important for managers of this critical function to develop a consistent communications and information exchange among the people – full- and part-time – that comprise the help desk organization.

PHYSICAL ASPECTS OF THE HELP DESK

Most people think of the help desk as being a customer service area where all the people have similar skill levels and work in the same room. This image was accurate in most organizations up until the early 1990s. In recent years, it has become practical to have help desk personnel logically, rather than physically located together. What this means is that the function performed by these people does not require them to be located in the same room. Technology can make them appear to be in a single location. It is important that the people who comprise the help desk work together as a team.

In the "good old days," most help desks supported only mainframe applications and HOST-attached hardware. A small staff could be trained in almost all hardware and software used in a company. With the broad scope of technology and applications used in companies, it is impossible to provide reasonable support with a small group of individuals. Unfortunately, it is not economical to assign experts in each area to work full-time on a help desk. An option is to have these subject matter experts assigned to other tasks and still available quickly to support users. A virtual help desk allows this to be possible.

Automatic Call Distribution (ACD) systems provide sharing of calls. The sophistication of today's ACD systems would allow a small group of full-time personnel to be located in a common area, and people at other locations could be added when needed. With networked ACD, it is possible to have people in other cities included on the help desk team. This has the added advantage of providing extended coverage by staffing in different time zones. The cost of multiple ACD systems, each with networking options, may at first seem cost-prohibitive. Do not rule it out on the initial cost without considering the long-term benefit and potential cost savings.

Having access to people during normal working hours in multiple time zones could prove very beneficial. For instance, during a particular period normal activity may dictate two full-time people. If problems occur, it may be necessary to add staff quickly for a short period of time. If this occurs outside the normal day shift in one time zone, but during prime time in another, it could make the solution more effective.

TOOLS

Many tools are available to support the help desk. A trip to any vendor exposition that addresses the needs of voice systems, call centers, help desks or computer telephony will provide you with more reading material than anyone would care to carry home. The important thing is to decide what the goals of your help desk should be and determine which tools are most suitable. From there, a quick review of the products should give some idea of what is available at an affordable price.

With the hype surrounding the Internet and Web browsers, many products focus on this area of technology. Like many other quick fixes that telecommunications managers and information technology face, it is important to look past the techno wizardry and consider the business case that would support the investment.

The primary tools that are essential for a successful help desk operation to solve these critical functions are:

- Handle the incoming call effectively
- Provide alarm reporting, if included in the help desk responsibilities
- Allow troubles and questions to be logged and tracked to conclusion
- Provide a means of quickly accessing high level support personnel
- Reporting information that can be used to analyze and improve the help desk operation

As described in the *Physical Aspects of the Help Desk* section, ACD is very effective in handling incoming calls from users. Not only do the users need to have their calls answered quickly, but support personnel must also have access to the people who work on the help desk. Using multiple call groups with different priorities assigned to specific dialed numbers, the ACD can also provide a means of support personnel gaining access to the help desk.

Alarms from systems should report to a centralized location. Depending on the size of the company and degree of technology employed, a network control center (NCC) separate from the help desk could be justified. In some operations, the NCC and help desk could be combined into a single operation. For our purpose, we will assume that separate functions are used. In that case, it is important that help desk personnel have some means of knowing the status of systems for which they provide support to the users. If the alarm and system status information is not readily available, time could easily be wasted searching for a problem that would otherwise be obvious.

There are several reasons to track troubles. One goal of a help desk is to aid in quick resolution to problems. Tracking troubles from the time a problem is first reported until it is resolved and the user is notified provides a measurement of the effectiveness of the operation. Changes to methods, tools and staffing can be evaluated to determine if the change was worthwhile. Rather than relying on memory, tracking can quickly identify repeat problems and possible solutions.

Many specialized software packages exist to provide tracking and reporting of troubles. These systems look very attractive, and some have a price tag that will make new car sticker shock pale by comparison. Do not automatically assume that the more you pay the better solution you will get. It is true that you may have a more sophisticated system if you are willing to pay more money. It is equally true that it will most likely *require* more input and analysis to provide the value. More importantly, some systems require more time and effort than it is worth for the value desired.

USING A SIMPLE DATABASE

Even a simple database created from a software suite may be suitable for tracking problems. If people who are experienced in creating databases are readily available, this could provide a good start to tracking. After more experience is gained, you could determine if more functionality is cost-jus-tified. At that point, an analysis could determine whether to expand the existing database to include new fields, reporting and functionality. If pur-chasing a system appears to be more desirable, the knowledge gained through a trial would improve the request for proposals.

It would be easier to determine what functions would be necessary, which ones are beneficial and which are unnecessary. The vendors are not in business to persuade you to buy the least costly solution. They are try-ing to persuade you to purchase the most sophisticated (read this to mean highest profit) system you can afford. It is your job to evaluate the business case and decide what makes sense and what is unnecessary.

Accessing second level support personnel can be accomplished through a number of methods. The method chosen depends on where these people reside, whether they are dedicated to support functions and whether they are employees or are provided through a service contract. The most effective method of accessing people quickly is by paging. Com-bining voice mail and paging allows help desk personnel to leave a message describing the problem in a mailbox, which is then programmed to page people.

In order to close the loop, a method should be implemented that will provide feedback to the help desk when the support person has received the page. This can be done with a procedure that requires the person to check in with the help desk. Remember that a separate ACD queue could provide support personnel with a higher priority for calls than users. Some systems could be programmed to provide automatic feedback. For instance, if a message were sent to a mailbox with a receipt requested when the message is read that would provide the caller — a help desk per-son in this case — with positive feedback that the message was heard.

If the mailbox is set to page upon receipt of a message and there is no response, the message will not be read. Therefore, no return receipt will be sent. This method works well to prove a message has been received. Unfor-tunately, it does not work as well with messages that are not heard. The person on the help desk must keep a ticket open to ensure that all requests for additional support have received attention.

COMMUNICATING WITH USERS

Do not overlook the benefit of providing users with information that can improve system knowledge and reduce the need to call the help desk. In the most basic form, messages should be sent to employees through com-pany publications, broadcast voice mail and e-mail to inform them of pend-ing changes or planned outages. It is also very useful to provide notification when problems occur. This may be more difficult if the means of providing the information (i.e., e-mail) is affected by the problem.

Bulletin boards and Web pages can provide users with a method of obtaining information and answers to frequently asked questions. If users know this information is readily available, it will reduce the number of calls for simple questions. Many questions, such as "How do I print on a printer in a different building?", can be answered with good internal Web pages or bulletin boards, then help desk personnel could spend time dealing with serious problems.

Combining some of the tools can increase the effectiveness immensely. For example, an IVR could be used to front end some of the calls. An experienced caller could select the appropriate choice from a menu and information could be provided without the intervention of a person. This is similar to the online, context-sensitive help available with many computer application programs. For problem resolution or specific help, the caller could select the appropriate choice, which then could page a specified person or group.

Most voice-mail systems have the ability for a voice menu that would operate similar to an IVR. If the support person was paged when necessary, the voice-mail message could provide information to the person who was paged. This would allow the user to describe a specific problem or ask a question without the interpretation problem that occurs when there is a third person (help desk person) involved.

There is no all-inclusive manual that will provide you with the appropriate tools for your company. Gather several people, including possibly a consultant, who have knowledge of the various tools. Start by defining the major goals for improvement in the help desk operation. Brainstorm some ideas to determine if some tools and combination of tools could potentially bring significant improvement.

Never rule out the systems that are presently in place. As stated above, most telephone systems include basic ACD. The integrated voice-mail systems include many features that could be used to improve the operation at little or no incremental cost. In fact, many times the expensive solutions may provide enhancements and options that will seldom be used.

SECURITY

There are two separate aspects to security. Protecting the access provided to help desk personnel from being available to others inside or outside the company. The second issue is that the help desk is the best place to focus users who have problems accessing the network or systems. Some method should be available to restore or change user passwords without compromising the security of the system.

Since help desk personnel may have access to systems beyond what average users are given, it is important to protect the access provided. In the case where all help desk personnel are in a common area this is easy. The area could be secured so that unauthorized personnel could not gain access to the workstations that have open access to systems. If alternate locations are used, the problem would most likely be controlled by procedures and trust in the employees to follow those procedures. Systems that time out would reduce the risk of someone leaving his workstation open into the network. Although this risk exists for all employees, it is likely that help desk personnel have access to a broader expanse of systems and into a greater depth than all but a few users.

ACCESS TO SECOND LEVEL SUPPORT PERSONNEL

As pointed out earlier, access to second level personnel is necessary to ensure timely response to user problems. If the people staffing the help desk are highly trained and experienced, access to second level people will not occur as frequently as it would if the help desk workers lack training or experience. Regardless of the frequency of escalating a problem to a second level support person, the response should be quick. By the time a decision has been made to escalate the problem, the user may already be frustrated by the wait for a solution. Do not prolong this waiting period with an ineffective method of contacting these people.

The most effective method of soliciting immediate support is to page the second level support people. In the most basic form, each person could carry a numeric pager and the help desk could dial the pager, leaving a callback number. Alphanumeric pagers allow the caller to leave a brief message. This can be an effective way to provide information without requiring the person to call back to the help desk. However, the caller must then type a message into a keyboard.

Another method would be to have a voice-mail system programmed to page people when messages are left in specific mailboxes. This paging function can be activated for all pages or only those marked urgent. With dedicated mailboxes used exclusively for immediate support requests, the former method is easiest. However, if individual user mailboxes are serving double-duty, it may be more practical to mark the support requests urgent when the message is left. Using a voice mailbox allows help desk personnel to leave messages easily that provide support person with information about the problem and can usually be accomplished quicker than using a keyboard. Another advantage is that information can easily be exchanged among support persons who have a need to communicate quickly while working on problems.

WIRELESS DATA TERMINALS

If detailed messages are regularly required when serious problems arise, wireless data terminals can be used. These devices can provide a means of two-way communication. In addition, some of the devices can be used as an interface device to equipment supported.

Second and third level support personnel do not have to be employees. Contractors can be used, especially at the third level support, to augment in-house staff. Although it is not important that users recognize whether employees or contractors are used, a well-run help desk operation should provide seamless connection among all support personnel, the help desk group and users.

If outside contractors are used as part of the support group, make sure there is a well-defined operating procedure and the contract supports the needs of the company. These arrangements can be very beneficial because they allow a company to have access to highly skilled people on short notice in a situation where there may not be sufficient need for a full-time person with the particular skills. However, the arrangement requires good procedure communications and cooperation among a variety of people in different organizations.

ORGANIZATION, TEAMWORK, AND GROWTH OPPORTUNITIES

As stated earlier in this chapter, a successful help desk operation starts by understanding the needs of the company. The role of the help desk must be clearly defined, and a mission statement must be developed. After that is done, it is important to promote an atmosphere of teamwork. The people who work in close proximity must naturally function as a team and be willing to help one another meet the common goals set. Although it may be more difficult to do when help desk personnel are located in diverse physical areas — especially if they are in different cities — it is equally important to promote teamwork among all these people.

The teamwork cannot stop with the people who answer the phones, monitor alarms, interface with users, and track problem progress. Second and third level support personnel are essential ingredients in successful problem resolution process.

Regular meetings and informal gatherings allow people to exchange ideas that can improve the process and methods used to support users. Informal gatherings generally improve communications and understanding among the people involved. If physical distance makes it impractical to gather these people together, videoconferencing can be used. Coffee mugs, T-shirts, or other special items that identify these people as part of a single customer support group will promote interaction and teamwork.

Anyone who manages a group of customer support people must accept the need for some variety in the work. It is useful if some degree of job rotation can be used to allow people to learn new skills, maintain enthusiasm and increase the interaction among the people. It is also important for the managers to provide opportunities for people to obtain additional training. People are encouraged to expand their technical and interpersonal skills with an eye toward advancement opportunities. Most people in the information technology field have a desire to learn new skills and move into more challenging positions. Help desk and second level support personnel are no different. Knowing there is an opportunity for advancement can increase the motivation level of at least the better people.

If a help desk manager considers this a job where the greatest challenge is to keep people answering phones and reporting and tracking problems, find someone else to do the job. If the manager sets a personal goal to improve the response with more job knowledge, better team work and development of people that can move upward in the organization, give him a bonus.

BRINGING IT ALL TOGETHER

Managing a successful help desk can be measured by the satisfaction of the users. Those users are looking for one place to call to get their problems resolved and questions answered in a timely manner. Proper staffing includes having the correct number of people, appropriate experience, and management that will get the most benefit of those people. Proper use of the tools is more important than the selection of the tools. Sophisticated tools can improve the operation, but only if they are understood and used in the best way.

Start with a mission statement, and make sure everything fits into that mission. If not, review the mission and conflicting idea. Which is incorrect? Either modify the mission statement or change the planned operation. You do not want to end up at the wrong destination.

Unlike a customer service operation that has the potential to generate revenue through additional sales, the help desk is usually viewed as only a cost of doing business. Always start with the base line cost for the minimum acceptable level of service. Cost for improved service should be built on that base. Make a comparison between the increased cost and added value.

147

SUMMARY

This will be a challenge, but it can be rewarding. There is a lot of frustration in dealing with problems every day, but there is a great deal of satisfaction in solving them. The bad news is that some users will never be happy. The good news is that most users that call for help are more impressed with a good effort and communications back to him than with the measured results. Measured results are necessary for the help desk manager to make sure the operation is always being improved and problem areas are quickly identified and eliminated. Quick response to users will take care of the level of satisfaction. Never forget to give users feedback.

Section III
The Network Providers

Chapter 10

The Impact of Regulatory Affairs on the Enterprise Network

Dr. Phyllis Bernt

INTRODUCTION

Regulation has always been important to telecommunications network managers. Regulatory rules have determined which providers could offer specific services, have delineated service quality requirements, have specified rates, and have outlined conditions of service provision. Network managers have had to understand the complexities of regulation to fully grasp the range of options available for getting effective services at optimum rates.

The need to understand regulatory issues has become even more important with the passage of the Telecommunications Act of 1996. That legislation, which was signed into law on February 8, 1996, promises increasing competition, new service options, and more flexibility for all consumers by breaking down some of the boundaries that have existed between services and between service providers. It is by no means certain that the promises of the Telecommunications Act will be realized; however, it is clear that network managers must be aware of the forces and conditions that led to its passage. The telecommunications landscape in the U.S. is a complex one; the Telecommunications Act of 1996 may make that landscape even more complex.

WHY REGULATION?

Telecommunications in the U.S. has been regulated as a public utility, that is, an industry that appears to have the characteristics of a natural monopoly and whose services appear to involve the public interest. The purpose of regulatory oversight is to ensure that the public utility does not abuse its position of market dominance by charging exorbitant rates, offering inferior service, or providing discriminatory service, and that the actions of the public utility further desired social policy goals. The Federal Communications Commission (FCC) and the 51 state utility commissions have exercised such oversight since the early part of the 20th century.

The existence and the authority of the FCC and the state commissions are granted by legislative action. The U.S. Congress, through passage of the Communications Act of 1934, created the FCC; the various state legislatures enacted legislation that established state regulatory commissions. The FCC and the state commission regulate telecommunications providers as common carriers. Common carriers are those entities that hold themselves out as being willing to provide service on a nondiscriminatory basis and at just and reasonable rates to all who are able to pay for the service. Common carriers, in return for these restrictions on rates and service provision, enjoy certain limitations on their liability. Specifically, telecommunications providers are not responsible for the content of the messages or information they transmit.

A Natural Monopoly

As providers of a public utility service, telecommunications carriers have faced stronger restrictions than those involved in simple common carriage. Telecommunications, until the last few decades, has been regarded as a natural monopoly, that is, a service involving such large economies of scale that competition does not appear feasible. Without viable competition, a monopoly provider can charge excessive rates, can provide inferior service, and can avoid innovation with few repercussions. It has been the responsibility of the FCC and the state commissions to replicate the benefits of competition by regulating rates and setting service standards.

In setting rates, the FCC and the state commissions traditionally sought to balance the interests of stockholders with those of consumers through the use of rate-of-return regulation. Under this regulatory method, rates were targeted to cover relevant costs and a reasonable return on investment; if the return appeared to exceed "reasonable" levels, rates were adjusted accordingly, thus benefiting consumers. Telecommunications is no longer regarded as a natural monopoly; competitors are emerging for every segment of the telecommunications industry. As competition has increased, the FCC and the state commissions have moved away from rate-of-return regulation and have adopted other methods, including the regulation of price movements (price cap regulation) or no rate regulation at all (interstate long distance, for example).

The state commissions and to some extent the FCC have also used regulatory oversight as a means of ensuring the attainment of social policy goals. State commissions, through rate regulation, have striven to keep residential local service rates low to foster universal telephone service. The FCC and the state commissions have mandated the averaging of toll rates so that the price of toll calls on low traffic routes is the same as the price of toll calls on high traffic routes of the same mileage. This geographic toll averaging has fostered universal service by ensuring affordable toll rates to geographically remote and sparsely populated areas. Whether these pricing approaches will be viable in a competitive environment is not clear, even though the Telecommunications Act of 1996 specifies the continuation of geographic toll averaging.

Dual Jurisdiction

Telecommunications services are provided across and within a complex series of boundaries. There are jurisdictional boundaries, there are boundary lines between services, and there are barriers separating providers. The jurisdictional boundaries are both within and between states.

Telecommunications services in the U.S. are regulated under a system of dual jurisdiction. The Communications Act of 1934 made it clear that the FCC jurisdiction would extend to interstate and international services; the Telecommunications Act of 1996 reaffirms that position. Intrastate telecommunications services fall under the purview of the state commissions. As a result, telecommunications circuits that cross a state boundary are governed by the FCC regulatory rules; circuits that are provided within a state fall under state commission oversight. Long-distance calls between a calling party in one state and a called party in another fall under FCC authority. Long-distance calls between parties in the same state (regardless of how the call is actually routed) are regulated by state commissions.

This system of dual jurisdiction has often been an uneasy one. Telecommunications facilities used for interstate services are often the same facilities that are used to provide intrastate services; the same loop plant, the same switch, and the same interoffice trunks can be used in providing an interstate call between Los Angeles and Seattle as well as in providing an intrastate call between Los Angeles and San Francisco. As long as the FCC and the state commissions approach these facilities in the same basic manner, there are few problems. If the FCC takes a significantly different approach than the state commissions, the result can be confusion and legal remedies. For example, the FCC determined that customer premise equipment (CPE) should be deregulated before the state commissions adopted that approach. The FCC has the power to preempt state commissions if it can show that the state commission rules would impede the FCC interstate agenda. State commissions can challenge preemption decisions in the courts. In the case of the deregulation of CPE, the FCC was able to prevail, and CPE was deregulated in both the interstate and intrastate jurisdictions.

In other cases, the state commissions have been able to defeat preemption efforts; the Louisiana utilities commission was able to defeat FCC preemption in setting depreciation rates for telecommunications carriers.

The FCC is also able to assume jurisdiction over new services that appear to be primarily interstate in nature. The FCC exercised preemptive authority over cellular services, for example, reserving the right to determine the structure of the cellular industry and the exclusive right to license cellular providers. The FCC argued that if cellular providers had to receive state authority to provide service, the establishment of a cellular industry would be severely impeded.

The Break Up of AT&T

The Modification of Final Judgment (MFJ) and the resulting breakup of AT&T introduced another jurisdictional boundary into the telecommunications landscape. To settle an antitrust suit by the Department of Justice, AT&T agreed to divest itself of its local telephone operations. This divestiture resulted in the creation of AT&T (the long-distance carrier) and of seven Regional Bell Operating Companies (RBOCs). According to the MFJ, the legal document outlining the rules governing the breakup of AT&T and the resulting rules and conditions governing the RBOCs, AT&T would keep the Long Lines, or long-distance facilities, and the RBOCs would keep the local loop plant, the local switching offices, and interoffice trunk facilities associated with the provision of local service and, within specified limits, short-haul toll services. The MFJ created a new geographic entity called a local access transport area (LATA), within which the RBOCs could provide service. While AT&T and the other long-distance carriers would provide service among these LATAs, the RBOCs would provide local service, short-haul toll, and access services within these LATAs.

The MFJ thus created another jurisdictional category for service provision. Most LATAs fall totally within one state; as a result, state commissions regulate most traffic and services that take place within LATAs. Since most states have more than one LATA, state commissions also regulate traffic and services that cross a LATA boundary but do not cross a state boundary. In those instances in which a LATA straddles a state boundary, the FCC has jurisdiction. The Telecommunications Act of 1996 provides for the end of LATA boundaries by eliminating restrictions on the RBOCs. When the RBOCs open their networks to competitors, they will be allowed to provide inter-LATA services, thus making the LATA an outmoded concept. The Telecommunications Act provides a detailed "competitive checklist" that the RBOCs must meet before they can rid themselves of inter-LATA restrictions. At this time no RBOC had successfully met the requirements outlined in the Telecommunications Act.

The existence of jurisdictional boundaries makes a network manager's job more complicated. Services that technically are the same may be priced differently and may be governed by different terms and conditions if they involve different jurisdictions. The type of service provider may also differ according to jurisdiction. Prior to the passage of the Telecommunications Act of 1996, and probably not until all the details of the act are implemented, local service could be offered by only a local telephone company, and toll service that crossed LATA boundaries could not be offered by an RBOC. The presence of jurisdictional differences can also offer the network manager some strategic opportunities. For example, some services may be offered at lower rates if they are interstate rather than intrastate in jurisdiction. Dedicated lines are an example of one category of services for which this has been the case. A network manager who configures a leased line network can pay interstate rates for that whole network if any portion, or "leg," crosses a state boundary.

Basic vs. Enhanced

In addition to jurisdictional boundaries, network managers must be aware of boundaries between categories of service. A fundamental distinction among services is that between enhanced services (also called information services) and basic services. The FCC determined after extensive deliberations during its computer inquiry proceedings that it would not regulate computer services. To determine what would be regulated and what would not, the FCC devised a definitional distinction. Basic services would be those that involved the transmission of a message; basic services would continue to be regulated. Enhanced services would be those that involved changing, or somehow affecting, a message; those services would not be subject to regulation. The Telecommunications Act of 1996 maintains this distinction between basic and enhanced services, ensuring that enhanced (or information) services will remain unregulated.

Despite the seeming clarity of this definition, drawing a clear distinction between computer services and telecommunications services has not always been a simple task because the two categories of services have been moving closer and closer together. The switches that are part of telecommunications networks are essentially computers; the circuits that connect many computers are telecommunications services. The Internet is an example of the intertwining of computer, or information, services with basic telecommunications services. The networks that connect Internet sites fall into the category of basic services, or telecommunications; the Internet sites themselves constitute enhanced, or information, services.

THE VARIOUS CATEGORIES OF REGULATED SERVICES

Not only are there distinctions drawn between basic and enhanced services, the basic services themselves are differentiated. There are several categories within basic services: local service, toll services, dedicated (or specialized) services, access, and wireless services. The billing approach, type of service provider, and regulatory body have tended to differ for each category of service.

Local Service

Local service is an intrastate service regulated by the state utility commissions. Local service is the basic building block of telecommunications services. Local service rates have included the connection from the customer location to the telephone switching office, a telephone number (or address on the public switched network), a directory listing, and the ability to place a call within a specified area without incurring a toll charge.

Local service is further subdivided into residential and business service. This distinction is significant from a billing standpoint. While most residential customers in the U.S. have flat-rate services, which allows them to make unlimited local calls for a monthly charge, business customers are increasingly being charged for local service under local measured service (LMS) arrangements. Businesses who have LMS are charged for local calling on a per-minute or per-message basis.

The distinction between local residential and local business service is significant even without LMS because of the wide disparity between residential and business rates. On the average, flat-rate business charges are three and a half times as great as residential rates. This disparity in charges between business and residential rates is part of a concerted effort to keep residential rates low, and therefore affordable to most residential subscribers, through a pattern of pricing cross subsidies. In effect, business rates help to subsidize residential charges.

Local service has traditionally been provided by the local telephone companies, which held an exclusive franchise for that service. In return for this monopoly position, the local telephone companies have been closely regulated concerning local rates and local rate structures. The introduction of competition into local service is expected to result in lower rates, especially for business customers.

Long-Distance Services

Long-distance service, or message toll service, is billed on a per-minute basis. Along with call duration, time of day and distance are taken into account in rating long-distance calls. Regular long-distance services are billed to the party originating the call.

The providers of long-distance services and the rates charged for these services are affected by regulatory policy considerations. Because of the MFJ, the RBOCs have been precluded from offering long-distance services that cross LATA boundaries; this tends to preclude interstate long-distance services as well. RBOCs have offered long-distance services that fall within a LATA. AT&T, MCI, and the other long-distance carriers offer interstate and inter-LATA long distance. In the early years after the breakup of AT&T, long-distance carriers were blocked from providing intra-LATA service by many state utility commissions. That is no longer the case, and long-distance carriers are allowed to compete for intra-LATA long-distance traffic in all states. Once the provisions of the Telecommunications Act of 1996 are fully implemented, all providers should be able to offer long-distance services in all jurisdictions.

Jurisdiction Determines Pricing

The pricing of long-distance services can vary greatly by jurisdiction. Interstate long-distance charges have decreased dramatically since the breakup of AT&T and the introduction of competition. One development that has caused the decline in long-distance rates has been the imposition of subscriber line charges. Business customers have paid $6 per month for every business line; that $6 had been built into long-distance charges. To lower long-distance charges further, the FCC has mandated that the $6 rate may increase to $9 over the next 2 or 3 years. Intrastate long-distance charges have not declined as dramatically, especially intra-LATA toll charges. Relatively higher intra-LATA toll charges have been the result of unwillingness on the part of state utility commissions to raise local rates. When local telephone companies have filed rate cases seeking to raise rates, state utility commissions have responded by allowing them to raise intra-LATA toll rates rather than local rates. In effect, intra-LATA toll rates have provided a subsidy for local rates.

Most business customers are able to purchase long-distance services at volume discounts.

Specialized Services

Long-distance services are switched services; they use the public switched telephone network (PSTN) from customer premise to customer premise, and they are billed on a usage basis. Specialized services, or dedicated services, involve facilities that are dedicated to the use of the specific customer. These dedicated lines are billed on a flat-rated, monthly basis; and, for large users, they are an economically efficient service option.

The pricing of dedicated lines varies by speed, or capacity. In the early days of analog services, dedicated lines were categorized by the type of use the line was capable of supporting. Dedicated lines varied from the simple "metallic" circuit, capable of transmitting only the simplest of message over a short distance, to the voice grade circuit, capable of transmitting conversations clearly, to the data circuit, capable of handling a fairly small amount of data information, to the circuits capable of handling closed circuit audio or video. These analog lines were billed according to the type of information they were engineered to handle and were billed on a mileage basis.

The billing of digital dedicated lines is not based on the type of information that will be transmitted. Digital dedicated lines are billed according to their speed or capacity. An important aspect of the pricing of dedicated lines is the crossover point between dedicated lines. For example, while a DS1 dedicated line is the equivalent of 24 DS0 lines, the pricing of the DS1 is much less than 24 times the price of one DS0 line. A network manager must determine at what point it becomes more economical to lease a DS1 rather than several DS0s. In the same manner, it is important to determine at which point a network manager should lease a DS3, which is the equivalent of 28 DS1s, rather than leasing several DS1s.

Dedicated lines have proved to be a financial boon to network managers because they can push a good deal of information over these lines without paying usage-based charges. Dedicated lines are also at times complex services to evaluate because of jurisdictional issues. Depending on the boundaries that the dedicated line crosses, a dedicated line can be local in jurisdiction, intra-LATA, inter-LATA, intrastate, or interstate. The jurisdiction of the dedicated line determines the price that is charged for the line, and also the type of provider that can offer the service. The intra-LATA prohibition has applied to the RBOCs for dedicated lines, as well as for long-distance services. If a network manager wishes to order a dedicated line that crosses a LATA boundary, the manager has had to go to an interexchange carrier such as an MCI or AT&T. For local and intra-LATA lines, the network manager has worked with an RBOC or independent local telephone company.

Access Services

The advent of long-distance competition brought with it a new category of service: access services. With the breakup of the Bell System and the creation of seven RBOCs came the creation of LATAs. These LATAs have been the serving territories within which the RBOCs provide local service and intra-LATA toll; they have also been the areas within which the RBOCs have provided interexchange carriers with access services. Access services encompass the use of RBOC facilities to reach subscribers. Interexchange carriers (AT&T, Sprint, MCI, etc.) pay RBOCs access charges for the use of the RBOC loop plant, local switching office, and interoffice trunk plant in the provision of inter-LATA long-distance and inter-LATA dedicated services.

The access service tariffs do not limit the provision of access services to interexchange carriers only; any entity can order from access tariffs. Because of the coordination problems involved in dealing with multiple RBOCs, most network managers purchase "retail" services from the interexchange carriers rather than buying "wholesale out of the access tariffs.

Wireless Services

Wireless services have been regulated differently from wireline services. The most common form of wireless service has been cellular service. The FCC in effect created the cellular industry by regulatory action. In the early 1980s, the FCC determined that cellular should be a duopoly, that is, that there should be two, and only two, cellular providers per area. The FCC divided the U.S. into metropolitan service areas (MSAs) and rural service areas (RSAs), and awarded two cellular licenses per MSA and RSA. Licenses were awarded by lottery; preference was given to the local telephone company in each area for one of the licenses.

The regulation of cellular service has been mostly at the federal level. In some states, state commissions regulate intrastate cellular traffic, but at the federal level, cellular service is not rate regulated.

The most significant development in wireless services is personal communications services (PCS). As with cellular service, the FCC is creating the PCS industry by regulatory proceedings. The PCS industry structure has been defined by the FCC, which has established a fairly complex pattern of PCS licensing service areas. PCS licenses are being awarded through an auction process, rather than by lottery. It does not appear that state commissions will have an active regulatory role with PCS; it does not appear that PCS will be rate regulated at the federal level. An interesting question about wireless services, including PCS, is what role they will play in the coming era of local competition. There is speculation that PCS might develop as a replacement for the wireline local loop. If that is the case, PCS may come under state commission authority as a local exchange service provider.

THE ROAD TOWARD COMPETITION

In 1950, telecommunications was a monopoly. AT&T, along with several hundred independent local telephone companies, provided a seamless PSTN. The telephone company owned every component required to place a telephone call: the premise equipment, the intrabuilding wiring, the loop plant, the switching offices, the interoffice trunks, and the toll switches. And it provided those components on a monopoly basis. Business customers seeking nonswitched, dedicated services rented lines from that same telephone company. By year 2000, there will be competitive provision of every one of those components. There will no longer be one PSTN; subscribers will have their choice of providers and their choice of networks.

The road to competition began at the peripheries of the PSTN (CPE and specialized services) and has been moving steadily into the heart of the public network: the local loop and the local telephone company switch.

Competition came into CPE with the FCC Carterfone decision in 1968. AT&T, as the monopoly telephone provider, had prohibited any customer-provided attachments to the telephone network, citing possible harm to the network; the FCC, in Carterphone, found this policy too restrictive and completed a series of proceedings that allowed customers to connect their own equipment to the network. Finally, with its Computer Inquiry II proceeding, the FCC decided that CPE would be deregulated effective Jan. 1, 1983.

Competition next came into specialized services, or dedicated line services. In 1959, the FCC allowed private use of microwave systems above 890 MHz; this was known as the Above 890 Decision. A company called Microwave Communications Inc. (MCI) filed with the FCC in 1963 for permission to provide point-to-point microwave dedicated line service between St. Louis and Chicago. The FCC granted the MCI request in 1969, and then in 1971 it adopted a policy of allowing the entry of new specialized carriers to compete for dedicated services. Once dedicated services were opened up to entry, the next step was competition for long-distance message toll, or switched services. When the FCC was at first reluctant to allow competition in regular long distance, MCI turned to the courts for relief on this issue. The courts found no validity in the argument that competition in long-distance markets would be counter to the public interest. The FCC began its own proceedings to examine the public interest aspects of long-distance competition and determined in its 1980 MTS/wide area telephone service (WATS) restructure proceeding that competition would now be the policy for long-distance service provision. The MFJ, with its provisions governing the breakup of the Bell System and its equal access arrangements, facilitated the move toward a competitive long-distance market.

The state commissions were not as quick to adopt a procompetitive policy toward CPE and long distance, but they have since followed suit. Even those states that might have been reluctant to adopt competition will have no choice but to move toward a fully competitive telecommunications environment because of the Telecommunications Act of 1996.

Competition in the Local Arena

The Telecommunications Act seeks to bring competition into all aspects of telecommunications, including the last major telecommunications monopoly: the local service arena. For decades, state commissions have granted local telephone companies an exclusive franchise to provide local service within a defined territory. In return for agreeing to restrictions on pricing flexibility and earning levels, the local telephone companies have had a monopoly within their local service areas. The Telecommunications

Act seeks to end that exclusive franchise and to open all services, including local service, to competitive entry. The act preempts the state commissions and takes away their power to block new entrants.

In many ways, competition in CPE and in specialized services was fairly easy to implement. Once a modular jack was developed and installed in all premises, a customer could plug in the instrument of his choice without disrupting the rest of the network. Dedicated lines are not an integral part of the PSTN; acquiring dedicated lines from common carriers other than the Bell System would not disrupt the arrangements surrounding the PSTN either. Even the competitive provision of long-distance service is, at least in theory, a fairly simple process. The RBOCs charge the long-distance carriers access charges for accumulating long-distance traffic from subscribers and delivering that traffic to the long-distance carrier of the customer's choice. The RBOCs deliver that traffic to the long-distance carriers at mutually agreed on points of presence. In a sense the long-distance carrier's point of presence is on the periphery of the PSTN.

Local service is a more complex undertaking. Local service entails the provision of a telephone number, access to operators and to directory assistance, a directory listing, access to emergency services, access to long-distance carriers, and other elements. To have competition in local service, competitors have to be able to provide all these elements on an equal basis. The Telecommunications Act in broad outline and the FCC in more detail through its proceedings and orders seek to establish procedures that will make it possible for a customer to change local providers without changing phone numbers (number portability) and without losing any of the significant elements that have comprised local service.

Keys to local competition are resale and interconnection. The Telecommunications Act and the FCC orders require the incumbent local telephone companies (the RBOCs and the independent telephone companies) to allow competitors to interconnect to their facilities and to resell their services. As an example of interconnection, a competitor can lease a local loop plant from a customer location right to the local telephone office; the competitor can then connect the loop plant to its own network. As an example of resale, a competitor can purchase local service from the local telephone company and resell it to a customer. For local competition to be viable, the rates for interconnection and for resale have to be low enough to encourage competition, but high enough to cover the relevant costs of the incumbent telephone company.

The Benefits of Competition

The goal of the Telecommunications Act is to bring the benefits of competition—innovation, efficiency, lower prices, and customer choice—to local service. Network managers should benefit greatly if viable local competition develops. The competitive local exchange carriers (CLECs) that are emerging are seeking to provide local service to business customers instead of to residential customers. Their motivation is obvious; business customers are large-volume users of telecommunications, including local services. The local rates charged to business customers by the incumbent local telephone companies have included subsidies for residential service. CLECs have pricing flexibility and the freedom to choose their markets. As a result, they can offer business customers lower rates.

It is not yet clear who the CLECs will be. One group that is beginning to emerge is composed of alternative service providers (sometimes also called competitive access providers). These alternative providers have built fiber networks in metropolitan areas and have provided specialized services to business customers. The Telecommunications Act makes it possible for these providers to expand their service offerings to their existing customer base and to provide a wider range of services to potential customers. Long-distance carriers may also be a possible source for CLECs. A long-distance carrier may find it attractive to become a one-stop service provider to its business customers by reselling local service and bundling those services with their long-distance services. Many industry players, in the wake of the Telecommunications Act, are positioning themselves, through mergers and acquisitions, to become full-service providers or to expand their geographic reach. The WorldCom Inc. acquisition of MCI creates a service provider capable of combining the provision of Internet access service with traditional long-distance services. The AT&T/Teleport merger combines the largest long-distance provider in the nation with an aggressive provider of competitive local service, thus providing AT&T with quick entry into the local service market. The mergers between RBOCs (the merger of NYNEX with Bell Atlantic and SBC with Pacific Telesis) and the proposed merger between Bell Atlantic and GTE will make it easier for business customers in multiple locations to receive their services from the same entity.

For network managers, local competition offers more options, the potential for lower prices, and the possibility of dealing with one provider for a multitude of services.

THE LOGISTICS OF REGULATION

Although telecommunications is becoming an increasingly competitive industry, regulators and regulatory procedures will not disappear in the foreseeable future. The Telecommunications Act precludes state commissions from implementing rules that could block emerging competition, but the act also gives state commissions a role in enforcing interconnection procedures and the authority to establish funds to support universal service efforts at the state level. At the federal level, the FCC has been active in

162

crafting the rules needed to make the vision outlined in the 1996 act a reality. Attaining viable local competition will not be an easy goal to achieve after so many decades of local monopoly; regulatory oversight will be required to ensure that the incumbent local exchange carriers (the RBOCs and the local telephone companies) do not abuse their dominant position and that the interests of consumers are protected in this period of industry transition.

Although the act bars state commissions from denying new entrants into the local service market, state commissions retain the authority to require those new entrants to be certified as carriers. State commissions also have the authority to require these new entrants to file tariffs and existing carriers to continue to file tariffs. Indeed, the Telecommunications Act of 1996 contains provisions allowing the tariffing of interconnection agreements between carriers.

The tariffing of services in an era of local competition may not be as extensive a process as in past years; however, tariffs will remain an important resource for network managers. Tariffs are, in effect, a surrogate for a contract. Tariffs outline the rights and the obligations of both the telecommunications carrier and the customer. Terms and conditions of service provision, installation schedules, and rates and charges have traditionally been listed in tariffs. The development of tariffs and changes to existing tariffs have been the result of lengthy state commission hearings, with significant consumer participation, and careful deliberation of extensive supporting materials presented by the telecommunications carrier. The tariffing process has been simplified and streamlined. Rate regulation is being replaced with incentive regulation; carriers are allowed to file new rates on short notice and without a hearing. Tariffs, however, continue to be valuable documents that network managers should be able to understand and use. Tariffs delineate the network manager's rights and options and can serve as a basis for complaint should those rights not be honored.

Another dimension of the regulatory process that is of great importance to network managers is the issue of service quality standards. Most, if not all, state commissions have established service quality standards for local telephone companies. These standards make clear how quickly companies must respond to service complaints and how quickly service outages must be remedied. The future of service quality standards in an era of competition is not clear. Theoretically, with robust competition, service quality standards should not be needed. How quickly robust competition will develop is not clear, however, and holding carriers—incumbents and new entrants alike—to quality standards may prove a valuable step on the road to local competition.

The focus of the regulatory process has changed during the past few years as rate regulation has been eased. The focus will continue to change as local competition unfolds. Rather than concentrating on specific rates or detailed services, regulators will focus their concerns on interconnection agreements and the enforcement of the other provisions needed to encourage the emergence of competition.

GLOBAL ISSUES

Telecommunication services are essential to the globalization of companies and of economies. (For more on global networks, see Chapter 12.) Companies that establish offices in multiple countries want to link those offices with voice, data, and imaging communication capabilities. Telecommunications services make those communications capabilities possible. Without telecommunications services and the resulting ability to move information across the globe at will, globalization would be a much more difficult and less attractive undertaking.

While telecommunications services are fueling globalization efforts, increasing globalization is having an impact on the provision of telecommunications services as well. Network managers for global organizations are pressing for the provision of comparable services delivered at comparable rates at all their locations. Countries seeking to attract global businesses are recognizing the importance of a developed telecommunications infrastructure capable of offering advanced services at attractive rates. The result has been a revolution in the approach to telecommunications services in all areas of the world.

Telecommunications in most countries has been regarded as a public utility, owned and operated by the government. In most nations, the norm has been government ownership of a monopoly PTT, a government agency responsible for the post office, the telegraph, and telecommunications services. In most nations, this arrangement has resulted in an insufficient infrastructure, lack of innovation, and little attention to customer service. Revenues raised from telecommunications have been used to subsidize the postal system, or other government enterprises, rather than being invested in infrastructure improvements. There have been few incentives for innovation or efficiencies. This approach is being replaced in most nations by privatization and the introduction of competition.

Most nations are disbanding their PTTs and separating the postal authority from the telecommunications system. They are also taking the further step of introducing some measure of privatization into telecommunications services. Some nations have made their telecommunications system a "parastatal" operation, owned by the government, but having a good deal of autonomy and freedom to operate. Other nations have sold shares in the telecommunications system to private investors but have retained some percentage of government ownership, and some nations have sold the entire telecommunications system to private inves-

164

tors. The result has been an infusion of capital for infrastructure development and more incentive for innovation and efficiency.

Attendant with privatization has been a move to introduce competition into various telecommunications services. The European Union has been at the forefront of these efforts, issuing directives requiring competition in CPE, in mobile services, and in data services, and, finally, competition in basic network services in most EU nations starting in 1998. Several countries have already adopted full-scale competition. For example, the U.K., which took its first step toward competition by adopting a duopoly approach in 1984, moved to full-blown competition in all telecommunications services in the early 1990s.

THE IMPACT OF TRADE POLICY

This move toward competition is being fueled by trade policy. Traditionally, international trade agreements have been seen as treaties involving tangible goods and agricultural products. The General Agreement on Tariffs and Trade (GATT) is an agreement signed by nations after lengthy negotiations concerning specific details of how these nations will sell one another wheat, steel, office furniture, and other commodities. The last round of GATT talks, the Uruguay Round, added to its deliberations the inclusion of trade in services. The result was the General Agreement on Trade in Services (GATS). Telecommunications has emerged as a key service covered in the GATS. The World Trade Organization (WTO) that replaced the GATT includes the GATS provisions. The inclusion of telecommunications under the trade umbrella is significant. Rather than being regarded as a public utility, telecommunications is now seen as an element of trade, as a commodity that can add to the economic health of a nation.

Even more significantly perhaps, the application of trade principles to telecommunications suggests that it is an economic sector that should be governed by free-market principles rather than by regulatory mandate. Trade principles like the most favored nation (MFN); the reciprocity rule, which requires that a concession by one party be met with a concession by the other party; the transparency rule, which requires that tariffs and rules be open and available to all; and the national principle rule, which requires that domestic competitors not be favored over foreign competitors operating in a country all tend toward the opening of telecommunications markets. The result should be a lowering of prices for international and domestic services, increased options such as international resale, and increasing similarity of services and rates across national boundaries.

THE INTERNATIONAL PRICING OF TELECOMMUNICATIONS

The pricing of telecommunications has been based on policy considerations rather than underlying costs. Many nations maintained low local rates by charging above-cost long-distance charges. Many countries subsidized their domestic rates by charging high international long-distance rates. Some countries had high rates for dedicated lines or did not even allow the provision of dedicated lines to keep customers on the PSTN. The forces of trade and the desire by many nations to attract business have led most nations to adopt some level of rate rebalancing and to liberalize their policies concerning dedicated lines.

International long-distance rates, in particular, have been declining, in part, in response to pressure from the U.S. The compensation arrangements between international common carriers have fueled a trade imbalance between the U.S. and many other nations. In this compensation arrangement, known as accounting and settlements, the carrier that handles the originating portion of the call compensates the carrier that terminates the call. Such an arrangement works well if the calling between nations is symmetric; however, since a larger portion of calls originate from the U.S. than terminate in the U.S., U.S. carriers have tended to pay out more in compensation than they have collected. The result is a trade imbalance of some size. This situation has caused the chairman of the FCC to put pressure on other nations to lower their international long-distance charges and thus stimulate calling to the U.S. The FCC chairman is also trying to decrease the amounts involved in the accounting and settlement compensation arrangements between nations.

The desire to avoid the accounting and settlement compensation arrangements, as well as a desire to attract international businesses, is fueling the creation of joint ventures and mergers by service providers. The opening of markets caused by the WTO process is facilitating this trend. Companies such as Sprint, Deutsche Telekom, and France Telecom have created a joint venture to attract international businesses by providing them, in effect, with one-stop international shopping. The British Telecom (BT)/MCI merger is another such example. The benefit of these joint ventures and mergers for network managers is evident; arrangements for international services are simplified.

The developments in global telecommunicationstrade issues, privatization, increasing competition, mergers, and joint ventures are tending to lower rates and provide network managers with more options. They are also tending to standardize services and service quality across national borders, a development that can make it much easier to design and manage a global network.

SUMMARY

Regulatory developments are increasingly important to network managers. The very structure of the telecommunications industry is being redrafted through legislation (such as the Telecommunications Act of 1996) and through regulatory proceedings at the FCC and in state commissions. Barriers between services and service providers are being eroded as RBOCs are striving to provide inter-LATA long-distance services and new entrants are emerging in the local services market. New services such as PCS are being defined by the FCC. Regulatory bodies are focusing on matters of industry structure and interconnection rather than on rates and service quality standards.

At the global level, governments are privatizing their former PTTs, competition is being adopted as the appropriate structure for telecommunications markets, and telecommunications services are being brought under the trade umbrella. New players are emerging, including joint ventures and mergers designed to give network managers the luxury of one-stop shopping for their international service needs.

Both domestically and internationally, the push is toward greater competition and more choices. Network managers face greater opportunities but also greater complexity as a result. It is more important than ever for network managers to be aware of new regulatory rules and approaches and what they mean for telecommunications service provision.

Chapter 11
Dealing with Carriers
Kimberly Russo

INTRODUCTION

Dealing with carriers is becoming more complex than ever before. The changing dynamic of the telecommunications industry has spawned a competitive environment with more companies vying for your business. This chapter focuses on the different types of carriers born at divestiture and the new entrants into the emerging competitive market.

Due to the increased market complexity, every network manager today needs to stay abreast of changes and to develop the skills needed to negotiate in this competitive environment. This chapter will give you the basic tools to determine which carriers are best suited to your needs based on the services they provide, the prices they charge, and the reliability they offer.

TYPES OF CARRIERS

Since divestiture, telecommunications carriers have traditionally been divided into categories based on the types of calls they are authorized to carry. As regulatory pressures subside and a competitive marketplace emerges, distinguishing telecommunications companies by the types of calls they carry is becoming more difficult. Call types once reserved for specific classifications of carriers are now being provided by companies once banned from those markets.

Local Exchange Carriers (LECs)

After divestiture, network managers needed to deal with several different carriers to get a full range of services and have all call types covered. LECs provided local service and the physical connection of the telecommunications network to your building. Because the LECs owned the tangible local loop infrastructure, the customer had no choice in determining which carrier provided local service.

LECs owned a monopolistic geographic territory and because of this, customers within that area had no other options available for local service. LECs also were the sole carriers of intralocal access transport area (intra-LATA) calls. LATAs are geographic boundaries set fairly arbitrarily at divestiture.

At that time, it was determined that only LECs could carry calls that originate and terminate within the same LATA. Conversely, any calls terminating outside the originating LATA (inter-LATA calls) were reserved as the domain of interexchange carriers (IXCs).

Today, the boundaries set forth at divestiture are becoming blurred as deregulation knocks down the barriers that previously constrained the carriers. IXCs and competitive LECs are entering the $96 billion local market, and LECs are providing long-distance service outside their local access areas while working to meet FCC requirements that would allow them to provide long-distance service within their local access areas.[1]

LECs include companies ranging from Mom and Pop shops to Fortune 500 corporations. Due to the diversity in size and number of customers served, the availability of technology from these LECs varies as much as their size. The most commonly known LECs are the Regional Bell Operating Companies (RBOCs), or the "baby bells." The RBOCs were split from AT&T at divestiture, creating seven new local phone companies known as Bell South Telecommunications, Bell Atlantic, Southwestern Bell Corp., Nynex, Pacific Telesis, U.S. West, and Ameritech. (Major alignments are under way.) Today, the RBOCs, as well as major independent LECs such as GTE, are jockeying for position as they begin their invasion of the IXC inter-LATA market. In 1996, the RBOCs accounted for 72% of total local revenues. With the IXCs planning their own attacks on the LEC territories, RBOCs are eager to fight back by taking their share of the $93 billion long-distance market.[2]

The usage charges for local service generally fall under one of three types, not all of which are available in every area. Network managers should be sure to investigate all the options available to them. If local usage is low, a measured or message rate local service is preferable. These services generally are offered at lower monthly rates with a per minute (measured) or per call (message) charge. If local usage is high, a flat rate local service is preferable. Although the monthly charge is generally higher, all local calls are provided at no additional charge. Flat-rate local service, however, is not available to businesses in many areas.

LECs also provide vertical services, also known as auxiliary or custom features. Vertical services include, but are not limited to voice message, circular and regular hunt groups, call forwarding, and speed dialing.

Competitive LECs

In the mid-1980s, competitive local exchange carriers (CLECs), then known as competitive access providers (CAPs) emerged. These carriers offered local service by building their own infrastructure to bypass the LEC and provide access directly to the IXC. CLECs that provide physical connection to customers via their own network are known as facilities-based carriers. Some of the earlier facilities-based carriers included MFS Intelenet, MCI Metro, and Teleport Communications Group, among others.

As the local market is deregulated, reselling of the LEC services is one of the primary ways of introducing competition into this former monopoly. The LECs are required to allow CLECs to purchase time on their networks at wholesale rates. The purchased block of time may then be sold by the competitor to business and residential customers. Reselling was decided by regulators to be the only way to introduce true competition because the cost of building the infrastructure necessary for facilities-based carriers is prohibitive, and rights of way for running lines is limited. LECs have therefore been required to reach interconnection agreements with their new competitors, allowing CLECs access to the already existing local loop. New entrants into the local market include the familiar long-distance carriers that have reached interconnection agreements with the LECs.

Traditionally, alternative carriers have been used by network managers for protection against service interruption. If BellSouth is the LEC for the area in which a network manager's facility is located, and that network manager also purchases service from a facilities-based CLEC, redundancy is created, which offers protection should one of the carriers experience a service outage. However, this level of protection does not exist if the chosen CLEC is a non-facilities-based carrier that is reselling time on the network owned by the LEC already serving the facility. A service outage in that case would likely affect both carriers.

Network managers should also note that as competition initially emerged, switching to a CLEC required a change in telephone number, since individual exchanges (NXXs) are assigned by the North American Numbering Plan Administration to specific LECs. Telecommunications networks route calls to their termination points by connecting to the carrier owning the dialed exchange. For connections to customers on alternative carrier networks to be routed properly, the customer was forced to change its exchange to one assigned to the chosen CLEC.

This situation is rapidly improving as numbers become "portable." Similar to 800 number portability, which began in May of 1993, the FCC has ordered that number portability for local service be available in the 100 largest cities by Dec. 31, 1998. In the meantime, interim number portability is being implemented to allow customers who wish to switch from their incumbent local exchange carrier (ILEC) to a CLEC to take their existing phone numbers with them. Methods of interim number portability include remote call forwarding, direct inward dial, and migration of an entire NXX from the ILEC to the CLEC. Number portability is not available if the customer is moving to a location outside the serving rate center of the NXX.

171

Exhibit 1.   Presubscribed Telephone Lines by Carrier

AT&T	10,177,257
MCI Telecommunications	22,938,608
Sprint	11,788,717
WorldCom Inc.	4,297,498
Excel Telecommunications	3,792,171
LCI Companies	2,244,192
Frontier Companies	2,050,019
SNET America Long Distance	783,135
GTE Long Distance Co.	733,558
Cable & Wireless Communications	625,367

From Trends in Telephone Service, Industry Analysis Division, Federal Communications Commission, February 1998.

Interexchange Carriers (IXCs)

IXCs are companies that since divestiture have provided long-distance services (any calls crossing LATA boundaries, or inter-LATA). The more well-known IXCs are the big three: AT&T, MCI, and Sprint. New competitors such as WorldCom Inc. (currently number four in number of presubscribed lines and is merging with MCI), Excel (number five), and thousands of others have gained market share over the past few years (Exhibit 1).

The new competitive environment is also allowing LECs, once banned from long-distance service, to enter the interexchange market. However, before LECs may provide long-distance service to customers in the local exchange area they serve, an FCC checklist ensuring fair competition on the local level must be fulfilled. Because of the absence of the go-ahead from the FCC to provide long-distance service to the existing customer base, the RBOCs have begun providing long-distance service outside of their own region, by forming such subsidiaries as U.S. West Long Distance, which has filed tariffs to provide interexchange service in Maryland, Missouri, and Arkansas, to name a few.

In addition to basic long-distance services, the IXCs provide dedicated access service, allowing the customer to bypass the LEC and connect directly to the IXC network. Dedicated services can include voice and data, and in the past they were typically huge, equipment heavy, private line networks set up by corporations to connect their multiple sites. Today, private lines have commonly been replaced by virtual networks, allowing dedicated access from the IXC to the customer without reserving specific bandwidth, lines, or equipment for them.

Some services are provided by both interexchange carriers for inter-LATA traffic and LECs for intra-LATA traffic. For example, most major LECs and IXCs currently provide frame relay in most of their service areas. In

172

addition, IXCs often provide similar vertical services to those available through the LECs.

METHODS OF SETTING RATES

The method of setting rates is a continually evolving process that has changed greatly over the past few years as we shift from a highly regulated to a highly competitive industry. Today, the competitiveness of the marketplace is the main factor in price setting. Regulated services, however, have always been affected by political motivations in the rate-setting process.

Rate of Return

Monopolistic services are typically regulated by the public utility commission (PUC) in each state, which must authorize rate increases. A carrier seeking a rate hike petitions the PUC for approval, and a series of hearings (also known as a "rate case") is held in which the carrier's financial reports and cost allocations are examined. Adversary financial and economic experts testify on behalf of both the carrier and the public interest.

The PUC commissioners determine if an increase in rates is warranted by calculating the carrier's costs plus a rate of return deemed fair by the commission. It is obviously in the interest of the petitioning carrier to show costs to be as high as possible. The state, on the other hand, argues that the utility's costs are not as high as presented. Once testimony is complete, a rate of return and subsequently the price change needed to satisfy that rate of return are set by the commission.

When the PUC approves raising rates, the increased charges have historically been applied to all the carrier offerings except basic residential local service. Occasionally, the rate increase for business services and vertical features does not satisfy the telephone company costs plus the approved rate of return. When this situation occurs, the residual amount is applied the residential local charges. For example, if the carrier costs are determined to be $10 million and the PUC has approved a 10% rate of return, the total amount of revenue to be generated is $11 million.

If raising rates for services other than the residential local market can bring revenue to $10.5 million, then the additional $500,000 would be the residual amount. This residual is collected by raising residential local rates by just the amount necessary for the carrier to collect the needed $500,000. This hesitance to increase residential local charges is largely a political decision. In many states, the PUC commissioners are elected officials.

For a publicly elected commissioner, approving an increase in prices for residential service means a likely defeat in the next election. In states where PUC commissioners are not chosen in public elections, they are generally appointed by the governor, which can also lead to decisions on rate increases based on political motivations. The regulated services of telephone companies are still often priced on a rate of return basis.

It is hypothesized that a deregulated local market will cause an increase in the rates for basic residential local exchange service because the rate of return process has kept these prices artificially low. Conversely, local rates for businesses may have been held artificially high, as they were assessed more than their share of the rate increases necessary to maintain a given rate of return. This is good news for network managers looking to benefit from the newly competitive local market.

Competitive Rates

In contrast to the rate of return method of setting pricing for utility services, today's marketplace allows prices to be set based on the competitiveness of the industry. Where consumers have a choice of carriers, standard economic models of a competitive marketplace apply. Many telecommunications services are becoming viewed as commodities, and carriers must meet the prices of competitors while maintaining profitability. Higher priced telephone companies must distinguish themselves as value-added providers through customer service, reliability, or technology if they hope to survive.

Like contenders in any other competitive industry, telecommunications carriers often set prices based on the services to which they hope to attract customers. Enticing customers with fixed monthly charges for all their usage is one way to do this, but network managers should be alert for changes in pricing structure, even once a contract is signed. These revisions will affect contract customers when their current term expires and they are investigating renewal. Keeping abreast of changes can save research time when the contract ends and renegotiation begins.

A prime example of potential price restructuring may be seen in the possibilities for the future of frame relay pricing. Currently, charges for this service from any of the big three are based on a fixed monthly rate as AT&T, MCI, and Sprint continue their efforts to draw customers to this high-technological service. Because of the fixed monthly rate, it is wise for customers to send as much of their traffic as possible via this service. Originally introduced as a data service, frame relay now carries voice traffic as well. Network managers have moved quickly to include their voice traffic in the fixed monthly frame relay rate. However, as revenue from voice services is cannibalized by the conversion to frame relay, it is possible that structure of frame relay pricing will change to a usage-based rate dependent on how much data and voice are transferred. This type of restructure could greatly affect the cost of a company's communications network, which network

174

Exhibit 2. Virtual Network Rate Comparison—Day Rates (Initial 18 s)

Mileage[a]	On-Network to On-Network			On-Network to Off-Network			Off-Network to Off-Network		
	SDN	VNET	VPN[b]	SDN	VNET	VPN[b]	SDN	VNET	VPN[b]
0–55	$0.0285	$0.0288	$0.0285	$0.0498	$0.0510	$0.0513	$0.0768	$0.0783	$0.0741
56–292	$0.0372	$0.0310	$0.0348	$0.0588	$0.0603	$0.0609	$0.0837	$0.0858	$0.0840
293–430	$0.0423	$0.0429	$0.0435	$0.0639	$0.0651	$0.0663	$0.0891	$0.0909	$0.0888
431–925	$0.0492	$0.0504	$0.0510	$0.0702	$0.0717	$0.0723	$0.0927	$0.0942	$0.0930
926–1910	$0.0540	$0.0549	$0.0558	$0.0762	$0.0774	$0.0783	$0.0972	$0.0990	$0.0983
1911–3000	$0.0588	$0.0603	$0.0645	$0.0780	$0.0795	$0.0819	$0.0972	$0.0990	$0.1010
3001–4250	$0.0660	$0.0669		$0.0879	$0.0894		$0.0972	$0.0990	
4251–5750	$0.0687	$0.0699		$0.0900	$0.0915		$0.0972	$0.0990	

[a] Mileage column is applicable to SDN and VNET only.
[b] VPN is not mileage sensitive. Instead the rates are tariffed in six bands. The appliable band depends on the area code of the originating point and the area code of the terminating point.

AT&T SDN rates effective Nov. 5, 1997, from AT&T Tariff FCC No. 1.
MCI VNET rates effective Nov. 15, 1997, from MCI Tariff FCC No. 1.
Sprint VPN rates effective Dec. 1, 1997, from Sprint Tariff FCC No. 5.

managers should be aware of when the change takes place and not when the contract is up for renewal.

NEGOTIATING WITH CARRIERS

There are many different tactics for saving money when choosing a carrier. There is, however, no escaping the fact that the higher your volume, the better the deal you will be able to negotiate.

Dedicated vs. Switched Access

First, changing from switched access to dedicated access can save money. Switched access means that the service from the IXC is being routed, or switched, through the LEC network and is considered off the IXC network. The LEC is charging the IXC for access to your site via the local network, and that cost is being passed on by the IXC to the consumer. Dedicated access means that your location or locations are set up on-network to the IXC, bypassing the LEC and charges associated with the LEC/IXC handoff of calls.

An example is the AT&T Software Defined Network (SDN) service. Currently, interstate charges for SDN when both the originating and terminating points are off-network locations are up to 270% of the rates charged if both points are on-network (Exhibit 2). Similar situations exist with Sprint and MCI equivalent services, Virtual Private Network (VPN) Service and VNET, respectively. If the sites of a corporation are in an off-network environment, subscribing to dedicated service for each location access can cut usage costs in half.

Exhibit 3. Long-Term and High-Volume Discount Examples of Frame Relay Service

Minimum Monthly Revenue Commitment ($)	Available Discounts				
	1 Year (%)	2 Years (%)	3 Years (%)	4 Years (%)	5 Years (%)
AT&T[a]					
2,000	3	4	7	12	17
5,000	5	6	10	15	18
10,000	7	8	12	19	22
18,000	8	10	16	23	26
25,000	8	12	19	25	28
50,000	9	13	20	26	30
MCI (Effective 2/19/96)[b]					
5,000	4	6	8	—	—
10,000	6	8	10	—	—
25,000	8	10	12	—	—
50,000	10	12	14	—	—
75,000	12	14	16	—	—
100,000	14	16	18	—	—

[a] From AT&T Tariff FCC No. 4.
[b] From MCI Tariff FCC No. 1.

Long-Term Agreements and High-Volume Discounts

Signing a long-term contract can also bring eligibility for big discounts, and high-volume users can arrange for even bigger discounts if they commit to spending a specified dollar figure each year. AT&T offers a 3 to 9% discount on its frame relay service for a 1-year contract, depending on the monthly revenue commitment level. A 5-year agreement brings those discounts to between 17 and 30%. MCI offers similar long-term, high-volume discounts on frame relay that range from 4 to 18%. MCI discounts require a minimum monthly revenue commitment of $5000. AT&T offers a monthly commitment as low as $2000. Further, the term discount from MCI goes out to only 3 years, as opposed to the AT&T 5-year schedule (Exhibit 3).

Network managers should calculate their expected minimum monthly usage, determine the longest length time for which they are comfortable signing a contract, and shop for a carrier with big discounts for the predetermined parameters.

Billing Increments

Another well-known way to bring down communications costs is by selecting a service that bills in small increments. If you are on a plan that charges per minute, each fraction thereof is billed as a full minute. On high-volume networks, this can add up to substantial unwarranted costs. A plan that bills in 6- or even 1-s increments, will allow you to pay an amount more closely related to the actual duration of the connection.

For example, carrier A charges a rate of 30 cents per minute. Carrier B charges 0.6 cents per second, which multiplies to a rate of 36 cents per minute. Carrier A appears to be the less expensive choice. However, consider a call with a duration of 1 min, 10 s. Carrier A would charge 60 cents. Carrier B would charge 42 cents. The difference adds up.

Talking to the Competition

Of course, in a competitive market, pitting one company against another can result in a lower price. Carriers are sensitive to the pressures of the marketplace and may lower their prices to win your business.

Reliability

Because efficient and immediate communication is vital to business, price cannot be the only factor on which a carrier is selected. No network manager wants to use a carrier unless its reliability is top notch. Factors such as outages, repair, and disaster recovery plans should be thoroughly investigated when negotiating a contract with any carrier. Investigate the network reliability and the guarantees offered by the carriers you are evaluating to ensure minimum downtime on your network.

For example, in the event of a frame relay access facility outage, the Sprint Frame Relay Disaster Recovery Service initiates a backup call into a different frame relay switch using a combination of the LEC switched line and Sprint Clarity Data Service. Sprint also guarantees a data delivery rate of 99% for domestic Burst Express Frame Relay Service. If the data delivery rate falls below 99%, Sprint evaluates the network and takes action to remedy the problem. Credits are given if the data delivery rate is not restored to the guaranteed level within 60 days.

Further, a Network Delay Service Level guarantee is offered by Sprint, ensuring customers that an end-to-end, one-way network delay average of 90 milliseconds (ms) for T1 access, 105 ms for 256K-bps access, and 150 ms for 56K-bps access will be maintained. These types of disaster recovery plans and service-level guarantees are available from many large telephone companies and should be a major consideration when choosing a carrier.

Contract Tariffs and Special Customer Arrangements

Contract tariffs can give you an idea of what kinds of deals other companies have been able to negotiate. This public information source tells you the cost, volume, term, features, etc. of contracts signed by the carrier with individual customers. Any other customer willing to commit to the same volume, terms, and conditions is entitled, by law, to receive the same contract. Unfortunately, this source of information is likely to disappear shortly. In October of 1996, the FCC proposed that all interstate interexchange services and contracts be "detariffed." The FCC request is being challenged in court, and the eighth U.S. Circuit Court of Appeals has postponed a decision until all petitions for reconsideration filed have been ruled on by the FCC. A decision on a petition to include a public information disclosure requirement, in which carriers must make rate information available to the public, is expected to be decided on by the FCC in late 1998.

Similar to contract tariffs, carriers can reach special customer arrangements with their patrons, which are usually added to a section of the basic tariff instead of being issued as individual contract tariff. Like contract tariffs, special customer arrangements may also be applicable to others parties willing to agree to the same terms and conditions. Because special customer arrangements can be found in many LEC and IXC tariffs, it is highly suggested that network managers do some research on what types of deals companies with similar requirements have been able to negotiate. Although this research is wise, it is also time consuming.

There are tens of thousands of contract tariffs and special customers arrangements filed by a wide variety of carriers, making research by the network manager long and tedious. One alternative to researching this yourself is hiring a consulting firm that specializes in finding the best contract deal based on the client's specific needs. These consultants have wide experience with contract tariffs and can search out information on what other customers in similar situations have negotiated. Armed with this data when meeting with perspective carriers, a network manager will know whether the proposal being offered by the carrier is a good one.

A majority of the information provided in this chapter in the section on negotiating with carriers is available in the tariffs filed by the carriers with the FCC and the state PUCs. Although deregulation is changing the scope of what is included in the tariffs, the most vital information can still be found. This is perhaps the best way to make true comparisons between what various carriers have to offer. Do keep in mind, though, that if your volume is high enough, a contract may be negotiated at substantially lower rates than those listed in the tariffs. There are several companies that specialize in providing copies of tariffs and databases of tariffed rates to the public. These companies are easily located on the World Wide Web.

REFERENCES

1. Trends in Telephone Service, Industry Analysis Division, Federal Communications Commission, February 1998.
2. Ibid.

Chapter 12
The Changing Global Telecommunications Marketplace

Christopher S. Cleveland

INTRODUCTION

The worldwide deployment of advanced facilities such as transoceanic fiber cables and digital switches, coupled with the emergence of alliances among national telecommunications (telecom) carriers, is dramatically reshaping the environment in which multinational corporations implement global networks and communicate internationally. This chapter will examine the worldwide deregulation of telecom and the industry's resulting realignment, the key services offered internationally, and the important considerations when building a global telecom network.

WORLDWIDE DEREGULATION

Historically, most countries operated postal, telegraph and telecom (PTT) authorities, which were government-operated departments that held strict monopolies over public switched telephone network (PSTN) service. PTTs kept telecom pricing artificially high, which served to cross-subsidize other government services such as postal services. Although telecom has long been a moneymaker, it did not usually rank high on governmental priority lists when competing with other national development projects for scarce resources. As a result, telecom service in most countries not only has been expensive, but it also has been less available and lower in quality than state-of-the-art technology would typically permit.

During the past few years, however, there has been a growing recognition that lower cost and more ubiquitous telecom services are instrumental in promoting economic growth, and that telecom deregulation and competition can contribute to that end. This recognition was borne out on Feb. 15, 1997 when 69 nations, which constitute 94% of the global telecom services market, agreed to a landmark World Trade Organization (WTO) agreement

0-8493-9990-4/99/$0.00+$.50
© 1999 by CRC Press LLC

to open their telecom markets to competition and outside investment. Although each signatory to the WTO agreement will institute its own formula on its own timetable for deregulation according to its national politics and priorities, the agreement firmly establishes a worldwide trend to transition telecom from a monopoly environment to one of competition.

The agreement will also strengthen the trend in cross-border acquisitions and investment. Since 1984, about 50 public telecommunications operators (PTOs, i.e., the former PTTs) have been separated from the governments and sold on public and private markets. The most significant privatizations are listed in Exhibit 1. The WTO agreement will remove many existing restrictions held by "holdout" governments that prohibit a company based in one country from acquiring a controlling stake in a dominant telephone carrier in another country. In parallel with the privatizations, many governments began to liberalize their telecom markets by permitting alternative carriers to compete with the former PTTs, now the dominant PTOs.

Countries usually move from a telecom monopoly to competition in a series of incremental steps. Value-added data services (VADS) are among the first to be deregulated; and, in fact, private international value-added network (IVAN) operators offer services such as X.25 in competition with the dominant PTOs in most industrialized countries today. This means that IVANs are permitted to lease private lines across country borders to connect to in-country X.25 switches and to enable users to bypass the PTO X.25 service.

In the next step, countries (i.e., the government telecom regulatory authorities) typically permit businesses to place both *voice* and data traffic on leased lines but stipulate that the voice must remain within a private network (i.e., that neither end of the leased line can "break out" onto the public network). This restriction aims to minimize revenue lost by the dominant PTO (in which the government often still has an ownership interest, or at least a political interest) when calls carried over the PSTN are instead rerouted over leased lines. However, enforcing compliance to this restriction usually proves difficult due to the "leaky PBX syndrome."

In the next step, governments permit alternative facilities-based infrastructure. This means that new carriers are given licenses to install transmission facilities and offer certain services in competition to the dominant PTO. Usually, alternative carriers are initially given permission to offer high-capacity services on a "wholesale" basis to other carriers in the country, such as mobile operators, cable television (CATV) providers or the dominant PTO itself. In some cases, the alternative carrier may also offer services directly to large end users, such as multinational corporations or governments.

Exhibit 1.   Principal PTO Privatizations

PTO/Country	Purchase Price ($ Million)	Years of Purchase	Major Investors and Investment Stakes Acquired (In Percentage)
Europe			
BT/U.K.	22,931	1984 1991 1993	Public shareholders purchased 100% in three tranches; U.K. government holds a "golden share"
Deutsche Telekom/Germany	13,360	1996	Public shareholders purchased about 23%; employees bought an additional 3%
TeleDanmark/Denmark	3,035	1994	Public shareholders purchased about 48%: employees bought additional 0.3%
KPN/the Netherlands	3,791	1994	30% sold on Amsterdam stock exchange
Belgacom/Belgium	2,400	1996	Consortium including Ameritech (40%), TeleDanmark (33%), and Singapore Telecom (27%) purchased 49% of Belgacom
Asia–Pacific			
NTT/Japan	70,469	1986 1987 1988	34.6% sold in domestic public offerings in three tranches
Singapore Telecom/Singapore	4,336	1993 1996	16.67% sold in public and private offerings in two tranches
Korea Telecom/South Korea	3,514	1993 1994 1996	28.8% sold in public offerings in three tranches
Telecom Corp./New Zealand	2,500	1990	Private sale to Ameritech and Bell Atlantic (50% each), with obligation to reduce their total stake to 24.9% after 3 years, which was accomplished
Latin America			
Telmex/Mexico	7,769	1990 through 1994	55.1% sold in total, of which 20.4% sold to consortium of Grupo Carso of Mexico, SBC of U.S., and France Telecom; SBC bought additional 5.1%, remaining 29.6% sold in public offering
Telefonica/Peru	3,202	1994 1996	61.6% sold in total; Telefonica of Spain purchased 35% of dominant long-distance and international carrier, ENTEL, and portion of the local telephone company, CPT; ENTEL and CPT merged to create Telefonica; additional 26.6% sold in public offering
CANTV/Venezuela	2,792	1991 1996	89% sold in total; private sale of 40% to Venworld consortium including GTE and AT&T, Telefonica of Spain, and two Venezuelan partners; 49% sold in public offering

From International Telecommunications Union.

In the final stage of opening the market, the regulator permits "simple re-sale," which is when a non-facilities-based third party offers switched voice services to the general public using leased private lines that break out on the PSTN on both ends. Simple resale is typically permitted initially for long-distance and international services and is usually followed by the opening of the market for all switched services. Generally, when a country permits simple resale, then competition in most or all other telecom ser-vice and equipment markets is also permitted.

Exhibits 2, 3, and 4 contain profiles of the competitive environments in Europe, the Asia–Pacific region, and Latin America, respectively. In these exhibits, the degrees of competition in PSTN, VADS, and transmission infra-structure are characterized as follows:

- **No or little competition**   Either a monopoly or a duopoly exists where one provider is overwhelmingly dominant.
- **Leader–follower competition**   The dominant carrier establishes market pricing and small competitors follow.
- **Incipient competition**   The dominant carrier and competitors exhib-it a greater degree of interdependence in pricing.
- **Full-fledged competition**   Competitors offer a comparable range of services at similar prices.

INDUSTRY REALIGNMENT

The ongoing deregulation of the telecom industry has led to the formation of global carrier alliances, the key players of which are AT&T WorldPart-ners, British Telecom (BT)/MCI Concert, and Global One. As of August 1998, AT&T and BT announced a new alliance to be called "AT&T Concert." In this announcement, AT&T stated that it plans to withdraw from the WorldPartners alliance. MCI previously stated it will withdraw from the Concert alliance based on its planned merger with WorldCom Inc.

However, it is expected that AT&T Concert will require more than 1 year to finalize, and the successful formation of the venture is dependent on a variety of U.S. and foreign regulatory approvals. For example, the European Commission will consider the degree of dominance that AT&T Concert would have in the trans-Atlantic and U.K. telephone markets before con-senting to the venture. Therefore, since AT&T Concert is far from a "done deal," this chapter will describe the current structures and participants of the global carrier alliances.

There are also so-called minialliances, which are regional in scope, and include Unisource in Europe or Telenordia in Scandinavia. Other global niche players include Cable & Wireless, which owns a "federation" of tele-phone companies around the world; and Société Internationale de Télé-communications Aéronautiques (SITA), which operates the largest private

Exhibit 2. Competitive Environment in 1998 in Representative European Countries

Competitive Indicator	France	Germany	Italy	Poland	Sweden	U.K.
Dominant PTO and ownership	France Telecom partially privatized	Deutsche Telekom partially privatized	Telecom Italia partially privatized	Telekomunacja Polska SA (TPSA) state-owned	Telia state-owned	British Telecom fully privatized
Principal competitors to dominant PTO	Cegetel, Netco, COLT, SIRIS AT&T Unisource, WorldCom/MFS, Equant, Infonet	Arcor, o.tel.o, Viag Interkom, Hermes/COLT, Cable & Wireless, WorldCom/MFS	Telemedia International, Infostrada, Unisource Italia, Albacom	Tel-Energo, NASK, BPT Telbank, Global One	Telenordia, Tele-2, Telecom Finland, WorldCom/MFS, Equant, Infonet	C&W Comms, AT&T Istel, Sprint U.K. Energis, Espirit, COLT/Hermes, WorldCom/MFS, Inonica
Public switched telephone services (local, national, and international)	Open entry and leader–follower competition	Open entry and leader–follower competition	Basically a monopoly with no or little competition	Basically a monopoly with no or little competition	Open entry and full-fledged competition	Open entry and full-fledged competition
Value-added data services (e.g., frame relay)	Open entry and incipient competition	Open entry and incipient competition	Entry with restrictions and leader–follower competition	Entry with restrictions and leader–follower competition	Open entry and full-fledged competition	Open entry and full-fledged competition
Provision of transmission infrastructure (e.g., fiber)	Open entry and leader–follower competition	Open entry and leader–follower competition	Basically a monopoly with no or little competition	Basically a monopoly with no or little competition	Open entry and full-fledged competition	Open entry and full-fledged competition

Exhibit 3. Competitive Environment in 1998 in Representative Asia–Pacific Countries

Competitive Indicator	Australia	Hong Kong	Indonesia	Japan	Philippines	South Korea
Dominant PTO and ownership	Telstra partially privatized	Hong Kong Telecom mostly privatized	PT Telekom; PT Indonsat; both partially privatized	NTT partially privatized; KDD fully privatized	Philippines Long Distance Telephone (PLDT) fully privatized	Korea Telecom fully privatized
Principal competitors to dominant PTO	Optus, Interlink Services, AAP Telecoms, BT Australasia, Equant, Infonet	New World Telecom, New T&T, Hutchison Communications, Global One, Infonet	Pramindo Ikat, PT Aplikanusa Lintasarta, Satelindo, Aria West Int'l.	IDC, ITJ, DDI, BT-NIS, Telway Japan NEC Corp.	Philcom, Capwire, Digitel, Globe Telecom, Eastern	SK Telecom, Dacom
Public switched telephone services (local, national, and international)	Open entry and full-fledged competition	Open entry and incipient competition	Entry with restrictions and leader-follower competition	Open entry and full-fledged competition	Open entry and full-fledged competition	Open entry and full-fledged competition
Value-added data services (e.g., frame relay)	Open entry and full-fledged competition	Open entry and full-fledged competition	Open entry and incipient competition	Open entry and full-fledged competition	Open entry and full-fledged competition	Open entry and full-fledged competition
Provision of transmission infrastructure (e.g., fiber)	Open entry and full-fledged competition	Open entry and incipient competition	Entry with restrictions and leader-follower competition	Open entry and full-fledged competition	Open entry and full-fledged competition	Open entry and incipient competition

Exhibit 4. Competitive Environment in 1998 in Canada and Representative Latin American Countries

Competitive Indicator	Argentina	Brazil	Canada	Chile	Mexico	Venezuela
Dominant PTO and ownership	Telecom Argentina Telefonica, both fully privatized; Telintar	Telebras; Embratel, both partially privatized	Stentor Alliance fully privatized; Teleglobe partially privatized	CTC; Entel, both partially privatized	Telmex fully privatized	CANTV fully privatized
Principal competitors to dominant PTO	Impsat Comsat International Ventures, Equant	Concert, Riograndense de Tele, AT&T WorldPartners Global One	AT&T Canada, MCI Canada, Sprint Canada, Rogers Network Services, ACC, Primus	VTR Larga Distancia, Telex Chile, Global One, Equant	Avantel, Alestra, Telinor, Bestel	MCI Venezuela, BT Concert, Impsat, Equant, Infonet
Public switched telephone services (local, national, and international)	Basically a monopoly with no or little competition	Basically a monopoly with no or little competition	Open entry and incipient competition	Open entry and full-fledged competition	Open entry and incipient competition	Basically a monopoly with no or little competition
Value-added data services (e.g., frame relay)	Open entry and incipient competition	Open with restrictions and leader–follower competition	Open entry and full-fledged competition	Open entry and full-fledged competition	Open entry and full-fledged competition	Open with restrictions and leader–follower competition
Provision of transmission infrastructure (e.g., fiber)	Open with restrictions and leader–follower competition	Basically a monopoly with no or little competition	Open entry and incipient competition	Open entry and full-fledged competition	Open entry and incipient competition	Basically a monopoly with no or little competition

185

value-added data network in the world on behalf of its 600 airline consortium members.

Carrier alliances aim to provide end-to-end communications to multinational corporations, governments, and other large users. Alliance portfolios include telecom services (e.g., virtual private networks [VPNs], X.25, frame relay, private lines, e-mail), a single point of contact (e.g., for networkwide accountability), unified billing options (e.g., choice of language and currency), unified network management (e.g., standardized network monitoring, trouble-ticketing, and fault correction), and network provisioning (e.g., standard time commitments for line installations).

The characteristics of the alliances are

- **Geographic expansion**   PTOs have established partnerships outside their own geographic territories, motivated by a desire to protect their home markets while acquiring low-cost access in areas outside their control, and by being able to claim global coverage.
- **Defensive nature**   Although the consortia espouse an aggressive market attitude, the core behavioral element of the participants is a defense of the home market.
- **Hardware compatibility**   PTOs tend to align along platform compatibilities due to the high cost of replacing existing networks and the difficulties in mixing incompatible platforms.
- **Restricted participation**   Although eager to gain access to new markets through partnerships, consortia partners have been careful to "protect" certain lines of business or certain customer relationships. There is a great eagerness to have partners, but not "at any cost."
- **Uneven market control**   Consortia partners are strongly entrenched in their home markets, but equally weak outside their home markets.

WorldPartners

AT&T was instrumental in setting up the WorldPartners global alliance in 1993. The WorldPartners ownership and distributor relationships are shown in Exhibit 5. Unisource is itself a joint venture of PTT Telecom Netherlands, Swiss PTT, and Sweden's Telia. By mid-1998, WorldPartners had rolled out virtual private voice network (VPVN) services to 21 countries in North America, Europe, and the Asia–Pacific region. WorldPartners also offers frame relay and private line services to the U.S. and Canada, 17 West European countries, 11 countries in the Asia–Pacific region, and Mexico and Israel. WorldPartners is currently building a new global telecom backbone network for a total of 400 customers in 30 countries.

Concert

Concert is a joint venture that as of August 1998 is 75.1% owned by BT and 24.9% by MCI, but that is subject to change once the acquisition of MCI by

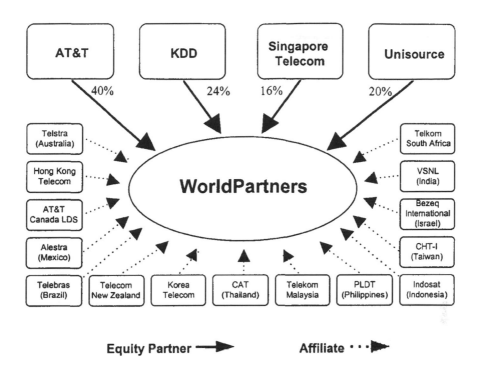

Equity Partner ➡   **Affiliate** ··▶

Exhibit 5.   WorldPartners Ownership and Distributor Relationships

WorldCom is completed. At that time, BT plans to buy out the MCI 25% stake in Concert (Exhibit 6). In 1998, Concert offered end-to-end X.25 service in 50 countries, frame relay in 37 countries, VPVN services in 17 countries, managed bandwidth services in 17 countries, and Internet access services in 13 countries. Concert claims more than 3000 multinational customers.

Concert has distributors in Italy (Albacom), Germany (Viag Interkom), the Netherlands (Telfort), Spain (BT Spain), Portugal (Comnexo), Denmark (TeleDanmark), Scandinavia (Telenordia), Norway (Telenor), Poland (BPT Telbank), Czech Republic (Eurotel), Gibtel (Gibralter), Austria (Management Data), Greece (Space Hellas), Hungary (HTC), Russia (Institute of Automated Systems), Japan (ITJ), Taiwan (PTT), South Korea (Samsung), the Philippines (GlobeCom), Indonesia (Indosat), Singapore (PTT), New Zealand (Clear), Malaysia (Telecom Malaysia), Thailand (PTT), Canada (Stentor), Israel (Tadiran), Oman (PTT), Kenya (PTT), Lebanon (Data Management), South Africa (Telkom), India (VSN), and Mexico (Avantel).

Global One

Global One had its beginnings when France Telecom and Deutsche Telekom merged their international units in a venture called Atlas. Atlas has

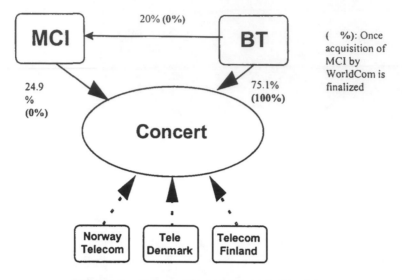

Exhibit 6.   Concert Ownership Relationships

since teamed with Sprint to form Global One. Each of the three Global One partners own one third of the Global One European unit. The Global One worldwide unit (operations outside Europe and the U.S.) is one half owned by Sprint and one half owned by France Telecom/Deutsche Telekom. Each partner is the sole operating partner in its home country, and the three partners are combining their strengths in marketing to the rest of the world (Exhibit 7).

Global One has X.25 nodes in 54 countries, frame relay nodes in 30 countries, VPVN nodes in 17 countries, and managed bandwidth offerings in 20 countries. The company claims more than 30,000 business customers and 2,900 employees.

KEY TELECOMMUNICATIONS SERVICES OFFERED GLOBALLY

This section reviews a range of traditional, newer, and developing technologies that either are in use by multinational users or are potentially useful to such users.

Traditional Telecom Technologies

Plain Old Telephone Service. In 1995, total plain old telephone service (POTS) lines worldwide reached 600 million, with more than 75 million new telephone numbers being created in that year. The world's telephones are distributed largely on the basis of country wealth. High-income countries such as the U.S. and Switzerland have teledensities (number of telephone

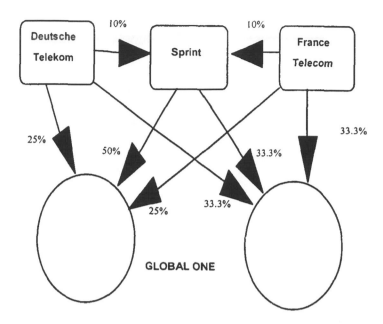

Exhibit 7. Global One Ownership Relationships

---

lines per 100 population) of about 60%. Middle income countries such as Hungary and Uruguay have teledensities around 20%. Low-income countries such as Nigeria or Mozambique have teledensities around 0.3%.

Telex. Telex is rapidly being replaced by lower cost, higher quality alternatives such as fax and e-mail. However, telex remains important in communicating to underserved areas of the world. For example, the International Telecommunications Union (ITU) estimates that from 1990 to 1995, telex was still growing in countries such as Bangladesh (telex use increased from 2,000 to 2,800 subscribers during the period), China (use increased from 13,000 to 16,000), and Haiti (use grew from 1,000 to 2,000). Even in underserved countries, the use of telex will eventually dwindle until it is no longer offered.

Fax. Theoretically, fax can be as ubiquitous around the world as POTS lines. The reason is that the quality of the vast majority of POTS lines worldwide—even telephone lines provided over antiquated facilities—will acceptably support Group III fax. The ITU estimates that in 1995 there were 2,500 fax machines in Azerbaijan, 600 in Cambodia, 1,400 in Ethiopia, 600 in Nepal, 1,300 in Tajikistan, 2,500 in Uganda, and 14,900 in Vietnam. However, Group IV fax requires 56K-bps connectivity and is available only in countries that have high-speed digital facilities.

189

Private Lines. An international private line is a bilateral service between two PTOs. It is possible to lease a private line between most countries worldwide, although circuit costs vary considerably depending on country pair. In past years, the end user ordered the respective half circuits from each PTO. Today, PTO joint marketing agreements are common whereby one PTO can make the necessary arrangements for both half circuits. This "one-stop shopping" provides the user with an end-to-end service and a single bill. Higher quality end-to-end service is offered by the carrier alliances and others under "managed bandwidth" offerings, which come with specified guarantees on circuit availability, backed up by financial penalties for nonperformance.

Public Data Networks. Public data networks (PDNs) using X.25 are available in more than 125 countries, including countries that are ordinarily difficult and expensive to communicate with such as Cameroon, Ivory Coast, Croatia, Ecuador, Estonia, Ethiopia, Fiji, Ghana, India, Kazakhstan, Kenya, Latvia, Mozambique, Nicaragua, Pakistan, Russia, Senegal, Sri Lanka, and Zimbabwe. PTOs originally built PDNs as domestic X.25 networks under a variety of hardware and software platforms. Later, X.75 "bridging" enabled packet interchange across multiple PTO X.25 networks. However, X.75 represents a "lowest common denominator" and often causes poor performance.

International Value-Added Networks. Due to the X.75 gateway problem, a PTO X.25 network may perform poorly with international traffic. The solution to this was to create "all-X.25" networks offering "seamless" X.25 service across country borders without X.75 gateways. This approach has been adopted by IVANs such as the IBM Global Network, and SITA and its commercial subsidiary, Equant. IVANs offer the convenience of a single supplier to multiple countries and comprehensive network management.

Analog Cellular Telephone. Analog mobile telephone technology was introduced in the early 1980s and preceded digital mobile technology by at least a decade. One of the earliest systems, the analog Nordic Mobile Telephone (NMT) system, was designed to support roaming between Denmark, Finland, Norway, and Sweden. However, the lack of a global standard for analog cellular resulted in a number of incompatible systems elsewhere and prevented international roaming on a large scale. The arrival of the digital cellular telephony, specifically the Global System for Mobile (GSM), brought global roaming closer to a reality, albeit a reality that is not here yet.

Newer Telecom Technologies

Virtual Private Networks for Voice. A virtual private network (VPN) provides a "private network" on public carrier facilities and is commonly offered by major PTOs and the carrier alliances. International virtual network calls to predetermined calling locations typically qualify for 7 to 40% discounts with respect to international direct distance dialing (IDDD), with the size of discount depending on calling patterns and volume levels. VPNs also offer enhanced calling features such as abbreviated dialing, call forwarding, and centralized billing. VPNs are offered by the carrier alliances and PTOs in most countries of Western Europe and the industrialized countries of the Asia–Pacific region. VPNs are increasingly being offered in Latin America (e.g., Brazil).

Calling Cards. Calling cards were rare outside North America until the early 1990s, but they are now offered by most major PTOs. Even PTOs in some developing countries have introduced calling cards, such as PTOs in Argentina, Bolivia, Bulgaria, and Senegal. Calling cards can be less expensive than the IDDD tariffs in high-tariff countries or in hotels that add a surcharge for calls. Often, though, such hotels will program their private branch exchanges (PBXs) to block calls to toll-free card numbers. Country direct services such as AT&T Direct are also becoming common in industrialized countries. AT&T Direct provides access to the AT&T U.S. dial tone from 130 countries.

Digital GSM Cellular Telephone. The GSM standard for digital cellular telephony was commercially introduced in 1992 by Finland's Oy Radiolinja. GSM spread throughout Europe and then to Africa, Asia, and the Pacific to become a de facto world standard. By 1996, there were 148 GSM networks in operation in 105 countries with some 25 million subscribers (about 18% of total cellular subscribers). Where GSM roaming agreements exist between PTOs, users carry either their GSM handset or subscriber identity module (SIM) smart card (for use in a rented GSM portable) when traveling abroad. Users who have roamed into another country are automatically picked up by that country's GSM operators. GSM roaming capability is widely available in Europe (accounting for 3 to 5% of all mobile calls in 1996), but is spotty in the rest of the world.

E-Mail. Today, more than 39 million personal computer (PC) users use e-mail (also referred to as electronic messaging) from at least one of three sources: (1) in-house corporate e-mail systems that rely on private networks for transport, (2) e-mail systems of on-line service providers such as America Online (AOL) or CompuServe, and (3) e-mail offerings of carriers such as ATT Easylink or MCI Mail. Although each of these e-mail services may be provided on a "private" network (e.g., AOL subscriber to AOL subscriber), they also interconnect via X.400 gateways to other service providers.

Carriers such as AT&T and MCI, and value-added providers such as IBM and GE Information Services (GEIS), offer public e-mail networks with a strong worldwide presence, a broad product line, a packaged solution, and a large base of subscribers. These carriers specialize in different applications of messaging. For example, GEIS offers electronic data interchange (EDI) in conjunction with its e-mail service. IBM is strong in e-mail application support. AT&T Easylink offers a full range of protocol conversion and technical options.

Integrated Services Digital Network (ISDN). This provides on-demand digital connectivity in some 50 countries in Western Europe and the Asia–Pacific region. ISDN is available in virutally all the industrialized countries and in certain developing countries such as Belarus, Croatia, Ecuador, Estonia, Peru, and Poland. ISDN basic rate interface (BRI) is sensitive to outside electromagnetic interference. Therefore, BRI lines cannot extend beyond 18,000 ft of their central office in the U.S.; otherwise, special ISDN extension devices must be employed. In many other countries, the ISDN is limited to approximately 10,000 ft from the central office.

Frame Relay Networks. Frame relay networks typically support data rates from 64K bps to 2M bps, whereas X.25 networks, with some exceptions, are generally limited to 256K bps (or 19.2K bps if local digital access circuits are not available). As a result, frame relay is often the technology of choice for local area network (LAN) interconnection and for client/server computing. Many dominant PTOs offer frame relay as part of their PDN offering.

The carrier alliances also offer frame relay. They cover their "home" territories well but typically have only a few frame relay nodes in countries outside their home territories. As an example, BT has far greater frame relay coverage in the U.K. than Concert has in South Africa. In South Africa, Concert interconnects with the dominant PTO (Telkom S.A.) frame relay domestic network in Johannesburg only. In another example, Deutsche Telekom operates 13 frame relay nodes in Germany, but Global One does not offer frame relay connections in South Africa at all.

Router-Based Networks. Router-based networks are offered by service providers such as the IBM Global Network and Infonet. IBM operates an IBM 6611-based router network called the Multi-Protocol Network (MPN), while Infonet operates a Cisco Systems Inc.-based router network called InfoLAN. Router networks carry Transmission Control Protocol (TCP)/ Internet Protocol (IP) traffic and are most often used to interconnect LANs. Router networks have a strong presence in Europe, especially in France, Germany, and the U.K. where ubiquitous domestic coverage is provided. Certain countries that are "difficult to reach" with advanced services, such as Greece, the Slovak Republic, and Israel, are served by router networks. Router networks are also gaining ground on the Pacific Rim, with a presence in countries such as Indonesia, Malaysia, and Thailand.

Very Small Aperture Terminals (VSATs). These networks derive their advantage in that multinational users can obtain international data services from a single vendor. In practice, this advantage is offset by two major restrictions. First, no vendor today offers a "global" VSAT service; instead, different vendors tend to have a strong presence in one or two world regions (e.g., MCI in South America, or France Telecom in Sub-Saharan Africa). Second, VSAT is often subject to local regulatory constraints, particularly in developing countries where PTOs take a dim view of the prospect that their facilities could be bypassed. Regulatory constraints take a number of forms, such as total prohibition (as in, Benin); prohibition of international VSAT (e.g., Bulgaria); imposition of heavy surcharges or licensing fees (e.g., Argentina); requirements that the VSAT equipment be owned, installed, or maintained by the PTO (e.g., Malaysia).

Developing Telecom Technologies

Mobile Satellite Systems (MSS). These enable users to make and receive calls through mobile handsets from virtually anywhere in the world. Although some geostationary systems are already in service, such as INMARSAT, most attention has focused on nongeostationary low earth orbit (LEO) or medium earth orbit (MEO) satellites systems. The LEO and MEO systems planned for deployment will provide global voice service coverage using cellular-sized handsets. LEO configurations typically involve several dozens or hundreds of satellites in orbits up to 1,500 km above the earth, and MEO systems are positioned in orbits at up to 10,000 km above the earth.

The most credible proponents of LEO systems include Iridium, Globalstar, and Teledesic. The most credible MEO proponents include Odyssey and ICO (previously known as Project 21 and Inmarsat-2000). The major LEO and MEO systems will use satellites having multiple high-power beams and will provide "cellular standard" telephony, fax, and a wide range of data and messaging services. The LEO and MEO systems will compete with terrestrial digital cellular and mobile systems. They are scheduled for global deployment in the 1998 to 2000 time frame.

However, LEO and MEO systems are costly to deploy and complex to maintain, and their performance may be inferior to terrestrial mobile systems. For instance, of the five systems mentioned earlier, only the high-end Teledesic plans to support fax and data rates above 4.8K bps. Moreover, services are also likely to be expensive, with voice calls costing up to $3 a minute or more. If this pricing structure is maintained, LEO and MEO services may compare unfavorably to terrestrial cellular alternatives, and even to traditional satellite alternatives such as Inmarsat. Inmarsat's latest terminal, the "mini-M," can be purchased for under $3000, and the associated calling charges are $2.40/min.

Exhibit 8.   Comparison of Transmission Vehicles to Send Documents from the U.S.

Communication Mode	Average Cost to Transmit 1 Page Each Day for 22 Working Days/Month ($)	Average Time to Transmit 1 Page Each Day for 22 Working Days/Month
Telex	200	66 min
International telephone/fax	165	110 min
Priority overnight mail	880	264 hr
Internet (local access included)	50	44 min

Asynchronous Transfer Mode (ATM) Networks. Carriers such as AT&T and MCI have begun to implement public ATM networks in the U.S., Europe, and Asia. In the U.K., BT has introduced an ATM service called CellStream. CellStream provides 34- and 155M-bps connectivity within the U.K. and to the U.S. In the Asia–Pacific region, Kokusai Denshin Denwa (KDD) of Japan began offering its Globalink ATM service in 1997 as a test service, with the intention of expanding it to a full-scale service after assessment of initial demand and verification of network control. Globalink is initially providing user access speeds of T1, 6M and 45M bps. At the outset, KDD is offering ATM service at three points of presence in the greater Tokyo metropolitan area, all three of which connect to the AT&T ATM service in the U.S.

Internet Service Providers (ISPs). These exist in a majority of the countries worldwide. ISP service charges are composed of two elements: (1) the usage charges for the telephone network, and (2) the ISP access charge. In most countries, the ISP access charge typically forms less than one half of the total cost of accessing the Internet. Countries having either low or no telephone usage charges usually have higher Internet take-up rates. For example, carriers in the U.S., Canada, and New Zealand include local calling in their flat-rate monthly subscription charges, and all three countries have high Internet penetration rates.

The Internet is an inexpensive means to move documents to and from the U.S. Cost and time comparisons between the Internet vs. other communication vehicles are shown in Exhibit 8.

However, for a corporation there are some distinct disadvantages in relying on the Internet too heavily for its communications needs. The first is the issue of security. A second disadvantage is the performance, reliability, and availability of the Internet (or lack thereof). The net effect of flat-rate pricing of most ISPs, coupled with the introduction of multimedia applications, has stimulated traffic to such an extent that the performance of the

Internet has suffered greatly. Therefore, the times shown in Exhibit 8 to send one page through the Internet should be understood to be the *best time* under optimum circumstances. During periods of severe Internet congestion, Internet e-mail can take much longer.

TELECOMMUNICATIONS ENVIRONMENTS AROUND THE WORLD

As a general rule, the quality of basic telecom services can vary from superior to extremely poor, depending not only on the particular country but also sometimes on the region within that country. Most developed and certain less developed countries have relatively new and highly reliable digital switching and transmission facilities connecting large cities and urban centers. Local circuits within these urban centers, or points outside of them, may vary extensively in quality and reliability.

Europe

In general, the Western and Northern European countries offer excellent services, and users experience little difficulty in operating networks or in procuring services. Most PTOs in the region are installing fiber at a rapid rate, not only between major cities for long-distance trunking but also within city metropolitan area networks (MANs). Despite progress, the overall quality of services in Southern Europe tends to be poorer and prices are higher than in Western/Northern Europe. This situation is improving, though. For example, Telecom Italia is upgrading its infrastructure to closely match the capabilities of its Western and Northern European neighbors. Italy's rate of teledensity has risen sharply since the late 1980s—from 34 to 44%.

Basic POTS, X.25, and analog leased-line services in Eastern Europe are usually satisfactory in major cities. However, advanced service offerings that are common in Western Europe such as digital leased lines, ISDN, frame relay, and ATM are not as available; or if they are available, they are offered on a case-by-case basis. Most countries in Eastern Europe are not expected to permit PSTN competition soon, although most now permit competition in VADS. Examples are Hungary, the Czech Republic, and the Slovak Republic. Some countries only allow a "quasi" form of competition. For example, the Bulgarian Telecommunications Company (BTC) owns 49% of the Global One subsidiary in Bulgaria, which "competes" with the BTC X.25 offering.

France. The competitive market in France is now intensifying. The principal facilities-based alternative to the dominant PTO France Telecom is Cegetel, which operates six local fiber networks in Paris and other cities. Cegetel is a subsidiary of Companie Generale de Eaux, BT, and Mannesmann of Germany. Eventually, Cegetel plans 20 local networks in France, which will be tied together with Cegetel's nationwide fiber network running along the French national railway, SNCF. Cegetel has an interconnection agreement with Concert for its international traffic.

COLT and WorldCom MFS also operate local fiber networks in Paris and have interconnection agreements with Hermes Europe and AT&T Unisource, respectively, to carry their international traffic. Hermes Europe operates a pan-European fiber network that provides wholesale capacity to established carriers, carrier alliances, cellular providers, IVANs, or multinational companies. Today, Hermes' network interconnects Paris, London, Brussels, Antwerp, Rotterdam, Amsterdam, and Frankfurt. Hermes Europe plans to connect 32 European cities by 2002 with its own fiber. In July 1998, WorldCom annnounced that it will build its own 2000-mi fiber network linking several European cities (including Paris).

Other significant competitors to France Telecom include Netco (a joint venture of Bouygues Telecom, Telecom Italia, and Veba of Germany), COLT (City of London Telecommunications, a U.K.-based alternative access provider), SIRIS (French distributor for AT&T Unisource), Equant (commercial networks subsidiary of SITA), and Infonet (the worldwide value-added network jointly owned by 10 PTOs.)

This new competition has prompted the dominant carrier, France Telecom, to rebalance its voice and data tariffs over the past 3 to 4 years. France Telecom's goal has been to reduce tariffs where it is vulnerable to new competition—high-capacity leased lines in urban areas and on long-distance trunking routes—and increase rates where it is likely to face the least new competition—local switched voice services.

Germany. The telecom market is changing quickly in Germany as well. The new German telecom laws requires Deutsche Telekom to begin offering copper or fiber on a wholesale basis to its competitors, which will reduce the chance for overcharging. This and other regulations have had a significant effect. Five years ago, Deutsche Telekom's leased line rates were among the highest in Europe. Since then, the PTO has slashed rates by 80%, bringing them to a level below the European average.

Currently, three main national facilities-based contenders compete with Deutsche Telekom: Arcor, o.tel.o, and Viag Interkom. Arcor is a joint venture of engineering firm Mannesmann, AT&T Unisource, and DBKom (a subsidiary of Germany's railway). O.tel.o is a joint venture of the conglomerate, Veba, with a unit of German utility, RWE. Viag Interkom is a joint venture of Viag (Germany's diversified utility), BT, and Norway's Telenor.

These players operate fiber networks among the major German cities, with Arcor having Germany's second largest digital network next to Deutsche Telekom. However, all these newcomers face the same problem: Their fiber backbones are not ubiquitous, and access networks from alternative

196

providers are still few. As a result, most leased lines sold by these carriers are rented from Deutsche Telekom.

Italy. Telecom Italia is the dominant VADS in Italy, and it has entered into local service provider (LSP) agreements with several of the carrier consortia and IVANs. One example is the IBM Global Network, which signed one such LSP agreement in 1997. Telecom Italia takes international frame relay traffic of the foreign carriers and delivers it within Italy. The principal VADS domestic carrier alternative to Telecom Italia is Infostrada, which is the Global One distributor in Italy and currently operates an X.25 and frame relay network across the country. Infostrada also offers closed-user group voice services and targets major multinational corporations and governmental entities.

Other competitors to Telecom Italia include Unisource Italia, which is the AT&T Unisource subsidiary in Italy, and Albacom, which is the Concert distributor in Italy. Another strong player in Italy is Telemedia International (actually a subsidiary of Telecom Italia), which provides international VADS.

Poland. Poland's state-owned PTO, Telekomunikacja Polska SA (TPSA), dominates most services. TPSA will be partly privatized in 1999, and it is lobbying the government to allow it to retain its monopoly status to command a higher privatization price. TPSA appears to be losing this argument. Tel-Energo, currently a local PSTN provider in certain areas not served by TPSA, has completed a nationwide fiber network running alongside the electric power distribution system. Tel-Energo will compete with TPSA when the long-distance market opens next year.

NASK is the Academic Research Computer Network that has been established by Poland's State Committee for Scientific Research. NASK provides Internet services to more than 1000 universities, scientific institutions, government organizations, and private companies. In 1997, NASK entered into an agreement with AT&T Unisource to provide international frame relay connections. Other competitors to TPSA include BPT Telbank (joint stock company owned by 21 Polish banks) and Global One.

Sweden. Sweden has one of the most open and competitive European telecom markets, which is second only to the U.K. market. Telia is the dominant PTO. The government not only permits but also encourages alternative facilities-based infrastructure in competition to Telia. Around the country, city councils have authorized and encouraged local utilities to run fiber under the streets and lease dark fiber to any of the current licensed carriers of telephone and leased line services.

Currently, Tele-2 (joint venture between Cable & Wireless and Kinnevik) is the chief competitor of Telia in terms of market share of PSTN services.

WorldCom/MFS operates a local fiber network in Stockholm, which is connected to WorldCom's pan-European frame relay network. There are 13 other local access providers also operating in Sweden. In the VADS market, Telenordia (joint venture of Norway's Telenor, TeleDanmark, and BT) is a significant competitor to Telia. Other competitors include Telecom Finland, Equant, and Infonet.

The United Kingdom. The U.K. spearheaded the European drive to liberalization as one of the most open telecom environments during the past decade. However, BT remains strongly dominant with an 80% share of the telephony market. The principal facilities-based alternative to BT is C&W Communications, which currently operates the Mercury long-distance network along with the CATV video and telephony infrastructure of its three CATV owners, Nynex, Videotron, and Bell Cable Media. The C&W Comm share of the telephony market is about 10%. Other operators—of which Vodafone is the largest—have 5% of the market. About ten major cable PTOs have taken up much of the remainder.

A particularly aggressive competitive U.K. player is Energis (owned by the National Power Grid), which runs a national fiber network that utilizes electric line rights-of-way. In 1997, Energis introduced international frame relay connections to 47 countries. There are also many providers of local fiber and microwave-based services. As an example, the COLT London local network extends 170 km and passes some 8000 buildings. COLT boasts 926 directly connected customers in 879 buildings. Signficant players in the VADS and voice services market include AT&T Istel, Sprint U.K., Espirit, Hermes, and WorldCom/MFS.

Asia–Pacific

Some of the most significant telecom industry changes are occurring in the Asia–Pacific region. Between 1990 and 1995, teledensity across the region grew by almost 10%, which is twice the rate of other world regions. Moreover, in developing Asia–Pacific countries, teledensity expanded during the same period at an annual rate of almost 30%. In countries like China, network growth has reached an annual average of 40%. Mobile and cellular markets in the region have also boomed during the period, expanding by 70% a year.

The top tier of countries in the region, Australia, Japan, Hong Kong, and Singapore, has modern infrastructures where users can obtain a full spectrum of voice and data services, including digital leased lines, frame relay, and IVPNs. The second tier of countries, including Malaysia, New Zealand, the Philippines, South Korea, Taiwan, and Thailand, has made significant strides toward improving infrastructures over the past few years. These countries generally offer state-of-the-art telecom facilities in the central business districts of major cities, although facilities in outlying areas are limited or poor in quality. The third tier includes countries such as China and Cambodia, which have a long way to go to modernize their infrastructures.

Australia. In Australia, facility-based Optus (jointly owned by Bell South, Cable & Wireless, and Optus Pty.) has attracted 20% of the domestic long-distance and international PSTN market from the dominant PTO, Telstra. Strong foreign carriers such as Telecom New Zealand, Singapore Telecom, and BT have entered the Australian PSTN market, which was completely opened to competition on July 1, 1997. Also, an entire group of new but smaller domestic competitors has also entered the PSTN market. The cellular market in Australia is served by three operators: Vodafone (95% owned by Vodafone of the U.K.), Optus, and Telstra.

Frame relay services are offered on a wide scale throughout the country by Interlink Services (partner of Telemedia International), AAP Telecoms (partner of WorldCom/MFS), BT Australasia (partner of Concert), Equant, and Infonet.

China. As of September 1996, China's Ministry of Posts and Telecommunications (MPT) provided about 65 million telephones, representing a teledensity of just under 6%. The principal rival to MPT is China United Telecommunications (China Unicom). China Unicom is owned by a coalition of the ministries of railways, electronics, and electric power, and it plans to have its own national network in place by 2005. MPT operates the X.25 networks, which have a total of 92,000 customers. CHINANET has been introduced as a national interactive computing network for videoconferencing, EDI, e-mail, videotex, and 800 service and card phones. Paging subscribers have reached 24 million, while mobile subscribers now number 6 million.

Hong Kong. In Hong Kong, the dominant PTO is Hong Kong Telecom, which is jointly owned by Cable & Wireless, China Telecom, and the public. Since 1995, three new PTOs have provided local telephone service in competition with Hong Kong Telecom: New T&T (owned by Wharf), New World Telephone, and Hutchison Communications (subsidiary of Hutchison Whampoa).

The fact that these new operators are providing local service is surprising considering (1) Hong Kong already has the highest teledensity in the region; (2) there is no long-distance market due to the small land size, and local calls are included with subscription charges; (3) there is already extensive competition in cellular calls; and (4) Hong Kong Telecom has a monopoly on international calls until 2006. However, proximity to mainland China and a large business market make Hong Kong's market attractive to new competitors such as these.

Japan. Japan's domestic market is dominated by Nippon Telegraph and Telephone (NTT) for domestic services and its international market by KDD. More than 1500 facilities-based and non-facilities-based operators compete in the market, particularly in VADS. The largest three competitors to NTT are DDI, Japan Telecom, and Teleway Japan—they have steadily undercut the NTT leading position, forcing prices down at a rapid pace. The largest competitors to KDD include International Digital Corp. (IDC) (owned by Cable & Wireless, AirTouch, Itochu, Toyota, and other investors) and International Telecom Japan (ITJ) (owned by 170 corporate investors, including BT and France Telecom).

In June 1999, NTT will be divided into a long-distance and international carrier and two regional local operators, under the umbrella of a holding company. Curbs on foreign ownership in NTT and KDD will also be lifted at that time. The NTT international company will compete with the three established international carriers, KDD, ITJ, and IDC. The long-distance and international carriers will also be allowed to compete in local markets.

Singapore. Singapore represents the leading edge of telecom carriers in the region. Due to its small size and prosperity, Singapore has created one of the most advanced infrastructures in the world. Singapore promotes itself as an "intelligent island," due to its large embedded base of fiber, digital switches, and intelligent networking facilities. All 30 or so central offices in Singapore are ISDN-capable, thus making Singapore one of the few countries where universal ISDN is a reality. In the cellular market, Mobil One, a consortium of local companies and Hong Kong Telecom (15% share), launched cellular service on the day the exclusive license of Singapore Telecom expired (April 1, 1997).

Latin America

Historically, services to and within Latin America have been handicapped by a lack of regional infrastructure. Until recently, satellites offered the only reliable connectivity between many Latin American countries, as well as between Latin America and North America or Europe. Indeed, many companies found that it was advantageous to locate the hub sites of their Latin American networks in U.S. cities such as Miami. In many instances, only two alternatives were available: (1) the PSTN—frequently unreliable even for basic telephony; or (2) Intelsat Business Service (IBS)—costly and often plagued by difficulties in obtaining in-country support.

Fortunately, the situation is improving. First, new operators such as Impsat and AmericaTel now offer international services. Second, increasing liberalization has led to the emergence of second national operators or alternate carriers. Third, new submarine fiber-optic cables are now connecting Latin American countries into the world's telecom infrastructure. Fourth, Latin America is increasing use of satellite VSATs with 24,000 VSATs installed. One promising new joint venture is Telefonica-Panamericana MCI (TPAM), which is 51% owned by Telefonica International SA (TISA) and 49% by MCI. TPAM plans to deploy a new fiber and microwave highway among Latin American capital cities in the 2001 to 2005 time frame.

Brazil. Except for cellular telephone and leased line resale for private networks, most telecom markets in Brazil remain closed to competition. However, in 1997, a new telecom law was passed that will redefine the industry structure. The telecom law requires the privatization and breakup of the local services monopoly provider, Telebras, into three regional landline companies: Telesp, Tele-Norte, and TeleCentro-South. Full competition among these new companies will be phased in by 2003. The long-distance and international carrier, Embratel, will also be privatized. After these privatizations, most telecom markets will be opened to competition. By the year 2000, one new local concession will be granted per region to compete with the new "baby bras" companies.

Brazil now has domestic fiber connecting Sao Paulo, Curitiba, Belo Horizonte, Brazilia, Goiania, Rio de Janeiro, Fortaleza, Curitiba, Florianopolis, and Porto Alegre for a route totaling 7,200 km of fiber and 123,000 voice circuits. Internationally, the 12,300-km Columbus II cable connects Brazil with the Caribbean, Mexico, the U.S., and Europe, and it has an interconnection at St. Thomas to Americas I. Because high-quality local alternatives have been unavailable in Brazil in the past, satellite VSATs have also been used advantageously in Brazil. Embratel kept a monopoly on VSAT until 1994, at which time the VSAT market was opened to resellers. Embratel retained its monopoly on VSAT space segment. Current VSAT providers include AT&T Tridom, GSI (Brazilian subsidiary of IBM), GE Spacenet's Skystar, and Gtech.

Chile. Chile was the first South American country to privatize its PTT and liberalize its telecom market. The Chilean government permitted Telefonica International to acquire controlling interest in the dominant local telephone company, Companiea de Telecoms de Chile (CTC), in 1990 and a significant majority of the dominant long-distance telephone company (Entel Chile). Today, the field of players in Chile's telecom markets has expanded to a point where competition is vigorous and margins are slim.

CTC is the dominant telephone provider with an estimated 90% of the local PSTN market, 34% of the long-distance market, and 22% of the international PSTN market. CTC was one of the first PTOs in South America to offer an all-digital network. It has also been expanding its network the most rapidly (17% growth of new subscriber lines in 1997.) Competitors such as Entel, VTR Larga Distancia (50% owned by SBC Corp.), and Telex Chile have also installed their own fiber facilities. Today, Chile enjoys the most advanced telecom infrastructure in South America

THE NETWORK PROVIDERS

Mexico. On Jan. 1, 1997, Mexico fully liberalized its telecom market. Telmex, Mexico's dominant PTO, and Telmex's many competitors have been rapidly expanding their fiber and microwave facilities. For example, Avantel (alliance of MCI, Telefonica, and Grupo Financiero Banamex) has invested $600 million in a "crystal triangle" of fiber among Mexico's three largest business centers—Mexico City, Monterrey, and Guadalajara. This network also links 30 other smaller Mexican cities. Alestra (joint venture of AT&T, Grupo Financiero Bancomer, and Grupo Alfa) has invested U.S. $450 million to install 2600 mi of fiber linking major cities. Bestel (joint venture between GST Global and Grupo Varo) has deployed 1365 mi of fiber in the states of Sonora and Sinaloa and in central Mexico.

A critical component of opening local markets to competition has been the auction of microwave licenses. With national point-to-point microwave, carriers can reach areas that are prohibitively expensive to reach with fiber and at the same time reduce their dependence on Telmex for resale connections to these areas. The government awarded a total of 80 microwave concessions to 19 carriers.

Venezuela. The privatization of Company Anonima Nacional de Telefonos de Venezuela (CANTV) was finalized in 1991, and it is 40% owned by a consortium of GTE (51%), Telefonica (16%), Electricidad de Caracas (16%), and VCIMC (17%). The impetus for privatization was an urgent need to improve the telecom infrastructure. In 1990, Venezuela's telephone exchanges were obsolete and transmission systems had deteriorated. CANTV has now significantly upgraded its infrastructure and completed fiber builds connecting Caracas with Venezuela's secondary cities. Internationally, the 7500-km Americas I fiber cable interconnects Brazil and Venezuela with the Caribbean and the U.S. A new fiber cable is planned to connect the U.S. Virgin Islands to interconnect St. Croix, Trinidad, Venezuela, Colombia, Panama, Ecuador, Peru, and Chile.

Africa

Africa has only 2% of the world's telephones despite having 12% of the world's population. Although network growth continues at 8% per year, that is much lower than other developing regions. The ITU noted the paradox that the African region has the lowest international telephone traffic per capita (less than 1 min/year), but it has the world's highest traffic per subscriber (200-plus min). The conclusion is that there is a huge pent-up demand. Mobile telephone service is the one bright spot for Africa. By early 1996, cellular systems operated in 23 African countries.

Africa faces enormous obstacles to telecom development. First, quality infrastructure is entirely lacking outside the central business districts of the capital cities. Great distances and preponderance of rural villages compound the problem of building infrastructure. Due to the rigors of terrain and climate, infrastructure is expensive to install, difficult to operate, and difficult to maintain. Special measures must be taken to protect equipment from heat, humidity, and dust. Copper wire is frequently stolen, even when buried. Moreover, there is a shortage of trained personnel to maintain microwave and telephone equipment.

Satellite communications represents one solution to Africa's telecom infrastructure problems. Intelsat has 46 African countries as shareholders and currently operates seven satellites that have coverage of the African continent. PanAmSat also serves Africa. WorldSpace plans to provide digital radio service to Africa on its AfriStar satellite, due for launch in the second quarter of 1998. Forthcoming LEO and MEO systems also plan African coverage.

EFFECT OF DEREGULATION ON END-USER PRICING

Deregulation and competition are combining to significantly reduce telecom pricing to end users in most countries. Many PTOs are now rebalancing their tariffs to increase local rates and decrease long-distance and international rates. PTOs have historically relied on international revenues to cross-subsidize the politically sensitive local calling rates. Under traditional bilateral agreements, two corresponding carriers compensate one another by a 50:50 division of the wholesale facilities or accounting rate per international traffic minute. The carrier that bills the call must pay this charge—called the settlement fee—to the terminating carrier. The originating carrier recoups this charge, plus a markup, through its tariff. Many PTOs—especially those in developing countries—have a vested interest in keeping accounting rates high.

The bilateral operating agreements provide for traffic from each PTO to be returned proportionally. For example, for each minute of traffic a carrier sends out to its correspondent, in theory, it should receive one in return. In this way, originating and return traffic are equal and no settlement payment is required. However, equivalent traffic in both directions is rarely seen. Since fewer international calls are made from PTOs with high international tariffs, the system favors these PTOs, which receive large net settlement payments from PTOs with low international tariffs. In any case, deregulation and the resulting competition are forcing both average per-minute pricing and accounting rates down over time, as shown in Exhibit 9.

CONTRACTING FOR A NEW GLOBAL NETWORK

Global corporate networks can be complex and can include technologies such as VPNs for voice and data, frame relay, X.25, ISDN, and private lines. Hardware elements can include routers, gateways, multiplexers, firewalls, IP telephony gateways, and remote access concentrators. Software can include router software, protocol stacks, and emulation utilities. A well-

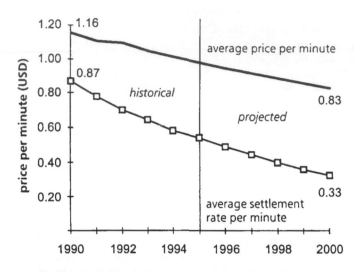

Exhibit 9. Trends in Per-Minute Pricing of International Call Rates & Settlement Rates (Source: International Telecommunications Union News 3/97, which Cited ITU/TeleGeography Inc., Direction of Traffic, 1996, Trends in International Telephone Traffic)

designed network should comply with accepted technology standards and open architectures and employ products with scalability and evolutionary migration paths. A well-designed network should also have the network management capability to monitor performance and utilization, diagnose and recover from outages, configure equipment remotely, and administer usage.

There is a five-step process for planning, designing, and choosing a carrier for a new international network. In this illustration, it is assumed that an international corporate network already exists but that the existing network needs to be redesigned or wholly upgraded. The five steps are discussed in turn.

Assess Current Network

First, assess the current network infrastructure, including architecture, technology, carrier services, and network management and support capabilities. Focus on wide area components, but LAN and desktop and server components should be reviewed as well to understand access needs. It may also be necessary to collect cost and traffic data for the existing voice, data, and video usage to provide carriers with statistics for current utilization.

Define New Network Requirements

Next, identify the corporation's strategic requirements for the new network. These derive from the company's business needs (e.g., new sites from acquisitions, data center relocations, and planned applications). It may also be necessary to review key business processes and to characterize the related information exchanges in terms of transaction patterns, connectivity, media, priority, volume, and other relevant criteria. The designer should translate these flows into estimates of traffic demand to determine capacity ranges that drive decisions among alternative transport service choices. This step includes determining protocol support, redundancy, security, interoperability, and scalability needs for each site.

Develop Initial Technical Design

A cost-effective network will make use of the most appropriate technologies in terms of initial implementation and ongoing operation. The network will typically be designed to support numerous applications, each with differing requirements in terms of network availability, latency, redundancy, etc. Further, the network will interconnect sites in countries with a variety of telecom infrastructures, market environments, and regulatory restrictions. The network should be designed to be reliable, fault-tolerant, and robust, and cost-effectively scalable.

Evaluate Carrier Alternatives

This step entails assessing carrier capabilities to implement and support the network. The carrier alliances (e.g., Concert, Global One, etc.) are a good place to begin with a set of inquiries, but other international network providers such as the IVANs and independent telephone companies (e.g., Cable & Wireless and NTT) should not be neglected. Users should tell the carriers what they would like to have. Some examples follow:

- **Cost** For the majority of large telecom users, cost is the single most important factor considered when evaluating a carrier service. As telecom becomes an increasingly important business resource, its cost levels rise. Customers with large telecom expenditures are aggressive in their demand for cost-effective solutions.
- **Reliability** Reliability has two dimensions. First, it is network reliability. Many customers have demanding reliability standards because their businesses are critically dependent on their network. For these users, reliability can be more important than cost. Second, carrier commitments in terms of promised responsiveness are critical. Reliability in this sense allows the customer to rely with certainty on what the vendor agrees to provide, such as implementation dates for new circuits.

205

- **One-stop shopping**   Customers often desire to procure their telecom services from a single source. For some users, this is a single source per country. For others, it means one supplier for the customer's worldwide network. The preference for the latter results from the expected savings from consolidating services onto a single bill with a single volume discount as well as the convenience of dealing through a single point of contact.
- **Seamless service**   Customers are not interested in the difficulties suppliers have in crossing national boundaries. They want a single network with end-to-end connectivity that can be easily monitored, managed, and repaired. Seamlessness is the ability to deliver consistent service levels and functionality across an entire worldwide network.
- **Proximity**   Customers operating worldwide often want their supplier or suppliers to offer locally based maintenance, operating support, and service with consistency.

Often companies will issue a request for proposals (RFP) for the new international network. First, the RFP should fully reflect the company's technical, geographic, application, service, management, implementation, and pricing requirements. Second, the RFP should be tightly specified to ensure that carrier responses can be compared in "apples-to-apples" fashion while at the same time allowing appropriate scope for creative vendor solutions. Third, the RFP should impose firm guidelines for carriers to provide detailed pricing information.

In a formal RFP process, the method of carrier selection and negotiation will depend on the complexity of the network design, the range of viable competing solutions, and the level of management control assigned to the service provider or providers. The company may pursue an abbreviated negotiation process or prefer a lengthier and more formal tender process.

CHOOSE A CARRIER AND IMPLEMENT NETWORK

After carrier proposals are received, a rigorous technical and financial analysis of the responses is invariably required because no vendor offers identical services and features. There are four major objectives to such an analysis:

1. Ensure that each proposal is complete and self-consistent.
2. Evaluate the comprehensiveness of each proposed solution.
3. Ensure that proposals conform with technical and regulatory practice in the countries where service is offered.
4. Compare each proposal in terms of individual pricing components and life cycle costs for the network.

After the proposal review process is completed, there are likely to be several meetings with one or more "finalist" carriers. After a carrier or carriers are selected, the user can move on to implementation of the new network.

SUMMARY

Telecom network facilities vary greatly between developed and developing or undeveloped countries. When looking at the world's telecom network as a whole, it is seen to be made up of "both old and new and a lot of in-between." For more than a century, the network's evolution—while dramatic in end result—has been accomplished in a piecemeal or patchwork fashion, with new technologies, facilities, and services being added incrementally as technology progressed, country wealth permitted, and demand for services increased. Newer facilities are heavily concentrated in industrialized nations, while older and obsolete facilities are found in developing countries.

Section IV
The Data Network

Chapter 13
Data Communications: The Physical Connections to the WAN

Dale Hibner

INTRODUCTION

When one discusses data communication today, the question to answer is what layer of the OSI Model will be discussed. For this chapter, the focus will be on the Physical Layer and some of the Datalink Layer. Thus, the discussion will be on the functional requirements, electrical/optical characteristics, and mechanical (wiring). The discussion must cover the delivery and recovery of bits. Although the purist will say that the physical media is not a part of the OSI Physical Layer, the requirements of the media must be considered and accommodated in the interface to the physical. The order of discussion is to look quickly at how this started, then how LANs work, then how to remotely connect to the LAN, and finally, what the future will hold.

FUNDAMENTALS

The basic element of data transmission is the binary digit or bit. The construct is a logical 1 and 0 or in truth tables, true and false. The transmission of a bit is not a phenomenon of the computer age. The use of dash and dot in Morse code is one implementation that pre-dates the information age. The use of machine readable transmitted codes are linked to the Baudot codes of teletypewriters and paper tapes. Today, the use of EBCDIC or ASCII takes care of the transmitted characters.

At the physical layer, the consideration is the structure of the path for transmission. Internal to the computer and for very close peripheral connections the data path is a parallel bus structure of 8, 16, 32, now 64 and soon 128 bits. The information is sent as a group of bits with one bit occu-

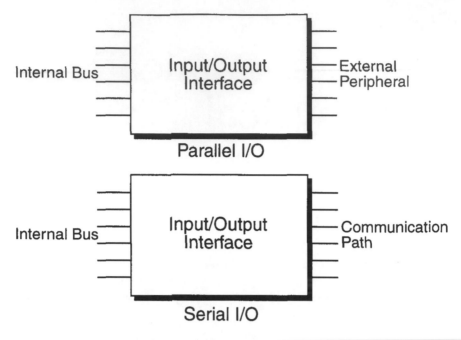

Exhibit 1.   Serial vs. Parallel Connections

pying each of the parallel lines. For any connections of communications that cover distance, like LAN and WAN, the external path is serial. That means the bits will follow one after the other from the source to the destination. The differences are illustrated in Exhibit 1.

To discuss the data communications and the path, a more complete understanding of the serial path is necessary. In parallel communications, the natural grouping is the number of parallel lines. Some form of grouping is also required for the bits as they traverse the serial path. The three methods of communicating on a serial bus are asynchronous, synchronous and isochronous. The difference between these methods is how each relates to timing. In the asynchronous case, the bits will flow usually in cluster without regard to any timing. File transfers using XMODEM are asynchronous. Synchronous communications on the other hand is absolutely timing dependent. The classic example of synchronous is a T1 trunk. Isochronous is a case where the communication path is asynchronous in its handling of bits but the application on each end is inherently timing dependent. An example of an isochronous transmission is video over FDDI II.

Exhibit 2 shows how the various methods appear relative to each other. Asynchronous and isochronous cases require the use of headers and trailers

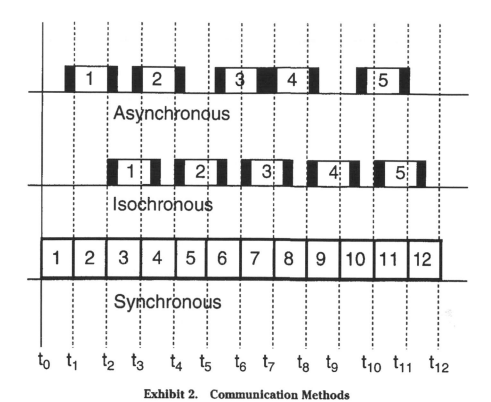

Exhibit 2. Communication Methods

for delineating the start and stop of each cluster of bits. In the simplest case, the start and stop are just an additional bit on each end of a character but within a frame, the header and trailer can be a set of octets (group of eight bits). Synchronous communications use the timing information to keep track of the bits within the data stream.

The physical characteristics of the media, twisted pair, coaxial cable and fiber optics, require the user to present the data stream in different formats for successful transmission. The frequency bandwidth of the media is the one measure that has defined the limits of what can be done. The general rule has been that the format of the signal will be digital for short distances or over fiber and analog for long distance.

When one thinks of a digital signal format, the intuitive outcome is a positive electrical signal for a "1" and no signal for a "0." The formal name for this representation is unipolar nonreturn-to-zero (NRZ). The nonreturn-to-zero has to do with the electrical signal staying at the appropriate level for the entire time that the logical bit is in that state. This is shown in the first signal of Exhibit 3.

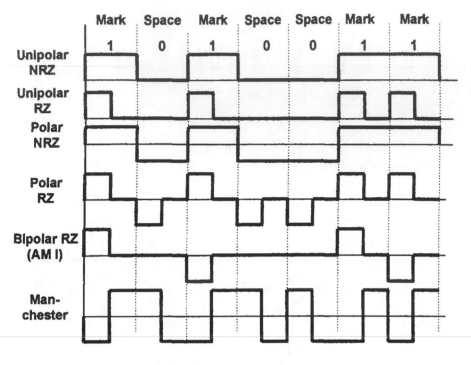

Exhibit 3. Signal Formats

The system of sending digital electrical signals that are unipolar tend over time to set up average or DC values that add unwanted voltages and currents. The polar signal formats therefore are needed for achieving average voltage or current values of zero.

Sending bits is only one part of the problem. Receiving and detecting the bits is the other part. If a continuous string of 1s or 0s are sent, the system can drift on the timing of the bits in the string which can result in loss of bit synchronization. Thus, a more reasonable digital signal would be the return-to-zero or RZ formats. The set of signals shown in Exhibit 3 give a small set of the choices for sending and receiving bits.

Two of the signals are significant for other reasons. The bipolar RZ is also know as alternate mark inversion (AMI). The AMI signal is the digital signal format used in T1 transmissions. Any occurrence of a 1 is either positive or negative where the positive 1 sets up the condition that the next 1 is negative and vice versa. The value of the format is two fold. The first is that AMI has the inherent capability to perform a single bit error detection. Any bit error will result in two sequential pulses with the same polarity. The second characteristic is that the relationship of information content

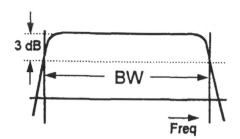

Exhibit 4.   Bandwidth

vs. the frequency bandwidth is the most efficient for a binary signal. The signal has a two bits per hertz relationship.

The second signal of significance is the Manchester code because it is used as one of the basic LAN signaling schemes. The value of this type of scheme is that the representation of the "1" and the "0" are mathematically orthogonal. That is, the signals are as far apart as is possible. Therefore, the ability of the receiver to distinguish the signals is as accurate as possible and the error rate is as low as possible.

The ability of any media to carry the maximum data rate in bits per second is constrained by the frequency bandwidth in hertz and the magnitude of the electrical noise as it relates to magnitude of the signal. Using these criteria one can mathematically determine the upper data rate limit of any channel. The frequency bandwidth of a channel is shown in Exhibit 4. The signal strength is constrained by the industry standards to an upper limit. Once noise is in the system, source is not easy to identify and reduce. So the only avenue for increasing the data rate limit is to increase the bandwidth and reduce the potential for noise to enter the system.

The best example of this is the category of unshielded twisted pair recognized by the standard EIA/TIA 568. As one proceeds up the categories from Category 1 to Category 5, the capacitive characteristics improve and the bandwidth is increased and the potential for noise is reduced. One thing to remember is that the data rate supported in each respective category is only guaranteed for up to 100 meters. The construction standards limit the horizontal distance from the wiring closet to the wall plate to 90 meters and allow 3 meters within the room. As the distance exceeds the standard distances, the bandwidth decreases and the data rate may not be supported.

The standard business installation practices today are to install Category 5 cabling for any data application. There is one school of thought that only Category 5 should be installed for all applications. As the Gigabit

Exhibit 5.   Category of UTP in EIA/TIA 568

Category	Grade	Data Rate	Usage
Category 1	Voice	1 Mbps	Plain old telephone
Category 2	Data	4 Mbps	Early token ring
Category 3	LAN	16 Mbps	Ethernet and token ring
Category 4	Super	20 Mbps	Specialty uses
Category 5	Hyper	100 Mbps	All new data installations
Category 7 (still in draft)		1 Gbps	Future high speed

Ethernet becomes more common, the installation practice may change. The cost differential from Category 5 to the new standard is not known and could be sufficient to warrant special installation only for those connections that will require the highest data rate.

LOCAL AREA NETWORKS (LAN)

The two classical LAN architectures are ethernet and token ring. Both have been accepted in business applications. The ethernet implementations are becoming the dominant form. Because token ring is the IBM solution to LANs, the businesses with a strong IBM connection are strong token ring supporters. There are reasons to still use token ring, however the new implementations of ethernet at the higher speeds and improved throughputs from switching hub environments have narrowed the range of reasons. As stated earlier, the wiring for LANs follow the entries in Exhibit 5 or, in new installations, are Category 5.

With the exception of some older existing implementations, both token ring and ethernet are now installed as physical star configurations and logical ring or bus configurations, respectively. The hubs or switches are the center of the star configurations with the logical structure existing within the hub or switch.

To implement the physical configuration, the workstations, PCs, and servers must have an access device internally which satisfies the functional requirements of the OSI physical and Datalink layers. The most common method used is to install a network interface card (NIC). PC manufacturers like Compaq are making ethernet interfaces part of the integrated motherboard in some models. The fact that ethernet is the LAN configuration being designed into the models says much about the relative distribution of ethernet vs. token ring.

One temptation is to compare speeds between ethernet and token ring. The simplest way is to use the system data transport speeds — 4 or 16M bps for Token Ring and 10M bps, 100M bps or soon 1G bps for ethernet. The reality is that these speeds are not achievable for data throughput.

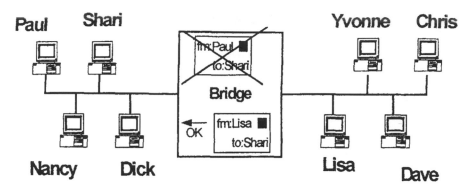

Exhibit 6.   Filtering Bridge Action

The more likely speeds for hub configurations are 3/14M bps for Token Ring and 6,60 or 600M bps for Ethernet. In addition, since LANs are inherently broadcast systems (i.e., every station on the subnet gets every packet), the data rate for any one user is much less. On average in a heavily used system, the per user data rate is the real data thoughput divided by the number of users on the subnet. The bursty nature of the data does not lend itself well to averages but one does need to consider the per user data rate. The trend for more and more multimedia with motion video can potentially turn all LANs into heavily used systems.

The introduction in the mid 1990s of switched LANs is the implementation that can achieve the highest throughput data rates. Each user has the dedicated use of his own connection to the switch and therefore, the potential to occupy the full system data rate. That means, instead of a throughput data rate for an Ethernet connection of 4–6M bps, the user can access almost 10M bps. This is because, unlike a hub, the switch has an internal data rate that is much higher than the system rate to accommodate the collision free connections.

Even with switched systems the broadcast nature of LANs can saturate the system because every station receives every packet. To reduce the amount of traffic that any one station has to receive, the LAN is segmented into subnets. Between the subnets, bridges filter the traffic and limit the number of stations that any one station has to receive (Exhibit 6). The bridge restricts the traffic by stopping the traffic from one station in the subnet destined for another station in the subnet from being delivered to the LAN subnets on the other side of the bridge. Further, the bridge only delivers the traffic destined for a station in the subnet from outside the subnet. Bridges are used when the LAN subnets are the same protocol — Ethernet to Ethernet and Token Ring to Token Ring.

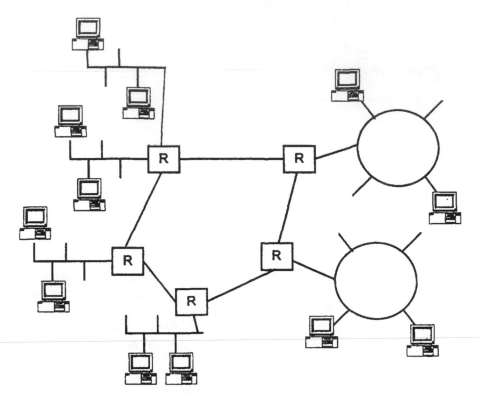

Exhibit 7.   A Routed LAN

Today, when the protocols are different the common solution is to use routers. Routers provide the capability to do the addressing and protocol conversions that are necessary for dissimilar LAN protocols. The additional capability of a router vs. an translating bridge is significant when compared to the minimal cost difference between a low end router and a translating bridge.

The routers are also used to direct traffic within homogeneous LANs that are large or complex. Large campus enterprise LANs usually include routers for ease of management and increased design flexibility. Whereas, a bridge tends to connect one subnet to one subnet, a router can interconnect many subnets. Routers also are used as the interface device between LANs and WANs. These routers are commonly called boundary or edge gateways. The advent of internet and intranet technologies has added to the routed network phenomenon. TCP/IP is critical to the success. The advantage of TCP/IP is the routing characteristics of the protocol and the ease of translation from the LAN world to the WAN world.

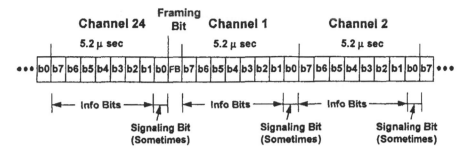

Exhibit 8. D4 Creates DS0 Format (8 bits x 8,000 bps)

WIDE AREA NETWORKS CONNECTIVITY

The purpose here is not to discuss the various WAN choices but to recognize the interconnectivy to a WAN. The only option for WAN access is to buy the service from a telephone company. Which company that is has changed with the advent of the Communications Act of 1996. Nevertheless, the basics are the same. For data communications, the service choice is likely to be digital because of the data rate advantage that digital offers over analog. Within a Telco the digital data rates are from 56K bps for a single channel up to 1.544M bps for a T1 and if necessary multiple T1's. Internationally, the data rates are 64K bps for a single channel up to 2.048M bps for an E-1.

Telcos are designed for delivery of voice communications which has synchronous delivery requirements. Any data communications through the Telco will use the circuits designed for voice which inherently requires a synchronous channel. The device that drives a digital signal over the telephone wires is the channel service unit (CSU) or digital service unit (DSU). The CSU/DSU also ensures the timing for the synchronous bit stream. The CSU/DSU must be present as the initial device for the digital WAN connection.

Occasionally, the input for the CSU/DSU is from a formatting device, the D4 channel bank. The D4 establishes the single channel format. This is normally the DS0 format that is associated with the digital voice. In Exhibit 8, the format of a single channel is the D4 output.

MULTIPLEXING

To capitalize on the cost of a single channel, the engineering solution is to make the path a shared path of more than one channel of digital information. The concept is multiplexing or muxing the information. Exhibit 9 displays the maturing of the process. Individual digital information streams can be combined by sharing the time available on the combined path. Each

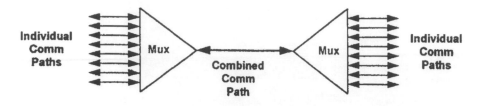

Exhibit 9. Multiplexing of Single Channels into One Path

individual signal owns the combined path for a formatted amount of time. The time available on the combined path is divided and shared. Thus, the name for this technique is time division multiplexing (TDM).

In the digital hierarchy of North America, the architecture of the multiplexing places 24 single channels in a shared path. This is the DS1 format used in the T1. The individual channels take 1/24th of the time available for the shared channel. The composite signal is synchronous digital traffic. In a DS0 format as it was created for voice, the single channel can only present its eight bits for 125 microseconds before a new eight bits of information has to be presented. Since the multiplexing is sharing, each additional channel has to fit directly next to the previous channel and the combined channels still only have 125 microseconds before the next set of data. With the 24 channels of the North American hierarchy, each single channel only has 5.2 microseconds dedicated to itself. In Europe, the number of channels sharing the single path is 30 individual information channels and two signaling channels.

Exhibit 10 shows the combined TDM channels of the DS1 format. The format groups the 24 channels into a frame. Each DS1 frame, including the framing bit, exists for 125 microseconds. The framing bit provides the frame synchronization. A framing bit by itself is not very useful. But when the receiver equipment views a group of frames looking for a sequence of framing bits in a specific pattern, 100011011100, the frames and the channels can be aligned and the synchronous pattern is maintained.

One of the characteristics of the voice network in the development of the digital transport was to use the least significant bits of all the DS0 channels in every sixth DS1 frame. The only reason to remember this bit of trivia is that the installed base of the telephone industry still has this technique of in-band signaling in some locations. Occasionally, for data applications the rates are restricted to the 56K bps instead of the full 64K bps that out-of-band signaling allows.

The choices in data communications will have 56K bps, 64K bps and T1 for some time to come. Even though the modern offerings for data now

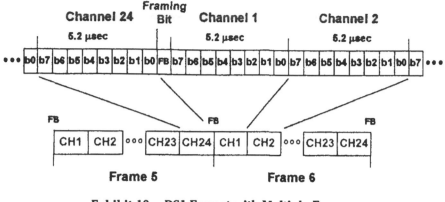

Exhibit 10.   DS1 Format with Multiple Frames

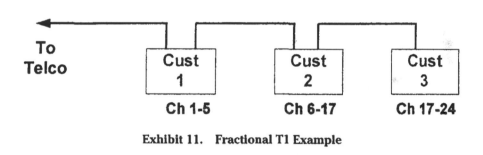

Exhibit 11.   Fractional T1 Example

include frame relay, the local access for the last mile will probably be the classical synchronous technology.

One variation for consideration is the use of fractional T1's. The reality of digital communication channels is that the costs for several single channels have a break point of approximately 14 before it is cost effective to move to a T1. Single channels are also expensive for the service provider. To reduce the overhead, telephone companies offer reduced quantities of grouped single channels in groups of less than 24 channels and less than 14. The concept is to provide a path for adjacent users by daisy-chaining the end users on a single T1 and taking advantage of installed, unused channels. Exhibit 11 shows how the connections might be made. The multiplexer at each site is a drop-and-insert mux. The only channels any user can access are the ones specifically dropped off at the location.

DATA COMMUNICATIONS IN REMOTE ACCESS

The discussion so far has been over the signal formats, LAN/WAN connectivity, and synchronous digital techniques. The last data communication to

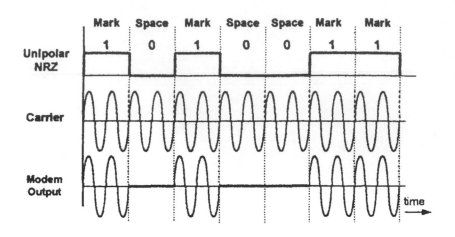

Exhibit 12.   ASK Format

discuss is how to gain access from remote locations. The choice for most locations does not include the above topics. The likely choice is analog plain old telephone service (POTS). The use of POTS as a data communication media causes a relook at the telephone analog channel. The signal formats shown in Exhibit 3 do not work very well as information carriers on a POTS line. Even the AMI format is limited with conditioned lines to about 12000 feet without repeaters. The standard states that RS-232 data cannot be guaranteed beyond 25 meters if sent in the digital format. This limit led to the use of many line drivers in the early days of computer terminals outside the computer room.

To overcome the limits in distance for digital data the use of modulator/demodulators (modems) is required. The principle employed is to recognize that the analog frequency content of voice within the 300–4000 hertz range propagates well in POTS and then make the data signal have the same propagation characteristics. The technique is to use the digital signal as the information and generate a frequency that will be the carrier. The simplest form of this technique is amplitude shift keying (ASK). This is shown in Exhibit 12. AM radio operates on a similar principle.

The view in Exhibit 12 is how the signals look relative to time. The limitation on how fast this scheme can pass data is dependent on the bandwidth that the composite modem signal occupies.

Exhibit 13 shows the amount of bandwidth that a recoverable signal needs. This ASK signal needs to have a bandwidth in hertz of three times the data rate in bit per second. With the voice channel bandwidth of 3600

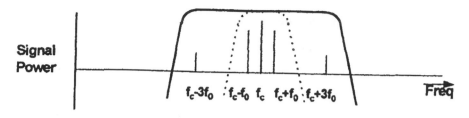

Exhibit 13. The Bandwidth View of an ASK Signal

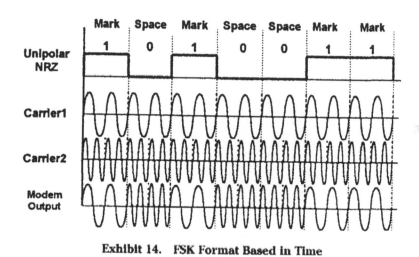

Exhibit 14. FSK Format Based in Time

hertz, the maximum data rate is 1200 bps for ASK. ASK is not a very efficient method for data communication transfer.

Other techniques were used like frequency shift keying (FSK). Exhibit 14 shows the scheme for FSK and the associated modem output. The bandwidth is not any more efficient.

To be successful the design had to be more creative. One way to achieve higher data rates in a modem is to increase the number of bits of information transmitted in a single time slot. This requires more than binary signaling formats or modulation schemes that can represent more than one bit.

Exhibit 15 gives a simple solution for the latter. The technique is phase shift keying (PSK). Where each transition in phase can represent two bits. Rather than the time plot, the more common representation is the constellation for a PSK signal.

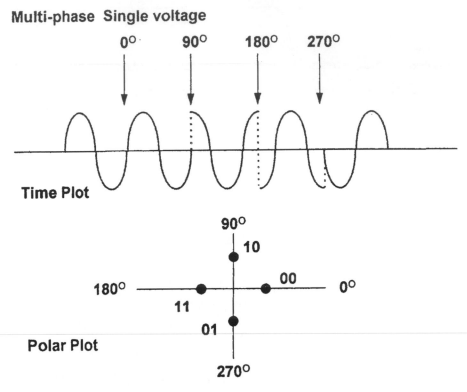

Exhibit 15. PSK Time Plot and Phase Amplitude Constellation

The typical modem today uses more complex signaling that shown in Exhibit 15. The constellation shown in Exhibit 16 is the 14.4K-bps V.33 standard. The bit patterns used in the modern modems are error correcting. The result is improved detection and therefore higher data rates.

SUMMARY

Claude Shannon, in his channel capacity theorem, offers only two avenues for technology to increase the data rate possible in the existing analog telephone system. One is to increase the bandwidth of the media used. The aging copper outside telephone plant does not offer much hope for even ISDN speeds. Second is to increase the signal to noise ratio. The noise will be a continuing problem for the same reason as an aged copper plant. Therefore, to increase speeds we have to increase signal strengths, but even there the increase in signal strength can increase interference (noise). The only hope for massive data rates to support data communication is the deployment and use of fiber optic. The fiber loop is becoming more and more ubiquitous and appears to be penetrating the last mile.

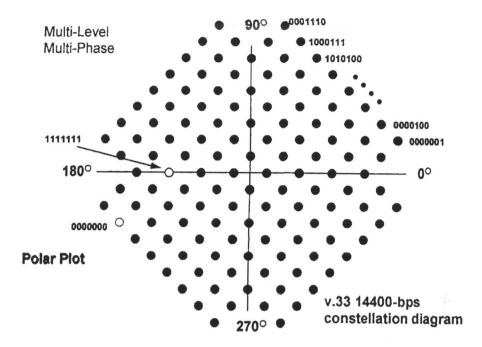

Exhibit 16. V.33 Constellation for 14.4K-bps

Chapter 14
Network Security: Firewalls Guard Intranets from Invasion

David Axner

INTRODUCTION

Companies are now more vulnerable to security breaches than ever before with their mass migration to the Internet to conduct business with their clients and to connect remote offices and telecommuters to corporate resources. The prevalence of computer crime now compels companies to adopt a proactive stance toward securing information assets.

What can companies do to safeguard their confidential information from unauthorized parties? How do unauthorized parties gain access to corporate networks? What methods are used to penetrate intranetworks? This chapter examines the methods used to access corporate intranets and ways in which to prevent intrusion.

WARNING

Your network is vulnerable to attack! Think of the Internet as an unregulated community roamed by unscrupulous characters called hackers. Who are hackers? They can range in age from kids to adults and often may be university students or software developers in the computer industry, which makes them quite sophisticated and knowledgeable. They can penetrate your network resources to browse through your sensitive documents, steal your information, and corrupt your databases.

What can be done to prevent attacks? Just as the kings of old built impenetrable walls and moats to secure their castles, today's corporate intranets can be secured by creating barriers between them and the Internet. A firewall is such a barrier which prevents unauthorized access to a protected network. And because security threats can also come from the inside, a firewall prevents your users from accessing unauthorized Internet services.

Passwords, the first line of defense and the simplest form of network security, were used to secure networks from unauthorized access before the Internet arrived. However, passwords are easily obtained by trial and error techniques, by stealing password files, or by tapping into legitimate telnet sessions. They offer no challenge to hackers.

ONE-TIME PASSWORDS

Handheld authenticators are inherently more secure, since they produce one-time passwords. They are used when logging on; the user enters both the generated password and a personal identification number (PIN). Although this technique offers greater protection, security issues transcend simple password protection. Security problems are inherent in all common Internet application programs. Simple Mail Transfer Protocol (SMTP) for example, includes a "Mail From" command that contains a return address.

There is no way to prove that the return address is genuine, enabling a user to send email anonymously. Mail messages sent in volume could overwhelm a network. Transmission Control Protocol/Information Protocol (TCP/IP), the transmission protocol of the Internet, conveys both source and destination addresses with files. A method called "IP Address Spoofing" changes the source address to make it appear as if the communication is coming from a trusted source.

Another way to attack a network is through a Domain Name Service (DNS). A DNS is a distributed database that maps host names with IP addresses. Using the DNS, hackers can find the IP address of trusted resources. It also gives hackers information about the size and structure of the intranet. By examining a specific financial project, for example, a hacker could determine the scope of the project by counting the number of computers named after the project.

ANOTHER SECURITY THREAT

File Transfer Protocol (FTP) presents another security issue. FTP enables an Internet user to download a file, public domain software, documents, and images. Using an anonymous FTP, an unauthorized person can retrieve files on an intranet file server.

Telnet provides direct access to computers connected to the Internet and, therefore, presents another security risk. Telnet connections from an external source should be authenticated by a challenge-response method to ensure their identity. Telnet connections typically depend on a one-time password based on either the DES algorithm or time.

Sendmail, a common software email package is another security risk as a result of the voluminous information associated with the program. Finger, a utility that emerged from the UNIX operating system, allows a user to find out about other users on the Internet. Finger presents an extreme security risk, since it allows hackers to gather information which they can use to penetrate a network. It is important to restrict the amount of information that can be accessed by a Finger request to safeguard a network.

FIREWALLS: HOW DO THEY WORK?

Firewalls defend networks from intrusion. They are barriers between trusted and untrusted networks, such as the Internet. Firewalls have evolved from a basic need to secure network resources against unauthorized access. The basic tenet of firewalls is *"that which is not expressly permitted is prohibited."* First generation firewalls used packet filtering to screen inbound and outbound traffic. Packet filters address the packet level of TCP/IP packets. A packet filter reads the source address of each incoming IP packet and compares it to a list of authorized addresses. It discards all packets with unauthorized addresses. Packet filters present a limited security measure and require substantial administration time. They do not isolate a trusted network from an untrusted one, since they provide a direct connection between the two networks. Packet filters provide the first line of security, but packet filtering alone cannot prevent a security breach.

As firewalls evolved to improve security, the circuit-level gateway emerged. Circuit-level gateways protect an internal network from outside intrusion by isolating it from an external network, such as the Internet. A gateway port acts as a proxy agent for external calls. It functions much like a post office box by providing a proxy address to outside callers. The agent verifies transmissions and accepts only authorized calls. It passes these calls onto the destination endstation or server on the intranet. For outbound calls, the gateway attaches the address of the agent port to each outbound packet to safeguard the true source address.

Because the gateway governs all inbound and outbound traffic, they are inherently secure. However, circuit-level gateways do not examine each packet of data. They accept multiple packets of data once address verification is done. Although this security method isolates the internal network from the Internet, it does not examine each packet for its contents, which may be destructive to internal network resources.

Application-level gateways, in addition to the functions performed by circuit-level gateways, examine the contents of each inbound or outbound packet as it passes through the gateway. This security measure precludes the possibility of a packet containing destructive data from entering the protected network. This is particularly important when receiving Internet email, since SMTP is not a secure protocol and is vulnerable. The gateway also prevents internal network users from accessing unauthorized Internet services that might subvert security. While this is the most secure method, it can cause response time delays and can be costly.

The firewall market is segmented into three tiers. First generation products form the lowest tier. These firewalls support packet filtering only, which presents a very limited measure of protection from attack. Second generation products form the second tier. These products shield an operating system from being breached; however, they do not totally prevent it, since they are deployed on stock operating systems, which present security loopholes. They add to packet filtering with circuit-level gateways and application-level gateways. Third generation products form the top tier and offer the highest level of security. These products contain all three of the basic security techniques, but what makes them more secure than second generation systems is their operating system architecture. Their OS has been stripped down to a kernel and modified or "hardened" to remove all added functionality that may impose security threats. The hardened kernel prevents penetration and manipulation of the OS. This technique makes third generation firewalls the most secure.

FIREWALL SOLUTIONS

A growing number of firewall solutions continues to emerge on the market. The four solutions presented here are from four early and prominent firewall providers with the largest market share. They are considered to be among the best solutions on the market.

Checkpoint Software Technologies Ltd. (Israel and Redwood City, CA) has the largest installed base of firewalls with over 6,000 units delivered. Its *Firewall 1* is a second generation firewall that employs a standard UNIX or Windows NT operating system. It consists of two firewall daemons and an inspection module. It can be installed on a dual-homed host or a server. The inspection module is loaded into the operating system kernel between the Data Link and Network layers. It intercepts and inspects all inbound and outbound packets on all interfaces.

It examines IP addresses, port numbers, and any other information, including information related to all higher layers and the data within the message based on the user's policy. A graphical user interface (GUI) enables users to define security policy and management using graphical tools from a single workstation. Gateway modules on internal network gateways limit traffic types between departments, containing internal traffic and preventing the spread of viruses or worms.

Logging and alerting features, executed from the network management station, log message statistics and alert the network manager to attempted break in. Tracking is selectable for every communication attempt and valid connection, including service attempted, action taken and related statistics plus protocol-specific information. Encryption keys and user names are included when applicable. A status monitor indicates the activity of each gateway in the system. Extended or additional log formats can be created via Script language. Logs can be viewed, queries made, and reports generated. Logged information is authenticated, encrypted and signed to secure the audited information. It is then stored in a condensed format to save disk space.

Firewall-1 Version 2.0 adds encryption for VPNs over the Internet, IP address translation, and client authentication for remote users and branch offices. V2.0 feature in-place selective encryption using DES and FWZI. Multiple encryption schemes are available and can be used concurrently. Firewall-1 generates and maintains all keys automatically using the Deffie-Hellman scheme. Public and private keys are generated for each encrypted communication. All encryption features are incorporated in Firewall-1's GUI Rule Base Editor and Log Viewer. However, encryption requires a Firewall-1 at both source and destination sites, unlike Secure Computing's approach. This is a distinct disadvantage.

Firewall-1 Version 2.1, just announced, adds support for its GUI for Windows NT and Windows 95 platforms. Its Management Module now allows a security manager to control Firewall-1 on Windows NT, Solaris 2, SunOS V4.0, HP-UX and Bay Networks routers. V2.1 also extends a VPN connection to remote users via SecuRemote, which loads on the remote PC or laptop under Windows 95 and encrypts TCP/IP communication to a remote Firewall-1 gateway before it passes to a network or Internet connection.

Raptor Systems Inc. of Waltham, MA, offers its *Eagle Version 4.0,* a third-generation firewall that employs a standard UNIX or Windows NT operating system and runs as an application-level gateway. It does not provide packet filtering nor does it provide a circuit-level gateway. The Eagle firewall uses proxy daemons and an authorization rule database to evaluate all connection attempts in or out of a secured network. Five proxy daemons handle connections; they include Telnet, FTP, Gopher, HTTP, and SMTP. In addition, two general-purpose daemons, Generic Service Passer (GSP) and Proxyd, handle other types of connection attempts, including NTP and NNTP.

Eagle's control process, which serves as the central database for Eagle, provides rule-based processing to handle connection attempts through any Internet protocol. Authorization rule thresholds, defined as limits of a rule, can be established for hosts, networks, domains, services, service access periods, users, or a combination of these factors via the Hawk GUI authorization window.

Suspicious Activity Monitoring (SAM) is an Eagle feature that uses rule thresholds and monitors all connections through the firewall. User created rules specify thresholds based on anticipated levels of access for each rule. A met or exceeded rule threshold by a connection attempt is logged and the administrator is alerted.

The Eagle firewall logs all network activity, which is accessible for viewing by an administrator. Log messages include date, time severity, computer names and IP addresses, and a description. Log files are automatically backed up on a daily basis.

The Eagle firewall supports transparent access of external connections for internal users, who can connect to outside systems via Telnet, FTP, SMTP, and HTTP. Conversely, transparent access is prohibited for external users. Authorization rules apply to both transparent and nontransparent access. Transparent access is supported only when allowed by a rule. A rule selected for a connection attempt that specifies no authentication allows the user to directly connect to the remote host. If a rule specifies an authentication type, the user is prompted in a manner similar to nontransparent operation.

The Eagle firewall disables several inherently insecure services at the application layer and at the operating system layer at installation. These services include IP packet forwarding, source routing, and NFS. The Eagle firewall uses the X server for its X Window System GUI, Hawk, but filters out any packets destined for the X server from remote hosts. Other network services that are automatically disabled include finger, bootd, tftpd, rlogind, timed, chargen, and echo. Depending on the platform, some kernal services are also disabled.

The Eagle Vulture program runs in background mode on all UNIX-based platforms. Because it does not have a secure operating system, such as BorderWare FireWall Server, Eagle is vulnerable to all UNIX security concerns. It monitors for suspicious processes running on a gateway and prevents any process that is not part of the underlying operating system, part of the Eagle software, or not specifically allowed by the Eagle administrator.

Secure Computing Corp. of St. Paul, MN, is the number two global supplier of firewalls and the largest network security company worldwide. Secure has shipped over 2,000 units worldwide. Its customers include government, education, healthcare, financial, and manufacturing. Secure Computing has partnered with Progressive Networks, Netscape, RSA, Cylink, FDS, DEC, and McAfee.

Secure Computing introduced Version 3.0 of its Sidewinder Security Server. Sidewinder runs on a UNIX workstation as a protected UNIX operating system. It operates as a circuit and application level gateway and does not support filtering. Version 3.0 includes Type Enforcement, encryption based on the IPSec standard, email filtering, JAVA Applet filtering, WebTrack Internet monitoring and filtering, an improved administration interface with a drag-and-drop graphical user interface, and client access authentication. Type Enforcement, an original feature of Sidewinder, contains restrictions that divide application or protocol domains and control the processes in each to prevent an attack on an Internet server from accessing domains serving internal protected networks.

Secure channels can be established between Sidewinder users connected to the Internet who load Secure Computing's BorderWare NETCourier on their PC. NETCourier provides IPsec-based encryption in addition to an enhanced mosaic Web browser for Windows 95 that includes PGP for email, FTP, Telnet, an attachment viewer, and a news reader. NETCourier is available as an encryption-only package for $129, or as a full service package for $199. Users can substantially improve the encryption performance of Sidewinder by using Cylink's ASIC-based SecureNode card, which fits into an ISA slot. email Filtering screens the content of incoming or outgoing mail messages and attached files based on keywords, binary format, or file size.

Keywords can identify sensitive client information, while binary filtering scans text patterns to ensure that it is not a virus or unauthorized information. Binary files or attachments can be rejected or flagged for later analysis. Java Applet filtering allows a user to reject a Java Applet originating from an unknown or unsecured site on the Internet. WebTrack enables users to control and monitor Internet use within the enterprise. It enables managers to eliminate nonbusiness activities within the workplace and preserves bandwidth for productive use. It logs all Internet access, reports usage statistics, and provides blocks for HTTP, FTP, GOPHER, and NNTP. Client access authentication is integrated into the Sidewinder's Authentication Services, which is based on the DES encryption standard and can support a variety of challenge/response hardware and software tokens for remote Internet access or dial-in. It also supports the standards TACACS+ (Terminal Access Control System) and RADIUS (Remote Authentication Dial-in User Service) protocols for dial-in access. A Sidewinder specific SNMP MIB supports the standard SNMP MIB II, enabling users to monitor Sidewinder from an SNMP network management station.

In December 1996, Secure Computing introduced version 4.0 of its third generation firewall server called *BorderWare Firewall Server,* which it acquired with the acquisition of Border Network Technologies. The BorderWare Firewall Server runs on a single standalone PC and functions as a black box; no source code is available so that it cannot be compromised. This advanced firewall has a hardened operating system consisting of a highly-modified kernel built from the ground up to ensure maximum security. By comparison, most firewalls use a stock operating system, such as UNIX or NT, which is vulnerable to security loopholes.

A secure operating system is essential to preclude vulnerability to attack. BorderWare FireWall Server 4.0 provides the combined security of packet filters, circuit-level gateways and application-level gateways to prevent a security breach. It features dual homing, which means it has separate logical circuits and security software for both the protected network side and the Internet side of the firewall to isolate the protected network from the Internet. Separate kernel-level packet filters exist on each interface, eliminating the need to wrap packet-filtering routers around it.

The filters automatically are configured as features are enabled or disabled. IP forwarding is disabled in the OS to prevent security breaches. Packets can only be exchanged between networks using a proxy agent. Source routing and ICMP redirects are disabled in the kernel, which considers source-routed packets to be insecure since their source can be disguised.

A BorderWare Firewall Server can be configured either locally or remotely, an important feature for administrators with geographically dispersed networks each connected to the Internet via a BorderWare Firewall Server. A network administrator can configure a remote firewall server by connecting to the Internet and, using a browser such as Netscape Communications Corp.'s Navigator, access a BorderWare Firewall Server on the Internet.

A Java configuration applet is automatically downloaded via HTTP from the server to the administrator's computer, which the administrator uses to configure the accessed firewall server. Java is platform independent and, therefore, runs on any computer. Access to the firewall server is protected and requires the use of a dynamic password authentication scheme, such as Enigma Logic's DES Gold or SecurID. (Enigma Logic was recently acquired by Secure Computing.)

Virtual Private Network (VPN), featured with Version 4.0 enables users to set up a secure private network using the Internet as a backbone. This provides substantial savings over the cost of multiple leased lines. Multiple user sites can be attached to the VPN, each via a firewall. The VPN safeguards data passed between user sites through public key encryption compliant with RSA-based encryption and includes the Data Encryption Standards (DES), triple DES, and RC5 encryption standards. Key to this feature is IPsec, an IETF standard, which automatically negotiates the encryption scheme to be used between the source and destination.

By using the IPsec standard, the BorderWare Firewall server can communicate over the Internet with any vendor's firewall that implements the IPsec standard. Secure Computing currently supports encrypted data over 56K-bps or T1 connections but plans to enhance this in the future with T3 connections.

The BorderWare Secure Server Net (SSN), another strong feature of Version 4.0, provides a solution to businesses that want to place services on the Internet, but want to secure these services with full firewall functionality. The advantage to this feature is that it supports any application server. The SSN feature, implemented by adding a third interface to the firewall, which isolates servers from the Internet, enables businesses to deploy any number of TCP/IP servers that provide application services. Secure Computing is the only firewall vendor which implements this unique solution.

BorderWare Version 4.0 also provides users with enhanced auditing and logging functions. Users can track Internet access, time, and transfers and can also obtain and create reports for chargebacks and tracking.

Trusted Information Systems (TIS) Inc. of Rockville, MD, developed its firewall, Gauntlet, based on its popular Internet Firewall Toolkit. Gauntlet Version 3.2, a second-generation firewall, employs a hardened UNIX or Windows NT operating system. Gauntlet's base operating system has been modified to disable IP forwarding, ICMP redirects, and source routed packets. It provides both packet-level and application-level filtering. While other firewall vendors take a black box approach to firewall design, TIS has taken a "crystal box" approach, meaning that its source code is distributed for assurance reviews by its customers, resellers, and other experts.

The crystal box approach offers some advantages; however, the system administrator must have significant UNIX or Windows NT and TCP/IP knowledge to administer the firewall. Gauntlet features dual homing and makes use of software proxies to isolate the internal network from the Internet. It also provides network address translation between the proxy address and internal network IP addresses to prevent knowledge of internal host and server addresses. Gauntlet's proxies support the following services: telnet, rlogin, FTP, SMTP & POP, HTTP, Gopher, X Window System (X11), Printer, and Remote Execution (Rsh), and for Sybase databases from Sybase, Inc. Proxies for RealAudio, which allows audio to be received from the Internet, and SQL*Net are optional. A proxy also acts as a patch panel for simple services in a one-to-one or one-to-many configuration. Through this plug gateway, Gauntlet supports Finger, Usenet News (NNTP), and Whois.

Java Guard, when activated by the network manager, blocks all Java and JavaScript code from crossing the firewall during an HTTP session, preventing an attack on the protected network using Java-coded programs.

Gauntlet prohibits Sendmail from running as a privileged process, since it is an unsecured service. Instead, Gauntlet provides an SMTP proxy which runs on an SMTP server on the firewall and gathers incoming mail. Sendmail is run as a nonprivileged process to parse addresses and to determine how to deliver mail. Gauntlet can be configured to act as a Post Office Protocol (POP) Version 3 access point for external users who want to access their e-mail via the Internet standard.

The use of an authentication server and authenticated circuit gateway enables the firewall manager to configure certain plug gateway services for availability on a per user basis after user authentication via security tokens or one-time password mechanisms. Additionally, Gauntlet functions as a secure server for Domain Name Service, Internet email, anonymous FTP, and HTTP.

Gauntlet supports transparent access of external connections for internal users, who can connect to outside systems using all permitted services through the firewall.

Gauntlet provides both Virtual Private Network (VPN) and Virtual Network Perimeter (VNP) functionality. As a VPN, it supports firewall-to-firewall IPsec-based encryption using the DES 56-bit scheme. A VNP is a network that appears to be a single protected network behind firewalls, which actually encompasses encrypted virtual links over untrusted networks.

The administration of all Gauntlet firewalls is performed from a central site using Gauntlet's enhanced GUI, which contains a standard HTML browser.

The Gauntlet PC Extender software option is for mobile users and telecommuters. It provides secure networking using the 56-bit DES encryption from a PC to a Gauntlet firewall, from the PC through the firewall, and from PC to PC. It runs on Windows 3.1 and Windows 95.

Firewall server characteristics are compared in Exhibit 1.

SUMMARY

The meteoric migration to the Internet by companies who want to use the medium to conduct their business has spawned a new business opportunity for network vendors — that of securing private networks from unauthorized access through the unprotected Internet. Passwords and packet filtering alone cannot prevent attacks on network resources. Outsiders can access and control a network through Internet TCP/IP protocols.

These protocols open the door to numerous security risks. Internet firewalls have evolved to counter these risks, securing networks from attacks through the Internet. A growing number of vendors now offer firewalls. No two are the same or use the same approach to network security. Each must be evaluated on its own merits.

Users should consider the following guidelines for firewall selection. Select a firewall that provides a circuit-level gateway to totally isolate a network from the Internet. It should also provide an application-level gateway, which examines each packet of data to safeguard an intranet from viruses and other forms of attack.

A firewall should also provide a secure (hardened kernel) operating system to prevent attempts for seizure and control. It must secure all internal network addresses from outside knowledge of them to prevent IP spoofing. User authentication using an authentication technique, such as Enigma Logic's DES Gold or SecurID, is essential to prevent network penetration by unauthorized persons. Encryption is necessary to set up a Virtual Private Network between firewalls over the Internet. However, a firewall that does not use IPsec for a VPN is not interoperable with other vendor firewalls. Message auditing, logging, tracking, and reporting aid network administrators in securing a network.

A secure server network connected to a firewall interface enables users to isolate their application servers from the Internet. Firewalls should also be easy to use through user transparency and GUIs. Simplified central management is essential to ease of management. Performance is also a key issue. Firewalls that limit network performance will cause users to circumvent them. All of these issues must be carefully weighed when evaluating a firewall to select the firewall that best meets the needs of the user.

Exhibit 1. Firewall Server Characteristics

Vendor/ Product	Platform (minimum)	Architecture	Kernel	Key Features	Authentication Schemes	Price/ Availability
Checkpoint Software Technologies Firewall-1 V2.1	Intel 486/Pentium; Sun Sparc or HP workstation; 16 MB RAM; 10 MB hard drive & NIC	Stateful Inspection (no circuit or application level gateway)	Windows NT; SunOS V4.1.3; Solaris 2.3/2.4/2.5; HP-UX 9&10	VPN encryption (DES); authentication; network address translation; auditing and logging	SecurID and S/Key	$4,990 (50-node LAN); $18,900 unlimited license; encryption module: $2,990/available now
Raptor Systems/Eagle V4.0	Sun Sparc, HP, or IBM RS/6000 workstation; 32 MB RAM; 1 GB hard drive; & NIC for Ethernet, Token Ring, or FDDI	Application-level gateway only (no packet filter or circuit-level gateway)	Windows NT; Sun OS V4.1.3/4; HP UX V9.0x; AIX V3.2	VPN DES & RC2 encryption; authentication; centralized management tool and GUI; suspicious activity monitoring w/alarms & reports	SecurID, S/Key, and CRYPTOcard	UNIX: $7,000–25,000; NTServer: $6,500–15,000
Secure Computing Corp./ BorderWare V4.0	Intel 486/Pentium; 16-32 MB RAM; 500 MB hard drive and NIC	Packet filter, circuit and application level gateways	Secured BSD UNIX	VPN– IPsec-based encryption- DES- 56 bit, triple DES, and RC5; authent-ication; Java-based remote config;tool; auditing and logging tool; Secure Server Net; Multiple Address Translation	Enigma Logic DES Gold, CryptoCard, and SecurID	$4,000–16,000/V4.0 available now

Vendor/Product	Hardware	Firewall Type	OS	Features	Authentication	Price
Secure Computing Corporation/Side winder 3.1	Pentium; 32 MB RAM min.; 2 GB hard drive and NIC	Circuit and application level gateway (no packet filter)	Secured BSD UNIX	VPN– IPsec-based encryption- RC4-40 bit, RC4-128 bit; and DES 56 bit; Type Enforcement; authentication; JAVA Applet filtering; E-mail filtering; auditing and logging tool; 4 network interfaces; Multiple Address Translation	CryptoCard, SecurID, ActiveCard, LOCKout DES, Digital Pathways Securenet Key	$6,900–29,900
Trusted Information Systems/Gauntlet V3.2	Intel Pentium P100; 16 MB RAM; 1.0 GB hard drive; 2 Ethernet NICs	Application level gateway (no packet filter or circuit-level gateway)	Windows NT; BSD/OS V2.1; Sun/OS V4.1.3/u3/4; HP-UX and other OS platforms	VPN- IPsec 56-bit DES; transparent access; supports all std. proxy servers; network address translation; Java Guard; auditing and report generation; alarms	SecurID, S/Key, SecurNet, CryptoCard. DigiPass, and Enigma Logic DES Gold	BSD/OS, Sun/OS, or HP-UX-$11,500/ available as of 9/96

Section V
The Voice Network

Chapter 15

Voice Network: Communications with the Sky-Is-the-Limit Versatility

Bryan Pickett

INTRODUCTION

For decades the voice network has been the bedrock of enterprise communications, determining much of the efficiency with which co-workers communicate with one another as well as the first impression received by outside callers.

The voice network is still the bedrock, but it is demonstrating a lot of exciting new abilities that boost productivity, make companies appear more receptive to callers, simplify employees' lives, and make the whole enterprise more effective. These new features rest on the digital technology that has taken over the private branch exchanges (PBXs) and key systems that provide telephone service within enterprises. Digital technology, built into voice switching and access fabrics, gives them the same kind of sky-is-the-limit versatility that it gives to data networks.

In fact, the two networks, voice and data, are increasingly cooperating in various tasks, further boosting the organization's effectiveness and the level of customer service it delivers.

Much of the bridging is done over a computer–telephony integration (CTI) interface, which is frequently used to integrate data operations with voice applications. Examples include a call center operation that retrieves customer files and presents them to customer service agents along with incoming calls, a voice-mail system that transfers recorded messages into data storage and then retrieves them for presentation in the voice format. Other CTI examples include a messaging system that combines presentation and retrieval of voice, fax, and e-mail messages; a desktop program on the PC that allows workers to make and receive telephone calls via keyboard or mouse commands; and a voice response unit (VRU) that collects customer commands on a keypad, then passes that string of commands, such as account number, to a call center agent.

THE VOICE NETWORK

A voice network serving an enterprise and owned by it can be thought of as similar in structure to a data network, consisting of five basic elements:

- **Servers** These one or more switches—PBXs or key systems—and perhaps adjunct applications software or processors handle specific tasks such as automatic call distribution and interactive voice response.
- **Clients** These telephone sets or terminals may vary widely in their features and capabilities. Although the switch serving them is probably digital, the telephones may be digital or analog (i.e., they may accept voice signals from the switch in either digital or analog form). Newer terminals might be PCs with telephone cards and software that provides a graphic user interface.
- **Local network fabric** The means of transmitting calls within the enterprise. This fabric may include copper, fiber, or radio links operating at rates from 56K bps up to T1 (1.5M bps) or even higher. In addition, the fabric may incorporate various network architectures (both voice and data may travel over the same links); various network protocols such as Integrated Services Digital Network (ISDN); and computer–telephony integration.
- **Wide area network (WAN) fabric** This is the means of transmitting calls outside of the enterprise or from one campus or location to another (often shared with data transmission). It may include the public switched telephone network (PSTN) and actual or virtual private networks (VPNs), operating at rates from 56K bps up to gigabit-per-second synchronous optical network (SONET) rates.
- **Network management** This involves network administration and maintenance, including provisioning of lines, troubleshooting, routine diagnostics, security, fraud detection, and traffic and performance monitoring.

An enterprise also may obtain voice services similar to those provided by such a private network from the local telephone service provider. This type of service, which is called Centrex, is provided by full-scale switches and facilities that are owned by the local exchange company (LEC) and are part of the PSTN. Centrex service emulates the features available from a private network. With this type of service, only the clients reside on customer premises. The servers, local and wide area access, and network management are the responsibility of the LEC, perhaps working with an interexchange carrier (IXC).

SERVERS

The heart of an enterprise private voice network is the switching system. This is normally a key system for smaller organizations or a PBX for larger ones.

Key systems typically serve just a few employees, beginning with two or three incoming lines, to several hundred employees with over 100 incoming lines. Key systems and PBXs share lines among extensions rather than providing an incoming line for each extension. Sharing is possible because not all employees will use their phones simultaneously; however, the number of lines should be carefully engineered to the number of users. Systems must be designed and sized to prevent incoming or outgoing calls from being blocked for lack of capacity, taking into account such parameters and events as maximum call length, busy day and busy hour, and disposition of call trafficking (intraoffice, interoffice, and incoming and outgoing call traffic.)

PBXs typically overlap with the upper range of key systems. They may handle only a few dozen incoming lines and fewer than 50 users at the low end; at the high end they may serve up to 50,000 users with several thousand incoming lines.

Smaller PBXs or key systems may be networked together or to a large central PBX to provide voice service among different buildings on a campus. This enables a very large organization such as a manufacturing or an office compound or a university or a hospital complex to have a single inbound number and presents a uniform interface to outside callers. The outlying buildings may be miles apart or spread around a city.

PBXs and key systems provide significant benefits in addition to a single inbound enterprisewide phone number. They enable employees to use a uniform dialing plan and dial one another within the enterprise with just four or five digits as well as to share trunks for both local and LCD services. They also provide uniform software-based calling features such as call forwarding, conference calling, caller line identification, and voice messaging, along with uniform access to these features.

How PBX traffic is handled is shown in Exhibit 1.

BASIC SYSTEM COMPONENTS

PBXs and key systems contain three major elements:

- **Terminal interface** This is composed of the line cards that terminate lines to individual extensions; trunk cards that terminate incoming PSTN or private trunks; miscellaneous service cards such as tone

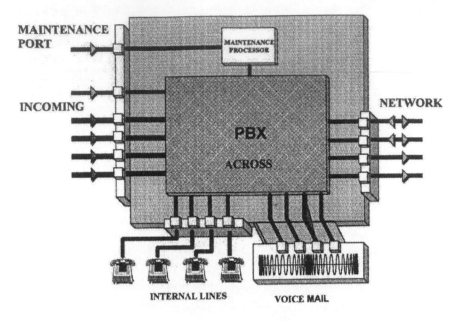

Exhibit 1. PBX Traffic

generator cards that generate dial tone, rings, and busy signals; and special announcement cards that play recorded announcements when activated by a call.

- **Switching fabric** This is the hardware and software that switches conversations between various terminal interfaces within the enterprise or between individual extensions and the trunks. Digital PBXs use the same technology as central office switches, called time division multiplexing (TDM) for converting analog voice signals into digital signals for transmission either to the central office switch or to another location. (The standard voice channel in public and private networks in North America is 64K bps.)
- **Control complex** This is the central processor and memory; it includes the software, which controls the operation of the switch. This control complex may also include adjunct software packages that perform various applications.

The switch may be linked to other switches in the enterprise network or to the PSTN by T1 lines or by ATM transmission, most commonly at 155M bps.

FITTING THE SYSTEM TO THE ENTERPRISE

PBXs and key systems should be carefully sized to fit the enterprise and provide room for growth. They should also offer features that match the needs of the specific enterprise. The five chief factors affecting the fit are

- **Configuration**   The particular types of software are loaded into the system, including operating software, feature packages, and other software specific to a given brand, model, and software release. The configuration may include software for particular applications.
- **System capacity**   This involves the number of calls likely to be made and the ability of the system to handle all calls even at peak hours. Systems do not usually have one line per extension, to save on expense, but should be designed for virtual nonblocking—in nearly all circumstances, no caller in or outbound should ever get a busy signal.
- **Processor speed and capacity**   The processor speed controls how quickly the PBX or key system can process requests for service, such as call connection; feature activation; and advanced applications such as automatic call distribution (ACD), messaging services, and network call routing.
- **Memory**   This should be adequate to serve operation requirements, system features, and individual features such as individual speed calling lists and personal directories.
- **Hardware**   The physical size of the system must be adequate to handle all the line cards, memory, and processing needed for the enterprise.

Each of these factors should be examined to ensure that a key system or PBX will successfully serve the enterprise. Together, they comprise the features and applications that can be provided or supported by the switch.

FEATURES AND APPLICATIONS

The primary tasks of the PBX or key system are to:

- **Route** incoming calls to the desired extension—or increasingly to the desired party anywhere on or off the premises
- **Convey** calls made by employees either within the system or out onto the enterprise private network or the PSTN
- **Provide** features that enable employees to handle calls effectively and efficiently

Digital PBXs and digital key systems typically offer hundreds of features that help companies and employees handle calls at the desktop, starting with basics such as call hold, call transfer, call forwarding, conference calling, speed dialing, and last number redial. (See the section on clients later in this chapter.) Some features may be represented by dedicated buttons on the telephone set; others can be accessed through programmable buttons or special codes interpreted by the PBX or key system. In addition, PBXs and key systems typically give each extension dual line appearances. Although an extension is in use, the switch can route a second call to it, the new call appearing as a call waiting indicator on the telephone set. The user can put the first call on hold and answer the second.

PBXs and key systems can usually work with caller ID to present the caller's number and often name on the telephone display screen. This enables the user to manage calls even more effectively. Other call management features available on PBXs and key systems offer capabilities such as setting up call hunt groups. (If one member of a group or department is on the phone, an incoming call will automatically be routed to a *predefined answering location.*)

Employees are usually given access to personal directories, which may be based in their own desk telephones, programmed in the switch's memory, or—*with a CTI interface*—on their PCs. Some PBXs and key systems work with display phones to guide users through telephone features. Research shows that this visual aid significantly increases use of call management features, and thus employee efficiency.

Today's PBXs and key systems go far beyond personal call management from the desk. They also can provide applications such as interactive voice response, automated call distribution, and messaging services that enable organizations to manage calls more efficiently on an enterprisewide basis. Some of these applications may be provided by applications modules or processors, perhaps PCs, linked to the PBX, or they may be integrated software modules that are part of the PBX itself.

Automatic Call Distribution

ACD distributes calls evenly among a group of employees set up to interact with incoming callers for a specific purpose. Examples are catalog sales, taking reservations or orders, or answering queries. Perhaps the most well-known applications are large telemarketing operations, call centers, or help desks.

The applications of ACD are increasing. Companies are using ACD to handle tasks such as making appointments, responding to account or help desk queries, and managing inventory—any business function that receives a significant number of incoming calls with a specific purpose can benefit from ACD capabilities.

ACD systems may support anywhere from just a few agents up to over 1000 agents. The agents may be located in different buildings, served by the same PBX or by geographically dispersed PBXs networked together. The ACD applications usually work with caller ID, so customer records or simply names and phone numbers can be automatically presented to the answering agent. Agents can even work at home using a telephone set that is linked back into the central call center.

ACD systems can offer a number of features that keep incoming callers satisfied and prevent call abandonment. For example, the system can play announcements while callers are on hold, informing them about specials or the estimated time they can expect to wait. The systems can also act as automated attendants, allowing callers to choose to remain on hold or go to an interactive voice response system, a specific extension, or a voice-mail system. With sophisticated CTI connections, customers are identified using their phone number, and as they are on hold, they can be treated to specialized messages or menu choices suited to their "customer profile."

Callers typically respond well to having a choice about how their individual calls are handled, and, of course, an associated interactive voice response system may well serve for many routine queries. Thresholds can be built in to the system to minimize delays while on hold or to divert calls to alternate queues, ensuring that no one waits too long. Alternatively, some companies may want to allow customers to leave a message instead of holding for long periods as a way to improve customer service and decrease 800-line charges. This increases customer satisfaction. ACD systems may also capture calling numbers for later callback if callers do hang up.

These systems can generate a variety of real-time and comprehensive historical reports that assist in call and call center management. For example, they can typically document busy hours and numbers of calls as well as calls answered, average time in queue, number of calls handled by individual agents, duration of time spent on each call, and number of abandoned calls. Such reports help managers to ensure that the right numbers of agents are available to handle calls. Managers can even reconfigure the call center in real time by linking in selected additional agents from other departments or locations to handle a sudden influx of calls. They can also correlate data, such as time spent on calls and sales generated, that may help supervisors measure effectiveness.

Customer-Defined Routing

Basic ACD systems manage calls like a queue at a bank—they allocate calls, in the order of arrival, to the next available agent or answering device. More advanced systems offer a variety of skill sets that work with an ACD system and caller ID or dialed number identification system (DNIS) to allow specific routing instructions to control the destination of individual calls, while still pooling ACD resources to ensure the most efficient use of all resources.

For example, the ACD system can give priority to long-distance calls, emergency calls, or calls to certain numbers—which is useful if, for example, preferred customers are given a specific number to dial. Calls to certain numbers (DNIS) or calls from certain areas or those associated with specific customer numbers can be sent to targeted agents, allowing selection of destination by variables such as skill sets of the agent or fluency in a foreign language. Different classes of callers, such as wholesalers and retail customers, can be routed to different agents so they do not wait in the same queue.

One typical application is routing by a credit card company of calls from its regular, gold, or platinum card holders to different groups of agents. Or a utility company might give priority during a power outage to calls from certain organizations, such as a hospital, defined as needing uninterrupted service. Calls from the outage area might be routed to an announcement giving specifics of service restoration that could give an expected wait time. This empowers the customer to hold or call back—increasing their satisfaction and decreasing 800 number costs.

Time of day and day of week can also be factored into routing instructions. Weekend calls might be routed to the help desk designated to take them or routed to receive a recorded announcement. Agents need not even be on the premises. Those in remote locations can become integral parts of the same call center through seamless reporting, call routing, and management structures.

Links to the call center can be extended from the PBX or central office via ISDN lines, which combine two voice and one data channel on an ordinary twisted copper wire pair. This type of wiring serves most residences, small businesses, and desktops within an enterprise. The ISDN line permits the simultaneous use of the remote agent's telephone and PC. This solution is especially appropriate for telecommuters and satellite offices.

Interactive Voice Response

Interactive voice response (IVR) systems are another important way to handle incoming calls within a call center or separate from it. An IVR system may also be offered as an adjunct to the PBX or key system or as an associated server. These systems can handle many types of calls that do not require human intervention, for example, queries about account balances, order status, prices, and product specifications. Since such calls can consume a significant portion of the service representatives' time, the IVR system can boost an enterprise's effectiveness and stimulate the best use of its resources.

In addition, an IVR system can increase customer satisfaction because callers can use it to complete transactions rather than leaving a voice-mail message that requires a follow-up call. Well-designed IVR systems can also be used for more complex transactions such as fund transfers and the taking or confirmation of orders. IVR systems can also offer such capabilities as automated speech recognition. Callers can simply speak their requests. Additionally, IVR systems can provide features such as multilingual capabilities and links to a fax service to provide a written confirmation of the transaction to the caller.

Increasingly, the IVR system is being used as the gateway into the call center. All callers are questioned by IVR and attend to routine business before opting to speak with an agent. IVR applications can even be used to interface to World Wide Web servers so that a bill pay program created on IVR can be used by the Web server to reduce development time and costs.

Voice Mail

Voice-mail capabilities can also extend the flexibility of the voice network. Voice mail can enable inbound callers to accomplish their business more easily and enable callers within the enterprise to work together more effectively.

Voice-mail systems now available go beyond simply recording messages for later playback. They also have the ability to act as an auto attendant, provide custom call routing, and offer additional messaging features such as priority notification and capture of calling numbers. If the caller tags a message as priority, for example, the PBX or key system may put it at the head of a queue of waiting messages and play it back first.

The system can also direct the recipient's telephone to indicate the presence of an urgent message. If the recipient is away from the office, he can direct that all messages with "urgent" tags be forwarded to another extension, an off-premise phone number, or a pager. Messages can also be forwarded after being heard to one or multiple extensions. Users can also direct the PBX or key system to send messages after them. Systems will try up to five different telephone numbers in sequence or automatically activate a pager.

To personalize handling of incoming calls, some voice-mail systems allow users to set up guest mailboxes for specific customers or clients; the users can personalize messages for specific clients. These mailboxes are linked to incoming numbers delivered by caller ID.

Key systems also provide automated attendant service through the voice-mail system, during or outside of business hours. Callers can be routed to their choice of extensions or individuals or to an operator. Outside of business hours, the system can continue to answer the phone and play announcements. Some systems can also reroute calls according to a programmed sequence if the dialed extension is busy or route incoming calls to specific extensions according to instructions defined for certain exchanges or incoming numbers.

Unified Messaging

PBXs and key systems may also help users manage voice, fax, and e-mail messages. Adjunct systems can enable users to handle voice as well as e-mail messages and faxes on their PCs, select both oral and written mes-

251

sages to be heard now or saved for later, direct selected voice messages to a phone, view entire fax or e-mail messages on the PC or just their beginnings, and manage messages in other ways. Users may send faxes from the PC to one or to many recipients and leave information in mailboxes to be faxed in response to customer inquiries.

Faxes and e-mail messages may be stored separately from voice mail to prevent voice mailboxes from being filled with written material. Unified messaging systems can also integrate voice calls with dialing via PC-based directories.

Adjunct servers may also support data services—even including multimedia conferencing—that travel over the Internet or other high-speed data networks to be delivered by the PBX to the user's desktop PC. Applications may be developed using the Microsoft Windows Telephony Application Programming Interface (TAPI) or Novell's Telephony Server Applications Programming Interface (TSAPI).

Personal Directories

Some systems also allow users to create personal directories that are stored in the system memory or in an associated PC accessed through a CTI interface. Such directories can contain names, phone numbers, and addresses of important contacts or customers, and information that people want at their fingertips, such as parts numbers or prices. Typically, the user pushes a button on the phone to bring the directory up to the display and then scrolls down to find an entry or, alternatively, keys in the first few letters of the name desired. Setting up directories can be made easier with the use of templates that are provided by some systems.

Wireless Service

PBXs and key systems also can support in-building wireless systems that allow employees to move around the building and still make and receive phone calls. The wireless system may be integrated with the PBX or key system so that calls to the user's regular desk phone extension are either routed to the wireless phone simultaneously or forwarded if the desk phone is not answered. Users can employ features such as call forwarding, conference calling, voice mail, call transfer and others. These wireless systems can work with Caller ID, so users can identify who is calling. They may also use a CTI link to access customer records, which appear on an associated PC or server, or access a corporate directory so they have telephone numbers at their fingertips while they roam.

The adjunct wireless system usually employs radio base stations throughout the premises, even including outdoor areas, such as a sales yard or walkways between buildings on a campus. Some systems cooperate with the public wireless carrier network so the same phone will be used by employees within the building and also outside as they are traveling.

Centrex Service

Some companies choose not to operate their own switches but obtain PBX-like features from their local telephone service provider. Such service is called Centrex, and it is delivered from the service provider's central office (CO) switch, which is part of the PSTN. Desktop call management features are to a great extent comparable to those available from a PBX or key system. For example, users can forward and transfer calls, set up a conference call, and see multiple line appearances. The central office switch may not, however, offer all features available in a PBX or key system.

Nonetheless, there are advantages to Centrex service. The enterprise does not need to get into the business of running a phone system, bear the capital costs of purchasing its own PBX or key system and lines and trucks, or dedicate space to the system. The LEC may be able to extend additional capacity when needed more easily than the enterprise can upgrade its private switch.

However, PBXs and key systems tend to have more features and capabilities, such as unified messaging, in-building wireless service, and extensive ACD and CCR options. Moreover, they tend to move more quickly with the times and technological developments than central office switches, so they offer more state-of-the-art features.

CLIENTS

Telephones for key and PBX systems range from simple units with one incoming line to complex sets with over 100 incoming lines that serve receptionists and call center operators. Sets may offer just basic capabilities or hundreds of features. Many now have screens and liquid crystal displays.

General Purpose Telephone Sets

General purpose sets range from the very basic to sets with a broad variety of features. The most basic—suitable perhaps for lobbies, cafeterias, warehouses, and other locations where people do not require many call management features—may have only one incoming line, a few features such as conference, transfer, call forward, and a few programmable buttons that can be set to dial extensions (e.g., security or front desk automatically).

Stepping up from this basic level, sets may have more programmable buttons, speakerphone, call timer, liquid crystal display, well over a hundred call-management features, personal directories, and additional call appearances. These more feature-rich phones may maintain a roster of the last incoming and outgoing calls, especially if the set works with caller ID to capture names and numbers of external callers. Names and extensions of internal callers are routinely displayed. With some phones, to return a call, the user just scrolls through the list of incoming calls and pushes a button.

Displays can range from a one-line alphanumeric screen that delivers simple messages such as "message waiting" or the number of the caller to a multiline display capable of delivering instructions on how to use various call-management features or presenting directory or call roster listings.

Telephone sets are also available for a wide variety of special purposes, such as call centers, operator or attendant consoles, and positions where a particularly smart phone is desired. ISDN hookups and links to PCs can also be incorporated into phone sets.

Call Center Sets

Sets designed for call centers may have displays that present a caller's name and other identifying information, allowing a personal greeting; jacks that accommodate the user's choice of headsets; dual headset jacks so supervisors can coach attendants; language options so information is available in the attendant's own language; and adapters that link the set to a PC or other server so customer files can be associated with calls.

Attendant Consoles

The attendant console should help the attendant guide calls through the organization efficiently. Sets designed for this position typically feature high-volume call handling, large directory, message center capabilities or links, and perhaps dial-by-name capabilities. These sets usually show line appearances for many or even all phones in a department or enterprise and indicate which one is busy.

ISDN Telephones

An ISDN set typically allows the user to link the phone to a desktop PC and make use of the two ISDN B-channels and perhaps the D-channel as well. The phone–PC link allows the user to carry on voice and data calls simultaneously, perhaps sharing data with a colleague, customer, or supplier while discussing the file.

Intelligent Telephones

Performance-oriented phones may help boost the productivity of busy managers and executives. These phones may offer aids to efficiency such as context-sensitive feature appearances—instructions or features appear only at the time they may be needed. For example, the option of transferring or forwarding a call only appears on a screen when the user is answer-

254

ing or on a call. An intelligent phone may also provide prompts and icons that guide the user through voice mail options.

Wireless Telephones

Wireless sets served by a PBX or key system through an adjunct wireless system can offer a wide range of call management features as well as data adapters and liquid crystal displays.

PCs and Workstations

Desktop PCs and workstations can be served through the PBX with the addition of a communications adapter that links the computer to a telephone via built-in RS232 or V.35 interfaces. These adapters can eliminate the need for dedicated data facilities, since data can be carried to the desk over standard telephone wiring. Adapters are also available that work with ISDN protocols.

LOCAL AREA ACCESS

The access fabric is considered to include both media for transporting signals and protocols for encoding them.

Media in a voice network may include both copper and fiber cabling as well as microwave and radio links. Wiring to the desk in the voice network is traditionally copper twisted pair; this is still a viable option even if broadband applications are delivered by the PBX to the desk. Twisted pair can carry hundreds of megabits per second of bandwidth. Fiber installed to the desk or floor may also carry voice along with data traffic. Microwave links are typically used in large private networks that traverse considerable distances and carry both voice and data traffic.

Radio links usually support digital wireless communications. They may operate according to various protocols, including code division multiple access (CDMA), time division multiple access (TDMA), or wavelength-division multiple access (WDMA). Some systems interwork with public digital wireless networks, which typically use either CDMA or TDMA.

Wiring architectures usually include the star design sometimes found in data networks. There are usually direct runs from the main distributing frame collocated with the PBX or key system or from intermediate distribution frames located in equipment closets on each floor or in other areas throughout the premises. The intermediate distribution frames are connected to the main frame by backbone risers.

Increasingly, voice networks may share facilities with data networks, and increasingly those networks include fiber capable of carrying very high transmission rates. It is not uncommon for very large enterprises to handle voice traffic over local area network (LAN) backbones operating at SONET rates of hundreds of megabits per second or even gigabits per second.

As transmission media are changing, so are transmission formats. Historically, PBXs and key systems have used the circuit-switched time division multiplexing (TDM) format employed in the PSTN, formatting signals into 64K-bps bit streams. These 64K-bps streams were usually multiplexed into a 24-channel 1.5M-bps signal, so that voice calls could be fed directly into that network. Now, however, as public networks are incorporating different types of transmission rates and protocols, some PBXs and even key systems are being equipped to interwork with systems and networks operating with those rates and protocols. Rather than just a single-purpose access fabric dedicated to the TDM format, these systems may have fabrics capable of handling signals in a variety of formats.

Some protocols and transmission rates, finding a place in the enterprise voice network, are asynchronous transfer mode (ATM), which is cell-switched and *usually* operates at 155M bps; circuit-switched SONET rates into the gigabits per second; and ISDN protocols. These operate from 128K bps up to 1.5M bps; and even from traditional data formats and speeds such as 16M-bps Token Ring, 10M-bps Ethernet, and Transmission Control Protocol (TCP)/Internet protocol (IP).

ISDN can provide great versatility, and it already uses the standard TDM 64K-bps increments. The basic service, called basic rate interface (BRI) provides two 64K-bps channels that may be used for voice or data, perhaps linking a telephone and PC. An additional low-capacity data channel, called the D-channel, may sometimes be used for control and signaling or even data transfers. PBXs and key systems may be able to supply ISDN bandwidth in 64K-bps increments up to the primary rate interface (PRI) limit of 1.5M bps, a full DS1 signal. This is enough capacity to accommodate many wideband applications such as multimedia, high-speed file transfer, or videoconferencing.

PBXs may also provide interfaces or buses to LANs operating under standard protocols such as Ethernet (10M bps), Token Ring (16M bps), and perhaps even fiber distributed data interface (FDDl [100M bps]). These interfaces work with a CTI interface (see later) to link data files and transactions to voice calls.

Perhaps the most important trend is the changeover that is beginning from circuit-switched to cell-switched transmission. Many enterprises are building cell-switched ATM networks to handle all traffic, including voice, data, and video. Voice over ATM is probably the direction of the future for the public network, stimulated in part by the trend to ATM for private enterprise networks, and ATM switches are being marketed for central offices. To be compatible with both public ATM networks as well as internal

256

ones, some PBXs are already equipped to interface with ATM or frame relay switches.

ATM switches are usually employed as edge switches, sitting at the edge of a local enterprise network and interfacing with either a public network or dedicated or virtual private circuits to an enterprise's other locations. ATM transport is becoming justifiably popular because of its tremendous capacity and because it can handle all kinds of traffic in any combination—voice, ISDN, video, fax, and all data formats. It gives the network manager the greatest flexibility.

Adjuncts to PBXs can consolidate all types of traffic and convert them to the cell-switched ATM or frame relay format. Among the features ATM systems offer is the ability to prioritize voice calls which cannot afford latency delays in transmission that are inherent in a cell-switched format. Eventually, this consolidation function will move directly into the PBX.

CTI Interface

A key part of a PBX or key system access fabric is likely to be a CTI interface, which links the phone to a PC, workstation, or server. This link is useful in a wide range of applications such as call centers, desktop videoconferencing, messaging, and wireless systems.

CTI interfaces may automatically identify a caller's telephone number, using caller ID or automatic number identification, and retrieve pertinent files from the PC or server. In call centers, they can work with ACD systems to bring up files while calls are being routed to call center representatives, enabling them to access a caller's account history, greet the caller by name, and transact necessary business immediately.

Having a customer's file available also enables businesses to deliver very personalized service. For example, a hotel or restaurant can offer to provide the same type of room or table the customer had on a previous visit, or a medical office can present a receptionist or nurse with a patient's file so the individual can immediately schedule an appointment or verify test results.

The CTI interface is also involved in linking messaging systems with a PBX, helping the system to bring faxes, e-mail, and voice mail together into one unified presentation. It is also an integral part of desktop videoconferencing, again linking the PC to the PBX, which handles the voice call. In addition, this interface may be used in wireless systems, allowing users to call into their home base to retrieve faxes or direct them to a nearby fax machine for printout.

WIDE AREA ACCESS

Wide area access links one location to another within a corporate private network or links the location or private network to a public local or long-distance network. It is similar to local area access, using the same formats and media, and it is following the same trends, particularly the change to cell-switched ATM transport.

Companies may establish dedicated private networks or virtual private networks (VPNs) that use public facilities. Economics may favor one or the other, depending on the amount of traffic between any two given sites. Typically, a public carrier will operate a "cloud" or backbone network, on which it sells a certain level of capacity as a virtual private network, perhaps with occasional higher levels permitted when demand soars (think of the first day of sales to popular concerts).

Either type of network may make use of switched facilities operating at rates from DS1 up to SONET gigabit levels. Voice signals may also travel over cell-switched ATM or frame relay facilities. WANs may also transmit voice via data protocols such as TCP/IP, for example, in the nascent trend to voice over the Internet. With the use of this technology, voice may also begin to be sent over corporate intranets.

NETWORK MANAGEMENT

Tools are available for many PBXs and key systems that give network managers a wide range of capabilities. Specific tools are available from various third-party vendors, or a comprehensive group may be available from the switch vendor itself. A comprehensive package from the vendor may make the management job simpler by working from the same database as the switch and by giving a unified picture of operations. Tools may employ an intuitive graphic user interface or commands based on strings of alphanumeric characters.

Management tools may handle tasks, including station management, call accounting, traffic and performance management, alarm management, call tracking, and maintenance.

Station Management

Station management includes configuration of phone sets, programming them with features and assigning directory numbers or terminal numbers for single or multiline sets, and adds, moves and changes. Station management tools may offer shortcuts, templates that can be established for configuring phones with features needed by specific groups of employees or job categories such as receptionist or salesperson. Then the manager simply calls up the template to provision a given phone. This is much easier than keying in commands to provision each feature on each phone. The tools may also offer options such as a menu of all available numbers or an automatic assignment of numbers. With some tools, station changes can be programmed off-line and then executed instantly, reducing downtime for users.

Call Accounting

Call accounting includes call detail recording, generation of call accounting reports, and toll fraud management. A call accounting package may record call details such as call duration, ring time, call frequency, and total use of phone by extension. It may also manage notification of certain alarms, perhaps even going down a list of phone numbers, including voice, fax, pager, and modem, to reach a system administrator. Alarms may be set to indicate when conditions are reached that may indicate security has been breached and fraud is present, for example, an unusual number of calls to a certain geographic area or from a given extension or department. Any such alarm may be continuously presented on a graphic interface.

Call detail recording can help telecommunications departments bill back phone charges to individual departments or help the company contain costs by generating complete reports that track phone usage, especially for long-distance calls. Call accounting programs can create and graph customized reports that include or exclude information such as date and time of call, cost, authorization code, and other criteria as desired.

Traffic and Performance Analysis

These tools report on usage of network resources such as trunks and network loops. Their analyses help the network manager monitor operations and detect problems before they affect service. Some tools also allow the manager to play out various scenarios for adding capacity or reconfiguring the network and to simulate their effects.

Alarm Management

These tools manage and report alarms, perhaps in graphic format. They may prioritize and sort alarms and set alarm thresholds. They can also create a log of all system events; summarize major, minor, and critical alarms; indicate when an alarm is being worked on; and filter alarms so only those needing action are brought to the attention of management personnel. Many PBXs now offer a Simple Network Management Protocol (SNMP) connection to the data network that allows a company to use one unified network management system to monitor all voice and data nodes in its network.

Call Tracking

Call tracking tools monitor calling patterns in part to detect fraud. They can deliver a wealth of information about how the voice network is being used to help forecast future needs and ensure that the current network is being used as efficiently as possible. For example, these tools can track the number and duration of calls to specific areas or countries, indicating when dedicated trunks might be an economy measure. They also can identify unusual calling patterns that might indicate toll fraud—unauthorized usage of a company's transmission facilities.

Maintenance

Maintenance tools provide information on the status or hardware and perform diagnostic tests. These tools may enable network personnel to identify individual hardware units such as line cards or trunks that are causing problems, run diagnostic tests, and enable and disable these devices.

The management tools may reside on a PC or workstation with a graphical user interface, and link to the PBX and other network elements via TCP/IP–Ethernet links or other protocols.

SUMMARY

The direction of voice networks in the future is already clear from the trends cited. Perhaps the most monumental are the changes in transport from circuit switched to cell switched. These primarily use ATM systems; the incredible versatility enabled by computer–telephony integration interfaces the extension of high-end features into even relatively small key systems, increasing involvement of the PBX or key system in a broad variety of operations, particularly those involving data.

Chapter 16

Planning a Cutover to a New Voice System

Thomas Osha

INTRODUCTION

Did you know that today, roughly 80% of a company's business is conducted using some form of telecommunications?

Your business communications systems are among your company's most vital tools for success. They are the critical link to your customers, suppliers, and employees. The companies that will succeed in the future marketplace are those that can take charge of existing and emerging technologies to gain a competitive advantage in their respective fields.

Because we rely so heavily on telecommunications for the majority of our business communications, it is imperative that our business communications systems be as productive as possible. The better the telecommunications system operates, the greater its ability to support the success of your business.

In many organizations, it is the network manager who is responsible for the operation, maintenance, and administration of the telecommunications systems and peripherals. And, because a company's telecommunications systems are such a crucial element of its operations, this position takes on increased significance and visibility anytime critical changes such as a major upgrade, addition, or the cutover to an entirely new system are undertaken.

This chapter will provide you with the insight and methodology necessary to plan and execute the cutover to a new voice communications system in a smooth and seamless manner without causing communications interruption or confusion in your organization.

Although this chapter focuses primarily on large scale voice systems, the planning elements and implementation checklist can be modified and applied to many types of communications installations.

0-8493-9990-4/99/$0.00+$.50
© 1999 by CRC Press LLC

IMPLEMENTATION BEGINS BEFORE THE SALE

Large scale voice systems are not impulse purchases. They are purchased for a reason; usually to satisfy a need, provide an application, or enable a company to communicate with its customers in a new way. In short, at the heart of the buying decision lies the business problem which prompted the need for a new voice system in the first place. Whatever the need: to interface with a voice mail or voice response system, to establish a call center, or just to handle routine calls in a more efficient manner, a successful implementation depends upon solving this underlying business problem as well as having a smooth cutover.

To ensure success, you should be as much a part of the buying cycle as possible. Even if you do not have the authority to specify, recommend, or approve the vendor or the model selected, as the future administrator, your input is valuable, but more importantly, the more you know about the system and its reasons for being purchased, the better equipped you are to smoothly implement the system.

For large scale telephone systems such as PBXs (private branch exchange), the purchase cycle is usually governed by an RFP (request for proposals). This document acts as a guide for fair comparisons among systems from different vendors. At its heart is a set of questions and conditions that represent the buyer's business problems and communications requirements. The vendor must answer these questions in the body of their proposal. Thus, in many ways, a well written RFP can function as a blueprint for your early implementation efforts.

Contained within the RFP response from your vendor of choice will be answers to many of the technical questions we will consider later in the chapter as well as descriptions of the system's features and design. The RFP and its corresponding response can be very useful in developing timelines and checklists for the project as well as serving as a guide to the original business problems and communications solutions.

IMPLEMENTATION KICKOFF

Once your organization signs a contract to purchase a new telecommunications system, the clock starts ticking. The contract generates a due date, which is normally 30 to 120 days (depending on system complexity) from the date of the contract. In this time, you must coordinate and direct the activities of a myriad of players, including: voice system vendor, local phone company, long distance vendor, building management, and system peripherals vendor.

In many cases you might also have to deal with: wiring contractors, electricians, architects, and software applications vendors. And, all of this coordination must be accomplished with great diligence. If even one detail is forgotten or late, the entire process can fall like a row of dominoes.

The best way to ensure that the literally hundreds of steps and details necessary to implement a new voice system are completed on time and in the proper order, is to hold an implementation kickoff meeting as soon as possible after the contract is signed. This meeting should bring together every vendor who will have a part, no matter how small, in the implementation as well as any employees of your company critical to the process.

As the project manager, you will lead the group in the two most crucial tasks to a successful cutover — the development of an implementation timeline and the assignment of roles and responsibilities to each of the participants. The Implementation Checklist (Exhibit 1) represents the four common phases of a voice system implementation and the required elements in each phase. This checklist is the focal point of the implementation kickoff meeting. With each of the vital participants present, all of the critical tasks can be assigned, from ordering and provisioning the network to the day of the cut activities.

As each task is assigned to a vendor or to a member of your staff, the number of days needed to complete the task should be estimated. Since many tasks can affect subsequent events, the order and timing of completion is important. For example, the long distance vendor is unable to test their service until the local telephone company finishes installing the trunks. But the local phone company cannot terminate the local trunks until the wiring contractor has finished installation of the cross connect field. However, the wiring vendor cannot finish the cross connect until the building management has completed the equipment room. Looked at in this light, it is easy to see how bottlenecks can occur and how projects can get behind schedule.

By developing an implementation timeline (Exhibit 2), all participants know their role and where their tasks fit into the implementation plan. Each person is now responsible for keeping their tasks on time so as not to jeopardize the timely completion of the project. In fact, many organizations include in their purchase agreements with vendors severe penalties for missing crucial deadlines.

After the initial meeting, you should hold weekly status meetings until the final week when they are held daily. These meetings serve to keep you informed of everyone's progress toward meeting their deadlines, as well as exposing any difficulties early enough to be dealt with before becoming major obstacles.

Let's look at the critical elements of the Implementation Checklist more closely and examine their importance to the voice system cutover.

Exhibit 1. System Cutover Implementation Checklist

Task	Responsibility
Contract accepted	Vendor/Customer
Floor plans obtained and marked	Vendor/Customer
System order transmitted and scheduled	Voice System Vendor
Network orders placed	Local Telephone Company
Customer kickoff meeting	Customer/All Vendors/Others
Equipment room requirements to customer	Voice System Vendor
Customer switch admin. training scheduled	Voice System Vendor
Customer adjunct training scheduled	Voice System Vendor
Software kickoff meeting	Customer/Voice System Vendor
Department coordinators training	Customer/Voice System Vendor
Station reviews	Customer/Voice System Vendor
System network trunking reviews	Customer/Voice System Vendor
Develop revised order (if required)	Customer/Voice System Vendor
Install wire	Wire Vendor
Equipment room preparation	Customer
Voice System materials arrive/inventory Technicians	Customer/Voice System
Install and test switch	Voice System Technicians
Install and test adjuncts	Peripheral Equipment Technicians
Initialize adjuncts	Peripheral Equipment Technicians
Install cross-connects	Wire Vendor/Voice System Techs
Print button labels	Voice System Vendor
Install and test sets	Voice System Technicians
Build System Master Disk	Voice System Vendor
Set-up Users training room	Voice System Vendor
End-user training	Voice System Trainer
Install trunks	Local Telephone Company
Integrated system test	Voice System Technicians
Cutover meeting	Customer/All Equipment Vendors
Cutover system	Voice System Technicians
Help desk	Customer/Voice System Vendor
Trouble resolution Technicians	Customer/Voice System
Remove old system	Voice System Technicians
Security review	Customer/Voice System Vendor
Post-cut meeting, if required	Customer/All

ORDER AND PROVISION NETWORK

As soon as the contract for the new voice system is executed, (which will result in an order for the system's various hardware components), you should begin working with your local telephone company account executive and long distance carrier account executive to start the network design and provisioning process.

Network trunks are your voice system's link to the outside world. Local trunks deliver dial tone and allow you to make and receive local calls. Inter-

Exhibit 2. System Cutover Implementation Timeline

Task	Duration
Contract Signed	0 days
Kickoff Meeting	1 day
Order & Provision Network	28 days
Equipment Room Preparation	10 days
Equipment Room Ready	3 days
Customer Switch Administration Training	10 days
Peripheral Administration Training	10 days
Station Reviews	1 day
System Ordered	0 days
Build and Ship	15 days
Install and Test PBX	5 days
Install and Test Peripherals	5 days
Install Cross Connects	1 day
Install and Test Sets	1 day
Install Trunks	5 days
End User Training	3 days
Cutover	1 day
In Service	1 day
Help Desk	1 day

exchange trunks carry long-distance traffic and inbound 800 number calls. There are also trunk lines which carry high speed data communications, link multiple voice systems together, or enable video applications. The number, type, and design of your system's trunking facilities will depend upon your organization's communications needs and business goals.

Your local telephone and long-distance account representatives have methods for studying your organization, determining the proper network elements, and engineering trunking and routing plans that fit your applications and communications needs.

Properly designing and provisioning network trunks for a PBX can be a complicated and time consuming process. Beyond just studying and analyzing your calling patterns and volumes, the local phone company will need to ensure that it has sufficient facilities running from its central office to your premises; and in the event that it does not, creating them.

On average, you should allow at least one month for trunk facilities to be designed, engineered, and installed. In certain cases, (i.e., moving into a newly constructed building where no previous trunk facilities existed) you may want to allow up to three months for this process. Even if you are staying in your present location, the cutover to a new voice system presents an excellent opportunity to review your current network resources, call volumes, and calling patterns.

EQUIPMENT ROOM PREPARATION

One of the keys to a successful cutover and an easy to administer, maintain, and expand, voice system is the timely completion of a well designed equipment room. Design and construction of a suitable equipment room is usually handled by the customer and can be your organization's most important contribution to a successful implementation.

Beyond just providing floor space for the PBX hardware, the are other factors which must be considered and will have an impact on the future operation of your system. While it is true that telecommunications equipment has gotten smaller and more forgiving in terms of its environmental requirements, smart planning is still required to prevent cutover delays and allow the equipment to perform to its fullest capacity.

Talk to any voice system vendor and you will learn that the majority of horror stories about installations gone awry revolve around the equipment room dimensions and environmental factors. Stories abound about rooms that are too small to hold the hardware or doorways too narrow to fit equipment through. One vendor showed up for a cutover and found a well designed equipment room — on the third floor of a building with no elevator. Another installed a PBX only to find that every day at 11:30 a.m., the PBX would shut down. It turns out the equipment room shared an electrical circuit with the lunch room. At lunchtime employees would begin using all six of the cafeteria's microwave ovens, causing electrical overload to the PBX.

Carefully researching the PBX's technical requirements contained in the RFP response and working closely with your vendor's technical support staff can prevent these types of costly and embarrassing mistakes. Here are some common technical considerations when constructing an equipment room:

ROOM DIMENSION

Besides just housing the PBX, your equipment room will probably need to serve other functions like providing system administrator workspace, room for storage of extra phones, and housing peripheral equipment. Plus, at some point, you may need to expand, upgrade, or add other application hardware to your system. All of this will require additional space.

Most typical PBXs are housed in cabinets the size of a common refrigerator. The number of cabinets is determined by the size and complexity of the system. The RFP response or your vendor will be able to tell you how many cabinets your system will have. But unlike refrigerators, PBX cabinets have doors on the front and back. Therefore, the cabinets must be positioned to allow for a clearance of about four feet front and back to enable access from both sides.

Basically, the equipment room should be large enough to hold twice the number of cabinets in your system, which leaves room for expansion; large enough to provide four feet of clearance front and back, which gives technicians access to the hardware; plus large enough to provide extra storage space for equipment, manuals, and other necessities. The room should also be large enough to comfortably accommodate three to four people working simultaneously.

ELECTRICAL REQUIREMENTS

As a sensitive piece of electronic equipment, your PBX will need a dedicated, reliable, clean source of power. Most PBXs require a dedicated 120 volt, 208 volt, 220 volt, or 240 volt circuit. The type of service is determined by your cabinet size and configuration. This circuit cannot be shared by any other equipment, cannot be controlled by a wall switch, and must be properly grounded. In addition to the PBX cabinet, are system administration terminals, remote access modems, and other miscellaneous pieces of equipment that will require common 110 volt circuits. It is advisable to install double the number of required outlets, and two additional 20 amp circuits to give you flexibility and expansion capacity.

Again, the RFP response and your vendor will be able to provide details about the power requirements of the telecommunications system and associated equipment. It is a good idea to check with every vendor, including your local telephone and long distance vendors, to ask about their power requirements. Many times data equipment, trunking equipment, and monitoring equipment have their own specific electrical requirements.

In critical installations, (hospitals, public safety, call centers), uninterrupted power supplies (UPS) and battery backup units are commonly installed. These units provide constant power levels to critical equipment in the event of a brown-out or total power failure. If a UPS system is part of your installation, remember to plan room to house the batteries which, depending on size and configuration, can be substantial.

Finally, be aware most PBXs and even some peripheral equipment do not use standard three-pronged electrical connectors. Most PBXs require special connectors and matched wall receptacles. It is advisable to have a professional electrician review your power requirements to ensure that you have the proper type and number of circuits, outlets, and connectors.

267

FLOORING REQUIREMENTS

Fortunately, as telecommunications systems have become smaller and lighter, the load distribution element of equipment room planning has largely become obsolete. Gone are the horror stories told of some unfortunate network manager who would install a four cabinet PBX on the first floor on Friday and come to work on Monday to find it sitting in the basement.

But, the one flooring issue that must be taken into consideration is electrostatic discharge (ESD). A PBX, like any piece of sensitive electronic equipment, is very susceptible to static electricity. Sudden discharges can frequently overload and burnout circuit cards in the PBX. Since circuit cards can cost from $1000 to $5000, depending on the type of card, ESD is a serious concern for network managers.

Fortunately, with some basic equipment room planning, ESD can be neutralized. The major cause of ESD is carpeted floors. Therefore, equipment rooms should be designed with concrete or linoleum floors to reduce the buildup of static electricity. Additionally, many equipment rooms will have static discharge mats inside each door. These mats pull the static electricity out of your body as you step from a carpeted surface onto them. With a little planning, an equipment room can safely be located in a variety of office locations providing that they have proper freight elevator service and meet the other room conditions discussed in this chapter.

SECURITY CONCERNS

For network managers, security has become a watchword of the 1990s. As telecommunications have become increasingly vital to an organization's operations, they must also be vigilantly protected from deliberate and accidental tampering.

Tightly controlling access to your equipment room is the most effective way of preventing physical security problems. Studies have shown that over half of system security violations are perpetrated by employees or others working inside the organization.

One of the more common security concerns stems from the ability of PBXs to transfer calls from an incoming set of trunks to an outgoing set of trunks. This feature can be useful in specialized remote access applications. But because of the danger of having outsiders use this feature to call into your system, then transfer to an outside line, which in effect becomes an unlimited "free" long distance line for the hacker, this feature is rarely enabled in most PBX installations.

However, there have been numerous reports of malevolent employees who, unbeknownst to the network manager, gain access to their company's equipment room and activate this feature for their own purposes; thus putting the PBX in danger of major toll fraud abuse. Unfortunately, this behavior is more common than one might think and instructions for enabling this feature on most models of PBX can be found on almost any internet site devoted to hacking. Restricting access to your PBX and peripheral equipment drastically reduces your exposure to malicious acts by insiders.

Another reason for limiting room access to only selected individuals is to maintain control over changes to your system or its components. These kinds of problems are usually caused by well meaning vendors whose technicians may make changes to the system during repairs or routine maintenance, then leave without telling the network manager what work was done.

This can result in problems in resolving cases of trouble or making feature changes. In most PBXs there are features which can counteract other features. If a technician activates one set of features, and the network manager unknowingly activates a different set of features the resulting compatibility error can take time to identify and correct.

To prevent this situation, establish a clear procedure for gaining access to the equipment room with all persons affected: your staff, facilities management, security, and each of your vendors. It is best to have the technician gain access to the room through the network manager. That way work to be performed can be discussed and the technician can be made aware of any special applications or unusual configurations in your PBX.

However, if there is such a room access arrangement, there should be two backup points of contact in addition to the network manager, such as a facilities manager, or a security manager. These individuals can give technicians room access to make important or emergency repairs in your absence. But they should always instruct the technician to leave you a note or voicemail describing the repairs or changes made.

Another physical security concern to take into consideration when designing an equipment room is handling fire suppression. A fire in your equipment room can destroy your PBX, cripple your business, and, of course, put your employees in danger. Therefore, the smallest hint of fire needs to be dealt with immediately and effectively.

Unfortunately, the sprinkler systems in use in most organizations today can do almost as much damage to a PBX as fire and are less effective against electrical fires. Therefore, most large equipment rooms install fire suppression systems that use halon gas instead of water to extinguish the fire. A halon system uses halon gas to displace the oxygen in the room, effectively smothering the fire. Once the fire has been extinguished, fresh air is pumped into the room and restoration work on the system can begin.

Halon systems are very effective, but because they are designed to remove all of the breathable air in a room, there are strict rules and codes regulating their installation and use. In some systems, warning lights and sirens are used to alert employees working inside the room to a fire condition, giving them a certain amount of time to leave the room before the gas discharges. Also, safety switches can be installed allowing employees to shutdown the system and prevent the gas discharge if necessary. These measures prevent employees from becoming trapped in the room and suffocating when the breathable air is removed by the halon gas. There are also regulations governing the airtightness of the equipment room, periodic inspection of the system, and the procedures for aerating the room after the system has been activated.

Most smaller equipment rooms with only one or two PBX cabinets may not need such a sophisticated fire fighting system. In this case, several fire extinguishers rated for electrical fires and placed in the proper positions around the room will suffice. Always be sure to check with your local fire marshall regarding the correct fire suppression system for your municipality and building category.

ENVIRONMENTAL CONCERNS

Although we have stated that today's PBXs are more forgiving in terms of environmental factors there are still some factors to take into consideration when designing your equipment room. As in the other parts of the building, heating, ventilation, and air conditioning (HVAC) also are important in the equipment room. Even though most PBXs have their own cooling fans, they are still susceptible to heat buildup in certain circumstances. The temperature threshold of a modern PBX can range from 50 to 85 degrees. Once the room temperature exceeds these thresholds, abnormalities may occur in the operation of the PBX or its adjuncts.

These "gremlins" sometimes can be extremely hard to locate and diagnose. Most telecommunications technicians cite examples of a PBX that misroutes or loses calls occasionally. The customer calls the repair center and the technician is dispatched. He arrives to find the network manager in the equipment room trying to find the problem.

They work for several hours trying to locate the problem. Meanwhile the PBX is operating normally. This situation is repeated several times, until one day the technician happens to be in the area and drops by to check the problem. He/she and the network manager enter the equipment room together, and find the temperature over 95 degrees. The technician realizes that whenever the network manager would enter the room, he/she would prop the door open to relieve the stuffiness. By the time the technician arrived, the room had cooled and the temperature had returned to within the threshold and the "gremlins" had disappeared.

To avoid this type of problem, install adequate heating, ventilation, and air conditioning to keep room temperatures at the same levels as the remainder of the building. Another environmental element that can cause problems for telecommunications systems is dust. As dust is pulled into the PBX cabinets by the cooling fans, it settles on circuit boards and can interfere with connection points between circuit boards.

Equipment rooms should be kept as dust free as possible. If possible, the room should be constructed without windows, without carpeting, and the air filters on the ventilation ducts supplying the room should be changed frequently. These measures should greatly reduce the amount of dust buildup. If you do notice dust in your system, do not use rags or dusters to clean electronic equipment. A can of compressed air can rid your equipment of dust without damaging fragile components or subjecting you to the risk of electrical shock.

One final environmental element that can easily be overlooked is lighting. Because the room is designed to hold equipment, architects usually do not spend much time planning lighting beyond a few fluorescent or incandescent fixtures. However, a PBX is composed of hundreds of very small circuit boards, cable connectors, and other components. When the network manager or system technicians are working on the cabinets, they often will need to be able to see in some very small spaces. For this reason, it is recommended that your equipment room be as well lighted as possible. A good equipment room lighting plan will include numerous fixtures, well placed to provide bright and even lighting throughout the room as well as moveable spot lights, used to see inside of cabinets and other small spaces.

BUILDING WIRING

Once the equipment room is completed, your wiring contractor will need to complete the plan for connecting each user's telephone to the PBX. This is usually accomplished through the use of a cross connect field between the PBX and the in-building wiring scheme. Generally, a cross connect has two sides, the port side and the station side. The port side represents each of the telephone ports in the PBX, and the station side represents each jack in the building. A phone is then connected to the system by a wire jumper running from the station side of the cross connect to the port side.

The type of wiring from the station side to each telephone will depend on several factors; the distance from cross connect to telephone jack, the type and function of the telephone set being used, and the type of wire needed. Early in the implementation process, you should arrange a meeting between your PBX vendor and your wiring contractor to discuss the system wiring requirements, size of the cross connect field, number of wire runs, quality, pairs of wires in each run, and jack type (RJ11, RJ45, etc.). They should also determine the number of port side cables that will run from the cross connect to the PBX cabinet.

Many successful network managers use these guidelines when designing a wiring scheme:

- To allow for future growth and flexibility of your voice system, you should design a cross connect field at least thirty percent larger than what you currently require.
- When calculating the number of wire runs, be sure to include several for the equipment room for phones and for testing purposes.
- When it comes to wire quality, always buy the best you can afford. Most PBXs require category three, four, or five wire. The better the wire, the more resistant it is to interference and the more flexibility you will have in the future.
- The same theory also holds true for the pairs of wires in each run. The more pairs in each run, the more flexibility you have for connecting phones.
- For instance, analog phones require a one pair wire run and digital phones require two or four pairs depending on the model. If you install one pair wherever you plan to place analog phones, those jacks will never be able to be used for any other type of phone.
- But if you install four pair runs everywhere, you can plug any type of phone into any jack and be assured of it working. A slightly larger investment up front can pay huge dividends later on when you upgrade phone sets, add new capabilities, like voice over data or video to phone sets, or reconfigure your office environment.
- Also, work with your wiring contractor to determine if the present wire can be reused in an existing building or in a new construction require wire to be installed before the drywall work is completed. These two steps can drastically reduce wiring costs.
- Finally, require that the cross connect field and each jack be clearly and understandably marked. This simple step can save time and money when future changes are needed or equipment is added.

SYSTEM ADMINISTRATOR TRAINING AND SUPPORT

Because it is so powerful, a PBX is also a very complicated piece of equipment. In most large organizations, one person is identified as the system administrator — the person with day-to-day responsibility for managing the telecommunications system. Several organizations also see this job as an extension of the network manager. Familiarity with personal computer interfaces and being comfortable with technology are two keys to being a successful system administrator. For this reason, network managers do make good system administrators.

The most crucial tool for success for whomever fills the position of system administrator is solid training on the voice system and all associated adjuncts. All major PBX vendors offer system administrator courses for their customers, covering the entire range of system capabilities, programming options, and maintenance and troubleshooting. The perfect time to attend this training is before the cutover, not after.

The more knowledgeable a system administrator is about the system, its design, features, and capabilities, the more valuable they are to the implementation project and especially the cutover day activities. A system administrator who is trained and "up to speed" prior to the cutover can be proactive, recognizing and heading off problems before they arise and can threaten a smooth cutover. A system administrator who is not trained can only rely on the knowledge of others and is purely in a reactive mode as problems arise and resources must be diverted from cutover activities to deal with them.

Beyond PBX training, you should attend training classes on as many of the system's adjuncts and peripherals as possible before the cutover. Depending on your system configuration, you may also need to attend training classes on the voicemail system, voice response system, call management system and software platforms like call accounting and contact management. Your equipment vendors can help you identify and register for the proper classes.

After you have been to the necessary training classes you should meet with your equipment vendors to plan the ongoing administration of the voice system. Duties such as routine maintenance, programming changes, moving users, running system reports, and simple troubleshooting are all commonly handled by the system administrator. The vendor provides technical support, advanced troubleshooting and repair, and upgrade and enhancement notification and installation.

You and your vendor should create a schedule of administrative activities to keep the system running smoothly, a set of escalation procedures that provide the system administrator vendor support for complicated maintenance and repair functions, and a vendor point of contact for receiving information about future upgrades and enhancements. Finally, both the vendor and the system administrator should identify an individual to serve as backup in their absence. This ensures that important activities and emergency repairs can take place when you are on vacation, at a conference, or otherwise unavailable.

STATION REVIEWS/SYSTEM PROGRAMMING

At the same time as the hardware elements are being planned, you should begin working with your voice system vendor to plan the software programming of the system. The system programming controls how the PBX handles calls, provides features to the users, and performs other functions.

In all but the smallest PBXs, the system programming and user setup is actually completed before the hardware is installed. This is accomplished by compiling all of the user profile and system programming information in a database, and using it to create a system configuration master disk. The process of creating this master disk is informally called conducting station reviews.

The station review is your opportunity to gather the information needed to program the system to meet each user's individual needs as well as setting overall system attributes. The station review is conducted by the system administrator and the PBX vendor. Using a station review form, (Exhibit 3), each user is interviewed to determine their communications needs and establish the features and functionality that will form their profile.

Exhibit 3. System Cutover Station Review Information Required

- User name
- Voice terminal type
- Extension number
- Call Pickup Groups
- Coverage Paths
- Fax/Modem/Off premises extension requirements
- Hunt Group information
- Voice terminal configurations (i.e., button assignments)
- Night service requirements
- Speed calling list information (i.e., who gets personal lists, who gets group lists, numbers for system list)
- Provide information on long distance network requirements (i.e., 800 numbers to be tested, configuration and specifications of long distance and local trunks)
- System parameters information (i.e., trunk-to-trunk transfer, call forwarding off-net, preferred feature access codes)
- Marked floor plans including extension number, set type, jack location
- ARS pattern information (call handling and routing information)

For each user, the following comprises their profile:

- Personal information — user name, office location, telephone set location, extension number, and telephone set type. In situations where the new voice system is replacing an older one, the previous extension numbers can usually be retained. Telephone set type is usually determined by a corporate standard determined by level in the organization or functional needs.
- Call answering information — call pickup groups, coverage paths, night service. Today's sophisticated PBXs have the ability to deliver calls to users in a variety of ways. Call pickup groups allow several

users to answer each others calls from any phone. They are useful for sales and support functions where several users cover for each other. Call coverage paths are the instructions which dictate where a call will go when it is not answered at the called station. When the called station is busy or does not answer, the call will ring at other selected stations. For instance, if a user is not at their desk, then a call for them would next ring at their secretary's phone, and if he/she was unavailable, the call would be directed to voicemail. Each user can have their own coverage path depending on their needs and personal preference. For systems where calls are first answered by a receptionist, night service enables calls to be delivered in another manner after hours or when the receptionist is unavailable.

- Button assignments — buttons can be customized for a user's individual preference. Combinations of call appearances, features buttons (redial, call forwarding, etc.), speed dial, or user programmable buttons can be set. Speed dial buttons can be set by the administrator for system wide use (branch offices, security, other commonly used numbers), or left to be programmed by the user.

The system profile comprises the following:

- Call routing — calls can be delivered over trunks in a variety of ways. Different long distance carriers have different rates at different times of the day. Intelligent routing in the PBX can deliver long distance calls over the most economical service depending on call type. There is also routing information that needs to be programmed to deliver 800 number calls to the proper destinations; sales, service, etc. If your PBX is part of a larger network of PBXs or uses private lines dedicated to your company, these need to be identified in the system programming. In short, the PBX must be told the number and kinds of trunks it has and what to do with incoming or outgoing calls on those trunks.

- System security — in the same manner that physical security in the equipment room is important, so to is it necessary to safeguard the system software from unauthorized use. Password protection should always be enabled on every system administration terminal and the password should be strictly guarded. Many PBXs have a password aging feature which forces the system administrator to change the password regularly, thus adding another level of protection. Toll restriction is another useful security feature. With the explosion of toll fraud committed against organizations, any ability that you have to limit your exposure to abuse should be utilized. Toll restriction features enable you to limit long distance calling access on a station by station basis. You may not want reception room phones to have any long distance access; you may limit conference rooms, break rooms, and other public areas to only 800 number access; and you may limit still other phones to only preapproved toll numbers (which can be programmed on a system wide

275

speed dial list). For employees who may gain access to the system remotely, either from home or the road, the monitoring and reporting features governing remote access should always be used. Regular reading of the remote access reports can discover abuse or hacking attempts. Some PBXs also have the ability to deny ports to certain phone numbers that originate unsuccessful or suspicious access attempts.

• System parameters — governs system wide features, report generation, and peripheral integration. A modern PBX is capable of delivering more than 200 features, a fraction of which appear on the users' phones. The remainder dictate how the system functions in different situations. Some features like, message waiting indication and send to coverage provide added functionality to all phones. Other features, such as dial plan definition and attendant routing define system operations. Still other features like hospitality service and shared tenant service are industry specific. And finally, features like trunk to trunk transfer and call forwarding outside the system pose some risks and should never be activated unless necessary and only then with security precautions in place. Because of the enormous flexibility of a PBX, you, with the help of your voice system vendor, have a broad range of system wide features to choose from to solve your business problems and meet your communications goals. System parameters is also where you select criteria for the system to conduct measurements and generate reports. In system administrator training you will learn the usefulness of traffic and threshold reports and how to use their data to keep your system running at peak efficiency. Finally, when adjuncts or other peripherals like voicemail or computer-telephony integrated workstations are present, the PBX must be told how to send and receive information from them. This allows several components from different manufacturers to operate as one seamless communication system.

INSTALLATION AND TESTING

Completion of the system master disk usually coincides with the arrival of the PBX hardware about one week before the cutover date. Once the equipment room is ready, technicians will begin installing the PBX hardware and any associated peripherals such as voicemail or a call management system.

Once the hardware installation is complete, each component is rigorously tested to ensure everything has been installed correctly, is working properly, and is communicating accurately. When the voice system technicians are satisfied the hardware installation and testing are complete, they will connect the PBX to the port side of the cross connect field and test those connections.

Next, phones will be placed on users' desks and in other specified locations. If there is a phone system already in place, the new phones will be placed next to the old ones. Tests are now run from the telephone sets to the station side of the cross connect field. Finally, when all connections are made and satisfactorily tested, the PBX is connected to the telephone company's line of demarcation; the point at which trunk service enters your building. Once these connections are established and tested, the voice system will be ready for the final cutover.

END USER TRAINING

At the same time that the hardware installation and testing is occurring, training sessions should be held for all employees on operating the new phone system. These sessions should last about 30 minutes and should deal with the basics of placing and receiving calls, what their new phone will look like and how it will work, simple features like hold, transfer, conference, send calls, and any specialized features specific to their workgroup or job.

Cutover day activities should be explained and all users should be given clear instructions on getting questions answered, problems resolved, and additional assistance in the first few days with the new system. It is also a good idea to give each user a booklet on how their model of phone works along with system wide information such as dialing instructions, group speed dial numbers, and how their coverage path works. These steps should alleviate noncritical calls to the help desk during and immediately after the cutover.

CUTOVER DAY

Once all of the hardware testing, trunk testing, and user training is complete, it is time to cutover the PBX. In many instances, this is done on a Friday evening after business hours to provide the maximum time for cutover and last minute modifications without affecting your business operations or inconveniencing your employees.

One set of technicians will begin to terminate the new trunks or redirect the old trunks on the line of demarcation and connect them to the PBX. The technicians then begin placing and receiving calls on all trunks, testing the lines and the PBX's call handling configuration.

Simultaneously, another set of technicians is activating each of the phones on the system. When each phone is connected, the technicians will restart the system using the system programming master disk. The system is now operating according to the information provided in the station review process. The user profile database also produces button labels for each phone set. These labels are installed and each extension is tested to ensure that its features match its station review profile.

The advantage of cutting a voice system at night or on a weekend is if any problems are encountered, they can be taken care of without affecting your business operations. And, the old phone system can be left in place for a few days, so that if a major service affecting problem surfaces, the trunks can be reattached to the old system preserving phone service until the problem is corrected.

When all technicians and the system administrator are satisfied that each segment of the new voice system is operating correctly and as designed, the local telephone central office releases the trunks and your new PBX is officially in service.

FIRST DAY ACTIVITIES

The first day of business operations under the new voice system is always a busy and exciting day for the system administrator and employees alike. As 1 users begin to use the new system and their new phone, small problems invariably surface. In most cases they are caused by mislabeled buttons on the phone, a user who has forgotten how to use a particular feature, or business needs that have changed since the station review.

To handle these problems and ensure that each one is corrected to the user's satisfaction, you should establish a help desk on your premises for the first few days under the new system. This help desk should be staffed by yourself, your backup system administrator, and technical support staff from each of your equipment vendors.

This group will be able to answer most questions that users have about how to use features in the system and on their phone. Programming changes and more complicated problems are placed on a "punch list." Technicians and the system administrator prioritize items in the list, (even in a midsize implementation the punch list can run several hundred, mostly minor items) and make the changes necessary to clear items from the list.

After a few days, or when help desk call volumes drop to almost zero, the help desk is closed and future questions are referred to the system administrator. Once the punch list has been cleared, the vendor support staff and technicians leave and the voice system is officially turned over to the system administrator.

GOING FORWARD

After you have officially taken charge of the voice communication system, you should immediately perform a system audit and backup. In a system audit you catalog every piece of equipment in your telecommunications system by recording the type of equipment, date of purchase, model and serial numbers, and vendor contact. You also record each system administration login ID and password for each system. Next record the circuit number of every trunk, remote access line, and the account codes of your long distance service. When you are finished, you have a document containing the specifications of each component of your telecommunications system. Now, anytime you need to troubleshoot a problem, talk with your vendor's technical support, or check for billing accuracy, you have all of the vital information in one place.

One copy of this document, minus the administration logins and passwords (which should be kept locked up when not in use), should be kept in a book next to the system administration terminal in your equipment room. Another copy, with the administration logins and passwords, should be kept in a secure place offsite or kept in a fireproof safe at your location. With this set of documents should be a full backup of the PBX translations. This is your disaster recovery kit.

As you have learned, installing the voice system hardware is only a small portion of a new system implementation. In the event of a major catastrophe — fire, flood, hurricane, destroying your entire system, the hardware can be replaced fairly quickly. But without the configuration and system translation information, reprogramming the system is a monumental task. Some vendors store your initial system master disk for use in such an emergency. But remember, the system master disk was made before the punch list changes were made, so you will still have some work to do before all system functionality is restored. Keeping a full set of system audit and backup information in a secure location can help you quickly recover from a major outage as well as more easily administer the system on a daily basis.

SUMMARY

The job of implementing and administering a PBX voice communications system is challenging and wide ranging. But, it helps to know that you are not in it alone. In many cities user groups have been established where system administrators can share information and ideas with each other, learn about enhancements and upgrades to their systems, and develop their network communications management skills.

During the implementation process, have your vendor register you for your local users group chapter and attend their meetings. You will probably gain valuable insight and learn how to avoid some problems that others have encountered, helping you to a successful implementation of your new voice communications system.

Chapter 17
Dealing with Telephone Toll Fraud
Ed Simonson and Jeff Dixon

INTRODUCTION

In the post-World War II eras, there was an explosive growth in the demand for telephones and long-distance communications services. Coin-operated telephones in the mid-1960s were targets of fraud. This illegal activity was perpetrated by the "blue box" of that era, a device that imitated the sound of coins dropping into the coin receiver. As primitive as this fraud was, the Bell system redesigned its coin telephone service to limit the effectiveness of the blue box. The race had begun. Hackers and "phreakers" (see p. 293) developed new tools, and the system responded with new controls.

In the late 1970s, stored program systems were introduced. The telephone industry was entering a new period, the age of the computer. Ultimately, this system became the largest computer ever built. Divestiture of the formerly regulated communications industry increased the speed of innovation. Judge Greene's Modified Final Judgment (MFJ) in 1984, which disbanded the Bell system, put technology and hackers on a high-speed collision course in the new community of Cyberspace.

Each innovation to increase revenue and service was followed by creative hacking that successfully exploited the system. This collision in 1992 occurred with a much publicized lawsuit between Mitsubishi and AT&T for a $1.5 million theft of service claim.

In the past seven years toll fraud has risen 1000%, making it a $5.6 billion a year industry.[2] With an average cost of $35,000 per occurrence, one can see the importance of telecommunications security. Long-distance carriers lose more than $3 million a day to toll fraud. The courts have decreed that whoever controls access to the network is responsible to the network for paying the bill.[1]

Today's technological innovations have gone farther than was ever expected when the Telecommunications Act of 1996 was passed. Voice over Internet Protocol (IP), proliferation of cellular phones, and computer–tele-

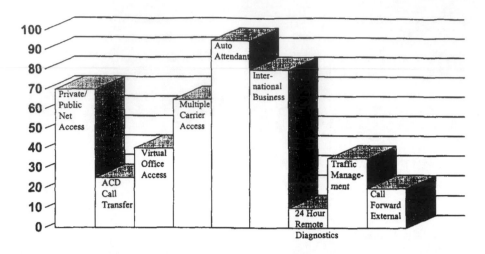

Exhibit 1.   Expense Model of Some Business Practices

phony integration, (CTI) to name a few, radically change the issues network managers have to understand managing their business.

With the integration of the computer and the telephone, opportunities for hackers and phreakers have increased tremendously. In addition, the business applications for which these networks are used also increase opportunities for hackers and phreakers. In pursuit of flexibility, network managers unwittingly open their network to hackers and phreakers.

CURRENT SITUATION

As we expand our communications capabilities and demands, new models for adapting to this growth have emerged. Rapidly changing business practices and philosophies such as virtual offices and telecommuting, coupled with the expansion of products being utilized, have changed the expense model (see Exhibit 1).

While total expenditures decreased, the percentage of the operating budget allocated to communications has increased, and corporate communication budgets are quickly reaching 5 to10% of operating expenses. With the expansion of network communications, increased attention is being paid to the laws surrounding this industry.

LEGISLATION AND LEGAL ENVIRONMENT

Prior to 1983, most communications service providers functioned as a natural monopoly and consumer protection was provided via federal or state tariffs. Under regulation, communication services were provided to end users via federal or state tariffs. The theory was that tariffs replace the natural controls of a competitive marketplace. The safety net formerly provided under governmental regulation has been eliminated through the 1984 deregulation of the telecom industry and the 1996 Federal Communications Act in the U.S.

Worldwide national telephone companies are rapidly privatizing. A deregulated telephone industry is bringing with it new opportunities and challenges. Competition dominates the U.S. market, and many services are now provided in a competitive environment. As a result, tariff law no longer protects consumers.

While as a nation we view competition with enthusiasm, consumers are discovering that the increase in business application choices is causing them to have less control of the process. The new responsibilities for network managers will be, in part, to establish the critical lines of communication throughout the company. This is no easy task considering the speed of technological advancements that seem to occur at a dizzying pace.

Cases have established a precedent for responsibility in contract law. The Federal Communications Commission (FCC) is responsible for providing rates and rules for the long-distance network. These have limited authority over the manufacture and installation of end-user equipment. The courts are building a body of case law that further separates toll charges and the customer owned and operated equipment.

Case Study

The case of AT&T vs. Jiffy Lube presented to the Communication Fraud Control Association by Mr. P. Coultier of AT&T, 1993.[3]

Facts—Jiffy Lube private branch exchange (PBX) with direct inward system access (DISA) was compromised. AT&T sued to collect $55,727.39 of outbound charges. Inbound calls were carried by MCI.

Jiffy Lube's contentions are

1. The calls originated at the computer hacker's location.
2. AT&T policy of holding customers liable is unjust because:
   a. AT&T fails to warn.
   b. AT&T is in a better position to implement control measures.
   c. AT&T failed to assist Jiffy Lube in tracking the callers.

Held—For AT&T:

"In arguing that the unauthorized calls originated not at Jiffy Lube's number, but at the unauthorized caller's number, Jiffy Lube ignores the fact that it created the vehicle and mechanism by which those long-distance calls became possible."

AT&T rules are not unjust and unreasonable practices under the Communications Act because such a conclusion would "...in effect, require AT&T to indemnify its customers for unauthorized calls and force it to absorb the costs associated with such calls."[2]

Note—Prejudgment interest at 8.15% compounded was awarded back to the date the charges became due.

TECHNOLOGY

Divestiture increased responsibility of network managers, making them accountable to their end users for growth and security. A few short years ago modems (modulators and demodulators) transmitted at the then dizzying speed of 300 baud over an analog network were distributed by copper. Now modems transmit as the modern PBX converts human voice into a digital signal and transmits both voice and data with equal deftness. The volume of information required when administering business applications on a modern PBX—with the new numbers, wireless, international access, and control of features and permissions—all too frequently resides in the ubiquitous Touch-Tone pad of an incoming caller.

The separate worlds of voice and data blur and disappear as we move into the year 2000 with mergers and acquisitions as in MCI with WorldCom Inc. and AT&T with TCI. Hackers have been holding discussions lately on their ability to obtain the public encryption key for the Data Encryption Standard (DES). An article printed by Reuters in June of 1998 has now confirmed this information. A researcher at Lucent Technologies Bell Labs has broken the standard encryption code used for electronic (e)-commerce, called secure sockets layer (SSL). By using a physical connection to a server computer operated by an Internet service provider, a hacker could send about a million carefully crafted messages to an e-commerce World Wide Web site operator, analyze the responses, and decode the message.

Today, 56K-bps Internet access is common from homes, and many commercial and government locations are connected via 1.54M-bps circuits distributed via fiber-optic digital services. This trend, coupled with the complex nature of today's networks, increasingly exposes a corporation to fraud.

REMOTE ACCESS THEFT (HACKING AND PHREAKING)

Any local area network (LAN), wide area network (WAN) or PBX system or network with its remote access or maintenance port and UNIX or C-based operating software is a prime target for manipulation and sabotage. With more service and technology comes more opportunity for illegal access to your system.

284

Every telecommunications system is a potential target for a hacker or phreaker. No manufacturer of communications systems develops and installs computerized systems that are impregnable to attack. Proactive attention to the potential loss must be constant and can control the severity of any hack.

When you select a PBX and implement that combination of business application features that best fit with your needs (i.e., Phonemail™, Call Detail Reporting (CDR), voice recognition, port security, access to 976 numbers), by nature of the flexibility built in to the system you create potential exposure to hacking and phreaking. More importantly, as the day-to-day changes are made, the overall design of the system is changed and creates further risks. The trade-off between security, convenience, and flexibility must be evaluated regularly.

Ultimately, it is the responsibility of all companies to configure their switch for security, monitoring, detection, and elimination of hacking opportunities. The changes initiated will need constant revision and updating. Cybercrooks live in a rapidly changing world.

WIRELESS

Wireless communication carries a special striking and unique niche in the domain of telephone fraud. All variations of wireless communication, by nature, are exposed through the airways. For instance, wireless transmissions yield to eavesdropping more than wire-based messages because they do not require a physical connection. The airways are public and available to anyone with the appropriate knowledge and equipment. Allegedly, General Manuel Noreiga was tracked down and arrested through the intelligence community's ability to monitor pager activity. Conversely, during Desert Storm the intelligence community was unable to monitor Sadam Hussein's command network because it was on a fiber network.

Changing frequencies, simplex one-way channels, and digital transmission help, but personal diligence is still required. With PBX wireless, the administrator must insure the company, and users' service interruptions and theft will be minimized. All wireless stations must have restricted classes of service that protect against unlimited access to your long-distance lines.

Examples of the compromise of wireless connections run from a prank to a theft of knowledge or information, a few of those that follow:

- Some hackers walk a residential street with a popular cordless telephone and flick the switch hook for dial tone; we will call that "walking for dollars."
- Others stealing the mobile identification number (MIN) and electronic serial number (ESN) from an analog cell telephone to place stolen calls.

- Some pranksters monitor the cellular network to eavesdrop on conversations.
- Others monitor the sideband signal at a microwave site to eavesdrop on private conversations. A University of California Regents meeting in 1995 was published in the *San Francisco Examiner* from a tape recording of the private meeting. The paper had received the transcript through a tape recording sent anonymously.
- Some hackers monitor cell telephone traffic to obtain voice mail and bank account passwords and access. Remember that analog conversations transmit dual tone multifrequency (DTMF) that is easily duplicated or recorded and then played back at the right time.
- PBX wireless sets pose two threats. The instrument may be duplicated by a third party disguised as an employee and used to gain access to your long-distance network. The conversation may be recorded, and the information may be used by thieves. A few years ago a picture was printed in the *National Geographic* magazine of the stock market in Turkey. The floor of the exchange uses many wireless and cellular telephones. The picture was of eavesdroppers outside of the exchange garnering illegal information by eavesdropping on trader information.
- Hackers reported in the *2600 Hacker Quarterly* that the SIMS chip in the European personal communications services (PCS) cell phone has been broken. They report that the security of the chip has been compromised, and they will monitor the PCS network.

This does not always work just for the hacker. For example, a well-known hacker, Kevin Mitnick, was tracked down and arrested by authorities using equipment that triangulated his cell telephone signal and led them to his location.

Wireless communications is a valuable business asset, and this segment of the industry market continues to grow. Such service has, for many people, become an essential part of our daily business and personal life. Attention to the security of the service and confidentiality of information exchanged over this medium should never be taken for granted.

RISKS[*]

Attacks on Department of Defense computer systems are an example of a serious and growing threat. The exact number of attacks cannot be readily determined because only a small portion is actually detected and reported. Defense Information Systems Agency (DISA) statistically reported data implies that defense may have experienced as many as 250,000 attacks in

---

[*] This information is reprinted from a report given to the Senate Select Committee on Intelligence, prepared by DISA and verified by a team of Pentagon security specialists as reported in 1998.

1996. DISA information also shows that attacks are successful 65% of the time and that the number of attacks is doubling each year, as Internet use increases along with the sophistication of hackers and their tools. At a minimum, these attacks are a multimillion-dollar nuisance to the government. At worst, they are a serious threat to national security.

The private sectors are faring no better. Independent studies indicate an explosive growth in intrusion with limited detection of the breeches. Theft of service includes "slamming" (the unauthorized changing of your long-distance carrier), clip-on fraud (physical intrusions and hard wire connections), traditional looping, and cellular or wireless eavesdropping. Network intrusion happens when and where it is least expected. The loss to the private sector has become so severe that the Federal Bureau of Investigation (FBI), which added this new category of crime to their national crime statistics, is now tracking the problem. The FBI and many local law enforcement agencies are providing electronic intrusion and remote unauthorized access to their agent field training.

Reports from industry sources state that $5.6 billion was stolen in 1996 from U.S. businesses. With at least the same level of growth in other countries, the problem is global and growing.

MANAGEMENT SOLUTIONS

There is perhaps no greater task for the network manager than the creation and acceptance of a viable communications policy. This policy must clearly state the acceptable use of company or departmental communications assets and the penalty for violating the policy deal with theft, damage, and fraudulent use of these assets. In addition, guidance must be given to departmental managers concerning purposes and expectations of these same outlets. A successful policy will have to address security or will always be in a reactionary, knee-jerk mode. With the reality of corporate funding, network managers need to make trade-offs. In most cases, they believe themselves to be trapped in a reactive mode and do the best they can. The reality, however, is that with a little investment in resources, network managers can begin to implement a proactive program.

Most reactive methods involve notifying the communications management team or the executive management team when a breech has occurred. The warning can come from internal reviews of call detail reporting (CDR) records or externally, from the carrier. The installation of a CDR system equipped with tracking software can be designed to warn management when calling parameters have been exceeded. Most long-distance carriers provide this service by monitoring traffic patterns and reporting changes in calling patterns.

The carrier records a normal traffic pattern for a given client and notifies the client when significant exceptions occur. Both methods alert the communication team of a possible intrusion to the system. Insist on seeing evidence that both your long-distance carrier and your local exchange carrier (LEC) will join your team. The carrier must have an adequate plan to identify theft of service and a client education program. The network manager has to then determine a solution quickly and make the corrections immediately with the carrier or carriers. Once that is completed and verified, it is time to assess the amount of loss, determine if there are any other exposures, and report back to management.

The proactive method is less painful, but it is tougher to get authorized because "there is no smoke"; however, it is much less costly by far in the long run to stop the hacker or phreaker before he gets into the system. By blocking access to system programming to reduce the threat of intrusion and then monitoring activity on a regular basis, the proactive network manager solves problems before they surface. This method also relies on the monitoring of the long-distance carrier and uses CDR after a thorough sweep of the software to ensure that the system stays clean.

By following a proactive method, the network manager is allowed to develop a plan to protect network assets. Experience has shown that network managers gain credibility for several reasons: First, they are well informed and knowledgeable about the issues, options, and risks with network security. Second, proposals for expenditures and strategies are debated on merits, not cost. Finally, with the support of upper management, network managers can take the steps necessary to protect not only their data networks, but also their voice systems.

The success from implementing this program is not necessarily seen as cost-reducing or revenue-producing, but as competent management of a valuable resource.

FIVE-STEP SOLUTION

The following is a proven five-step proactive solution for fraud prevention that is cost-effective and provides a road map for management of communications systems. This basic outline may be utilized as a framework for prevention and management control in today's environment. Neither this nor any other guide is a guarantee that a company will be immune to fraud.

The five steps are

1. Create, adopt, and implement a corporate telecommunications policy.
2. Review the software configuration of your current system.
3. Install an approved third-party device to stop unauthorized access.

288

4. Reprogram the system software to remove identified security vulnerabilities.
5. Establish a standard for system monitoring and conduct systematic review audits on a regular scheduled basis.

Step 1—Create, adopt, and implement a corporate communications policy. The most critical element is the backing and trust of upper management. Researching the issues and presenting a comprehensive policy to the officers of an organization places the network manager in the position of a valued and trusted employee. Obtaining upper management support for implementing a policy statement begins an education process to solicit organizational understanding of the concerns of running a communications system securely in today's environment.

Step 2—Review the software configuration of the current system. The business application of "user-friendly" features makes a telecommunications system vulnerable to hacker or phreaker attacks. Review the current software configuration to uncover security risks that may have crept into the system. Evaluate the specific business needs and design a level of service that fits the company policy and business requirements. This process will become a balancing act because security and service may be at odds. Thus, this is the reason for a policy on unauthorized remote access. Consult with a service provider and long-distance carrier because most service offerings may be offered in a secure fashion.

Step 3—Install an approved third-party device to stop unauthorized access. It is mere child's play for high-technology thieves to find and gain remote access to maintenance or administrative ports. A security device that blocks unwanted remote dial-up access is suggested for the system. The requirements for a protection device are that it allows the protected system to dial out to report trouble, does not auto answer with the log-in sequence of the protected system, is an approved device capable of working with the system supplier or system maintainer, and is able to allow access from many remote sites.

Disconnecting or not installing the remote device is not a viable option. A modern system automatically dials the specified service supplier and requests repair service, and 80% of trouble reports are cleared remotely. Some manufacturers routinely dial in to the systems that they maintain at night to perform automated routine maintenance.

Step 4—Reprogram the system software to remove identified security vulnerabilities. After completing the preceding business case, begin reprogramming the system. This process eliminates pre-existing security concerns and secures the system against future attacks. This stage of managing the system requires the implementation of system standardization and configuration management.

Step 5—Establish a standard for system monitoring and conduct systematic review audits on a regular scheduled basis. The only way to protect against Cyberspace fraud is to ensure that the proper safeguards are in place at all times. Due diligence means that the parameters established in step four must be maintained and monitored. All trunk information must be shared with your long-distance and local carriers. The carrier must be provided with a 24-hour call out list for emergencies. Staff must be provided with a list of supplier's numbers for around-the-clock assistance. CDR should be installed and the system configuration should be verified at least once a month to ensure conformity with the established benchmark.

THE FUTURE

One actively pursues a secure environment in the unregulated and unprotected world of Cyberspace. A colleague has suggested that unauthorized remote access and theft of service is the "AIDS" of the communications industry: "It cannot happen to me." The immediate past and the foreseeable future do agree. It can and will happen to anyone who is not protected. There is no silver bullet to protect anyone, but hard work and diligence will yield results.

Networks in today's environment are expanding rapidly. With the latest round of mergers on Wall Street, the major players are lining up to the dominant provider to the public and private sectors for Internet connectivity, intranet/Internet access and design, far-reaching voice services, easy data access, and encryption-based security.

The advent and adolescence of CTI services, Internet telephony—voice over IP, is uniting once discreet data networks with a common platform and is taking telephony into the computer age by allowing circuit-switched telephone calls to become packet-switched phone calls. This enables both voice and video services to travel alongside data in our network environment. The latest telephony advancements are in the area of integrated switching, a high capacity public switched telephone network (PSTN) to Transmission Control Protocol (TCP)/IP link integrating advanced smart router switching, combined with asynchronous transfer mode (ATM), IP telephony, and TCP/IP technologies.

As telephony technology grows with amazing acceleration, the security structure to support business application use lags profoundly. As this gap expands, so does the risk to today's network manager. In many instances, the security has yet to be developed. We continually see that packet filtering, proxies, and encryption fail to keep our networks secure. It is the legal responsibility of the network gatekeeper to control access and to limit all but legitimate use of technology's new resources.

SECURITY AUDIT SAMPLE

Departmental Issues

1. Do you have a corporate policy in place that addresses telecommunications fraud? The single most important element in combating fraud is to have upper management support for your efforts.
2. Do you currently have protection from your long-distance carrier? Contact your carrier and verify its plan and the conditions of your coverage. Document your carrier's monitoring program and its expected delay in notifying you of potential loss.

Physical Security

Does the telephone equipment room have:

1. A commercial grade lock? Ensure that all telephone equipment rooms are secured with commercial grade locks.
2. Limited authorized access? Limit access to telephone personnel only. Avoid using the telephone room as a storage area for other departments.
3. Keys kept in a secure place? Develop effective key control systems.

Trunks

Are any two-way or outgoing trunk dials accessible? Most trunks are accessed via automatic route selection (ARS) and are not required to be accessed directly. Many times during the installation or maintenance process, this feature is activated and then left open and unsecured.

Call Detail Recording

Are you tracking in- and outgoing traffic via:

1. CDR? Activate CDR on all trunks. This creates an "instant check" for compliance to your established parameters (i.e., the next time you check your trunk permissions and find that CDR is not active you know that unauthorized changes have been made).
2. Traffic reports? Analyze traffic reports for unusual calling activity.
3. Monthly system review? Analyze traffic reports for unusual calling activity.

Stations

1. Is a facility access test call number assigned? The facility access test call dial code allows station users to directly access specific trunk ports. This feature will go around class of restriction and facility restriction levels.

2. Do any stations have call forward external or call forward off-net capabilities? With call forward external enabled, your users can call forward to 9-1 and then make long-distance calls all day from home by dialing their own extensions. Class of service for voice mail and auto attendant should be call forward external denied (CFXD). Call forward external allowed should be changed to *deny* unless absolutely necessary.

DISA

1. Is the direct inward system access (DISA) or *remote access* feature activated? This is a very popular way toll fraud occurs. Hackers will find or create DISA and then utilize the system to dial out. Considering the seriousness of the problem, DISA should be deactivated.
2. If you have DISA activated, are the ports protected (dial back, voice recognition)? Most features may be activated in a secure fashion including DISA. Voice recognition provides a user-friendly interface for this feature, and it is relatively secure.

Voice Mail

Is the voice mail or auto attendant maintenance port-protected? Protect remote access to the program and remote access to the PBX. Make sure that your voice mail is protected in your voice-mail software from dialing any trunk route access code, flexible feature codes, and unnecessary first dialed digits. Restrict everything except valid four-digit extension numbers. Apply this to voice mail, voice menus, and auto attendant through dial and operator revert features.

FREQUENTLY ASKED QUESTIONS

1. When I get hacked, who is going to pay for the calls? Your company is responsible for all charges incurred on your system. Recent court decisions and filed tariffs make you, not the carrier, responsible for the security of your PBX.
2. Who are these people and why are they stealing calls? Today, communications theft is perpetrated from remote distances by highly skilled, technologically sophisticated criminals who have little fear of being detected, let alone apprehended or prosecuted. These criminals conduct a growing business selling access to unsuspecting buyers or connecting your service to "party services" all over the world. Some thieves may be part of an international crime ring whose purpose is to steal your corporate assets. What began as an intellectual pursuit has turned criminal.
3. Why do the carriers not write off these charges? Today, fraudulent calls are placed over many different interexchange carriers (IXC);

each carrier must pay that portion of the call handled by them. When the call is placed to an international location, the *domestic carrier must pay* the foreign carrier regardless of the fraud. Court cases, divestiture, and FCC rulings prevent carriers from writing off calls. *You, the end user, must control access and egress to your systems.*

4. Why is identifying or stopping the fraudulent calls the customer's responsibility? Only the customer can differentiate legitimate calls from fraudulent ones. The long-distance carriers do not have the skill, access, or permission to work on your PBX, the vehicle that hackers use to perpetrate theft. Just as it is your responsibility to lock your home or office, it is also your responsibility to establish security to stop telecommunications fraud and telephone abuse.

5. How will the hacker find my system? Several methods are used:
   - Criminals pay for a PBX maintenance port number and password.
   - Hackers "scan" using autodialers to find systems equipped with modems, autoattendant, voice mail, or other phreaking opportunities.
   - A major carrier recently investigated a young woman who allegedly was receiving $6 per hour to scan for targets using a demon dialer.

6. How do I justify the expense of corrective action when we have not suffered a loss? Past performance is not an indicator of present threats. The equipment and the motivation to perpetrate this criminal activity did not exist a few years ago. Imagine attempting to explain to the early settlers in a covered wagon the U.S. freeway system, or explain to a rural builder of windmills that the windmill would be a popular alternative energy source. Interesting statistics from the Department of Defense have reported:

Number of Attacks	Reported Year
53	1992
115	1993
225	1994
559	1995

Only one hacker attack in every 150 is reported. Information security–computer attacks at the Department of Defense pose increasing risks. GAO/AIMD-96-84 TeleDesign Management Inc. recommends that the executive management be educated about the pitfalls of not protecting assets. As your first step enlist management support by implementing a corporate policy on unauthorized access.

7. What is a phreaker? A phreaker exploits the omission of security controls in your system or cons your employees for access. The phreaker steals from your system without the need to change any of

293

your system parameters. The only tools required to be a very good phreaker are patience and *social engineering* (con artist) skills.

8. How does a hacker gain access to my system? Hackers use computerized calling programs, automatic dialers, and sophisticated software to break your system's security and pass codes. Hackers attempt to gain access in the following order:
   a. Remote maintenance administration port
   b. Voice mail
   c. Automated attendant
   d. Remote access or DISA

9. Why is it important to protect my maintenance administration port? Hackers gain access to your software to program your system for their benefit. Hackers may install back doors to circumvent normal system protection that allows attackers unauthorized access in the future.

10. How do hackers know which PBX type and brand of voice mail I am using? Hackers identify the type of PBX by the log-in procedure used for each system. Hackers recognize the various voice-mail systems by the default digitized voice recordings.

11. How does a hacker use my voice mail? Hackers and phreakers both use voice mail systems:
    a. Through your voice mail the hacker or phreaker is able to use your PBX to access your long-distance network.
    b. Your voice mail might also be used as a "bulletin board" to distribute stolen credit card and other hacker-related information.
    c. Hackers and phreakers may change your greeting to accept third-party billing charges.
    d. Some voice-mail systems may be capable of sidestepping PBX security.

12. I understand why a large user must be concerned, but I am a small business in a rural community. Why should hacker and phreaker activity concern me? Hackers use autodialers to search entire area codes to find systems to hack. Normally they do know who or where their victims are. No one is safe, and smaller companies may be less able to absorb the average loss of from $10,000 to $80,000 per incident.

13. What happens when a hacker finds my maintenance administration port? Information on how to use your system is sold to a "call sell operator" who sells calls over your system to whomever wishes to place calls. The access may be sold to an international crime ring for voice or fax calls.

14. What is "fax back fraud?" Fax back fraud happens when the system accepts incoming requests for catalogs, product information or investment opportunities. These requests are stored with a callback number. During off-peak hours the system delivers the requested

information by way of a callback. The company sending out the information pays for the call. International Cyberspace criminals requested information that is transmitted to an international pay per call number (at least $3.95/min) and you pay the bill.

15. What is different about fax theft from other forms of fraudulent activity? There are three major differences with this case:

    a. The call is harder to detect because it is processed as data not voice.

    b. An international organization is required.

    c. The theft has migrated and expanded in form and severity.

16. What do you mean that the theft has migrated? When first discovered, the theft required a victim to have fax back service. The thieves then migrated to "looping through a PBX." Now they are using cheap throw-away fax machines and "clip-on fraud" to attack buildings. The thief places an incoming call to a target system in the U.S. He dials out to a "pay per call" number in a foreign country. He does not need fax back service and is in control of the origination and termination of the call. Criminals are buying inexpensive portable fax machines and clipping them on to exposed telephone wires. They call the international number and charge $400 or $500 worth of stolen calls to the victim.

17. What can we do to protect ourselves from Cybercriminals and con artists? This is one disaster that is very predictable and equally preventable. Hackers and phreakers are easily stopped from breaking in to a system. However, *they are very difficult to evict*. Form "a security watch" team that includes a security specialist, your long-distance carrier, your local exchange, and your service provider. Do *not let the management of your company be taken by surprise*.

SUMMARY

Vice networks are being replaced with virtual private networks (VPN). Older communications systems (pre-1983) are being replaced with new enhanced and improved systems, feature rich for your business application needs. The Old World embraced the ethics of hard work and the values of "Thou shalt not steal." The emerging world of Cyberspace is approaching rapidly with different ethics and values. We live with a foot in each world, where business ethics and social values are not universal and are often disregarded for ego gratification or financial gain.

The Department of Defense conducted Tiger Team Attacks and statistically reported that out of 8932 attempted break-ins, 393 were discovered and only 86 were stopped. In 1998, an elite team of government computer professionals proved that the Pentagon's computers were vulnerable to hacker attacks. *It all begins with a telephone call.*

Remember that you will be a victim. You do control the severity of the attack.

Notes

1. Reported by Telecommunications Advisors Inc. for 1996.
2. AT&T vs. Chartways Technology, file #E8872, 8/93, and United Artists Payphone Corp. vs. New York Telephone Co., file #E9181, 8/93.
3. Jiffy Lube Case summarized by Mr. Pete Coultier, AT&T, 1993. With permission.

Section VI
New Technologies

Chapter 18
Emerging High-Bandwidth Networks

Kevin M. Groom and Frank M. Groom

INTRODUCTION

Corporate users are increasingly demanding faster transport speed. This is driven by the type of media being employed and shared among workers, such as documents, images, and training material. This material is being augmented by e-mail communication and increasingly by desktop video-conferencing. Further, the access to traditional transaction data applications on servers and requests and responses from client/server applications continue to be a primary driver for network connectivity.

As personal computers (PCs) and workstations come equipped with fast Peripheral Component Interconnect (PCI) buses that can deliver data to networks at 100M bps and greater speeds; have powerful Pentium II, Power PC, or Alpha central processing units (CPUs); and have 6- to 11-Gb hard drives, the user is demanding faster transport to feed these powerful data engines. Moreover, the distribution of large data and application servers is now augmented by groupware servers such as Lotus Notes storing documents and data and World Wide Web servers storing Hypertext Markup Language (HTML) marked-up pages for access with browsers.

To transport information among increasingly diverse and distributed processors, sharply greater bandwidth is required. As the trend for workers to spend many of their hours working from home or on the road continues, fast home access to corporate information is becoming an equal partner in the high-bandwidth business environment.

Asymmetrical digital subscriber line (ADSL) high bandwidth to the home worker has emerged from trials by the Regional Bell Operating Companies (RBOCs) and is being offered in a gradual rollout in the 1998-2000 period. ADSL is the newest and most promising high bandwidth connection technology for access from the home. Asynchronous transfer mode (ATM) of 100M bps and Gigabit Ethernet are the emerging network technologies in the office. Frame relay is the fastest growing wide area connection technology,

0-8493-9990-4/99/$0.00+$.50
© 1999 by CRC Press LLC

and the beginnings of a demand for ATM is emerging. Both frame relay and ATM are the prime interexchange carrier services offered to bridge city, state, and the national locations. Finally, world high-bandwidth connection services are emerging as corporations attempt to meld their national networks into a blend of high-bandwidth connectivity provided by such consortiums as AT&T's World Partners Frame Relay Consortium, which partner to deliver integrated world frame relay service.

HIGH-BANDWIDTH LOCAL ACCESS FOR THE HOME

Telephone, cable, and satellite companies have concentrated significant attention on basic residential connectivity. Initially, home entertainment was the application that was expected to drive customer demand for higher speed connectivity. However, with the emergence of vast interest and usage of the Internet, industry sights have turned to Internet access, work-at-home situations, and remote access to standard business Ethernet, Internet Protocol (IP), or ATM local area networks (LANs).

The general classification for the telephone company's product direction is termed digital subscriber line (DSL) service. DSL service has a basic intent of delivering higher bandwidth transport over the in-place twisted pair telephone loop plant that extends to each residence, while placing a modem on each end of the loop, one at the subscriber's location, and one at telephone central office switch center. The local loop tends to have between 20 and 33 bridge taps along the line. About 20% of installed lines have loading coils as well.

This gives problems to other services, such as Integrated Services Digital Network (ISDN), and limits the number of telephone lines that are ISDN equitable. DSL services—due to their more modern modulation techniques, digital signal processors, and isolation of the voice traffic to the low end of the frequency spectrum—are impervious to the bridge and load coil situation, thus allowing direct usage of a large percentage of the currently existing twisted pair local loop wire. It is estimated that 85% of U.S. households could be connected through DSL service with no modification of the wire pair with an equivalent 30 to 50% of such wire being ISDN capable. Among the array of DSL services that have been defined, telephone companies have targeted ADSL and high bit–rate digital subscriber line (HDSL) services as having the most customer demand potential.

XDSL Speeds and Services

The complete array of DSL services and the traditional modem service are presented in Exhibit 1. These are ADSL, HDSL, very high bit rate digital subscriber line (VDSL), and symmetric digital subscriber line (SDSL) service.

Exhibit 1. Digital Subscriber User Service Array

Type	Data Rate	Mode	Use
Modem	28.8, 34.6, 56.4K bps	Duplex	Minimum remove
DSL	160K bps	Duplex	ISDN
ADSL	1.5–9M bps	Simple down	Internet
16–640K bps	Duplex up	Work home	
HDSL	768K bps	Duplex down	Symmetric
768K bps	Duplex up	Computer use	
SDSL	384K bps Up/D	Duplex	Minimum data
VDSL	13–52M bps	Duplex down	Heavy data processing
1.5–2.3M bps	Duplex up		

The ADSL forum has defined a standard model to be followed by telephone companies and equipment suppliers to construct an ADSL connection and to offer ADSL services. The loop plant twisted pair wire is expected to remain unchanged. Distances beyond 3.5 mi from a central office will be connected by means of a T1 line that will span the longer distance to arrive within a reasonable distance to a residence community. ADSL places a splitter at both ends of the local loop line as well as an ADSL transmission unit (ATU-C at the central office and ATU-R at the residence).

The purpose of the modems is to modulate higher speed data and video on the line. The splitter allows the plain old telephone service (POTS) telephone conversation to be modulated separately on the line after the data and video and to be isolated from these transmissions. At the central office, the telephone conversation is split off from the higher speed data and video and sent directly to a line module of the central office switch, such as a traditional analog transmission. These ATU modems and the splitters are portrayed in Exhibit 2.

The modems on each end modulate the traffic into very high speed (above 138 kHz to 1.1 GHz), medium speed (from 30 to 138 kHz) with the overlap accommodated by echo cancellation. The POTS telephone connection sits as it always has at the bottom frequency between 0 and 4 kHz. A guard band of 24 kHz separates the voice traffic from the higher speed frequencies.

ADSL is an asymmetrical connection service. The downstream traffic is designed to be significantly faster than the upstream traffic. The service is intended for an audience with asymmetrical needs. Video-on-demand service has a limited and relatively slow request traffic, followed by massive and continuous downstream flow of a video movie. Internet traffic has been observed to follow the same pattern, with a browser-based seek request for information, followed by a sizable series of text, image, video, and sound clip information flowing downstream. ADSL can have this asymmet-

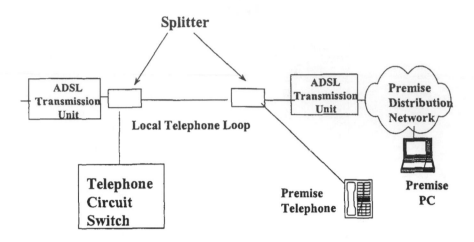

Exhibit 2. The Standard Reference Model for ADSL Service

rical connection set up in a range from 1.5M bps downstream coupled with 64K bps upstream from the residence, to 6.1M bps downstream and 640K bps upstream.

There are four basic transmission modes for ADSL service:

1. Packet mode is essentially Transmission Control Protocol (TCP)/IP over a home Ethernet, which requires an Ethernet card in each home or remote office PC and twisted pair wire to connect to the ADSL home modem. This mode is ideal for home access to the Internet and for connection to a corporate network.
2. Cell-based ATM employs an ATM card in each home or remote office PC and is suited for remote office connection to a corporate ATM network by means of a telephone company ATM network. This connection is desirable for multimedia, videoconferencing, or home or office delivery of real-time training material.
3. Bit synchronization mode will be employed for streamed video to the home such as with video-on-demand service.
4. POTS mode is reserved for voice telephone traffic.

EMERGING OFFICE AND BUILDING CONNECTIVITY

Corporations are requiring increased bandwidth to connect to servers in the worker's building or across the campus, as well as to the distant location of other workers in the corporation. Simultaneously, they have an investment in older PCs, Ethernets and hubs, and software such as Novell Inc.'s NetWare. To modernize their investments and satisfy a diverse set of

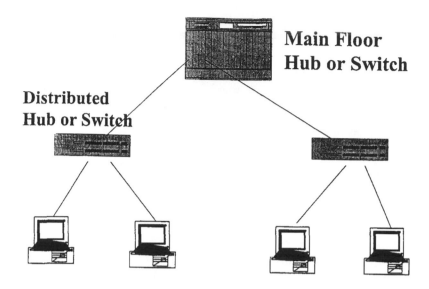

Main Floor Hub or Switch

Distributed Hub or Switch

Exhibit 3. The Distributed Simple Hubs Connected by a Smart Switching Hub

needs, they need to accommodate both the current network technology and the emerging high-bandwidth technology.

Current Office Connectivity and Building Backbones

Most corporations have already interconnected workgroups of users on a particular floor of an office building through an intelligent hub. Up to 100 or 120 users can be connected to a hub by means of category three or five twisted pair wire over distances of no more than 100 m (330 ft). These users can then be bridged to other hubs on the same or other floors. Such interconnected office workers can share common laser printers, e-mail, file servers, and applications through their shared and commonly managed LAN hub.

To minimize the investment in intelligent hubs (which cost between $10,000 and $20,000, depending on their configuration) and to extend the user's connection beyond 100-m distance limitation, cheaper "dumb" or distributed hubs supporting up to 20 PCs can be placed close to workers for their subgroup interconnection. The distributed hubs can then be linked to a more distant floor hub by means of coaxial cable or fiber. The stacking of these simple hubs and connecting them to a central switching hub for the floor is portrayed in Exhibit 3.

These traditional building connections are now under pressure from a number of advanced applications. In particular, the use of multimedia and desktop videoconferencing is driving bandwidth demands to the desktop

Exhibit 4. Varying Bandwidth Requirements for Media Types

Media Type	Bandwidth (bps)
Entertainment video–real-time play	3,000,000
Videoconference	128–356,000
Image visualization–real time	50–80,000
Engineering image	90,000
Voice	64,000
Sound	176,000–700,000
Stereo	1,400,000
Fax	64,000

for special-case users. However, the big impetus for desktop bandwidth is the movement from personal desktop computing toward network and workgroup computing. Much of desktop usage involves sending and receiving transactions over the local network to office, building, campus, and national and international servers. To meet this demand, simple office Ethernets have been upgraded first to switched 10M-bps Ethernet, which has minimum contention, and then to 100M-bps switched Ethernet. As companies rapidly move to switched Ethernet and Token Ring LANs to reduce Ethernet collisions and the latency both experience and many move to 100M-bps Fast Ethernet on the floor, there is a general movement toward replacing the more expensive and complicated router-based fiber distributed data interface (FDDI) backbones with a single 100M-bps Fast Ethernet switch and placing a Fast Ethernet exit card in each floor hub or switch.

ATM DESKTOP CONNECTIVITY

ATM to the desktop is driven by the requirement for a variety of media to be delivered over the same connection to the desktop applications and disk storage. Exhibit 4 presents the range of information sizes and speeds required for the variety of multimedia that might be delivered. Sound and motion video pose the additional requirement that they must have rapid, yet unvarying delivery speed with no lags or variation. In many cases, this mixed set of media types must be delivered simultaneously in an intermixed stream over a common connection and used as a unit by the destination device.

Further, many of the individual media types require compression algorithms unique to the individual media type to be performed at the source and destination sites to squeeze the volume of information into any reasonable delivery protocol.

Only ATM provides the bandwidth reservation with guaranteed quality of service and a fast enough transfer rate to deliver these varying types of

304

media to the desktop in a satisfactory fashion. In contrast, fast Ethernet provides high-speed and high-quality data transmission but cannot guarantee the delivery rate for individual media types. Many believe that a moderately loaded (less than 50% of capacity) 100M-bps Ethernet can carry multimedia to the desktop over the last 100 m if ATM is used for the wider backbone network.

ATM BUILDING BACKBONE NETWORKS

Unless ATM is provided all the way to ATM-equipped desktop PCs, ATM backbone networks provide only high bandwidth without the quality of service features, classes of service, and bandwidth guarantees for which ATM was created. As a backbone network, ATM competes with the newer 100M-bps and 1G-bps Ethernet and the older FDDI protocols purely on speed, simplicity of the protocol, and cost.

The simplicity and cost factors are the strength of Fast Ethernet. FDDI strength is in its embedded base and proven capability, while multimedia such as picture, video, desktop videoconferencing, and group document delivery are the features requiring ATM. If multimedia is employed locally and wide area ATM connection is provided by an interchange carrier to other distant ATM networked sites, building connectivity is moving to Fast Ethernet. ATM becomes the vehicle for interconnecting the buildings of a campus.

Where ATM is employed as building or campus backbone interconnecting 10M- or 100-bps Ethernet floor LANs, ATM acts as a bridging service and requires the employment of three LAN emulation servers, including the LAN emulation server itself, the LAN emulation configuration server, and a broadcast unknown server.

FDDI Backbone Network

The standard for campus backbone networks has been an FDDI network constructed with routers interconnected by dual fiber rings. The hubs that interconnect workgroups and workers on a given floor are connected to the FDDI by fiber links that span the greater distance from the floor to a central FDDI router. Either a passive fiber card or a full FDDI card can be placed in the hub to gain access to the backbone.

If the passive card is used, connection to the ring is at 10 or 16M bps. If the full FDDI card is placed in the hub, the connection speed from the hub to the ring router is at 100M bps. An FDDI ring is created by placing two FDDI cards (in some cases a single four-port card can be employed) in a set of routers. These routers are then interconnected by a set of dual fiber cable to form a building or campus ring. A third FDDI card or passive fiber card is placed in the router to link back to the LAN hub. Such an FDDI back-

305

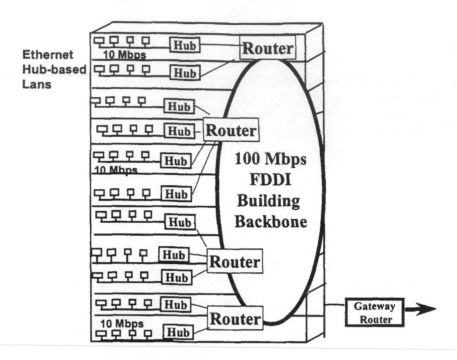

Exhibit 5. Connecting Hubs to a Router-based FDDI Building Backbone

bone connection is portrayed in Exhibit 5, with hubs serving as the office access to the backbone ring.

HIGH-BANDWIDTH CAMPUS BACKBONE NETWORKS

Looking more closely at a campus situation, we can see quite clearly how the placement of a limited set of switches can be more cost-effective than employing router-based, shared-bandwidth, FDDI backbones. The complete FDDI campus backbone is then constructed by placing a router with two FDDI cards in the first floor of each building and stringing dual sets of multimode fiber around the campus, from building to building connected to a router in each building. One of the routers on the ring can serve as a gateway router to off-campus networks and to the Internet. Otherwise a server is connected to the ring to perform the gateway function.

Fast Ethernet Backbone Networks

To access an FDDI ring from a hub we either need to encapsulate our LAN-addressed packet inside an FDDI-addressed packet, termed "tunneling" the LAN packet, or we need to translate Ethernet to FDDI and then back to Ethernet on the other end of the ring. This complexity, delay, and

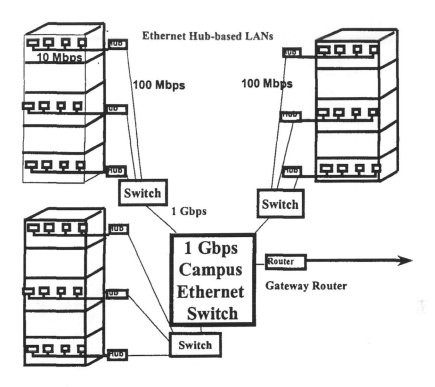

Exhibit 6. 1G-bps Interbuilding Campus Backbone Network

cost in such translation has led to the creation of a faster version of the standard LAN protocol, Ethernet.

Although only Pentium-class computers (or PowerPC computers) workstations can make use of 100M-bps Fast Ethernet, it is quickly finding a home as a fast backbone network connecting 10M-bps Ethernet switches. Ethernet at 100M bps can serve as fast transport between switching hubs or Ethernet switches or it can serve as a complete building backbone.

Further, Fast Ethernet can serve as fast campus backbone network interconnecting Fast Ethernet building backbones. Fast Ethernet can replace FDDI as both a building and a campus backbone, offers the same transport speed of 100M bps in a nonshared fashion, and maintains the same protocol and addressing throughout the complete campus network. The simplicity of this design as well as its low cost is quickly persuading companies to convert to this structure as an extension of what they already have installed (Exhibit 6).

In early release, prior to the promised 1998 standard specifications from the Gigabit Ethernet Alliance, a number of vendors have offered Gigabit

Ethernet switches for campus and large building backbone networks. These switches employ a hybrid protocol with Layer 2 media access control (MAC) remaining traditional Ethernet, while Layer 1 is the fiber channel protocol using either multimode or single mode fiber. Gigabit Ethernet is designed to interconnect 100M-bps Fast Ethernet switches and thus will be a strong competitor to existing FDDI and the emerging ATM backbone networks.

ATM Backbones

ATM switches can be used to create a backbone network that cross-connects the hubs that interconnect the floor traffic. These ATM switches can be used to construct a building backbone network or extended to create a campuswide backbone network, much as can be constructed with FDDI and Fast Ethernet.

ATM in the Building

When an ATM switch is used to cross-connect floor hubs, an ATM access module must be placed in each hub, and a set of LAN emulation servers must be connected to the backbone ATM switches. Traditional Ethernet or Token Ring LAN packets are then segmented into ATM cells by the access modules. The access module then requests an address translation from the ATM LAN emulation servers in the backbone and then readdresses the cells with ATM addresses to traverse the ATM network to the destination Ethernet segment. The reverse of this process is then performed by the ATM access module in the receiving hub. These ATM access modules, commonly called Proxy LAN emulation clients (LECs), act as bridging devices to bridge the traffic flowing from an Ethernet network to an ATM network, and bridging back again on the egress side.

ATM Campus Backbone

When the complete campus requires very high bandwidth to interconnect the buildings (155M or 622M bps) and multimedia traffic is being transported, a set of ATM switches can be placed at the heart of the campus with media, application, and file servers centrally attached to the backbone switches. These servers attract much of the traffic over the network and thus require very high entry speed between the servers and the network. LAN emulation servers are usually moved out from the building backbone to the campus ATM backbones when most of the traffic flows across campus generally supporting up to 1000 users (Exhibit 7).

Where larger communities are served, multiple separate LAN emulation servers can be created, specialized to a particular set of buildings. High-performance workgroups are separated from the regular LAN connections in the buildings and interconnected with their own workgroup ATM switch,

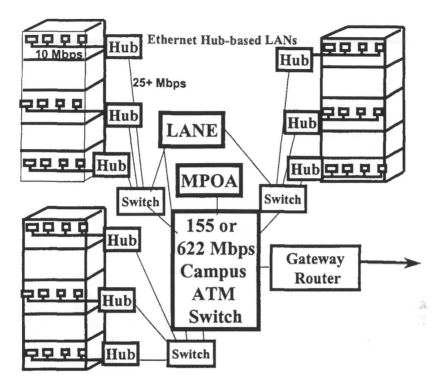

Exhibit 7. An ATM Switch Connecting Ethernet Switching Hubs

which is then directly attached either to the campus or to a building ATM backbone network.

AVAILABLE WIDE AREA NETWORK CHOICES

Traditionally, access from the campus to wide area networking has been performed by employing a gateway router that can bridge local and wide area networks (WANs), perform required packet reformatting, and address translations and interpretations. T1 bridged routers, frame relay, and ATM networks are the current prime choices for providing high bandwidth across a wide area.

The conventional WAN is router-based, providing TCP/IP connectivity. The network is constructed as a set of autonomous networks that are interconnected by border routers. Such a network is accessed by a gateway router from individual buildings or campuses.

The individual routers that make up a TCP/IP WAN have traditionally been connected by full or fractionalized private T1 lines that have been leased from the telephone companies. Each router link requires such a connection and frequently a mesh of such lines connects all the routers. Usually the routers are located at the sending building locations, with the T1 links spanning the distance between the individual routers, providing an asynchronous bridging function.

Interconnecting many gateway routers to form an IP mesh network becomes very expensive as the distance grows. Each connection is composed of the two links on both ends to the public cross-connect network and the multiplexed usage of the public backbone over the distance to be traversed. More frequently, these building gateway routers connect only to a single central site for an application server, e-mail store-and-forward, Web sites, and a corporate file server. In this case, the private lines between the routers can be eliminated, since most traffic goes to one central site. When occasionally traffic must go end site to end site, the central router can route the traffic back over the connecting destination end site to the central router.

This network architecture, although it eliminates the interrouter connecting private lines, still creates a number of problems. First, there are a large number of links required from the distant locations to the central site. These links are very costly, each incurring many thousands of dollars per month based on the distance covered, the speed of the link, and the number of carrier companies employed in the interlinking. The farther the distance, the larger the cost. Since these separate links are not combined into a network service, these connections are difficult to manage.

A frame relay network should provide significant savings over an equivalent private line network. By employing a frame relay network to connect many locations to a central site, 20% savings should be achievable compared to a standard private line design regardless of the comparable speed used. This is regardless of whether we compare a 64K-bps private line to frame relay 64K-bps service or a 1.5M-bps private line vs. 1.5M-bps frame relay service.

Furthermore, for the many-to-many requirement, a still larger savings should be achievable approaching a 30% reduction. Frame relay service still requires the customer to lease at full price a short, private line access link to the location of the edge relay switch of the vendor. However, significant savings should be achievable over the long-haul distance with frame relay service. This results from the opportunity to statistically share the facilities and from dramatically reducing the number of individual, long-distance, end-to-end, private line links required to connect each end customer site to all the others in a many-to-many connection.

On the other hand, benefits from network management services can be achieved if the frame relay service is provided by one carrier and only short private lines connect users at each end point. Top quality network

310

management can be achieved, since the network and its facilities are all under one carrier's control.

Using Public Frame Relay Networking to Bridge Locations

Frame relay addresses the problems raised by a national connection. Frame relay service does this by substituting a national, high-speed, public, packet-switched, shared network for the many individual private lines that would normally need to be established. Although private line links must be established from each location to the closest entry point of the national frame relay network, these links are decidedly shorter and thus much less expensive. A short T1 link to a connection may be $500 for a full 1.5M bps down to $200/month for a 32- to 64K-bps subchannel of a private line. A T1 private line from New York to Seattle, on the other hand, would cost thousands of dollars a month, mostly from the distance charges.

Charges for frame relay have been dropping. Since the public frame relay network is a shared-use network, the pricing is reduced. Ideally, frame relay is intended to be an on-demand, pay-as-you-use network with dramatically reduced price compared with building your own private network with long and leased T1 private lines. Ideally, the public frame relay network would be the equivalent of a dial-up high-speed packet network. This is considered to be a switched virtual circuit (SVC) network in terms. Such a presubscribed and pay-as-you-use public data network would require the carrier provider, on receiving a call setup message from your router, to dynamically pick each sequential link in the path of the end-to-end frame relay network that you would utilize.

Further, the carrier would need to dynamically update the route selection table in each node in the frame relay network that you temporarily use to create a virtual path for your transmission. This is projected to reduce a user's national network connectivity cost by up to 70% over a national, dedicated, private line network. Unfortunately, this dynamic update of switch tables is not yet a reality. What is offered is the ability to contract for a stated period of time a "temporarily permanent virtual path" or a permanent virtual circuit (PVC) in terms.

On placing an order with the carrier and leasing a line to the carrier's point of presence (POP) closest to each of your sites a company can have a 24-hr/day, 30 days/month, shared piece of a public high-speed network. This permanently shared piece of the network costs about 80% of what a private line network would cost. In fact, the distance portion of the private line facility is a shared portion of the carrier's digital cross-connect network anyway, with your portion being prereserved as a PVC. Exhibit 8 represents a frame relay network established as a set of PVCs.

Public Frame Relay Network

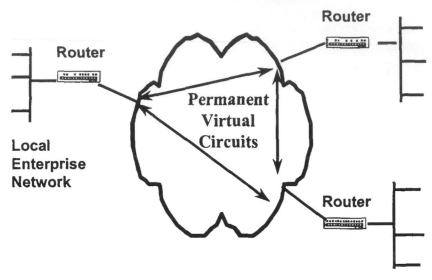

Exhibit 8.   Frame Relay Network Composed of Permanent Virtual Circuits

To establish a "permanent circuit" between sites 1, 2, and 3, one of two modes of operation would be employed. In the standard approach, the customer would subscribe with the carrier for PVCs from site 1 to site 2, from site 1 to site 3, and from site 2 to site 3. The carrier would then provide the customer a set of frame relay addresses to place in the customer's router. This router will then translate the IP addresses to frame relay addresses and place these new addresses in each packet prior to sending them to the frame relay network to be forwarded to a specific site.

These temporary addresses are called data link control identifiers (DLCIs). Each port can specify up to 1024 DLCIs—in other words, up to 1024 PVCs per port. Fortunately, frame relay is a fully duplexed, bidirectional network requiring only one setup to establish both directions of the communication (differing from its big brother network, ATM, which requires a separate call setup for each direction of the communication path). However, like ATM, frame relay employs a different DLCI address at each end of the link (and unseen by the subscriber, a whole string of sequential DLCIs for each link along the way to the destination final leg link). To send a packet from site 1 to site 2, the customer's router must place DLCI 100 in every packet.

Customer participation in frame relay addressing has been considered enough of a hurdle that many carriers offer the preferred option of the carrier creating the frame relay addresses for the customer using the carrier's within-network router and database to perform the translation from IP to DLCI addresses. Under this option, the customer submits IP packets with IP addresses from the customer's router to the carrier's router (which is on the edge of the frame relay network). The carrier's router will then perform the address translation on both ends of the frame relay network, with the customer sending and receiving standard IP packets with which they have years of experience. As far as the customer perceives, with this approach frame relay is merely an extension of the local IP networks.

Interfacing Frame Relay with Other Networks

Since frame relay is a carrier-provided network service, existing protocols (such as the widely popular IP protocol, the IBM Systems Network Architecture [SNA], the Telco ISDN), and even voice can be carried over it with a significant reduction in cost and the added advantage of having a carrier-managed wide area linkage.

Frame Relay and ATM Interworking

The ATM and frame relay forums have approved two methods by which these two networks can be interconnected. Under network interworking, devices on the frame relay network must be knowledgeable about the ATM network and capable of performing the frame relay to ATM mapping. This includes the mapping for the frame relay service-specific convergence sublayer (FR-SSCS) functions of the ATM, AAL-5 adaptation layer at the upper portion of the ATM Layer 2 protocol. In another frame relay/ATM interworking method, the service interworking method, devices on both the ATM and frame relay networks are not required to know anything about the other network protocol.

To customer premise equipment (CPE) on a frame relay network, the entire network appears as frame relay. The same is true of CPE on the ATM network. To accomplish this protocol isolation, an FR/ATM interworking function (IWF) has been defined and performed by a device sitting as a bridge between the two networks. The IWF node must translate frame relay DLCI addresses to ATM virtual path indicators (VPIs) and virtual channel indicators (VCIs). Current public wide area frame relay and ATM offerings are provided only by setting up PVCs. In the future, it is anticipated that both frame relay and ATM networking will also be offered as "on-demand, pay-as-you-use" SVC services. Both call–setup messaging and dynamic route allocation must then be handled by the IWF interface unit for both sides of the connection.

This will be a sizable task. Exhibit 9 depicts frame relay connecting local networks to a wide area ATM network through a standard IWF node. This

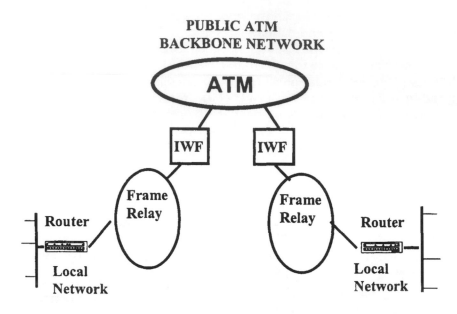

PUBLIC ATM
BACKBONE NETWORK

Exhibit 9.   Frame Relay as Regional Access to an ATM Wide Area Backbone

IWF node, usually a router with frame relay and ATM access cards, and the IWF address conversion and packet segmentation software.

In the early stages of ATM and frame relay interworking, most prefer to think of ATM as a low-level physical connection technology employed by frame relay service. In fact, much of public frame relay has been implemented by the RBOCs and the interexchange carriers (IE) with ATM as the actual transporting vehicle. The customer buys frame relay service, but that service is provided with an ATM backbone. Ultimately, frame relay and ATM will be considered as two services, each with its own special audience and employing IWF interconnection points as the translation and interconnection nodes between the two network protocols.

Frame relay service was designed as a data-only networking scheme due to the bursty nature of data, which in the past was incompatible with the continuous flow required for voice traffic. Now many companies are beginning to recognize the savings they could gain by employing their frame relay network to carry voice traffic along with their data traffic. Voice savings of 25 to 30% have been incurred by connecting a company's PBX to a common multimedia access switch that is shared with the company's data traffic.

The approach taken is to first convert the analog voice to digital form using sampling and pulse code modulation resulting in 8-b words at a 64-bps transfer rate. This digital representation is then compressed to remove

314

pauses and hesitation (Bell estimates the average pause time per call at 2.5 s). This compressed, digitally represented voice set of bytes is then placed into packets (about 4000 bytes per packet), addressed to the appropriate destination, and sent forward on a 64K-bps link to the frame relay network. At the receiving end it is desirable to set up large buffers so the message can be reassembled with all the pauses and hesitations as they originally occurred. Generally, frame relay does not provide the same quality of voice as the public circuit switched telephone network, but for many businesses, the cost savings and management capability of voice over frame relay will override the modest quality degradation.

ATM NETWORKS: PUBLIC CARRIERS AS VIRTUAL CIRCUIT PROVIDERS

Where a company has achieved the speed and quality of service (QoS) control of transmission locally and wishes to connect dispersed locations and still maintain ATM speed and the QoS features, a public carrier's ATM networking service can be contracted to provide continuous ATM service that can be used in creating an end-to-end wide area ATM connection. Moreover, the complete range of ATM speeds from 51M to 622M bps can be publicly contracted for this wide area ATM connection. However, only the establishment of a permanent connection (PVC service) is currently publicly provided by most public carriers, although AT&T has announced a SVC ATM service.

With carrier-provided wide area PVC ATM service, businesses use the carrier as if it were providing a private line connection between their sites. They preestablish a 155M-bps PVC from one location to the other. The two end-point ATM switches treat the public connection as if it where a private line between the locations. Although they locally, dynamically create SVC connections, when they bridge sites using the public ATM network, they do not attempt to dynamically set up a circuit over the public network. What they do is only route the traffic to an available, preestablished PVC as if they were switching to a line connecting the sites.

The switches on each end dynamically establish their connection and disconnection locally, but the public connection is always available for use as a link between the local ATM switch port much like a permanently leased line. Either a single IXC (such as AT&T) or an RBOC telephone company (such as Ameritech) can provide the wide area ATM PVC connecting service.

PUBLIC CARRIERS PROVIDE JOINT ATM NETWORK

An RBOC can provide a local ATM PVC connection. However, when a company needs to cross the country, one has some choice in the connection. One can establish the PVC service either with an IXC—such as AT&T, Sprint, or MCI—or with a mixture of an IEC and two RBOCs. A major problem may occur when a business wishes to employ a mixture of carriers to create an end-to-end ATM network. The two local carriers need to create links to the national IXC, and the three companies need to set up a set of end-to-end PVCs that create a link across the multiple carriers to the destination. This is a difficult circuit to set up initially, and it is virtually impossible to manage as a unit today due to the reluctance of the carriers to allow management across their boundaries.

EMERGING GLOBAL OPTIONS

Partnering is the strategy employed by the carriers to create global high-bandwidth connection, such as the planned AT&T and British Telecom (BT) agreement.

Sprint, France Telecom, and Deutsche Telekom have established Globe l as their joint world communication vehicle. Beyond using the carrier consortia, organizations—such as Sandia Laboratories in Arizona—are using 155M-bps ATM satellite links to interconnect their site to a number of national supercomputer research centers such as that at the University of Illinois, and to laboratories such as Lawrence Livermore in California. Sandia establishes two one-way links (one in each direction) and can interconnect locations without the problems of establishing long fiber connections to a land-based ATM network. Motorola has announced its own satellite network for providing global 56K-bps to 155M-bps data connection to and from any location on the globe.

SUMMARY

Users continue to seek faster networks for metropolitan, national, and international connection. As users, equipped with high-performance computers seek to transport more information and multimedia over faster local networks, the push for high-speed corporate networks increases. This has led toward Fast Ethernet and ATM for the local interconnection.

Moreover, the national and global distribution of corporations and a requirement to communicate with suppliers and customers, as well as distant corporate employees at a speed equivalent to local connection, are driving the deployment of fiber-based connection locally, nationally, and globally and the employment of ATM and soon 1-Gbps Ethernet protocols. As more complicated applications with distributed databases and Web server-based information are added to corporate networks, the endless cycle requiring more speed to more locations will continue.

Chapter 19
The Internet as an Alternative to the Corporate Network

Larry L. Learn

INTRODUCTION

No technological development—including the advent of personal computers (PCs) and their derivative local are networks (LANs) and wide area networks (WANs)—has made a more significant impact on the corporate
network scene in such a brief period of time than has the Internet[1] and its
associated World Wide Web.[2] No development been as problematic for network managers. Bringing an organization into the Internet community has
in many ways been a Faustian contract for the network manager. Although
there are many substantial benefits to be gained from the Internet, there
are also good and substantial reasons for network managers to approach
the Internet with some trepidation.

However, now is not the time to be faint of heart. This new technology, if
used correctly, presents unprecedented opportunities for new and improved global marketing and sales, greatly enhanced customer and user
support, and greatly facilitated communications within an organization
(e.g., enterprisewide electronic mail, and remote-agent online access to corporate data and applications), as well as with customers, suppliers and alliance partners (e.g., electronic commerce [e-commerce]). Timely access to
vast stores of external information (e.g., current government regulations,
government contract opportunities, financial, scientific and technical data,
patent and legal data, and current competitor information) critical to ongoing corporate operations constitutes a valuable corporate asset.

The technology provides many new opportunities to streamline internal communications and management functions, to integrate diverse corporate operations and systems (particularly in a dynamic era of
downsizings, *restructurings*, *divestitures*, *mergers*, and *acquisitions*), and in
both the short- and long-term, to optimize the cost and effectiveness of

0-8493-9990-4/99/$0.00+$.50
© 1999 by CRC Press LLC

marketing and sales, operations, and support efforts. It also enables the enterprise to capitalize on the many opportunities provided by the emerging field of e-commerce. Although Internet-based *telephony* (Internet Protocol [IP] telephony)[3] may not be quite up to corporate quality standards now, the day that corporate voice traffic can be effectively routed over the data network is not far in the future. In addition, the technology may be good enough for many voice applications today, holding the promise of significant cost savings in the corporate telephony budget.

Since the Internet is often viewed as a telecommunications and networking technology, it can strategically position the network management function as a keystone between numerous highly visible corporate efforts, each with the potential for substantial positive business results.

THE INTERNET AS A PARADIGM

Reading the current literature, one encounters a sometimes confusing menagerie of Internet-related apparitions: Internet, intranet, Web, and the more recent very high speed Backbone Network Service (vBNS)[4] and Internet2[5] among but a few. From the network manager's perspective, it is constructive to view the Internet as an IP-based transport infrastructure over which IP packets travel from a variety of higher level protocol implementations, the most prevalent of which is the so-called Transport Control Protocol (TCP) suite.[6]

This TCP/IP–transport paradigm is supported by an ever-growing number of networked applications, not the least of which is the evolving network computer model,[7] wherein PCs are replaced with less expensive devices that depend on the network for their basic function. The Internet paradigm enables the network manager to focus on network infrastructure and management, providing a common framework for accommodation of various current and evolving applications in a consistent and compatible manner. In so doing, the network manager can create the potential to generate added economies of scale and to dilute essential overhead costs.

The Internet has been generally associated with the wide-open, IP-based, network-of-networks that includes the myriad of global networks and computers shared by millions of users and applications worldwide (e.g., public, shared, comparatively inexpensive, highly accessible, but more variable, and less secure than a private network). At the opposite end of the network spectrum, intranets typically consist of private networks of telecommunications channels and computers specific to an individual organization, or to at least a restricted community of related organizations (e.g., controlled, access-restricted, more manageable and predictable, and more secure, but more expensive than the Internet) following the same IP-based model. Between these extremes exists a variety of intranet-like networks that may use virtual private network facilities (i.e., physically

318

shared, but logically private) for interconnection of some or all network nodes, or that may actually use the Internet itself to construct some or all these virtual private network (VPN) links. Although the IP-based applications platform can be identical for both Internet and intranet, obvious differences include issues such as management control, security, performance and reliability, and cost.

Characterizing the Internet as a paradigm and not necessarily as a physical network entity leads inevitably to at least two positive consequences for the network manager:

1. There is recognition that the network question does not need to be, in fact should not be, formulated in terms of Internet vs. corporate network (i.e., the Internet as an alternative to a corporate network), but rather in terms of a continuum of compatible transport infrastructure alternatives that can be brought under the influence, if not always the complete control, of the network management function.
2. There is flexibility to manage this continuum of facilities to bring many new and worthwhile opportunities to play within the corporate network environment (i.e., the enterprise), while simultaneously optimizing cost and performance for a wide variety of applications needs. This paradigm should define the role of the Internet within the enterprise network environment.

GROWTH

The public Internet is literally exploding. Many of the same forces are driving demands on intranets as well. The number of national Internet backbones within the U.S. is believed to have grown from 9 at the end of 1996 to 37 in 1997—an approximate 411% annual rate of increase. During the same period of time, the number of Internet service providers (ISPs) in the U.S. grew from around 1447 to 4300 (a 297% increase), and from 1500 to 2000 in Europe (a 133% increase). At the end of 1997, there were believed to be 7500 ISPs worldwide. Currently, around 20 million U.S. homes have Internet access, and that number is expected to double to 40 million by the turn of the century (an approximate 42% compounded annual increase).

AT&T has invested over $300 million to augment its Internet backbone facilities; GTE invested $616 million to acquire a 15,000-mi network from BBN Corp.; and Quest capitalized over $7 billion in a new coast-to-coast fiber network.[8] The MCI Internet backbone alone is claimed to carry an aggregate in excess of 1120 terabits (1120 trillion bits) per week. To put this into concrete terms, to view 1120 terabits, you would have to watch the motion picture *Star Wars* 24 hr/day for nine straight years—the movie being about 24 billion bits in size.[9] The message is clear: *growth and scalability* are very important to modern enterprise network design and implementation, as well as a serious concern within the public Internet infrastructure.

SCALABILITY

At first glance, adequate network transport capability would seem to be a simple matter of cost. Reliable transport at rates from analog line speeds, upward through T1 (1.5M bps), T3 (45M bps), OC-3 (155M bps), OC-12 (622M bps), and beyond are now available for a price. Although some higher speed facilities may be currently unavailable in isolated areas, this situation is rapidly improving. However, the carrier network infrastructure often does not scale (i.e., accommodate incremental capacity increases) well. Adding the next increment of needed capacity to a circuit may require the purchase of a huge jump in bandwidth with significant related additional cost.

Underlying protocols (e.g., X.25,[10] frame relay,[11] switched multimegabit data services [SMDS][12]) and network routers/switches may also prove problematic as speeds increase. Unfortunately, accommodation of growth and scalability is seldom a simple issue of a bigger pipe or a bigger box. Fortunately, newer protocols such as asynchronous transfer mode (ATM),[13,14] scale much better; they also provide enhanced functionality and performance, presenting an opportunity for network managers to address many scalability issues through protocol (e.g., ATM) migration.

LOCAL INFRASTRUCTURE

Installed building cabling and wiring may also be inadequate to accommodate today's (or tomorrow's) higher bandpass requirements, particularly above 100M bps. Yet, these bandpass demands are being driven in many organizations by the evolving applications (e.g., the Web and IP-based Internet telephony and videoconferencing). Newer structured wiring systems (e.g., EIA/TIA-568A)[15] will readily handle rates upward of OC-3, and at least one vendor[16] now certifies its (proprietary) category 5 (CAT5) structured wiring systems for up to OC-12 rates running ATM.

Fiber to the desktop is also an option, but it may prove to be a more expensive and less flexible solution, particularly when workstation interface hardware and software application costs are considered. A hierarchical (i.e., tiered) approach using fiber backbone (and within multistory environments, fiber riser) and CAT5 distribution (i.e., horizontal) wiring in support of the TCP/IP paradigm is a solution now often employed in buildingwide and campuswide networks. Local wiring and cabling systems and their implications for the workstation environment should surely be assessed, and should become an element of future network–facilities planning.

Addressing

The current 32-b IP address space (IPv4) in theory supports upward of 4.3 billion (2 + 32) unique host and client computer IP addresses, seemingly more than enough to accommodate all worldwide Internet addressing needs. However, the practices of reserving certain address classes for specific functions (e.g., multicasting)[17] and issuing addresses to organizations in various sized blocks (e.g., 24-b Class A, 16-b Class B, or 8-b Class C, rather than as individual addresses) are not optimally efficient. Worldwide, IP address exhaustion is rapidly approaching, although there currently exists some disagreement about exactly when this exhaustion will occur.

A new IP addressing scheme being called IP next generation (Ipng[18]; also called IPv6) is on the horizon, and it incorporates many improvements a 128-b address field, providing the potential for more than $3.4 \times 10 + 38$ (i.e., 10 followed with 38 zeros) unique addresses, a practically inexhaustible supply of IP addresses for the future. Switches and routers must be able to capitalize on the new protocol; and network managers would be well-advised to review current network systems as well as anticipated new systems to ensure compatibility and compliance with evolving (e.g., IPv6) protocols.[19]

Routers and Switches

Routers and switches—the network traffic cops—can also be problematic as network speed and traffic increase. Although a treatise can be written on selection and implementation of routers and switches, areas worthy of note include (1) capacity, (2) capability and reliability, (3) flexibility, and (4) cost. Since these devices generally represent a significant financial investment, it is desirable that this investment be protected (i.e., physical lifetime equal or exceed economic lifetime). They should provide a growth path to accommodate both present and anticipated future traffic requirements, and the flexibility to accommodate evolving protocols (e.g., IPv6) and functions. A financially viable upgrade strategy to accommodate evolving hardware interfaces (e.g., to support frame relay, SMDS, ATM, Gigabit Ethernet[20]) is very desirable.

Unfortunately, router capacity seldom scales linearly with either traffic volume or channel speed. Accommodating increasing traffic volume and port speeds often requires ever-increasing message queue depths, buffer memory requirements, and processor power to manage the additional process overhead. Typically, these system aspects scale exponentially with channel speed. The protocols themselves and their specific implementation (e.g., software vs. hardware) can also have a dramatic effect on scalability within routers and switches. Although it is probably unrealistic to presume that a network manager can totally avoid these problems, careful planning and the provision of flexibility to take advantage of evolving technology can go a long way toward avoiding many potential problems. The most appropriate time to address issues of future capacity and capability, reliability, and flexibility of switches and routers is with vendors before these systems are purchased and implemented. Consideration of options

321

and alternatives for network growth and evolution in advance of need is certainly desirable, particularly in the shadow of the rapidly evolving Internet platform.

Control

The network manager's spectrum of control includes

1. Network elements and aspects that can be directly affected by the manager
2. Those elements that the manager can directly or indirectly influence
3. Elements that are typically beyond the control or influence of the manager

Generally speaking, intranets provide the manager with the greatest degree of control at the greatest cost, while the public Internet can cost considerably less but often leaves the manager with far less control. As we will see, the Internet paradigm can afford the manager the flexibility to better optimize between elements of control and cost.

Security

Interconnection with the public Internet will clearly increase external security risks, but these are but one facet of overall network security. Security threats can (and do) originate from inside as well as outside an organization. Although external threats (e.g., hackers, industrial espionage or sabotage, and theft of data or service) have received much attention in the popular press, less publicized internal threats are probably more common with equally deleterious outcomes. Internal threats most commonly result from inadvertent deleterious events, for example, innocent human error or software failure (i.e., bugs, equipment failure, environmental factors, or large or small physical disasters). Disgruntled employees (or exemployees) are another common source of internally precipitated deleterious outcomes. Internet-related security risks should be appropriately addressed as still another element in an overall security and risk avoidance and mitigation program, should be kept in perspective, and should not be allowed to be inflated beyond their true significance.

Firewalls

Firewalls can provide a degree of protection against unauthorized penetration from outside, and they should be seriously considered if interconnections with the public Internet are contemplated. Generally speaking, firewall products stand between the external network (extranet) and the protected internal network and most frequently afford some form of IP address filtering.[21] These filters commonly work by examining the header of the IP packet and making pass or fail decisions based on the source and

322

destination IP addresses. In this way, the risk of access by unauthorized users can be reduced.

Unfortunately, source and destination information within packets can be falsified (spoofed); and other more sophisticated infiltration strategies can be executed, leading to escalating warfare between evermore sophisticated (and expensive) firewall products on the one hand and evermore devious potential interlopers on the other hand. This process inevitably leads to a stalemate, with the firewall technology generally acknowledged to serve the function of reducing the population of potential infiltrators (i.e., "raising the bar"), but never totally eliminating the potential threat. Thus, the network manager must resolve to balance risks, potential consequences, and costs within a delicate operational equation.

Encryption

Other security-related concerns, particularly within the global arena or in situations where the public Internet is utilized, include confidentiality (i.e., secrecy of message content), integrity (i.e., assurance that message content has not been purposely or inadvertently altered), and authenticity (i.e., assurance that the message originator is actually as claimed) of electronic messages. Modern encryption-based technologies[22] provide highly effective (but far from perfect) mechanisms to ensure these aspects of security. Technically and economically suitable encryption technologies are commercially available for domestic use,[23,24] but with few exceptions, adequate encryption is currently unavailable with international communications due primarily to U.S. government encryption export policies and restrictions.[25] This is a highly dynamic political environment that may well change for the better within the foreseeable future[26] and should be carefully monitored.

It is interesting to observe some individuals. They would readily hand over their credit card number to an unfamiliar gas station attendant or sales clerk. They would also have no compunction about writing a credit card or bank account number on a personal check that may be seen by untold numbers of unknown clerical or bank employees, but they become paranoid about having the same information somehow intercepted from the Internet. This is not to make light of legitimate security concerns.

It is merely to point out that we live in a world filled with risks and that the best strategies for dealing with this world are based on a considered and rational assessment of these various risks followed by appropriate and measured responses to control or mitigate them. It would be unfortunate indeed for an organization to pass up the substantial potential benefits afforded by Internet access due to an exaggerated perception of Internet-connectivity-related risks that, in reality, can be substantially mitigated.

Performance and Reliability

Network performance (e.g., responsiveness and throughput) and reliability (e.g., data integrity, consistency of performance, and availability) are important network considerations. The Internet paradigm affords the network manager the opportunity to optimize costs while meeting reliability-related and performance-related criteria by selective utilization of the public Internet, private intranet, or other IP-compatible transmission facilities.

Traffic with stringent reliability or performance requirements might be selectively routed over an intranet, while traffic with less stringent requirements might just as easily be directed through the public Internet to remote locations. This would thus reserve the typically more expensive intranet bandpass for the more demanding traffic, all with relative transparency to the IP-based application. Also, traffic from a specific network node or application might be routed over the intranet on certain occasions and over the Internet on other occasions.

Internet-based network bandpass management schemes involving the dynamic overflow of lower priority traffic from the intranet to the Internet during periods of potential intranet congestion are also possible. Dynamic overflow routing can also provide a mechanism for network hardening, the ability of the network to function (albeit, at potentially reduced levels of service) during periods of intranet (or Internet) outage by routing traffic away from the malfunctioning network element.

INTERNET-BASED VIRTUAL PRIVATE NETWORKS

Today's technology[27] affords the network manager the potential to economically carve out a virtual intranet from the broader public Internet. Remote sites can be accommodated in a nearly transparent manner using the Internet, where performance may not be a serious concern, or more commonly, where simple economics would otherwise prohibit the interconnection of the remote site using private facilities.

The general concept is to connect via the public Internet, cooperating nodes that may combine compression, encryption, and authentication. The armored payload of the IP packet exchanged between these nodes is used to ensure a secure, private, and transparent communications channel. This technology can also be used to support certain legacy protocols (e.g., Internet packet exchange [IPX][28]) as well as ATM, in addition to standard IP packets. Such devices usually provide a transparent communications channel to network devices within the confines of the local network (e.g., appear to be simple private lines).

DIVERSITY

Diversity exists when the failure of a single network element (e.g., transmission channel or network switch) does not result in an interruption of network service. Alternate routing between an intranet and the Internet can provide an element of diversity, but the flexibility provided by the Internet paradigm can be further extended to provide additional elements of diversity. ISP failures can be readily accommodated by interconnecting with multiple ISPs. During normal operations, traffic volume is typically shared between the ISPs, thus optimizing bandpass utilization, performance, and cost.

During periods of abnormal performance by an ISP, traffic can be routed to the remaining ISP or ISPs, thus maintaining network functionality (albeit at potentially reduced levels of service when inadequate reserve bandpass to accommodate the full traffic load may have been provisioned on the remaining facilities). Where essential, levels of performance can be preserved at some additional cost through provisioning of additional reserve bandpass. Since the Internet was originally designed with military applications in mind, a network based on the Internet paradigm provides the network manager with unusual flexibility to design a highly redundant and reliable network and often at a cost far less than would be required within other network architectures.

BROWSER-BASED NETWORK MANAGEMENT

Within the Internet paradigm, network management can be enhanced and simplified through the use of browser-based network management technology.[29] In a typical installation, an inexpensive network–management server is deployed within the network, which provides convenient access via the network itself (or via a local console) to network management information, exploration, and control functions across the enterprise using a generic Web browser client.[30,31]

Browser-based network management typically provides multivendor hardware support within a single unified network–management platform by taking advantage of the simple network management protocol (SNMP).[32] Particularly within multivendor environments, browser-based clients provide the ability to simply log on to the network from any convenient workstation (including remote access via the public Internet where authorized).

Using a multiplatform (e.g., Windows, Unix, Macintosh) compatible Web browser, the network manager can in a consistent and uniform manner check the configuration and status of network–resident devices provided by multiple vendors. Network managers can also access and analyze network status information (e.g., alarms, traps, traffic and utilization statistics, and device state conditions) across different network platforms. And by using an efficient and consistent graphical user interface (GUI), they execute authorized configuration and control functions. This approach can provide a significant improvement over many current enterprise–network management methodologies (e.g., proprietary management platform), particularly when more than one network–equipment vendor might be involved.

As with other applications within the Internet paradigm, the many benefits provided by ease of access can also present increased vulnerability to surreptitious acts. Within the server itself, most systems provide rigorous log-on security procedures to thwart unauthorized access and permit the network manager to reserve certain more sensitive control functions to a subset of authorized users. In addition, when access is provided via the public Internet, intruders must first successfully penetrate any firewall precautions in place within the network environment before gaining access to the log-on functions of the network–management server, further decreasing the potential for unauthorized access. As with other aspects of the Internet paradigm, the benefits typically significantly exceed the risks, but the network manager must, nonetheless, be mindful of the resultant vulnerabilities.

Browser-based network management technology, particularly immediate remote access by off-site network–management technical personnel (e.g., from home, or on the road, via a home PC or laptop computer and a local ISP network), can significantly expedite resolution of network-related problems. The technology can also provide a valuable opportunity for the network manager to enhance, streamline, and simplify network support operations. In particular, this can be done where potential procurement and installation of network elements from multiple vendors might both allow the network manager to optimize network functionality by choosing the most appropriate equipment for specific network applications, regardless of vendor, and to leverage network budgets through advantageous utilization of competitive procurement practices.

QUALITY OF SERVICE

A notable deficiency inherent in the current Internet paradigm, particularly within the public Internet environment, is the inability of the network to readily distinguish among traffic from competing applications and to provide accommodation in routing and resource utilization based on special needs of specific applications. For example, a large file transfer application may be highly intolerant of any data packet loss and require a significant amount of average network bandpass but be relatively insensitive to data-packet transport latency or bursts and pauses in data-packet arrival (i.e., interpacket arrival times).

Conversely, an interactive terminal session may require minimum average bandpass but be particularly sensitive to packet transport latency and data-packet loss. On the other hand, an audiotransmission application might be adequately served by moderate average bandpass and be somewhat tolerant of nominal data-packet loss or corruption but be particularly sensitive to both transport latency and interpacket delivery times. A videoconferencing application, while being moderately insensitive to data-packet loss or corruption, might require relatively large average bandpass, low packet transport latency, and predictable interpacket arrival times.

The ability to queue and route data packets on the basis of relative priority and reliability parameters is frequently referred to as quality of service.[33] Both ATM[34] and the frame relay[35] protocol specifications make provision for designating priority within the transmitted data unit (i.e., cell or frame). Evolving internetworking standards accommodate the transmission of IP packets over ATM and frame relay, including provision for quality of service.[36] Several major carriers make multiple levels of Internet service based on quality of service priorities widely available to ISPs[37] and already incorporate quality of service capability within their international backbone networks. However, carriers and ISPs alike have other nontechnical motivations for moving toward the implementation of quality of service.

With the rapidly growing commercial presence on the public Internet, performance has become an important issue. The quality of service provides a ready-made strategy for meeting more rigorous performance criteria within a price-sensitive market by providing a convenient means whereby the ISP or carrier can deliver several levels of premium service products at various levels of additional cost to the subscriber—analogous to airmail, first class, parcel post, etc.—within the postal system.

At the network and ISP level, quality of service holds the illusive promise of allowing enhanced bandpass management and the potential for the network manager to integrate a wider range of applications onto the network, thus generating greater economies of scale and reducing redundant network costs while preserving (or enhancing) needed levels of performance on an application class by application class basis. However, the real promise of quality of service lies with its extension into the application architecture itself. Evolving protocols such as the Resource Reservation Protocol (RSVP)[38] allow an individual enabled application to request a bandwidth reservation from its host PC, which passes the request upstream to the RSVP-equipped routers along the information path, thus providing an end-to-end reservation.

Moving toward implementation of such enabled applications, however, may prove more problematic for network managers within some organizational structures than merely providing the inherent network support function for these evolving application capabilities. Nonetheless, these applications capabilities provide sufficient promise that they should at least be appropriately considered within the network planning and development process.

INTERNET VOICE TELEPHONY

The Internet paradigm provides the network manager with the potential to capitalize on evolving Internet-based telephony applications.[39] Internet-based voice telephony—the ability to place and receive voice telephone-like calls over the Internet using PCs—initially evolved as mainly a hobby-ist's technology. Over time the technology has advanced to the level where nominally acceptable voice quality can be produced. While at the present time, the technology may not be quite ready for prime time within the business sector; it continues to evolve.[40]

The prospect of RSVP-like capabilities[41] provides great promise for the technology in the foreseeable future. In the meantime, the technology might prove to be of acceptable quality to replace or supplement certain existing telephony needs (e.g., particularly expensive international calls among business colleagues) within the enterprise network environment. IP telephony is also evolving to fill a niche in "remote agent" call center applications where "computer–telephony integration" (CTI)[42] and "telecommuting" are combining to support "virtual call center" applications[43] within an ever increasingly problematic employment marketplace.

WEB-BASED COMPUTER–TELEPHONY INTEGRATION

Probably of more interest to the network manager is the penetration of the Web into the call center environment. As the Web plays an ever larger role in many call centers, Web-based CTI,[44,45] can empower a customer (or prospective customer) to merely click on a Web page icon, enter a telephone number in a browser dialog box, and be connected to a call center representative over the voice network.

Such integrated applications (i.e., Web server, private branch exchange [PBX]/automatic call distributor [ACD], corporate database computer) can also allow the call center agent to dynamically view the same Web screen that the customer sees, information concerning the customer or related products and service from internal databases, and simultaneously converse with the customer on the voice line—a powerful sales and service application. Web-based CTI applications are also available that enable a Web user to perform such functions as scheduling or creating telephone conference calls without operator intervention,[46] as well as other useful CTI-based applications. Web-based CTI would appear to provide yet additional potential derivative benefits from the Internet paradigm for the network manager.

VIDEOCONFERENCING AND COLLABORATION

Internet-based desktop videoconferencing and collaboration applications[47] are becoming available, although the technology is still somewhat nascent. Web-based videoconferencing and collaboration applications[48] are also debuting, with at least some of these incorporating quality of service functionality at the workstation level, making this a very promising evolving technology as enterprise networks migrate toward incorporation of quality of service. The prospect of viable videoconferencing and collaboration at the desktop level across the enterprise, or possibly extended through the public Internet to include videoconferencing and collaboration with suppliers, alliance partners, or even customers can be very attractive. The Internet paradigm provides the essential underpinnings for the network manager to capitalize on these evolving technologies.

ELECTRONIC COMMERCE

According to U.S. authorities, Internet-based e-commerce is poised to become the "United States' most active trade vehicle within a decade."[49] On-line commerce was zero in 1992 and is expected to zoom to $300 billion by 2002.[50] Although electronic data interchange (EDI)[51] has made significant contributions toward streamlining the business purchase and sales process, it is nonetheless a somewhat "static" mechanism that is more akin to a catalog sales paradigm. E-commerce, on the other hand, tends to provide a more "dynamic" and "interactive" paradigm.

Many organizations are currently looking to e-commerce as a marketing and sales mechanism targeted toward the skyrocketing numbers of new Internet users (i.e., the electronic storefront), and there certainly have been examples of spectacular success along these lines.[52] Nonetheless, this may not be where the technology ultimately comes to leave its most significant mark. E-commerce encompasses both downstream (i.e., retail and customer sales) and upstream (i.e., supplier) marketing channels. In the future, the capabilities of this technology may well reshape the concept of competition from the downstream sales and marketing channel to the upstream supply channel. In the future, the more successful business may be the one that better masters fulfilling its supply needs through the dynamic processes of e-commerce, rather than the business that maintains its downstream market channels but falls behind the times when it comes to exploiting upstream channels.

There still remain, however, a number of currently unresolved issues surrounding e-commerce. These include

1. Evolving legal structures and frameworks (e.g., Universal Commercial Code (UCC) for e-commerce)[53]
2. Evolving tariff and tax issues[54,55]
3. Privacy, security, and encryption issues[56]
4. Potential for government regulation
5. Intellectual property rights and protections[57]

The economic and political forces driving e-commerce will, no doubt, push these issues to early resolution, and much progress has already been made. The good news is that from the network infrastructure perspective, the Internet paradigm strongly supports e-commerce applications. Implementation of this paradigm will empower the enterprise (and hopefully, the network management function) to reap optimum advantage of evolving e-commerce opportunities.

PRIVACY-RELATED ISSUES

A presence on the Internet-based Web can be utilized to acquire valuable marketing-related information. It can be akin to a flower that is visited by a parade of busy bees with each bee taking some nectar, but probably without any awareness of the others, and also leaving a record of their visits by depositing bits of pollen. However, collection of various user-specific (i.e., personal) information, particularly without the user's knowledge or consent, can raise issues of propriety as well as privacy.

This practice can be even more problematic when children—who are "surfing the 'net" in ever-increasing numbers (often unsupervised by a responsible adult)—contribute to the information that is collected. The common practice of collecting information in this manner, and subsequently using it for marketing or sales-related activities (particularly selling the information, or products derived from the information, e.g., qualified mailing lists) has attracted the attention of privacy advocates, government regulators, and legislators alike.[58]

In an effort to avoid government regulation of the Internet and to avoid potential impediments to retail sales over the Web (e.g., consumer reluctance to conduct e-commerce for fear of surrendering personal information to surreptitious uses), there have been several attempts by the information industry (as well as by others) toward self-regulation.

The general thrust of these efforts has focused on:

1. Disclosure (i.e., what information, if any, is collected, and what use might be made of this information)
2. The opportunity for an individual to "opt out" of having his personal information collected
3. A commitment not to collect information from or about minors (except possibly where explicitly authorized by a parent or other responsible adult supervisor)

Typically, information that might be collected for the sole purpose of billing, shipping, etc. is permitted (although the fact of the collection of such information would still be disclosed). Typical of such guidelines is the International Chamber of Commerce (ICC) Revised Guidelines on Advertising and Marketing on the Internet.[59]

Organizations that maintain a presence on the Web, whether or not they engage in e-commerce, are encouraged to:

1. Formulate and formally adopt a "privacy policy" relating to their information gathering and use activities
2. Conspicuously post on their Web site, in keeping with the tenets of their privacy policy, their information gathering and use practices in a public "privacy statement" (area currently the focus of both regulators and legislators)
3. Keep abreast of potentially evolving legislation or regulations concerning collection or use of personal information

SUMMARY

The Internet should not be viewed from the perspective of an alternative to the corporate network, but rather the corporate network might better be viewed in the light of an underlying TCP/IP-based Internet paradigm. By incorporating an underlying TCP/IP-based transport infrastructure, the network manager can create the foundation for an integrated enterprise network capable of supporting and evolving with today's and tomorrow's evermore demanding applications. By capitalizing on both intranet and Internet models, the paradigm allows the manager to more readily balance benefits and costs, accommodate existing and emerging applications, and plan for a smoother transition into the future. Such a paradigm might also encourage a more strategic role for the network manager within the broader enterprise.

Notes

1. The Internet Society; "http://info.isoc.org/"
2. The World Wide Web Consortium (W3C); "http://www.w3.org/pub/WWW/Consortium/"
3. Using IP Telephony To Bypass Local Phone Monopolies; "http://www.phonezone.inter.net/tutorial/telco-bypass.htm"
4. Very High Speed Backbone Network Service; "http://www.vbns.net/"
5. Internet2 Project; "http://www.internet2.edu/"
6. The Internet Protocol Suite-TCP/IP; "http://kafka.uvic.ca/~svanmoss/FA345/TCP.IP.HTML"
7. Network Computer Reference Profile; "http://www.nc.ihost.com/nc_ref_profile.html"
8. MCI Internet Factsheet; "http://www.mci.com/mcisearch/aboutus/company/news/wcom/internet.shtml"
9. MCI News: Internet Policy Vision; "http://www.mci.com/mcisearch/aboutus/company/news/internetpolicy/basics.shtml"
10. Summary of ITU-T Recommendation X.25; "http://www.itu.int/itudoc/itu-t/rec/x/x1-199/s_x25_e_49468.html"
11. Frame Relay Tutorial; "http://www.telastro.demon.co.uk/fr_idx.htm"
12. An Introduction to SMDS; "http://www.ja.net/documents/NetworkNews/Issue40/SMDS/SMDS.html"
13. ATM Tutorial; "http://www.telastro.demon.co.uk/ATM_idx.htm"
14. Zahir Ebrahim, A Brief Tutorial on ATM; "http://juggler.lanl.gov/lanp/atm.tutorial.html"
15. Standards for Communications Cabling-Appendix A (EIA/TIA-568+TSB-40 Implementation); "http://www.computersource1.com/standard.htm"
16. Lucent Technologies, Systimax SCS; "http://www.lucent.com/netsys/systimax/"

17. The IP Multicast Initiative; "http://www.ipmulticast.com/"
18. TCP/IP and IPv6; "http://www.telastro.demon.co.uk/ip_idx.htm"
19. IP Next Generation (IPng); "http://playground.sun.com/ipng/"
20. The Emerging Gigabit Ethernet Standard IEEE 802.3z; "http://www.gigabit-ethernet.org/technology/whitepapers/gige/standard.html"
21. Interactive Network Design Manual: Internet Firewall Essentials; "http://techweb.cmp.com/nc/netdesign/wall2.html"
22. Encryption Technology; "http://www.campbell.org/issues/encrypt.htm"
23. Officials within the Clinton administration have encouraged Congress to enact legislation that would restrict domestic use of encryption technology or mandate so-called "trap doors" to enable authorities to easily intercept domestically encrypted messages: FBI Documents on Encryption; "http://www.epic.org/crypto/ban/fbi_dox/"
24. Legislation is currently pending that would prohibit government interference with domestic use of encryption: H.R.695-Security and Freedom Through Encryption (SAFE) Act [Sec. 2]; "http://jya.com/hr105-108-pt5.htm"
25. White House Memo on Encryption Export Policy; "http://www.bxa.doc.gov/Encryption/m961115.htm"
26. Pending legislation would relax U.S. export restrictions on encryption technology: H.R.695-Security and Freedom Through Encryption (SAFE) Act [Sec. 3]; "http://jya.com/hr105-108-pt5.htm"
27. RedCreek Communications Inc. Ravlin; "http://www.trustednetworks.com/"
28. Novell IPX; "http://www.cisco.com/warp/public/535/1.html"
29. Asante IntraSpection; "http://www.intraspection.com/"
30. Netscape Navigator/Communicator, "http://home.netscape.com/"
31. Microsoft Internet Explorer, "http://www.microsoft.com/"
32. SNMP-Simple Network Managment Protocol; "http://www.rad.com/networks/1995/snmp/snmp.htm"
33. Quality of Service: Delivering QoS on the Internet and in Corporate Networks; "http://www.employees.org/~ferguson/QoS.html"
34. Anatasios Dagiuklas, Bee J. Tye, and Mohammad Ghanbari, The Impact of UPC (Usage Parameter Control) on the QoS of VBR Video in ATM Networks; "http://senanet.com/epy/23/www/pc1.htm"
35. Norm Al Dude and N. Erd, On The Subject of Frame Relay; "http://www.datacomm-us.com/technow/scan04/scan04.html"
36. Anthony Alles, ATM Internetworking; "http://www-europe.cisco.com/warp/public/614/12.html"
37. Cisco Enables Premium Services for Internet Service Providers Worldwide; "http://www.cisco.com/warp/public/146/2019.html"
38. Stefanie Wilkinson, Boundless Bandwidth, "PCWeek" (Online); "http://www.pcweek.com/mgmt/0513/13dmain.html"
39. VocalTec, Internet Phone; "http://www.vocaltec.com/"
40. Lucent outlines IP telephony strategy; "http://search.zdnet.com/pcweek/news/0504/07mluce.html"
41. RSVP-Resource Reservation Protocol; "http://www.rad.com/networks/1997/rsvp/rsvp_toc.html#TOC"
42. CTI Software Overview; "http://www.phonezone.inter.net/phonezone/tutorial/cti-overview.htm"
43. NetSpeak ITEL(tm) Call Center; "http://www.netspeak.com/"
44. Sprint, Give Me a Call; "http://www.sprint.com:80/college/s_call.html"
45. AT&T, InstantAnswers; "http://www.att.com/features/0896/callmenow.html"
46. Sprint, Sprint Internet Conference Center (SM); "http://www.sprintconf.com/"
47. Microsoft, Net Meeting; "http://www.microsoft.com/netmeeting/"
48. First Virtual, Media Operating Software (MOS); "http://www.fvc.com/products/MOS.html"
49. White House Memo: A Framework for Global Electronic Commerce; "http://www.whitehouse.gov/WH/New/Commerce/index.html"
50. Andrew Zajac, In On-Line Access, A Great Divide, *Chicago Tribune*, (June 22, 1998, Sec 3, p. 1); "http://chicago.tribune.com/splash/article/0,1051,SAV-9806220001,00.html"
51. Welcome to the EDI Tutorial!; "http://www.getradeweb.com/pub-html/EdiBasicTutorial/EdiTutIx.html"

52. A classic example of a successful organization exploiting the "electronic store front" paradigm is Amazon.com, Inc.: "http://www.amazon.com"
53. Uniform Electronic Transactions Act {DRAFT-1998 March 23}; "http:// www.law.upenn.edu/library/ulc/uecicta/eta398.htm"
54. S.442-Internet Tax Freedom Act; "http://jya.com/s442.htm"
55. H.R.3529-Internet Tax Freedom Act; "http://thomas.loc.gov/cgi-bin/query/z?c105:h.r.3529:"
56. H.R.695-Security and Freedom Through Encryption (SAFE) Act; "http://jya.com/hr105-108-pt5.htm"
57. H.R.2281-WIPO Copyright Treaties Implementation Act; "http://dev.abanet.org/intelprop/hr2281.html"
58. Privacy and the NII: Safeguarding Telecommunications-Related Personal Information; "http://www.ntia.doc.gov/ntiahome/privwhitepaper.html"
59. International Chamber of Commerce, 38 Cour Albert 1er, 75008 Paris, France: ICC Revised Guidelines on Advertising and Marketing on the Internet; "http://www.iccwbo.org/Commissions/Marketing/Internet_Guidelines.html"

Chapter 20

The Role of Wireless in Corporate Communications

Dr. George Thomas

Cellular phones, personal pagers, mobile data modems, wireless e-mail, personal digital assistants, and a plethora of other wireless devices and services have become indispensable productivity tools for managers on the move in today's corporate world. Our purpose in this chapter is to present a quick review of the state of the art in wireless technology for the corporate users.

Instead of tracing the history of the development of wireless communications from its roots, we shall use the introduction of the relatively modern Advanced Mobile Phone Service (AMPS) as our starting point. Introduced in the U.S. in 1982, AMPS embodied an innovative idea from Bell Telephone Laboratories, namely, spatial frequency reuse through a cellular architecture. In this system, a mobile telephone service area is divided into a number of adjacent cells of about 20 to 30 mi in diameter. Each cell has a base station at its center and a set of frequencies assigned to it. It is graphically convenient to represent the cells as nonoverlapping regular hexagons as in Exhibit 1.

However, somewhat overlapping circles superscribing the hexagons would have been closer to reality, and in actual fact each service area is an irregular shaped region depending on local terrain. The AMPS operates in the 800-MHz band (more about frequency spectra in the next section), using 832 two-way channel pairs, each channel being 30 kHz wide. Mobiles within one service area are dynamically assigned a pair of available frequencies for communication with the base station and onward to other mobiles through the base station. The neighboring cells around this cell are all assigned different sets of frequencies. However, a given set of frequencies may be simultaneously assigned to a number of cells that are far enough apart so that there is no mutual interference among these cells. As

0-8493-9990-4/99/$0.00+$.50
© 1999 by CRC Press LLC

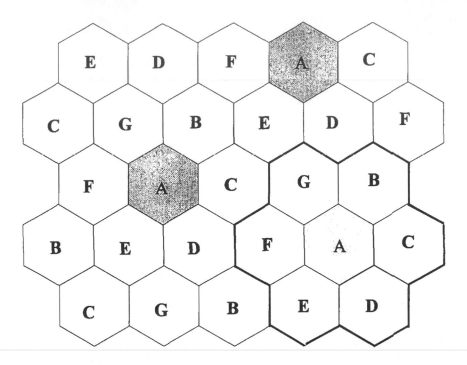

Exhibit 1. Seven-cell Frequency Reuse Pattern. The Frequency Sets A Through G are Reused Spatially Such That the Same Frequency Set (e.g. A) is Reused at Sufficiently Large Distances

---

shown in Exhibit 1, AMPS used a seven-cell frequency reuse pattern where any pair of cells using the same set of frequencies is separated by a distance of at least about two cell diameters.

The power of the cellular concept lies in its ability to use low-power transmitters and recursively reuse the same frequencies over nonadjacent regions, thereby increasing the coverage area and overall capacity to arbitrarily large levels. As an example, if a service area of 100-mi radius is covered by a single base station transmitter using a pool of 100 frequency channels, we would need a high power transmitter that can radiate enough power on each of those frequencies to cover the 100-mi radius. (This is clearly even more difficult to achieve for the mobile units than the fixed base station.) Besides, at any given time only a single mobile unit could use each one of those 100 frequencies. However, if we divide the service area into 100 cells of 10-mi radius and assign 10 frequencies to each cell, then the radiated power requirements would diminish as the square of the distance (i.e. by a factor of 100 in our example). More importantly, each frequency is reused about 10 times within the service area, so any one fre-

336

quency channel may simultaneously be used by 10 mobiles, in 10 different cells. The total call-carrying capacity has been boosted by a factor of ten.

Mobiles communicate with the base station and not directly with other mobiles even if they happen to momentarily share the same cell. The base stations are connected by fixed links to a mobile switching center (MSC). The "switching" (i.e., the routing of the call from the calling mobile to the called unit) takes place at the MSC. The called unit may be another mobile or a subscriber to the public switched telephone network (PSTN).

Mobiles moving across cell boundaries can continue with an ongoing call by acquiring a new pair of frequencies from the newly entered cell and relinquishing the frequencies that belonged to the cell just exited. This is accomplished by a procedure called handoff. The brief interruption is hardly noticeable for voice calls. In cells with heavy traffic, it may occasionally be that an entering mobile with an ongoing call will not be able to find a free frequency pair for ready handoff. In such a case the call is dropped. Good system engineering takes into account the projected maximum traffic levels and ensures that the probability of such call dropping is extremely small.

A less obvious strength of the cellular approach is in cell-splitting for capacity increase. In high-density urban centers or along heavily used highways, a single large cell 10 or 20 mi in diameter will not usually have enough frequency channels to support the large demands. In such cases, the cell may be divided into subcells and frequency reuse may be used among the subcells to increase the total traffic carrying capacity. An example of this plan is in Exhibit 2.

The spectacular success of the AMPS stimulated demands for even higher capacities, better quality, and newer services. Several later generation systems have emerged in response to these needs. Digital AMPS (D-AMPS) uses time division multiple access (TDMA) and voice digitization using the same 30-KHz channels of AMPS. The Telecommunications Industries Association Interim Standard IS-54 describes this approach. Alternatively, the IS-95 standard represents a code division multiple access (CDMA) system deployed by Qualcomm, which has claimed superior performance when used with dynamic power control and sectorized antennas.

Groupe Special Mobile (GSM) (also known more recently as Global System for Mobile Communications) was originally developed in Europe as an advanced mobile phone service with the chief attraction that one phone should work all over Europe across national boundaries. It uses two 25-MHz channels in the 900-MHz band, divided into 125 channels, each 200 kHz wide. TDMA is used, with voice digitized at 13K bps using a method known as linear predictive coding. Briefly, both TDMA and CDMA are available today as two strong competitors in the advanced mobile phone service mar-

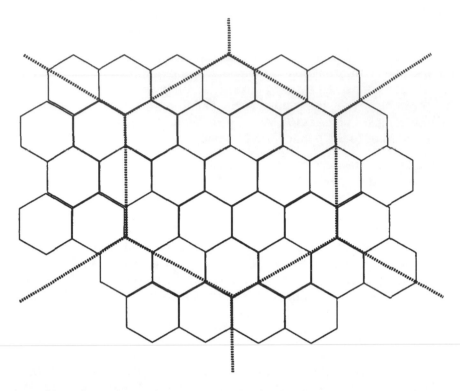

Exhibit 2. Cell Splitting—One Large Cell is Divided Into a Number of Smaller Subcells to Enhance Frequency Reuse and Increase Traffic Capacity

---

ket. These technologies also migrate easily to the emerging personal communications services (PCS) market. PCS is discussed in a later section.

REGULATORY AND SPECTRUM COORDINATION ASPECTS

The radio spectrum has been recognized as a natural resource whose utilization needs to be coordinated and controlled. In the U.S., this coordination responsibility has been assigned to the Federal Communications Commission (FCC), which was created as a consequence of the landmark Communications Act of 1934. The FCC has broad authority over all areas of radio spectrum usage, including spectrum allocation, rule making, licensing, product certification, and spectrum monitoring. The FCC serves as the single focal point for all aspects of use of the radio spectrum in the U.S., except for federal government uses whose oversight rests with the National Telecommunications and Information Agency (NTIA). Additionally, the FCC also represents U.S. interests in global radio spectrum management in the International Telecommunications Union (ITU).

Requests for new or revised allocations of spectrum are initiated by petitions for rule making submitted to the FCC by interested parties. The FCC responds by issuing a request for comments and soliciting comments and replies from all interested parties. Later the FCC issues a notice of proposed rule making or a notice of inquiry. After another round of comments and replies, the FCC either rules in favor of the notice by issuing a report and order or it rules against the proposal in the notice in the form of a memorandum opinion and order.

In addition to playing a traditional role of spectrum coordination and management for conventional uses of the radio spectrum, the FCC has played very innovative roles in opening up new spectral bands for commercial utilization of emerging new wireless applications. The series of spectrum auctions for PCS is the strongest case in point. Another example relevant to the wireless scene is the Pioneers' Preference Policy, which encourages early disclosure of innovative uses of the spectrum by rewarding the innovators with preferential treatment in ensuing spectrum allocations. An enlightened FCC has been at the core of some revolutions in the wireless and PCS arena.

Revised Allocations of the Radio Spectrum

Revised allocations made by FCC in 1994 have set aside large bandwidths for PCS applications in the 1800-MHz band. Specifically, the 140-MHz band from 1850 to 1990 MHz was divided into three segments. A 20-MHz band for unlicensed PCS was sandwiched between two bands each 60 MHz wide for licensed PCS operations. Each of the licensed bands was carved up into three 15-MHz blocks, labeled A, B, and C; and three 5-MHz blocks labeled D, E, and F (Exhibit 3). Additionally two more 20-MHz blocks were allocated in the bands 2130 to 2150 MHz and 2180 to 2200 MHz. Further, allocations were made in the 900-MHz band for narrowband PCS such as paging services.

Ten-year licenses for use of the newly allocated PCS spectrum blocks were auctioned by FCC during 1995 and 1996. Licenses were specific to clearly defined major trade areas (MTAs) and basic trade areas (BTAs), which roughly compare in size to a state and a city, respectively. Not only the traditional major players in the telecommunications and wireless business but also a number of new entrants secured these licenses. FCC has stipulated build-out requirements for the PCS licensees.

Emerging New Uses of the Unlicensed Band

FCC rules are organized and published according to a numbering system consisting of "parts" numbered from 0 through 100. For example, part 22 deals with public mobile services and part 95 deals with personal radio services. Of particular interest to emerging wireless applications is part

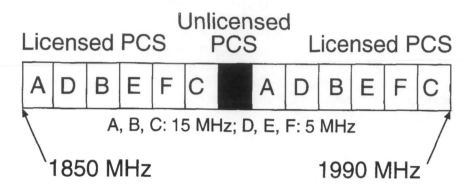

Exhibit 3.   1800-MHz PCS Spectrum

15, radio frequency devices. These rules cover the cases where uninten-
tional radiation (e.g., small DC motor appliances emitting radio frequency
interference) or incidental radiation (e.g., microwave ovens and garage
door openers emitting low power radio signals by design) are allowed
without individual licenses. Essentially these devices are constrained to
operate at low power levels such as 0.75 mW, so as to minimize interference to other occupants of the band. However, spread-spectrum devices
are allowed unlicensed operation with up to 1 W of output power. Unlicensed part 15 devices are also expected to tolerate any interference from
other higher priority and higher power licensed devices that may operate
in the same band.

A number of consumer technologies have successfully exploited part 15
unlicensed mode of operation, most typically using the industrial, scientific, and medical (ISM) band (902 to 928 MHz, 2400 to 2483.5 MHz, 5725 to
5850 MHz, and 24.00 to 24.25 GHz). Cordless phones, wireless private branch
exchanges (PBXs) and wireless local area networks (LANs) are specific examples of exploitation of part 15 provisions. With the deregulation in the
telecommunications industry, there are proposals for a variety of services to
homes, with wireless access into the buildings via Part 15 technologies.

WIRELESS LOCAL AREA NETWORKS

Wireless LANs typically operate over two different media: radio and infrared. We will discuss both in this section.

Radio LANs

Radio LANs use a radio frequency band to interconnect the elements of
a LAN. This tetherless option for local area networking has found much favor not only because of mobility of the elements but also because of

avoiding expensive in-building wiring and simplifying the physical layer issues related to network upgrades and reconfiguration. Radio LANs tend to be designed for one of the four transmission technologies: narrowband frequency modulation (FM), low-power radio, spread-spectrum radio, and microwave radio.

Narrowband FM radio LAN connectivity makes use of low-bandwidth channels (12.5 or 25 kHz) within the 450- to 470-MHz licensed band, with a maximum power limit of 2 W. Data rates of 9600 kbps are typical but throughputs tend to be lower because of the automatic repeat request (ARQ) and retransmission protocol required because of the multipath fading effects. The narrowband transmissions are also prone to cochannel and adjacent channel interferences. In spite of these, the small-sized and inexpensive narrowband FM radio with a good coverage range in both indoor and outdoor applications is a choice technology for low-speed applications such as wireless bar code scanners for inventory control, ID tag verification, etc.

Low-power radio technology is a typical choice for very short range applications (about 50-m range) where part 15 unlicensed operation of transmitters of power typically not exceeding 1 mW becomes feasible in the previously mentioned ISM bands (900 MHz; 2.4, 5.8, and 24 GHz). This is an attractive option for many in-building applications where the transmitter devices need not be individually licensed and where the transmission is well confined inside the building. The adverse effects of interference and multipath fading can be effectively contained by use of dynamic channel allocation (DCA) where the best transmit frequency out of a pool is selected dynamically based on the interference environment.

Spread-spectrum technology distributes the signal power over a much wider bandwidth than in conventional techniques, thereby reducing the power per unit bandwidth to very low values. This allows other systems to see less interference into themselves, and the special properties of spread spectrum resist interference from other users. More details on spread spectrum are given in a later section. Spread spectrum has been the most popular technology for exploitation of the part 15 rules. Growing out of the 900-MHz band, there have lately been an increasing number of wireless LAN and wireless digital PBX product offerings in the 2.4-GHz band. In these bands, the highest priority is for licensed operations supporting truly industrial, scientific, and medical applications (such as industrial plywood dryers, ultrasonic humidifiers, and medical diathermy equipment). Also naval radar, automatic vehicle monitoring, and amateur radio operations in these bands enjoy a higher priority to spread-spectrum wireless products. One reason for the current interest in the 2.4-GHz band is that it is at present much less encumbered with these other high priority operations. A second reason is that unlike the U.S., the 900-MHz band is heavily in use in Europe by the GSM system, which we will discuss later.

Microwave radio is a unique technology choice for wireless LAN, exemplified by the Altair product line from Motorola Inc. By using licensed operation at 18 MHz, Altair offers high-speed wireless LAN services over a 17.5-mi radius, supporting 10M-bps Ethernet LAN connectivity over 15M-bps radio links. Altair technology uses an intelligent six-sector antenna that can be electronically directed toward the direction of the strongest received signal. The licensed operation affords reliability and protection from interferences. With a somewhat high price tag, this product is aimed at high-end applications.

Infrared LANs

Infrared LANs are an interesting alternative to radio LANs. Infrared technology is relatively simple and inexpensive. The links are typically point to point. However, transmitted power can be scattered off a diffuser to achieve broadcast connectivity over a small area such as a room. Data transmission is accomplished by simple on–off modulation, using relatively inexpensive infrared light-emitting diodes (LEDs) and diode detectors. Battery power consumption on the portables is very low compared to the radio counterparts. Infrared data communications standards are guided by the Infrared Data Association (IrDA), a consortium of concerned industries formed in 1993. The IrDA standards envisage infrared data links operating at speeds up to 115.2K bps. Many personal and handheld devices use infrared links. However, we will not pursue the infrared option further in this chapter.

Spread-Spectrum LANs in the Unlicensed Bands

In this section we summarize the basic facts about spread spectrum. The key idea is that a data signal occupying a relatively small bandwidth can be "spread" over a much larger bandwidth by using a suitable "pseudorandom" spreading sequence. For example, each bit in a 1M-bps data stream can be replaced by a 100-b spreading code sequence, so that the transmission rate becomes 100M bps (Exhibit 4). The total transmitter power, for example, 1 W, is now spread thinner over the larger bandwidth. As such this lower power per unit bandwidth dumps less interference energy into other coexisting users. Besides, the pseudorandom spreading code only appears to be random; it is known perfectly to the intended receiver that uses this sequence to "despread" the spread-spectrum signal. While the despreading operation regenerates the desired (1M-bps) signal, it also spreads out other unwanted signal spectra by a factor of 100, so that the received signal to noise ratio has an advantage by a factor of 100 (Exhibit 5).

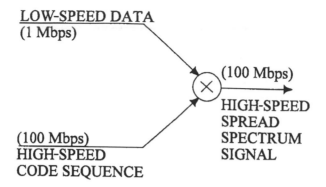

Exhibit 4. **Direct Sequence Spread Spectrum—Low-speed Data is Multiplied by a High-speed Spread Spectrum Code Sequence to Generate the Spread Spectrum Signal**

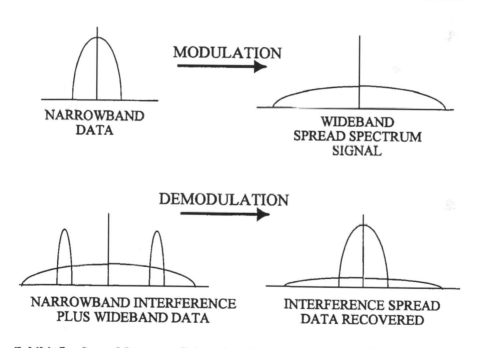

Exhibit 5. **Spread Spectrum Principle—The Spread Spectrum Demodulator Spreads Out Narrowband Interference While Recovering the Original Narrowband Signal by Correlation Techniques Based on the Properties of the Spreading Code Sequence**

Spread-spectrum technology is thus well known to afford low-power, low-interference transmissions without sacrificing signal to noise ratio, and to allow coexistence of a number of simultaneous users of the same physical channel at the same time without adverse multiaccess interference. In this latter multiaccess context, the terminology CDMA is more prevalent, emphasizing that it is the spreading code rather than time or frequency diversity that separates the multiple users. The origins of spread spectrum can be traced to secure military communications, where its other attributes of low probability of unauthorized detection and resistance to jamming play important roles. Its inherent code-based security (whereby a receiver that does not know the transmitting pseudorandom code cannot receive the signal) is important not only to military but also to civilian wireless communications.

Spread-spectrum systems utilize one of two different spreading technologies: direct sequence and frequency hopping. The example we had earlier typifies the direct sequence approach, where each bit is directly spread by a spreading sequence. The bandwidth of the spread signal is actually much larger than the original bandwidth. Frequency hopping takes a radically different approach. It does not physically expand the data signal bandwidth, for example, to 100 MHz. Instead it randomly hops among a hundred 1-MHz channels according to a pseudorandom hopping pattern. To an alien receiver, the entire 100×1-MHz band appears occupied, while a legitimate receiver that possesses the exact hopping pattern used by the transmitter can track the transmission from channel to channel and recover the data sequence (Exhibit 6).

The choice between the two technologies is guided by a number of factors. First, in typical mobile radio applications, a base station receives signals from transmitters that are at different distances. The received signal strengths are in inverse proportion to the squared distance. In direct sequence spread spectrum this "near–far effect" is known to penalize receivers located relatively farther away from the receiver. Reverse power control, where the receiver uses a reverse channel to control the transmit powers of the mobiles in accordance with their distances, is an effective but an expensive solution. Frequency hopping, on the other hand, is known to be much less prone to near–far effects.

However, frequency hopping spread-spectrum systems need very fast ("frequency-agile") tunable oscillators that can hop from channel to channel at speeds at least a fraction of the data rate ("slow" frequency hopping) or even at rates equal to or faster than the bit rate ("fast" frequency hopping). Such frequency agility is a technological challenge and tends to limit the data rate in frequency hopped spread spectrum. Further, direct sequence and frequency hopping spread-spectrum systems tolerate narrowband interference differently. In the ISM band, a licensed, non-spread-

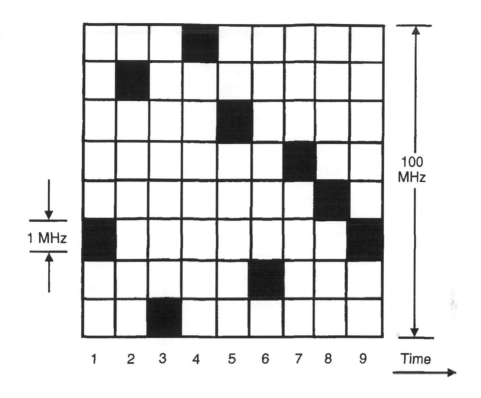

Exhibit 6. Frequency-hopping Spread Spectrum

spectrum user appears as a relatively high-power, narrowband interference to a spread-spectrum user. Frequency hopping is found more tolerant to such interference.

Based on the preceding considerations, there have been both types of spread-spectrum products offered for the wireless data market. As an example, the Omnipoint spread-spectrum product line offers a basic TDMA system with 8K bps (voice) to 500K bps (data) per user. The use of spread spectrum in the Omnipoint system is solely to provide tolerance to interference. On the other hand, Metricom's Ricochet system, typically deployed for campus-wide networking of portable computers, uses a frequency hopping system with 163 channels, each carrying 56K-bps user data on 77K-bps radio channels. Ricochet uses frequency hopping for multiaccess connectivity. The Qualcomm CDMA system is an example of a direct sequence spread-spectrum system with reverse power control.

Operation of spread-spectrum systems in the unlicensed bands is of course governed by relevant FCC rules. Maximum transmitted power is lim-

345

ited to 1 W (compared with typically 1 mW or less for non-spread-spectrum transmissions). Direct sequence systems are required to use a spreading factor of at least ten. For frequency hopping systems, this factor must be at least 50 in the 900-MHz band and at least 75 in the higher (2.4- and 5.8-GHz) bands. Also the hopping patterns are required to use all channels equally frequently. The "dwell time," the time spent in each channel in each hop, is not to exceed 400 ms over any 20-s interval for the 900-MHz systems. For those in the 2.4- and 5.8-GHz bands, the maximum is 400 ms over 30 s.

Wireless LAN Standards: IEEE 802.11

The Institute of Electrical and Electronics Engineers (IEEE) has been fostering the development of a Wireless LAN standard named IEEE 802.11. It focuses primarily on the 2.4-GHz band, with 1M bps data rate. International acceptance and multivendor interoperability of wireless LANs are foreseen as a result of these standards.

Technically, the 802.11 standard bases itself on a medium access control (MAC) protocol based on Carrier Sense Multiple Access with Collision Avoidance (CSMA/CA) plus acknowledgments for correctly received packets. Both infrared and spread-spectrum radio are available as the physical transmission medium. For spread spectrum, both direct sequence and frequency hopping techniques are available. The IEEE standards committee finalized the draft standard in mid-1996 and the standardization process was completed in 1997.

WIRELESS WIDE AREA NETWORKS FOR CORPORATE DATA NETWORKING

While wireless LANs add mobility and portability to the corporate work environment locally, wireless technology can also enhance the wide area networking (WAN) options for corporate networks. Next we briefly survey several key technologies and services in this arena.

Specialized Mobile Radio (SMR)

In the late 1970s, the Federal Communications Commission (FCC) decided to reallocate some of the ultrahigh frequency television (UHF TV) channels so as to make room in the 900-MHz band for two services: cellular radio and specialized mobile radio (SMR) services. It was envisaged that SMR services would be one option for providing two-way radio voice networking among mobile fleets. These are based on the concept of dynamically assigning radio channels among groups of intercommunicating mobiles, using a pool of 25-kHz radio channels licensed to a particular service area. Call requests go on a signaling channel to a controller that identifies unused radio channels from the pool of 5 to 20 channels (Exhibit 7).

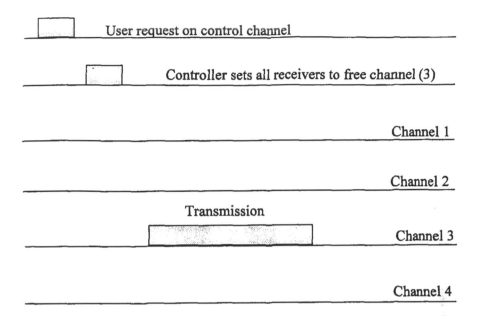

User request on control channel

Controller sets all receivers to free channel (3)

Channel 1

Channel 2

Transmission

Channel 3

Channel 4

Exhibit 7. Typical SMR Sequence of Events—The Controller Sets All Receivers of a Desired User Group to One of the Available Frequency Channels

The controller then commands all transceivers belonging to the requested group to tune to this assigned frequency. On call completion, the channel is returned to the pool of available radio channels. With a modestly sized pool of frequencies, SMR services can thus cater to a large number of groups of users. SMR licenses are awarded specific to a region of operation. However, SMR service providers (e.g., NexTel) have been able to acquire licenses for contiguous regions spanning wide areas and to offer "roaming" facilities over large geographic areas. Thus, SMR presents a viable option for many voice (and data) networking needs of corporate users. In addition, businesses involved with fleet management, delivery-and-pickup, and field service operations are typical examples of users of SMR services.

In digital SMR (DSMR), each of the conventional 25-kHz channels is divided into three or six digital voice channels. In enhanced SMR (ESMR), the 25-kHz channel is operated as a TDMA system with six time slots. This factor-of-six enhancement in capacity is further boosted fivefold by using a cellular architecture with frequency reuse. Thus, ESMR achieves a 30-fold increase in capacity vs. plain analog SMR. Apart from capacity enhancement, the support of digital data transmission and other additional services (such as roaming, call waiting, and three-way calling) make ESMR very attractive for several corporate communications needs.

347

Advanced Radio Data Information Service (ARDIS)

ARDIS originated in 1990 as a wireless data network built by Motorola Inc. for IBM to support its field service operations. However, it has grown into a nationwide network of over 1300 base stations covering most U.S. business areas and providing access to non-IBM users as well on a commercial basis. Nationwide roaming has been available since 1993. Most of ARDIS non-IBM clientele also are in field support operations for various corporations. A main strength of ARDIS is excellent in-building penetration, a feature necessitated by the needs of service crews working inside buildings.

ARDIS uses 25-kHz duplex radio channels in the 900-MHz band with 4800-bps data rate. Base stations with 40 W transmit power provide coverage over 15- to 20-mi radius. Mobile radios within this service area radiate up to 4 W of power. Lightweight InfoTAC personal and messaging units from Motorola form the bulk of the mobile units in the ARDIS network. Base stations and mobile units supporting higher speeds (19,200 bps) are being introduced.

ARDIS uses centralized network control (Exhibit 8). Base stations communicate to radio controllers, which in turn eventually route all messages to a central network control center (NCC). From here, the data packets are switched to land line links to the respective customer headquarters. ARDIS uses a tariff rate based on the number of packets. Tariff rates are typically in the 10 to 20 cents-per-packet range, with packet sizes limited from 256 to 512 bytes.

RAM Mobile Data/Mobitex

Mobitex is an international specification for wireless voice and data communications. In the U.S., RAM Mobile Data operates a data-only Mobitex-based network with major support from BellSouth. Additional support has been provided by Intel Corp., Lotus Development Corp., AT&T Radio-Mail Corp., Simware, and Oracle Corp. for various aspects including wireless e-mail and database applications. RAM Mobile has over 800 base stations in the top 100 business service areas in the U.S. By using an FCC waiver to SMR rules and taking advantage of an early entry into the field, RAM Mobile has successfully built up and maintained its presence in such urban niches as business and convention centers, airports and hotel districts. Its radio links support 8000-bps data rate over 12.5-kHz channels in the 800-MHz band.

RAM Mobile data network is comparatively more decentralized than ARDIS. Messages between mobiles within the same base station coverage area are switched locally. Only billing and administrative and control messages go up to the highest level of the hierarchical network. RAM Mobile also limits packets to modest sizes and has a tariff structure including a flat fee plus a proportional usage cost of a few cents per packet.

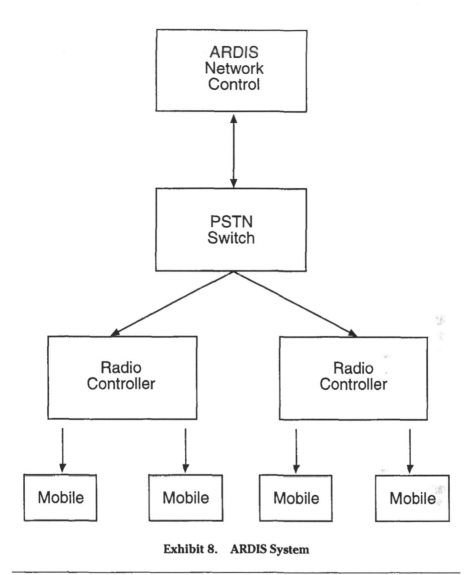

Exhibit 8.   ARDIS System

Cellular Digital Packet Data (CDPD)

CDPD is a new and ingenious technology that utilizes the idle channels in the existing cellular telephone networks to transmit wireless packet data on a low-priority basis. Pioneered by IBM and McCaw Cellular, CDPD standardization and other activities are now championed by the CDPD forum, which consists of other interested cellular operators and users.

Recall that a cellular telephone base station operates a pool of radio channels that it assigns to mobile cell phone users who transit through its service area from time to time. A CDPD mobile unit within that service area uses one of the unused channels in the pool (if any) to transmit several packets of wireless data while the channel is available. A newly arriving cell phone user may cause the base station to deny further use of the channel to the CDPD mobile, until another channel becomes free for temporary use by the CDPD mobile (Exhibit 9). In fact, CDPD systems can use "sniffer" antennas to detect the brief gap between termination of one call on a frequency and the "immediate" allocation of this frequency to another voice call. This brief gap is sufficient for CDPD to push a few packets through. Despite this sporadic, nonguaranteed availability of the channel, CDPD has the advantage that the radio system infrastructure is already in place and that service can be deployed with a minimum of delay. Thus, CDPD has been a major technology wave in the wireless data networks area.

CDPD radio link data rate is 19,200 bps, but this includes heavy use of error correction coding and other overheads. The user throughput is further lowered by the sporadic availability of the channel, typical data throughputs being as low as 2400 bps. Clear-cut tariffs have not emerged but the expectation is that a per-packet pricing formula will emerge.

The preexisting cellular telephone network that is a major strength of the CDPD proposal, has also been its drawback. Cellular telephone networks are licensed on a regional basis. Different operators dominate different area. Weaving a near-national CDPD network will thus involve the goodwill of a number of cellular service providers. These parties have displayed varying levels of support for the CDPD concept. Thus, in reality, national CDPD network service offerings have not appeared as quickly as had been expected.

PAGING NETWORKS

The earliest paging networks consisted of lightweight, portable devices that could be simply addressed by frequency and code. Its purpose was to merely reach the addressee and prompt him to the nearest phone or other conventional communication device. Applications abound in hospitals, on shop floors, and at convention centers. It was expected that the proliferation of cellular telephone services would obviate the paging services market. However, paging services have registered continued growth in spite of the availability of cell phones. One reason for this is probably that cellular phone tariffs are based on air time, so that both incoming and outgoing calls are chargeable. Subscribers therefore have found it more economical to use a pager to be alerted to incoming calls that they can answer selectively from the cell phone.

One-Way Paging

One-way paging involves routing of a simple alert signal or a brief alphanumeric message to a particular receiver within the service area. Nationwide

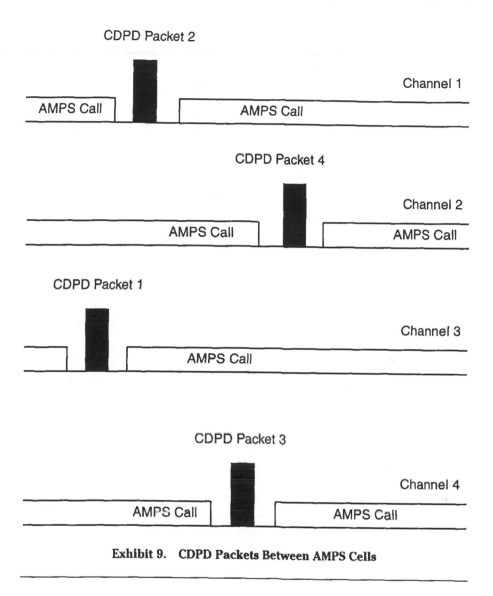

Exhibit 9. CDPD Packets Between AMPS Cells

paging networks receive paging calls at a national center from where it is beamed via satellite to a number of regional retransmission towers. Each of these retransmission towers simultaneously rebroadcast the same signal locally. Coverage regions of several towers overlap so that the same signal arrives from different angles at any given point. This enhances reachability and ensures a very high probability of successful message delivery.

This is important in one-way systems where there is no feedback and no chance for retransmission of unsuccessful messages. Multiple copies of the same signal on the same frequency arriving from different sources consti-

351

tute the standard "multipath" environment that tends to limit the data rate. In today's practical systems at least 1200 bps is found feasible, which is sufficient for the low-rate messaging needs in the present application.

SkyTel's SkyPage nationwide paging service is a notable example, operating in the 900-MHz UHF band. SkyTel also operates an enhanced SkyWord service that supports transmission of short text messages. The Motorola Electronic Mail Broadcast to a Roaming Computer (EMBARC) is another leading provider of paging and short text message delivery service nationwide. Motorola also has the FLEX technology that has become a de facto standard for high-performance paging protocols. FLEX can operate at 1600-, 3200-, or 6400-bps data rates.

A distinctive feature of FLEX compared to earlier protocols is that transmission is synchronous using a periodic pattern of 128 fixed-length frames. Transmitted every minute are 32 frames. Of the 32-frame sequences, 4 constitute a FLEX cycle that repeats periodically. Data, when present, is encapsulated into these frames. Unlike older pager technologies, the page receivers do not have to constantly monitor the channel for any messages addressed to it, thus causing constant battery drain. Instead, FLEX pagers periodically look for an alert pattern at a designated point in the received signal stream but otherwise stay dormant and thus conserve battery power.

Two-Way Messaging

Two-way messaging is an outgrowth of one-way paging. It allows the paging receiver to at least confirm receipt of the page and possibly also attach a brief response message. In early systems, the pager could respond with a numeric code that corresponded to one of a set of preselected responses. Advanced two-way messaging systems envisage true alphanumeric response capability for the pager. Motorola's reFLEX has noted much success in this direction. By using a 50-kHz channel, reFLEX supports 12,800 to 25,600 bps data transmission rate to the pager and up to 9,600 bps on a return link from the pager. Motorola's latest offering in this line is in FLEXion, which supports two-way voice messaging. A very large number of service providers nationally and worldwide have adopted the FLEX family of paging protocols for a variety of applications.

PERSONAL DIGITAL ASSISTANTS

We shall use the term personal digital assistants (PDAs) to denote generically a number of handheld devices that have appeared in the market under various other names such as personal communicators, personal information managers, and so forth. The Apple Computer Inc. Newton and the 3Com Corp. PalmPilot are just two examples. PDAs are lightweight, handheld devices, ranging in price from $300 to $1000 or more. They are aimed at business travelers who need an integrated, miniature information environment that can move with them. Pen-based text input with character recognition and touch-sensitive screens with icons and simulated keyboards are almost the norm. Common utilities such as appointment book, calendar, address book, spreadsheet, database, basic word processing, e-mail, and cell phone dial-up are typically supported. Despite a sluggish start, these devices are expected to eventually become a major segment of wireless consumer products for the corporate user.

Apple's Newton is recognized as a pioneer product in the field. The 15-oz handheld device measuring 5×7 in. has a Reduced Instruction Set Computer (RISC) processor running an object-oriented operating system, and it is designed for very low battery drain. Newton runs useful application programs such as note pad, card file, and calendar. It features pen-based input with handwriting recognition software and certain intelligence and learning features that allow it to personalize itself to the user. An infrared port allows data transfer at 19,200 bps at close proximity and a Personal Computer Memory Card International Association (PCMCIA) slot allows modem, pager, and wireless interconnection to the outside world. Newton found acceptance not only as a productivity enhancement tool for traveling executives but also as a handy integrated information management tool for a variety of applications such as inventory management in warehouses and facilities management in large convention centers. However, as a result of Apple's reorientation of its product line focus, Newtons have not been in production since early 1998.

There are other successful entrants into the PDA market. The PalmPilot from 3Com has earned a sizeable market share, competing with similar products from Hewlett-Packard Co., Casio, NEC, Philips, Sharp, and others. While PalmPilot runs on its own operating system (Palm OS), many competing products are beginning to embrace Microsoft Corp.'s Windows CE (Consumer Electronics) as a common platform. Downsized versions of most of the familiar Microsoft suite of applications, including e-mail and World Wide Web browsing, are available on these palmtop computers with wireless links to the outside world.

The Casio Z-7000 is a PDA product available through the Radio Shack retail chain and is comparable to similar products from Tandy and Sharp. With an infrared data port and a PCMCIA slot for external access, the Z-7000 can interact with external databases. It has a low-speed, low-power processor (compared to Newton) and hence has very low power consumption, thereby enabling prolonged operation on batteries. It uses an icon-based operating system and manages a display that can mix text and freehand drawings with ease. In fact, the pen-input drawings can be erased stroke by stroke just as the character input by using the backspace key. In addition to the usual utilities, these devices variously support dictionary and thesaurus, spell checker, language translators, and financial packages.

Simon is a PDA product developed by IBM and marketed by Bell South, 8×2.5 in. in size and weighing 18 oz. Its liquid crystal display (LCD) presents a simulated cell phone key pad that can be activated by touch. It can also display a QWERTY keyboard that can take alphanumeric input by touch. It also has another novel input mode, the predictive keyboard, which displays six large keys representing characters that are statistically most likely to follow the previous inputs. Simon has Group III fax capability for transmitting text and handwritten material.

Sony's Magic Link is another high-end PDA product that offers a variety of useful features. It features both a pager and a dial-up modem, giving the user the flexibility to choose the more economical option. In addition to the standard amenities (cardfiles, scheduler, notepad, etc.), Magic Link has an infrared port for short-range data exchange, a PCMCIA slot, a fax capability, and a voice recording feature with built-in microphone and speaker. Magic Link runs on the Magic Cap operating system from General Magic Corp., and uses the Telescript remote programming language. Telescript creates smart agents (self-contained messages that include remotely executable programs). These agents are preauthorized to negotiate with other agents and systems within specified parameter limits. For example, instead of two human users exchanging several messages back and forth until a mutually agreeable meeting time can be scheduled, an intelligent agent can be launched with authority to agree for the earliest available time within a prescribed time window. The agent returns after some time with the appropriate result.

PERSONAL COMMUNICATION SERVICES

The widespread availability of mobile phone services and portable wireless devices for both in-building and outdoor communications naturally gave shape to the dream of an integrated wireless system where one single personal, handheld, cordless device (with one single universally portable phone number) can access the network form anywhere in the world at any time. Several partial realizations of this obviously archetypal model are being actively developed and deployed by various providers, all under the general stamp of PCS.

One notable track of product development in PCS has been in advanced versions of cordless phones themselves. The first generation cordless telephones, CT1, used analog transmission in the high-frequency (HF) band (specifically 49 MHz in the U.S., operating under FCC part 15 rules) and were mostly for in-home use as a simple replacement for the cord linking the phone base to the handset.

A major technological improvement came with the second-generation cordless phones, CT2, which uses digital technology, specifically, digitized voice and TDMA transmission. In addition to offering better performance as cordless phones for home use, CT2 also led to digital PBXs and also to new services such as cordless access to the PSTN through wireless access points installed in public places (i.e., a wireless equivalent of a pay phone). This was further advanced by CT2-Plus, developed by Nortel (formerly Northern Telecom). CT2-Plus added such features as user mobility support from one cell to another, capability for reception of incoming calls and data transmission support.

CT3, developed by Ericsson, improves on the handoff performance of CT2-Plus. In the latter, cell-to-cell handoff is not smooth, and a perceptible disruption occurs when the transition occurs. CT3 improves this by constantly monitoring other channels during its idle time in the TDMA transmission sequence. Also CT3 uses picocells (i.e., cells of very small diameter with low transmission power levels) to achieve higher capacity and better performance. The digital european cordless technology (DECT) standards evolved in large measure from the developmental efforts for CT3. DECT has spectrum allocations covering all Europe in the 1800-MHz band. Further, the DCS-1800 is another TDMA system that is a modification of the GSM system for PCS services. In the U.S., both TDMA and CDMA systems are in use.

In the U.S., the FCC has allocated additional spectrum for PCS in the 1.7- to 2.3-GHz band. This spectrum was auctioned region-wise in 1995 and 1996 and raised several billions of dollars for the government. However, this spectrum is already occupied by other users who are to be moved to other frequency bands.

GLOBAL MOBILE SATELLITE SERVICES

Mobile satellite services (MSS) is an area where significant growth in wireless technology is foreseen. Geostationary satellites have proved their value in providing universal service coverage to a large area at once. Operating from equatorial orbits at 22,000 mi in altitude, these satellites move at the same angular speed as the rotation of the earth and hence appear relatively stationary to a ground-based observer. Geostationary satellites thus serve as very tall microwave relay towers. Their accessibility to small handheld communicators is severely limited by the demand for transmit power necessitated by the very large distance.

At lower altitudes (of a few thousands to several hundreds of miles), the power requirement can be drastically reduced, thus making it possible for low-power portable and handheld devices to reach the satellite directly. The satellite beam toward the earth (for both transmission and reception) can be organized in the familiar cellular fashion (Exhibit 10). Not only does this afford capacity enhancement by frequency reuse, but it also concentrates power into narrow cell-sized beams, thereby reducing the required sizes of the portable antennas.

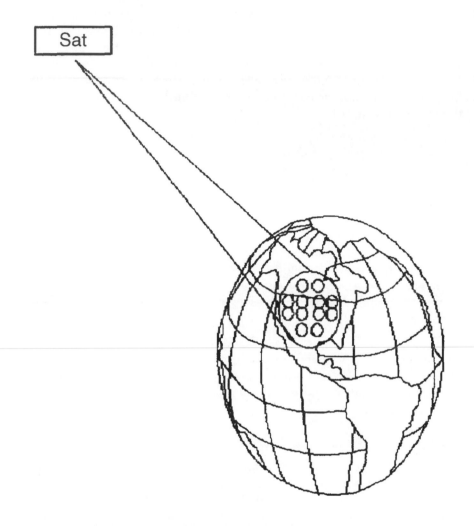

Exhibit 10.   Cellular Beams for Mobile Satellite Service

A pioneering vision from Motorola, now taking shape as Project Iridium, envisages a constellation of 66 satellites in polar orbits of about a 500-mi altitude (Exhibit 11). Each satellite beams a 48-cell pattern with 12-cell frequency reuse. Each cell will have about a 300-mi diameter on the surface of the earth. As these satellites orbit the earth, they present a moving pattern of cells to a fixed ground-based user, in contrast with the familiar case of mobile users in a fixed cellular frequency allocation in terrestrial mobile radio. Iridium design ensures that at any time any point on the earth will see at least one satellite not more than about 1500 miles away. TDMA channels of 2400 bps will support both data and voice transmissions. The satellite links to the mobiles are in the L-band (1.6 GHz) while the satellite links to larger terrestrial stations are in the Ka band (20 to 30 GHz). A unique feature of Iridium is intersatellite links. A call received by one satellite can be passed on to adjacent satellites via these intersatellite links until it reaches a satellite that can reach the called party. If the called party belongs to the terrestrial public switched telephone network, the call is downlinked to one of several Iridium gateways around the world. Iridium system is expected to be operational in late 1998.

Globalstar is another mobile satellite venture by Qualcomm and Loral that is expected to go into service in 1999. Eight circular orbits of about 880 mi in altitude carry 48 satellites that together cover almost 98% of the populated areas of the earth. Globalstar system architecture is more conservative and does not use intersatellite links or onboard processing and switching. Instead, all calls are downlinked to Globalstar gateways around the world and distributed from there over the PSTN. If the called party is another Globalstar handheld unit, the call is uplinked to a satellite in that region and the satellite beams it down to the intended subscriber. Globalstar will use Qualcomm CDMA technology for higher capacity and better voice quality.

Iridium and Globalstar are the apparent leaders in what are called low earth orbit (LEO) satellite systems. The LEO satellites are further subdivided into "little" LEOs and "big" LEOs. Iridium and Globalstar are big LEOs, relatively larger-sized satellites in relatively higher orbits, typically supporting voice communications among handheld receivers. The little LEO satellites are smaller in size and occupy lower altitude orbits, and they tend to cater primarily to data services. Orbcomm, a venture by the Orbital Sciences Corp., and Teledesic by Microsoft and McCaw Cellular are the prime examples. The main focus of Orbcomm is on global messaging and data communications. Teledesic hopes to provide Internet download data rates of up to 64M bps directly from satellite to computers.

At higher altitudes, well above the Van Allen radiation belt, there are proposals to operate medium earth orbit (MEO) satellite systems. An example is the 14-satellite ICO Global Communications system being implemented by Inmarsat. ICO satellites use orbital altitudes of about 6500 miles. There are also geostationary earth orbit (GEO) satellite systems being developed to support mobile communications in various parts of the world.

Mobile satellite systems have the advantage that they can bring instant wide area coverage and roaming capabilities. Systems such as Iridium offer the promise of one phone operable worldwide. However, satellite systems tend to be costlier. Iridium phones are expected to cost about $3000 initially, and calls are expected to cost about $3 per minute. The one-phone convenience will have to face the multiphone economics.

Exhibit 11.   Iridium Satellite Constellation

RADIO LOCATION SERVICES

One of the lesser noticed wireless markets of interest to the corporate community is in radio determination of position. A number of portable or car-mounted devices have appeared that provide accurate position location and route direction services for the mobile user. These devices typically make use of the global positioning system (GPS) satellites. Signals from a number of GPS satellites visible from any point on the earth can be processed to provide accurate determination of the longitude, attitude, and elevation of the GPS receiver. Handheld GPS receivers under $200 have appeared in the market. Many PC/laptop-based map programs (e.g., Street Atlas by Delorme) are capable of receiving GPS signals and marking the position on the map automatically. Such tracking systems are finding applications in other areas such as fleet management. One may expect newer PDAs appearing in the market with these sophisticated position location features.

Video over Wireless

Video communications has been well known to be bandwidth-intensive, while wireless communications has been perennially in shortage of bandwidth. Wider bandwidth allocations alleviate this problem from one end, while advances in digital video compression offer some allowances from the other. Thus, the stage is being set for wireless video to and from mobile platforms. The applications are certainly not of the entertainment variety. Instead one can foresee use of wireless and mobile video transmission in mobile videoconferencing, monitoring and surveillance, and medical and military applications. The finalized Motion Picture Experts Group (MPEG) standards embody the current state of the art in digital video compression. MPEG-1 accomplishes "VCR-quality" video compression for the CD-ROM medium, typically at about 1.5M bps average bit rate. The MPEG-II standards cover video and associated audio compression at higher quality and at various data rates from 4 to 20M bps. Even the 1.5M bps rate of MPEG-1 is considered too large for wireless bandwidths. Work is in progress on a new set of standards, MPEG-4, for very low rate video compression for applications including mobile video.

SUMMARY

We have briefly reviewed many facets of emerging new wireless technologies that potentially have impacts on the corporate communications scenario. These technologies are poised to make fundamental changes in how business in transacted. Although cell phones, pagers, and PDAs may only peripherally enhance the "comfort level" in the way business is transacted today, new technologies such as wireless access to the Internet and transport of real-time full-motion video over such channels will foster radically new ways of transacting business. The traditionally "wirebound" telecommunications infrastructure is being untethered. The heights to which it can now rise will certainly be an exciting spectacle to watch.

Chapter 21
Telecommuting: Distributed Work Programs

Richard A. Bellaver

INTRODUCTION

The time has come to make the art of telecommuting and its synonyms, the virtual office, or telework, into a science. Benefits for the employee and to the company are available. Several million contract or regular full-time or part-time people now are active participants in either formal or informal programs. Obviously the technology to make these concepts viable is here; however, more important than the technology needed to make these programs work is the change in management style needed to get the full benefits of these new working arrangements. Several companies have more than three years of experience with employees in satellite centers, hoteling, or working at home. This experience shows that corporate policies are affected by these changes and must be considered before attempting to take advantage of the new arrangements.

Government and nature have added the required emphasis to prove the practicality of the *virtual* corporation. The U.S. Clean Air Act attempted to force large companies in the nation's smoggiest cities to cut commuting by 25% and to have in effect plans for "employee trip reduction." Although federal legislation has eased up on its demands, many companies had already started to comply. Nature intervened in the form of the January 1994 southern California earthquake.

This natural disaster showed that distributed work can be a lasting environment not just a passing fad. According to Pacific Bell, 1300 workers had their commuting routine changed by the quake; nine out of ten who took advantage of the company telecommuting relief package were still working at home a year later even though most of the roads were cleared by then.

Does this mean that every company should start a telecommuting program? Much investment and much management preparation must take

0-8493-9990-4/99/$0.00+$.50

place before a company should get involved. Not everyone and not every job is a good candidate for distribution. Questionnaires for employees and job evaluation techniques can be used to examine the fit. While business re-engineering should consider work distribution in the redesign of basic business processes, a company must first look to its basic policies concerning evaluation of employees and supervision.

A change to a form of absentee production means that supervisors must establish specific objective outputs that can be measured to prove the value of an employee's activities. This management skill, as well as the skill of giving instructions and taking status over the telephone, may have to be learned before going to a virtual office plan. Many companies may not be ready for such a change to their corporate culture.

TYPES OF PROGRAMS

Telecommuting involves the use of technology to replace the need for employees to travel to or work from a conventional office. The concept is to move the work to the employee instead of vice versa. Also included, and a fact that cannot be forgotten, is that organization of the work, its social parameters, and management of employees so involved must also be considered.

Traditionally management people have "taken work home" through the years. Many more have attempted to overlap travel time by doing something work-oriented while on the road. New technology has assisted this effort greatly. The use of networks to send hard copy messages (e-mail) as well as voice has been practical for many years. Some types of work have traditionally been done out of the office.

People who repair large appliances spend a good deal of the day away from the company office (the exception being the Maytag repairman) only coming in for dispatch. Now some companies are having these people remain at home handling scheduling, parts ordering, and distribution from their home computers; and making schedule changes using cell phones for voice and facsimile to the truck. Due to the lack of official criteria for measuring the numbers of telecommutters, the estimates of the number vary from as little as 2 to as high as 45 million Americans.

Formal Programs

The conference board estimates that only about 15 to 20% of U.S. companies practicing telework have formal programs. Formal programs are characterized by specific policies encouraging the program and usually a specific agreement between the company and every employee that participates. Formal programs are specific about who owns equipment and how it is maintained, and in some cases they involve management review and approval of the remote work site. Some formal programs are conditions of employment, involve specific training, test grades, and are part of official employment documentation.

Informal programs are much more common and are identified by as little as word of mouth encouragement or enhancement to flexible working hour arrangements. Some training for the employee on how to set up an office or deal with vendors of communications equipment is usually provided even in informal programs. Hardware and software may be recommended and possibly may be some financial assistance toward its acquisition even in informal programs.

In the downsizing trend of the past few years we have seen a good deal of outsourcing and the use of temporary workers. These methods of providing human productivity are also a part of the telework equation. The opportunity to use people for short-term needs without having to provide space and equipment is very inviting. Usually the arrangement for these contract workers is developed on an individual basis and is a formal arrangement.

The American Telecommuting Association has developed a checklist to determine how suitable an employee is for telecommuting. The list of 33 questions, called the Affinity Index, is based on a three-point Likert scale; some of the questions it asks include Am I about as happy with my work as most people I know? Do I usually meet all of my responsibilities? When I finish a job, am I usually satisfied with the results? A score of over 80 indicates a person is a prime candidate to be a successful telecommuter. Less than 20 indicates special effort and training will be required to be successful.

BENEFITS OF "DISTRIBUTED WORK"

Other than compliance with the various laws, there are more positive benefits for business to look at distributing work. There is the ability to recruit employees who cannot work "normal" hours or cannot commute because of disabilities. There is the possibility to provide better customer service by working the "off hours." There is the capability to cut down on moves associated with organizational changes or promotions. Growth can be managed faster. Distant resources can be tapped.

There are reduced space requirements at the central site. There is the ability to differentiate through knowledge and innovation growth. There is enhanced reputation of being a human resources leading edge company. Finally, there is increased individual productivity. Estimates vary on the increase. Some early studies of small manager groups indicate the number could be as high as 30%. More conservative and consistent estimates indicate as high as a 15% improvement could be realized.

Employee benefits sometimes center around the family, allowing a more flexible schedule, or the elimination of payments and insurance for one car. Many people feel the ecological aspects are beneficial enough, but some look for less expense for clothes or even lunches. Some employees just like to work by themselves or have caregiving responsibilities. Many people would like to be able to commute independent of where they live or send their children to school. In our present world any way to lessen stress, such as the reduction of fighting traffic, is considered positive.

Although full-time distributed work does not usually involve upper level managers, the president of a Cincinnati-based data services company, quoted in *Managing Office Technology* magazine, says, "My job was mostly brain work. I spent my time in the office on the phone, tending to voice mail or e-mail, doing research and making decisions on corporate strategy. Over time I realized that these duties could be done anywhere." He now does them between November and April in the Florida Keys.

Company Experience

The people of a California advertising agency went virtual when they opened a new building. This company has probably done the fastest job of converting their corporate culture because of the opportunity to design and build a structure specifically tailored to virtual concepts. The interior design of the building, only about a block from the beach, reflects an interesting philosophy as stated by one of the executives, "Work is something you do, not a place to go."

This company is into the practice of "hoteling," assigning shared space to individual people based on a reservation system. Along with the 300 to 900 sq ft of "project room" space, comes a large table, several conventional phones, a speakerphone, a desktop computer, and a video tape deck with monitor—the equipment needed to do intellectual work as well as to put on presentations for customers. Workers are able to engage in company mail, look at databases, and contact customers by phone from home or their cars using portable devices.

Most employees can be reached by pager. Although the program is quite formal, some procedures have not been demanded. Executives are expected to maintain their calendars online, but it is not part of an agreement. However, missing a meeting due to failure to check the mechanized calendar is not permitted.

Spend More Time with Customers

Spending more time with the customer is the chief motivation behind a large computer company's telecommuting effort. It has about 20,000 employees in the U.S. who participate in what is called "mobile computing," a concept designed to increase productivity, improve relationships, and save time and expense. Employees are given laptop computers with local area network (LAN) and long-distance dial connectivity software programs.

Other support includes pagers, fax, and cellular tools. Major cost reductions have come in the form of less real estate, heating, cooling, and maintenance, and fewer phones, computers, and other equipment in the individual offices. The company usually does not break out these savings, but it is assumed that they are in the millions. Most of the people doing mobile computing are in sales and service, but others are in manufacturing, development, research, and staff support.

Many of the company offices around the country have implemented this formal program of mobile computing based on pilots conducted in Indiana and Florida in the early 1990s. Individual offices remain in most company complexes, but they are few. In most cases, there is an open concept with work spaces, computers, and phones assigned to employees who come to their base locations to work or meet with peers or managers. The ratio of employees to office is generally 4:1, and in some locations it is 10:1. Employee surveys show 75% of the employees have benefited from less commuting expense by being mobile, and studies show that mobile computing allows marketing representatives to spend an average of three more hours each week with customers.

One East Coast company has about two years of experience with telecommuting. Some people are away from the office 80% of the time. They have home terminals and voice mail transfers to the home, and some have pagers. The workers have one group meeting a week in the office. They still need to come in for U.S. mail and some supplies. The expense of telecommuting is doing very well vs. office space, and the work is still providing quality results. At another location, the company has converted a former warehouse complex into a telecommuting center. The employees of four former office facilities were assigned to the remodeled space. The hoteling concept is used except that the 450 resident spaces are segregated from the space of the 630 hotelers. Only 110 workstations are available for the hotelers. "Manager rooms" are available, and there is shared meeting space. Services are provided to both groups by a third resident organization.

A Phased Approach

A formal program involving a phased approach to telecommuting was piloted by the information systems (IS) organization of a large insurance company. This company knew that not all jobs are appropriate for telecommuting. The jobs included in the pilot were measurable, contained relatively little face-to-face communication, did not require access to office equipment or files, and involved thinking tasks. The employees wishing to participate needed to have a minimum of 1 year of employment. They were allowed to volunteer, but they did not participate unless approved by management.

- Phase 1   Specific IS positions were identified by management as full-time telecommuting jobs. The positions were allocated to the IS divisions based on population and filled through the a job opportunities program. In the first quarter of the year, the people selected began telecommuting.
- Phase 2   In the second quarter, the opportunity to telecommute was offered on a part-time basis to IS officers and managers. Approximately 100 positions were identified as 3 days at home and 2 days in the office part-time.
- Phase 3   In the following year, telecommuting was designated as a corporate program and was adopted by several other business groups, which substantially increased the numbers of professionals and the types of jobs identified for telecommuting.

Consulting firms would seem to be ideal candidates, and several are active participants using virtual office concepts. One such firm has been hoteling in its Chicago office since June of 1992. If a consultant or an accountant wants to reserve office space, it must be done a least a day in advance. Everything needed to do the proscribed work, including personal belongings, will be set up beforehand. In Los Angeles, another global consulting firm started a pilot program in 1993 for 40 of its 200 executives. Based on early feedback and continual input from the participants, both consulting firms were able to overcome psychological space possession problems and poor utilization of the reservation system, and they feel they are on the right track.

Another company is now in the process of standardizing its internal networks and platform specifically in light of telecommuting. Many of the company's customers have gotten into virtual offices on a quick need-to-do basis, like planning to close downtown offices during the Atlanta Olympics.

One firm is looking at what is really needed for the long run. How many databases are going to be accessed from home? What type of bandwidth will be needed for graphics? How does wireless fit into the equation? The test bed for the newly designed platform and network will be in the firm's new technology park in suburban Chicago.

A PILOT PROGRAM

According to the AT&T publication, *Telecommuting Connection*, in one of the most measured trials in the U.S., AT&T and the state of Arizona conducted a pilot program with 134 telecommuters and 70 supervisors. During the trial, telecommuters worked 1 day/week at home. After 6 months they logged 97,078 mi, avoiding the generation of 1.9 tons of vehicle-related pollutants. They saved 3,705 h of drive time and $10,372 in travel expenses.

Approximately eight out of ten participants said telecommuting better equipped them to work at personal peak times, become better organized, and plan more effectively. Of the supervisors reporting, 95% acknowledged adequate communication with their staff, and 80% said that telecommuting increased employee productivity.

Almost two thirds of all nonparticipants would telecommute if given the opportunity. In 1992, the state of Arizona and AT&T were selected to receive a national Environmental Achievement award. Since the initial trial, the number of AT&T and state commuters has grown to 648, and in 1993 they drove an estimated 1 million fewer commuter miles and avoided generating 20 tons of air pollution.

Second Thoughts

Not all companies are moving as aggressively as those mentioned earlier. A brewing company in Milwaukee, as a part of a program of its parent organization, conducted a pilot of a "telecommuting work option" in August and September 1994. The program was very expensive because each employee was equipped with a total home office.

Some preliminary findings indicated that such an extensive set up was not required, women viewed the program more positively than men, and distractions arose in those households where children were home for the summer months. The latter situation improved in September when school started. The company did not include telecommuting as part of their compliance plan for the Clean Air Act; however, it may conduct expanded pilots as part of future "work/life" initiatives.

CORPORATE INVESTMENT

As brought out earlier by the brewery's experience, companies react to the potential investment of telecommuting in different ways. For those that want to provide relatively high-speed lines because of database access or videoconferencing requirements, Integrated Services Digital Network (ISDN) is the most common service used. More commonly regular telephone lines are used. In many cases, a second line is paid for by the employer. This second line is satisfactory for Internet access, fax, limited file downloads, and certainly voice transmission.

Many times a speakerphone is provided. Once the circuitry is determined, decisions must be made as to the equipment, not just type and capacity but ownership, maintenance responsibilities, and even safety. If the program is formal, most of these arrangement are documented in the telecommuting agreement. The agreement can go so far as to the specific times the equipment must be available for access from the office. Children cannot use the second line to call their friends.

Some companies consider the value of telecommuting to the employee as benefit enough and do not accept any responsibility for the expense. A central Indiana data processing firm has had 45 employees working from their homes for several years. The company does not pay for telephone service, but it will help the employee finance the purchase of a computer. This three-shift operation has the normal turnover of employees but never has a problem replacing them. If a worker wants a second line into the house for emergency purposes, it is his responsibility. In all cases a hardware and software platform must be standardized for telecommuting to work to best advantage. The data entry function of the Indiana company used dial-up service and a modem pool. This approach has been around for years and for relatively slow speed works well. This particular company uses proprietary software with built-in security, since the data transmitted is sensitive.

There are many software packages available over the counter that can perform the transmission function well, and some have a form of security built in. More companies are allowing employees access to LANs. Corporate standards have generally been established before this takes place so that the home workstation looks just like any centralized station to the host or router. Security must be considered carefully and a software firewall constructed if there is any possibility of abuse of the system or its data.

Some companies have considered use of the Internet as a means of providing a work-at-home environment. E-mail through the Internet, as well as through commercial online services, is used by many employees. The lack of security is a serious problem and in most cases has kept the use of the Internet from serious consideration as a major vehicle to carry telework traffic.

Change in Management Style

For those companies moving ahead, the most difficult part of establishing a virtual environment has been the changes required to their management style. Many managers have talked of "management by objective" for years, but now the job must be precisely defined to make telecommuting successful. Managers must learn how to give meaningful assignments over the telephone without seeing body language or observing whether the subordinate makes notes. Management by "walking around" must be modified to "calling around."

The ideals of participatory management are embedded in the new style. Along with more faith in the workers' abilities goes more participation in the decision of how the work is to be done. It will be necessary for a manager to provide access to more background information and information about the problem than in the past. For a remote worker to be a self-starter, the data to find one's own way must be available. In the past some managers wanted to keep data to themselves to retain the power the data possessed; this kind of management will not work with remote workers. Managers will also have to learn how to get along with fewer strokes from their subordinates. The old model of the boss getting the credit for everything goes out the window.

For well-defined projects, the supervisor must establish the goals, provide the tools, and get out of the way. For more complex projects more status communication must be built in at each milestone and a good definition of the next portion to be completed must be agreed on. The team concepts of total quality management are compatible with these management characteristics, and even the dreaded reengineering should consider the aspects of virtual office. The idea of testing your employees to do the right thing is implicit. There must be an investment in management training to shift the corporate culture to accomplish benefits from telecommuting.

If the internal communications model of a company is conversations around the water cooler or coffee pot, a new method, involving possibly an electronic bulletin board, must be developed. If most business gets done at power lunches or breakfasts, the locations might have to be shifted or the times juggled. If a manager lives for the hubbub of the typing pool, you may have to provide a white noise machine. All these aspects must be considered in formulating a virtual office plan.

In conjunction with the previously mentioned consulting firm that moved to the suburbs, a pilot project was established in which lessons learned were shared with all other parts of the organization worldwide offices. While studying many different facets of telecommuting, the research was primarily focused on three areas: planning, teaming, and communications. A variety of methods also were used to collect information and assess the program's progress. For example, focus groups were conducted with supervisors of telecommuters as well as the staff that technically supports them. All the data gathered was analyzed; and those found valid were used to reinforce the program or make modifications.

The Best Employees

Not everyone is suited to be a telecommuter. Of course, trust is the key link between company and an absent employee, but most of the other attributes of good employees are found in good telecommuters. Those who require little supervision are usually the ones who keep up to date on their work load. They are well-organized, tend to look for more work to do, and are the best team players. This latter characteristic may seem contradictory; however, the good team players are those who keep the communications links open. Naturally, people best suited to telecommuting are those who are

369

willing to accept the use of technology and undergo the training necessary. Respect for technology is necessary—love is not required. Your company nerds may not be the best telecommuters.

In an attempt to get an impression of employee's beliefs about the benefits of telecommuting, a study was conducted to evaluate the effects of telecommuting from seven standpoints. The results, appearing in *The Journal of Computer Information Systems*, showed:

- Quality of life   Employees believed that telecommuting had a significant positive effect on their quality of family life, social life, job satisfaction, and physical well-being.
- Environment   There were significant positive effects on pollution, traffic congestion, and road accidents.
- Career development   This showed negative effects on peer interaction, career opportunities, acquisition of new skills, and accessibility to managers.
- Productivity   This was expected to improve slightly.
- Management and control   Input from managers in the areas of ability to manage, supervise, and coordinate were slightly negative.
- Company appeal   There was a slight positive effect on employment longevity, morale, interpersonal trust, company reputation, and ability to attract employees.
- Society   Employees believed that telecommuting would capitalize on wider diversity by bringing disadvantaged people (handicapped, elderly, and women with children) into the work force.

One of the drawbacks documented about telecommuting is isolation. Moving experienced employees from the social contacts of office work has a negative effect on some workers over time. Many plans that called for no office visits or very limited returns to the "old office" have had to be modified to include extra attention to the social aspects of work. Some aspects of isolation can be eased by additional voice contact with the homebound employee, more bulletin board activity, or even possibly support group meetings outside the office environment.

In some cases, the number of days per week for each employee to be in the office has had to be increased. Some people are not suited to telecommuting at all. Questionnaires need to be used to discover employees' desire to telecommute. Supervisory experience should be consulted for present workers, and possibly some psychological testing should be done before deciding on which specific employees should work at home.

The Best Jobs

As with employees, not all jobs are suitable to be done at home. Work functions that are easily understood and long in duration are the best to teleport. Data entry and many clerical jobs are good candidates. Programming is good, provided it can be well-defined and tested independently.

Outward dialing telemarketing is widely done from people's homes. Telemarketing easily fits the criteria of a job that can be well-defined and is easily measured. The number of calls and the number of sales can be easily matched. Provided training is properly administered and maintained, telemarketing is an excellent candidate.

Research is another good function to be done remotely. Many reporters do their interviews using laptops and later enter the data to the editor automatically via a home communications device. Of course, travel demands are one of the biggest reasons to equip and train management people in the art of telecommuting.

Cell phones, laptops, and even fax machines move from limousine to taxi to airplane to hotel desk with a minimum of interruption. Many higher level managers are accustomed to working in this environment; however, they have usually been supported by an office full of people. The thought of calling from an airplane to a subordinate's boat in the middle of the day might be somewhat upsetting.

Changes in Corporate Policy

Most companies with formal plans have a specific written telecommuting policy, secure agreements from employees, and gather data during the telecommuting activity. Most formal programs are not started without a trial or pilot program. Legal advice may be useful to determine ownership of equipment supplied to the home and possible safety requirements.

It may even help to look at zoning laws for potential difficulties. An employee may live in a different municipality with different laws than at the company office. Unions have been concerned about potential effects of telecommuting on their membership. A union, which probably has the most experience with mechanization, has formalized its concerns in a set of demands for employers. Exhibit 1 lists requirements for the Communications Workers of America (CWA).

Exhibit 1.   Communications Workers of America Telecommuting Requirements

Equal pay and benefits
Work to be done in the office for at least two days a week
No more than two visits a month to home by a manager with a 24-hour notice
The company to supply equipment and materials
The company to reimburse for higher utility and insurance costs
The union having the right to inspect the home for safety and ergonomics
Telecommuters being able to see all routine job openings

It can be seen that the union is protecting against the possibility of several abuses with these rules. The union also is attempting to protect against isolation of employees and making sure equal opportunity for advancement is available even though the employee is absent.

Because of the new way of evaluating productivity, new pay programs may be required and management evaluation processes may need to be updated. Workers may be concerned about their career advancement when they are absent from the office, so human resources people need to be involved early and continuously. Important human resources procedures, such as time reporting, telephone expense, and use of other home resources must be spelled out in the telecommuting policy statement or the employee agreement.

One of the consulting firms mentioned previously is developing principles and guidelines for its pilot that are expected to serve as blueprints for the future telecommuting programs. While not viewing telecommuting as a substitute for child or elder care, the company would like to develop a framework flexible enough to enable people to use the program as a tool in helping them balance their professional and personal lives. Core hours will be identified, which means the company can expect the employee to be available during specific hours at a home telephone number. It is also very important for companies to have a thorough understanding of insurance liability and human resource issues that can arise as a result of this initiative.

Steps to Be Taken

If a company is interested in becoming a virtual corporation, there are some steps that can be taken today. Just as total quality management methodology advises, a task force of different levels of the organization and different attitudes about telecommuting should be established to examine the situation. This group should look at all aspects even including the safety, comfort, and security of potential home offices. The subject of isolation should be considered when determining how many days per week the program should incorporate and what types of additional communications means need to be considered.

People with authority to do something with the results should be included on the team. People within the company who have some experience with the subject should be included. Consultants can be used, but experienced employees are the best resource. Vendors of telecommuting products and services may provide many services including assistance in network sizing, job requirements, and even employee questionnaires.

The company must establish the policies that will be needed as early as possible. Policies can be tested during a pilot phase. The question of ownership of equipment and how maintenance will be handled should be addressed. These concerns are better thought about up front before experience dictates a problem. Experience can be used to modify the practices later.

Companies must learn about the technology, its use, and its cost. It is best to sample employees' opinions and attitudes. If the attitude and the culture seem compatible, it is proper to set up a pilot with specific objectives and specific means of measurement. It is then up to the company to select the proper jobs, the proper people, and the proper managers and to give the virtual corporation a try.

AGENCIES AND ASSOCIATIONS

Home Office Association of America Inc.
909 Third Avenue
New York, NY 01122
(800) 908-4622
FAX: (800) 315-4622

The International Telework Association
Telecommuting Advisory Council
204 E Street, Northeast
Washington, DC 20002
(202) 547-6157
FAX: (202) 546-3289

For World Wide Web links to sites that follow use:
http://www.ameritech.com/products/custom/topic/archive/1997_11/related.html

The Basics of Telecommuting
Home Office Association of America
Alternative Work Environments
Telecommuting & the Home Office @Escape Artist.com
PS Enterprises
Transportation Implications of Telecommuting (TMIP)
Go Green
The Age of Telecommuting
   Smart Valley Telecommuting Guide

Chapter 22

Operating Teleconferencing Systems (Audio, Audiographics/ Multimedia, and Video)

S. Ann Earon

INTRODUCTION

Teleconferencing, defined as groups of people communicating electronically from locations separated by distance and/or time, is a technology that has existed for many years and has changed and matured during its existence.

While many people think of teleconferencing as a new industry, its roots — the first applications — go back to the early 1930s. The emergence of teleconferencing on a wider scale is based on the coupling of two major factors: better teleconferencing technologies and the current socioeconomic climate. Teleconferencing is an industry marked by new technologies, new applications, and new suppliers. Many organizations are assessing or implementing teleconferencing as a new management tool.

Basic questions asked about teleconferencing are: can this technology be used to effectively increase productivity and reduce travel; and what changes in working, communicating, and managing habits will it require? To assist in answering these questions one must first understand that meetings are typically called to: discuss ideas, disseminate information, delegate work, give presentations, inspect objects, resolve conflict, seek information, and solve problems.

Undesirable characteristics of meetings frequently include: absence of appropriate people, difficulty in coordination, excessive length, high travel expenses, lack of structure, poor communications, and slow information exchange. Teleconferencing is a cost-effective and efficient alternative to many face-to-face meetings. It is an extremely effective tool for conducting important decision-making or problem-solving meetings that might not otherwise be held. It can reduce unproductive travel time, optimize attendance and access to scarce talent, and provide an excellent education and training medium. In other words, teleconferencing can significantly increase productivity and efficiency, improve management communication at all levels, and significantly enhance business opportunities when used appropriately.

TELECONFERENCING TERMS

Teleconferencing can be discussed in four basic categories:

1. Audioconferencing
2. Audiographics/Multimedia Conferencing
3. Videoconferencing
4. Computer Conferencing.

Audioconferencing

Audioconferencing is voice communication between three or more people from multiple locations. A variety of equipment might be involved including common telephone handsets, speakerphones for use by small groups, special open microphone and speaker systems for large groups, and any of these alternatives incorporated into specially designed teleconferencing rooms.

Audiographics/Multimedia

Audiographics and multimedia conferencing provide for transmission of speech and written communications, as well as real-time modification of written information sent via graphic displays, electronic blackboards, and tele-writing equipment. The most recent advances in this area incorporate evolving standards for data sharing and allowing individuals to share computer files and annotate information.

Videoconferencing

Motion video systems show pictures of people and objects and allow you to hear and see them in real time. Cameras can be speaker activated or provide continuous presence. The signal can be analog or digital for transmission purposes. These systems are now available as room or group systems and at the desktop.

Computer Conferencing

Computer conferencing uses a personal computer to facilitate communications among people at (generally) scattered locations. Messages can be viewed when received or stored for later retrieval. Additional features can be provided for keeping participants up-to-date, for maintaining a transcript of on-going conferences, and for providing voting capability.

GENERIC BENEFITS

The generic benefits of teleconferencing can be put into two categories: quantitative and qualitative. While many of the benefits of teleconferencing are difficult to quantify, it is still important to examine them with relationship to their relevance to efficient corporate operations. The easiest benefit to quantify is that teleconferencing supplements and/or displaces direct travel costs. By using teleconferencing the need for travel can be displaced in some situations. However, travel displacement represents a small percentage of the benefits of teleconferencing.

The use of teleconferencing to supplement travel is a more likely occurrence, e.g., accessing remote locations. Qualitative benefits are as important as quantitative benefits. Teleconferencing increases productivity and efficiency, improves management communication, and enhances business opportunities.

Increases Productivity

The use of teleconferencing has the potential of increasing productivity and efficiency by reducing unproductive travel time, preventing meeting delays, creating shorter and more structured meetings, and allowing for greater participation

A Booz–Allen study found that from the time one knows a meeting is needed to the actual time the meeting takes place, on the average, two weeks of time passes. By using teleconferencing, arrangements can be made more quickly and those individuals not physically able to attend the meeting may "attend" by telephone or video.

The use of teleconferencing requires individuals to prepare themselves for proper and effective use of the medium. This preparation results in individuals learning to better plan their meetings and waste less time in unnecessary discussions during the meeting. Teleconferencing also allows for an increased number of participants. It is difficult to send all individuals to a distant meeting. Often only one or two individuals are sent. When these people return to their work location, they often hold additional meetings to brief those who did not travel. With teleconferencing, all individuals who need to attend a meeting can do so regardless of their location.

377

Improves Management Communication

Teleconferencing enables management to increase their participation in a greater number of critical meetings. This results in greater interaction between all management levels and increases the flexibility managers have in attending a variety of meetings even while traveling.

Enhances Business Opportunities

The use of teleconferencing can enhance business opportunities. The more teleconferencing is used and the more comfortable people feel using it, the more applications are developed to fill specific needs.

Teleconferencing can be used to enhance customer service and provide a competitive advantage. Teleconferencing facilitates the timely exchange of essential information. Experts can be called as needed and their critical input obtained more quickly. Teleconferencing also allows individuals to time-share scarce talent. With rapid access to information, teleconferencing enhances the speed and accuracy of the decision-making process. Teleconferencing can also be used as an education and training tool to present valuable information about a product, service, or situation as it is needed.

GENERIC APPLICATIONS

The following information (Exhibit 1) is provided to show applications that apply to specific types of teleconferencing. This is by no means an exhaustive list, but rather highlights a variety of uses for teleconferencing.

Standards and Compatibility Issues

The videoconferencing market is not at the point where all one has to do is ask for your videoconferencing numbers and then dial you. As the facsimile market was several years ago, when one needed to know the type of fax machine and group number, videoconferencing is today. As soon as standards were available for "Group Three Fax" the market exploded. Standards are still an issue in videoconferencing and data collaboration today. However, the International Telecommunications Union (ITU) is quickly eliminating the restraints that exist. The combination of the H.320 audio/video standard, and the T.120 audiographics standard will drive videoconferencing, especially at the desktop, to a level of interoperability that is as transparent to users as fax machines are today.

H.320. H.320 is an international standard for audio and videoconferencing that includes a collection of specifications: H.261 for video, H.221 for communications protocol and framing, H.242 for call set-up, and several audio specifications (G.711, G.722, and G.728). H.320 emphasizes switched digital telecommunications networks, such as ISDN and Switched — 56 lines, for group videoconferencing and audio. H.320 was not designed with

378

Exhibit 1. Applications for Specific Types of Telemarketing

Management/Administrative	Product/Service
Budget reviews	Customer professional development
Executive conferences	Equipment trouble-shooting
Labor negotiations	Media promotion
Management development	New product information
Personnel matters	Product discussions
Planning meetings	Product announcements
Recruitment	Public relations
Strategy sessions	Trade rhows
Subsidiary relations	
Training sessions	**Engineering**
	Project coordination
Financial	Staff engineering sessions
Accounting, billing discussions	
After hours data transmission	**Manufacturing**
Computer programming design	Manufacturing trial appraisals
Data processing discussions	Inventory control meetings
Mergers, acquisitions, and divestitures	Meetings with suppliers
New stock offerings	Project coordination
Sales/Marketing	
Marketing coordination	
Marketing presentations	
Sales organization meetings	

asynchronous networks in mind, like the LAN. Two additional standards have emerged to address local area networks (LANs) and the plain old telephone system (POTS) that use analog lines.

H.323. This standard is an extension of H.320 that allows for videoconferencing over LANs. Because it is based on the Real-Time Protocol (RTP/RTCP), H.323 can also be applied to video over the Internet.

H.324. This standard allows simultaneous two-way video, audio, and data transfer over POTS (analog) lines.

T.120. T.120 is a standard for multimedia exchange. While H.320 provides a basic means for graphics transfer, T.120 supports high resolutions, annotation, pointing, and application sharing. By using a PC platform, users can share and manipulate information as if they were in the same room.

Audioconferencing

The most widely used form of teleconferencing is the audioconference. It is so easy to use and widely accepted that, in many cases, the audioconference is taken for granted and not given recognition as the most significant form of teleconferencing technologies. Without audio, a videoconference is nothing but a silent picture.

Although telephone calls are taken for granted, the technology for audio and audioconferencing is not necessarily simple. Important considerations for successful audioconferencing include:

- Room acoustics (What does the room "sound" like?)
- Transmission lines (How does the sound get from one location to another?)
- Terminal equipment (What hardware is required to conduct and audioconference?)

Room Acoustics

When holding an audioconference, several factors must be considered. The obvious ones include:

- Will the room accommodate the number of people in the meeting?
- Is there a phone in the room?
- Is there an electrical outlet available?

Less obvious considerations relate to room acoustics: echo, reverberation, and noise.

Echo   An echo is a repetition of the original sound, as if one was speaking in a cavern.

Reverberation   Reverberation is actually multiple echoes with a short time between each. These multiple echoes are perceived as sound "bouncing around" the room and will be heard as a hollowness in the voice or a "rain barrel" effect at the distant end.

Noise   All rooms contain noise, even when empty. The ambient noise may be caused by heating, ventilation, and air conditioning systems. This seems to be like a rushing noise or a rumble from the units. Other ambient noise is produced by office equipment (VCRs, Overhead Projectors, etc.), lighting fixtures, and outside noise (traffic, bathrooms, elevators). For effective audioconferencing the ambient noise should be as low as possible.

TRANSMISSION LINES

The quality of the transmission line is crucial to the success of an audioconference. A regular dial-up telephone line is often all that is needed to conduct a successful audioconference. Be wary of some of the lines available off a PBX, as they frequently do not offer the same quality as an analog telephone line.

While many people use their telephone systems for three-way conference calls, and sometimes up to ten sites, a multipoint conference often requires an audio bridge to link sites together. The bridge connects the sites and controls the audio level. A number of telephone companies and bridging service companies offer multipoint audioconferencing services. Calls can be established through an operator or on a dial-up basis.

TERMINAL EQUIPMENT

Audioconferencing products can be categorized as simplex, quasi-duplex, or full-duplex, depending on the interactivity and interruptibility of conference connections. All systems include microphones, speakers, and a table-top control unit.

Simplex — With a simplex system, while one person is talking the other person cannot interrupt, except during a pause or by being significantly louder. Simplex equipment is generally low priced, but no longer used as often as full duplex systems, which in recent years have become widely available and cost effective.

Quasi Duplex Systems — This approach improves on simplex technology by incorporating very fast switching between send and receive voice channels. The sensitive switching allows for natural interruptions without shouting. Again, while a number of these systems still exist in the marketplace, buyers today are usually purchasing full duplex systems.

Full Duplex Systems — Full duplex systems provide the same kind of interaction one gets from the telephone. Users can interrupt one another at any time. Communication seems as natural as being with the person. Full duplex systems work best in rooms free of echoes, reverberation, and noise.

Audiographics/Multimedia Conferencing

An audiographic conference combines audio communications with images. The use of electronic "whiteboards" and tele-writing tablets is not new, as these items have been used for years. What is new is the proliferation of PC-based systems that allow for the sharing of documents, whiteboarding, real-time annotation, and application sharing. This proliferation has come about with the advent of the T.120 standards (see standards section of this document). In the next two years, more and more firms will be offering products and software that are developed based on the T.120 standard. The intent is to allow users to collaborate on work as if they were in the same room.

Multimedia conferencing is being positioned as the technology that will make the "virtual conference room" a reality. Marketing, engineering, distributors, outside suppliers, and customers can collaborate on a project, from various parts of the world, without leaving their offices or homes.

The future of multimedia conferencing depends on the development of easy-to-use systems which provide better communications and more competitive ways of working together. The challenges for multimedia conferencing include the development of applications and the provision of real-time interactive connectivity at all levels.

Videoconferencing (From the Room to the Desktop)

Videoconferencing began in 1964 with the introduction of the AT&T Picturephone at the World's Fair. Unfortunately, no one could afford the bandwidth needed to operate the unit. In the early 1980s the first videoconferencing codec was introduced for business use. It was the size of a refrigerator and cost approximately $150,000 per unit, with a minimum of two needed.

Since that time the technology advancements have made videoconferencing not only small in size, with the capabilities of a codec on a chip on a board, but also reasonably priced — both for the hardware and the network. Videoconferencing equipment now ranges from capability on a PC, to roll-about systems, to permanent rooms. Prices range from under $1,000 for many desktop systems to a range of $10,000–$75,000 for group systems.

The early adopters of the technology were the federal government and Fortune 100 companies. Today all industries use videoconferencing and the market has expanded to small and mid-sized organizations. With the advent of desktop videoconferencing the technology has expanded to telecommuters and the home market. The growth of videoconferencing has been propelled by decreasing equipment costs, improvement in technology, adoption of standards, and deployment of digital networks.

Videoconferencing allows people in different locations to conduct business as if they were in the same room. No longer considered a technology for the future, videoconferencing has a positive impact on the way organizations conduct business today. Videoconferencing is a proven technology which provides both quantifiable and qualitative benefits. However, a videoconference is not a face-to-face meeting. To be effective while planning and holding a videoconference there are a number of tips to follow. These can be divided into four areas: planning, room preparation, effective meetings, and meeting etiquette.

PLANNING

To be effective, videoconferencing takes proper, prior planning, particularly as your conferences include more than two locations. The more time you allot to planning your videoconference, the better the chances the time slots you seek will be available (Exhibit 2). Be sure you take into consideration time zone differences or you may find some of your participants do not join the

Exhibit 2.   Videoconference Planning Tips

- Identify a meeting date and time with participants.
- Distribute an agenda with meeting date and time noted.
- Plan for time zone differences.
- Reserve the appropriate conference rooms at all locations.
- List attendees and site leaders with telephone numbers.
- Obtain telephone number and video numbers in each room.
- Confirm network and bridging (if needed) availability.
- Prepare visual aids
  - Use bold 16-point type face or larger when preparing visual aids with approximately six words per line and six lines per page, landscape orientation. Black lettering on a white background is best.
  - Know the document camera's graphics capabilities.
- Confirm the planned attendance of all individuals.

---

meeting on time. Also be sure to get the telephone number in the video room in case you need to call someone there should you have any trouble. Large font size on graphics materials is important since without it participants will not be able to see the image clearly even if they try to do so by getting closer to the screen! Having a fax machine near the videoconferencing room is also helpful when last minute information needs to be distributed.

ROOM PREPARATION

Ideally, prior to installing your videoconferencing equipment your room was treated to ensure proper lighting, sound, and HVAC (heating, ventilating, and air-conditioning). Whether or not this was done, you can maximize the effectiveness of your videoconference by turning on all lights so individuals appear evenly illuminated, avoiding the "raccoon eye" look.

If the room you are in has windows, close all blinds. Turn off any extra fans. Be sure all the equipment you need for your conference is in the room and in working order. The table should face the video monitors so everyone is equidistant from the camera. This results in all participants being the same size image to the distant end.

Videoconferencing Room Preparation

- Prepare the room at least 15 minutes prior to the scheduled conference and prepare a test of the video equipment.
- If there are windows in the video room, keep curtains, blinds, etc. closed.
- Make sure all appropriate lighting is on.
- Set camera presets prior to the meeting.
- Provide any additional equipment needed for the meeting (slides, charts, etc.)

EFFECTIVE MEETINGS

Like face-to-face meetings, videoconferences should be well prepared. The difference between a face-to-face meeting and a videoconference is that meetings that are not properly prepared appear worse on videoconferencing.

All participants should be introduced, even those who may not appear in the camera image. It is helpful to have a sign at each site identifying that location. This way as each site comes on the screen others know with whom they are speaking. This is particularly important in a multipoint conference.

HOW TO RUN EFFECTIVE VIDEOCONFERENCING MEETINGS

Meeting Etiquette

Meeting etiquette is particularly important in a videoconference for without it chaos begins to reign. This is especially true in multipoint conferences. Be sure to mute your microphone when another site is speaking. Be aware of the transmission delay. (If a good joke is told those at your end will laugh before those at the distant end hear the punch line.) Avoid making rapid movements during a videoconference. The equipment works based on what moves. The more movement, the harder the equipment must perform. Looking like television anchor people is not necessary, but wearing muted colors and solids produces better images.

Videoconference Participant Tips and Meeting Etiquette

- Arrive on time.
- Act and speak naturally.
- Be aware of the transmission delay, and pause for others to comment.
- Always mute your system when dialing in on a multipoint call until you need to make a comment.
- Do not cough into microphones, shuffle papers, tap objects, or carry on side conversations; mute microphone as necessary.
- Sit still, do not swivel in your chair.
- Avoid making rapid movements during the call.
- Direct questions to individuals or locations.
- Avoid clothing with overly detailed patterns.
- Avoid bright, flashy jewelry that reflects light.
- Wear blue or pastel-colored shirts instead of white.
- Wear a solid medium-to-dark suit jacket.

As videoconference usage within your organization continues to grow, the above guidelines should prove helpful in ensuring successful meetings using videoconferencing.

Transmission Techniques and Protocols

A number of forces are driving the need for network improvements. As the number of users in an enterprise network grows, the available bandwidth continues to shrink. Some devices, like video and data conferencing devices, consume more bandwidth than others.

When videoconferencing was initially adopted by end users in the early 1980s, the bandwidth used by most was a T1 line offering 1.544 megabits of data. The picture at any less than this speed was not acceptable. As codec algorithms improved, the needed bandwidth dropped. Users began to hold conferences at half the original speed (768K bps). Soon ISDN and Switched-56 networks were introduced. The magic of a device called an inverse multiplexer (I-MUX) allowed users to vary the bandwidth needed based on the amount of information (number of people, type of data shared) in a call.

Codecs continued to improve and users settled on multiples of 56 or ISDN (usually at 112/128K bps or 336/384K bps) for their calls. Technology continues to improve and today many people are holding video calls over the plain old telephone system (POTS) analog lines. While others are now using their LANs or ATM. Following is an explanation of the technologies being used.

ISDN. Integrated Services Digital Network is very suitable for videoconferencing. It supports isochronous (where timing is derived from the signal carrying the data) data transmission and bandwidth is guaranteed once the connection is made. In the early 1990s firms began to use ISDN for videoconferencing and added an inverse multiplexer (I-MUX) to allow them to alter the number of channels needed during a call. ISDN became readily available globally and cost-effective for most videoconferences. ISDN, however, can be an issue when deploying videoconferencing on a widescale basis to the desktop. The issues relate to large scale bandwidth availability to the desktop and the cost of providing the bandwidth to each desk.

Switched 56. Like ISDN, Switched 56 traffic travels over the same physical infrastructure, and provides a two channel call for videoconferencing. However, the bandwidth for Switched 56 is limited to 56K bps as opposed to 64K bps for ISDN. Switched 56 is an older technology with decreasing significance, except in those areas where ISDN is not available.

POTS. The plain old telephone system (POTS) is the most widely used bandwidth today. Regular telephone calls use the POTS network. Unfortunately, the bandwidth available does not support the quality of videoconferencing wanted by most businesses. However, a number of video devices are now on the market that use a POTS line. Their price and ease of use have become of interest to the average consumer and with the popularity of the Internet, many people are experiencing videoconferencing for the first time using a POTS line.

LAN. The nature of local area network (LAN) traffic has changed over the years. The ability to process high resolution images and complex data applications translates into larger and larger files going across the network. As the machines communicate faster and contain more data, shared LANs slow down and network performance decreases. Networks must now be more than fast, they also must be accurate. Video and multimedia data need to be fast, accurate, and realtime.

ATM. ATM has been considered the LAN of the future. It provides a high-bandwidth solution with advantages such as quality of service, security, and accounting. ATM supports transmission speeds from 45M bps (megabits per second) to 622M bps and perhaps even higher. It is intended primarily as a backbone network. ATM's major limitation is cost and lack of availability. It is in the early stages of testing and deployment and may or may not be a widely available transport in the near future.

STEPS TO SUCCESSFUL IMPLEMENTATION

For many people, teleconferencing is still a new way to conduct business. It is unrealistic to assume that once a system is installed users will immediately flock to use it. One way of looking at teleconferencing is to equate it to a personal computer (PC). When PCs first entered the marketplace no one was expected to immediately sit down and use them to solve all business problems. Instead, most users found a learning curve associated with the hardware and with each software package.

The same holds true for teleconferencing. Users look at a technology that will improve productivity, increase the use of subject matter experts, and allow meetings to be held when needed. These are all factors that are difficult to quantify and place a dollar value on. Yet many users are discovering that teleconferencing is a business advantage.

How is a successful teleconferencing system implemented? The answer is by concentrating on the human factors as well as the hardware. Let the business needs drive the technology, not the reverse.

There are seven important steps to successful teleconferencing:

1. Needs assessment
2. System design
3. System management
4. Internal promotion
5. User training

6. Usage tracking
7. System expansion

1. Needs Assessment

Begin by conducting a needs assessment to determine how potential users of the system presently conduct business.

A needs assessment will provide data needed to develop an economic justification showing what the system will cost and what its rate of return will be for the organization in terms of dollars and other, less quantifiable benefits. It provides input into the system design phase by identifying key locations and functions to be served and the specific equipment to meet the needs. A thorough needs assessment assures that once the system is installed, it will be used effectively because it is designed to meet the requirements of the organization. A needs assessment also provides input into long-range plans for eventual system expansion.

2. System Design

The system design is based on information obtained during the needs assessment phase. Specific equipment is selected to support the identified needs, and facilities are selected, designed, and constructed.

It is important not to design the system before the needs assessment is completed or to ignore the results. It is not uncommon to hear that an organization installed a particular teleconferencing system because the chief executive officer heard that another organization had the same type of system.

3. System Management

Once the appropriate system is designed it is important to consider how it will be managed. Will users call one central number for reserving the facilities? Will someone be responsible for each site and available at any time to provide assistance to users? System management deals with all aspects associated with reservations and room operations.

Organizations should consider developing guidelines for room operations. These guidelines are a ready reference for individuals wishing to use the room and a permanent copy should be placed by the equipment. A separate user guide should be available for participants to take with them.

4. Internal Promotion

An often overlooked problem is how to be sure the system will be used once it is installed. The answer is an active, ongoing promotion campaign. If users are not made aware that a teleconferencing system exists and how it can be used effectively there will be little usage. Users need to be told how and why they can benefit from teleconferencing, and the promotion effort must be ongoing.

To do this, consider using a variety of media. People react differently to different types of media. Poster, flyers, memo pads, travel inserts, and other print material may appeal to one type of person while another reacts more favorably to videotapes or CD-ROMs. Hearing about the successes of others often causes people who have not used a system to try it.

5. User Training

Most vendors provide technical, maintenance training and general user training to help users understand how to operate the system. Unfortunately, one important aspect of training is frequently overlooked — application training. Organizations are repeatedly finding that usage of a teleconferencing system often drops once the initial newness has worn off. Many teleconferencing systems have been installed with one particular application in mind and no forethought given to future uses of the system. Developing potential applications, along with conducting a needs assessment, will help users prepare for ongoing system use.

6. Usage Tracking

A usage tracking system will provide valuable information for evaluating the effectiveness of a teleconferencing system and for monitoring room and equipment use. This system also will monitor system utilization over a period of time, help to determine system strengths and weaknesses, and gauge user satisfaction.

Information gathered by a usage tracking system also will provide the data to develop justification for the current system and for future expansion. Users should consider the following areas of usage tracking:

- reservation system data
- post-meeting questionnaires
- participant surveys
- telephone interviews
- travel questionnaire and trip data, and
- reports to management.

7. System Expansion

Based on the success of the initial system, expansion of the system will need to be addressed. The development of a guideline for system expansion is undertaken in this phase. A system expansion guideline might contain the following chapters:

- introduction and general information
- audioconferencing
- audiographic/multimedia conferencing
- videoconferencing
- conducting a needs assessment
- usage tracking and evaluation
- applications.

It is important to consider all the elements needed for a successful teleconferencing system. Using teleconferencing is an advantage because it improves the ability to meet, wherever and whenever.

SUMMARY

The teleconferencing market is real and, although some people are concerned that the growth has not happened as quickly as they would have liked or was projected, it is a technology with proven applications and cost benefits.

The future for teleconferencing is bright. Connectivity issues are being addressed, standards are in place, and vendors are quickly building products. Eventually a video conversation will be as available as an audio call. Not only will it be available from a desktop or group system, but it will also be available from a stand-alone video telephone set and a television. Both these devices are offered today, but neither has a wide market share — yet. In time, as has happened with the fax machine, people will wonder how they lived without audio, audiographics/multimedia and videoconferencing.

Section VII
Support for the Network Manager

Chapter 23
Evaluating the Information Technology Outsourcing Option

Kenneth Harnisch

Although no formal universal definition exists, outsourcing is generally agreed to mean the transfer of resources, control, and functional management from an internal organization to an external one. In the world of information technology (IT), outsourcing means the acquisition and transfer of telecommunications and data networking functionality—often including client resources, assets, and network management capabilities—from an internal client organization to an external IT services expert or provider.

The client in an outsourced IT relationship is more than likely a large organization whose requirements for a given type of specialized service or function cannot be met in-house, or whose business focus and strategy cannot support the continuance of providing such expertise internally. The outsourcer can be any telecommunications entity, such as a worldwide network services provider, an equipment manufacturer, or a local common carrier. Outsourcers can also be third parties with no formal affiliation to any of the former, but with a proven track record for negotiating and managing outsourcing contracts involving systems management, network management, and other associated telecommunications functionality.

Outsourcing in its various forms has existed for many years. Automatic Data Processing Inc. (ADP), for example, has processed payroll and provided tax services to its client base for decades. Many firms have successfully outsourced support functions such as security, cafeteria services, housekeeping, and the like. In the world of IT, however, outsourcing is a relatively recent concept, given its initial impetus after the 1968 Carterphone decision and its greatest after divestiture of the Bell System in 1984.

0-8493-9990-4/99/$0.00+$.50
© 1999 by CRC Press LLC

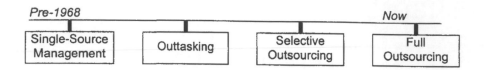

Exhibit 1.   Evolution of Service Options in the IT Industry, Pre-Carterphone to Now

Prior to Carterphone, companies usually maintained small telecommunications staffs whose primary responsibility was to negotiate local service from a Bell Operating Company (BOC), and long-distance services from AT&T Long Lines. The chief task of these support staffs was to minimize costs and maximize service quality. Options were limited, and vendor choices were virtually nonexistent.

Carterphone changed the landscape dynamically. Suddenly, options were available in terms of technologies, equipment providers, and most of all, cost. The subsequent divestiture of the Bell System encouraged a revolution in communications technology and industry management, the most dramatic being the passing of responsibility for corporate telecommunications management from the provider to the client.

Since then, the pace of the technology revolution has accelerated at a breakneck pace. Technologies change rapidly (a computer company, in one of its ads, admits "that a seven-year old plane is younger than a one-year old server"). In a global marketplace, with multiple vendors and myriad services, the most sophisticated IT managers are often overwhelmed by choices and decisions that may have significant impacts on their corporate bottom lines.

Today, the need to keep technology current and complex worldwide networks up and running 100% of the time has dramatically changed the relationship between service provider and client. Over time, by using a variety of vendor-provided service options, management of the client's network has shifted increasingly from the organization itself to hired experts and consultants, or network service and equipment providers (Exhibit 1).

The technological revolution now under way will undoubtedly accelerate this trend, because the need to manage sophisticated networks will require expertise and resources that many large organizations do not and will not possess. Some form of outsourcing in the IT world may well become the rule rather than the exception.

- **Single-source management**   Service quality and cost watchdog function interfacing with sole source telecommunications service provider.

- **Outtasking** Contract and tariff arrangement to supply specific or specialized telecommunications services (i.e., network monitoring and management, maintenance, etc.) for client-owned network, with control retained by client.
- **Selective outsourcing** Transfer of control and management for specific telecommunications functionality to external service provider, affiliate, or consultant (i.e., help desk; legacy systems administration; fault isolation and resolution; equipment moves, adds, and changes, etc.).
- **Full outsourcing** Complete transfer of assets, resource and control and management over whole or sectionalized components of client-owned networks to external service provider, affiliate, or consultant.

Note: The relationship of service options to chronology does not hold for all outsourcing entities. The various forms of service options shown earlier reflect trends in the IT industries, and they may not be applicable to related industries or outsourcing in general.

WHY COMPANIES OUTSOURCE

Outsourcing is never a decision to be entered into lightly. In any outsourcing arrangement, there can be significant organizational changes, dislocation of people, transfer of company-owned assets, and long-term contractual relationships with the outsourcer. Still, outsourcing, which was estimated to be an $18.5 billion market in 1995, is anticipated to grow in excess of $42 billion by the year 2000.

Studies of outsourcing decisions made by large organizations indicate there are clear reasons why companies outsource part or all of their operations. Those reasons—and the anticipated benefits—can be codified as follows:

- **Improving company focus** This allows companies to focus on core businesses while outsourcing day-to-day operations to external suppliers.
- **Accessing world-class capabilities** Outsourcing providers, by their nature, bring expertise, technology, methodologies, and resources to bear that the client company cannot expect to emulate.
- **Accelerating re-engineering benefits** Re-engineering is the fundamental rethinking and retooling of business processes to effect positive changes to company costs, quality, service, and speed. An outsourcer reengineered to world-class standards brings expertise to the client, which the client may not be able to access or afford internally.
- **Sharing risks** Clients will outsource to an outside vendor to alleviate the risks associated with sustaining technological improvements. The client will outsource to off-load the cost of risk to a strategic partner.
- **Free resources for other purposes** Every organization has limits to resources. Outsourcing permits an organization to refocus those re-

sources on core businesses that have a greater return to the client from its customer base.

- **Making capital funds available**   Outsourcing can reduce the need of the client to invest capital funds in noncore business functions.
- **Cash infusion**   Outsourcing often involves the transfer of assets from the client to the outsourcer, which may result in a significant one-time cash payment to the client.
- **Reducing and controlling operating costs***   The advantages of specialization or greater economies of scale that the outsourcer can bring to the client can and does reduce and control client cost, and they are clearly the preeminent tactical reason most organizations outsource. (For a discussion of cost considerations in outsourcing arrangements, see the next section of this chapter.)
- **Resources not available internally***   Companies either do not have or do not plan to hire resources necessary to manage critical or noncritical components of their operation. Outsourcers with proven track records in management of these components provide a viable and attractive alternative to building such expertise internally.
- **Function difficult to manage or out of control**   Outsourcing is an option for areas of the client's operation deemed difficult to manage or out of control. *Caution:* Outsourcing the problem area does not negate the responsibility of internal management for the problem area or address the underlying causes of the difficulty as they existed prior to the outsourcing contract.

COST CONTROL AS A FACTOR IN OUTSOURCING

According to the Outsourcing Institute, "The single most important tactical reason for outsourcing is to reduce and control operating costs."[1]

Cost reduction and control does not mean the *absence* of costs. One of the myths about outsourcing is that it always drives down cost, which is flatly untrue. There are trade-offs in any outsourcing agreement, and although outsourcing can and does provide services more cost effectively to the client in most cases, requirements for improved service levels and better quality of services to end-user customers have a price tag that can translate into *higher* costs, at least in the short term.

Nevertheless, cost reduction and control is usually the most critical value point the outsourcer brings to the client. The outsourcer leverages economies of scale inherent in its operation against the real and presumed costs, which the client might otherwise incur if he were to develop the expertise

---

* While all the reasons listed here have application to outsourcing in the IT industry, those identified with asterisks (*) are usually cited as being most important to the decision to outsource IT management functions to an external service provider.

Exhibit 2. Cost Control Elements in the Outsourcing Process

Element	Description
Cost avoidance	Effective management of existing or legacy systems to extend shelf life and minimize need for additional expenditures; avoids capital investments and operating expenses
Cost reduction	Reduction of operating expenses by diminishing or divesting recurring expense items or operations; leverages outsourcer's inherent economies-of-scale
Cost containment	Stabilization of operating expenses by contracting with outside supplier at fixed rates or imposing rigid expense limitations on internal resources
Asset liquidation	Converting fixed assets into cash by selling them to outsourcer or third party; having outsourcer provide management services for them under contract at a recurring management fee
Predictability	The ability to accurately determine or anticipate costs over time for planning and budgeting purposes

internally. In the IT universe specifically, the astonishing pace of the technology revolution, the threat of competition, and the advent of the global marketplace makes the costs of start-up and "keep-up" daunting to even the most intrepid organization. In this fluid and rapidly changing environment costs can become—and are—prohibitive, volatile, and unpredictable.

Cost Control Elements

For the client organization, understanding the specific cost elements involved in outsourcing decisions is critical to understanding the process of cost control. As Exhibit 2 illustrates, cost control represents a complex set of these elements, each with its own inherent benefits and limitations.

Outsourcers do not necessarily sell their services by emphasizing their specialties in managing individual cost control elements, though obviously some have developed a reputation for focusing on one or two areas that may be extremely attractive to the client. Cost considerations can make or break a decision to outsource by an organization. The best outsourcers have the flexibility to manage most, if not all, elements of cost control, or to ally themselves with strategic partners whose expertise can make up for any shortcomings the outsourcers might have. It is critical for the client's and outsourcer's ongoing relationship to know which elements of cost control are driving the decision-making process at all times.

COST CONSIDERATIONS IN OUTSOURCING FOR THE INFORMATION TECHNOLOGY INDUSTRY

The volatility of the technology revolution underscores the IT client's continuing apprehensions about costs of doing business in the present and in

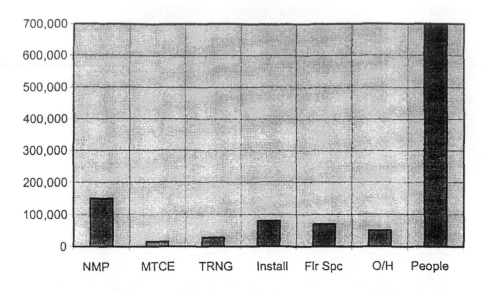

Exhibit 3.   Client's Network Management Costs

the future. Day-to-day costs for managing present networks and keeping them running are already substantial. The costs of network downtime, on which many IT management careers may hinge, can be exorbitant. Future costs are a big question to many IT managers, and they have driven decisions to outsource some or all the network as a result.

Network Management Costs

In Exhibit 3, cost elements involved in running a network requiring support 7 days a week, 24 hours a day were calculated as being approximately $1.09 million.[2] The following assumptions were used in this calculation:

- People—six to seven full time, with loaded salary rates of $100,000 per annum
- Network management platform (NMP)—$100,000 to 150,000
- Maintenance—calculated as 10% of NMP platform
- Recurring training—$4,000 per person per year
- Installation/project management—$800 per site (assumes 100-site network)
- Floor space for six to seven people—$50/sq ft (approximately)
- Overhead/miscellaneous expenses—$50,000

Network Downtime

A primary consideration for IT management has to be the actual cost of network downtime. These costs can vary by industry, making outsourcing

Exhibit 4. Downtime Costs for Various Industries

Business	Industry	Cost Range (per hr)	Average Cost (per hr)
Brokerage operations	Finance	$5.6–7.3 Million	$6.45 Million
Credit card and sales authorization	Finance	$2.2–3.1 Million	$2.6 Million
Pay-for-view	Media	$67–233 Thousand	$150 Thousand
Home shopping (TV)	Retail	$87–140 Thousand	$113 Thousand
Catalog sales	Retail	$60–120 Thousand	$90 Thousand
Airline reservations	Transportation	$67–112 Thousand	$89.5 Thousand
Tele-ticket sales	Media	$56–82 Thousand	$69 Thousand
Package shipping	Transportation	$24.5–32 Thousand	$28 Thousand
ATM fees	Finance	$12–17 Thousand	$14.5 Thousand

decisions predicated on downtime more important for some industry elements than for others. As Exhibit 4 indicates, those costs can be severe for high-volume financial industries and less so for retail and transportation companies, but they are significant in all cases for only an hour's average outage.

Costs Not Quantified

Not quantifiable in this model are unknown future costs for the following:

- **Resource** Additional qualified people who may be needed to manage a new application or technology
- **Training** Costs of keeping current staff abreast of the new changes, in excess of budgeted recurring training costs
- **Physical plant improvements** Necessary to house support staff and equipment, including costs such as insurance, rent, security, and utilities
- **Capital investment** Dollars invested in new tools, techniques, and equipment that may be necessary to support and manage new technologies
- **Maintenance** Keeping availability and quality of network services at optimum levels during all phases of technology improvements

These last series of costs, somewhat predictable in previous years due to the manageable pace of technological change, are today as volatile as the technologies that drive them. The rate of change, the unknown costs associated with managing it, and the client's fear of not being able to manage either make outsourcing a more attractive option for the IT manager than it was in the past.

BENEFITS AND RISKS OF IT OUTSOURCING

Costs aside, IT managers must take a hard look at outsourcing without glorifying its anticipated benefits or minimizing its potential risks for their organization. In most cases, the *perceived* benefits of outsourcing are not in dispute by either party. It is the perception of the risks of outsourcing, by the client specifically, and an absence of empathy or response to them by the outsourcer that most often contributes to the collapse of negotiations and a "no contract" decision. Understanding and managing the risk equation is necessary to both client and outsourcer throughout the often arduous process of outsourcing negotiation.

Benefits

For both outsourcer and client in the IT environment, the benefits of outsourcing are amplified in a marketplace where some form of universal outsourcing may soon become the norm. The benefits to the entrepreneurial consultant or management facilitator are obvious in terms of client satisfaction, reputation, and increased profit. For the large network provider or equipment manufacturer, outsourcing may be a necessary step to retaining millions of dollars in current or future company business. In fact, protection of embedded revenue is the reason most of these nontraditional outsourcers got into the business in the first place.

For the client, the benefits of outsourcing, some previously detailed in this chapter, include the following considerations for high-end managers of the business:

- Outsourcing support organizations make the core business more attractive to potential "mergers and acquisitions" suitors.
- Outsourcing is preferable to downsizing.
- Outsourcing cost centers improve the prospect of measuring true contribution of profit centers in remaining business.
- Outsourcing forces a tighter linking of business strategy and IT via the necessity to "vendor manage" the outsourcer.

The ability to support the client through the pace of rapid technological change, to "manage through the revolution" as one network outsourcer puts it, along with the relief promised to existing cost structures and limited resources, are collectively cited as the other key determinants when client IT management assesses the benefits of outsourcing.

Risks of Outsourcing

"If all parachutes opened without a hitch," someone once said, "there would be a lot more skydivers."

Outsourcing carries with it substantial risk, more for the client than to the outsourcer, but significant for both. The risk can vary from business to business, from company to company. It is less complicated for a business, for example, to outsource nonstrategic functions such as security, cafeteria services, payroll, grounds keeping, and mail services than the computers, peripherals, and the networks over which they communicate. This is especially true when the client sees the network as a differentiator in corporate business strategy, not merely a commodity.

For that reason alone, it is critical for both clients and outsourcers to appreciate the unique risks attendant to outsourcing in the IT industry, mainly:

- **Loss of strategic control**   Internal management of a vital part of the company's business is outsourced, changing the relationship between the IT manager and internal customer-focused organizations. In communications-intensive industries (airlines, car rental agencies, home shopping clubs, etc.), loss of control is seen to be more important than potential cost savings.
- **Hidden risk to outsourcer**   Internal customer organizations tend to be demanding of high service levels without appreciation of the "real" costs of providing them.
- **Responsiveness to needs of internal customers**   The client is more aware of the specialized needs of internal customers than the outsourcer. This is critical to companies that manage IT for internal profit centers or end-user-focused "centers of excellence." In effecting economies of scale, and with an eye to profit, the outsourcer may try to provide "cookie cutter" services in strict accordance with the contract, thus antagonizing the client's internal end-user support organizations.
- **Security**   Network security is always an issue when an outsourcer assumes control. To the extent that sensitive information is stored in outsourced systems and travels through network switches, the risks of intrusion, information loss, and alteration must weigh on the decision to outsource. For this reason, financial institutions and research organizations were considered very poor prospects for outsourcing. For this reason, too, many larger-scale outsourcers have introduced security products and services such as encryption and managed firewall services into their suite of outsourcing services and solutions to assuage this vital client concern.
- **Competition for resources**   Generally not a consideration when IT services are provided internally to single departments or heterogeneous organizations, but an outsourcer may support multiple client organizations. In the event of disaster or localized failure, an outsourcer's resources may be strained, and services "budgeted" to the client organizations may be without appreciation of their value to the client.
- **Strategic direction**   Long-term contracts (which are the hallmark of outsourcing deals) and the presence of an outsourcer may impede management initiatives to become involved in mergers, acquisitions, or restructuring. The client's ability to control the outsourcer's resources is significantly less than his own, and it affects decisions to "rightsize" or downsize.

In addition, the IT client may have to consider these lesser, but insubstantial, risks when determining the ability of outsourcing to meet its requirements as a provider:

- Difficulties in benchmarking initial contracts
- High exit or switching costs
- The fixed nature of long-term contracts
- Cultural conflicts
- Possibility of weak management
- Hidden costs
- Hidden partners (both parties)
- Loss of innovative capacity by the client
- Fuzzy focus

TO OUTSOURCE OR NOT: DECISION MAKING IN THE IT INDUSTRY

Outsourcing, at the least, is an *emotional* decision. It involves contracting with an external supplier to assume control and management of tasks and resources that the organization may have had in-house for many years, and the disruption or dissolution of lines of communication that may have been in place between internal client organizations and IT management for nearly as long. It is not a decision made easily, and it is not one to be left solely to middle management, who may have a personal stake in its outcome. *Any* decision to outsource, to be valid, must have the continuous buy-in and support of top client management, for without it, the decision-making process may be mired in trivial details that lose sight of the strategic reasons the company chose to outsource in the first place.

The Client: The Process of Decision

For the IT client and, indeed, for all potential outsourcing customers, the *process* of decision making involves the following finite steps, each weighed carefully and each involving discussions, assessment, reassessment, amendment, and agreement. This is a formal and informal process that may take *years* to finalize, depending on the criticality of the function or functions being outsourced by the client.

- **Making the outsourcing decision** Deciding, after weighing the factors involved, that outsourcing makes the most sense to address a strategic or tactical need.
- **Identifying capable vendors** Determining which range of outsourcers fits the critical criteria necessary to manage the network.
- **Selecting the "best value" vendor** Determining which vendor best meets the company's strategic needs. (*Note:* Cost is not necessarily the dominant factor in this decision.)
- **Negotiating and arranging contract and statement of work** Negotiating length and terms of the contract; articulating and formalizing

benchmarking goals and establishing clear service levels for all aspects of the outsourced network.

- **Transition management**   Making the change from client to outsourcer management as minimally disruptive as possible.
- **Monitoring effort and verifing output**   Continuous assessment of vendor performance against established benchmarks and service levels; renegotiation and contract clarification if necessary to clear up problem areas in post contract phases.

Minimizing Risk in the Decision Processes

The client deciding to outsource will *always* seek to minimize risks and the upheavals that outsourcing can cause internal staff and operations. Few rumors are more disruptive to morale than the one that an outsourcer is being sought to assume some role in the company's operations. Staff members who believe themselves most affected by outsourcing tend to become insular and will look to themselves and their careers more than they will a business they often feel is turning its back on them. This can have a significantly negative effect on business if the decision is dragged out over a long period of time. For IT clients, such morale problems can materially affect the efficient operation of the network. For this reason, few clients decide to fully outsource at the outset of the decision process unless some compelling cause, such as poor financials, makes it imperative.

Clients often take steps to minimize the risks attendant to outsourcing while they study it for further application in the business. These steps reduce the "trauma" of outsourcing, and give the client information necessary to analyze the future value of outsourcing to other aspects of the organization. These steps are specific to IT, but they can be applicable to other outsourcing applications as well:

- **Incremental outsourcing**   Outsourcing noncritical sections of the network or organization first, rather than outsourcing entirely.
- **Hard learning**   Using experience to determine which components of the organization or network are running most or least efficiently and making the outsourcing decision accordingly.
- **Strategic**   The key determinant to outsourcing a network or its resources. (How valuable is the network and IT to company strategy and what portions of it can most readily be turned over to external management at least risk to the client's business focus?)

The major factors for managers of an IT organization to consider when outsourcing components of its network are

- Is the network a differentiator of company business strategy and focus or is it a commodity?

403

Exhibit 5. Factors in IT Network Outsourcing

Keep In-House		Outsource	
Factor	Positioning	Factor	Positioning
Business positioning impact	High	Business positioning impact	Low
Link to business strategy	High	Link to business strategy	Low
Future business uncertainty	High	Future business uncertainty	Low
Technology maturity	Low	Technology maturity	High
Level of IT integration	High	Level of IT integration	Low
In-house expertise	High	In-house expertise	Low

- Conversely, what is the relationship between the IT activity and service and the business strategy? The more critical the network is, the less willing the client will be to fully and completely outsource.

Other factors that leverage the outsourcing decision include

- The degree of uncertainty about the future business environment
- Level of IT integration into day-to-day client operations
- In-house capability relative to that available on the external market
- Estimated internal costs (labor, material, time, etc.) of providing the service and expertise
- Advantages and problems of internal task performance
- Advantages and problems of external task performance
- Strategic advantages and disadvantages of outsourcing work

As noted, studies such as these take time, and the resulting decisions involve many layers of management, not all of whom may buy in to the need to perform that task in a time frame expeditious to the outsourcer or the client's own top management. Fear and foot dragging are common obstacles to the outsourcer who is dealing with client middle managers.

To Decide to Outsource: Best Cases

Although not foolproof, a client can use the following decision framework to determine whether or not to outsource components of the network if all other factors in the decision are seen to be roughly equal (Exhibit 5).

Of course, most IT outsourcing decisions involve factors more complex than those presented in this table. For example, few organizations provide such a neat fit for this criteria. Other factors involved (business strategy, technology, cost containment, or control efforts) may be more compelling to the client in the decision process. Nevertheless, a table such as this, used for objective analysis of existing client capabilities, can provide a good starting point for discussion and debate.

THE VENDOR

The process of finding the right outsourcing vendor is critical to the decision to outsource. In most cases, this is *not* a serial process, begun only after the decision to outsource is made. An IT client who has a preexisting relationship with an outsourcer, a network service provider, an interexchange company, a local telephone company, or a well-positioned third-party consultant will often try to tailor a decision to outsource to meet the favored vendor's strengths. For all its drawbacks, it is nevertheless a process appealing to many potential clients, since it usually involves contracting service with a known quantity and reduces many of the uncertainties (and angst) attendant to outsourcing.

In cases where this relationship is insufficient to the need (i.e., the client's requirements cannot be met by the vendor of choice) or where the client has no preset prejudices for or against an outsourcer, the decision may involve competitive bidding; issuance of requests for proposals (RFPs) and requests for information (RFI); and round after round of internal meetings, debates, assessments, and decisions.

The technology revolution has had its greatest impact on IT client-vendor choices because even long-term relationships cannot match the importance of finding the right vendor if the client has concerns about network obsolescence, cost control, expertise, and economies of scale. In this environment, selection of the *best-fitting* outsourcing vendor becomes extremely critical.

Deciding on the Vendor: Factors

The more critical the network is to business strategy, the more important confirmation of the following factors is to the ultimate vendor choice:

- **Expertise** Question A-1: Does the vendor have the necessary skill and experience to manage the operation effectively?
- **Commitment** The vendor must demonstrate a strong commitment to the business of outsourcing and be ready to provide strong contractual assurance of that commitment.
- **Viability** Sound past and present financial performance, history in the business, and vision for growing the business are factors that the client should look for in the outsourcer.
- **Track record** The critical nature of the client–outsourcer relationship makes the track record of the outsourcer a key component in the decision process. Past and current business with the outsourcer can provide a benchmark for both a valid assessment of performance and a determinant of future behavior. Testimonials and references can be equally valid if the client and the vendor do not have an existing relationship.

405

- **Survivability**   The vendor must be able to weather business reversals, downturns, loss of key personnel, and demands on its resources, while demonstrating a continuation of high-quality service throughout.

Deciding on the Vendor: Best Value Outsourcing

Like the griffin or the unicorn, there is no such animal as the "perfect" IT outsourcer. Outsourcers come in all shapes and sizes, have expertise that is often tailored to specific networks or their components, and have strategic approaches to outsourcing that are markedly different from each other. In the end, only the client who is doing the outsourcing can make the determination which vendor or vendors are most compatible with client needs and strategies.

Nevertheless, a good initial assessment of outsourcers' capabilities is in their ability to meet the strategic requirements that are driving the client's outsourcing decision. It is the client who makes this decision, hopefully, not clouded by fear or favor. Subjective judgments in outsourcing have long-term ramifications, which may negatively impact the outsourcing partnership between client and vendor.

Chief factors in outsourcing IT (and vendor selection), outside of costs, include the following:

- **Access to world-class capabilities**   The client must look to an outsourcer to provide expertise and presence in marketplaces or arenas where the client cannot. In IT, this usually involves outsourcing specific areas such as network monitoring and management, fault isolation and resolution, security, and disaster recovery. *Potential trade-off* is loss of control and internal expertise, making the client more vendor dependent.
- **Shared risks**   The vendor is willing to share the financial risks of outsourcing with the client. *Potential trade-offs* are hidden costs and long-term contracts that may limit the client's ability to strategically manage the business.
- **Accelerated re-engineering benefits**   The vendor brings acknowledged expertise in tools, techniques, and resources to bear on client networks, saving money and ensuring access to trained resources and continuing modernity of network components. *Potential trade-offs* include loss of network control, and limiting client options to change networks themselves or contract with third parties for network services.

HOW THE IT OUTSOURCER MANAGES RISK AND DECISION

All risk is not the client's alone. If outsourcing is not a decision entered into lightly by the client, it is also not a business for the fainthearted or the company seeking short-term returns. It costs millions of dollars to create an IT outsourcing organization and millions more to engage clients in what is often an arduous process of negotiation and renegotiation until a contract is signed. Once involved, outsourcers are exposed contractually and may well sacrifice future business if they cannot live up to negotiated service levels. Contract terms and conditions may be privileged information. Still, anecdotal evidence about poor service provided by an outsourcer traded during a client industry conference can have a devastating long-term effect on future business.

The best outsourcers understand all aspects of the outsourcing business, including the pitfalls. For that reason, the best outsourcers will learn from past mistakes and involve themselves in a process of continuous quality improvement. Some will walk away from lucrative business opportunities because they understand the risks of winning are greater than the risks of playing. Some outsourcers, preferred beforehand by the client, have nevertheless decided not to participate in an opportunity because their reasoned assessment is that there is no reward in victory. Hard learning may be a concept more applicable to vendors, which have been involved in numerous unsuccessful outsourcing opportunities, than it is to clients, who usually have not.

Bid or No Bid

IT outsourcers have a stake in making sure the risk and decision process is structured in such a way that it protects them from long, fruitless negotiations and endless give and take sessions with the client. To that end, many outsourcers have developed a sequence of bid or no bid checkpoints that can benchmark quality client opportunities in advance of the costs required to engage them. Based on a point value system, the client is evaluated for its relationship with the outsourcer, the outsourcer's assessment of the opportunity, and the risk management requirements, all of which are weighted toward a bid or no bid decision.

Some of the questions an outsourcer will ask itself in this detailed process are the following:

- Client relationship
  - Have good executive relationships been established with the client?
  - Is there a clear champion or sponsor for the opportunity within the client's top executive ranks?
  - Are the outsourcer's marketing and operations management aware of, and does it support, the opportunity?
- Opportunity assessment
  - Will this opportunity provide benefit to the client?
  - Is there a well-defined "win" strategy?
  - Was the outsourcer able to influence the RFP?

- — Has the outsourcer assessed all operational risks involved in the opportunity?
- — Who is the competition?
- — If teaming, are the team members stable, financially viable, and reliable?
- — Why does the outsourcer want this business?
- Risk management
  - — Does the outsourcer have a good financial profile of the client?
  - — What is the purpose and value of the outsourced organization to the client's overall business strategy?
  - — Have business cases been prepared, analyzed, and approved?
  - — What is the anticipated length and costs associated with "due diligence"?[3]

Note: Other bid or no bid decision points may vary from outsourcer to outsourcer.

Depending on the answers to these questions, especially the ones the outsourcer asks candidly of itself and its own organization, an outsourcer can generally reach an intelligent bid or no bid decision.

The Slow Dance: The Aftermath of Winning

A bid decision is not the end of the transaction for the outsourcer nor is awarding the contract the end for the client. What follows a successful notification to bid is usually a long slow dance, a sluggish waltz between two reluctant partners who often feel quite uncomfortable together and are bound to step on each other's toes a few times in the lengthy process to follow.

For the client, awarding the contract allows time to reflect on issues that may have been glossed over in the process to find a successful bidder. For the outsourcer, the client may now seem like an obstructionist, all too willing in the wake of contract signing to question minute aspects of the deal and the methods by which the vendor will be performing the contracted services.

This "re-look" after the fact is a somewhat natural reaction. The problem is that postbid second-guessing may spawn a series of rancorous dealings between outsourcer and client that may spill over into their postcontractual relationship. Some of this is unavoidable but is merely a response to the ordinary tensions of negotiation. However, there are clear-cut signs that an outsourcing deal, though well-intended and mutually supported, may be heading for disaster. Three of the most notable signs are discussed in the following section.

Warning Signs of Impending Failure

Signs that an outsourcing deal may be headed for eventual disaster and bad feelings between the client and the outsourcer are varied, but these three have been identified as sure signs the contracted outsourcing deal may be doomed before it even gets under way:

- **Intense involvement of middle level management, especially financial and legal, in the relationship** Although financial and legal issues have a critical role to play in supporting client management, surveys done by the Outsourcing Institute indicate a deal is in trouble if these issues dominate the postcontract discussions. This is an indication that the strategic reasons for outsourcing are being overshadowed by detail. Since the key to a successful outsourcing relationship is the partnership between client and outsourcer, the quagmire of numbers, terms, and conditions can have the effect of damaging this relationship before it really begins, ensuring an ultimate breakdown of the relationship.

- **Vendors not prequalified** In too many cases, vendors are chosen for reasons that are subjective, reflecting a client's personal preferences, or because they were low bidders. In IT outsourcing especially, cost of the deal is secondary to the vendor's technical expertise; knowledge; willingness to learn the client's business; and compatibility with the client's in-house technical expertise, management, physical plant, and resources. Price, after all, is only one element of cost, and illusory savings at the bid level may well be offset by excessive costs in postcontract operations and performance.

- **Short-term benefits dominating as decision factors** Since cash infusions through asset transfer and resolution of resource constraints are short-term benefits to the client that may be offset in the long term when lower operating expenses, access to better or expanded skills, and improved company focus on the part of the outsourcer cannot or are not being met. Short-term benefits are critical decision points to the client. However, they can have trade-offs that compromise the longer term success of the deal.

Successful Outsourcing: Steps in a Winning Process

As noted, the pace and scope of the technology revolution almost demands that IT client and vendor cooperate closely from the outset, since some form of network outsourcing is becoming the rule, not the exception. The need to compete in the client's core business lines makes it imperative that the network supporting it is kept current and is kept running and that the expertise necessary to run the network is always available.

That point is rapidly being reached when only the large outsourcing organizations can support such technological fluidity, since the costs of maintaining internal client resources are becoming prohibitive. The market is there if the outsourcers can do what it takes to win it and hold to.

A successful outsourcing relationship involves a joint clarity of purpose and minimizing risk. Underscoring that is the trust that must develop between client and vendor for the relationship to be successful. To that end, the following are seen to be key factors in successful IT outsourcing contracts:

- **Coordination**   There should be an open three-way communication among the outsourcer, the IT management, and the client organizations that use the network to transact business.
- **Length of contract**   The contract should be long enough for the outsourcer to be successful, but short enough for the client to retain the ability to manage through changes in the business.
- **Clear service levels**   Service levels must be articulated early, guaranteed by contract, managed, and reported on at regular intervals.
- **Control**   The client should retain control of these two aspects for the relationship to be successful: management of the vendor through the IT organization and management of the internal relationships between itself, the vendor, and the end-user organizations. The latter should *never* be completely ceded by the client, in fact.
- **Single-point-of-contact (SPOC)**   This is critical to ensuring service requests are focused, articulate, cost-effective, and purposeful.
- **Accountability**   The outsourcer must know to whom he is accountable in the client's organization for all levels of service delivery. (*See* SPOC.)
- **Benchmarking**   The vendor should be gauged against "best-in-class" industry standards for assurances of high-quality network performance and management.
- **Business processes alignment**   The client must realign internal business processes to acknowledge the reality of the outsourcer's presence and to manage it.

How the Outsourcer Can Help the Client

As noted, the risks of outsourcing are significant to both client and vendor. This is especially true in the IT universe where technological advances are forcing decisions on wary enterprises who, all things considered, would rather not be faced with the choice. For the client, risk is in the loss of control, the displacement of people, and the transfer of both assets and responsibility to a third party that may be competent but certainly does not know the ins and outs of the business that it has just been contracted to manage.

For the outsourcer, the risk is in the high cost of dealing with a reluctant partner, of having a reputation tarnished by poor performance, and in the uncertainty that attaches itself to any endeavor where technological change and volatility are the norms. The technology revolution may be breathtaking to watch for those businesses not involved in it directly. For most large enterprises, however, it can mean disaster if not planned and managed with care and competence.

For the high-end network services provider, common carrier, or equipment manufacturer, outsourcing represents a golden opportunity to keep and grow business that might otherwise be lost to price discounters and start-up entrepreneurs. For the most part, full IT outsourcing is provided by companies that have tremendous size, world-class facilities, global presence, demonstrated investment in training and resource, and most of all, vision. The best outsourcers in the 21st century will have to possess all these qualities, managing change through flexible service options and continuous processes of self-improvement that reduce negotiation cycle time, demonstrating superior network management capabilities and above all being are continually responsive to the client's needs and apprehensions.

In the process of outsourcing, the vendor can support the client by understanding the risks involved for the client and by managing them effectively. This means the outsourcer will actively seek to partner with the client as soon as possible in the process and make every effort to thoroughly learn the client's business. To the extent possible, the business objectives of the client and the supplier metrics of the outsourcer must be aligned so that measurements of progress use the same yardsticks and service improvement can be a concurrent process for client and supplier.

Specifically, the outsourcer can support the client by:

- Writing clear, comprehensive statements of work that demonstrate response to the business objectives articulated by the client in the beginning of the process.
- Setting, in conjunction with the client, specific service levels for overall network and financial performance.
- Demonstrating flexibility, being willing to assume control of disparate network components with varieties of available options, including hybrid mixtures of centralized off-site management and on-site presence.
- Respecting the client's personnel, codes of conduct, and property; and abiding by client's rules and regulations when on-site.
- Attending joint client–supplier informational meetings to keep client personnel apprised of the scope of the proposed contract and responding frankly and forthrightly to concerns expressed by a resource who may be in line to become part of the outsourcer's staff.
- Concretely detailing the scope of "normal" work and providing price schedules and firm guidelines for performance of work done out of scope.

- Drafting and articulating transition plans early in the process and sharing them with the client.
- Forming postcontract operations management teams early in the process and involving them in the transition process in advance of the "cutover."
- Defining client–vendor responsibilities clearly to avoid overlap and confusion.
- Having regularly scheduled meetings to evaluate ongoing performance.
- Specifying processes by which performance shortfalls can be measured, responded to, and resolved.
- Providing clear and detailed costs for contract modifications and improvements.

CONCLUSION

In the world of IT management, outsourcing presents an opportunity for the large and stable company to make sense of a truly remarkable revolution in technology, products, and services. The client–supplier partnership is vital to the success of any outsourcing arrangement, but it involves great risk. Because the risks of outsourcing are significant, both vendor and client can make use of careful analysis and planning techniques to minimize the consequences of risk. Clear lines of communication and objective self-examination by both parties before saying yes can be of great benefit to the success of the IT outsourcing process.

An Afterword: The Future of IT Outsourcing

In the late 1990s, changes in the global economy, specifically the Asian financial crisis and the concurrent boom in the American domestic economy, raised questions about the value of outsourcing during these specific kinds of economic upheavals. In the case of the former, questions were raised about the wisdom of signing long-term outsourcing agreements in the face of unexpected events, such as the unanticipated decline of the Asian stock markets, which may saddle companies with long-term fixed costs when they are seeking ways to shrink costs to survive.

In the case of the American economic boom, the quandary is almost paradoxically opposite. Why outsource in flush times, some executives wonder, when the company is prospering and many are expanding work forces to keep up with growing demand? It would seem in the case of such success that the chief reason for outsourcing—cost control—does not qualify in periods of expansion and increased employee productivity.

The answer in both cases is that outsourcing is a viable client initiative whether times are good or bad. Some low-technological industries may indeed decide they can afford to keep certain operations in-house during

412

times of economic boom or bust. However, for companies that are thinking of outsourcing network management during these economic swing times, the key factors in making the outsourcing decision have less to do with cost than they do with the need to keep the network running smoothly. The trade-off favors the outsourcer in either calculation.

Cost control is the key element in deciding whether to outsource in the IT industry. However, the main subelements in cost control involve the outsourcer's ability to provide levels of expertise (and thus, economies of scale) that the company does not have internally, or more importantly, cannot afford over time. In the long term, whether the economy is good or bad, it is a safe bet to assume that technology will not sit still, and that a company rocked by economic downturns or blessed with economic success will still have the responsibility to (1) keep current with the rapid pace of technological change; (2) direct scarce resources to the primary goal of securing the company's competitive edge by "sticking to the knitting;" and (3) keep its products, information, and services flowing unfettered to both internal and external organizations who rely on it to keep the company sound and profitable.

The most successful IT clients are the ones that realize that network management is critical to their operation whether times are fair or foul, economically. The most successful IT outsourcers are those that can manage those networks at less cost and more efficiently than the clients can themselves.

This, in a nutshell, is the essence of IT outsourcing.

Notes

1. Newsletter, The Outsourcing Institute, 1/23/97.
2. Various sources, including AT&T, Hewlett-Packard Co., and Dean & Co.
3. Due diligence is the outsourcer's process of exploration and discovery of the client's organization, finances, etc., which is standard in most outsourcing contracts.

Chapter 24
Writing an Effective Request for Proposals
Douglas R. Ballou

INTRODUCTION

The purpose of this chapter is to explore the importance of the telecommunications request for proposals (RFP) in a large business environment. In this chapter the reasons for creating an RFP are examined. The size of the RFP, writing the RFP, RFP content, RFP distribution, and response expectations are discussed.

DEFINITIONS

According to Newton's *Telecom Dictionary* (paraphrased), a request for proposals is a "detailed document prepared by a buyer defining requirements for service and equipment. The document is sent to one or several vendors for review and a detailed response. The vendor's response is typically binding on the vendor. That is, the vendor will be obligated to deliver what is described in the RFP response, at the stated conditions, and at the stated prices."

Other documents are sometimes preliminary to the RFP. These documents are the request for information (RFI) and the request for quotes (RFQ). These documents are usually very basic, short in length, and used when the customer is unfamiliar with the vendor community, offered products, and associated pricing. The RFQ can also be used to establish project budgetary guidelines. However, in most cases, companies forgo the RFI and RFQ effort and direct their energies toward the more comprehensive RFP process.

Another RFP-related process is called the invitation to bid (ITB). Generally associated with government, the major purpose of this process is to receive the lowest bid for the system described. ITB procedures and terms are very rigid, and vendor competency and product quality appear to be secondary. Many examples of unsatisfactory results and problems that go unresolved for years are proof that the ITB process leaves much to be desired. Fortunately, the current government trend is toward the more favorable and flexible RFP.

REQUEST FOR PROPOSALS CONSIDERATIONS

At what point does an RFP become a consideration? An RFP should be considered at any point that the user wants an assurance that all vendors are responding to exactly the same information. This applies to small systems and large systems alike. Usually the only difference is that the large system RFP is weightier and more complex. RFPs can be as few as 4 to 5 pages (anything less is usually meaningless) or as large as 100 pages and beyond.

The size of the RFP is dictated by the amount of information that the user must *convey* to potential vendors. The information must be meaningful and specific. Size is added to the document if that document is intended to also serve as the final contract (terms, conditions, etc.). *Otherwise, the documents are treated separately. In the event of a conflict between any of the bid documents, the terms of the RFP will control, except and to the extent expressly and specifically modified by the terms of any attachments or change documents.*

While developing the RFP, it is important to consider the responder's point of view. That is, the weight of the RFP must be proportional to the size, complexity, and value of the proposed system. Since vendors must allocate resources and costs to bid responses, it must make business sense for that vendor to participate in the bidding process. For example, it is unlikely that a vendor would respond to a 50-page RFP for a $30,000 key system, but it might if it were a $200,000 private branch exchange (PBX).

The vendor must also have a reasonable expectation of winning the bid. A user's worst nightmare is to spend a large amount of time putting together a quality RFP and have only the weak vendors or no one respond to it. While creating the specification, the potential vendors must be foremost in the author's mind. *In the event that all vendor responses are unacceptable, it should be clearly stated in the "contract award" area of the RFP that the organization is under "no obligation to award a contract under this RFP."*

Major changes in the telecommunications system and network design of any organization of size are very visible *to users and to management.* These changes are visible during the planning process, visible during cutover, and visible after acceptance. The typical capital expense associated with the *change process* usually is large enough for everyone to take notice. The new system will likely have such an impact on the firm that upper management will want assurances that the system and its design will support the organizational strategic plan, both short and long term. To the extent allowed, this plan should be the foundation when writing the RFP.

REQUEST FOR PROPOSALS ORGANIZATION

There are multiple ways to organize an RFP. Some methodologies work better than others. The methodologies that work best are those that are logical, relevant, and simple. The following is one RFP structure that has been very successful and has been well received by both the large and small vendor communities. Guidelines for writing the RFP are included under each category.

Section 1.0: General

This section begins with a strong statement of purpose and describes what is contained in the RFP. This is followed by an abstract that describes the company, its structure, its lines of business, and its strategies. Next is a bidder qualification statement that usually begins as follows: *"In responding to this RFP, bidder represents that bidder's company possesses the capabilities, hardware, software and personnel necessary to provide an efficient and successful installation of properly operating equipment. Bidder must also ensure continued maintenance and support of all proposed systems by the bidder's trained and certified personnel, and available parts, all over a ten (10) year period."*

A subsection entitled "Bidder Company Profile Requirements" is important. Its purpose is to ensure that the responding companies are qualified. Such limitations may be "5 years in business," "revenues must exceed $100 million per annum," "bidder must demonstrate financial soundness," "bidder must be an authorized distributor of the proposed product," and so on. It also serves to limit the number of responses received *to a manageable number of quality companies.*

It is important that there be a statement dictating that the selected contractor *must* be a single point of contact *for any problems or outages. This arrangement will, in most cases, eliminate agonizing "finger-pointing" situations that delay problem resolution and extend outages.*

Finally, mandatory pre-bid conferences are strongly urged. If elected, date, time, and location must be clearly spelled out in boldface type in the RFP. The benefit of the mandatory conference is that vendor interest can be clearly identified. *It indicates the maximum number of responses that will be received. Of course, there is no guarantee that all or any of the vendors at the conference will respond. Because the conference is mandatory,* if a vendor does not attend the project briefing, the vendor is not eligible to respond to the RFP.

Section 2.0: Proposal Process

The purpose of this second section is to provide the project timetable beginning with the date that the RFP is issued to the date of system cutover. The vendor's acceptance of the RFP timetable means that the vendor is able to do the work and has the resources to complete the cutover from the old system to the new one at the specified date.

Also in this section are the specific rules for handling vendor questions. If information is provided to one vendor, the same information must be provided to all others. It is recommended that responses to questions be in writing (facsimile, e-mail, letter, etc.). For legal purposes, all vendors must be treated equally and without bias. It creates a level playing field and is also good business. Instructions (delivery address, day, date, and time) for user receipt of RFP responses on the specified due date are also included in this section. Sealed bidding processes, if applicable, are also described. Finally, a general statement is made about the factors and methodology that will be used to select the winning contractor.

Section 3.0: Terms and Conditions

This section addresses some of the legal issues that are part and parcel of the RFP. Discussed are the binding nature of the agreement, related contracts, governing laws, severability, hardware requirements, claims, indemnity, limitation of liability and remedies, risk of loss, handling of travel expenses, Equal Employment Opportunity, prevailing wages, compliance with the law, permits, confidentiality, drug-free and smoke-free working environment, invoice methodology, assignment, standards of performance and acceptance, maintenance (general), warranties, response time, ownership of software, and so on.

Section 4.0: Proposal Content

This section establishes the "order of things" for the vendors' RFP responses. The goal is to standardize responses so that specific information can be found in a specific section of every bidder's response. This is a significant first step toward eliminating the need to search for information in a vendor's RFP. A typical "Table of Contents" might appear as follows. A brief explanation accompanies each tab name.

Tab 1: Executive Summary and Cover Letter. This includes the recommendation and a brief description of the product and the scope of services to be provided. A positive commitment to ensure that the overall system implementation is successful must be made. *Bidders must verify* that submitted pricing will be good for at least 120 days.

Tab 2: Manufacturer's Profile. If the bidder is not the manufacturer, the bidder must demonstrate the quality of the manufacturer. Information might include years in business, market share, profitability, product strategies, number of employees, management strength, and so on.

Tab 3: Bidder Profile (If Different from Tab 2). Information might include a brief organizational background, date of incorporation, annual revenue, statement of profitability, number of employees, number of certified tech-

418

nicians, manufacturer affiliations, industry experience, relationship with respective manufacturers, *experience* with proposed system(s), etc.

Tab 4: Bidder References. Require a minimum of four references. Systems must be of the same type and software level and must be similar in configuration and size. It is preferred that at least two of the references be in *close proximity to the installation site.*

Tab 5: Key Personnel Profile Summaries. The intent of this section is to ensure that the key personnel working on the project have the knowledge and experience necessary for a professional installation. Information must include a request for three references for which these individuals have successfully completed a project of similar size and scope to the one being proposed. Key personnel shall include project manager, customer support representative for each site, field technician for each site, training personnel, technical support manager, and peripheral experts.

Tab 6: System Capabilities, Present and Future. This section must include descriptive literature that provides a general overview of the capabilities of the hardware and software contained in the bidder's response. Evidence of a strong migration path toward advanced present and future capabilities is important.

Tab 7: Technical Documentation. Technical information on all recommended products must be provided. The intent is to be able to evaluate the products recommended from a technical point of view. *The level of technical detail required should be clearly defined.*

Tab 8: Bidder Response Information. This section is the placement for the original RFP. Bidders' responses are inserted immediately underneath the appropriate paragraph. This section also instructs the bidders as to what word processing software should be used in the response, since a *disk* containing the bidders' response is requested for global search purposes.

Tab 9: Implementation and Training Plans with Time Line. This section requests that a sample milestone chart or time line be provided. It must include the bidder's best estimate for cutover. Details such as lead time following *contract* signature, training intervals, and so on are important. If specific project planning software, such as Microsoft Project, is required, *it should be so stated in* this section. *The importance of professional training and a quality training program is paramount to implementation success.*

Tab 10: Warranty and Maintenance Plan. The bidder shall provide a detailed description of its warranty, service process, and maintenance plan options. A description of the bidder's service dispatch and management system can prove enlightening. Sample agreements *and pricing* must be provided in this section.

Tab 11: Cost Summary. A general cost summary is requested in this section. General categories will include the cost of PBX equipment and peripherals and separately the cost of installation for each item. Leasing terms are to be included in this section. Maintenance costs after the warranty period for each item must also be included. A purchase agreement should be inserted under this tab.

Tab 12: Options and Expansion Cost Summary. This section must provide detailed itemized components and pricing for the proposed system and all proposed peripherals. *Itemized pricing down to the component level is mandatory.* The bidder's proposal shall include costs for all hardware, software, and services recommended. In addition, the bidder shall provide an itemized list with prices for spare and post-cutover equipment. Such pricing shall be fixed for a specific period of time (e.g., 36 months).

Tab 13: Proof of Insurance. Selected contractor and subcontractors shall carry and furnish evidence of insurance against liability for death, injury, and damage to property caused by the selected contractor, its employees, and agents. Specific language and requirements should be addressed by the user's legal and insurance departments.

Tab 14: Bond Submittals. The organization's bonding requirements must be stated in this section. Requirements might include a 100% performance bond, a 100% labor and materials bond, and a 100% maintenance and guarantee bond for a specific period of time.

Tab 15: Bidder's Checklist. This final tab is reserved for a user-created list of key subjects with space allowed for the bidder to provide associated page numbers. *The page numbers will identify the specific location of the subject response in the bidders document.* Key subjects might include equipment room design; heating, ventilating, and air-conditioning (HVAC); battery backup; automatic call distribution (ACD); interactive voice response (IVR); and so on. Checklist response is mandatory.

Section 5.0: Project Description, Overview

This section provides an overview of the project. It usually restates the purpose of the effort and provides project direction for the bidder. It may refer to the organization's long-range plan with some detail. Project requirements are listed. Terms such as "forward architecture," "transparency," and "advanced technology" are often used. The physical layout is described.

The number of buildings, associated addresses, and environment (college campus, hospital campus, high-rise, etc.) is listed. If there is construction in progress or planned, scope and timetables are stated. Inside wiring issues usually prove to be important. Campus wiring logically follows if applicable. Some statement of voice, data, imaging, and videoconferencing applications may be in order. There is also a description of what new equipment (PBX, voice mail, IVR, ACD, call accounting, etc.) will be required at designated sites.

Usually, a statement of anticipated networking infrastructure is also submitted. For example, the network must have an open architecture and be based on industry standards so that all functionality is accessible to any user through standard interfaces and protocols. Network management from a single centralized location may be an important requirement. Other points might include coordinated dialing plan, integrated and networked voice mail, centralized attendant service (CAS), look-ahead ACD routing, and transparent networking between sites for present and more advanced multimedia technology.

Section 6.0: System Requirements

This section provides the detail necessary for the contractor to supply an accurate bid. The scope of the project is stated in detail. Requirements are listed with appropriate explanation. Requirements might include redundancy, Integrated Services Digital Network (ISDN) primary rate interface (PRI) capability, advanced data communications and multimedia capabilities, local area network (LAN) capability, video to the desktop, applications programming interface (API), network security, and so on. "Working," "equipped," and "wired for" capacities are quantified and include the number of specific trunks, number of stations, number and types of telephones, number of consoles, etc. This section also lists the specific details and functionality associated with ACD, ACD reporting, IVR, IVR reporting, call accounting, voice mail and automated attendant, and so on.

Section 7.0: General Conditions

This section addresses standards for installation, wiring standards, requirements for engineering, patching and painting, fire stopping, disaster management, training and documentation requirements, security, safety, project management, etc.

Section 8.0: Evaluation of Proposals

This section provides a description of the process used to evaluate submitted proposals and to select the winning bidder. Each organization generally has its own methodology. This process is usually a side-by-side comparison of eligible vendors and their recommendations. It is a weighted comparison that generally emphasizes three general categories. They are (1) proposed equipment, (2) manufacturer or vendor strength *and support*, and (3) cost. This process is usually very structured, includes an interview process to finalize selection, and emphasizes objectivity in the event of an audit.

Section 9.0: Attachments

This section includes any attachments that may be required. Typical attachments are contracts, forms, and blueprints.

ADMINISTERING THE RFP

Once the RFP is ready for distribution, a distribution list is created. This list will consist of the strongest vendors that are qualified to provide and implement the required product and software configuration. For those who are not familiar with the telecommunications industry, some research may be required to identify qualified vendors. Familiar telecommunications vendors will know who their competition is and will usually share that information. Regional communications organizations and consultants are also sources of *vendor* information.

When dealing with government agencies, including education, it is important to know that the government usually mandates a period of time, usually 2 to 4 weeks, that RFP availability must be appropriately advertised in the local papers. This procedure is intended to provide an equal opportunity for all interested companies, if qualified, to respond to the RFP.

Purchasing departments generally prefer three bid responses, but issuing three RFPs is no guarantee that three responses will be returned. As a result, usually a minimum distribution of four to five RFPs will achieve the desired result. To make it easier for vendors to respond, it is recommended that a disk with the RFP be provided with the directed hard copy. Weekly contact with all potential bidders to answer questions or remind them of the deadline will reflect a good level of interest and make response more likely.

REQUEST FOR PROPOSALS RESPONSE EXPECTATIONS

The measure of success for the RFP process is the number of responses received, the quality of the companies that respond, the quality of the responses, and of course a successful cutover. Much will also depend on the relationship that the user has with the respective vendors. A quick scan of the RFP responses will immediately reveal if the RFP guidelines were followed. If the RFP instructions were followed by the bidder, finding the necessary information to make the required side-by-side comparisons to select the finalists should prove to be relatively straightforward.

CONCLUSION

The RFP documents the organization's new system requirements. It is a statement of purpose and illustrates strategic direction. It clearly spells out and quantifies what is needed. It serves to provide a level playing field in that all vendors receive the same information at the same time. Rules of the RFP provide a communications protocol between user and vendor.

In short, the RFP process makes order out of chaos. The creation of an RFP is one of the most difficult, yet one of the most important, tasks in a telecommunications project. It literally sets the foundation for success or failure in the organization's goal to select and implement a new telecommunications system.

Chapter 25

Tapping the Experience Resources of Consultants

Michael G. Zivich

Throughout the last few decades, the changing face of telecommunications has served to increase the need for telecommunications consultants. The Bell System, with AT&T at its head, had maintained a legal monopoly on telecommunications equipment and services throughout the majority of the 20th century. Since the choices were limited with little variance on the price, the responsibility for telecommunications within a company fell to individuals with other primary duties such as the office or purchasing manager. In the latter part of this century, decisions and regulations made at the federal level introduced competition into both the equipment and service sides of the industry.

Effective at the beginning of 1984, the Justice Department Consent Decree, Modified Final Judgment, broke up the Bell System into seven regional operating telephone companies and AT&T. It heralded the end of monopolistic telecommunications on the national level. Today, the last bastion of the telecommunications monopoly in the U.S., local telephone service, is in the process of being dismantled. Internationally, other countries and regional consortia are following suit. Mergers, both domestically and internationally, are creating an ever-changing telecommunications infrastructure.

These changes in the telecommunications regulatory structure have created a major increase in competition between existing telecommunications vendors and new entrants who appear on the scene with increasing frequency. Over time, a number of these new entrants along with some of the old line vendors have exited the marketplace or have merged with each

0-8493-9990-4/99/$0.00+$.50
© 1999 by CRC Press LLC

other or with foreign companies. This increase in competition has spawned a vast array of new products and services, plus a great increase in the intricacy of the pricing structures and contracts. All this, plus the increasing complexity and turnover in the technologies involved, has been responsible for the expansion of the need for telecommunications expertise within companies and the rapid growth in the numbers and demand for telecommunications consultants over the last two decades.

Telecommunications consultants first provided assistance to Bell System users in determining if they were being properly billed for equipment and services. For this service, the consultant usually received a percentage of the savings that resulted from any discovered discrepancy. This type of consulting service continues today. As competition was introduced into the telecommunications marketplace, along with changing regulations at the federal and state levels and with technology turnover times shortening logarithmically, demand for new consulting services increased.

Consultants then began to provide new services designed to assist companies in sorting out everything necessary to arrive at the best and most cost-efficient telecommunications purchase and management decisions. Consulting organizations range in size from subsidiaries of large accounting firms to businesses with only one or two consultants. These smaller firms make up the vast majority of today's telecommunications consulting industry.

WHY USE CONSULTANTS

Along with the megachanges within the telecommunications industry, this is a time of great change within companies that utilize telecommunications. As competition becomes global and budgets continue to shrink, companies are downsizing, right-sizing, and re-engineering. The ranks of staffing within telecommunications, as well as other departments, are becoming thinner and possibly less experienced, as those individuals with the most experience are being phased out.

This situation is making it much more difficult for organizations to accomplish assigned projects. As a result it is much more relevant to consider the use of consultants with the knowledge and expertise to provide support in areas with which telecommunications staffs are not familiar. Additionally, the telecommunications staff may already be overburdened with operational tasks and projects or there may be a need for expert representation at a remote location when schedules and travel budgets do not permit many extended trips.

All these reasons serve as incentives to bring in consultants to help meet the goals and expectations of companies. Of course, consultants can, on the surface, appear to be expensive, charging not only for their time but also for other expenses such as travel and postage. But how expensive are they? Companies would incur many of the same types of expenses to accomplish a project on their own. Also, the consulting fees are one-time expenses that can be offset by the salary and benefit costs for the time that would have been spent by the telecommunications staff.

These points being considered, the overall impact to the company's bottom line, may not be that great. Additionally, the increased productivity that the use of consultants can provide, along with the potential reduction of the time it takes to complete a project, should also not be overlooked. When budgetary figures for an upcoming project are required, it might be appropriate to include money for consulting services. Be prepared to justify these funds with the costs that would be incurred by the telecommunications staff without the support of consultant services.

CONSULTING FIRMS AND SERVICES

As mentioned earlier, consulting firms vary in size from large accounting and management organizations down to independent businesses consisting of one or two individuals. The larger firms are typically utilized for major projects involving multiple locations domestically and internationally. These types of projects may include acquisitions and their assimilation into a company's telecommunications infrastructure, creation of strategic plans, and studies of emerging technologies.

The smaller consulting firms are often utilized for projects more narrow in scope. The procurement and installation of a private branch exchange (PBX) for a new or existing location, assisting in the selection of a telecommunications common carrier and the negotiations of a new contract, and the assessment of telecommunications organizational structures within a company often are capably handled by smaller consulting firms.

Some of the most common consultant service specialties include telecommunications services and tariffs, equipment procurement and installation, wiring, billing, project management, and integration. A consulting firm may concentrate on one or more of these specialties or tackle any project offered them across the entire spectrum. Additionally, a consultant may concentrate on one or a few individual industries such as the telemarketing, financial, transportation, or health care industries.

The *telecommunications services and tariffs* specialty encompasses all the service offerings and tariffs of interlocal access and transport area (inter-LATA) and interstate common carriers such as AT&T, MCI, and Sprint, plus those of the local telephone companies. These include all the switched services such as long-distance, local calling, toll-free (800, 888, 887, etc.) service; wide area telephone service (WATS), very small aperture terminal (VSAT) and satellite offerings, the dedicated analog and digital circuits used for voice and data services; and dedicated, virtual, and hybrid networks.

Studies of existing or predicted traffic may also be included to determine the proper number and type of circuits or trunks required to maintain an acceptable level of service. There are consultants with experience in this area who specialize in the selection of switched and dedicated network providers. They assist the client company with the negotiation of contracts and as an additional service keep them informed of tariff changes that might affect strategies and costs.

The *equipment specialty* encompasses all items of equipment used for both voice and data communications. This includes PBXs, automatic call distributors (ACDs), smaller business (key) systems, Centrex, voice mail and automated attendant systems, computer–telephony integration (CTI) systems, predictive dialers, channel service units (CSUs) and data service units (DSUs), multiplexers, modems, and local area network (LAN) equipment (including servers, routers, and PCs).

The *wiring specialty* concentrates on building and campus networking infrastructures. This involves the type of medium used, such as shielded and unshielded twisted pair copper wire, coaxial cable, optical cable, or radio frequency (RF) devices such as infrared and microwave systems. Also included in this category are the design of the network, selection and procurement of the medium, installation, and management systems.

The *billing specialty* concerns the audit of existing bills from carriers, local telephone companies, and voice and data equipment vendors. These audits seek to identify mistakes concerning services improperly billed, discontinued services not removed from bills, inappropriate taxes being levied, and in some instances alternate services available at less cost. The usual method of compensation involves a percentage of the retroactive and ongoing savings for a defined period of time.

Many consultants will offer to manage the project that was the catalyst for their retention in the first place. Project management services can be beneficial to clients with little expertise, time, or small staffs. Having already been involved in the design or selection of the systems being installed, the consultant is in an excellent position to carry a project to completion. There are multitudes of details, which, if neglected, can spell disaster for a project. The consultant, representing the client's interests at the job site, can help ensure that the telecommunications vendors and their subcontractors as well as the building trades complete their work on time and to the specifications.

The *integration specialty* is usually considered to be an area that specializes in aspects of some or all the preceding specialties. Integration skills may be necessary because of the project requirement to create a network

428

or system that will handle voice and data across an entire company or division of a company from the desktop. In many cases, services in this area will also involve management tools and issues.

HOW TO FIND A CONSULTANT

To find a number of consultants who might be solicited to submit a bid for your project, references such as the "Business-to-Business" telephone directory can be utilized. Check with local chambers of commerce or growth associations for recommendations. Make inquiries with professional telecommunications organizations such as the International Communications Association (ICA) and professional societies such as the Society of Telecommunications Consultants and the Association of Telecommunications Professionals. Ask for lists and references of consultants who specialize in the areas of interest required by the project.

The telecommunications and network staff has usually met contemporaries through membership in professional associations and by attending educational programs and user groups. These individuals should be consulted for their experiences and references. Inquiries can also be made through vendors with whom the telecommunications staff has an ongoing professional relationship or who offer products that would be utilized in the project.

Many vendors have consultant liaison programs and are capable and willing to supply lists of consultants by specialty, location, or other criteria. If it has not already been initiated, a reference file should be started containing the consultant solicitations received over time. As a result of these solicitations, meetings might be arranged with some firms to have a relationship established prior to the time there is a need. Professional journals should be checked for advertisements. Finally, go into Cyberspace and consult the Internet utilizing search engines such as Alta Vista, Excite, Lycos, Magellan, and Yahoo.

WHAT TO LOOK FOR IN A CONSULTANT

A consultant is a vendor of telecommunications services and, possibly, of products. Therefore, expectations will be similar to those when conducting a search for a telecommunications equipment vendor, a long-distance provider, or local service provider.

- What services does the consultant offer?
- In what areas does the consultant claim to have the most experience?
- How long has the consulting firm been in business?
- How stable does the consulting company appear to be?

429

- If it is expected that the project will take an extended period to complete, does the consultancy have multiple members of like and sufficient expertise?
- What are the rates for the consultant's services?
- Can the consultant supply a list of similar projects completed, plus the names and phone numbers of client references for some of those projects?
- Do the recommendations of products and services by the consultant appear to be biased toward a particular vendor that might indicate a possible conflict of interest because of an affiliation between the two entities?
- Is the consultant a member of any professional organizations?
- Has the consultant published any articles in professional journals or been utilized as an expert by any governmental body?
- Is the consulting firm organized in a manner that will facilitate coordination, communications, and ability to manage multiple tasks and organizations during the project?
- Finally, when meeting with the individual or individuals proposed to be assigned to the project, what are the impressions of their professional demeanor and abilities to communicate?

IS THIS CONSULTANT THE RIGHT ONE?

Once the choices have been narrowed, how are individual consultants checked out? Start by re-examining the literature that has been received from the consultant. Require a presentation. During the discussions, keep in mind that many of the same questions and tactics that are used for interviewing potential new employees are applicable in this situation. Ask direct and detailed questions about anything not understood:

- Does the consultant appear to be current with the required technologies and the telecommunications industry in general?
- What are the opinions of the consultant concerning regulatory issues and future industry trends?
- Have any statements been made by the consultant that are known to be incorrect?
- Does the interviewer believe that he knows more than the consultant does?

While the telecommunications staff concentrates on the business issues, the legal staff should be examining the offered contract, including any and all attachments.

Call the references supplied and ask specific questions concerning the performance of the consultant. Include questions that would help form an opinion of the consultant's level of general and specific technical knowledge, including the products and services required for the project. Find out about the consultant's ability to deliver a quality product on time and within the quoted prices, the perceived level of honesty, the oral and written communications capabilities, and whether the referenced client would hire the consultant again.

HIRING THE CONSULTANT

Once a consultant has been selected, an agreement must be completed. Keep in mind that any agreement is subject to negotiation. A good consultant is interested in pleasing the client. Satisfaction leads to repeat business and referrals. However, also consider that consultants must protect their own interests. Therefore, an agreement should be crafted that will result in a win–win situation for both parties.

There can be an agreement to operate with no formal document. This situation, while the easiest to consummate because it avoids company policies that are invoked with the creation of a contract, is dangerous to both the consultant and the client. When a disagreement occurs, there is no written document that can serve to settle the dispute. The client may not get the project completed. The consultant may not get paid.

A *letter of agreement* or intent is usually a simple document that indicates the scope of the work, the time frames involved, the compensation expected, and the provisions for termination of the agreement. It may avoid some of the more detailed and time-consuming company contract policies and may be appropriate for small projects such as traffic studies. The letter of agreement can also be useful if follow-up work is awarded to a consultant on completion of a project or if there has been a continuing and satisfactory relationship between the parties in the past. If any dispute arises, it will serve as a legal document.

A *formal agreement* or contract, if required, can be lengthy and cumbersome. Company policies concerning competitive bidding, budgets, and legal reviews will all serve to slow down the approval process. Be sure to allow sufficient time for these delays in the planning process since, with more parties involved, greater scrutiny is possible. However, a good contract spells out all the details and protects both the client and the consultant. It should definitely be considered for projects that are large, costly, or lengthy. Also, a formal agreement might be appropriate for a first-time relationship. Be sure that any attachments, addenda, and exhibits that are part of the contract are referenced in the main body of the agreement.

Some of the central elements of a formal agreement follow. The exact order in which they appear and the detail concerning each element may vary depending on the project, the wishes and concerns of both parties, and the policies of the company.

- **The parties** Both the client and the consultant are identified along with their locations and the date of the agreement.
- **Term** The length of time the agreement will be in effect is given. The term may exceed the indicated length of the project. Sometimes master agreements are created that outline the general terms of business conduct between the consultant and the client company with individual projects and their details being added as addenda. This strategy is useful when a continuing relationship is anticipated and can lock in favorable terms. It can also reduce the time it will take for additional project approvals, as only the new addenda are submitted for review because the master agreement has already gone through the approval process.
- **Scope** The project is identified and defined.
- **Provided services** A detailed breakdown of the services should be provided, which is sometimes included in an attachment or exhibit to the agreement.
- **Confidential information** Both parties agree as to what constitutes information that is confidential in nature, how it will be protected, and what the duration is.
- **Associates** The ability of the consultant to employ the services of others outside of his own organization is defined and quantified. (This clause may be more likely to appear in agreements with smaller consulting organizations.)
- **Access** This means the needs of the consultant to obtain access to a client's sites, the method by which such access will be requested, and the restrictions (if any) under which the consultant must operate while at the client's site.
- **Compensation** The type of compensation (hourly, flat fee, etc.), the rate or amount, and the details for additional compensation are stated.
- **Expenses** Reimbursement for expenses that are in addition to the actual work performed such as travel, lodging, and blueprint copies are detailed either as part of the compensation clause or as a separate clause.
- **Invoices** The method of billing, the payment of work performed, and any other expenses are included. The time frames for submission of invoices and the payment are also covered in this clause. Again, this clause may be separate or included in the compensation clause.
- **Default** This includes circumstances that, if occurring, would constitute default of the contract by either party. Methods of notification of the default, time for correction or remedy allowed, and penalties to be imposed are covered in this section.
- **Termination** The details concerning the ability of and circumstances by which either party can terminate the agreement are stated.
- **Governing law** This identifies the state under which whose laws govern the content and performance of this agreement.

432

- **Acceptance** The signatures of the individuals authorized to represent both parties and the dates signed appear near or at the end of the document. It is wise to execute at least two copies of the agreement with original signatures and retain one for the project file.

An agreement can specify a flat fee for the work performed or establish an hourly rate. When the hourly rate format is selected, it may be appropriate to provide limits by specifying the number of hours that the project will take or by establishing a "not to exceed" price. Both formats have some limitations and drawbacks.

A consultant who agrees to a flat fee or a not-to-exceed price may charge the client the maximum amount regardless of how much effort that was required. The same problem exists with an hourly rate because the consultant can claim hours that were not actually expended. Also, larger consulting firms will usually assign portions of the project to junior associates and administrative assistants. While negotiating the agreement, the client should inquire as to the involvement of these types of individuals and opt for a reduced hourly rate for their services.

Conversely, some projects are extremely difficult to quantify in terms of the time necessary to complete them. Also, events unforeseen by either party may occur that will throw the estimates off and increase the amount of time required to complete the project. Because of this, a consultant may tend to overestimate the time necessary to complete a project or require the inclusion of language providing for the ability to exceed the estimate. The client may wish to refuse payment if the work accomplished is not satisfactory. However, the consultant may not agree with this stipulation because it is very subjective and could be abused by the client.

MANAGING THE PROJECT

For the duration of the project, and especially if it is a long and complicated one, it is appropriate for the client to initiate the following procedures by which the consultant's progress can be gauged:

- **Milestones**, determined by time and accomplishment, can be set up in the agreement.
- **Scheduled meetings** with the consultant, which may include members of the clients' telecommunications staff, vendors, and contractors, can be established.
- **Impromptu meetings** should be called if events dictate.

The consultant can be required to submit regular reports, and the agreement can be used to specify their content and frequency. If appropriate, the agreement can require the consultant to be present at the project site either for specific events or on a regular basis. The decision-making ability and general authority granted the consultant should be determined in advance and, if appropriate, be incorporated into the agreement. The consultant should be responsible to a single individual representing the client, typically the network manager or the project manager. This manager is responsible for establishing the project guidelines, acting as liaison between the consultant and the client company, and fulfilling the consultant's requests for information and support throughout the life of the project.

CONCLUSION

In the final analysis, consideration of the information contained in this chapter, coupled with the quoted costs and delivery guarantees, should assist in making an informed decision as to the best consultant for the particular job. When negotiating the terms of an agreement, understanding that just as there are good and bad consultants, there are good and bad clients, will aid in the appreciation of the requests from consultants for some security and guarantees of payment.

Consultants are powerful tools that can be utilized by companies to accomplish their goals. They bring technical knowledge, experience, and understanding to the project that may be missing or in short supply at the client company. In fact, consultants are used quite frequently by some companies to accomplish various tasks and jobs. The network manager can, in the proper circumstances, utilize the consultant's insights and recommendations to support a position. Amazingly, company management may hold a consultant's opinion and recommendation in higher esteem than when the same conclusions are espoused by a member of the company's networking staff.

Properly used, the services offered by consultants can be of great benefit to a company in general and to telecommunications and network managers in particular.

Chapter 26
Budgeting in a Telecommunications Environment

Ron Kovac

INTRODUCTION

Budgeting is a lot like breathing. We cannot survive without either, and they both are something we tend to overlook. Certainly both do not create a stimulating conversation or have the "sex appeal" of other telecommunications functions, but both are essential functions of the network manager. Budgeting is an essential tool, a tool that allows a department or organization to predict and plan, two critical elements of any entity. Budgeting is a tool at a manager's disposal, not something that tells us what to do, but something that we use to get a job done.

In this chapter we will address the art and science of budgeting in the telecommunications arena. This will be done by addressing some of the common misperceptions and questions that managers have concerning budgeting, such as: What is a budget and why do I have to do one? What are all these budgeting sheets and expense reports given to me? Can budgeting be made any easier? Are there different, better ways to do budgeting? Why does it take so much time to do budgeting? How come I never get the budget I want? How can I improve my chances of getting my budget approved? These will be explored.

WHY DO A BUDGET?

At one point budgets were strictly financial documents stating *what is*. Budgets have evolved to become a policy and financial plan. Budgets are a financial expression of a department's planning and direction and essentially the goals of the department manager. Are budgets really necessary? The answer is, of course, a resounding yes. For any entity, whether a household or a business, if there are more spending demands than there are funding sources, budgeting is a required tool.

0-8493-9990-4/99/$0.00+$.50
© 1999 by CRC Press LLC

Many misconceptions surround budgeting. Each of these misconceptions can cause the telecommunications manager to lose focus, and therefore the budget tug-of-war results. This further leads to the reinforcement of the misconceptions and a vicious downward cycle. Let us look at some of these misconceptions:

1. **My department is critical and must be funded.** Never has the chasm between senior management and technology been greater. Our field is so complex that many practicing professionals have difficulties understanding the regulatory and technical environment, let alone the acronyms. Senior management usually does not have a clue about what telecommunications does for the organization and therefore cannot make appropriate budget decisions. Unless provided the business purpose and business justification of telecommunications, senior management will reduce the debate to one of two questions: (1) What does it cost? or (2) How much will we save? Each of these is inappropriate in making the best telecommunications decisions, especially strategic ones. The key concept must be business and not the technical concepts with which we are familiar.

2. **It is not my job.** We are all comfortable in the technical dimensions of our field, but unfortunately our budget training is usually minimal or nonexistent. Budgeting may not be the primary role of a network manager; yet, it is an inescapable part of the job. Understanding the basic process of budgeting can assist tremendously in obtaining the budget we desire.

3. **Budgeting and accounting are just numbers on paper.** Budgeting and accounting are different. While accounting is for external reporting and is retrospective in nature, budgeting is for internal management of the organization and is proactive. Although both accounting and budgeting deal with numbers, they are not number games. Budgeting involves every part of an organization and is the lifeblood on a department.

4. **Senior management does not understand.** If they do not, it is our fault for not creating an environment for them to understand. Telecommunications costs are usually significant, and senior management needs to understand what these expenses provide for the organization in business concepts but not technical concepts. The "understanding" gap can be closed, but it takes an understanding and proactive network manager.

These misconceptions must first be recognized and then attenuated for telecommunications to be funded properly. This is the job of the network manager. One must always keep in mind that competition for funds can be fierce, and our field—being highly complex—needs to be understood. Budgeting is a process that can be won, and won by the department manager.

Exhibit 1.   Self Test: Are You and Your Organization Doing the Right Thing?

Your Organization	Yes	No	Sometimes
1. Does your organization possess a written budget selection process?			
2. Is the process widely known?			
3. Is the process followed?			
4. Are there clearly defined requirements that budgets must meet?			
5. Are budget justifications required to demonstrate linkage with business objectives?			
6. Are budgets ranked based on benefit, cost, or risk criteria?			
7. Does senior management base its decisions on these rankings?			
8. Are approved projects scheduled for regular review by senior management?			
9. Are review meetings automatically scheduled with senior management when a key deliverable is not met?			
10. Is all the preceding information disseminated and freely available?			

Your Budget Process	Yes	No	Sometimes
1. Do you have a defined and repeatable process for monitoring and reviewing your budgets?			
2. Is data being used to track unit and project performance against estimates that were used to justify the budget?			
3. Does the process define who is accountable for acting on review decisions?			
4. Do reports contain review results issued to key personnel?			
5. Does the process define how open action items are to be addressed?			
6. Are budget items tied to key business objectives?			
7. Are deficiencies submitted to senior management for a decision about what to do with the issue?			
8. Is this information being fed back to decision makers to help make future decisions?			
9. Does the organization have a defined, documented process for conducting postimplementation review of projects?			
10. Have project benefits been quantified?			
11. Have project benefits been reported to senior management?			
12. Is the budget shared with staff in the department?			
13. Is there accountability for all items in the budget?			

Exhibit 1 depicts two self-assessment tests that may help in establishing the correct course of action.

WHAT IS THE PURPOSE OF BUDGETS?

Budgets have three essential purposes—planning, evaluation, and control. Budgets are used to plan a department's action, for example: Can I hire a new staff member? How many nodes must be bought? What type of management system can I buy? Budgets put your plan onto paper and allow others to rally behind your plan (both staff and management). The planning function of budgets also stops the end-of-the-year panic that results from not budgeting. In organizations with no budget plan, they often realize in their last quarter that expenses have exceeded revenue and harsh cost-cutting measures are usually put in place (across the board cuts, staff reductions). Budgeting, through planning, inhibits this harsh knee-jerk reaction and promotes an orderly year.

Budgets also form a basis for evaluation. Since you put your plan on paper with the justification for the expenses, now you will be held accountable for these outcomes. This is positive because it defines parameters for your department and therefore limits erroneous blame and direction.

Budgets also control. Budgets define and therefore control actions. A voice communications manager may be allotted a pool of money for staffing, and he cannot hire beyond that limit. Flexibility is allotted in how the money is spent, but a cap is in place. This allows individual department decision making within the parameters defined by the budget. On another positive note, this can also limit outside parties from distracting you from your budgeted and stated goals.

ARE THERE DIFFERENT WAYS TO DO BUDGETING?

There are as many variations of budgets as there are types of automobiles. Although true in principle, the choices you will likely have will be few because the organization you work for, its philosophy, and its senior management will usually select the budget type it is comfortable with. This not withstanding, a review of the various budget types and their attributes and detriments can prove beneficial because you can influence and possibly change over time the budget type that you will have to execute.

There are essentially four basic types of budgets. Although each begins with the same raw material, an estimation of costs, the purposes diverge after that. These budget types and a brief discussion of each follow:

- **Line-item budgeting** With a line-item budget, each individual expense (such as software costs) is documented and brought forward for approval as part of a total package. Line-item budgets show their worth over time in that each expense category can be tracked and accurate projection of the future can be made from past data. The detailing of each line item allows budget practitioners to examine incremental changes over time and to identify appropriation trends. For example, if telecommunications line costs for the 1996 year were $250,000 and for 1997 were $275,000, a 10% increase can clearly be shown. Was this increase due to increased number of lines or rate increases? This needs to be highlighted in the justification. Surely, the budget reviewers will question the 10% increase given that the rate of inflation is not that great, and the common news media notes that telecommunications costs are decreasing due to competition.

- **Program budgeting** Unlike line-item budgets, program budgets bring forth expenses related around individual programs. For example, the budget for Internet access could be a single program. Within that program budget would be line costs, Internet service provider (ISP) costs, personnel costs, etc. The advantage of this type of budgeting is that it forces an examination of program goals and objectives, and in some cases clarifies program performance and outcome. The downside is that this examination could bring to the forefront programs that are best left in the background. Outsourcing decisions may also be an outcome from this. Seeing one figure for a single program may lead to looking for a cheaper way to accomplish the objective (outsourcing).

- **Zero-based budgeting** Unlike the previous two budget types, zero-based budgeting does not start with item expenses but with a clean slate. Zero-based budgeting questions the very essence of a department or program to determine its worth and value to the organization. With this clean slate, the goals, objectives, and deliverables of the department are used as the foundation to determine costs. The upside to this type of budgeting is the fresh look at old methods used to accomplish a goal. For example, you may have always used a maintenance contract for the private branch exchange (PBX), but after wiping the slate clean and reviewing the various options you may determine that, due to technological changes, securing a new PBX with a time and material contract would be cheaper and more efficient to meet your voice objective. The downside of this type of budget is that it requires extensive amounts of upfront work and time for the budget preparer.

- **Performance-based budgeting** The newest of the budget types is performance-based budgeting. With this type of budgeting, performance objectives are used to make budget-related decisions. For example, if in last year's budget you noted an expense figure to accomplish the provisioning of increased bandwidth to all parties in the organization and you did not complete the task, future funding will most likely be cancelled.

Although not a type of budget, a budget model that is coming to the forefront today is partner-based budgeting. This budgeting model allows business units to form partnerships and share common expenses (such as telecommunications expenses). For example, in a local area network (LAN) environment, the telecommunications department would control common expenses for the LAN (wiring, switches, routers, and support personnel), and the end users would control expenses for the departmental personal computers (PCs) and printers. The budget would be submitted as one (named, for example, LAN budget) and would be controlled by both the telecommunications department and the end-user department. Typically a separate committee, made up of representatives of all affected departments, would have joint budget making and monitoring authority over this budget. This model is gaining favor because it is ending the tug-of-war between departments for tight budget resources.

WHAT NEEDS TO GO INTO A BUDGET?

Now that the purpose and types of budget are known, the next logical question is: What goes into a budget? Telecommunications and networking budget items are of two general categories: *fixed cost* items and *variable cost* items.

Fixed cost items are not affected by usage or department activity and are often contractually fixed. Figures for locked-in cost items come from negotiated contracts and are highly predictable. For example, if management and staff have negotiated a 6% raise, you would take current staff salary figures and raise them 6% to determine the cost for next year. Multiyear contracts add to this predictability.

Fixed cost line items include

- **Salaries and benefits for the telecommunications staff** These are to include accrued vacation and sick time, which must be accounted for.
- **Floor space and related utilities** These usually transfer to another arm of the organization and usually charge by square footage or number of personnel.
- **Maintenance contract costs** Assuming you have selected maintenance contracts on your equipment, each piece of equipment in the department needs to be listed with its associated expense. This may include the PBX, routers, typewriters, and all other hardware or software in the department.
- **Line fixed costs** These are charges from vendors for the various lines (voice, data, and video) that occur within the department.
- **Other contractual costs** There may be costs for disaster recovery contract or contracts, legal retainers, etc.

Variable cost items are more difficult to work with because of their sensitivity to the amount of activity and use. For example, you will need to include a cost for long-distance service (certainly affected by use) as a budget line item. The cost for long-distance service will vary dependent on your marketing efforts, clients, and number of company employees. An estimate can be determined based on a review of past similar efforts. For example, if the firm is contemplating adding four more marketing personnel and the cost per marketing personnel for long-distance service is historically $500, you will need to budget $2000 more to this item next year.

Additionally, variable cost line items are usually subject to price changes. These should be factored into the item amount. Variable cost line items could include

- Voice expenses
  - Long-distance service
  - 800 Number use
  - Moves, adds, and changes
- Data expenses
  - ISDN line use
  - Frame relay use
  - Moves, adds, and changes
- Mailing and shipping charges
- Repairs not covered by maintenance contracts
- Consulting expenses
- Installation charges

To make budgeting easier and more accurate, it is better to have fixed expenses rather than variable expenses. Unfortunately, in today's fast-paced environment, this is not common. Additionally, information systems and telecommunications systems should respond to corporate needs and not dictate them. Accordingly, the science and methodology of budgeting often becomes an art. Some strategies to use include

- If the price increase is unknown (contract still in negotiation or a variable regulatory environment), budget a 10% increase in that line item.
- Keep your ears to the ground for all organizational activities. If you hear of a corporate merger in the wings, you may want to budget anticipated expenses for this. Your success in this arena will rely on your ability to know what the organization is thinking (at *all* levels).
- It is wiser to have money left over at the end than to have to go looking for more funds midyear. Poor budgeting has wrecked many a career.
- Plan for the unexpected. Even with the science of the budget template, and the maticulous planning and forecasting by management, expenses will come up during the fiscal year that are unpredictable (acts of God, acts of the board of directors). Budgeting for these unexpected expenses in a contingency or rainy day fund is prudent because it stops return trips to the budget trough. Some organizations formally allow for this as a line-item budget expense; others see this as a poor budget practice. If you happen to work for the latter type of company, it is suggested that some contingency money be built into the budget in obscure ways.

The preceding points are targeted at the development of a department budget, but oftentimes a network manager will be required to develop a project budget. A project budget is a microversion of a department budget. Project budgets are handled quickly to respond to a corporation need and will usually be put under a *project heading*. For example, the organization may desire to provide remote access to all its employees to improve its competitive edge. The network manager will be asked to draw up a projected budget for this. Exhibit 2 is a draft project budget for this example.

THE INFAMOUS BUDGET CYCLE

It is very difficult to be specific in detailing dates and steps in the budgeting process because this is usually dictated by specific organizational guidelines. Although each organization has varying steps and timelines in the budgeting cycle, typically the phases of budget are similar across organizations. These phases will be discussed later, but it is strongly recommended that those who are responsible for budgeting get the details and specific dates that the organization promulgates and that these are incorporated into the budgeting responsibility of the position.

Phases of the budget cycle

Phases of the budget cycle include

- Strategic planning meetings (determine goals and directions)
- Determination of preliminary budget (estimate of what it will cost to accomplish goals)
- Running the preliminary budget up the flagpole (garner support)
- Adjustment phase (interim correction)
- Creation of the final budget (putting the pieces together)
- Selling the budget
- Monitoring the budget

Strategic Direction Setting

As noted earlier, budgeting is a tool to accomplish departmental tasks. One must first start with defining the departmental tasks and their strategic directions. Depending on management style of the organization and the manager, this can be a single-person task or a divisional task. It is recommended that involvement be sought from each unit in the division because this will aid selling the budget in later steps, and it will also aid in creating a unified staff.

In the divisional planning model, each unit within the division would be represented at planning meetings. The planning meetings would coalesce the departmental thoughts for the upcoming year. For example, the following could be reviewed:

Exhibit 2. Sample Draft Project Budget

Widgets Inc.
Project budget request and justification
Fiscal year 1999

Title: Remote access for staff
Number: 3439-343
Description: A project aimed at providing remote access for all management and
 professional staff for Widgets Inc. (75 people).
Priority: High
Start date: January 1, 1999
Responsible manager: John Q. Doe (Jdoe@Widgets.com)
End date: December 1, 1999

Risk assessment (possible negatives from doing the project)
1. Possible security breaches
2. All staff desiring access
3. Runaway costs

Threat assessment (possible negatives from not doing the project)
1. Loss of competitive edge due to lack of communication with staff
2. Loss of contact with staff as they travel
3. Loss of international contracts

Action plan and milestones

Milestone	Start	End	Responsibility
Conduct RFP	2/1	3/1	RK
Install equipment	3/1	4/1	JK
Test security	4/1	4/15	PAK
Turn on system	4/15	12/1	KAK
Monitor and adjust	4/15	12/1	KAK

Budget estimate
Personnel	
Employees (2.0)	$ 39,000
Contract (1.0)	$ 45,000
Equipment	
Hardware	$ 430,000
Software	$ 200,000
Contractual services	$ 175,000
Miscellaneous	$ 57,000
Indirect costs	
Administrative	$ 45,000
Infrastructure	$ 30,000
Communication	$ 34,000
Miscellaneous	$ 23,000
Total project cost for fiscal year 1999	$ 1,250,000

- What customer needs are being considered?
- What new technology is available to make our operation more efficient?
- What special projects will carry over the year?
- What impact will service-level agreements have on operation?

The final outcome of this phase is a detailed strategic plan with objectives, timelines, necessary software, hardware, and personnel to accomplish the tasks. Minimum effort should be put in developing costs for each of these items; instead the efforts should be put on strategic planning of divisional goals. Some prioritizing and coalescing should take place, but a solidified, coherent, and unified strategic plan is the intended outcome of this stage.

Creation of Preliminary Budget

Based on the results of the previous step, and mixed with details of past budget and projected equipment needs, a preliminary budget needs to be created. This preliminary budget should be detailed by line items mentioned previously. This step involves putting a price tag on each of the necessary elements. This step is detailed and involves a fair amount of research and "guesstimation." For example, a new management system might be proposed in the strategic plan to meet the service-level agreements being put forward by the company, and estimated costs would need to be derived for hardware, software, increased personnel, and maintenance.

Run the Plan "Up the Flagpole"

In this stage the preliminary budget, in strategic objective form and dollar amount, should be presented to upper management. Upper management may not be aware of what your division is contemplating and can give early indications if the direction and costs are appropriate. This stage is trying to prevent the embarrassment of a budget being discredited by a single statement such as: "We are looking at zero percent budget growth," or "Did you see the merger memo?" This stage also solicits preliminary support from upper management to pave the way for final budget approval.

Adjustment Phase

Based on the feedback from the previous stage, some (possibly a lot) adjustment may be necessary. In the previous stage, the budget was run up the flagpole, and the number of people who salute it affects on how much you modify it. This is a one- to two-person job of prioritizing, shifting, and assessing support level for each strategic initiative of the division.

Creation of the Final Budget

The final plan, a result of the previous adjustment phase has two essential parts—the justification and the price tag. The justification section (strategic initiatives, in business terms) and deliverable items must match up with business objectives to be sold. If the decision makers are to be convinced and see the necessity of your objectives, they must see the business outcomes. Once this occurs, the selling of the price tag will come easier. The price tag section is merely the capital needed to accomplish the goals. The price tag will be arranged in the budget type appropriate to the organization (line-item, zero-based, etc.)

Selling of the Plan

Because of the importance of this phase, the next section provides the details of selling the budget plan.

Maintenance of the Budget

When the budget is approved, it is not the end. Now the budget must be monitored and controlled throughout the course of the budget (usually a year). This involves a fair amount of monitoring and attention.

Most beginning managers are surprised about the amount of time and attention the budget process takes. Typically the process can last a good part of the year, with budget maintenance lasting throughout the year.

SELLING YOUR BUDGET

A discussion of budget would not be complete without a discussion of selling the budget. Many a well-formed budget has failed due to poor presentation. Not everybody will inherently understand the importance of the telecommunications budget, and it is the manager's job to justify and sell the budget to both upper management and the staff. Both parties must support the budget for it to be approved and succeed.

In selling a budget, or for that matter any idea, these three key questions need to be kept in mind:

- What are the basic points of my message (budget)?
- What will be the substance of the message (budget)?
- What organizational style should I use?

In attacking these questions, some basic steps must first be taken.

Understand the Audience

Enough cannot be said here. Too often presentations fail because there is a lack of communication between the parties. If you are presenting to upper management do *not* expect it to understand technical terms or concepts. It is being paid to look at the big picture and needs *you* to interpret the technical terms and directions into items that it can understand.

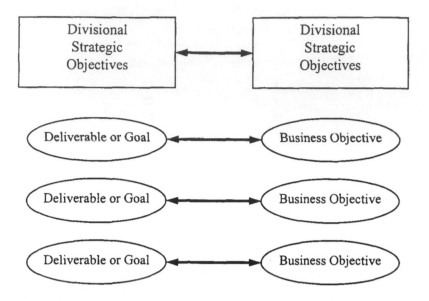

Exhibit 3.   Alignment of Divisional Objectives with Business Objectives

Prepare an Outline Organized Around the Business Objectives. The first step would be to include *only* what is necessary for understanding and rely on upper management's questions to fill in any gaps. For example, you do not need to go through each maintenance contact (and its price) to get through the points of rising amounts of equipment and the need to maintain this equipment.

Points to include are the alignment of the budget with the business objective, the major categories of the budget, the approach to your budgeting, the key deliverables and schedules that the budget will allow, and the mechanisms in which you will monitor the success of the deliverables (Exhibit 3).

Flush Out each Key Point with only the Necessary Detail. For each major category of budget, what amount is being requested and why? Typically items are divided between personnel costs and equipment. There are differing sensitivities to each of these, and corporations appear more willing to spend on one-time hardware than to make a long-term commitment to staffing needs.

Put Together the Data. Usually two things will have to be assembled, a budget justification with written documents and usually a presentation. Use the budget detail to prepare a short, eye-appealing presentation that will focus on the business essence and not the details. The justification, short and to the point, should:

- Be two to three pages in length (depending on organizational conditions)
- Use bullet points to convey the essence
- Use many individual section headings
- Use language that is clear and to the point (less is more). For example,
  — Do not use: *The Project is critical.*
  Use: **This project will allow the...**
  — Do not use: *We will allow Internet access.*
  Use: **Internet access for 200 people will be completed.**
  — Do not use: *Sometime during the third quarter.*
  Use: *The project will end in September of 1999.*

DOES MY STAFF NEED TO KNOW ABOUT THE BUDGET?

Not only does your budget put parameters and directions to your department, but it also does so to each staff member. Staff, to be fully engaged, should have input to the budget and, at a minimum, should be aware of the budgeting process and its outcome. This will alleviate many questions and concerns and, therefore, focus staff efforts on completing this year's tasks and garnering support for next year's budget. Selling the budget to the staff has the same steps as the previous section but special attention needs to be paid to the "know your audience" section. You can expect staff members to understand the technical terms and directions, but you cannot expect them to see "organizationally."

CONTEMPORARY ISSUES THAT CAN AFFECT YOUR BUDGET

There are certain contemporary issues that may need to be included in your budget thinking. These issues affect, or can affect, the department's actions and therefore its budget. Briefly the issues are discussed next.

Year 2000

More often called the Year 2000 issue, this has most companies scurrying to verify that the information infrastructure of the company will not come to a screeching halt when the year 2000 is reached. According to the Meta Group, 75% of its customers expect the Year 2000 issue to affect what and how they do things. In affecting the information services field intensely, the year 2000 will also affect the telecommunications field. PBXs, routers, and management systems all are subject to the Year 2000 issue; and contact with the vendor needs to be made to verify that they are year 2000 compliant. Especially vulnerable are scripts and software programs written by internal staff. All equipment and software that maintains a date field is subject to Year 2000 dangers. Expenses should be budgeted for consultants to explore your vulnerability, for programmers to fix the problems, for new hardware or software upgrades to become year 2000 compliant, and even for contingency expenses to be allocated if disaster strikes in the year 2000.

Security

In these days of Internet and global access, network and host security has become a prime concern to information and telecommunications professionals. Use of a firewall or a virtual private network (VPN) are two popular strategies to gain this security without unduly restricting work flow and access. Both of these strategies require budgeted expenses for equipment, software, personnel, and maintenance.

Purchase or Lease

With rapidly changing technology and low interest rates, many companies are looking to lease rather than to purchase equipment (and even services). Although either way is usually a fixed expense, the amortization and capitalization of the strategy is different and takes some long-range budget thinking to reach any educated conclusion.

According to the equipment leasing association, 85% of all U.S. businesses lease or finance some or all their equipment. The advantage of leasing is that you preserve capital for day-to-day expenses and for other company needs. Additionally, lease payments are flexible in that they can be structured to match the unique needs of your business, and you get the equipment you need when you need it. You lease first and after two years you can either purchase your leased equipment or buy the newest and greatest piece. Of course, there are disadvantages. You do not own the equipment, the leasing company does, and you need to maintain it carefully. Additionally, cost of ownership maybe higher with leasing.

The Regulatory Environment

Due to the seed of telecommunications deregulation in the 1980s and the resultant changes of today, the regulatory environment is causing changes in the telecommunications industry that match in importance the introduction of new technologies (see Section 6). From a budgeting perspective, these changes are usually good. For example, frame relay has offered increased flexibility for data communication at a decreased cost. The move of Regional Bell Operating Companies (RBOCs) to open up local access to get into the long-distance market has usually offered new options, players, and reduced costs for local access. An effective network manager needs to watch the tide of the regulatory environment and anticipate budget effects on the department. Luckily, from a budget perspective these are usually for the better.

MAKING BUDGETING EASIER: USING TECHNOLOGY AS A TOOL

In today's day and age, it is almost impossible to meet budgeting needs without the use of technological tools. Technology allows for:

- The quick adaptation of budget figures to compensate for fast changing needs.
- The ability to create effective presentation, in various forms, for key decision makers.
- The ability to benchmark and track budget figures over time.
- Ease in monitoring the budget (luckily, the drudgery of budgeting being taken away by the selfless obedience and accuracy of computers).

Ultimately, departmental budget data will have to interface with the corporate accounting system. These systems, sometimes called enterprise resource planning (ERP) systems are large in scope and include accounts payable, payroll, accounts receivable, inventory and maintenance, general ledger, and usually a module in budgeting. Although these systems are the corporate standards and the way to integrate the various divisions together, they usually do not allow for flexibility in budgeting and playing "what-if scenarios." There are three possible approaches to this dilemma:

1. Use the ERP system budgeting tools and live with their idiosyncratic behaviors and limitations. You can compensate, or work around them, by doing a lot of "paper and pencil" outside work.
2. Develop your own budget tools. By using an off-the-shelf spreadsheet package, such as Excel or Lotus 1-2-3, develop the framework for your budget. These packages have good graphic packages incorporated so that the graphs and charts you will need for presentations will be relatively easy to create. This tack allows you the greatest flexibility but demands a fairly good working knowledge of spreadsheets, charting, and graphing. The danger here is integration. To make integration smooth, and therefore less time consuming, make sure the spreadsheet package integrates with the ERP system. The integration must occur on the downloading end (ability to pull the budget account numbers and codes from the ERPS) and the uploading end (ability to put your budget figures and account codes, once finalized, into the ERPS). Exhibit 4 shows an example of a homegrown spreadsheet budget.
3. Select an off-the-shelf budgeting package. Many packages exist for budget creation and maintenance, and they advertise their ability to integrate with *any* other package (such as an ERP system). Many of these packages are full-feature accounting software (most of the elements of an ERP system) and can be used by your department as a stand-alone package. Other packages are targeted at budgeting only and were created to allow the flexibility of a spreadsheet pack-

Exhibit 4. Homegrown Spreadsheet Budget

Administrative computer services—A610-7710		
1996–1997 Appropriations	Preliminary Appropriations (29.67 FTE)	1997–1998 Estimates (27.83 FTE)
Personal services		
Instructional	$ 205,111	$ 196,055
Noninstructional	$ 687,365	$ 606,965
Equipment	$ 6,500	$ 6,500
Supplies and materials	$ 111,819	$ 111,819
Contractual	$ 620,630	$ 620,630
Telephone telecommunications	$ 90,636	$ 90,636
Services from districts	$ 148,859	$ 150,384
Fringe	$ 270,593	$ 221,241
Total direct expense	$ 2,141,513	$ 2,234,987
Transfer charges		
Transfer to other funds	$ 7,513	$ 8,268
Operation and maintenance	$ 42,726	$ 41,504
Transportation	$ 38,362	$ 33,994
Central services	$ 31,697	$ 27,139
RIC support service	$ 237,513	$ 216,673
Total program expenses	$ 2,499,324	$ 2,543,945
Less transfer credits from other service programs	$ 139,485	$ 144,321
Net expenses	$ 2,359,839	$ 2,453,240
Revenue		
Charges to components	$ 1,280,991	$ 1,204,231
Charges to other BOCES	$ 984,385	$ 827,948
Other revenues	$ 68,666	$ 26,186
Total revenue	$ 2,334,042	$ 2,453,240

age but not demand the intimate working knowledge of them. These products often have features that support sophisticated decision reporting, data mining, and easy reporting to end users. The list in Exhibit 5 includes some of the more popular packages.

Whatever approach is taken, enssure that the technology package integrates both departmental and corporate wide. For example, for an international firm, currency differences and exchange rates must be taken into consideration. Additionally, language barriers may also have to be handled.

Exhibit 5. Budgeting Software Tools

Product	Description	Platform	Number	Vendor
One-Write Plus	Full-featured accounting package	Windows	1-800-388-4344	NEBS
Business Maestro	Data collection, analysis and budgeting	Windows	1-800-366-5111	Planet Corp.
SAS Solution	Financial budgeting and planning	Windows	1-919-677-8000	SAS Institute
Pillar	Budget design and planning	Windows, Macintosh	1-800-286-8000	Hyperion Corp.

CONCLUSION

Although budgeting does not have the appeal of other facets of the telecommunications and networking profession, it is the lifeblood of the operation. The knowledge of basic budget types and tactics can aid a manager immensely in the creation of a winning budget. Additionally, once a manager realizes that he has to compete for and sell the budget, a competitive revelation takes hold.

In these fast changing and fierce budget times, no where is it more important to succeed them in budgeting and therefore in helping the organization succeed in its strategic plans.

Chapter 27
Managing Data on the Network: Data Warehousing

Richard A. Bellaver

INTRODUCTION

Chapter 4 deals with the evolution of application processing on the network. This chapter will deal with the storage, identification, and quality of data *in* the network. New opportunities to develop corporate databases and share data across companies are technologically feasible, and many companies are starting to evolve data processing systems to take advantage of networking and other new technologies under the name of data warehousing.

These phenomena and the obsession with "quality" in American industry are having profound effects on company data processing (DP) planning. The practicality of distributed DP and the desire to take advantage of the latest technology have led many companies to concentrate on cleaning up the databases and restructuring the processing. This twofold approach provides a challenge to both corporate DP and business planning communities. The difficulty for planners lies in an apparent inconsistency in the "quality" definition in DP. Are the advertising-type descriptions of processing (e.g., new, improved, faster) in conflict with the historical descriptions of data (e.g., identifiable, complete, accurate)?

In those companies undergoing mergers or acquisitions, bringing together diverse DP systems, organizations, and methodologies provides an even more challenging opportunity. Even some of the large, more stable DP organizations have experienced the accordion effect of centralization vs. decentralization leading to a similar "clean it up and make it better situation." A look at an evolution of the strategies concerning system architecture can be an aid to meeting such a challenge. By definition, a computer system architecture is the logical structure and relationship of the data and application functions used to satisfy a company's business requirements. This chapter describes a practical architectural evolution that can lead to

0-8493-9990-4/99/$0.00+$.50
© 1999 by CRC Press LLC

quality-based DP and that includes both definitions while emphasizing the data aspects of quality. It will also go into the nontechnical problems in sharing data that may be more severe than the technical ones.

Data can be a most valuable asset to a business, and technology can allow access to that data faster than ever; however, there must be a logical approach to the establishment of data quality procedures before the benefits of warehousing can be attained. At a minimum, interdepartmental battles about ownership of data must be fought, new chargeback algorithms must be accepted, and managers will probably have to learn at least new coding structures if not new languages. An examination of the present systems of many companies will establish a base for comparison.

CURRENT ARCHITECTURE

Even with the advent of client/server and unbridled growth in the use of personal computers (PCs), the current architecture of many large computer systems can generally be defined as mainframe oriented, stand alone, and data redundant. This situation did not happen by accident. The early approach to DP for most large companies was to search for projects based on economy of scale. For example, companies looked for large, team-sized applications. Usually, for order clerks or bill investigators, manual training methods and procedures had been standardized to achieve the last measure of efficiency. Computer mechanization followed the model of these standard operating procedures.

Very large, procedurally (organizationally) oriented systems were built based on the need to increase operational productivity. Generally, the systems used for ordering, dispatching, billing, inventory control, financial control, and many other business functions have been developed using the most efficient technology for both hardware and software. That technology in the past was basically large mainframes.

In many cases, a total systems approach to mechanization was implemented with that organizational orientation. All the data needed to solve a business problem was isolated. The workgroups that needed access to the mechanized process were identified, and the rules of the data, the processing, and the communications to solve the specific problem were defined and implemented into one system.

As depicted in Exhibit 1, if data A were necessary to support process 1, they were acquired, edited, and stored. If the same data were needed for process 2, they were also acquired, edited, and stored. At best, the data was passed off-line from 1 to N, then still edited according to process N rules, and stored again (usually in a new format). As a result of the magnitude of the process, the large volume of data, or the limitation of hardware and software capabilities, all aspects of each system were tightly

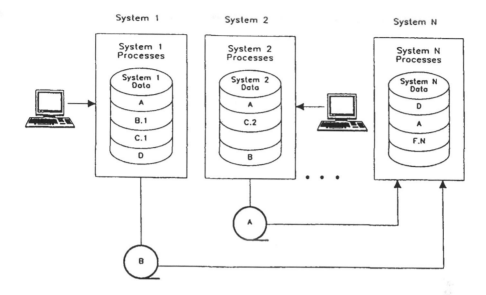

Exhibit 1. Current Architecture

integrated to ensure efficiency of processing time and data storage charges. The cost justification of the project was usually based on increasing human productivity. User departments that paid for the development and the use of the systems reduced cost by reducing human resources. User departments had a very proprietary interest in both the data and the supporting processing system.

The state of the art, especially the limitations of database management systems and communications software, also left its mark on the current architecture. In many cases, systems developed were efficient, monolithic, inflexible, end-to-end special-purpose procedure "speeder-uppers" owned by various departments. The computer implementations matched the work, the work matched the organizations, and a degree of stasis was obtained. However, over time, most organizations are subject to significant change.

To contain costs as a corporation moves forward (especially toward centralization or integration), there is a need to increase partnering of organizations while sharing resources and data are required. Technology cost structure changes and user needs become more sophisticated. Unfortunately to meet this change, most current architectures are characterized by:

- Many large stand-alone systems
- Individual communications networks

- Data configured differently for each process
- Redundant functionality and data
- Inability of organizations and systems to access other organizations' systems and data
- A nonquality situation

THE OPPORTUNITIES AND THE CHALLENGES

The current architecture picture looks pretty bleak. Must everything be thrown out and started over to clean up and restructure? Economics answers that question. Not many companies have the resources to rearchitect their systems from scratch. Cost-effective ways must be found to establish targets for architectural migration. System architecture strategies must provide a transition from the current status to a more flexible architecture that supports organizations and systems working together. These strategies must also maximize the advantage of:

- Increasing capabilities of large and small processors
- Networking capabilities
- Less complicated programming techniques
- Concentration on quality data

The latter point should be emphasized for a simple reason. Data is more permanent than processing. Data is also what ties the corporation together. Some organizations would not talk to each other at all if they did not have to exchange data. Business functionality, although basic, can usually be handled in a variety of ways, but the data needed is usually stable. (After all, humans ran the business before computers.) Improvement of the processing aspects of data processing cannot make up for the lack of historically defined quality of the data. The emphasis of quality for data can be achieved by trapping required data as close to its source as possible and leaving it in its barest form. The long-range goal must then be to have systems designed around the provision of quality data. There are several interim targets that can be used along the way.

An analysis of existing vs. long-range target systems architecture yields the following steps for maximizing productivity of existing resources while building target system architectures:

- Search and destroy—eliminating redundancy of functionality and data
- Surround—adding flexibility to present systems
- Quality data—designing, planning, and implementing architecture for data quality and long-term flexibility

SEARCH AND DESTROY: ELIMINATE REDUNDANCY

The first architectural strategy is to eliminate functional duplication and redundancy on an application-by-application basis. Financial and administrative systems are normally a high priority because of the need for common bookkeeping processes, payroll, and personnel systems. In merged companies, whole systems of the current architecture are subject to elimination. However, usually, under the pressure of time requirements, systems are patched together and new feeder systems are created. Pure duplication in the systems that support operations is usually more difficult to find because the organizations coming together do not quite perform exactly the same tasks.

In some cases, a company is still determining which operations should be merged and which should be kept separated during DP consolidation. Usually, not a great number of whole systems can be eliminated or can much major functionality be disabled, but costs can be reduced by eliminating any duplication of less-than-whole systems or major functions. That is difficult because the current architectures are normally quite inflexible and costly to modify. Therefore, it is ordinarily determined at merge time that the largest part of the current architecture be continued for some period of time.

This determination seems quite appropriate at the time. However, company operations start to change. Some of the work done by separate organizational entities starts to be done by consolidated groups. People then do work that requires them to get data from multiple systems in the current architecture. A strategy has to be developed that can allow users to get to multiple old systems from the same terminal to do their work functions.

DEFINING CORE DATA

The first of the new traumas facing the convert manager is the definition of corporate or "core" data. Core data in the smallest component (usually third normal form) is that essential to the functionality of the business. It is not financial report data, organizational data, or even necessarily previously defined customer data (that data with which the manager is familiar). It may not be the previously most used data or most redundantly stored data, although the later is probably good indicators. Core data cannot be defined until the company's business functions are well-defined.

This is a difficult task that must involve interdepartmental or corporate planners. The task is too important to be left to DP planners. Business functions are distinct from departmental goals or even business objectives. Business functions are the detail of what the business does and how it does it. Hard looks at business functions result in strange new descriptors for the work of the organization generally under the headings of management control, operations, support, and planning. Only after these overall functions are broken down can planners really determine what data is necessary to perform the functions and determine where to find the source of highest quality data.

The science of data analysis is becoming better defined each day, but the art of agreement as to what data belong to departments and what is core is ill-defined. The practice of charging back the costs of DP to the user has reduced DP budgets over the years while bringing in more hardware and software, but it has also engendered a very proprietary feeling toward systems and data on the part of the users. Individual departments say because they paid for the conversion, processing, and storage, they own the data. Upper management intervention is usually required to settle many arguments and establish the general rules for the shared use of data. As if upper management intervention was not traumatic enough, the reason for defining core data is to share it. This is not always recognized by all participants, which leads to psychological manifestations such as sibling rivalry or who has the biggest ego (or budget).

THE DATA ENGINE

Once it is agreed what should be core or shared, that data must go through three steps before storage (Exhibit 2):

1. The one source of the smallest component of the data must be identified. Basically this step determines from where and how the basic data will enter the storage system. This step is essential in establishing the quality framework of the system. The rules for data integrity must be established here.
2. Standard identification and the catalog structure must be determined. The user must understand and identify the data. The use of "directories" seems to be a way to solve this problem. (see below.)
3. A standard output interface must be defined. The calling terminology and the access rules to the data must be spelled out fully.

The preceding three steps are usually performed by technicians, but the result generates some syntax that must be understood by managers to get the full benefit of core data. Learning new language and codes has great psychological ramifications.

WHAT IS A DIRECTORY?

A directory is a specialized repository that contains lists of system users and their access rights. It also functions as a kind of network white pages, giving users a simple way to locate applications, print services, and other computing resources. The directory also plays a role in system administration, providing information technology (IT) managers a listing of all the hardware and software assets in a far-flung enterprise. Most important, a

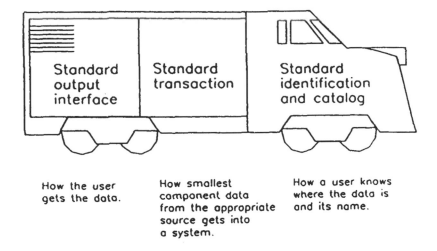

| How the user gets the data. | How smallest component data from the appropriate source gets into a system. | How a user knows where the data is and its name. |

Exhibit 2.   Engine for Quality Data

directory is a tool to integrate applications and business units that have functioned as stand-alone systems in the past.

The first widely adopted directory technology was based on the X.500 standard developed by the Consultative Committee on International Telephone and Telegraph's (CCITT) international standards organization. X.500 is a directory service that includes a model for naming users and system resources, a method for computer systems to exchange directory information, and a way of authenticating users. Although a number of information systems (IS) shops adopted X.500 products, the service failed to live up to its potential largely because it was difficult to implement.

In 1994, the Internet Engineering Task Force issued the first version of the Lightweight Directory Access Protocol (LDAP) standard, a smaller, more efficient version of X.500 (developed at the University of Michigan) that lets clients access and manage information in a centralized directory service. Some 40 vendors have decided to support LDAP since 1996, and the standard is now in its third generation. The primary reason behind its growing acceptance is that LDAP takes up less memory and uses fewer processing resources than X.500.

Today, directories exist in a multitude of applications ranging from a network operating system and asset management system to e-mail and database applications. The cost of implementing and administrating these disparate and often proprietary directories is great. That is why many companies are moving to implement a single, master directory that can integrate these diverse systems. The business value of a unified directory is

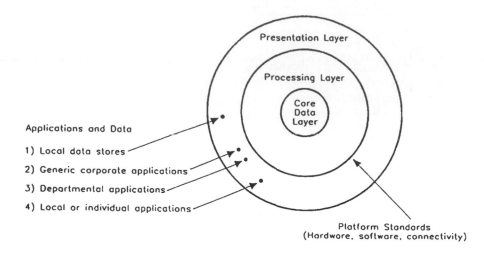

Exhibit 3. Conceptual Model

compelling: It is the elimination of redundancy and the automation of business processes across an entire enterprise.

SURROUND-INCREASE FLEXIBILITY OF PRESENT SYSTEMS

In addition to accessing multiple systems functionality from the same terminal to increase flexibility, there is a desire to distribute the data of those systems for the users to add their own functionality. The Gartner Group has developed a rather complex seven-stage model depicting the evolution to a client/server architecture. Exhibit 3 shows a more simplified model indicating the shift from a single-purpose DP system (in many cases, that is a current corporate architecture on a mainframe) through a separation of some processing (which may include a minicomputer or smart terminals) leading to a networked system with the possible use of all the processing tools with access to data that could be stored almost anywhere in the network.

Currently available computer hardware, software, and network products can be used to accomplish a partial distribution of DP on a step-by-step basis. Large mainframe systems can be accessed without renetworking every terminal and without multiple log-on and log-off procedures. A minicomputer can be programmed to emulate the current terminal and mainframe interface. Data can be accessed using the current data management schema. This can be done with the same or enhanced security requirements with little additional communications time. In addition, with the use of different communications and database management software, file segments or whole files can be downloaded for different local processing.

The surround approach can be implemented with minimum complications to present mainframe processing or database software. The present application programs require modest modifications; some "add-on" programming is required to meet interface standards. Local area networking (LAN) technology helps resolve communication delays. The distribution of minicomputer and storage devices can provide resources for local development and capability for additional centrally developed systems such as electronic mail (e-mail) and office automation. With the use of a tightly controlled standards process for software distribution and data security, there is potential for departmental reports processing, site-oriented database administration, or other user-generated programming at each site or from a combination of sites. However, this would mean additional costs.

The great advantage to the surround approach is that it decreases the need for mainframe program modification. It leaves the current mainframe databases as they are. New user functionality can recreated using minicomputer-based programming that can be generated faster and cheaper than mainframe programs can be enhanced. By not having to get into mainframe languages or database management systems for every change required by users, analysts and programmers can have more time to apply their knowledge and experience to developing a long-term view of systems architecture.

QUALITY DATA STRUCTURE

The "search" portion of search and destroy takes a detailed look at the processing and data of the current architecture. Surround uses what is learned in search and links data and processing and attempts to meet changed business needs. The long-term view should introduce the concept of a functional orientation as opposed to the traditional organizational approach to doing business. The theory is to examine what functions are required to best serve the needs of the corporation's customers and then to determine how best to accomplish those functions. A functional model of the corporation should be constructed. When the functional model is understood, the data needed to support the business functions must be defined and the source described. The data must then be standardized and a corporate data catalog built to ensure that the data is of the highest quality and stays that way.

SEPARATE THE DATA FROM THE PROCESSING

Close examination of the data in most current system architectures indicates several potential barriers to data quality. The search to eliminate functional redundancy usually identifies significant data redundancy or apparent redundancy. There are multiple systems storing the same data (see Exhibit 1) but coming from different sources. There are multiple systems storing different data from the same source. There are systems deriving and storing summarized data from detail for one business purpose and other systems deriving and storing a somewhat different summarization to be used by a different business function.

Although data editing and quality checking were stressed when individual systems were built, the combination of data that may be used for new organizations for different business purposes was not preplanned or coordinated. An obvious problem with the current architecture is the cost of resources for processing and storage for the redundant data. The more serious problem, however, is the lack of confidence generated when a user confronts nonmatching data while trying to solve a customer problem. Redundant data or apparent redundancy is not quality data. Use of poor quality data causes slow reaction to customer needs and poor customer satisfaction. Resolution of the data redundancy and quality problem is simple—separate the data from the processing and build a data engine as mentioned earlier.

CONCEPTUAL MODEL

Thinking about data separated from processing leads to a layered approach. This approach is feasible only through well-defined, strictly enforced standards dealing with hardware, software, and connectivity. These rules form a standard operating environment that must be in place to allow access to shared data. A conceptual systems model depicts three layers:

- The core data necessary to accomplish business functions
- Processing of transactions necessary to get core data into and out of databases
- Presentation or other manipulation of core or local data required by the user (Exhibit 3)

SUPPORTING TECHNOLOGY

The conceptual model does not imply any specific hardware implementation, but certain inferences can be derived based on changing technology. In the current architecture, terminals connected to mainframes are used to gather, edit, and store data (see Exhibit 4). Mainframe programming formats reports and rearranges data on terminal screens. Mainframes summarize and restore data. All DP and presentation are done by mainframe programming. With capabilities of new technology, opportunities are available to use mainframes, minicomputers, and PCs to greater advantage through networking.

To store core data in the smallest logical component, find the data, and provide all the required derivations, it will be necessary to use complex relational data structures and the directories mentioned earlier. The process-

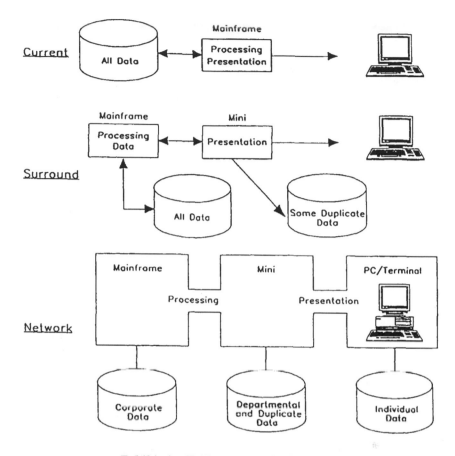

Exhibit 4.   Technological Architecture

ing power required (even with special database machines) indicates that mainframes may be required to build and maintain large shared databases. However, the processing of that data, or the manipulation of the transactions that get the data into and out of the system, could be done with minicomputers.

THE STEAK OR THE SIZZLE?

Once consistent quality data is available, presentation—the way data looks on output can be driven closer to the user to provide flexibility. All the formatting of the data can be done outside the mainframe, thereby reducing the load on the communications facility. (Terminal emulation mode requires that all screen format characters, as well as data, be exchanged with the mainframe. Studies indicate that by sending only data, communications requirements can be cut by orders of magnitude.) The programming

463

could be done in a minicomputer for a group of users to analyze data in the same manner or in a networked PC if the display is for an individual.

Although this new technological approach (the processing definition of quality) is important to architectural planning, it is more important to analyze functions and data required for functions before jumping to the technology. The surround approach and the uses of new technology will produce some better efficiencies and add some flexibility at a reasonable cost (if local enhancement capabilities are very carefully accounted for), but the quality roadblock cannot be eliminated unless corporate data is standardized and made available for all processing. In the long run, a redesign of major systems around the use of quality data is required. A combination of moving to new technology while achieving quality data is ideal.

IMPLEMENTATING DATA WAREHOUSING STRATEGY

The idea of redesigning major systems around quality data or anything else seems to be an anathema in these days of cutbacks. A greater problem is that data planning is difficult on a corporate scope. The whole is too big even for the best corporate and DP planners. However, planning done on an organizational basis will bring about another generation of new, improved, faster nonquality systems. It is possible to identify clusters of data to single source and start sharing. Search will identify data that is currently being shared. Savings achieved in elimination of redundancy in the reduction process can be used to pay for extra hardware needed for the surround process.

Each of these strategies refines the data sharing process until it becomes practical (either through cost justification or some less tangible value judgment) to separate certain specific data and build a data engine. It is impractical to reimplement most operational support systems at one time to make a great leap forward. The better plan is to move from the current architecture to a series of interim architectures, each becoming more quality data oriented (Exhibit 5).

Search and destroy should be pursued not only to save money but also to identify and to start the elimination of redundant data. A logical separation can begin with implementation of the surround approach for specific functions. Most of this hardware can remain in place to transfer to processors in the conceptual model. Concentration on quality data can begin by examining each new mechanization project in light of its use of standard core data.

As practical clusters of data are identified, data engines should be designed that provide the storage structure and distribution of corporate data using the presently installed mainframes. All present database systems should be examined to determine modifications needed for interim data

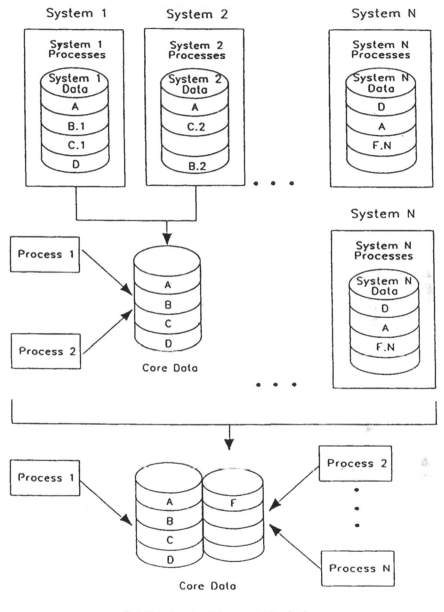

Exhibit 5.   Architectural Evolution

systems and methods for converting and merging data into the next generation of engines. Over time, with new systems and high priority modification required by present systems, the goal of quality data can be reached.

All aspects of quality are important to DP, but data quality is essential. Current systems architectures do not support economical data sharing or take advantage of new technology. Future systems will be designed around the use of quality data stored in the smallest component and available for all processing. Networking will provide the advantages of the best properties of mainframes, minicomputers, and PCs. Surround structures are an interim approach, providing continuing use of the current architecture while laying the hardware base for the transition to transaction and presentation processing of the future. A plan of migration can be developed targeting an ever-increasing sharing of data until the future design can be realized.

UNDER WHICH SHELL IS THE PEA?

The technical architecture of the evolved storage structure shows the repository of core data, but it also implies that core data can be duplicated so that departmental and individual data can be defined. This means that after definition of core data there must be further definitions of the storage structure. Core data will be used for traditional corporate DP, that is, turning the data into information for corporate reports, payroll, etc. However, the data in this information (output or presentation format) will never be kept in a corporate information base. Only the data will be kept. Summarization will never be retained in the corporate database, but just generated on output. Customer bills will never be found in bill format in the corporate database. Storage backup will be less data-intensive and cost less, but users must now address that database with the proper language to retrieve year to date or quarterly results or to create a bill status when handling customer inquiries. A hard copy of a customer bill will never be retained. Archiving, if the media is cheap enough (microform or laser storage technology), can be on an information basis.

"What if..." games will now be done outside the mainframe on departmental processors (if the data must be shared) or all the way out on individual PCs. Departmental data, not needed for corporate processing (i.e., team sales results, training information, bowling scores, etc.), can reside only at the departmental level. Corporate data can be duplicated and reside at the departmental level if aging information is applied by the departmental processors when the data are downloaded. (Warnings that the data was downloaded at a certain time or the data is valid only until a certain time must be applied.)

MORE COMPLICATIONS

Individual or private data and individual programs will be stored only in PCs with the tightest security precautions to avoid upward contamination. Mail or announcement services will originate at the PC and can still be hubbed on mainframes, depending on the communications networking scheme, but any storage on mainframes will be physically separated from corporate data. Formatted data such as expense vouchers will be input from the PC, but only corporate required data will be passed up the line. Other data will be kept in departmental files or even locally. If it is appropriate to disburse from the departmental level, the check creation or an electronic funds transfer can take place there (hopefully speeding up the process) with only financial data going to corporate. Decentralization with centralized quality data will gain a new meaning.

The psychology of change impact of such a data and information processing hierarchy as described is traumatic. Besides the knowledge of the standard identification of data needed (new codes and language) for sharing, an understanding of the storage hierarchy must be in place. Individual managers must understand what data will be shared and where to find it. They must also understand how to legitimately avoid the sharing of data. Auditors, as will the managers, will no longer be able to pull hard copies of vouchers from departmental files. They must know how to navigate to the farthest ends of the storage structure to get all the comments added by originators.

Storage pricing structures will vary greatly, depending on the location and utilization of data. New chargeback allocations will have to be developed. All this takes place after the trauma of core data definition with all its internecine battles and, yes, even the need for top management involvement in really determining the functions of the business, have been faced. These factors must be understood by all before it is appropriate to move ahead.

CONCLUSION

The concept and data warehousing create a new set of promises of quality, strategic impact, and even cost savings available to potential users. If managers are not interested in these promises, the paper glut will force them finally to use new systems. The need to prepare users for the psychological aspects of the great opportunities has never been so important. Companies must be prepared to face the challenges and the time required to do all the interdepartmental planning work required to gain the potential advantages.

Chapter 28
The Art and Science of Project Management

Antoinette Z. Hubbard

INTRODUCTION

Over the past 15 years, telecommunications has meant many things to people. When one looks at college curricula, telecommunications turns up as media production, speech, television, recording, broadcasting, and (very infrequently) the study of telephony in its voice and data varieties. The author has always known it as the diligent and seemingly miraculous installation of those phone and computer systems and networks that connect us to the world.

The true excitement is the challenge that readers of this chapter have experienced or are about to experience—the successful planning and implementation of telecommunications projects, on time, within budget (reasonably), and with specifications that match the needs and requirements of the users. This chapter consists of two sections: the art of project management and the science of project management:

> The *art* encompasses the skills, relationships, organizational understandings, and leadership insights, which have proved themselves to be useful resources in the design of projects.

> The *science* encompasses the tools, planning capabilities, technical understandings, and managerial attributes that complement and reinforce the art.

The balance, the understanding, and the knowledge of people, planning, product, and process create successful outcomes in the projects that lie ahead.

This chapter will discuss the science and art of project management, describing and defining a project, project management concepts, and attributes of a project manager and team members. The chapter will also

0-8493-9990-4/99/$0.00+$.50
© 1999 by CRC Press LLC

provide checklists and tables that present key words and steps in a project. The reader will need to begin to collect the materials, documents, and templates that specifically assist in the actual execution of a project. The intention of the author is that this chapter will be the framework to assist the project manager in organizing and implementing a successful telecommunications project.

THE SCIENCE

What Is a Project?

The most useful concept a network manager can begin with is the definition of a project. A clear understanding of the meaning and attributes of a project will contribute to the orientation of management as to why the work that is about to be done is different, thereby requiring a different framework for support, budgeting, resource allocation, and reward.

A project is an allocation of resources directed toward a specific objective following a planned, organized approach (Leintz and Rea). A project is any set of activities and tasks that consume resources (people, money, and equipment); and has a specific objective to be completed within certain specifications with a defined start and end dates, and funding limits (Kerzner). A project has a beginning and an end. A project can be recognized by its objectives:

1. **Attainable**   The objective identifies a target that can be reasonably achieved given the time and resource constraints of the project. If the objective is set too high, credibility is destroyed.
2. **Definitive**   The objective spells out in concrete terms what is to be achieved and to what degree. The results to be attained are clearly defined.
3. **Quantifiable**   It specifies a yardstick for completion that can be identified by all concerned, especially those responsible for its achievement. The establishment of measurable objectives is mandatory so that performance can be compared to a standard.
4. **Specific duration**   It defines the time parameters within which the task is to be achieved. This is necessary for evaluation of the project's progress and completion.

A typical objective will be a statement such as the following:

- To move the purchasing department into the vacant area in the administrative building by Jan. 1, 2000 at a cost not to exceed $72,000
- To buy a house by the end of the summer with four bedrooms, two baths, and a small yard (continuing with list of specific items) at a cost not to exceed $150,000

It is not a project objective:

- To graduate from college

470

- To run a business
- To be a project manager

The clear statement of project objectives ensures that the end product meets customers' requirements, specifies results, and forms the foundation for the entire planning process (including the responsibility matrix). Project objectives are reviewed frequently and help identify changes that fall outside the original scope. The objectives determine if the project has reached its successful conclusion.

The unwillingness to take the time and effort to struggle with specific definitions of a project or problems that a project will address leads to difficulties and hinders the successful implementation and management of the project. This is the seed for the beginning of failure or the achievement of success. If you do not know where you are going, any map will do. However, you may not arrive where you thought you were headed.

Finally, a project is differentiated from the work that is normally done in that it has uniqueness about it. The scope of a project is not something that is done as a regular activity in the workplace (accounting, payroll, sales, and marketing), although every department may have projects that mark a one-time activity that contributes to change or enhancement of the basic processes of the department. Although the installation of each network or system may have many similar elements, every design is a new beginning subject to the same planning and definition that has been discussed. A wise project manager develops a database of templates and resources that assists this planning and respects that each system requires a new set of eyes and time to differentiate this installation from the last successful implementation.

What Is Project Management?

Project management is the application of traditional management processes toward the successful achievement of the stated project objective. The traditional tasks of management are usually seen as:

1. **Planning** Choosing courses of action to follow and identifying, evaluating, and selecting resources that will achieve the objectives.
2. **Organizing** Bringing all the assets of an organization together into a proper relationship to achieve the objectives.
3. **Implementing** Putting into effect the plans and organization that will achieve the objectives.
4. **Controlling** Monitoring the results that will ensure the accomplishment of the objectives.
5. **Coordinating** Bringing all the parts of an organization into a single harmonious working unit to achieve the objectives.

Exhibit 1. Phases of a Project

Start Up (5%)	Planning (20%)	Growth (30%)	Production (30%)	Shutdown (15%)
Concept	Budgeting	Resourcing	Auditing	Evaluating
Research	Scheduling	Allocating	Implementing	Terminating
Study	Resourcing	Monitoring	Testing	Divesting
Thinking	Allocating	Controlling	Training	Rewarding
Defining	Controlling	Communicating	Documenting	Acknowledging
Design	Marketing	Replanning	Acknowledging	Celebrating
Approval		Problem solving	Verifying	
Buy-in			Integrating	

Each project manager will find different ways to implement the previously mentioned characteristics, but there are certain common attributes and phases that are part of the project management process, as shown in Exhibit 1.

The network project manager finds tools and methods that assist the implementation of these attributes, but the author will present some checklists in the chapter that will be helpful in making these processes more real.

It is important to recognize that a project must begin with a clear definition of the problem or innovation that the project will address. This clarity allows upper management to understand and support the proposed solution. The most dangerous part of a project is its beginning. Most project teams and organizations refuse to take the time to carefully and completely understand and plan projects.

A typical retrospective on a project would look like 10% planning and 90% implementation because that is where "the real work" is (and in most business cultures the reward—attention for putting out fires and running around in response to crisis is a better way of being recognized.) A successful and less stressful project is 90% planning and 10% implementation; there is less attention, but it is ultimately more healthful, restful, and beneficial to the team members.

What is a System?

All projects take place in real time with real people in real settings. To successfully plan, implement, and work with projects, a project manager must expand definitions and awareness beyond a simple solution. Working with a systems understanding the project takes in an appreciation of more elements that could affect the success of the project.

A system is a series of interrelated parts bound together to form unity or wholeness for the achievement of an identified objective. Systems thinking stresses interdisciplinary relationships and interactions. Its goal is to keep units of the system working together to achieve systemwide goals. In looking at the world, the project manager can break it up into three parts so it is easier to name some of the players and influences:

1. **The internal**   The influences with which the project manager has direct control or direct contact include, for example, assets, product (major output of the group and major product of the organization), objectives, labor force (skills, work standards, objectives), and management.
2. **The immediate external**   The influences with which the project manager has indirect control and direct contact include the stockholders with their ethics and expectations, the creditors, the competitors, the customers, and the unions.
3. **The general external**   The environment with which the project manager may have indirect contact and indirect control includes government, general public, markets, consumer wants and needs, technology, ecology (such as issues of scarcity, inequality, waste, and pollution) and finally economic conditions.

Systems weave in and out. They are interconnected and affect one another. They exist together in the way that the proverbial butterfly flutter creates a monsoon in India. The more the project manager works to understand and name them, acknowledge them, or be aware of them in the planning and definition of the project, the more successful the project will be.

A project is an exciting possibility. Its challenges are the complete definition of the problem or solution—the willingness to use a systems thinking approach by recognizing all parties involved and the effects of one system on another. Included are the effective use of resources by a commitment to planning and communication, the motivation of the project team, and the recognition and appreciation at the conclusion.

What Does a Telecommunications Project Look Like?

Every useful project begins with defining the problem and its proposed solutions. In the beginning of the *conceptual* (start-up) phase, a telecommunications or network manager begins with a needs assessment and a statement of the present situation (Exhibit 2).

The positioning of the telecommunications function, structure, and charter through the effective use of assessment tools and measures will be vital to the success of achieving individual project goals. Staff members, consultants, and previous studies can be resources for creating methodologies for the phases of needs assessment. Telecommunications programs at universities might be very interested in providing student interns for the development and implementation of the assessment phase.

473

Exhibit 2.   Needs Assessment

Where Are We? Environmental Assessment	*What Could We Do?* Examine Strategic Risks, Alternatives, and Contingencies	*How Do We Get There?* Proposed Solutions
Current business	Leading edge	Project planning
Current uses	Proactive	Education
Current system	Conservative	Leadership
Hardware	Reactive	Priorities
Software	Develop conceptual	Technical
Site analysis	alternatives	Financial
Problems	Develop configuration and	Strategic
Billings	migration plans	Request for informational
Traffic studies	Develop planning horizons	development and analysis
Benchmark costs	Develop assumptions	

Why Change? Identify Critical Issues, Strategic Objectives, Opportunities	*What Should We Do?* Develop Feasibility Studies	
Increase profits	Organization	
Increase productivity	Vendors	
Reduce and avoid costs	Funding	
Integration	Standards	
New business lines	Cost/benefit	
Growth	Policies	
	Architecture	
	Capital expense	
	Client relationships	
	Risk evaluation	

The planning phase flows from much of the information that has been collected and discussed in the start-up. If the project has received management support, the telecommunications or network manager continues into the definition process and issues a full request for proposals (RFP) (bid specification). The telecommunications manager composes the RFP so that at the end of the bidding process, he is able to determine for the project:

1. Firm identification of the human and nonhuman resources required
2. Final system performance requirements
3. Detailed plans to support the system
4. Determination of the realistic cost, schedule, and performance requirements
5. Identification of those areas of the system in which high risk and uncertainty exist, and delineation of plans for further exploration of those areas

6. Definition of intersystem and intrasystem interfaces
7. Definition of necessary support systems
8. Identification and initial preparation of the documents required to support the system, such as policies, procedures, job descriptions, budget and funding papers and memoranda

A typical RFP would include (also see Chapter 24):

1. General conditions (a brief statement of business conditions from the needs assessment, what can appropriately be seen by people not in the company)
2. Request for information about the bidding company
3. Hardware and software requirements
4. Optional requirements
5. Cutover requirements
6. Maintenance conditions
7. Repair and replacement
8. Room layout
9. Customer list
10. Technical data on proposed system
11. General comments
12. Pricing
13. Training

At the end of the RFP evaluation the telecommunications manager now understands the system technology, flexibility, reliability, and design. There has been a complete analysis of alternatives, both technical and financial. Contract negotiations have been concluded and the contract has been awarded. The growth and production phases begin.

During this time the project manager is responsible for:

1. Completing the detailed plans conceived and defined during the preceding phases
2. Identification and management of the resources required to facilitate the production processes, such as labor, supplies, and funds
3. Verification of system specifications
4. Beginning of production, construction, and installation
5. Final preparation of essential procedural documents (invoices, schedules for training, etc.)
6. Monitoring the progress of the system installation
7. Communicating essential material in a timely fashion
8. Documenting the process, success, and issues of the project
9. Tracking actual costs to estimate
10. Being fully present during the final stages of installation and cutover (see Chapter 16)
11. Acknowledging the work done by staff and supplier

Although in most telecommunications projects the supplier has con-tracted for the installation, the successful projects proceed with the full in-volvement and participation of the telecommunications or network manager.

At the end of the project, the telecommunications manager is responsi-ble for acceptance and delivery of the system into the operational aspects of the company (shutdown of the project).

The manager can then evaluate:

1. Use of system results by the intended user
2. Actual integration of the project's product or service into existing organizational systems
3. Evaluation of the technical, social, and economic aspects of the project to meet actual operating conditions
4. Provision of feedback to organizational planners concerned with de-veloping new projects and systems
5. Development of "lessons" learned from system project to include major problems encountered and their solutions, new or improved management techniques, recommendations for future research, rec-ommendations for future projects, and references for supplier

The flow of a project can be summarized as follows:

1. **Proposed innovation or problem**
2. **Definition of solution by using systems theory** (internal, immediate external, and general external)
3. **Develop detailed project plan** (project manager team, vendor, cli-ents, and others)
4. **Phases of a project** (start-up, growth, production, shutdown)
5. **End of project** (placing system into daily working of company and keeping the notes)

Tools and References

The ability to identify the problem as completely as possible by using systems awareness, the willingness to take the time and effort to plan, a solid understanding and appreciation of the field, and the commitment to manage are the primary skills that will establish a project in reality and pro-duction.

The traditional project management concepts such as program evalua-tion review technique (PERT), Gantt charts, and work breakdown structure (WBS) are based on the full definition of the project scope. The best re-sources for a complete understanding of these methods can be found in *Project Management*, the encyclopedic and valuable reference by Harold Kerzner. Excellent online references are Project Management Institute, *www.pmi.org*, and Center for International Project and Program Management, *http//shaw.iol.ie/%7Emattewar/CIPPM/index.html*. Interesting reference sites are *www.projectmanagement.com*, *www.pmnetwork.com*, and www.4pm.com (online classes for a fee and references). Finally with regard to software, all software packages are only as good as your planning process and awareness of *all* of the elements of your project. *PCWorld* has an excellent World Wide Web site that discusses many of the existing *packages (www.pcworld.com/software/accounting—financial/articles/oct97/ 1510p176f.html)*. If your planning is incomplete, inaccurate, and uninspired, no software package will be good enough to fix your project. The science of project management is the ability to fix concretely as many of the details of the processes that will compose the project and determine the relationships of these elements. Only then is the telecommunications network manager ready to use the software package and begin the art of project management.

THE ART

The art of project management begins with self. Many years ago in an unnamed and forgotten article, the author came across a list of attributes that reflected creativity. The list seemed to reflect perfectly the qualities needed to be a successful project manager: openness to experience, independence, self-confidence, willingness to risk, sense of humor and playfulness, sensitivity, lack of a feeling of being threatened, personal courage, unconventionality, flexibility, preference for complexity, goal orientation, originality, self-reliance, persistence, curiosity, vision, self-assertion, acceptance of disorder, tolerance for ambiguity, motivation, and inclination for the offbeat.

One of the most useful skills a project manager can have is an awareness of his own strengths and differences.

To put together an effective project team, the project manager needs to be able to assess what capabilities are present, who has them, how those gifts work with one another, and how the differing types complement one another. This chapter is not a psychological study, but the most helpful reference for these understandings is the use of the Myers–Briggs Type Inventory or the Keirsey–Bates Temperament Sorter. The Myers–Briggs must be officially administered, but *Please Understand Me* (Keirsey) provides a thoughtful beginning. Often people in technical companies may feel uncomfortable with these ideas, but it is most helpful to understand that issues with communication and understanding come from a genuine difference with solutions available. *The People Process* (Hollister) also provides hints and useful readings for portraying the differences among team members.

477

Once differences and similarities are understood, listening and communicating in ways that reach one another will be significant. Taking the time to understand how well one hears and responds appropriately reduces stress and friction within the team. *Listening Styles Profile* and *Communication Skills Profile* are two workbooks that provide both self-assessment understanding and insight into improvement (*http://www.pfeiffer.com*).

All improvement leads to better team interaction and better team performance. The project manager must nurture a climate in which the members are committed to the program, have open communication among members, experience a low degree of detrimental interpersonal and intergroup conflict, and commit themselves to the performance of the tasks at hand.

A group of young professionals when asked to determine the characteristics of an exciting working team responded:

1. A clear vision and consistency as demonstrated by an understanding of roles and responsibilities augmented by quantifiable goals
2. Responsive and collaborative members who valued information sharing and were willing to work and were determined to succeed
3. Decisive atmosphere in which relevant details, analysis, problem solving, and imagination contribute to the continuation of the solution
4. Appreciation of organization with time management, multitasking, focus, record keeping, and feedback kept the group on task
5. Comfortable creativity where the members expressed new ideas in safety, with humor was present, and a sense of celebration
6. Open communications with recognition of individual strengths and utilization of these strengths
7. A leadership environment that is tolerant and encouraging and balances structure with direction and openness

The project manager can reflect on these criteria and see that the basis for success begins with the capability to plan thoroughly and disseminate the planning process adequately. Team members want to understand and to contribute.

In summary, the art of project management is in the willingness to discover and applaud our similarities and differences. A team is a group of people working for a common objective and knowing what each person contributes to the success of the endeavor. A group of people with a common objective is a line of people waiting for a movie. A team is the nine baseball players on the field with different skills and positions, and yet each with the intention of winning. Understanding the parts of the people who make up the team is as important as understanding the phases of a project. The use and recognition of both aspects of project management will contribute to a project's successful outcome.

CONCLUSION

The list of common project pitfalls contains the following: definition of problem, planning, personnel, communication, client orientation, scheduling, upper management support, company organizational structure, design, human factors, cost controls, change in scope, logistics, and project termination. By going back through this chapter, the reader can avail himself of the skills and assets that can be used to offset the problems that are encountered during the course of a project. Planning, management techniques, systems thinking, understanding the phases of a project (including its ending), self-awareness, recognition of the different attributes and skills of team members, proper reinforcement of the team, and continued communication among all identified partners of the project all are tools and skills that will bring the network manager to a successful end of one project and inspire the enthusiasm to embrace another.

Notes

Gilbreath, Robert, *Winning at Project Management*, John Wiley & Sons, New York, 1986. (This book is well-written and documents in plain English many project pitfalls.)

Hollister, Pam, *The People Process*, ISBN 0-88390-328-8.

Keirsey, David, *Please Understand Me*, ISBN 0-9606954-0-0.

Kerzner, Harold, *Project Management*, Van Nostrand Reinhold, 1998. (This is the expensive ($60) encyclopedia of project management.)

Lewis, James, *Fundamentals of Project Management*, AMACOM, 1997, ISBN 0-8144-7835-2.

Lientz, Bennett P. and Rea, Kathryn, P. *Project Management for the 21st Century*, Academic Press, Harcourt Brace, 1995.

Lipnack, Jessica and Stamps, Jeffrey, *The Age of the Network*, John Wiley & Sons, New York, 1994.

Reddy, Brendan, *Intervention Skills*, Pfeiffer & Company, San Diego, CA, 1994. (This book is an excellent introduction to ideas about group process.)

Schrage, Michael, *No More Teams!* Currency Doubleday, 1995.

Weinberg, Gerald, *Becoming a Technical Leader*, Dorset House Publishing, New York, 1986. (This is a wonderfully written, enjoyable, and applicable book.)

Section VIII
Education Support for the Network Manager

Chapter 29
Educating Aspiring Network Managers

John M. Lusa

INTRODUCTION

The breakup of AT&T in 1984 was just one of the reasons at that point in time that created a big demand for professionals with telecommunications and networking experience. Principal among the other reasons was the growing use of computer networks. Much of the traffic generated by computers was running over the same infrastructure as the voice traffic.

Not only did divestiture leave using institutions to their own devices in running their own telephone systems, but it also occurred while they were just learning to build local area networks (LANs) and wide area networks (WANs) to hook them together. The strategic uses of the voice and data networks were becoming more generally recognized. Divestiture and the explosive growth of both voice and data communications resulted in a shortage of skilled and knowledgeable people to run these fast-growing networks.

VISIONARY ACADEMICS

Visionary academics at the University of Colorado in 1971 saw an early educational need in the telecommunications industry beyond just electrical engineering. So, with the help of a number of industry executives and advisors, the first interdisciplinary master degree telecommunications program was established. The program has celebrated well over a quarter century of success.

There is no doubt that the huge explosion in professional employment opportunities in the telecommunications field is now being matched by educational opportunities at all levels of education. Today, hundreds of various types of institutions throughout the U.S. and Canada have followed the lead of the University of Colorado and are offering a variety of degrees and certificates related to telecommunications and computer networking.

For the most part, early telecommunications education consisted of getting an electrical engineering degree and specializing in telecommunications systems. However, there was a number of pioneering universities in the U.S. that recognized the need for telecommunications professionals with interdisciplinary skills. Although the need for engineers is still great and schools continue to ratchet up these programs, it is recognized that professionals with management and other technical skills are in demand as well.

TECHNICAL AND MANAGEMENT TRAINING

Now numerous programs are geared to include both technical and management training. Some approach the problem from an engineering discipline, while others come from a business heritage. For instance, the University of San Francisco offers a telecommunications track in its master of business administration (MBA) program. In preparation for this chapter, a survey was conducted among those U.S. institutions offering graduate and 4-year undergraduate programs. The study shows a growing trend to provide graduates with management and technical skills, as well as engineering qualifications. Some 26% of bachelor degree graduates now enter the telecommunications industry in management positions, and 46% enter technical-type positions, while 28% are hired as engineers. For master graduates, management placement jumps to 43%, while technical position placement is 39% and engineering placement is 18%.

Most of the university programs reported having systems laboratories. A number of programs offered internships for students as well. These internships usually occur during long breaks from classes, such as during the summer period.

In addition to the University of Colorado, other early adopters of telecommunications education were two Texas universities, Southern Methodist University (SMU) and Texas A&M University. SMU established its undergraduate telecommunications program just two years after Colorado. Texas A&M's College of Engineering established its program in 1976 to prepare students to become telecommunications analysts and technologists in both voice and data communications.

INTERDISCIPLINARY TRAINING

Although its telecommunications program is not as large as that of the University of Colorado, Texas A&M has both an undergraduate and a master program. The master program is an interdisciplinary technical management plan through one of four different schools at the university: engineering, business, administration, computer science, and management information systems.

Texas A&M is among the handful of universities to receive accreditation from the Technology Accreditation Commission of the Accreditation Board for Engineering and Technology (TAC/ABET). The other is the Rochester Institute of Technology in New York.

Many university programs aggressively include interdisciplinary aspects of technology management into their telecommunications curricula. This trend has helped bridge the gap between those who develop technology and those who have to manage it. Dr. Ray Steele, founding director of the Center for Information and Communications Sciences (a master program established in 1985) at Ball State University in Muncie, IN, says that the 1996 federal telecommunications legislation has had a great impact on the industry and has created a great deal of additional employment activity.

MANAGEMENT PROGRAMS

From the survey of university telecommunications programs, it was learned that over half of the programs offer some type of engineering education. However, the majority of graduates are from management-type programs such as Ball State or interdisciplinary programs such as the University of Colorado. At the undergraduate level, most institutions offer telecommunications engineering programs, while some such as Ohio University and State University of New York (SUNY) Institute of Technology are more management and technically oriented.

The Ball State program provides training in voice, data, videoconferencing, and multimedia. Its first graduating class had just a handful of students. Now the program graduates well over 50 a year with virtually a 100% placement rate. Dozens of prospective employers annually send interviewers to campus. Dr. Steele, the director, explains that his master candidates get "specialized education in the same manner as a law or medical school." To be accepted by Ball State, all candidates are required to write a paper on their professional aspirations. Dr. Steele points out that candidates soon learn that the pace is fast. He says, "We develop graduates with a broad understanding of technology and the industry."

The Ball State program has been a trailblazer for other university programs. To keep the Ball State program on track, Dr. Steele and his faculty rely heavily on contacts with industry. He maintains a large and active advisory board, as well as a fellows board. They not only provide advice but also donate equipment and systems for use in the laboratories and spend time mentoring the students. Dr. Steele points out that the Ball State program takes the extra step of helping its students develop professional and social skills as a way of enhancing professional relationships and careers.

Although much of this knowledge is obtained through classroom work, Dr. Steele explains that "students get involved in real-world projects with participating vendors and user organizations." He adds, "Many of the projects are also revenue producing for the center." For Ball State, placing practically all its graduates in good-paying management, technical, or consulting positions is the norm. All the universities in the survey showed similar rates of success. For instance, Professor Carol Richardson, chair of the Telecommunications Engineering program at the Rochester (NY) Institute of Technology, reports that bachelor graduates who have chosen the management option receive excellent starting salaries.

In the Rochester program, according to Professor Richardson, the undergraduate bachelor of science program in telecommunications and engineering technology has accreditation from TAC/ABET. She adds, "All students must complete a required cooperative work experience, starting in their junior year. They alternate between six months of classes and six months of work over a three-year period."

A NEW BREED

Ohio University's J. Warren McClure School of Communications Systems Management represents the new breed of undergraduate management-style programs that have spawned since divestiture. Dr. Phyllis Bernt, former director of the school and now associate dean of the College of Communications in Athens, OH, explains that a progressive journalism faculty saw the future and was responsible for the founding of the school. The faculty members were inspired by the use of satellites by Gannet Publishing, the publisher of *USA Today.* She said, "They also saw that with the rise of the interconnect market and with the talk of electronic publishing, things were going to be changing drastically."

Interestingly, the curriculum was literally put together by a committee from across the campus. Interpersonal skills, communications, business, and journalism were all represented. Early on they agreed that it would be a multidisciplinary degree program. "The goal was to combine technical competence with strategic vision," Dr. Bernt explained.

At the start, she said, "This program was very much a voice-oriented program. Now it has added a heavy data component, and we are moving into wireless and video." The school has built a well-equipped voice and data lab. She added, "I think the career opportunities for future graduates will continue to grow. Every year since I have been here, we have added new employers and new segments of the industry to our list of employers of our graduates." She said graduates need to have a grasp of a broader span of technologies and will need to understand the whole issue of market structure much more clearly because of the converging of technologies. As do a number of other programs, Ohio University offers internships to its undergraduates.

GRANTS FOR UNIVERSITIES

Help for developing university programs has come from a number of sources. One of the more important has been the encouragement, direct assistance, and financial support from the International Communications Association (ICA), an influential group of network and telecommunications managers in large business and institutional organizations. It has been directly responsible for grants of thousands of dollars to more than 30 university programs over the years. In addition, its members have worked closely with the programs as advisors. Many of the university programs listed in the appendix of this chapter (those with astericks) are associated with the ICA.

Equipment and systems from vendor organizations are funneled to universities through the ICA as well. The user influence on the university programs has been crucial and enormous. The ICA formally set up an educational foundation in 1989 to dispense its assistance and grants to universities. The association has also been generous in funding faculty and students attendance at its annual conferences. Free booth space is also provided to give an opportunity for association members and students to meet ICA members and industry contacts.

The advisory board concept is not unique to Ball State, of course. For instance, ICA maintains a roster of universities that become eligible for possible assistance from the association. One of the requirements of being included on this roster is to maintain an advisory board.

INDUSTRY ADVICE

A well-known name in the industry and a long-time ICA member, Phil Evans, the telecommunications director for Perot Systems Corp., keeps popping up when universities need help with telecommunications curricula. Evans always seems to be where the action is. He has held top telecommunications positions at Ashland Oil and FMC Corp., and now at Perot Systems. A former ICA president, Evans has also been active over the years in the ICA educational program.

Evans was involved in helping to develop curricula at the earliest university telecommunications programs in the U.S. They include the University of Colorado, Texas A&M (his alma mater), and SMU. He has played a key role with a number of other university telecommunications programs, as well. They include the University of Kansas, George Washington University, University of Houston, Ohio University, and Southwest Louisiana University. He continues to serve on the advisory boards at the University of Colorado, Texas A&M, and Southwest Louisiana University.

Obviously, Evans is in a position to comment on the value of a telecommunications education. He points out that it may be difficult to quantify,

487

"but undeniably (a telecom education) is an asset to all graduates who chose to put that education to good use." Interestingly, in the three decades he has been involved with university telecommunications programs, he finds more new advisory board members are now graduates from the university telecommunications programs. "They are up-and-coming leaders in their companies," he says.

He is fully aware of the "immediate value the graduates of telecom programs bring to their new employers, as contrasted to the longer "familiarization" time for graduates from traditional engineering programs." Evans says that another "measure of value is the percentage of graduates who land jobs upon graduation." He explains that it is almost 100% within a short time, and the pay equals or exceeds that of electrical engineers.

What should the university programs include in their curricula? He suggests, "privatization and deregulation, the business management embracing world rather than local markets, new applications of technologies to enable new business methods and markets, virtual office for telecommutters, and security for financial transactions over the network."

CONCLUSION

University telecommunications programs have enhanced their stature considerably. They represent a focal point for educators, employers of new graduates, and the telecommunications industry. With the fast growing use of telecommunications and the resultant growth of the industry itself, universities will continue to play a key and growing role in providing the entry-level technical and management professionals skilled in telecommunications technology.

APPENDIX

What follows is a list of universities and colleges in the U.S. and Canada offering engineering, and technical and management training in telecommunications and computer networks:

> **Arizona State University**, Department of Communications, Tempe, AZ. Bachelor and master programs, technical and management orientation. (609) 965-5011.
> * **Ball State University**, Center for Information and Communication Sciences, Muncie, IN. Master program, management orientation. Provides actual work projects, as well as laboratories in data, voice, multimedia, and video. (765) 285-1889, FAX: (765) 285-1889.
> **British Columbia Institute of Technology**, Barnaby, BC, Canada. Diploma of technology. Electronics technology, analyzing analog and digital networks. (604) 432-8251.

* **California State University of Chico**, Department of Communication Design, Chico, CA. Bachelor program, technical and management. Offers internships. (916) 898-4626, FAX (916) 898-6824.

Camosun College, Electronics Engineering Technology, Victoria, BC, Canada. Diploma in electronic engineering. (604) 370-4433.

Carleton University, Department of Systems and Computer, Ottawa, ON, Canada. Bachelor, master, and doctorate programs; technology and management programs. (613) 520-5740.

Carnegie Mellon University, Engineering and Public Policy in Telecommunications, Pittsburgh, PA. Master in information networking. (412) 268-3436.

Centennial College, Telecommunications Management, Scarborough, ON, Canada. Certificate in telecommunications management. (416) 289-4718.

* **Christian Brothers University**, Center for Telecommunications and Information Systems, Memphis, TN. Bachelor in telecommunications and masters in engineering management. (901) 321-3571, FAX: (901) 722-0580.

* **City University of New York**, Center for Public Policy in Telecommunications and Information Systems, New York, NY. Doctorate in computer science. (212) 642-2984, FAX: (212) 642-2959.

Columbia University, Center for Telecommunications Research, New York, NY. Master of communications and master of management of information and communications media. (212) 854-4222.

Conestoga College of Applied Arts, Electronics Engineering Technology/Telecommunications Systems, Kitchener, ON, Canada. Diploma in technology. (519) 748-5220.

* **Devry Institute of Technology, Telecommunications**, Irving, TX. Bachelor in telecommunications. (214) 929-6777, FAX: (214) 929-6778.

Duke University, Department of Electrical and Computer Engineering, Durham, NC. Master in telecommunications and computer networks in association with European universities. (919) 660-5442.

* **George Washington University**, Graduate Telecommunications Program, Washington, D.C. Master in telecommunications and doctorate in public policy. (202) 994-3989, FAX: (202) 994-0022.

Georgia Institute of Technology, Department of Electrical Engineering, Atlanta, GA. Bachelor, master, and doctorate programs in computer science and electrical engineering. (404) 894-3187.

* **Golden Gate University**, School of Telecommunications and Industry, San Francisco, CA. Master and bachelor programs in technology and management. (415) 442-6540, FAX: (415) 442-7049.

Holland College Royalty Center, Telecommunications Technology, Computer Studies Division, Charlottetown, PEI, Canada. Diploma in telecommunications and data communications. (902) 566-9372.

Humber College, Teleprocessing and Networking, Etobicoke, ON, Canada. Bachelor in teleprocessing techniques.(416) 675-3111.

* **Illinois State University**, Applied Computer Science Department, Normal, IL. Bachelor in telecommunications management. Interdisciplinary program and internships offered. (309) 438-8146, FAX: (309) 438-5113.

Indiana University, Department of Telecommunications, Bloomington, IN. Bachelor, master, and doctorate degrees in various telecommunications management disciplines. (812) 855-6895.

McGill University, Montreal, PQ, Canada. Bachelor of commerce with a technical and conceptual foundation in the design and analysis of organizational information systems. (514) 398-4065.

* **Michigan State University**, Department of Telecommunications, East Lansing, MI. Bachelor, master, and doctorate degrees in engineering and management disciplines. (517) 355-4451, FAX: (517) 355-1292.

Mount Royal College, Telecommunications Management, Calgary, AB, Canada. Diploma in telecommunications. A 3-year program. (403) 240-6111.

National University, San Diego, CA. Master in telecommunications from adult education program. (800) 628-8648.

New York City Technical College, Division of Engineering Technology, Brooklyn, NY. Associate and bachelor degrees in telecommunications management. (718) 260-5000.

New York Institute of Technology, Telecommunications Management, Old Westbury, NY. Associate and bachelor degrees in technology and management disciplines. (516) 686-7931.

* **New York University**, Interactive Telecommunications Program, New York, NY. Master of professional studies. (212) 998-1888, FAX: (212) 998-1898.

Northern Alberta Institute of Technology, Telecommunications Engineering Technology, Edmonton, AB, Canada. Diploma in telecommunications engineering. (403) 471-7818.

Northwestern University, Interdepartmental program, Evanston, IL. Master in telecommunications science, management, and policy. Summer internships are available. (708) 491-7531.

* **Ohio University**, J. Warren McClure School of Communications Systems Management, Athens, OH. Now offered is a bachelor in communications. A master program is proposed. Voice and data laboratories are available. Internships provided to students. (740) 593-4889, FAX: (740) 593-4891.

Oklahoma State University, Graduate College, Stillwater, OK. Master in telecommunications management. Interdisciplinary with business, engineering, and arts and sciences. An associate degree is also available. (405) 744-9000.

* **Pace University**, School of Computer Science and Information Systems, White Plains, NY. Telecommunications management orientation. Various bachelor and master degrees in information systems, telecommunications, and computer science are offered. Cooperative educational programs are available. (212) 346-1871, FAX: (212) 346-1863.
* **Rochester Institute of Technology**, Telecommunications (Electrical) Engineering Technology, Rochester, NY. Associate degree in applied science electrical technology with telecommunications option and bachelor of science in telecommunications engineering technology. Cooperative education with industry provided. TAC/ABET accredited. (716) 475-2179, FAX: (716) 475-2178.
* **Ryerson Polytechnic University**, Telecommunications Management, Toronto, ON, Canada. Bachelor in administration and information management with telecommunications specialization and a certificate in telecommunications management. (416) 979-5000, ext. 6740; FAX: (416) 979-5249.

  Saint Lawrence College, Telecommunications Management, Brockville, ON, Canada. MBA in telecommunications management. (613) 345-0660.
* **Saint Mary's University of Minnesota**, School of Graduate Studies, Minneapolis, MN. Bachelor and master degrees in telecommunications management and related subjects. (612) 874-9877, ext. 178; FAX: (612) 870-7666. Certificate program: (612) 853-5686, FAX: (612) 853-4409.

  Sault College of Applied Arts and Technology, School of Engineering, Sault Ste. Marie, ON, Canada. Diploma in Electronic Engineering. (705) 759-2554.

  Sheridan College of Applied Arts and Technology, Sheridan College Telecom Management Program, Oakville, ON, Canada. Certificate in telecommunications management. (905) 845-9430.

  Simon Fraser University, Communications Department, Burnaby, BC, Canada. Master in communications. (604) 291-3520.
* **Southern Methodist University**, School of Engineering and Applied Science, Dallas, TX. Associate and bachelor degrees in various telecommunications orientations. (214) 768-3113, FAX: (214) 768-3573.
* **Stevens Institute of Technology**, Department of Electrical and Computer Engineering, Hoboken, NJ. Certificate in telecommunications management, master degree in telecommunications management and a doctorate in telecommunications management. (201) 216-8938, FAX: (201) 216-8246.
* **SUNY Institute of Technology at Utica/Rome**, Institute of Technology, Telecommunications Program, Utica, NY. Bachelor and master degrees in telecommunications. Interdisciplinary programs. (315) 792-7149, FAX: (315) 792-7800.

Syracuse University, Telecommunications and Network Management, Syracuse, NY. Master degree in telecommunications and network management. (315) 443-2911.

Technical University of Nova Scotia, Department of Electrical and Computer Engineering, Halifax, NS, Canada. Offers bachelor, master, and doctorate programs in engineering or applied science. (902) 420-7721.

* **Texas A&M University**, Department of Engineering Technology, Telecom Course, College Station, TX. Bachelor, (409) 847-9396, FAX: (409) 845-5966; and master, (409) 845-5169, FAX: (409) 845-9396, in telecommunications. Master degree includes management courses from MBA program.

University of Alabama Tuscaloosa, Department of Telecommunications and Film, Tuscaloosa, AL. Master degree in communications technology and doctorate of education in communications policy. (205) 348-6300.

University of Alberta, Department of Electrical and Computer Engineering, Edmonton, AB, Canada. Bachelor, master, and doctorate programs in engineering. (403) 492-3332.

University of British Columbia, Vancouver, BC, Canada. Bachelor, master, and doctorate degrees in information systems. Management orientation. (604) 822-8395.

* **University of Colorado at Boulder**, Interdisciplinary Telecom Program, Boulder, CO. Associate, bachelor, and master programs in electrical engineering and MBA. Interdisciplinary and international orientation. Provide internships. Oldest master program. (303) 492-8225, FAX: (303) 492-1112.

* **University of Denver**, Telecommunications, Denver, CO. Certificate, bachelor or master programs in telecommunications. An interdisciplinary and nontraditional program. (303) 871-3964, FAX: (303) 871-4047.

* **University of Houston-Clear Lake**, School of Natural and Applied Science, Houston, TX. Telecommunications option for bachelor or master degrees in computer science. (281) 283-3879, FAX: (281) 283-3870.

* **University of Kansas**, Telecommunication and Information Sciences Laboratory, Lawrence, KS. Bachelor, master, or doctorate programs in electrical engineering or computer science. (913) 864-7762, FAX: (913) 864-7789.

University of Maryland, College Park, MD. Master program in telecommunications. Designed for midcareer professionals. (301) 405-3683, Fax (301) 405-3751.

* **University of Miami**, School of Business Administration, Coral Gables, FL. Master. (305) 284-5161, FAX: (305) 284-5161.

* **University of Mississippi**, Center for Telecommunications, University, MS. Bachelor of engineering in telecommunications. (601) 232-7779, FAX: (601) 232-7796.

* **University of Missouri-Kansas City**, Computer Science-Telecommunications Program, Kansas City, MO. Bachelor in computer science and telecommunications, master in telecommunications, and doctorate in computer networking and telecommunications. Internships are available. (816) 235-2399.
* **University of Nebraska-Kearney**, Telecommunications Program, Department of Industrial Technology, Kearney, NE. Bachelor. (308) 865-8504, FAX: (308) 865-8976.

   University of New Brunswick, Business Administration, Fredericton, NB, Canada. Bachelor and master programs in business administration with technology orientation. (506) 453-4869.

   University of Ottawa, Computer Science, Ottawa, ON, Canada. Bachelor, master, and doctorate programs in computer science with emphasis on computer networking. (613) 562-5826.
* **University of Pittsburgh**, Department of Information Science in Telecommunications, Pittsburgh, PA. Certificate and master degree in telecommunications. Internships available. (412) 624-9432, FAX: (412) 624-5231.
* **University of San Francisco**, Mclaren College of Business Telecom Management and Policy, San Francisco, CA. Master degree in business administration with emphasis in telecommunications. (415) 422-6711, FAX: (415) 422-2502.
* **University of Southwestern Louisiana**, Department of Electrical and Computer Engineering, Center for Telecom, Layfayette, LA. Bachelor in electrical engineering with telecommunications option and master in telecommunications. Master degree is interdisciplinary. Internships are offered. (318) 482-6472, FAX: (318) 482-6687.

   University of Toronto, Information Studies (MIST), Toronto, ON, Canada. Master and doctorate degrees in information studies. (416) 978-3234.

   Washington University, Information Management Program, School of Engineering and Applied Science, St. Louis, MO. Bachelor and master of information management and master of telecommunications management. (314) 935-5484, FAX: (314) 935-5449.

   West Virginia University, Department of Education Program in Telecommunications, Morgantown, WV. Master of education in communications technology and doctorate of education in communications policy. (304) 293-2852.
* **Western Michigan University**, Telecommunications management program, Kalamazoo, MI. Bachelor and master degrees. (616) 387-3182, FAX: (616) 387-3990.

---

* Affiliated with International Communications Association.

Chapter 30
Staying Updated with Media, Shows, and Seminars

John M. Lusa

INTRODUCTION

In the networking industry where six months is a long time, keeping abreast of fast-changing technology enhancements is imperative. Those who deal with enterprise networks cannot really rest on their laurels even after they have updated their networks with what they think is an infusion of the latest technological developments.

Technology executives and network managers need a well thought out proactive plan to contend with the tidal wave flood of information that continually spews forth. A great amount of information is created on a daily basis, so much so that it can literally be overwhelming to a lonely technology user. What complicates the situation even more is that the source of technological information is varied and widespread. It includes trade publications, World Wide Web sites, vendor literature, vendor presentations, vendor user groups, nonaffiliated user associations, trade shows, conferences, and seminars.

Keeping a copy of this publication, *The Network Manager's Handbook*, close by is a start. However, more is needed. A program for keeping up might be considered a big part of your personnel training plan or simply an information gathering plan. In either case, it should be given formal financial support and be included in your departmental budget.

FORMAL PLAN

The important point is to have a formal plan to separate the wheat from the chaff. There is so much information being generated, and not all of it is applicable to your network operation. Regardless of the size of your staff, it is probably a good idea to divide up the responsibility among all the members of your team or department. Possibly set aside a time during regularly scheduled weekly or monthly staff meetings to review the information collected.

In any case, what you and your staff are seeking is to optimize your valuable time and to avoid duplicating your efforts. At the same time, you need to set up a system to distribute the applicable information among your staff members. For instance, divide up responsibility for the various trade publications that you and your staff receive. The most prevalent complaint heard from technology professionals is that they receive too many publications and there is not time to read them all. That is true. Thus, assign publications to various staff members to read and they can report out what they found important to other staff members.

There is quite a bit of duplication among these sources of information. That is another pertinent reason for dividing up responsibility. This division of labor may also be along subject matter lines, depending on the work specialty of staff members (i.e., software, hardware, disaster recovery systems, network management systems, network security, and many others). This same type of arrangement can be made with vendor presentations, trade shows, seminars, and conferences.

The various types of information sources are reviewed in the following paragraphs. They are not an exhaustive study of the topics but are meant as starting points for developing an effective training and information gathering program.

TRADE AND TECHNICAL PUBLICATIONS

Paid vs. Controlled

A wide range and number of publications are available to managers and technologists in charge of their enterprise's information and networking systems. The first difference to be noticed is that they have either paid or controlled (nonpaid) circulation. In actuality, controlled means free.

There is no particular pattern as to the type of publication and its method of circulation. The fact that a publication is paid or free does not necessarily reflect its quality. On one hand, anyone can buy a subscription to a paid circulation, while a controlled circulation requires a completion of a lengthy questionnaire once a year.

Those publications that require readers to pay for a subscription tend to have a more eclectic reading audience. In actuality they will write their editorial content with a particular audience in mind. For instance, the weekly newspaper, *Computerworld*, is paid circulation and its readers are generally in charge of large enterprise information systems.

Network World and *Internet Week* (formerly *Communications Week*) on the other hand, are controlled circulation weekly newspapers. Controlled circulation means publishers control who reads their papers. Generally, they seek readers who are in charge of or operate large enterprise networks. The purpose of their yearly questionnaires is to weed out those not qualified to read the magazine. In this manner, they can guarantee to their advertisers a specific type of audience.

There might be some concern on the readers' part about the unbiased viability of the editorial content of paid vs. controlled publications. Even though it may appear that paid subscriptions are less influenced by advertiser pressure, it is not necessarily true. Revenue from subscriptions represents only a small percentage of the overall revenue, generally in the range of 10 to 20%. Most of the remainder is from advertising revenue. As a result, selecting a paid circulation is no assurance you will receive objective and nonbiased editorial content.

Association Publications

There is a third type of circulation orientation for publications. This type falls into the broad classification of association publications. These are less numerous than the other types, but have an important role in the scheme of things.

These publications tend to be more focused on member interests and generally carry less advertising than independent publications. An example of an association publication is the *Communication of the ACM*, which is published by the Association for Computing Machinery. The editorial staffs of the association publications are a varying mixture of paid professional journalists and association members.

Publication Content

Within the context of information systems or networking technology, publications range in editorial content from general news to specialized, as well as from management to technical. Most tabloid-sized publications tend to be news-oriented. On the other hand, slick formatted magazines vary from news to specialized technical.

InfoWorld is a weekly tabloid that provides both news and product information for personal computer (PC) and local area network (LAN) users, while *Information Week* is a slick weekly magazine that emphasizes mostly topics of interest to information systems management, with very little emphasis on product information. *Government Computer News* essentially delivers what its title indicates.

See Appendix B for contact information on a number of selected publications.

TRADE SHOWS

A common form of information gathering is to attend an industry show. There are a number of them. Some are large and general in nature, such as the ComNet show, held annually during midwinter in Washington, D.C. In 1998, ComNet debuted a West Coast version in San Francisco. Another large show is Netwold+Interop, held twice a year, generally in Las Vegas and Atlanta, with more emphasis on networking, LAN, and interoperability. Both shows have international versions, held in other countries. Specific information on those shows and others follow this section of the chapter.

First some advice on getting the most out of trade show attendance follows.

Effective Show Going

Haphazard, unfocused attendance at trade shows is both a waste of time and costly, while effective trade show participation can generate profitable information for a person individually and for the enterprise network organization. Whether one person or a group attends a trade show, the basic fundamentals for optimizing are the same with a few differences.

The key to effective trade show attendance is preplanning well in advance of the show. One thing you can depend on is that leading shows are scheduled well ahead of time. This gives attendees an opportunity to plan their participation. Early registration usually means a lower conference fee if one is a part of the show and many times free entry to the exhibition.

Preplanning includes investigating airfares. The larger shows usually have made special arrangements with a number of airlines for special rates. Early registrants also have an early opportunity to reserve the less expensive hotels. Considering how little time is spent at a hotel while at a trade show, there is not much to gain from staying at the more expensive hotels. Keep in mind that the larger trade shows usually provide shuttle bus service from all show-affiliated hotels to the exhibit hall. An important advantage of early registration is that most shows now mail the show badge and registration material to attendees in advance of the show. Avoiding the registration line at the show can be a big time-saver.

Effective attendance requires having specific goals in mind of what is expected to be learned from a show or conference. Select the exhibitors that are to be visited. Look up their booth numbers and put them in some form of priority and order. Keep in mind that if you are also attending any conference sessions, this takes away from your exhibit floor time. If more than one person from an organization is attending, divide up the responsibility in the same manner suggested earlier for publications.

Decide in advance which group of vendors each person is to visit. Gather literature, if you wish, but keep in mind that you can only carry so much. Do not hesitate to ask the exhibitors to send you literature. Plan daily meetings with your colleagues to compare notes. If you plan to attend conference sessions, you need to schedule them carefully, keeping in mind that they are usually held at the same time the exhibit floor is open. Some shows will have openings in the conference schedule to provide a limited amount of time to view the exhibit floor.

The following is a partial list of shows of interest to network managers. Without exception, these shows are publicized and advertised in industry publications.

Trade Shows for Network Managers

ComNet. This important show for network and information system, managers was founded in 1979 and is held in January or early February annually in the Convention Center, Washington, D.C. Owned by International Data Group (IDG), it attracts over 40,000 management-oriented visitors and has a full range of conference sessions, tutorials, and keynote addresses directed to them. More than 500 companies are represented in the huge exhibition halls, taking every available inch of space in the center. An early fall version is now held in San Francisco.

For show information, contact: ComNet, 1400 Providence Highway, P.O. Box 9103, Norwood, MA 02062-9103; (800) 545-3976, FAX: (617) 440-0359, or www.comnetexpo.com.

Networld+Interop. This is another important show that was founded in 1986 as the Transmission Control Protocol (TCP)/Internet Protocol (IP) Interoperability (Interop) conference. A few years ago it merged with the LAN-focused Networld show and is now offered twice annually, usually in the fall in Atlanta and in the spring in Las Vegas. Without any doubt, this is the premier networking show. In excess of 40,000 attend both versions of the show, with well over 500 networking companies in huge exhibit halls. This show tends to attract those who are more technologically oriented and are the implementers of networks from LANs to WANs. The show is owned by Softbank Exposition and Conference Co.

For show information, contact Networld+Interop, P.O. Box 5855, San Mateo, CA 94402-0855; (800) 488-2883, FAX: (415) 525-0199, or www.interop.com.

SUPERCOMM. This huge industry show is primarily directed at telephone companies and communication carriers, but it has a strong end-user orientation as well. The International Communications Association conducts it annual conference in conjunction with it. In addition, there are a large number of exhibitors in a special section of interest to end users.

499

Overall, there were 650 exhibitors at the most recent show. This annual show changes it venue. Most recently it appeared in Atlanta, GA. Other recent sites have been in New Orleans, LA; Dallas, TX; and Anaheim, CA. Sponsors are the Telecommunications Industry Association and the United States Telephone Association.

For show information, contact SUPERCOMM, 2500 Wilson Boulevard, Suite 300, Arlington, VA 22201; (800) 278-7372, FAX: (703) 903-7746, or www.super-comm.com.

CMA Telcom. This is a respected regional show that is always held in the New York Hilton & Towers Hotel, New York, NY, and is sponsored by Communications Managers Association, a group of telecommunications and network managers of large enterprises in the New York metropolitan area. The show includes a conference and fairly large exhibition hall.

For show information, contact CMA Telecom, 1201 Mt. Kemble Avenue, Morristown, NJ 07960-6628; (800) 262-3976, FAX: (201) 425-0777, or www.cma.org.

Other Shows of Importance

TCA, sponsored by Telecommunications Association, was held in late summer of 1998 in Reno, NV. Contact TCA Office, 74 New Montgomery, Suite 30, San Francisco, CA 94105-3411; (415) 777-4647, FAX: (415) 777-5295, or www.tca.org.

Call Center, sponsored by Technology for Call Center Solutions, was held in Los Angeles during the spring of 1998. Contact Technology Marketing Corp., 1 Technology Plaza, Norwalk, CT 66854; (800) 243-6002, FAX: (203) 863-22845, or www.tmcnet.com.

INTER COMM is an annual congress and exhibition for communication and IT executives. In early 1999 the show is to be held in Vancouver, Canada, and is to be sponsored by Horizon House Publications, 685 Canton Street, Norwood, MA 20262; (781) 769-9750, FAX: (781) 255-9211, or www.intercomm99.com.

ITCA annual Teleconferencing Convention and Exhibition, sponsored by the International Teleconferencing Association, was held in Washington, D.C., early in the summer of 1998. Contact ITC, 1650 Tysons Boulevard, Suite 200, McLean, VA 22102; (703) 506-3280, FAX: (703) 506-3266.

Telecon Teleconferencing Users Conference is produced by Applied Business TeleCommunications and sponsored by U.S. Distance Learning Association, P.O. Box 5106, San Ramon, CA 94583; (800) 829-3400, FAX: (405) 743-3426, or www.usdla.org/telecon.html.

Computer Telephony Expo is sponsored by *Computer Telephony* magazine, 12 West 21st Street, New York, NY 10010; (800) 999-0345, FAX: (212) 691-1191, or www.ctexpo.com.

CONFERENCES AND SEMINARS

Trade shows tend to be megaevents with big halls, big crowds, and dozens of sessions and tutorials. As valuable as they are, they can be intimidating to approach and frustrating to effective information gathering. It is difficult to attend a big show and not come away thinking you may have missed something. On the other hand, there are focused seminars and conferences with a limited number of attendees and held in quiet, comfortable settings. These events tend to deal within a narrow focus of technology. They provide an opportunity to hone in on a topic or area of interest with a great deal of efficiency.

The sponsors and producers of these specialized seminars and conferences represent a wide range of interests. They include vendors, specialized trainers, consultants, research firms, associations, and even universities. The fees for the specialized training vehicles range from a few hundred dollars for a day or two to thousands at an exotic resort.

The value of these events is not so much in how much is charged but in the quality of the instructional staff and presenters and their affiliations. Interestingly, once you place your name on the circulation list of either a controlled or paid publication you become a target of the promotion. It thus becomes important to evaluate the instructors and their track records. The affiliation of the seminar producers is not necessarily an indication of their value. Being independent or affiliated with a university, an association, a publisher, or a vendor is not necessarily an indicator of value.

The real value of these types of training devices is the ability to come up to speed quickly on a new or unfamiliar technology. Generally, the class or session sizes are small enough for some individual attention. Many of the seminars provide actual hands-on instruction. Thus, the value is determined not as much by the cost, whether in the hundreds or thousands of dollars, but in how that instruction fits your needs at a particular moment in time.

It might be more cost-effective to train one of your own staffers rather than trying to hire someone with that experience. With the number of seminars and conferences that are available, it is becoming easy enough to match one that fits your objectives and need.

Generally, the course fee or tuition includes a course binder, meals, and supplies in cases of a hands-on situation. Discounts may be provided for multiple registrations. Some seminar providers and consultants will bring the instruction on-site if there are enough students to make it worthwhile. This arrangement has the value of saving traveling and accommodation expenses. The big disadvantage of an on-site program is that students may slip away from the training sessions to perform their regular duties, as a result, missing some valuable instruction.

501

What follows is just a sampling. This list is not meant to be all inclusive, but to provide some idea of the various types of instructional programs that are available.

Understanding Computer Telephony Integrations is presented in various cities by Advanced Information Technologies, 150 Clove Road, P.O. Box 401, Little Falls, NJ 47424-0401. It is a two-day interactive seminar for $895. (800) 882-8684, or www.iqpc.com/ait.

Understanding Voice/Data Communications is presented in various cities by Alexander Hamilton Institute, 306 High Street, P.O. Box 994, Hackettstown, NJ 07840. It is a two-day seminar for $695. (908) 852-3699, FAX: (908)852-2751, or www.ahinst.com.

Hands-On Network Training is presented in various cities by American Research Group Inc., 114 Edinburgh South, Suite 200, P.O. Box 1039, Cary, NC 27512. For the two- to five-day program in over 40 courses, prices range from $995 for two days to $1695 for 5 days. (919) 461-8600, FAX: (919) 461-8646, or www.arg.com.

Seminars in Network Technologies are presented in various cities by BCR Enterprises Inc., 950 York Road, Suite 203, Hinsdale, IL 60421-2939. Hands-on instruction is offered. Prices range from $1095 for a two-day course to $1595 for a four-day course. (800) 227-1234, FAX: (630) 323-5324, or www.bcr.com.

Integrated Hands-On Networking Seminars are presented in various cities by KAZCOM, 1006 Rene Court, Park Ridge, IL 60068. It also offers TCP/IP certification and computer-based training. Prices range from $795 for two days to $1075 for three days. (800) 444-0543, FAX: (847) 692-5792, or www.kazteach.com.

Telecommunications for the Business Professional is a two-day workshop for $745 in various cities held by The Pelorus Group, 33 Second Street, Suite J, Raritan, NJ 08869; (908) 707-1121, FAX: (908) 707-1135.

Summer program on contemporary networking issues at the University of Colorado is a six-day program sponsored by the International Communications Association, 2735 Villa Creek Drive, Suite 200, Dallas, TX 752234-7419. (800) 422-4636, FAX: (972) 488-9985.

Fundamentals of Telecommunications is a 2-day, $995 seminar in various cities, sponsored by Data-Tech Institute, P.O. Box 2429, Clifton, NJ 07015. (201) 478-5400, FAX: (201) 478-4418, or www.datatech.com.

Telecommunications seminars are presented in various cities by Bellcore, TEC, Room F100, 6200 Route 53, Lisle, IL 60532. Prices vary starting at $695 for two days to $1195 for three days. Off-site instruction is available. (800) 832-2463, FAX: (630) 960-6160, or www.bellcore.com.

Technical seminars are one-day seminars on networking subjects presented in various cities by *Network World* magazine, Professional Development Group, 161 Worcester Road, Framingham, MA 01701-9172.

Price is $450. (800) 643-4668, FAX: (508) 820-1283, or www.nwfusion.com/ seminars.

Webtorials on Frame Relay, ATM, and other subjects also include specialized on-site training. These are distributed by Networking Associates, 2707 Lake Forest Drive, Greensboro, NC 27408. (336) 288-3858, FAX: (336) 370-1437, or www.webtorials.com.

USING RESEARCH FIRMS

Another effective method for gathering technology information is to have others do it for you. There are a number of firms that specialize in researching and disseminating high-technology topics. They are quoted quite often in the technology press as well as the general business press.

These research firms specialize in identifying user needs, analyzing technology vendors, assessing technology, and interpreting market trends. Generally, they do this in support of client needs for strategic planning, business development, and industry marketing requirements. They operate and offer their services in a variety of ways.

Clients can subscribe to a full range of services to assist in making key decisions. This advice can come in the form of extensive reports on selected technology subjects, customized briefings, conferences, symposia, audioconferences, videoconferences, and vendor exhibitions. Clients may also receive late-breaking news, analysis, flash reports, and other information through faxes, e-mail, the Web, CD-ROMs, Lotus Notes, and even telephone calls, depending on the subscribed level of service.

The full range of services can cost tens of thousands of dollars a year. For those clients whose information systems and networking budgets are in the millions of dollars a year, subscribing to these research services may represent a necessary investment to maintain a competitive system and to protect against obsolescence.

It is possible to take advantage of major research without subscribing to the full range of services offered by research firms. Specific technology reports are available for a few thousand dollars, or it may be possible to attend specific briefings or symposia. Some firms may offer separate services or individual reports or will customize their services to fit a client's needs. Most of the major firms operate throughout the world and maintain global offices. Some of the leading firms follow:

Aberdeen Group Inc., One Boston Place, Boston, MA 02108. (617) 723-7890, FAX: (617) 723-7897, or www.aberdeen.com.
Datapro USA, 600 Delran Parkway, Delran, NJ 08075. (800) 328-2776, FAX: (609) 764-2812, or www.datapro.com.
Forrester Research Inc., 1033 Massachusetts Avenue, Cambridge, MA 02138. (617) 497-7090, FAX: (617) 868-0577, or www.forrester.com.

Gartner Group Inc., 56 Top Gallant Road, Stamford, CT 06904-2212. (203) 964-0096, FAX: (203) 316-1100, or www.gartner.com.
International Data Corp., 5 Speen Street, Framingham, MA 01701. (508) 872-8200, FAX: (508) 935-4015, or www.idcresearch.com.
Meta Group Inc., 208 Harbor Drive, Stamford, CT. (203) 973-6700 or www.Metagroup.com.
Yankee Group, 200 Portland Street, Boston, MA 02114-1715. (617) 956-5000, FAX: (617) 956-5004, or www.yankeegroup.com.

Section IX
Appendices

Appendix A
Selected Vendors and Manufacturers in the Networking and Communications Industries

3Com Corp.
P.O. Box 58145
5400 Bayfront Plaza
Santa Clara, CA 95052
(408) 764-5000
FAX: (408) 764-5001

3Com Broadband Access Division
(formerly OnStream Networks)
3393 Octavius Drive
Santa Clara, CA 95054
(408) 727-4545
FAX: (408) 727-5151

Acacia Networks
650 Suffolk Street
Lowell, MA 01854
(508) 458-7200
FAX: (508) 458-4277
www.abirnet.com

ACC (Advanced Computer Communications)
340 Storke Road
Santa Barbara, CA 93117
(805) 685-4455
FAX: (805) 685-4465
info@acc.com

Acclaim Communications Inc.
5000 Old Ironsides Drive
Santa Clara, CA 95054
(408) 327-0100
FAX: (408) 327-0106
Inffo@aaclaim.com

Accord Video Telecommunications
45 Executive Drive
Plainview, NY 11803
(516) 349-8100
FAX: (516) 349-8101

ACE*COMM
209 Perry Parkway
Gaithersburg, MD 20877
(301) 258-9850
FAX: (301) 921-0434
info@acec.com

ACT Networks Inc.
188 Camino Ruiz
Camarillo, CA 93012
(805) 388-2474
FAX: (805) 987-2105
www.acti.com

Adaptec Inc.
691 South Milpitas Boulevard
Milpitas, CA 95035
(408) 945-8600
FAX: (408) 262-2533

ADC Kentrox
14375 Northwest Science Park Drive
Portland, OR 97229
(503) 643-1681
FAX: (503) 641-3341
info@kentrox.com
www.kentrox.com

ADP Autonet
175 Jackson Place
Ann Arbor, MI 48103
(313) 769-6800
FAX: (313) 995-6458

Adtech Inc.
3465 Waialae Avenue, Suite 200
Honolulu, HI 96816
(808) 734-3300
FAX: (808) 734-7100
contact@adtech-inc.com

ADTRAN
901 Explorer Boulevard
Huntsville, AL 35806
(205) 971-8000
FAX: (205) 971-8699

Alcoa Fujikura Ltd.
P.O. Box 3127
Spartanburg, SC 29304
(864) 433-0333
FAX: (864) 433-5353
afifiber@ssw.alcoa.com

American Power Conversion (APC)
132 Fairgrounds Road
West Kingston, RI 02892
(401) 789-5735
FAX: (401) 788-2739

American Technology Labs Inc.
10097 Tyler Place, Suite 1
Ijamsville, MD 21754
(301) 695-1547
FAX: (301) 874-3465
info@atli.com

Ameritech
225 West Randolph, Suite 17C
Chicago, IL 60606
(800) 840-8444
FAX: (312) 364-3485
www.ameritech.com

AMP
P.O. Box 3608
Harrisburg, PA 17105
(800) 835-7240
FAX: (910) 727-5735

Andrew Corp.
10500 West 143rd Street
Orland Park, IL 60462
(708) 349-3300 or (800) 328-2696
FAX: (708) 349-5673
www.andrew.com

Applied Photonic Devices Inc.
P.O. Box 118
Danielson, CT 06239
(800) 774-1248
FAX: (860) 774-2571

Ascend Communications Inc.
One Ascend Plaza
1701 Harbor Bay Parkway
Alameda, CA 94502-3002
(510) 7696001 or (800) 621-9578
FAX: (510) 747-2635

Ascom Timeplex
400 Chestnut Ridge Road
Woodcliff Lake, NJ 07675
(201) 391-1111
FAX: (201) 391-0852

Astrocom Corporation
2700 Summer Street
Northeast Minneapolis, MN 55413-2820
(612) 378-7800
FAX: (612) 378-1070
info@astrocorp.com

AT&T
400A Pierce Street
Somerset, NJ 08873
(908) 356-1790
FAX: (908) 356-3392

AT&T Capital Corp.
1830 West Airfield Drive
DFW Airport, TX 85261
(800) 874-71 23
FAX: (972) 456-4002
ids@attcapital.com

Avetel Inc.
2009 Renaissance Boulevard
King of Prussia, PA 19406-2763
(610) 239-7300
FAX: (610) 278-6668

Bay Networks Inc.
8 Federal Street
Billerica, MA 01821
(508) 670-8888
FAX: (508) 436-8442
www.baynetworks.com

BDM International Inc.
1501 BDM Way
McLean, VA 22102-3204
(800) 955-2361
FAX: (703) 848-6101

Belden Wire and Cable Co.
2200 U.S. Highway 27 South
Richmond, IN 47374
(317) 983-5200 or (800) 235-3362
FAX: (317) 983-5257

Bellcore
8 Corporate Place
Piscataway, NJ 08854
(800) 521-2673, in New Jersey
  (908) 699-5800
www.bellcore.com

Bellsouth
3535 Colonnade Parkway
Birmingham, AL 35243
(205) 977-5215
FAX: (205) 977-1513

Berk Tek
132 White Oak Road
New Holland, PA 17557
(717) 354-6200
FAX: (717) 354-7944

Biscom Inc.
321 Billerica Road
Chelmsford, MA 01824
(508) 250-1800
FAX: (508) 250-4449
sales@biscom.com
www.biscom.com

Black Box Corp.
1000 Park Drive
Lawrence, PA 15102
(412) 873-6812
FAX: (412) 873-6817

Branch DataComm
2127 Espey Court, Suite 110
Crofton, MD 21114
(410) 451-2077
FAX: (410) 451-2080

BTR Telecom
Division RIA Electronic Inc.
P.O. Box 447
430 Industrial Way
West Eatontown, NJ 07724
(888) 722-5625
FAX: (908) 389-9066

Bull Information Systems
Technology Park Drive
Billerica, MA 01821
(800) 285-5727
FAX: (508) 294-6109
www-ism.bull.com/ism

C & L Communications Inc.
26254 I-H West
Boerne, TX 78006
(210) 698-3380
FAX: (210) 698-0077

Cablesoft Inc.
1156 West Shore Drive
Arlington Heights, IL 60004
(847) 797-1300:
FAX: (847) 342-9663
cablesoftk@aol.com

Cabletron Systems
35 Industrial Way
Rochester, NH 03867
(603) 332-9400
www.cabletron.com

CACI Products Co.
3333 North Torrey Pines Court
La Jolla, CA 92037
(619) 824-5200
FAX: (619) 457-1184

Cambio Networks Inc.
(formerly ISICAD)
4800 Great America Parkway,
  Suite 415
Santa Clara, CA 95054
(408) 567-1400
FAX: (408) 567-1401
info@cambio.com

Canoga Perkins Corp.
21012 Lassen Street
Chatsworth, CA 91311
(818) 718-6300
FAX: (818) 718-6312

Carrier Access Corp.
5395 Pearl Parkway
Boulder, CO 80301
(303) 442-5455
FAX: (303) 546-9724

Cascade Communications Corp.
5 Carlisle Road
Westford, MA 01886
(508) 692-2600
FAX: (508) 692-5052
http://www.casc.com

Chatsworth Product Inc.
9541 Mason Avenue
Chatsworth, CA 91311-5201
(818) 882-8595
FAX: (818) 718-0473

Chesilvale Electronics Ltd.
222 Antelope Drive
P.O. Box 1317
Sedona, AZ 86339-1317
(520) 282-6180
FAX: (520) 282-7270

**Chromatic Technologies/Helix/
  HiTemp Cables Inc.**
20 Forge Park
Franklin, MA 02038
(508) 541-7100
FAX: (508) 541-8122

Cisco Systems Inc.
170 West Tasman Drive
San Jose, CA 95134
(408) 526-4000
FAX: (408) 526-4100

Coastcom
1151 Harbor Bay Parkway
Alameda, CA 94502
(510) 523-6000
FAX: (510) 523-6150

ComByte USA
5415 Easton Drive No. 101
Springfield, VA 22151-3455
(703) 866-0000 or (800) 446-3634
FAX: (703) 750-3779
combyte@beryls.com

CommScope
3642 U.S. Highway
70 East Claremont, NC 28610
(704) 459-5000
FAX: (704) 459-5099

Communication Devices Inc.
1 Forstmann Court
Clifton, NJ 07011
(201) 772-6997 or (800) 359-8561
FAX: (201) 772-0747
info@commdevices com
www.com mdevices.com

Compaq Computer Corp.
20555 State Highway 249
Houston, TX 77070
(713) 370-0670
FAX: (713) 514-1740
www.compaq.com

CompuServe Network Services
5000 Britton Road
Hilliard, OH 43026
(614) 723-1070
FAX: (614) 723-1643

Compuware Corp.
31440 Northwestern Highway
Farmington Hills, MI 48334
(810) 737-7300
FAX: (810) 737-7513

Computer Associates International Inc.
One Computer Associates Plaza
Islandia, NY 11788
(516) 342-5224
FAX: (516) 342-6866
www.cai.com

Comtest Inc.
600 West Germantown Pike,
  Suite 400
Plymouth Meeting, PA 19462-1046
(610) 940-1710 or (800) 940-1710
FAX: (215) 619-8811
www.comtest-int.com

Comtrol Corp.
900 Long Lake Road, No. 210
Saint Paul, MN 55112
(612) 631-7654
FAX: (612) 631-8117
info@comtrol.com

Concord Communications Inc.
33 Boston Post Road West
Marlboro, MA 01752
(508) 460-4646
FAX: (508) 481-9772
info@concord.com
www.concord.com

CrossComm Corp.
450 Donald Lynch Boulevard
Marlboro, MA 01752
(508) 229-5300 or (800)`701-4220
FAX: (508) 229-5535
www.crosscom.com

511

CUBIC VideoComm
9333 Balboa Avenue
San Diego, CA 92123
(619) 505-2030
FAX: (619) 505-1508

Cubix Corp.
2800 Lockheed Way
Carson City, NV 89706
(702) 888-1000 or (800) 829-0550
FAX: (702) 888-1001
www.cubix.com

CXR Telcom
2040 Fortune Drive, Suite 102
San Jose, CA 95131
(408) 435-8520
FAX: (408) 435-1276

Cybex Computer Products Corp.
4912 Research Drive
Huntsville, AL 35805
(205) 430-4000
FAX: (205) 430-4030

Cylink Corp.
910 Hermosa Court
Sunnyvale, CA 94086
(408) 735-5800
FAX: (408) 735-6643
info@cycon.com
www.cylink.com

Data Communications Technologies
2200 Gateway Centre Boulevard
Morrisville, NC 27560
(919) 462-6540
FAX: (919) 462-0300

Data Labs Inc.
444 North Frederick Avenue,
Suite 240
Gaithersburg, MD 20877
(301) 840-8578
FAX: (301) 990-1344

Datacom Technologies
11001 31st Place West
Everett, WA 98204
(206) 355-0590 or (800) 468-5557
FAX: (206) 290-1600
www.datacomtech.com

Datacomm Management Sciences Inc.
25 Van Zant Street
East Norwalk, CT 06855-1790
(203) 838-7183
FAX: (203) 838-1751
dmsmtrx@aol.com

Datakey Inc.
407 West Travelers Trail
Burnsville, MN 55337
(612) 890-6850 or (888) DATAKEY
FAX: (612) 890-2726
sales@datakey.com

Data Race Inc.
12400 Network Boulevard
San Antonio, TX 78249
(210) 263-2000 or (800) 329-7223
FAX: (210) 263-3075
sismktg@datarace.com
www.datarace.com

Digicom Systems Inc.
188 Topaz Street
Milpitas, CA 95055
(408) 262-1277
FAX: (408) 262-1390
www.digicomsys.com

Digital Equipment Corp./Network Division
Digital Drive
Merrimack, NH 03054
(603) 884-3110
FAX: (603) 884-5299

Digital Lightwave Inc.
601 Cleveland Street, Fifth Floor
Clearwater, FL 34615
(813) 442-6677
FAX: (813) 442-5660

Digital Link Corp.
217 Humbolt Court
Sunnyvale, CA 94089
(408) 745-6200
FAX: (408) 745-6250
www.dl.com

Digitech Industries Inc.
P.O. Box 2267
55 Kenosia Avenue
Danbury, CT 06813-2267
(203) 797-2676
FAX: (203) 797-2682

Dynatech Communications Inc.
12560 Darby Brooke Court
Woodbridge, VA 22192
(703) 494-1400
FAX: (703) 494-1920
www.dynatech.com

Eastern Research
225 Executive Drive
Moorestown, NJ 08057
(609) 273-6622
FAX: (609) 273
info@erinc.com
www.erinc.com

e-Net Inc.
12800 Middlebrook Road, Suite 200
Germantown, MD 20874-5204
(301) 601-8700
FAX: (301) 601-8777

Eicon Technology
14755 Preston Road, Suite 620
Dallas, TX 75244
(214) 239-32770
FAX: (792) 404-9314
www.eicon.com

Emcor Products/Crenlo Inc.
1600 4th Avenue Northwest
Rochester, MN 55901
(507) 289-3371
FAX: (507) 287-3405

Epilogue Technology Corp.
10501 Montgomery Northeast,
    Suite 250
Albuquerque, NM 87111
(505) 271-9933
FAX: (505) 271-9798
www.epilogue.com

EQUANT
3100 Cumberland Circle
Atlanta, GA 30339
(770) 612-4700
FAX: (770) 612-4710

Equinox Systems Inc.
One Equinox Way
Sunrise, FL 33351-6709
(800) 275-3500
FAX: (954) 746-9101

Ericsson Inc.
1010 East Arapaho Road
Richardson, TX 75083
Research Triangle Park, NC 27
(972) 583-0000 or (800) 227-3663
FAX: (972) 889-9846
www.ericsson.com

Essex Group Inc.
1710 Wall Street
P.O. Box 1750
Fort Wayne, IN 46801
(219) 461-4000
FAX: (219) 461-5660

FastComm Communications
45472 Holiday Drive
Sterling, VA 20166
(703) 318-7755
FAX: (703) 787-4625
info@fastcomm.com
www.fastcomm.com

Fenton Technologies Corp.
229 Laurel Road East
Northport, NY 11731
(800) 735-5877
FAX: (516) 261-0108
info@fentonups.com

Fiberdyne Labs Inc.
P.O. Box 906
Herkimer, NY 13350
(315) 866-0310
FAX: (315) 866-0341
www.fiberdyne.com

Fibertron Corp.
4601 Locust Lane, Suite 101
Harrisburg, PA 17109
(717) 652-6565
FAX: (717) 652-6677

Fluke Corp.
6920 Seaway Boulevard
Everett, WA 98203
(800) 443-5853
FAX: (206) 356-5043
www.fluke.com/nettools/

FORE Systems Inc.
174 Thorn Hill Road
Warrendale, PA 15086
(888) 404-0444
FAX: (412) 635-3625
info@fore.com
info@fore.com

France Telecom
1270 Avenue of the Americas
New York, NY 10020
(212) 332-2146
FAX: (212) 245-8605
www.francetelecom.com

Frederick Engineering Inc.
10200 Old Columbia Road
Columbia, MD 21046
(410) 290-9000
FAX: (410) 381-7180
fe@infocomm.net
www.fe.engr.com

Frontier Software
321 Billerica Road
Chelmsford, MA 01824
(508) 244-4000
FAX: (508) 244-4004
www.frontier.com

Gandalf Systems Corp.
501 Delran Parkway
Delran, NJ 08075
(800) GANDALF
FAX: (609) 461-4074
sales.queries@gandalf.ca
www.gandalf.ca

General Cable Corp.
4 Tesseneer Drive
Highland Heights, KY 41076
(606) 572-8000 or (800) 424-5666
FAX: (800) 547-8249

General DataComm Inc.
1579 Straits Turnpike
Middlebury, CT 06762-1299
(203) 574-1118
FAX: (203) 758-9468
www.gdc.com

General Signal Networks
13000 Midlantic Drive
Mount Laurel, NJ 08054
(609) 234-7900
FAX: (609) 778-8700
www.gsnetworks.com

GigaLabs Inc.
290 Santa Ana Court
Sunnyvale, CA 94086
(408) 481-3030
FAX: (408) 481-3045
info@gigalabs.com
www.gigalabs.com

GL Communications Inc.
841-F Quince Orchard Boulevard
Gaithersburg, MD 20878
(301) 670-4784
FAX: (301) 926-8234
gl-info@gl.com
www.gl.com/glcomm/

GN Nettest
6611 Bay Circle No. 190
Norcross, GA 30071
(770) 446-2665 or (800) 262-8835
FAX: (770) 446-2730
www.gnnettest.com

Graybar
34 North Meramec Avenue
Clayton, MO 63105
(314) 512-9200
FAX: (314) 512-9288

GRC International
1900 Gallows Road
Vienna, VA 22182
(703) 506-5000
FAX: (703) 893-0443
networkvue@grci.com

Hadax Electronics Inc.
310 Phillips Avenue South
Hackensack, NJ 07606
(201) 807-1155
FAX: (201) 807-1782
hadax@hadax.com
www.hadax.com

Hewlett Packard Co.
3000 Hanover Street
Palo Alto, CA 94304
(415) 857-1501 or (800) 752-5518
www.hp.com

Hitachi Internetworking
3101 Tasman Drive
Santa Clara, CA 95054
(408) 970-7024 or (800) HITACHI
FAX: (408) 988-0778
hi.customer@hitachi.com
www.internetworking.hitachi.com

Hubbell Premise Wiring
14 Lord's Hill Road
Stonington, CT 06378
(800) 626-0005
FAX: (860) 535-8328
salesinfo@hubbell-premise.com

Hughes Network Systems
11717 Exploration Lane
Germantown, MD 20876
(301) 428-5500 or (800) 467-3278
FAX (301) 428-1868
info@hns.com
www.hns.com

IBM Corp.
1001 Winstead Drive
Cary, NC 27513
(919) 301-3200
FAX: (919) 301-3055
wgeorgi@vnet.ibm.com

IdentiComm
5909 Hamilton Boulevard
Wescosville, PA 18106
(888) 667-7440
FAX: (610) 391-1343
simplify@identicomm.com
www.identicomm.com

Intel Corp.
5200 Northeast Elam Young
  Parkway
Hillsboro, OR 97124
(503) 264-7354 or (800) 538-3373
www.intel.com/comm-net/sns

Interconnect Systems Group Inc.
15 East Uwchlan Avenue
Exton, PA 19341
(610) 524-9622
FAX: (610) 524-9007

Interlink Technologies
1005 Sussex Boulevard
Broomall, PA 19008
(610) 328-0930
FAX: (610) 543-3055

International Data Sciences Inc.
475 Jefferson Boulevard
Warwick, RI 02886
(401) 737-9900
FAX: (401) 737-9911
idsdata@businesson.com

International Microwave Corp.
25 Van Zant Street
East Norwalk, CT 06855
(203) 857-4222
FAX: (203) 857-4234

Interphase Corp.
13800 Senlac
Dallas, TX 75234
(214) 654-5000
FAX: (214) 654-5500
fastnet@iphase.com
www.iphase.com

ISDNet Inc.
900 Lafayette Street, Suite 410
Santa Clara, CA 95050
(408) 260-3080
FAX: (408) 260-3090
www.isdnet.com

Jensen Tools Inc.
7815 South 46th Street
Phoenix, AZ 85044-5399
(800) 426-1194
FAX: (800) 366-9662

Jones Futurex Inc.
3715 Atherton Road
Rocklin, CA 95765
(916) 632-3456
FAX: (916) 632-3445

LANart Corp.
145 Rosemary Street
Needham, MA 02194
(617) 444-1994 or (800) 292-1994
FAX: (617) 444-3692
sales@lanart.com
www.lanart.com

LANCAST
12 Murphy Drive
Nashua, NH 03062
(603) 880-1833
FAX: (603) 881-9888
lancastl@aol.com

Lantronix
15353 Barranca Parkway
Irvine, CA 92618
(714) 453-3990
FAX: (714) 453-3995
www.lantronix.com

Larscom Inc.
4600 Patrick Henry Drive
Santa Clara, CA 95054
(408) 988-6600
FAX: (408) 986-8690
info@larscom.com
www.larscom.com

LCI International
8180 Greensboro Drive, Suite 800
McLean, VA 22102
(800) LCI-1911
FAX: (614) 798-6093

LDDS WorldCom
515 East Amite
Jackson, MS 39201
(601) 360-8600
FAX: (601) 974-8450
info@wcom.com
www.wcom.com

Learning Tree International
1805 Library Street
Reston, VA 20190
(800) 843-8733
FAX: (800) 709-6405

LeeMah DataCom Corp.
6200 Paseo Padre Parkway
Fremont, CA 94555-3601
(510) 608-0600
FAX: (510) 608-0688
www.leemah.com

Leviton Telcom
2222-222nd Street Southeast
Bothell, WA 98021
(206) 486-2222
FAX: (206) 487-9486

The Light Brigade Inc.
7691 South 180th Street
Kent, WA 98032
(206) 251-1240
FAX: (206) 251-1245
admin@lightbrigade.com

Linear Switch Corp.
225 Executive Drive, Unit 5
Moorestown, NJ 08057
(609) 273-8555
FAX: (609) 273-0522
www.viinc.com

Litton-FiberCom
3353 Orange Avenue, Northeast
Roanoke, VA 24012
(540) 342-6700
FAX: (540) 342-5961
info@fibercom.com

Lucent Technologies
600 Mountain Avenue
Murray Hill, NJ 07974-0636
(908) 582-8500
FAX: (908) 508-2576
(888) 4LUCENT
www.lucent.com

Madge Networks
2310 North First Street
San Jose, CA 95131-1011
(800) 876-2343
FAX: (408) 955-0970
www.madge.com

MCI
901 International Parkway
Richardson, TX 75081
(214) 498-1000
www.mci.com

Methode Electronics Inc.
7444 West Wilson Avenue
Chicago, IL 60656
(708) 867-9600
FAX: (708) 867-4140

MFS Communications Co. Inc.
55 South Market Street, Suite 1250
San Jose, CA 95113
(408) 975-2200
FAX: (408) 975-2210
info@mfst.com
www.mfst.com

MICOM Communications Corp.
4100 Los Angeles Avenue
Simi Valley, CA 93063
(805) 583-8600
FAX: (805) 583-1997
info@micom.com
www.micom.com

Microdyne Corp.
3601 Eisenhower Avenue
Alexandria, VA 22304
(703) 329-3700 or (800) 255-3967
FAX: (703) 329-3722
www.mcdy.com

MicroFrame Inc.
21 Meridian Road
Edison, NJ 08820
(908) 494-4440
FAX: (908) 494-4570

Microsoft Corp.
One Microsoft Way
Redmond, WA 98052
(206) 882-8080
FAX: (206) 936-7329
www.microsoft.com

Microtest Inc.
4747 North 22nd Street
Phoenix, AZ 85016
(602) 952-6400
FAX: (602) 952-6490
www.microtest.com

MIL3
3400 International Drive Northwest
Washington, DC 20008
(202) 364-4700
FAX: (202) 364-8554
info@mil3.com
www.mil3.com

Mitel Corp.
350 Legget Drive
P.O. Box 13089
Kanata, ON K2K 1X3
Canada
(613) 592-2122
FAX: (613) 591-2321
www.mitel.com

Mitsubishi Electronics America
5665 Plaza Drive
Cypress, CA 90630
(800) 843-2515
FAX: (714) 236-6339

MOD-TAP
285 Ayer Road
Harvard, MA 01451
(508) 772-5630
FAX: (508) 772-2011
www.mod-tap.com

Mohawk/CDT
9 Mohawk Drive
Leominster, MA 01453
(508) 537-9961
FAX: (508) 537-4358
sales@mohawk-cdt.com

Motorola Inc.
1303 East Algonquin Road
Schaumburg, IL 60196
(847) 576-5000 or (800) MOTOROL
ul792@e-mail.mot.com
www.mot.com

Multi-Tech Systems
2205 Woodale Drive
Mounds View, MN 55112
(612) 785-3500
FAX: (612) 785-9874
sales@multitech.com
www.multitech.com

Multilink Inc.
587 Ternes Avenue
Elyria, OH 44035
(216) 366-6966
FAX: (216) 366-6802
www.multilink.com

N.E.T.
800 Saginaw Drive
Redwood City, CA 94063
(415) 366-4400
FAX: (415) 366-5675
www.net.com

NBase Communications Inc.
8943 Fulbright Avenue
Chatsworth, CA 91311
(818) 773-0900 or (800) 858-7815
FAX: (818) 773-0906
info@nbase.com
www.nbase.com

NEC America Inc.
1555 West Walnut Hill Lane
Irving, TX 75038
(972) 518-5000
FAX: (972) 518-4982

Netcom Systems
20500 Nordhoff Street
Chatsworth, CA 91311
(818) 700-5100
FAX: (818) 709-7881
www.netcomsystems.com

NetEdge Systems Inc.
P.O. Box 14993
Research Triangle Park, NC 27709-
4993
(919) 991-9000
FAX: (919) 991-9060
www.netedge.com

Netlink Inc., a Cabletron Company
1881 Worcester Road
Framingham, MA 01701
(508) 879-6306
FAX: (508) 872-8136
info@netlink.com
www.netlink.com

NetManage Inc.
10725 North De Anza Boulevard
Cupertino, CA 95014
(408) 973-7171
FAX: (408) 257-8789
www.netmanage.com

NETRIX Corp.
13595 Dulles Technology Drive
Herndon, VA 20171-3424
(703) 793-2030
FAX: (703) 742-0523

Netscape Communications Corp.
501 East Middlefield Road
Mountain View, CA 94566
(415) 254-1900
FAX: (415) 528-4125

NetSoft/NSA
31 Technology Drive
Irvine, CA 92718
(800) 352-3270
FAX: (714) 753-0810
www.netsoft.com

NETSYS Technologies Inc.
100 Hamilton Avenue, Suite 175
Palo Alto, CA 94301
(415) 833-7500
FAX: (415) 833-7597
info@netsystech.com
www.netsystech.com

Network Analysis Center Inc.
45 Executive Drive, Suite GL3
Plainview, NY 11803
(516) 576-3200
FAX: (516) 576-3269
www.nacmind.com

Network Communications Corp.
5501 Green Valley Drive
Bloomington, MN 55437
(612) 844-0584
FAX: (612) 844-0487

Network General Corp.
4200 Bohannon Drive
Menlo Park, CA 94025
(415) 473-2000
FAX: (415) 473-2555 or (800) 764-3337
suggestions@ngc.com
www.ngc.com

Newbridge Networks
593 Herndon Parkway
Herndon, VA 20170
(800) 343-3600
FAX: (703) 471-7080
www.vivid.newbridge.com

Nippon Telegraph & Telephone Corp. (NTT)
101 Park Avenue, 41st Floor
New York, NY 10178
(212) 808-2239
FAX: (212) 661-1078
www.ipo.nttinfo.ntt.op

Nortel
4001 East Chapel Hill-Nelson
  Highway
Department 4355
Research Triangle Park, NC 27709
(800) 4-NORTEL
FAX: (800) 598-6726
www.nortel.com

Northrop Grumman Canada Ltd.
777 Walker's Line
Burlington, ON L7N 2G1
Canada
(905) 333-6000
FAX: (905) 333-6050

Novell Inc.
1555 North Technology Way
Orem, UT 84097-2399
(801) 222-6000 or (800) 453-1267
www.novell.com

Noyes Fiber Systems
Eastgate Park P.O. Box 398
Laconia, NH 03247
(603) 528-7780
FAX: (603) 528-2025

Nuera Communications Inc.
10445 Pacific Center Court
San Diego, CA 92121
(619) 625-2400
FAX: (619) 625-2422
info@nuera.com
www.nuera.com

Objective Systems Integrators
100 Blue Ravine Road
Folsom, CA 95630
(916) 353-2400
FAX: (916) 353-2417
www.osi.com

ODS Inc.
1101 East Arapaho
Richardson, TX 75081
(888) ODS-7770
FAX: (972) 301-3893

Olicom Inc.
900 East Park Boulevard, Suite 250
Plano, TX 75074
(800) 20LICOM
FAX: (972) 423-7261

Optical Cable Corp.
P.O. Box 11967
Roanoke, VA 24022-1967
(540) 265-0690
FAX: (540) 265-0724
www.occfiber.com

Orion Atlantic
2440 Research Boulevard, Suite 400
Rockville, MD 22094
(301) 258-3345
FAX: (301) 258-3222

Ortronics
595 Greenhaven Road
Pawcatuck, CT 06379
(860) 599-5555
FAX: (860) 599-0714
connect@ortronics.com
www.ortronocs.com

OST Inc.
14225 Sullyfield Circle
Chantilly, VA 22021
(703) 817-0400
FAX: (703) 817-0402
ecb@fastcomm.com

PairGain Technologies
14402 Franklin Avenue
Tustin, CA 92780
(714) 832-9922
FAX: (714) 832-9924
www.pairgain.com

Pan Dacom
 Telecommunications Inc.
200 Cottontail Lane
Somerset, NJ 08873
(908) 271-8680
FAX: (908) 271-8689
pandacom@worldnet.att.net

Panduit
17301 South Ridgeland Avenue
Tinley Park, IL 60477
(708) 532-1800
FAX: (708) 532-3998

Paradyne
8545 126th Avenue North
Largo, FL 33773
(813) 530-2000 or (800) 482-3333
FAX: (813) 530-2103
www.paradyne.com

Paragon Networks International
800 Main Street South
Southbury, CT 06488
(203) 264-4800
FAX: (203) 264-4808
marketing@paragon-networks.com
www.paragon-networks.com

Paralon Technologies Inc.
700 Fifth Avenue, Suite 6101
Seattle, WA 98104-5061
(206) 674-4800 or (800) PARALON
FAX: (206) 674-4801
info@paralon.com

Performance Technologies Inc.
315 Science Parkway
Rochester, NY 14620
(716) 256-0200
FAX: (716) 256-0791
http://process.com.com.perftech

Persoft Inc.
465 Science Drive
Madison, Wl 53711
(608) 273-6000
FAX: (608) 273-8227
www.persoft.com

Phillips Business Information Inc.
Telecom News & Information
 Services
1201 Seven Locks Road, Suite 300
Potomac, MD 20854
(301) 340-1520
FAX: (301) 424-4297

Phillips Communications &
 Equipment
P.O. Box 6160
Charlottesville, VA 22906
(804) 985-3600 or (800) 999-4123
FAX: (804) 985-2006
www.phillipscom.com

Proteon Inc.
9 Technology Drive
Westboro, MA 01581
(508) 898-2899 or (800) 545-7464
FAX: (508) 366-8901
pro@proteon.com
www.proteon.com

PSINet Inc
510 Nuntmar Park Drive
Herndon, VA 22066
(703) 904-4200
FAX: (703) 904-4200
info.psi.net
www.psi.net

Pulse Communications
2900 Towerview Road
Herndon, VA 22071
(703) 471-2900 or (800) 841-1005
FAX: (703) 478-7052
www.pulse.com

Racal Data Group
1601 North Harrison Parkway
Sunrise, FL 33323
(800) RACAL-55
www.racal.com/rdg

RAD Data Communications
900 Corporate Drive
Mahwah, NJ 07430
(201) 529-1100
FAX: (201) 529-5777
market@radusa.com
www.rad.com

Radcom Equipment Inc.
900 Corporate Drive
Mahwah, NJ 07430
(201) 529-2020
FAX: (201) 529-0808
www.radcom-inc.com

RADVision Inc.
900 Corporate Drive
Mahwah, NJ 07430
(201) 529-4300
FAX: (201) 529-3516

Raptor Systems Inc.
69 Hickory Drive
Waltham, MA 02154
(617) 487-6700
FAX: (617) 890-6523
www.raptor.com

SAS Institute Inc.
SAS Campus Drive
Cary, NC 27513
(919) 677-8000
FAX: (919) 677-4444
software@sas.sas.com
www.sas.com

Scope Communications Inc.
100 Otis Street
Northboro, MA 01532
(508) 393-1236
FAX: (508) 393-2213

Shiva Corp.
28 Crosby Drive
Bedford, MA 01730
(508) 788-1539 or (800) 977-4482
www.shiva.com

Shomiti Systems
2099 Gateway Place, Suite 220
San Jose, CA 95110
(408) 437-3940
FAX: (408) 437-4041
info@shomiti.com
www.shomiti.com

Siecor Corp./Corning Inc.
P.O. Box 489
489 Seicor Park
Hickory, NC 28603
(704) 327-5900 or (800) 743-2675
FAX: (704) 327-5973

Siemens
4900 Old Ironside Drive
Santa Clara, CA 95054
(408) 492-2000
FAX: (408) 492-3430
www.siemensrolm,com/info

Siemens Energy & Automation
3333 Old Milton Parkway
Alpharetta, GA 30202
(770) 751-4822
FAX: (770) 751-2203

The Siemon Company
76 Westbury Park Road
Watertown, CT 06795
(860) 274-2523
FAX: (860) 945-4225
www.siemon.com

SilCom Technology
5620 Timberlea Boulevard
Mississauga, ON L4W 4M6
Canada
(905) 238-8822
FAX: (905) 238-4976
silcom@silcomtech.com
www.silcomtech.com

SolCom Systems Inc.
1801 Robert Fulton Drive, Suite 400
Reston, VA 20191
(703) 758-6722
FAX: (703) 758-3568
info@solcomsystems.com

Sony Electronics Inc.
3 Paragon Drive
Montvale, NJ 07645-1735
(800) 686-7669 or (201) 930-6964
FAX: (201) 358-4215
www.sony.com

Sourcecom Corp.
5388 North Sterling Center Drive
Westlake Village, CA 91361
(818) 735-3500
FAX: (818) 735-3505
www.source.com

South Hills Datacomm
760 Beechnut Drive
Pittsburgh, PA 15205
(412) 921-9000
FAX: (412) 921-2254

Southwestern Bell
One Bell Center
St. Louis, MO 63101-3099
(314) 235-2027
FAX: 314-331-1600

Sprint
5420 LBJ Freeway, Suite 1700
Dallas, TX 75240
(972) 405-5000
FAX: (972) 405-5891
www.sprint.com

Stallion Technologies Inc.
2880 Research Park Drive, Suite 160
Soquel, CA 95073
(408) 477-0440
FAX: (408) 477-0444
www.stallion.com

Stanford Telecom
1761 Business Center Drive
Reston, VA 20164
(703) 438-8000
FAX: (703) 438-8112
info@sed.stel.com

**StorageTek, Network Systems
  Group**
7600 Boone Avenue North
Minneapolis, MN 55428
(612) 424-4888
FAX: (612) 424-2853

Sun Mircosystems Inc.
2550 Garcia Avenue
Mountain View, CA 94043
(415) 960-1300
FAX: (415) 786-8394
www.sun.com

Sync Research
40 Parker
Irvine, CA 92618
(714) 588-2070
FAX: (714) 588-2080

SysKonnect Inc.
1922 Zanker Road
San Jose, CA 95112
(408) 437-3800 or (800) SK2-FDDI
FAX: (408) 437-3866
www.syskonnect.com

Technical Communications Corp.
100 Domino Drive
Concord, MA 01742-2892
(508) 287-51009
FAX: (508) 371-1280
info@tccsecure.com

Technocrats International Inc.
246 Snug Harbor Station
Duxbury, MA 02331
(800) 231-2667
FAX: (800) 977-4345

Tektronix Inc.
P.O. Box 500
Howard Vollum Park
Beaverton, OR 97077
(503) 627-4753
(800) 547-8949
FAX: (503) 627-3678
www.tek.com

Telco Research
616 Marriott Drive
Nashville, TN 37214
(615) 872-9000
FAX: (615) 231-6144

Telebit Corp.
One Executive Drive
Chelmsford, MA 01824
(508) 441-2181 or (800) telebit
FAX: (508) 441-9060
info@telebit.com
www.telebit.com

Tekelec
26580 West Agoura Road
Calabasas, CA 91302
(818) 880-5656
FAX: (818) 880-6993
info@tekelec.com
www.tekelec.com

Telco Systems Inc.
63 Nahatan Street
Norwood, MA 02062
(617) 551-0300
FAX: (617) 551-0539
www.telco.com

Telecom Analysis Systems Inc.
34 Industrial Way East
Eatontown, NJ 07724
(908) 544-8700
FAX: (908) 544-8347

TELEMATE Software Inc.
4250 Perimeter Park South,
  Suite 200
Atlanta, GA 30341-1201
(770) 936-3700 or (770) 773-4000
FAX: (770) 936-3710
info@telemate.com

Telenetworks
625 Second Street, Suite 100
Petaluma, CA 94952
FAX: (707) 773-4099
www.telenetworks.com

Telect
2111 North Molter Road
Liberty Lake, WA 99019
(509) 926-6000
FAX: (509) 926-8915
getinfo@telect.com
www.telect.com

Telematic-ECI Telecom
1201 West Cypress Creek Road
Fort Lauderdale, FL 33309
(954) 772-3070
FAX: (954) 351-4405
www.telematics.com

Telemax Corp.
1833 Centre Point Drive, Suite 115
Naperville, IL 60563
(630) 505-1234
FAX: (630) 505-0943

Teleport Communications Group
Two Teleport Drive
Staten Island, NY 10311-1004
(718) 355-2082

Tellabs Inc.
4951 Indiana Avenue
Lisle, IL 60532
(630) 378-8800
FAX: (630) 852-7346
www.tellabs.com

Thomas & Betts Telecom Group
1555 Lynnfield Road
Memphis, TN 38119
(901) 682-8221 or (800) 888-0211
FAX: (901) 680-5139

TimeStep Corp.
362 Terry Fox Drive
Kanata, ON K2 K 2 P5
Canada
(613) 599-3610 or (800) 383-8211
FAX: (613) 599-3617
info@timestep.com
www.timestep.com

Tivoli Systems
9442 Capitol of Texas Highway North
Austin, TX 78759
(512) 794-9070
FAX: (512) 794-0623
www.tivoli.com

Transition Networks Inc.
6475 City West Parkway
Minneapolis, MN 55344
(612) 941-7600 or (800) LAN-WANS
FAX: (612) 941-2322
info@transition.com
www.transtion.com

Trend Communications Inc.
12030 Sunrise Valley Drive, Suite 324
Reston, VA 20191
(703) 391-6040
FAX: (703) 391-6026
www.trendcomms.com

Tripp Lite
500 North Orleans
Chicago, IL 60610,
(312) 755-5400
FAX: (312) 644-6505
info%tripplite@mcimail.com

TSL Division, Brite Voice Systems
50 Broad Street, 14th Floor
New York, NY 10004
(212) 248-2000
FAX: (212) 248-4500
www.brite.com/tsl

TTC (Telecommunications Techniques Corp.)
20400 Observation Drive
Germantown, MD 20876
(301) 353-1550 or (800) 638-2049
FAX: (301) 353-0234
www.ttc.com

TxPORT, a Division of Danahe
127 Jetplex Circle
Madison, AL 35758
(800) 926-0085
FAX: (205) 772-3388
info@txport.com

U.S. Robotics
6201 West Oakton Avenue
Morton Grove, IL 60053
(800) USR-CORP
FAX: (847) 933-5800
sales@usr.com
www.usr.com

UB Networks
3900 Freedom Circle
Santa Clara, CA 95054
(408) 496-0111
FAX: (408) 970-7300
www.ub.com

Unisys
P.O. Box 500
Blue Bell, PA 19424
(215) 986-4011
FAX: (215) 986-6850
www.unisys.com

Universal Power Systems Inc.
212 Waples Mill Road
Fairfax, VA 22030-7404
(703) 352-8644
FAX: (703) 352-8648
info@upsi.com

UUNet Technologies
3060 Williams Drive
Fairfax, VA 22031-4648
(800) 4UU-NET4
FAX: (703) 206-5601
info@uu.net
www.uu.net

VCON
17130 North Dallas Parkway No. 210
Dallas, TX 75248
(972) 735-9001
FAX: (972) 735-9099

Verilink Corp.
145 Baytech Drive
San Jose, CA 95134
(408) 945-1199
FAX: (408) 262-6290
www.verilink.com

VideoServer Inc.
63 Third Avenue
Burlington, MA 10803
(617) 229-2000
FAX: (617) 505-2101
www.videoserver.com

Visual Networks Inc.
2092 Gaither Road
Rockville, MD 20850
(301) 208-6784
FAX: (301) 258-5137
info@visual.mctec.com
www.visualnetworks.com

Visual Telephone International
69 Wesley Street South
Hackensack, NJ 07606
(201) 525-0777
FAX: (201) 457-0400
www.vistele.com

Walker & Associates Inc.
7129 Old Highway 52
Welcome, NC 27347
(910) 731-6391 or (800) 472-1746
FAX: (910) 731-6973
www.walkerassoc.com

Wandel & Goltermann
1030 Swabia Court
Research Triangle Park, NC 27516
(919) 941-5730
FAX: (919) 941-5751
solutions@wg.com
www.wg.com

Western Telematic Inc.
5 Sterling
Irvine, CA 92618
(714) 586-9950
FAX: (714) 583-9514
info@westtel.com

Westinghouse Communications
902 Brinton Road
Pittsburgh, PA 15221
(412) 244-6558
FAX: (412) 244-6666

Xylan Corp.
22679 West Agoura Road
Calabasas, CA 91302
(818) 880-3500 or (800) 99-XYLAN
FAX: (818) 880-3505
www.xylan.com

ZyXEL
4920 East La Palma Avenue
Anaheim, CA 92808
(714) 693-0808 or (800) 255-4101
FAX: (714) 693-8811
sales@xyxel.com
www/xyzel.com

Appendix B
Selected Periodicals in the Networking and Communications Industries

America's Network
201 E. Sandpointe Avenue, Suite 600
Santa Ana, CA 92707-8700
(714) 513-8400
FAX: (714) 513-8634
1-800-346-0086
www.americasnetwork.com

Auerbach Publications
2000 NW Corporate Boulevard
Boca Raton, FL 33431
(212) 297-9176
FAX: (212) 297-9176
www.auerbach-publications.com

BackOffice Magazine
10 Tara Boulevard, 5th Floor
Nashua, NH 03062-2801
(603) 891-9297
FAX: (603) 891-9297
www.backoffice.com

Business Communications Review
950 York Road
Hinsdale, IL 60521-2939
(630) 986-1432 or (800) 227-12234
FAX: (630) 323-5324
www.bcr.com

Cabling Installation & Maintenance
10 Tara Boulevard
Nashua, NH 03062-2801
(603) 891-0123
FAX: (603) 891-0587
www.cable-install.com

CIO
492 Old Connecticut Path
Framingham, MA 01701
(508) 872-8200
www.cio.com

Cisco World
12416 Haymeadow Drive
Austin, TX 78750
(512) 250-9023 or (800) 678-9724
FAX: (512) 331-3900
cisco@pcinews.com
www.pcinews.com/pci

Client/Server Computing Magazine
One Research Drive
Westborough, MA 01581
(508) 366-2031
FAX: (508) 836-4732

Communications News
2504 North Tamiami Trail
Nokomis, FL 34275
(941) 966-9521
FAX: (941) 966-2590
nelpub@lx.netcom.com
www.comnews.com

Computer Reseller News
600 Community Drive
Manhasset, NY 11030
(516) 562-5000
www.cm.com

Computer Telephony Magazine
12 West 21st Street
New York, NY 10010
(212) 691-8215
FAX: (212) 961-1191
www.computer.telephony-
magazine.com

Computerworld
500 Old Connecticut Path
Framingham, MA 01701
(508) 879-0700
www.computerworld.com

Data Communications Magazine
600 Community Drive
Manhasset. NY 11030
(516) 562-5000
www.data.com

ENT
Enterprise Systems Journal
Cardinal Business Media
1300 Virginia Drive
Fort Washington, PA 19034
(215) 643-8000
FAX: (215) 643-8099
www.cardinal.com

Federal Computer Week
3110 Fairview Park Drive, Suite 1040
Falls Church, VA 22042
(703) 876-5100

Government Computer News
8601 George Avenue, Suite 300
Silver Spring, MD 20910
(301) 650-2195
FAX: (301) 650-2112

InfoWorld
155 Bovet Road, Suite 800
San Mateo, CA 94402
(415) 572-7341
www.infoworld.com

Information Week
600 Community Drive
Manhasset, NY 11030
(516)-562-5000
www.informationweek.com

Inter@ctive Week
100 Quentin Roosevelt Boulevard
Garden City, NY 11530
(516) 229-3700
FAX: (516) 229-3777

Internet Week
600 Community Drive
Manhasset, NY 10020
(516) 562-1000
www.interwk.com

Internet World
Internet Shopper
Web Developer
Web Week
Meccklermedia
20 Ketchum Street
Westport, CT 06880
(203) 226-6967
FAX: (203) 454-5840
www.internet.com

INTERNETWORK
1300 Virginia Drive
Fort Washington, PA 19034
(215) 643-8000
FAX: (215) 643-8099

LAN Magazine
600 Harrison Street
San Francisco, CA 94107
(415) 905-2200 or (800) 227-4675
FAX: (415) 905-2234
www.mfi.com

LAN Times
1900 O'Farrell Street, Suite 200
San Mateo, CA 94403
(415) 513-6800
FAX: (415) 513-6985
www.lantimes.com

Lightwave
10 Tara Boulevard, 5th Floor
Nashua, NH 03062-2801
891-0123

Network Computing
600 Community Drive
Manhasset, NY 11030
(516) 562-5000
www.networkcomputing.com

Network Magazine
600 Harrison Street
San Francisco, CA 94107
(415) 905-2200
www.network-mag.com

Network World
161 Worcester Road
Framingham, MA 01701
(508) 875-6400
www.netfusion.com
nwcirc@nww.com

PC Magazine
One Park Avenue
New York, NY 10016
(212) 503-5100
FAX: (212) 503-5519

PCWeek
1 Park Avenue
New York, NY 10016
(212) 503-5928
FAX: (212) 503-5495

Phillips Business Info Inc.
1201 Seven Locks Road, Suite 300
Potomac, MD 20854
(301) 340-7788
FAX: (301) 424-0176
www.TelecomWeb.com

tele.com Magazine
1221 Avenue of the Americas
41st Floor
New York, NY 10020
(212) 512-4454
www.teledotcom.com

tele.com
600 Community Drive
Manhasset, NY 11030
(516) 562-5000
www.teledotcom.com

Telecommunications Magazine
685 Canton Street
Norwood, MA 02062
(617) 769-9750
FAX: (617) 762-9071
www.telecoms-mag.com

Telecommunications Reports
1333 H Street Sorthwest, Suite 200
  West Tower
Washington, DC 20005
(202) 842-3022
FAX: (202) 842-3023

TELECONNECT Magazine
12 West 21st Street
New York, NY 10010
(212) 691-8215
FAX: (212) 691-1191

Telephony Magazine
One IBM Plaza, No. 2300
Chicago, IL 60611
(312) 595-1080
FAX: (312) 595-0295

APPENDICES

UNIX REVIEW
600 Harrison Street
San Francisco, CA 94107
(800) 227-4675
FAX: (415) 905-2234
www.mfi.com

Ziff-Davis Inc.
One Park Avenue
New York, NY 10016
(212) 503-3500
FAX: (212) 503-5495
www.ziffdavis.com

Appendix C
Glossary

ACD
Automatic call distributor is a private branch exchange (PBX)-related switching system to automatically distribute incoming calls to a group of agents and to hold calls in a queue of if all answering positions are busy.

ADPCM
Adaptive differential pulse code modulation is a method for coding voice channels at 32K bps to double the capacity of a T1 circuit from 24 to 48 channels.

ADSL
Asymmetrical digital subscriber line is a high-speed digital service offered by carriers.

Aggregator
An aggregator is a company that commits to a volume and term for long-distance service with the hope of reselling it to other users.

Algorithm
This is a set of processes in a computer program used to solve a problem with a given set of steps.

Alternate Access Carrier (AAC)
This is a common carrier that builds a local access network (LAN), generally a fiber-optic loop in a metropolitan area, to provide access service to interexchange carrier circuits.

Alternate Routing
Generally, this is the ability of a PBX, or a switch of some sort, to establish alternate paths over more than one circuit group.

Amplitude Distortion
This is any variance in the relative level of different frequencies within the band of a communications transmission channel.

Analog
A voice transmission mode, not digital, transmits information in its original form by converting it to a continuously variable electrical signal.

AOS

Alternate Operator Service is a telecommunications company that offers operator-handled call services and billing to hotels and customer-owned coin telephone providers. Among its services are third-number, collect, and credit card calls.

ARS

Automatic route selection is a software feature of PBXs and hybrids that selects the appropriate trunk route for a call to use as determined by digits dialed and the caller's class of service.

ASCII

American standard code for information interexchange is a seven-bit (7-b) (plus one parity bit) coding system used for encoding a defined set of characters for transmission over a data network.

Asynchronous

This refers to a means of transmitting data over a network wherein each character contains a start and stop bit to keep the transmitting and receiving terminals in synchronization with each other.

ATM

Known as asynchronous transfer mode, it is a CCITT standard for a broadband connection-oriented switching service for data, voice, and video information carried in 48-byte cells with a 5-byte header (*see* CCITT).

Audiotex

This voice-mail service prompts callers for the desired service and delivers information in audio form.

Automatic Number Identification

This identifies the caller delivered from the calling station to the interexchange carrier for billing purposes.

Backbone Cable

This cabling connects a main distributing frame to intermediate distributing frames located in telecommunications closets.

Backplane

The wiring in a card carrier interconnects circuit packs and equipment.

Balun

This device converts the unbalanced wiring of a coaxial terminal system to a balanced twisted pair system.

Bandwidth

This is the range of frequencies a communications channel is capable of carrying without excessive attenuation.

Baseband

A baseband is a form of modulation in which data signals are pulsed directly on the transmission medium without frequency division.

Baud

This refers to the speed at which communications devices transmit information and is not necessarily related to bits per second number, although the two are related.

BER

Bit error rate is the ratio of bits transmitted in error to the total bits transmitted on the line.

Bit Rate

This is the speed at which bits are transmitted on a circuit; usually expressed in bits per second, bit stream is a continuous string of bits transmitted serially in time.

Blocking

This switching system condition occurs when no circuits are available to complete a call. In this situation, a busy signal is returned to the caller.

BRI

Basic rate interface, the basic ISDN service, consists of two 64K bps information or bearer channels and one 16K bps data signaling channel (*see* ISDN).

Bridge

This is a device that contains circuitry to interconnect networks with a common set of higher level protocols, generally between LANs (*see* LAN).

Broadband

This is a form of LAN modulation where multiple channels are formed by dividing the transmission medium into distinct frequency segments.

Busy Hour

This is a peak load period used when designing network capacity.

Byte

A byte is a sequence of eight bits (8 b) and is the smallest usable unit in memory.

Callback Queuing

A trunk queuing system is when the switch signals a user that all trunks are busy and will call back when a trunk is available.

Call Sequencer

This unit is similar to an automatic call distributor. It answers calls, informs agent of which call arrived first, holds callers in queue, and provides some statistical information.

CCITT
Consultative Committee on International Telephone and Telegraph is an international committee that sets telephone, telegraph, and data communications standards. It is a committee of the International Telecommunications Union (ITU) in Geneva, Switzerland.

CCS
This is a measure of network load in that 36 hundred call seconds (CCS) represent 100% occupancy of a circuit or piece of equipment.

Centralized Attendant Service
This is a PBX feature that routes calls from a multi-PBX system to a central answering location where attendants have access to features of the larger system.

Centrex
This central office feature provided by the local exchange carrier (LEC) provides service equivalent to having a PBX on the user's site service. Incoming calls are directed to extensions without operator intervention.

Channel Bank
This device, similar to a multiplexer, is capable of consolidating separate slow-speed voice or data circuits onto a larger circuit, such as a T1.

CIO
The chief information officer is responsible for technology deployment within an organization.

CIR
Committed information rate in a frame relay or ATM network is the speed the carrier guarantees to provide. Frames above the CIR are carried on a permissive basis up to the port speed but may be discarded.

Circuit Switching
This is a method of network access in which terminal devices are connected by switching. In a circuit switched network, the terminals have full real-time access to one another.

CLASS
Custom local area signaling service is a series of featured services offered by local carriers to its subscribers.

Class of Service
This classification system controls the features, calling privileges, and restrictions the user is assigned from a telecommunications system.

CLEC
The competitive local exchange carrier that is emerging as a result of the Telecommunications Act of 1996 seeks to provide local service to business customers instead of residential customers.

CODEC

This coder and decoder is a device used to convert analog signals to digital and vice versa.

Collision

This condition is present when two or more terminals are in contention during simultaneous network access attempt.

Concentrator

This data communications device subdivides a channel into a larger number of data channels.

Conditioning

This is a special treatment given to transmission circuits to make them suitable for high-speed data communication.

Contention

This occurs during multiple access to a network in which the network capacity is allocated on a "first come, first served" basis.

Cost of Money

This is the composite cost of capital used as the discount rate in a financial study.

CPE

Customer premise equipment is situated on the user's premises and is connected to the voice or data network.

CPU

A central processing unit, often referred to as the "brain," is the logic chip where all the computing takes place.

Critical Path

This tool is used in project management techniques and is the duration based on the sum of the individual tasks and their dependencies. The critical path is the shortest period a project can be accomplished.

Cross-Connect

This is a wired connection between two or more elements of a telecommunications network.

Cross Talk

This is unwanted crossing of signals from two separate transmission paths.

CSU

A channel service unit is an apparatus that interfaces to digital circuits from telecommunications carrier to enable digital communications without a modem. This is used with a data service unit (DSU) when the user device lacks complete digital line interface capability.

Cutover
This is a changeover procedure from an existing to a new telecommunications system.

DACS
A digital access and cross-connect system is a digital switching device for routing T1 lines and DS0 portions of lines among multiple T1 ports.

Data Layer Link
The Open Systems Interconnection (OSI) layer is responsible for data transfer across a single physical connection or a series of bridged connections.

Data Line Monitor
This a data line device that bridges the data line and observes the condition of data, addressing, protocols, and other conditions.

dBm
This measure of signal power as compared to one milliwatt (1 mW) or 1/1000 W of power is used to express power levels.

DCE
Data circuit-terminating equipment is designed to establish and terminate a connection to a network and condition the input and output of data terminal equipment (DTE) for transmission over the network

Delphi
This is a forecasting method in which several knowledgeable individuals make forecasts derived by a trained analyst from a weighted average.

Demarcation Point
This is the point where customer-owned wiring and equipment interface with the circuits from a telecommunications carrier.

Diagnostics
These are test programs used for error and fault detection.

Digital
This is a mode of transmission in which information is coded in binary form on the network.

Discounted Payback Period
This involves the number of years in which a cash flow is discounted at an organization's cost of money and repaying an initial investment.

Distribution Frame
This framework-holding terminal block is used to interconnect cable and equipment and to provide test access.

Downlink
This is the transmission path from a satellite to an earth station.

DSL
A digital subscriber line is a high-speed digital service offered by carriers.

DSU
A data service unit interfaces data terminal equipment (DTE) to a line connecting to a dataport channel unit and allows digital communications without a modem. This service unit can be used with a CSU when data terminal equipment (DTE) lacks complete digital line interface capability.

DS0
Digital signal level 0 or 64K bps is the worldwide standard speed for digitized voice channels.

DS1
A circuit operating at digital signal level 1 at 1.544M bps is also known as a T1 circuit in the U.S. and some other countries. In Europe it is referred to as E-1 and these circuits operate at 2.048M bps.

DTE
Data terminal equipment is any type of computer, peripheral, or terminal that can be used for originating or receiving data over a communication channel.

DTMF
Dual tone multifrequency (or Touch-Tone, a trademark of AT&T) is a signaling method used between the station and the central office consisting of a push button dial that emits dual-tone encoded signals.

E and M Signaling
This is an arrangement that uses separate leads, called E Lead and M Lead, for signaling and supervisory purposes at the point of interface with connected equipment.

Earth Station
This includes the ground radio equipment, antenna, and satellite communication control circuitry that are used to provide access from terrestrial circuits to satellite capacity.

Echo Canceler
This electronic device processes any echo signal and cancels it out to prevent annoyance during transmission.

E-mail
This service allows text-form messages and attached files to be stored in a central file and retrieved with a modem-equipped terminal.

Encryption
This refers to enciphering or encoding data.

Erlang
A unit of network load, 1 erlang equals 36 CCS and represents 100% occupancy of a circuit or piece of equipment.

Error-Free Seconds
This is the number of seconds per unit of time that a carrier guarantees the circuit will be free of errors.

ESF
Extended superframe (DS1) carrier framing format provides 64K bps clear channel capability, error checking, and other data transmission features.

Ethernet
This proprietary contention bus network was developed by Xerox Corp., Digital Equipment Corp., and Intel Corp. and was issued as the Institute of Electrical and Electronics Engineers (IEEE) 802.3 standard.

Facility-Based Carrier
This refers to a telecommunications services company that owns and operates its own network of switches and transmission equipment.

Fax on Demand
A fax-on-demand system retrieves the information from a database and automatically faxes it to the caller.

FCC
The U.S. Federal Communications Commission, an independent government agency created by the Communications Act of 1934, regulates interstate and foreign wire and broadcast communications.

FDDI
Fiber distributed data interface is a network standard whose underlying medium is fiber-optic cable and topology is a dual-attached, counterrotating Token Ring.

Feasibility Analysis
This is a procedure for evaluating the technical and economic effectiveness of various alternatives.

Filter
This is a process or device that screens incoming information for definite characteristics and allows a subset of that information to pass through it.

Firewall
This device protects a network by screening and filtering incoming and outgoing data packets so as to determine who or what can enter or leave a network.

Foreign Exchange Service
This special service connects CPE located in one telephone exchange with switching equipment located in another.

Fractional T1
This is a carrier service offered for users who do not need all 24 channels in a T1 service.

Frame Relay
This is a switching technique operating in a packet mode where error-checking mode is permitted end-to-end instead of on each individual link. This also refers to a "fast packet" data transport service that has more capacity and throughput than X.25 but less than ATM. The service transports frames of information. Price is based on three elements: committed information rate (CIR), access circuit, and port speed.

FTP
File transfer protocol allows remote viewing of file directories as well as transfer of files in either direction across a TCP/IP network (*see* TCP/IP).

Full-Duplex
This is a data communication circuit over which data can be sent simultaneously in both directions.

Gantt Chart
This is a project management chart that shows the duration of tasks as horizontal bar charts on a timescale, with the length of the bar representing the duration of the task.

Gateway
This is a system used to interconnect networks by converting the protocols of each network to those used by the other.

GATT
The General Agreement on Tariffs and Trade is an agreement signed by nations after lengthy negotiations about specific details of how member nations will sell one another commodities.

Gauge
This is the physical size of an electrical conductor, such as a cable, as specified by American Wire Gauge (AWG) standards.

GoS
Grade of service is the percentage of time or probability that a call will be blocked in a network. It is also known as a quality indicator used in transmission measurements to specify the quality of a circuit based on both noise and loss.

Groupware
This is software designed to help teams or groups of people work together.

GSM

Groupe Special Mobile, also known more recently as Global System for Mobile Communications, was originally developed in Europe as an advanced mobile phone service for Europe.

GUI

Graphical user interface is software designed to make applications easier to use by giving them all the same look and feel, usually involving a mouse to move a pointer on the computer screen.

Half-Duplex

Data can be sent in only one direction at a time over this communications circuit.

Handshaking

Signaling between two communications devices on a link to set up communications between them is known as handshaking.

HDSL

High bit–rate digital subscriber line services are offered by carriers.

High Usage Groups

These are trunk groups that are established between two switching machines to serve as the path of first choice between the machines and to handle the bulk of the traffic.

Holding Time

This is the average length of time per call that calls in a group of circuits are off hook.

IDDD

International direct distance dial is a standard international call dialed by the user.

Inside Wiring

This is wiring on the customer's premises between the telephones and the demarcation point.

Interface

This is the connection between two systems.

ITU

International Telecommunications Union is an agency of the United Nations responsible for setting telecommunications standards.

IP

Internet Protocol is the network layer protocol for the Internet.

ISDN
Integrated Services Digital Network is a set of standards promulgated by ITU to prescribe standard interfaces to a switched digital network. Implementation varies in the U.S. but is fairly consistent in Europe.

ISP
Internet service provider.

IVAN
This refers to an international value-added network.

IVPN
International virtual private network is provisioned on public carrier facilities. It can mean a carrier network offering used by many customers of a carrier.

IVR
Interactive voice response, also known as voice response unit (VRU), equipment acts as an automatic telecommunications front end for a computer system enabling callers to conduct their own transactions.

IXC
An interexchange carrier provides long-distance service between LATAs (*see* LATA).

Key Telephone System
This is a small telephone system that allows several central office lines to be accessed from multiple telephone sets.

LAN
A local area network is a medium- to high-speed data communications network restricted to a room, floor or building. LANs that run between neighboring buildings are often called campus networks.

LATA
A local access transport area is a geographic boundary within which Regional Bell Operating Companies are permitted to offer long-distance traffic.

LCR
Least-cost routing is a PBX feature that selects the most economical route to a destination based on the cost of the service.

Leased Line
An unswitched telecommunications channel is leased to an organization for its exclusive use.

LEC
A local exchange carrier is an operating telephone company that serves a particular franchised area.

LEO
Low earth orbit satellite system.

Life Cycle Analysis
This is an analysis in which all cash flows are identified over the life of the project and discounted to their present value at the organization's cost of money.

Line Conditioning
This is a service offered by common carriers to reduce delay, noise, and amplitude distortion to produce transmission of higher data speeds.

Loopback Test
This is a test applied to a full-duplex circuit, main distributing frame (MDF). The cable rack is used to terminate all distribution and trunk cables in a central office or PBX.

MEO
Medium earth orbit satellites system.

MFJ
Modification of Final Judgment resulted in the breakup of AT&T in 1984.

MIB
Management information base is a database item contained in an SNMP-compatible device to define the object that is to be managed (*see* SNMP).

Microwave
This high-frequency, high-capacity radio system is usually used to carry multiple voice channels between two points as an alternative to a terrestrial system.

Modeling
This is a system for designing a network from a series of mathematical formulas that describe the behavior of various network elements.

Modem
This modulator–demodulator unit is used to convert analog signals to digital form and vice versa.

Modem Pool
This pool of modems centrally located and available through a PBX or LAN provides off-net data transmission from terminals without modems.

MTBF
Mean time between failures is the average time a device or system operates without failing.

MTTR
Mean time to repair is the average time required to repair a failed device or system.

Multidrop

This is a circuit dedicated to communications among multiple terminals connected to the same circuit.

Multiline Hunt

This is the ability of a switch to connect incoming calls to another number in a group when other numbers in that group are busy.

Multimode

This large-diameter optical fiber permits more light paths (or modes) in the fiber core.

Multiplexer

This device is used for combining several lower speed channels into a higher speed channel.

Net Present Value

This is the algebraic sum of all discounted cash flows less the initial investment.

Node

This major point in a network is where lines from many sources meet and may be switched.

Octet

The group of 8 b is also known as a byte, although a byte can have other than 8 b.

Off-Hook

A signaling state in a line or trunk is off-hook when it is working or busy.

ONA

Open network architecture provides the interfaces to enable service providers to connect to the public switched telephone network.

OSI

Open systems interconnection is a seven-layer international data communications protocol model that specifies standard interfaces vendors can use to facilitate computer network communications.

Outsourcing

This refers to contracting out some or all of an organization's communications operations with the hope of leading to cost savings. The term is often used to cover any corporate activity that is contracted out.

Packet

This unit of data information consists of header, information, error detection, and trailer records.

APPENDICES

Packet Switching
This form of data communications breaks a data stream into small sections, sends them separately by the best available channels, and reassembles the original data stream at its destination.

PAD
Packet assembler/disassembler is a device used on a packet-switched network to assemble information into packets and to convert received packets into a continuous data stream for further processing.

Parity
This is a bit or series of bits appended to a character or block of characters to ensure that the information received is the same as the information that was sent. Parity is used for error detection.

PBX
A private branch exchange is an automatic switching system dedicated to telephone and data use in a private communications network.

PCM
Pulse code modulation is a digital modulation method to encode a voice signal into an 8-bit digital word representing the amplitude of each pulse.

PERT
A program evaluation and review technique developed by the U.S. Navy after World War II is a method of displaying relationships between tasks in a project in graphic form.

Poisson
This is a curve that describes the distribution of arrival times at the input to a service queue.

Polling
In this network-sharing method, remote terminals send traffic on receipt of a polling message from the host.

POP
A point-of-presence is where the interexchange carrier (IXC) end of a long-distance circuit ends at a central office.

POTS
Plain old telephone service usually refers to basic analog telephone service.

PRI
A primary rate interface is a 1.544M-bps information-carrying channel that furnishes ISDN services to end users. It consists of 23 bearer channels and 1 signaling channel in the U.S. and 30 bearer channels in Europe.

544

Protocol

This is a formal description of messages to be exchanged and rules to be followed for two or more systems to exchange information, generally in a networking situation.

Private Line

This can be a dedicated, full-time communications channel provided to a customer for exclusive use.

Project Management

This is the application of traditional management processes toward the successful achievement of the stated project objective.

Protocol

The term refers to the conventions used in a network for establishing communications compatibility between terminals and for maintaining the line discipline while they are connected to the network.

Protocol Analyzer

This data communications testing unit set enables a network engineer to observe bit patterns in a data transmission, trap specific patterns and to simulate network elements.

Protocol Converter

This device converts one communications protocol to another.

PSTN (or PSN)

Public switched telephone network is a standard public telephone network used to carry voice or facsimile and potentially low-speed data traffic.

PTO

Public telecommunications operator.

PTT

This is a government agency responsible for post office, telegraph, and telecommunications services.

PVC

A permanent virtual circuit is defined in software and functions as if a hardware path is in place.

Queuing

This is the holding of calls in queue when a trunk group is busy. It completes them in turn when an idle circuit is available.

RBOCs

Regional Bell Operating Companies were split from AT&T at divesture, creating the seven new local phone companies.

Remote Access
This is the ability to dial in to a computer over a local telephone number using a number of digital access techniques.

Reseller
This is an organization that purchases transmission capability and resells it to the end user.

RFI
A request for information is issued by prospective purchasers to determine if a product or service is available and what its major features are.

RFP
A request for proposals is for specific proposals on a product or service where there are significant differences among products that make it necessary to choose the product on the basis of several different factors.

RFQ
A request for quotations is for price quotations on a product or service for which there is little difference in quality or features among competitors.

RJ-11
A standard four-conductor jack and plug arrangement typically is used for connecting a standard telephone to inside wiring.

RMON
Remote monitoring is a network management function that enables the manager to monitor network functions from a remote management workstation.

Router
This electronic transmission device routes data packets to destinations.

Server
This is a device in a distributed computing network that provides specialized services such as file, print, and modem or fax pool services.

Singlemode Fiber
This optical fiber has a core so small that only a single light path is present. Even so, singlemode fiber provides the greater transmission bandwidth.

SMDR
Station message detail recording is available through a port on a PBX and provides information such as called and calling station, time of day, and duration of long-distance calls. It is usually connected to a call accounting system.

SNMP
The simple network management protocol provides a means to monitor and set computer network configurations and runtime parameters. It is now an established standard.

SONET
Synchronous optical network is a protocol for high-speed networks.

Spread Spectrum
This radio frequency (RF) technology distributes the signal power over a much wider bandwidth than in conventional techniques, thereby reducing the power per unit bandwidth to very low values.

Statistical Multiplexing
This is a form of data multiplexing in which the time on a communications channel is assigned to terminals when they are ready to transmit.

STTS
A shared telecommunications tenant service refers to that provided by a building to tenants or businesses. The service usually consists of local and long-distance services; adds, moves, and changes; maintenance service; and other telecommunications-related services.

Synchronous
This is a protocol of transmitting data over a network, where the sending and receiving terminals are kept in synchronization with each other by a clock signal embedded in the data.

TCP
Transmission Control Protocol is the major transport protocol in the Internet suite of protocols.

TCP/IP
This connection-oriented developed transmission control protocol was developed for the Internet. Now it is commonly used in WANs (*see* WAN).

TDM
Time division multiplexing is commonly used in T1 multiplexers.

10Base-T
This is a LAN signaling baseband protocol operating at 10 bps over twisted pair.

Trunk
This telecommunications channel between switching systems is equipped with terminating and signaling equipment.

Uplink
This is the transmission path from an earth station to a satellite.

Value-Added Network
This data network adds various processing services such as error correction and storage to the basic function of transporting data.

Virtual Circuit

This is a circuit established between two communicating devices by assigning a logical path over which data can flow. A virtual circuit can be either permanent, in which terminals are assigned a permanent path, or switched, in which the circuit is re-established each time a terminal has data to send.

Virtual Network

This can be a switched voice or data network offered by interexchange carriers that provides service similar to a private voice network. Virtual networks offer reduced rates.

Voice Mail

This is a service that allows voice messages to be stored digitally in secondary storage and retrieved remotely by dialing access and identification codes.

Voice Messaging

This is the use of digital technology on voice networks to record and play back messages (*see* Voice Mail).

Voice Response Unit (VRU)

This device collects customer commands on a keypad and then passes the string of commands to a call center agent.

VPN

Virtual private network generally uses the Internet as the device to connect two remote sites.

VSAT

This very small aperture terminal is a small diameter (typically 1.8 to 2.4 m) satellite earth station situated at the customer premise site and used for data, video, and occasionally voice communications.

WAN

A wide area network consists of leased and private circuits for voice and data service, generally being operated by private, governmental, and institutional organizations.

WATS

Wide area telephone service is a bulk-rated long-distance telephone service. Its price is based on usage and the state in which the calls terminate.

Wiring Closet

This is the junction between backbone and horizontal cabling.

Workstation

This is a powerful PC often used for scientific applications.

WTO
The World Trade Organization.

WWW
World Wide Web.

X.25
This is a data packet switching and transmission standard that has dominated international data communications for 25 years. It became popular in Europe because of its error-correcting procedures. It is an ITU standard for low-speed packet switching used as a lower cost alternative to leased lines in many WANs.

X.400
This e-mail addressing standard was formulated by the ITU and is supported by most European PTTs.

About the Editor

John M. Lusa is a visiting associate professor for the Center for Information and Communication Sciences, a graduate school at Ball State University in Muncie, IN, where he teaches marketing and telecommunications management. He is also the principal in International Communications, his consulting firm in Centerville (a suburb of Dayton), OH. He also writes about telecommunications and networking for a number of publications and has been project editor for some major magazine supplements. John retired as a publisher and editor-in-chief at PennWell Publishing Co. (Westford, MA), where he headed a number of publications in the networking and communications fields. Prior to that, he was a vice president, publisher, and editor-in-chief of a publication for information system executives, published by Hitchcock Publishing (Wheaton, IL), an ABC Publishing subsidiary at the time. He is a journalism graduate of Ohio University and has an MBA from the University of Dayton. You can reach him at jmlusa@compuserve.com. John is active in the Association for Telecommunication Professionals in Columbus, OH, and is a retired colonel in the U.S. Army Reserves.

Index

Printed and bound by CPI Group (UK) Ltd, Croydon, CR0 4YY

22/10/2024

01777622-0016